COMPLETE
CHRISTIAN
CLASSICS

Volume One

edited by
OWEN COLLINS

HarperCollins*Publishers*

HarperCollins*Religious*
Part of HarperCollins*Publishers*
77–85 Fulham Palace Road, London W6 8JB

First published in Great Britain in 1999 by HarperCollins*Publishers*

Compilation © 1999 Owen Collins

10 9 8 7 6 5 4 3 2 1

Owen Collins asserts the moral right
to be identified as the editor and compiler of this work

A catalogue record for this book
is available from the British Library

ISBN 0 00 628122 2

Printed and bound in Great Britain by
Creative Print and Design (Wales), Ebbw Vale

CONTENTS

—✠—

ON LOVING GOD

by

—✛ ST BERNARD OF CLAIRVAUX ✛—

Based on a translation by Edmund G. Gardner, first published, 1929

DEDICATION
To the illustrious Lord Haimeric:
Bernard, called Abbot of Clairvaus, wisheth long life in the Lord and death in the Lord

Hitherto you have been wont to seek prayers from me, not the solving of problems; although I count myself sufficient for neither. My profession shows that, if not my conversation; and to speak truth, I lack the diligence and the ability that are most essential. Yet I am glad that you turn again for spiritual counsel, instead of busying yourself about carnal matters: I only wish you had gone to some one better equipped than I am. Still, learned and simple give the same excuse and one can hardly tell whether it comes from modesty or from ignorance, unless obedience to the task assigned shall reveal. So, take from my poverty what I can give you, lest I should seem to play the philosopher, by reason of my silence. Only, I do not promise to answer other questions you may raise. This one, as to loving God, I will deal with as He shall teach me; for it is sweetest, it can be handled most safely, and it will be most profitable. Keep the others for wiser men.

CONTENTS

✝ CHAPTER 1 ✝
Why we should love God and the measure of that love

You want me to tell you why God is to be loved and how much. I answer, the reason for loving God is God Himself; and the measure of love due to Him is immeasurable love. Is this plain? Doubtless, to a thoughtful man; but I am debtor to the unwise also. A word to the wise is sufficient; but I must consider simple folk too. Therefore I set myself joyfully to explain more in detail what is meant above.

We are to love God for Himself, because of a twofold reason; nothing is more reasonable, nothing more profitable. When one asks, Why should I love God? he may mean, What is lovely in God? or What shall I gain by loving God? In either case, the same sufficient cause of love exists, namely, God Himself.

And first, of His title to our love. Could any title be greater than this, that He gave Himself for us unworthy wretches? And being God, what better gift could He offer than Himself? Hence, if one seeks for God's claim upon our love here is the chiefest: Because He first loved us (1 John 4:19).

Ought He not to be loved in return, when we think who loved, whom He loved, and how much He loved? For who is He that loved? The same of whom every spirit testifies: 'Thou art my God: my goods are nothing unto Thee' (Ps. 16:2, Vulg.). And is not His love that wonderful charity which 'seeketh not her own' (1 Cor.13:5)? But for whom was such unutterable love made manifest? The apostle tells us: 'When we were enemies, we were reconciled to God by the death of His Son' (Rom. 5:10). So it was God who loved us, loved us freely, and loved us while yet we were enemies. And how great was this love of His? St. John answers: 'God so loved the world that He gave His only-begotten Son, that whosoever believeth in Him should not perish, but have everlasting life' (John 3:16). St. Paul adds: 'He spared not His own Son, but delivered Him up for us all' (Rom. 8:32); and the Son says of Himself, 'Greater love hath no man than this, that a man lay down his life for his friends' (John 15:13).

This is the claim which God the holy, the supreme, the omnipotent, has upon men, defiled and base and weak. Some one may urge that this is true of mankind, but not of angels. True, since for angels it was not needful. He who succoured men in their time of need, preserved angels from such need; and even as His love for sinful men wrought wondrously in them so that they should not remain sinful, so that same love which in equal measure He poured out upon angels kept them altogether free from sin.

✝ CHAPTER 2 ✝

On loving God. How much God deserves love from man in recognition of His gifts, both material and spiritual: and how these gifts should be cherished without neglect of the Giver

Those who admit the truth of what I have said know, I am sure, why we are bound to love God. But if unbelievers will not grant it, their ingratitude is at once confounded by His innumerable benefits, lavished on our race, and plainly discerned by the senses. Who is it that gives food to all flesh, light to every eye, air to all that breathe? It would be foolish to begin a catalogue, since I have just called them innumerable: but I name, as notable instances, food, sunlight and air; not because they are God's best gifts, but because they are essential to bodily life. Man must seek in his own higher nature for the highest gifts; and these are dignity, wisdom and virtue. By dignity I mean free will, whereby he not only excels all other earthly creatures, but has dominion over them. Wisdom is the power whereby he recognizes this dignity, and perceives also that it is no accomplishment of his own. And virtue impels man to seek eagerly for Him who is man's Source, and to lay fast hold on Him when He has been found.

Now, these three best gifts have each a twofold character. Dignity appears not only as the prerogative of human nature, but also as the cause of that fear and dread of man which is upon every beast of the earth. Wisdom perceives this distinction, but owns that though in us, it is, like all good qualities, not of us. And lastly, virtue moves us to search eagerly for an Author, and, when we have found Him, teaches us to cling to Him yet more eagerly. Consider too that dignity without wisdom is nothing worth; and wisdom is harmful without virtue, as this argument following shows: There is no glory in having a gift without knowing it. But to know only that you have it, without knowing that it is not of yourself that you have it, means self-glorying, but no true glory in God. And so the apostle says to men in such cases, 'What hast thou that thou didst not receive? Now, if thou didst receive it, why dost thou glory as if thou hadst not received it? (1 Cor. 4:7). He asks, Why dost thou glory? but goes on, as if thou hadst not received it, showing that the guilt is not in glorying over a possession, but in glorying as though it had not been received. And rightly such glorying is called vain-glory, since it has not the solid foundation of truth. The apostle shows how to discern the true glory from the false, when he says, He that glorieth, let him glory in the Lord, that is, in the Truth, since our Lord is Truth (1 Cor. 1:31; John 14:6).

We must know, then, what we are, and that it is not of ourselves that we are what we are. Unless we know this thoroughly, either we shall not glory at all, or our glorying will be vain. Finally, it is written, 'If thou know not, go thy way forth by the footsteps of the flock' (Cant. 1:8).

And this is right. For man, being in honour, if he know not his own honour, may fitly be compared, because of such ignorance, to the beasts that perish. Not knowing himself as the creature that is distinguished from the irrational brutes by the possession of reason, he commences to be confounded with them because, ignorant of his own true glory which is within, he is led captive by his curiosity, and concerns himself with external, sensual things. So he is made to resemble the lower orders by not knowing that he has been more highly endowed than they.

We must be on our guard against this ignorance. We must not rank ourselves too low; and with still greater care we must see that we do not think of ourselves more highly than we ought to think, as happens when we foolishly impute to ourselves whatever good may be in us. But far more than either of these kinds of ignorance, we must hate and shun that presumption which would lead us to glory in goods not our own, knowing that they are not of ourselves but of God, and yet not fearing to rob God of the honour due unto Him. For mere ignorance, as in the first instance, does not glory at all; and mere wisdom, as in the second, while it has a kind of glory, yet does not glory in the Lord. In the third evil case, however, man sins not in ignorance but deliberately, usurping the glory which belongs to God. And this arrogance is a more grievous and deadly fault than the ignorance of the second, since it contemns God, while the other knows Him not. Ignorance is brutal, arrogance is devilish. Pride only, the chief of all iniquities, can make us treat gifts as if they were rightful attributes of our nature, and, while receiving benefits, rob our Benefactor of His due glory.

Wherefore to dignity and wisdom we must add virtue, the proper fruit of them both. Virtue seeks and finds Him who is the Author and Giver of all good, and who must be in all things glorified; otherwise, one who knows what is right yet fails to perform it, will be beaten with many stripes (Luke 12:47). Why? you may ask. Because he has failed to put his knowledge to good effect, but rather has imagined mischief upon his bed (Ps. 36:4); like a wicked servant, he has turned aside to seize the glory which, his own knowledge assured him, belonged only to his good Lord and Master. It is plain, therefore, that dignity without wisdom is useless and that wisdom without virtue is accursed. But when one possesses virtue, then wisdom and dignity are not dangerous but blessed. Such a man calls on God and lauds Him, confessing from a full heart, 'Not unto us, O Lord, not unto us, but unto Thy name give glory' (Ps. 115:1). Which is to say, 'O Lord, we claim no knowledge, no distinction for ourselves; all is Thine, since from Thee all things do come.'

But we have digressed too far in the wish to prove that even those who know not Christ are sufficiently admonished by the natural law, and by their own endowments of soul and body, to love God for God's own sake. To sum up: what infidel does not know that he has received light, air, food – all things necessary for his own body's life – from Him alone who giveth food to all flesh (Ps. 136:25), who maketh His sun to rise on the evil and on the good, and sendeth rain on the just and on the unjust (Matt. 5:45). Who is so impious as to attribute the peculiar eminence of humanity to any other except to Him who saith, in Genesis, 'Let us make man in Our image, after Our likeness' (Gen. 1:26)? Who else could be the Bestower of wisdom, but He that teacheth man knowledge (Ps. 94:10)? Who else could bestow virtue except the Lord of virtue? Therefore even the infidel who knows not Christ but does at least know himself, is bound to love God for God's own sake. He is unpardonable if he does not love the Lord his God with all his heart, and with all his soul, and with all his mind; for his own innate justice and common sense cry out from within that he is bound wholly to love God, from whom he has received all things. But it is hard, nay rather, impossible, for a man by his own strength or in the power of free will to render all things to God from whom they came, without rather turning them aside, each to his own account, even as it is written, 'For all seek their own' (Phil. 2:21); and again, 'The imagination of man's heart is evil from his youth' (Gen. 8:21).

✛ CHAPTER 3 ✛

What greater incentives Christians have, more than the heathen, to love God

The faithful know how much need they have of Jesus and Him crucified; but though they wonder and rejoice at the ineffable love made manifest in Him, they are not daunted at having no more than their own poor souls to give in return for such great and condescending charity. They love all the more, because they know themselves to be loved so exceedingly; but to whom little is given the same loveth little (Luke 7:47). Neither Jew nor pagan feels the pangs of love as doth the Church, which saith, 'Stay me with flagons, comfort me with apples; for I am sick of love' (Cant. 2:5). She beholds King Solomon, with the crown wherewith his mother crowned him in the day of his espousals; she sees the Sole-begotten of the Father bearing the heavy burden of His Cross; she sees the Lord of all power and might bruised and spat upon, the Author of life and glory transfixed with nails, smitten by the lance, overwhelmed with mockery, and at last laying down His precious life for His friends. Contemplating this the sword of love pierces through her own soul also and she cries aloud, 'Stay me with flagons, comfort me with apples; for I am sick of love.' The fruits which the Spouse gathers from the Tree of Life in the midst of the garden of her Beloved, are pomegranates (Cant. 4:13), borrowing their taste from the Bread of heaven, and their colour from the Blood of Christ. She sees death dying and its author overthrown: she beholds captivity led captive from hell to earth, from earth to heaven, so 'that at the name of Jesus every knee should bow, of things in heaven and things in earth and things under the earth' (Phil. 2:10). The earth under the ancient curse brought forth thorns and thistles; but now the Church beholds it laughing with flowers and restored by the grace of a new benediction. Mindful of the verse 'My heart danceth for joy, and in my song will I praise Him' she refreshes herself with the fruits of His Passion which she gathers from the Tree of the Cross, and with the flowers of His Resurrection whose fragrance invites the frequent visits of her Spouse.

Then it is that He exclaims, 'Behold thou art fair, My beloved, yea pleasant: also our bed is green' (Cant. 1:16). She shows her desire for His coming and whence she hopes to obtain it; not because of her own merits but because of the flowers of that field which God hath blessed. Christ who willed to be conceived and brought up in Nazareth, that is, the town of branches, delights in such blossoms. Pleased by such heavenly fragrance the bridegroom rejoices to revisit the heart's chamber when He finds it adorned with fruits and decked with flowers – that is, meditating on the mystery of His Passion or on the glory of His Resurrection.

The tokens of the Passion we recognize as the fruitage of the ages of the past, appearing in the fullness of time during the reign of sin and death (Gal. 4:4). But it is the glory of the

Resurrection, in the new springtime of regenerating grace, that the fresh flowers of the later age come forth, whose fruit shall be given without measure at the general resurrection, when time shall be no more. And so it is written, 'The winter is past, the rain is over and gone, the flowers appear on the earth' (Cant. 2:11ff); signifying that summer has come back with Him who dissolves icy death into the spring of a new life and says, 'Behold, I make all things new' (Rev. 21:5). His Body sown in the grave has blossomed in the Resurrection (1 Cor. 15:42); and in like manner our valleys and fields which were barren or frozen, as if dead, glow with reviving life and warmth.

The Father of Christ who makes all things new, is well pleased with the freshness of those flowers and fruits, and the beauty of the field which breathes forth such heavenly fragrance; and He says in benediction, 'See, the smell of My Son is as the smell of a field which the Lord hath blessed' (Gen. 27:27). Blessed to overflowing, indeed, since of His fullness have all we received (John 1:16). But the Bride may come when she pleases and gather flowers and fruits therewith to adorn the inmost recesses of her conscience; that the Bridegroom when He cometh may find the chamber of her heart redolent with perfume.

So it behoves us, if we would have Christ for a frequent guest, to fill our hearts with faithful meditations on the mercy He showed in dying for us, and on His mighty power in rising again from the dead. To this David testified when he sang, 'God spake once, and twice I have also heard the same; that power belongeth unto God; and that Thou, Lord, art merciful (Ps. 62:11–12). And surely there is proof enough and to spare in that Christ died for our sins and rose again for our justification, and ascended into heaven that He might protect us from on high, and sent the Holy Spirit for our comfort. Hereafter He will come again for the consummation of our bliss. In His Death He displayed His mercy, in His Resurrection His power; both combine to manifest His glory.

The Bride desires to be stayed with flagons and comforted with apples, because she knows how easily the warmth of love can languish and grow cold; but such helps are only until she has entered into the bride chamber. There she will receive His long-desired caresses even as she sighs, 'His left hand is under my head and His right hand doth embrace me' (Cant. 2:6). Then she will perceive how far the embrace of the right hand excels all sweetness, and that the left hand with which He at first caressed her cannot be compared to it. She will understand what she has heard: 'It is the spirit that quickeneth; the flesh profiteth nothing' (John 6:63). She will prove what she hath read: 'My memorial is sweeter than honey, and mine inheritance than the honey-comb' (Ecclus. 24:20). What is written elsewhere, 'The memorial of Thine abundant kindness shall be showed' (Ps. 145:7), refers doubtless to those of whom the Psalmist had said just before: 'One generation shall praise Thy works unto another and declare Thy power' (Ps. 145:4). Among us on the earth there is His memory; but in the Kingdom of heaven His very Presence. That Presence is the joy of those who have already attained to beatitude; the memory is the comfort of us who are still wayfarers, journeying towards the Fatherland.

✝ CHAPTER 4 ✝

Of those who find comfort in the recollection of God, or are fittest for His love

But it will be well to note what class of people takes comfort in the thought of God. Surely not that perverse and crooked generation to whom it was said, 'Woe unto you that are rich; for ye have received your consolation' (Luke 6:24). Rather, those who can say with truth, 'My soul refuseth comfort' (Ps. 77:2). For it is meet that those who are not satisfied by the present should be sustained by the thought of the future, and that the contemplation of eternal happiness should solace those who scorn to drink from the river of transitory joys. That is the generation of them that seek the Lord, even of them that seek, not their own, but the face of the God of Jacob. To them that long for the presence of the living God, the thought of Him is sweetest itself: but there is no satiety, rather an ever-increasing appetite, even as the Scripture bears witness, 'they that eat me shall yet be hungry' (Ecclus. 24:21); and if the one an-hungred spake, 'When I awake up after Thy likeness, I shall be satisfied with it.' Yea, blessed even now are they which do hunger and thirst after righteousness, for they, and they only, shall be filled. Woe to you, wicked and perverse generation; woe to you, foolish and abandoned people, who hate Christ's memory, and dread His second Advent! Well may you fear, who will not now seek deliverance from the snare of the hunter; because 'they that will be rich fall into temptation and a snare, and into many foolish and hurtful lusts' (1 Tim. 6:9). In that day we shall not escape the dreadful sentence of condemnation, 'Depart from Me, ye cursed, into everlasting fire' (Matt. 25:41). O dreadful sentence indeed, O hard saying! How much harder to bear than that other saying which we repeat daily in church, in memory of the Passion: 'Whoso eateth My flesh and drinketh My blood hath eternal life' (John 6:54). That signifies, whoso honours My death and after My example mortifies his members which are upon the earth (Col. 3:5) shall have eternal life, even as the apostle says, 'If we suffer, we shall also reign with Him' (2 Tim. 2:12). And yet many even today recoil from these words and go away, saying by their action if not with their lips, 'This is a hard saying; who can hear it?' (John 6:60). 'A generation that set not their heart aright, and whose spirit cleaveth not steadfastly unto God' (Ps. 78:8), but chooseth rather to trust in uncertain riches, it is disturbed at the very name of the Cross, and counts the memory of the Passion intolerable. How can such sustain the burden of that fearful sentence, 'Depart from Me, ye cursed, into everlasting fire, prepared for the devil and his angels'? 'On whomsoever that stone shall fall it will grind him to powder' (Luke 20:18); but 'the generation of the faithful shall be blessed' (Ps. 112:2), since, like the apostle, they labour that whether present or absent they may be accepted of the Lord (2 Cor. 5:9). At the last day they too shall hear the Judge pronounce their award, 'Come, ye blessed of My Father, inherit the kingdom prepared for you from the foundation of the world' (Matt. 25:34).

In that day those who set not their hearts aright will feel, too late, how easy is Christ's yoke, to which they would not bend their necks and how light His burden, in comparison with the pains they must then endure. O wretched slaves of Mammon, you cannot glory in the Cross of our Lord Jesus Christ while you trust in treasures laid up on earth: you cannot taste and see how gracious the Lord is, while you are hungering for gold. If you have not rejoiced at the thought of His coming, that day will be indeed a day of wrath to you.

But the believing soul longs and faints for God; she rests sweetly in the contemplation of Him. She glories in the reproach of the Cross, until the glory of His face shall be revealed. Like the Bride, the dove of Christ, that is covered with silver wings (Ps. 68:13), white with innocence and purity, she reposes in the thought of Thine abundant kindness, Lord Jesus; and above all she longs for that day when in the joyful splendour of Thy saints, gleaming with the radiance of the Beatific Vision, her feathers shall be like gold, resplendent with the joy of Thy countenance.

Rightly then may she exult, 'His left hand is under my head and His right hand doth embrace me.' The left hand signifies the memory of that matchless love, which moved Him to lay down His life for His friends; and the right hand is the Beatific Vision which He hath promised to His own, and the delight they have in His presence. The Psalmist sings rapturously, 'At Thy right hand there is pleasure for evermore' (Ps. 16:11): so we are warranted in explaining the right hand as that divine and deifying joy of His presence.

Rightly too is that wondrous and ever-memorable love symbolized as His left hand, upon which the Bride rests her head until iniquity be done away: for He sustains the purpose of her mind, lest it should be turned aside to earthly, carnal desires. For the flesh wars against the spirit: 'The corruptible body presseth down the soul, and the earthly tabernacle weigheth down the mind that museth upon many things' (Wis. 9:15). What could result from the contemplation of compassion so marvellous and so undeserved, favour so free and so well attested, kindness so unexpected, clemency so unconquerable, grace so amazing except that the soul should withdraw from all sinful affections, reject all that is inconsistent with God's love, and yield herself wholly to heavenly things? No wonder is it that the Bride, moved by the perfume of these unctions, runs swiftly, all on fire with love, yet reckons herself as loving all too little in return for the Bridegroom's love. And rightly, since it is no great matter that a little dust should be all consumed with love of that Majesty which loved her first and which revealed itself as wholly bent on saving her. For 'God so loved the world that He gave His only-begotten Son, that whosoever believeth in Him should not perish but have everlasting life' (John 3:16). This sets forth the Father's love. But 'He hath poured out His soul unto death,' was written of the Son (Isa. 53:12). And of the Holy Spirit it is said, 'The Comforter which is the Holy Ghost whom the Father will send in My name, He shall teach you all things, and bring all things to your remembrance, whatsoever I have said unto you' (John 14:26). It is plain, therefore, that God loves us, and loves us with all His heart; for the Holy Trinity altogether loves us, if we may venture so to speak of the infinite and incomprehensible Godhead who is essentially one.

✝ CHAPTER 5 ✝

Of the Christian's debt of love, how great it is

From the contemplation of what has been said, we see plainly that God is to be loved, and that He has a just claim upon our love. But the infidel does not acknowledge the Son of God, and so he can know neither the Father nor the Holy Spirit; for he that honoureth not the Son, honoureth not the Father which sent Him, nor the Spirit whom He hath sent (John 5:23). He knows less of God than we; no wonder that he loves God less. This much he understands at least – that he owes all he is to his Creator. But how will it be with me? For I know that my God is not merely the bounteous Bestower of my life, the generous Provider for all my needs, the pitiful Consoler of all my sorrows, the wise Guide of my course: but that He is far more than all that. He saves me with an abundant deliverance: He is my eternal Preserver, the portion of my inheritance, my glory. Even so it is written, 'With Him is plenteous redemption' (Ps. 130:7); and again, 'He entered in once into the holy place, having obtained eternal redemption for us' (Heb. 9:12). Of His salvation it is written, 'He forsaketh not His that be godly; but they are preserved for ever' (Ps. 37:28); and of His bounty, 'Good measure, pressed down and shaken together, and running over, shall men give into your bosom' (Luke 6:38); and in another place, 'Eye hath not seen nor ear heard, neither have entered into the heart of man, those things which God hath prepared for them that love Him' (1 Cor. 2:9). He will glorify us, even as the apostle beareth witness, saying, 'We look for the Saviour, the Lord Jesus Christ, who shall change our vile body that it may be fashioned like unto His glorious body' (Phil. 3:20–21); and again, 'I reckon that the sufferings of this present time are not worthy to be compared with the glory which shall be revealed in us' (Rom. 8:18); and once more, 'Our light affliction, which is but for a moment, worketh for us a far more exceeding and eternal weight of glory; while we look not at the things which are seen, but at the things which are not seen (2 Cor. 4:17-18).

'What shall I render unto the Lord for all His benefits towards me?' (Ps. 116:12). Reason and natural justice alike move me to give up myself wholly to loving Him to whom I owe all that I have and am. But faith shows me that I should love Him far more than I love myself, as I come to realize that He hath given me not my own life only, but even Himself. Yet, before the time of full revelation had come, before the Word was made flesh, died on the Cross, came forth from the grave, and returned to His Father; before God had shown us how much He loved us by all this plenitude of grace, the commandment had been uttered, 'Thou shalt love the Lord thy God with all thine heart, and with all thy soul and with all thy might' (Deut. 6:5), that is, with all thy being, all thy knowledge, all thy powers. And it was not unjust for God to claim this from His own work and gifts. Why should not the creature love his Creator, who gave him the power to love? Why should he not love Him with all his being, since it is by His gift alone that he can do anything that is good? It was God's creative grace that out of nothingness raised us to the dignity of manhood; and from this appears our duty to love Him, and the justice of His claim to that love. But how infinitely is the benefit increased when we bethink ourselves of His fulfilment of the promise, 'thou, Lord, shalt save both man and beast: how excellent is Thy mercy, O Lord!' (Ps. 36:6-7). For we, who 'turned our glory into the similitude of a calf that eateth hay' (Ps. 106:20), by our evil deeds debased ourselves so that we might be compared unto the beasts that perish. I owe all that I am to Him who made me: but how can I pay my debt to Him who redeemed me, and in such wondrous wise? Creation was not so vast a work as redemption; for it is written of man and of all things that were made, 'He spake the word, and they were made' (Ps. 148:5). But to redeem that creation which sprang into being at His word, how much He spake, what wonders He wrought, what hardships He endured, what shames He suffered! Therefore what reward shall I give unto the Lord for all the benefits which He hath done unto me? In the first creation He gave me myself; but in His new creation He gave me Himself, and by that gift restored to me the self that I had lost. Created first and then restored, I owe Him myself twice over in return for myself. But what have I to offer Him for the gift of Himself? Could I multiply myself a thousand-fold and then give Him all, what would that be in comparison with God?

CHAPTER 6

A brief summary

Admit that God deserves to be loved very much, yea, boundlessly, because He loved us first, He infinite and we nothing, loved us, miserable sinners, with a love so great and so free. This is why I said at the beginning that the measure of our love to God is to love immeasurably. For since our love is toward God, who is infinite and immeasurable, how can we bound or limit the love we owe Him? Besides, our love is not a gift but a debt. And since it is the Godhead who loves us, Himself boundless, eternal, supreme love, of whose greatness there is no end, yea, and His wisdom is infinite, whose peace passeth all understanding; since it is He who loves us, I say, can we think of repaying Him grudgingly? 'I will love Thee, O Lord, my strength. The Lord is my rock and my fortress and my deliverer, my God, my strength, in whom I will trust' (Ps. 18:1–2). He is all that I need, all that I long for. My God and my help, I will love Thee for Thy great goodness; not so much as I might, surely, but as much as I can. I cannot love Thee as Thou deservest to be loved, for I cannot love Thee more than my own feebleness permits. I will love Thee more when Thou deemest me worthy to receive greater capacity for loving; yet never so perfectly as Thou hast deserved of me. 'Thine eyes did see my substance, yet being imperfect; and in Thy book all my members were written' (Ps. 139:16). Yet Thou recordest in that book all who do what they can, even though they cannot do what they ought. Surely I have said enough to show how God should be loved and why. But who has felt, who can know, who express, how much we should love him.

CHAPTER 7

Of love toward God not without reward: and how the hunger of man's heart cannot be satisfied with earthly things

And now let us consider what profit we shall have from loving God. Even though our knowledge of this is imperfect, still that is better than to ignore it altogether. I have already said (when it was a question of wherefore and in what manner God should be loved) that there was a double reason constraining us: His right and our advantage. Having written as best I can, though unworthily, of God's right to be loved. I have still to treat of the recompense which that love brings. For although God would be loved without respect of reward, yet He wills not to leave love unrewarded. True charity cannot be left destitute, even though she is unselfish and seeketh not her own (1 Cor. 13:5). Love is an affection of the soul, not a contract: it cannot rise from a mere agreement, nor is it so to be gained. It is spontaneous in its origin and impulse; and true love is its own satisfaction. It has its reward; but that reward is the object beloved. For whatever you seem to love, if it is on account of something else, what you do really love is that something else, not the apparent object of desire. St. Paul did not preach the Gospel that he might earn his bread; he ate that he might be strengthened for his ministry. What he loved was not bread, but the Gospel. True love does not demand a reward, but it deserves one. Surely no one offers to pay for love; yet some recompense is due to one who loves, and if his love endures he will doubtless receive it.

On a lower plane of action, it is the reluctant, not the eager, whom we urge by promises of reward. Who would think of paying a man to do what he was yearning to do already? For instance no one would hire a hungry man to eat, or a thirsty man to drink, or a mother to nurse her own child. Who would think of bribing a farmer to dress his own vineyard, or to dig about his orchard, or to rebuild his house? So, all the more, one who loves God truly asks no other recompense than God Himself; for if he should demand anything else it would be the prize that he loved and not God.

It is natural for a man to desire what he reckons better than that which he has already, and be satisfied with nothing which lacks that special quality which he misses. Thus, if it is for her beauty that he loves his wife, he will cast longing eyes after a fairer woman. If he is clad in a rich garment, he will covet a costlier one; and no matter how rich he may be he will envy a man richer than himself. Do we not see people every day, endowed with vast estates, who keep on joining field to field, dreaming of wider boundaries for their lands? Those who dwell in palaces are ever adding house to house, continually building up and tearing down, remodelling and changing. Men in high places are driven by insatiable ambition to clutch at still greater prizes. And nowhere is there any final satisfaction, because nothing there can be defined as absolutely the best or highest. But it is natural that nothing should content a man's desires but the very best, as he reckons it. Is it not, then, mad folly always to be craving for things which can never quiet our longings, much less satisfy them? No matter how many such things one has, he is always lusting after what he has not; never at peace, he sighs for new possessions. Discontented, he spends himself in fruitless toil, and finds only weariness in the evanescent and unreal pleasures of the world. In his greediness, he counts all that he has clutched as nothing in comparison with what is beyond his grasp, and loses all pleasure in his actual possessions by longing after what he has not, yet covets. No man can ever hope to own all things. Even the little one does possess is got only with toil and is held in fear; since each is certain to lose what he hath when God's day, appointed though unrevealed, shall come. But the perverted will struggles towards the ultimate good by devious ways, yearning after satisfaction, yet led astray by vanity and deceived by wickedness. Ah, if you wish to attain to the consummation of all desire, so that nothing unfulfilled will be left, why weary yourself with fruitless efforts, running hither and thither, only to die long before the goal is reached?

It is so that these impious ones wander in a circle, longing after something to gratify their yearnings, yet madly rejecting that which alone can bring them to their desired end, not by exhaustion but by attainment. They wear themselves out in vain travail, without reaching their blessed consummation, because they delight in creatures, not in the Creator. They want to traverse creation, trying all things one by one, rather than think of coming to Him who is Lord of all. And if their utmost longing were realized, so that they should have all the world for their own, yet without possessing Him who is the Author of all being, then the same law of their desires would make them contemn what they had and restlessly seek Him whom they still lacked, that is, God Himself. Rest is in Him alone. Man knows no peace in the world; but he has no disturbance when he is with God. And so the soul says with confidence, 'Whom have I in heaven but Thee; and there is none upon earth that I desire in comparison of Thee. God is the strength of my heart, and my portion for ever. It is good for me to hold me fast by God, to put my trust in the Lord God' (Ps. 73:25ff). Even by this way one would eventually come to God, if only he might have time to test all lesser goods in turn.

11

But life is too short, strength too feeble, and competitors too many, for that course to be practicable. One could never reach the end, though he were to weary himself with the long effort and fruitless toil of testing everything that might seem desirable. It would be far easier and better to make the assay in imagination rather than in experiment. For the mind is swifter in operation and keener in discrimination than the bodily senses, to this very purpose that it may go before the sensuous affections so that they may cleave to nothing which the mind has found worthless. And so it is written, 'Prove all things: hold fast that which is good' (1 Thess. 5:21). Which is to say that right judgment should prepare the way for the heart. Otherwise we may not ascend into the hill of the Lord nor rise up in His holy place (Ps. 24:3). We should have no profit in possessing a rational mind if we were to follow the impulse of the senses, like brute beasts, with no regard at all to reason. Those whom reason does not guide in their course may indeed run, but not in the appointed race-track, neglecting the apostolic counsel, 'So run that ye may obtain'. For how could they obtain the prize who put that last of all in their endeavour and run round after everything else first?

But as for the righteous man, it is not so with him. He remembers the condemnation pronounced on the multitude who wander after vanity, who travel the broad way that leads to death (Matt. 7:13); and he chooses the King's highway, turning aside neither to the right hand nor to the left (Num. 20:17), even as the prophet saith, 'The way of the just is uprightness (Isa. 26:7). Warned by wholesome counsel he shuns the perilous road, and heeds the direction that shortens the search, forbidding covetousness and commanding that he sell all that he hath and give to the poor (Matt. 19:21). Blessed, truly, are the poor, for theirs is the Kingdom of Heaven (Matt. 5:3). They which run in a race, run all, but distinction is made among the racers. 'The Lord knoweth the way of the righteous: and the way of the ungodly shall perish' (Ps. 1:6). 'A small thing that the righteous hath is better than great riches of the ungodly' (Ps. 37.16). Even as the Preacher saith, and the fool discovereth, 'He that loveth silver shall not be satisfied with silver' (Eccles. 5:10). But Christ saith, 'Blessed are they which do hunger and thirst after righteousness, for they shall be filled' (Matt. 5:6). Righteousness is the natural and essential food of the soul, which can no more be satisfied by earthly treasures than the hunger of the body can be satisfied by air. If you should see a starving man standing with mouth open to the wind, inhaling draughts of air as if in hope of gratifying his hunger, you would think him lunatic. But it is no less foolish to imagine that the soul can be satisfied with worldly things which only inflate it without feeding it. What have spiritual gifts to do with carnal appetites, or carnal with spiritual? Praise the Lord, O my soul: who satisfieth thy mouth with good things (Ps. 103:1ff). He bestows bounty immeasurable; He provokes thee to good, He preserves thee in goodness; He prevents, He sustains, He fills thee. He moves thee to longing, and it is He for whom thou longest.

I have said already that the motive for loving God is God Himself. And I spoke truly, for He is as well the efficient cause as the final object of our love. He gives the occasion for love, He creates the affection, He brings the desire to good effect. He is such that love to Him is a natural due; and so hope in Him is natural, since our present love would be vain did we not hope to love Him perfectly some day. Our love is prepared and rewarded by His. He loves us first, out of His great tenderness; then we are bound to repay Him with love; and we are permitted to cherish exultant hopes in Him. 'He is rich unto all that call upon Him' (Rom. 10:12), yet He has no gift for them better than Himself. He gives Himself as prize and reward: He is the refreshment of holy soul, the ransom of those in captivity. 'The Lord is good unto them that wait for Him' (Lam. 3:25). What will He be then to those who gain His presence? But here is a paradox, that no one can seek the Lord who has not already found Him. It is Thy will, O God, to be found that Thou mayest be sought, to be sought that Thou mayest the more truly be found. But though Thou canst be sought and found, Thou canst not be forestalled. For if we say, 'Early shall my prayer come before Thee' (Ps. 88:13), yet doubtless all prayer would be lukewarm unless it was animated by Thine inspiration.

We have spoken of the consummation of love towards God: now to consider whence such love begins.

✛ CHAPTER 8 ✛

Of the first degree of love: wherein man loves God for self's sake

Love is one of the four natural affections, which it is needless to name since everyone knows them. And because love is natural, it is only right to love the Author of nature first of all. Hence comes the first and great commandment, 'Thou shalt love the Lord thy God.' But nature is so frail and weak that necessity compels her to love herself first; and this is carnal love, wherewith man loves himself first and selfishly, as it is written, 'That was not first which is spiritual but that which is natural; and afterward that which is spiritual' (1 Cor. 15:46). This is not as the precept ordains but as nature directs: 'No man ever yet hated his own flesh' (Eph. 5:29). But if, as is likely, this same love should grow excessive and, refusing to be contained within the restraining banks of necessity, should overflow into the fields of voluptuousness, then a command checks the flood, as if by a dike: 'Thou shalt love thy neighbour as thyself'. And this is right: for he who shares our nature should share our love, itself the fruit of nature. Wherefore if a man find it a burden, I will not say only to relieve his brother's needs, but to minister to his brother's pleasures, let him mortify those same affections in himself, lest he become a transgressor. He may cherish himself as tenderly as he chooses, if only he remembers to show the same indulgence to his neighbour. This is the curb of temperance imposed on thee, O man, by the law of life and conscience, lest thou shouldest follow thine own lusts to destruction, or become enslaved by those passions which are the enemies of thy true welfare. Far better divide thine enjoyments with thy neighbour than with these enemies. And if, after the counsel of the son of Sirach, thou goest not after thy desires but refrainest thyself from thine appetites (Ecclus. 18:30); if according to the apostolic precept having food and raiment thou art therewith content (1 Tim. 6:8), then thou wilt find it easy to abstain from fleshly lusts which war against the soul, and to divide with thy neighbours what thou hast refused to thine own desires. That is a temperate and righteous love which practices self-denial in order to minister to a brother's necessity. So our selfish love grows truly social, when it includes our neighbours in its circle.

But if thou art reduced to want by such benevolence, what then? What indeed, except to pray with all confidence unto Him who giveth to all men liberally and upbraideth not (James 1:5), who openeth His hand and filleth all things living with plenteousness (Ps. 145:16). For doubtless He that giveth to most men more than they need will not fail thee as to the necessaries of life, even as He hath promised: 'Seek ye the Kingdom of God, and all those things shall be added unto you' (Luke 12:31). God freely promises all things needful to those who deny themselves for love of their neighbours; and to bear the yoke of modesty and sobriety, rather than to let sin reign in our mortal body (Rom. 6:12), that is indeed to seek the Kingdom of God and to implore His aid against the tyranny of sin. It is surely justice to share our natural gifts with those who share our nature.

But if we are to love our neighbours as we ought, we must have regard to God also: for it is only in God that we can pay that debt of love aright. Now a man cannot love his neighbours in God, except he love God Himself; wherefore we must love God first, in order to love our neighbours in Him. This too, like all good things, is the Lord's doing, that we should love Him, for He hath endowed us with the possibility of love. He who created nature sustains it; nature is so constituted that its Maker is its protector for ever. Without Him nature could not have begun to be; without Him it could not subsist at all. That we might not be ignorant of this, or vainly attribute to ourselves the beneficence of our Creator, God has determined in the depths of His wise counsel that we should be subject to tribulations. So when man's strength fails and God comes to his aid, it is meet and right that man, rescued by God's hand, should glorify Him, as it is written, 'Call upon Me in the time of trouble; so will I hear thee, and thou shalt praise Me' (Ps. 50:15). In such wise, man, animal and carnal by nature, and loving only himself, begins to love God by reason of that very self-love; since he learns that in God he can accomplish all things that are good, and that without God he can do nothing.

✝ CHAPTER 9 ✝

Of the second and third degrees of love

So then in the beginning man loves God, not for God's sake, but for his own. It is something for him to know how little he can do by himself and how much by God's help, and in that knowledge to order himself rightly towards God, his sure support. But when tribulations, recurring again and again, constrain him to turn to God for unfailing help, would not even a heart as hard as iron, as cold as marble, be softened by the goodness of such a Saviour, so that he would love God not altogether selfishly, but because He is God? Let frequent troubles drive us to frequent supplications; and surely, tasting, we must see how gracious the Lord is (Ps. 34:8). Thereupon His goodness once realized draws us to love Him unselfishly, yet more than our own needs impel us to love Him selfishly: even as the Samaritans told the woman who announced that it was Christ who was at the well: 'Now we believe, not because of thy saying: for we have heard Him ourselves, and know that this is indeed the Christ, the saviour of the world' (John 4:42). We likewise bear the same witness to our own fleshly nature, saying, 'No longer do we love God because of our necessity, but because we have tasted and seen how gracious the Lord is.' Our temporal wants have a speech of their own, proclaiming the benefits they have received from God's favour. Once this is recognized it will not be hard to fulfil the commandment touching love to our neighbours; for whosoever loves God aright loves all God's creatures. Such love is pure, and finds no burden in the precept bidding us purify our souls, in obeying the truth through the Spirit unto unfeigned love of the brethren (1 Peter 1:22). Loving as he ought, he counts that command only just. Such love is thankworthy, since it is spontaneous; pure, since it is shown not in word nor tongue, but in deed and truth (1 John 3:18); just, since it repays what it has received. Whoso loves in this fashion, loves even as he is loved, and seeks no more his own but the things which are Christ's, even as Jesus sought not His own welfare, but ours, or rather ourselves. Such was the psalmist's love when he sang: 'O give thanks unto the Lord, for He is gracious' (Ps. 118:1). Whosoever praises God for His essential goodness, and not merely because of the benefits He has bestowed, does really love God for God's sake, and not selfishly. The psalmist was not speaking of such love when he said: 'So long as thou doest well unto thyself, men will speak good of thee'(Ps. 49:18). The third degree of love, we have now seen, is to love God on His own account, solely because He is God.

<h3 style="text-align:center">✝ CHAPTER 10 ✝</h3>

Of the fourth degree of love: wherein man does not even love self save for God's sake

How blessed is he who reaches the fourth degree of love, wherein one loves himself only in God! Thy righteousness standeth like the strong mountains, O God. Such love as this is God's hill, in the which it pleaseth Him to dwell. 'Who shall ascend into the hill of the Lord?' 'O that I had wings like a dove; for then would I flee away and be at rest.' 'At Salem is His tabernacle; and His dwelling in Sion.' 'Woe is me, that I am constrained to dwell with Mesech!' (Ps. 24:3; 55:6; 76:2; 120:5). When shall this flesh and blood, this earthen vessel which is my soul's tabernacle, attain thereto? When shall my soul, rapt with divine love and altogether self-forgetting, yea, become like a broken vessel, yearn wholly for God, and, joined unto the Lord, be one spirit with Him? When shall she exclaim, 'My flesh and my heart faileth; but God is the strength of my heart and my portion for ever' (Ps. 73:26). I would count him blessed and holy to whom such rapture has been vouchsafed in this mortal life, for even an instant to lose thyself, as if thou wert emptied and lost and swallowed up in God, is no human love; it is celestial. But if sometimes a poor mortal feels that heavenly joy for a rapturous moment, then this wretched life envies his happiness, the malice of daily trifles disturbs him, this body of death weighs him down, the needs of the flesh are imperative, the weakness of corruption fails him, and above all brotherly love calls him back to duty. Alas! that voice summons him to re-enter his own round of existence; and he must ever cry out lamentably, 'O Lord, I am oppressed: undertake for me' (Isa. 38:14); and again, 'O wretched man that I am! who shall deliver me from the body of this death?' (Rom. 7:24).

Seeing that the Scripture saith, God has made all for His own glory (Isa. 43:7), surely His creatures ought to conform themselves, as much as they can, to His will. In Him should all our affections centre, so that in all things we should seek only to do His will, not to please ourselves. And real happiness will come, not in gratifying our desires or in gaining transient pleasures, but in accomplishing God's will for us: even as we pray every day: 'Thy will be done in earth as it is in heaven' (Matt. 6:10). O chaste and holy love! O sweet and gracious affection! O pure and cleansed purpose, thoroughly washed and purged from any admixture of selfishness, and sweetened by contact with the divine will! To reach this state is to become godlike. As a drop of water poured into wine loses itself, and takes the colour and savour of wine; or as a bar of iron, heated red-hot, becomes like fire itself, forgetting its own nature; or as the air, radiant with sunbeams, seems not so much to be illuminated as to be light itself; so in the saints all human affections melt away by some unspeakable transmutation into the will of God. For how could God be all in all, if anything merely human remained in man? The substance will endure, but in another beauty, a higher power, a greater glory. When will that be? Who will see, who possess it? 'When shall I come to appear before the presence of God?' (Ps. 42:2). 'My heart hath talked of Thee, Seek ye My face: Thy face, Lord, will I seek' (Ps. 27:8). Lord, thinkest Thou that I, even I shall see Thy holy temple?

In this life, I think, we cannot fully and perfectly obey that precept 'Thou shalt love the Lord thy God with all thy heart, and with all thy soul, and with all thy strength, and with all thy mind' (Luke 10:27). For here the heart must take thought for the body; and the soul must energize the flesh; and the strength must guard itself from impairment. And by God's favour, must seek to increase. It is therefore impossible to offer up all our being to God, to yearn altogether for His face, so long as we must accommodate our purposes and aspirations to these fragile, sickly bodies of ours. Wherefore the soul may hope to possess the fourth degree of love, or rather to be possessed by it, only when it has been clothed upon with that spiritual and immortal body, which will be perfect, peaceful, lovely, and in everything wholly subjected to the spirit. And to this degree no human effort can attain: it is in God's power to give it to whom He wills. Then the soul will easily reach that highest stage, because no lusts of the flesh will retard its eager entrance into the joy of its Lord, and no troubles will disturb its peace. May we not think that the holy martyrs enjoyed this grace, in some degree at least, before they laid down their victorious bodies? Surely that was immeasurable strength of love which enraptured their souls, enabling them to laugh at fleshly torments and to yield their lives gladly. But even though the frightful pain could not destroy their peace of mind, it must have impaired somewhat its perfection.

✝ CHAPTER 11 ✝

Of the attainment of this perfection of love only at the resurrection

What of the souls already released from their bodies? We believe that they are overwhelmed in that vast sea of eternal light and of luminous eternity. But no one denies that they still hope and desire to receive their bodies again: whence it is plain that they are not yet wholly transformed, and that something of self remains yet unsurrendered. Not until death is swallowed up in victory, and perennial light overflows the uttermost bounds of darkness, not until celestial glory clothes our bodies, can our souls be freed entirely from self and give themselves up to God. For until then souls are bound to bodies, if not by a vital connection of sense, still by natural affection; so that without their bodies they cannot attain to their perfect consummation, nor would they if they could. And although there is no defect in the soul itself before the restoration of its body, since it has already attained to the highest state of which it is by itself capable, yet the spirit would not yearn for reunion with the flesh if without the flesh it could be consummated.

And finally, 'Right dear in the sight of the Lord is the death of His saints' (Ps. 116:15). But if their death is precious, what must such a life as theirs be! No wonder that the body shall seem to add fresh glory to the spirit; for though it is weak and mortal, it has availed not a little for mutual help. How truly he spake who said, 'All things work together for good to them that love God' (Rom. 8:28). The body is a help to the soul that loves God, even when it is ill, even when it is dead, and all the more when it is raised again from the dead: for illness is an aid to penitence; death is the gate of rest; and the resurrection will bring consummation. So, rightly, the soul would not be perfected without the body, since she recognizes that in every condition it has been needful to her good.

The flesh then is a good and faithful comrade for a good soul: since even when it is a burden it assists; when the help ceases, the burden ceases too; and when once more the assistance begins, there is no longer a burden. The first state is toilsome, but fruitful; the second is idle, but not monotonous: the third is glorious. Hear how the Bridegroom in Canticles bids us to this threefold progress: 'Eat, O friends; drink, yea, drink abundantly, O beloved' (Cant. 5:1). He offers food to those who are labouring with bodily toil; then He calls the resting souls whose bodies are laid aside, to drink; and finally He urges those who have resumed their bodies to drink abundantly. Surely those He styles 'beloved' must overflow with charity; and that is the difference between them and the others, whom He calls not 'beloved' but 'friends'. Those who yet groan in the body are dear to Him, according to the love that they have; those released from the bonds of flesh are dearer because they have become readier and abler to love than hitherto. But beyond either of these classes are those whom He calls 'beloved': for they have received the second garment, that is, their glorified bodies, so that now nothing of self remains to hinder or disturb them, and they yield themselves eagerly and entirely to loving God. This cannot be so with the others; for the first have the weight of the body to bear, and the second desires the body again with something of selfish expectation.

At first then the faithful soul eats her bread, but alas! in the sweat of her face. Dwelling in the flesh, she walks as yet by faith, which must work through love. As faith without words is dead, so work itself is food for her; even as our Lord saith, 'My meat is to do the will of Him that sent Me' (John 4:34). When the flesh is laid aside she eats no more the bread of carefulness, but is allowed to drink deeply of the wine of love, as if after a repast. But the wine is not yet unmingled; even as the Bridegroom saith in another place, 'I have drunk My wine with My milk' (Cant. 5:1). For the soul mixes with the wine of God's love the milk of natural affection, that is, the desire for her body and its glorification. She glows with the wine of holy love which she has drunk; but she is not yet all on fire, for she has tempered the potency of that wine with milk. The unmingled wine would enrapture the soul and make her wholly unconscious of self; but here is no such transport for she is still desirous of her body. When that desire is appeased, when the one lack is supplied, what should hinder her then from yielding herself utterly to God, losing her own likeness and being made like unto Him? At last she attains to that chalice of the heavenly wisdom, of which it is written, 'My cup shall be full.' Now indeed she is refreshed with the abundance of the house of God, where all selfish, carking care is done away, and where, for ever safe, she drinks the fruit of the vine, new and pure, with Christ in the Kingdom of His Father (Matt. 26:29).

It is Wisdom who spreads this threefold supper where all the repast is love; Wisdom who feeds the toilers, who gives drink to those who rest, who floods with rapture those that reign with Christ. Even as at an earthly banquet custom and nature serve meat first and then wine, so here. Before death, while we are still in mortal flesh, we eat the labours of our hands, we swallow with an effort the food so gained; but after death, we shall begin eagerly to drink in the spiritual life and finally, reunited to our bodies, and rejoicing in fullness of delight, we shall be refreshed with immortality. This is what the Bridegroom means when He saith: 'Eat, O friends; drink, yea, drink abundantly, O beloved.' Eat before death; begin to drink after death; drink abundantly after the resurrection. Rightly are they called beloved who have drunk abundantly of love; rightly do they drink abundantly who are worthy to be brought to the marriage supper of the Lamb, eating and drinking at His table in His Kingdom (Rev. 19:9; Luke 22:30). At that supper, He shall present to Himself a glorious Church, not having spot, or wrinkle, or any such thing (Eph. 5:27). Then truly shall He refresh His beloved; then He shall give them drink of His pleasures, as out of the river (Ps. 36:8). While the Bridegroom clasps the Bride in tender, pure embrace, then the rivers of the flood thereof shall make glad the city of God (Ps. 46:4). And this refers to the Son of God Himself, who will come forth and serve them, even as He hath promised; so that in that day the righteous shall be glad and rejoice before God: they shall also be merry and joyful (Ps. 68:3). Here indeed is appeasement without weariness: here never-quenched thirst for knowledge, without distress; here eternal and infinite desire which knows no want; here, finally, is that sober inebriation which comes not from drinking new wine but from enjoying God (Acts 2:13). The fourth degree of love is attained for ever when we love God only and supremely, when we do not even love ourselves except for God's sake; so that He Himself is the reward of them that love Him, the everlasting reward of an everlasting love.

✝ CHAPTER 12 ✝

Of love: out of a letter to the Carthusians

I remember writing a letter to the holy Carthusian brethren, wherein I discussed these degrees of love, and spoke of charity in other words, although not in another sense, than here. It may be well to repeat a portion of that letter, since it is easier to copy than to dictate anew.

To love our neighbours' welfare as much as our own: that is true and sincere charity out of a pure heart, and of a good conscience, and of faith unfeigned (1 Tim. 1:5). Whosoever loves his own prosperity only is proved thereby not to love good for its own sake, since he loves it on his own account. And so he cannot sing with the psalmist, 'O give thanks unto the Lord, for He is gracious' (Ps. 118:1). Such a man would praise God, not because He is goodness, but because He has been good to him: he could take to himself the reproach of the same writer, 'So long as Thou doest well unto him, he will speak good of Thee' (Ps. 49:18, Vulg.). One praises God because He is mighty, another because He is gracious, yet another solely because He is essential goodness. The first is a slave and fears for himself; the second is greedy, desiring further benefits; but the third is a son who honours his Father. He who fears, he who profits, are both concerned about self-interest. Only in the son is that charity which seeketh not her own (1 Cor. 13:5). Wherefore I take this saying, 'The law of the Lord is an undefiled law, converting the soul' (Ps. 19:7) to be of charity; because charity alone is able to turn the soul away from love of self and of the world to pure love of God. Neither fear nor self-interest can convert the soul. They may change the appearance, perhaps even the conduct, but never the object of supreme desire. Sometimes a slave may do God's work; but because he does not toil voluntarily, he remains in bondage. So a mercenary may serve God, but because he puts a price on his service, he is enchained by his own greediness. For where there is self-interest there is isolation; and such isolation is like the dark corner of a room where dust and rust befoul. Fear is the motive which constrains the slave; greed binds the selfish man, by which he is tempted when he is drawn away by his own lust and enticed (James 1:14). But neither fear nor self-interest is undefiled, nor can they convert the soul. Only charity can convert the soul, freeing it from unworthy motives.

Next, I call it undefined because it never keeps back anything of its own for itself. When a man boasts of nothing as his very own, surely all that he has is God's; and what is God's cannot be unclean. The undefiled law of the Lord is that love which bids men seek not their own, but every man another's wealth. It is called the law of the Lord as much because He lives in accordance with it as because no man has it except by gift from Him. Nor is it improper to say that even God lives by law, when that law is the law of love. For what preserves the glorious and ineffable Unity of the blessed Trinity, except love? Charity, the law of the Lord, joins the Three Persons into the unity of the Godhead and unites the holy Trinity in the bond of peace. Do not suppose me to imply that charity exists as an accidental quality of Deity; for whatever could be conceived of as wanting in the divine Nature is not God. No, it is the very substance of the Godhead; and my assertion is neither novel nor extraordinary, since St. John says, 'God is love' (1 John 4:8). One may therefore say with truth that love is at once God and the gift of God, essential love imparting the quality of love. Where the word refers to the Giver, it is the name of His very being; where the gift is meant, it is the name of a quality. Love is the eternal law whereby the universe was created and is ruled. Since all things are ordered in measure and number and weight, and nothing is left outside the realm of law, that universal law cannot itself be without a law, which is itself. So love though it did not create itself, does surely govern itself by its own decree.

✝ CHAPTER 13 ✝

Of the law of self-will and desire, of slaves and hirelings

Furthermore, the slave and the hireling have a law, not from the Lord, but of their own contriving; the one does not love God, the other loves something else more than God. They have a law of their own, not of God, I say; yet it is subject to the law of the Lord. For though they can make laws for themselves, they cannot supplant the changeless order of the eternal law. Each man is a law unto himself, when he sets up his will against the universal law, perversely striving to rival his Creator, to be wholly independent, making his will his only law. What a heavy and burdensome yoke upon all the sons of Adam, bowing down our necks, so that our life draweth nigh unto hell. 'O wretched man that I am! Who shall deliver me from the body of this death?' (Rom. 7:24). I am weighed down, I am almost overwhelmed, so that 'If the Lord had not helped me, it had not failed but my soul had been put to silence' (Ps. 94:17). Job was groaning under this load when he lamented: 'Why hast Thou set me as a mark against Thee, so that I am a burden to myself?' (Job 7:20). He was a burden to himself through the law which was of his own devising: yet he could not escape God's law, for he was set as a mark against God. The eternal law of righteousness ordains that he who will not submit to God's sweet rule shall suffer the bitter tyranny of self: but he who wears the easy yoke and light burden of love (Matt. 11:30) will escape the intolerable weight of his own self-will. Wondrously and justly does that eternal law retain rebels in subjection, so that they are unable to escape. They are subject to God's power, yet deprived of happiness with Him, unable to dwell with God in light and rest and glory everlasting. O Lord my God, 'why dost Thou not pardon my transgression and take away mine iniquity?' (Job 7:21). Then freed from the weight of my own will, I can breathe easily under the light burden of love. I shall not be coerced by fear, nor allured by mercenary desires; for I shall be led by the Spirit of God, that free Spirit whereby Thy sons are led, which beareth witness with my spirit that I am among the children of God (Rom. 8:16). So shall I be under that law which is Thine; and as Thou art, so shall I be in the world. Whosoever do what the apostle bids, 'Owe no man anything, but to love one another' (Rom. 13:8), are doubtless even in this life conformed to God's likeness: they are neither slaves nor hirelings but sons.

✝ CHAPTER 14 ✝
Of the law of the love of sons

Now the children have their law, even though it is written, 'The law is not made for a righteous man' (1 Tim. 1:9). For it must be remembered that there is one law having to do with the spirit of servitude, given to fear, and another with the spirit of liberty, given in tenderness. The children are not constrained by the first, yet they could not exist without the second: even as St. Paul writes, 'Ye have not received the spirit of bondage again to fear; but ye have received the spirit of adoption, whereby we cry, Abba, Father' (Rom. 8:15). And again to show that that same righteous man was not under the law, he says: 'To them that are under the law, I became as under the law, that I might gain them that are under the law; to them that are without law, as without law (being not without law to God, but under the law to Christ)' (1 Cor. 9:20–21). So it is rightly said, not that the righteous do not have a law, but, 'The law is not made for a righteous man', that is, it is not imposed on rebels but freely given to those willingly obedient, by Him whose goodness established it. Wherefore the Lord saith meekly: 'Take My yoke upon you', which may be paraphrased thus: 'I do not force it on you, if you are reluctant; but if you will you may bear it. Otherwise it will be weariness, not rest, that you shall find for your souls.'

Love is a good and pleasant law; it is not only easy to bear, but it makes the laws of slaves and hirelings tolerable; not destroying but completing them; as the Lord saith: 'I am not come to destroy the law, but to fulfill' (Matt. 5:17). It tempers the fear of the slave, it regulates the desires of the hireling, it mitigates the severity of each. Love is never without fear, but it is godly fear. Love is never without desire, but it is lawful desire. So love perfects the law of service by infusing devotion; it perfects the law of wages by restraining covetousness. Devotion mixed with fear does not destroy it, but purges it. Then the burden of fear which was intolerable while it was only servile, becomes tolerable; and the fear itself remains ever pure and filial. For though we read: 'Perfect love casteth out fear' (1 John 4:18), we understand by that the suffering which is never absent from servile fear, the cause being put for the effect, as often elsewhere. So, too, self-interest is restrained within due bounds when love supervenes; for then it rejects evil things altogether, prefers better things to those merely good, and cares for the good only on account of the better. In like manner, by God's grace, it will come about that man will love his body and all things pertaining to his body, for the sake of his soul. He will love his soul for God's sake; and he will love God for Himself alone.

✝ CHAPTER 15 ✝

Of the four degrees of love, and of the blessed state of the heavenly Fatherland

Nevertheless, since we are carnal and are born of the lust of the flesh, it must be that our desire and our love shall have its beginning in the flesh. But rightly guided by the grace of God through these degrees, it will have its consummation in the spirit: for that was not first which is spiritual but that which is natural; and afterward that which is spiritual (1 Cor. 15:46). And we must bear the image of the earthly first, before we can bear the image of the heavenly. At first, man loves himself for his own sake. That is the flesh, which can appreciate nothing beyond itself. Next, he perceives that he cannot exist by himself, and so begins by faith to seek after God, and to love Him as something necessary to his own welfare. That is the second degree, to love God, not for God's sake, but selfishly. But when he has learned to worship God and to seek Him aright, meditating on God, reading God's Word, praying and obeying His commandments, he comes gradually to know what God is, and finds Him altogether lovely. So, having tasted and seen how gracious the Lord is (Ps. 34:8), he advances to the third degree, when he loves God, not merely as his benefactor but as God. Surely he must remain long in this state; and I know not whether it would be possible to make further progress in this life to that fourth degree and perfect condition wherein man loves himself solely for God's sake. Let any who have attained so far bear record; I confess it seems beyond my powers. Doubtless it will be reached when the good and faithful servant shall have entered into the joy of his Lord (Matt. 25:21), and been satisfied with the plenteousness of God's house (Ps. 36:8). For then in wondrous wise he will forget himself and as if delivered from self, he will grow wholly God's. Joined unto the Lord, he will then be one spirit with Him (1 Cor. 6:17). This was what the prophet meant, I think, when he said: 'I will go forth in the strength of the Lord God: and will make mention of Thy righteousness only' (Ps. 71:16). Surely he knew that when he should go forth in the spiritual strength of the Lord, he would have been freed from the infirmities of the flesh, and would have nothing carnal to think of, but would be wholly filled in his spirit with the righteousness of the Lord.

In that day the members of Christ can say of themselves what St. Paul testified concerning their Head: 'Yea, though we have known Christ after the flesh, yet now henceforth know we Him no more' (2 Cor. 5:16). None shall thereafter know himself after the flesh; for 'flesh and blood cannot inherit the Kingdom of God' (1 Cor. 15:50). Not that there will be no true substance of the flesh, but all carnal needs will be taken away, and the love of the flesh will be swallowed up in the love of the spirit, so that our weak human affections will be made divinely strong. Then the net of charity which as it is drawn through the great and wide sea doth not cease to gather every kind of fish, will be drawn to the shore; and the bad will be cast away, while only the good will be kept (Matt. 13:48). In this life the net of all-including love gathers every kind of fish into its wide folds, becoming all things to all men, sharing adversity or prosperity, rejoicing with them that do rejoice, and weeping with them that weep (Rom. 12:15). But when the net is drawn to shore, whatever causes pain will be rejected, like the bad fish, while only what is pleasant and joyous will be kept. Do you not recall how St. Paul said: 'Who is weak and I am not weak? Who is offended and I burn not?' And yet weakness and offence were far from him. So too he bewailed many which had sinned already and had not repented, though he was neither the sinner nor the penitent. But there is a city made glad by the rivers of the flood of grace (Ps. 46:4), and whose gates the Lord loveth more than all the dwellings of Jacob (Ps. 87:2). In it is no place for lamentation over those condemned to everlasting fire, prepared for the devil and his angels (Matt. 25:41). In these earthly dwellings, though men may rejoice, yet they have still other battles to fight, other mortal perils to undergo. But in the heavenly Fatherland no sorrow nor sadness can enter: as it is written, 'The habitation of all rejoicing ones is in Thee' (Ps. 87:7, Vulg.); and again, 'Everlasting joy shall be unto them' (Isa. 61:7). Nor could they recall things piteous, for then they will make mention of God's righteousness only. Accordingly, there will be no need for the exercise of compassion, for no misery will be there to inspire pity.

THE INSTITUTES OF THE CHRISTIAN RELIGION

by

 JOHN CALVIN

Based on a translation by Henry Beveridge, first published in 1845

CONTENTS

✛ PART I ✛

KNOWING GOD AND OURSELVES

✛ BOOK ONE ✛

THE KNOWLEDGE OF GOD THE CREATOR

✛ PART II ✛

GOD'S WORD AND GOD'S SPIRIT

✛ PART I ✛

KNOWING GOD AND OURSELVES

✛ BOOK ONE ✛

THE KNOWLEDGE OF GOD THE CREATOR

✛ CHAPTER 1 ✛
The knowledge of God and of ourselves mutually connected
Nature of the connection.

Sections
1. The sum of true wisdom – the knowledge of God and of ourselves. Effects of the latter.
2. Effects of the knowledge of God, in humbling our pride, unveiling our hypocrisy, demonstrating the absolute perfections of God, and our own utter helplessness.
3. Effects of the knowledge of God illustrated by the examples (1) of holy patriarchs, (2) of holy angels, (3) of the sun and moon.

1. Our wisdom, in so far as it ought to be deemed true and solid Wisdom, consists almost entirely of two parts: the knowledge of God and of ourselves. But as these are connected together by many ties, it is not easy to determine which of the two precedes and gives birth to the other. For, in the first place, no man can survey himself without forthwith turning his thoughts towards the God in whom he lives and moves; because it is perfectly obvious, that the endowments which we possess cannot possibly be from ourselves; nay, that our very being is nothing else than subsistence in God alone. In the second place, those blessings which unceasingly distill to us from heaven, are like streams conducting us to the fountain. Here, again, the infinitude of good which resides in God becomes more apparent from our poverty. In particular, the miserable ruin into which the revolt of the first man has plunged us, compels us to turn our eyes upwards; not only that while hungry and famishing we may thence ask what we want, but being aroused by fear may learn humility. For as there exists in man something like a world of misery, and ever since we were stript of the divine attire our naked shame discloses an immense series of disgraceful properties every man, being stung by the consciousness of his own unhappiness, in this way necessarily obtains at least some knowledge of God. Thus, our feeling of ignorance, vanity, want, weakness, in short, depravity and corruption, reminds us, that in the Lord, and none but He, dwell the true light of wisdom, solid virtue, exuberant goodness. We are accordingly urged by our own evil things to consider the good things of God;

and, indeed, we cannot aspire to Him in earnest until we have begun to be displeased with ourselves. For what man is not disposed to rest in himself? Who, in fact, does not thus rest, so long as he is unknown to himself; that is, so long as he is contented with his own endowments, and unconscious or unmindful of his misery? Every person, therefore, on coming to the knowledge of himself, is not only urged to seek God, but is also led as by the hand to find him.

2.   On the other hand, it is evident that man never attains to a true self-knowledge until he has previously contemplated the face of God, and come down after such contemplation to look into himself. For (such is our innate pride) we always seem to ourselves just, and upright, and wise, and holy, until we are convinced, by clear evidence, of our injustice, vileness, folly, and impurity. Convinced, however, we are not, if we look to ourselves only, and not to the Lord also – He being the only standard by the application of which this conviction can be produced. For, since we are all naturally prone to hypocrisy, any empty semblance of righteousness is quite enough to satisfy us instead of righteousness itself. And since nothing appears within us or around us that is not tainted with very great impurity, so long as we keep our mind within the confines of human pollution, anything which is in some small degree less defiled delights us as if it were most pure just as an eye, to which nothing but black had been previously presented, deems an object of a whitish, or even of a brownish hue, to be perfectly white. Nay, the bodily sense may furnish a still stronger illustration of the extent to which we are deluded in estimating the powers of the mind. If, at mid-day, we either look down to the ground, or on the surrounding objects which lie open to our view, we think ourselves endued with a very strong and piercing eyesight; but when we look up to the sun, and gaze at it unveiled, the sight which did excellently well for the earth is instantly so dazzled and confounded by the refulgence, as to oblige us to confess that our acuteness in discerning terrestrial objects is mere dimness when applied to the sun. Thus too, it happens in estimating our spiritual qualities. So long as we do not look beyond the earth, we are quite pleased with our own righteousness, wisdom, and virtue; we address ourselves in the most flattering terms, and seem only less than demigods. But should we once begin to raise our thoughts to God, and reflect what kind of Being he is, and how absolute the perfection of that righteousness, and wisdom, and virtue, to which, as a standard, we are bound to be conformed, what formerly delighted us by its false show of righteousness will become polluted with the greatest iniquity; what strangely imposed upon us under the name of wisdom will disgust by its extreme folly; and what presented the appearance of virtuous energy will be condemned as the most miserable impotence. So far are those qualities in us, which seem most perfect, from corresponding to the divine purity.

3.   Hence that dread and amazement with which as Scripture uniformly relates, holy men were struck and overwhelmed whenever they beheld the presence of God. When we see those who previously stood firm and secure so quaking with terror, that the fear of death takes hold of them, nay, they are, in a manner, swallowed up and annihilated, the inference to be drawn is that men are never duly touched and impressed with a conviction of their insignificance, until they have contrasted themselves with the majesty of God. Frequent examples of this consternation occur both in the book of Judges and the Prophetical Writings; so much so, that it was a common expression among the people of God, 'We shall die, for we have seen the Lord.' Hence the book of Job, also, in humbling men under a conviction of their folly, feebleness, and

pollution, always derives its chief argument from descriptions of the Divine wisdom, virtue, and purity. Nor without cause: for we see Abraham the readier to acknowledge himself but dust and ashes the nearer he approaches to behold the glory of the Lord, and Elijah unable to wait with unveiled face for His approach; so dreadful is the sight. And what can man do, man who is but rottenness and a worm, when even the Cherubim themselves must veil their faces in very terror? To this, undoubtedly, the prophet Isaiah refers, when he says (Isa. 24:23), 'The moon shall be confounded, and the sun ashamed, when the Lord of Hosts shall reign'; i.e., when he shall exhibit his refulgence, and give a nearer view of it, the brightest objects will, in comparison, be covered with darkness. But though the knowledge of God and the knowledge of ourselves are bound together by a mutual tie, due arrangement requires that we treat of the former in the first place, and then descend to the latter.

✚ CHAPTER 2 ✚

What it is to know God. Tendency of this knowledge.

Sections

1. The knowledge of God the Creator defined. The substance of this knowledge, and the use to be made of it.
2. Further illustration of the use, together with a necessary reproof of vain curiosity, and refutation of the Epicureans. The character of God as it appears to the pious mind, contrasted with the absurd views of the Epicureans. Religion defined.

1. By the knowledge of God, I understand that by which we not only conceive that there is some God, but also apprehend what it is for our interest, and conducive to his glory, what, in short, it is befitting to know concerning him. For, properly speaking, we cannot say that God is known where there is no religion or piety. I am not now referring to that species of knowledge by which men, in themselves lost and under curse, apprehend God as a Redeemer in Christ the Mediator. I speak only of that simple and primitive knowledge, to which the mere course of nature would have conducted us, had Adam stood upright. For although no man will now, in the present ruin of the human race, perceive God to be either a father, or the author of salvation, or propitious in any respect, until Christ interpose to make our peace; still it is one thing to perceive that God our Maker supports us by his power, rules us by his providence, fosters us by his goodness, and visits us with all kinds of blessings, and another thing to embrace the grace of reconciliation offered to us in Christ. Since, then, the Lord first appears, as well in the creation of the world as in the general doctrine of Scripture, simply as a Creator, and afterwards as a Redeemer in Christ – a twofold knowledge of him hence arises: of these the former is now to be considered, the latter will afterwards follow in its order. But although our mind cannot conceive of God, without rendering some worship to him, it will not, however, be sufficient simply to hold that he is the only being whom all ought to worship and adore, unless we are also persuaded that he is the fountain of all goodness, and that we must seek everything in him, and in none but him. My meaning is: we must be persuaded not only that as he once formed the world, so he sustains it by his boundless power, governs it by his wisdom, preserves

it by his goodness, in particular, rules the human race with justice and judgment, bears with them in mercy, shields them by his protection; but also that not a particle of light, or wisdom, or justice, or power, or rectitude, or genuine truth, will anywhere be found, which does not flow from him, and of which he is not the cause; in this way we must learn to expect and ask all things from him, and thankfully ascribe to him whatever we receive. For this sense of the divine perfections is the proper master to teach us piety, out of which religion springs. By piety I mean that union of reverence and love to God which the knowledge of his benefits inspires. For, until men feel that they owe everything to God, that they are cherished by his paternal care, and that he is the author of all their blessings, so that nought is to be looked for away from him, they will never submit to him in voluntary obedience; nay, unless they place their entire happiness in him, they will never yield up their whole selves to him in truth and sincerity.

   2. Those, therefore, who, in considering this question, propose to inquire what the essence of God is, only delude us with frigid speculations, it being much more our interest to know what kind of being God is, and what things are agreeable to his nature. For, of what use is it to join Epicures in acknowledging some God who has cast off the care of the world, and only delights himself in ease? What avails it, in short, to know a God with whom we have nothing to do? The effect of our knowledge rather ought to be, *first*, to teach us reverence and fear; and, *secondly*, to induce us, under its guidance and teaching, to ask every good thing from him, and, when it is received, ascribe it to him. For how can the idea of God enter your mind without instantly giving rise to the thought, that since you are his workmanship, you are bound, by the very law of creation, to submit to his authority? – that your life is due to him? – that whatever you do ought to have reference to him? If so, it undoubtedly follows that your life is sadly corrupted, if it is not framed in obedience to him, since his will ought to be the law of our lives. On the other hand, your idea of his nature is not clear unless you acknowledge him to be the origin and fountain of all goodness. Hence would arise both confidence in him, and a desire of cleaving to him, did not the depravity of the human mind lead it away from the proper course of investigation. For, first of all, the pious mind does not devise for itself any kind of God, but looks alone to the one true God; nor does it feign for him any character it pleases, but is contented to have him in the character in which he manifests himself always guarding, with the utmost diligences against transgressing his will, and wandering, with daring presumptions from the right path. He by whom God is thus known perceiving how he governs all things, confides in him as his guardian and protector, and casts himself entirely upon his faithfulness, perceiving him to be the source of every blessing, if he is in any strait or feels any want, he instantly recurs to his protection and trusts to his aid, persuaded that he is good and merciful, he reclines upon him with sure confidence, and doubts not that, in the divine clemency, a remedy will be provided for his every time of need, acknowledging him as his Father and his Lord he considers himself bound to have respect to his authority in all things, to reverence his majesty, aim at the advancement of his glory, and obey his commands, regarding him as a just judge, armed with severity to punish crimes, he keeps the judgment-seat always in his view. Standing in awe of it, he curbs himself, and fears to provoke his anger. Nevertheless, he is not so terrified by an apprehension of judgment as to wish he could withdraw himself, even if the means of escape lay before him; nay, he embraces him not less as the avenger of wickedness than as the rewarder of the righteous; because he perceives that it equally appertains to his glory to store up punishment for the one, and eternal life for the other. Besides, it is not the mere fear of punishment that restrains him from sin. Loving and revering God as his father, honouring and obeying him as his master, although there were no hell, he would revolt at the very idea of offending him.

Such is pure and genuine religion, namely, confidence in God coupled with serious fear – fear, which both includes in it willing reverence, and brings along with it such legitimate worship as is prescribed by the law. And it ought to be more carefully considered that all men promiscuously do homage to God, but very few truly reverence him. On all hands there is abundance of ostentatious ceremonies, but sincerity of heart is rare.

✝ CHAPTER 3 ✝
The knowledge of God naturally implanted in the human mind.

Sections

1. The knowledge of God being manifested to all makes the reprobate without excuse. Universal belief and acknowledgment of the existence of God.

1. That there exists in the human minds and indeed by natural instinct, some sense of Deity, we hold to be beyond dispute, since God himself, to prevent any man from pretending ignorance, has endued all men with some idea of his Godhead, the memory of which he constantly renews and occasionally enlarges, that all to a man being aware that there is a God, and that he is their Maker, may be condemned by their own conscience when they neither worship him nor consecrate their lives to his service. Certainly, if there is any quarter where it may be supposed that God is unknown, the most likely for such an instance to exist is among the dullest tribes farthest removed from civilisation. But, as a heathen tells us, there is no nation so barbarous, no race so brutish, as not to be imbued with the conviction that there is a God. Even those who, in other respects, seem to differ least from the lower animals, constantly retain some sense of religion; so thoroughly has this common conviction possessed the mind, so firmly is it stamped on the breasts of all men. Since, then, there never has been, from the very first, any quarter of the globe, any city, any household even, without religion, this amounts to a tacit confession, that a sense of Deity is inscribed on every heart. Nay, even idolatry is ample evidence of this fact. For we know how reluctant man is to lower himself, in order to set other creatures above him. Therefore, when he chooses to worship wood and stone rather than be thought to have no God, it is evident how very strong this impression of a Deity must be; since it is more difficult to obliterate it from the mind of man, than to break down the feelings of his nature – these certainly being broken down, when, in opposition to his natural haughtiness, he spontaneously humbles himself before the meanest object as an act of reverence to God.

✝ CHAPTER 4 ✝

The knowledge of God stifled or corrupted, ignorantly or maliciously.

Sections

1. The knowledge of God suppressed by ignorance, many falling away into superstition. Such persons, however, inexcusable, because their error is accompanied with pride and stubbornness.
2. Stubbornness the companion of impiety.
3. No pretext can justify superstition. This proved, first, from reason; and, secondly, from Scripture.
4. The wicked never willingly come into the presence of God. Hence their hypocrisy. Hence, too, their sense of Deity leads to no good result.

1. But though experience testifies that a seed of religion is divinely sown in all, scarcely one in a hundred is found who cherishes it in his heart, and not one in whom it grows to maturity so far is it from yielding fruit in its season. Moreover, while some lose themselves in superstitious observances, and others, of set purpose, wickedly revolt from God, the result is that, in regard to the true knowledge of him, all are so degenerate, that in no part of the world can genuine godliness be found. In saying that some fall away into superstition, I mean not to insinuate that their excessive absurdity frees them from guilt; for the blindness under which they labour is almost invariably accompanied with vain pride and stubbornness. Mingled vanity and pride appear in this, that when miserable men do seek after God, instead of ascending higher than themselves as they ought to do, they measure him by their own carnal stupidity, and, neglecting solid inquiry, fly off to indulge their curiosity in vain speculation. Hence, they do not conceive of him in the character in which he is manifested, but imagine him to be whatever their own rashness has devised. This abyss standing open, they cannot move one footstep without rushing headlong to destruction. With such an idea of God, nothing which they may attempt to offer in the way of worship or obedience can have any value in his sight, because it is not him they worship, but, instead of him, the dream and figment of their own heart. This corrupt procedure is admirably described by Paul, when he says, that 'thinking to be wise, they became fools' (Rom. 1:22). He had previously said that 'they became vain in their imaginations', but lest any should suppose them blameless, he afterwards adds that they were deservedly blinded, because, not contented with sober inquiry, because, arrogating to themselves more than they have any title to do, they of their own accord court darkness, nay, bewitch themselves with perverse, empty show. Hence it is that their folly, the result not only of vain curiosity, but of licentious desire and overweening confidence in the pursuit of forbidden knowledge, cannot be excused.

2. The expression of David (Pss. 14:1; 53:1), 'The fool hath said in his heart, There is no God,' is primarily applied to those who, as will shortly farther appear, stifle the light of nature, and intentionally stupefy themselves. We see many, after they have become hardened in a daring course of sin, madly banishing all remembrance of God, though spontaneously suggested to them from within, by natural sense. To show how detestable this madness is, the Psalmist introduces them as distinctly denying that there is a God, because although they do

not disown his essence, they rob him of his justice and providence, and represent him as sitting idly in heaven. Nothing being less accordant with the nature of God than to cast off the government of the world, leaving it to chance, and so to wink at the crimes of men that they may wanton with impunity in evil courses; it follows, that every man who indulges in security, after extinguishing all fear of divine judgment, virtually denies that there is a God. As a just punishment of the wicked, after they have closed their own eyes, God makes their hearts dull and heavy, and hence, seeing, they see not. David, indeed, is the best interpreter of his own meaning, when he says elsewhere, the wicked has 'no fear of God before his eyes' (Ps. 36:1); and, again, 'He has said in his heart, God has forgotten; he hideth his face; he will never see it.' Thus, although they are forced to acknowledge that there is some God, they, however, rob him of his glory by denying his power. For, as Paul declares, 'If we believe not, he abideth faithful, he cannot deny himself' (2 Tim. 2:13); so those who feign to themselves a dead and dumb idol, are truly said to deny God. It is, moreover, to be observed, that though they struggle with their own convictions, and would fain not only banish God from their minds, but from heaven also, their stupefaction is never so complete as to secure them from being occasionally dragged before the divine tribunal. Still, as no fear restrains them from rushing violently in the face of God, so long as they are hurried on by that blind impulse, it cannot be denied that their prevailing state of mind in regard to him is brutish oblivion.

3. In this way, the vain pretext which many employ to clothe their superstition is over-thrown. They deem it enough that they have some kind of zeal for religion, how preposterous soever it may be, not observing that true religion must be conformable to the will of God as its unerring standard; that he can never deny himself, and is no spectre, to be metamorphosed at each individual's caprice. It is easy to see how superstition, with its false glosses, mocks God, while it tries to please him. Usually fastening merely on things on which he has declared he sets no value, it either contemptuously overlooks, or even undisguisedly rejects, the things which he expressly enjoins, or in which we are assured that he takes pleasure. Those, therefore, who set up a fictitious worship, merely worship and adore their own delirious fancies; indeed, they would never dare so to trifle with God, had they not previously fashioned him after their own childish conceits. Hence that vague and wandering opinion of Deity is declared by an apostle to be ignorance of God: 'Howbeit, then, when ye knew not God, ye did service unto them which by nature are no gods.' And he elsewhere declares, that the Ephesians were 'without God' (Eph. 2:12) at the time when they wandered without any correct knowledge of him. It makes little difference, at least in this respect, whether you hold the existence of one God, or a plurality of gods, since, in both cases alike, by departing from the true God, you have nothing left but an execrable idol. It remains, therefore, to conclude with Lactantius (*Instit. Div.* Lib. 1:2, 6), 'No religion is genuine that is not in accordance with truth.'

4. To this fault they add a second – that when they do think of God it is against their will; never approaching him without being dragged into his presence, and when there, instead of the voluntary fear flowing from reverence of the divine majesty, feeling only that forced and servile fear which divine judgment extorts, judgment which, from the impossibility of escape, they are compelled to dread, but which, while they dread, they at the same time also hate. To impiety, and to it alone, the saying of Statius properly applies: 'Fear first brought gods into the world' (*Theb.* Lib. 1). Those whose inclinations are at variance with the justice of God, knowing

that his tribunal has been erected for the punishment of transgression, earnestly wish that that tribunal were overthrown. Under the influence of this feeling they are actually warring against God, justice being one of his essential attributes. Perceiving that they are always within reach of his power, that resistance and evasion are alike impossible, they fear and tremble. Accordingly, to avoid the appearance of condemning a majesty by which all are overawed, they have recourse to some species of religious observance, never ceasing meanwhile to defile themselves with every kind of vice, and add crime to crime, until they have broken the holy law of the Lord in every one of its requirements, and set his whole righteousness at nought; at all events, they are not so restrained by their semblance of fear as not to luxuriate and take pleasure in iniquity, choosing rather to indulge their carnal propensities than to curb them with the bridle of the Holy Spirit. But since this shadow of religion (it scarcely even deserves to be called a shadow) is false and vain, it is easy to infer how much this confused knowledge of God differs from that piety which is instilled into the breasts of believers, and from which alone true religion springs. And yet hypocrites would fain, by means of tortuous windings, make a show of being near to God at the very time they are fleeing from him. For while the whole life ought to be one perpetual course of obedience, they rebel without fear in almost all their actions, and seek to appease him with a few paltry sacrifices; while they ought to serve him with integrity of heart and holiness of life, they endeavour to procure his favour by means of frivolous devices and punctilios of no value. Nay, they take greater license in their grovelling indulgences, because they imagine that they can fulfil their duty to him by preposterous expiations; in short, while their confidence ought to have been fixed upon him, they put him aside, and rest in themselves or the creatures. At length they bewilder themselves in such a maze of error, that the darkness of ignorance obscures, and ultimately extinguishes, those sparks which were designed to show them the glory of God. Still, however, the conviction that there is some Deity continues to exist, like a plant which can never be completely eradicated, though so corrupt, that it is only capable of producing the worst of fruit. Nay, we have still stronger evidence of the proposition for which I now contend – that a sense of Deity is naturally engraven on the human heart, in the fact, that the very reprobate are forced to acknowledge it. When at their ease, they can jest about God, and talk pertly and loquaciously in disparagement of his power; but should despair, from any cause, overtake them, it will stimulate them to seek him, and dictate ejaculatory prayers, proving that they were not entirely ignorant of God, but had perversely suppressed feelings which ought to have been earlier manifested.

✝ CHAPTER 5 ✝

The knowledge of God conspicuous in the creation, and
continual government of the world.

This chapter consists of two parts: (1) The former, which occupies the first ten sections, divides all the works of God into two great classes, and elucidates the knowledge of God as displayed in each class. The one class is treated of in the first six, and the other in the four following sections: (2) The latter part of the chapter shows, that, in consequence of the extreme stupidity of men, those manifestations of God, however perspicuous, lead to no useful result. This latter part, which commences at the eleventh section, is continued to the end of the chapter.

Sections

1. The invisible and incomprehensible essence of God, to a certain extent, made visible in his works.
2. This declared by the first class of works – the admirable motions of the heavens and the earth, the symmetry of the human body, and the connection of its parts; in short, the various objects which are presented to every eye.
11. The second part of the chapter, which describes the stupidity both of learned and unlearned, in ascribing the whole order of things, and the admirable arrangements of divine Providence, to fortune.
14. Though irradiated by the wondrous glories of creation, we cease not to follow our own ways.
15. Our conduct altogether inexcusable, the dullness of perception being attributable to ourselves, while we are fully reminded of the true path, both by the structure and the government of the world.

1. Since the perfection of blessedness consists in the knowledge of God, he has been pleased, in order that none might be excluded from the means of obtaining felicity, not only to deposit in our minds that seed of religion of which we have already spoken, but so to manifest his perfections in the whole structure of the universe, and daily place himself in our view, that we cannot open our eyes without being compelled to behold him. His essence, indeed, is incomprehensible, utterly transcending all human thought; but on each of his works his glory is engraven in characters so bright, so distinct, and so illustrious, that none, however dull and illiterate, can plead ignorance as their excuse. Hence, with perfect truth, the Psalmist exclaims, 'He covereth himself with light as with a garment' (Ps. 104:2); as if he had said, that God for the first time was arrayed in visible attire when, in the creation of the world, he displayed those glorious banners, on which, to whatever side we turn, we behold his perfections visibly portrayed. In the same place, the Psalmist aptly compares the expanded heavens to his royal tent, and says, 'He layeth the beams of his chambers in the waters, maketh the clouds his chariot, and walketh upon the wings of the wind', sending forth the winds and lightnings as his swift messengers. And because the glory of his power and wisdom is more refulgent in the firmament, it is frequently designated as his palace. And, first, wherever you turn your eyes, there is no portion of the world, however minute, that does not exhibit at least some sparks of beauty; while it is impossible to contemplate the vast and beautiful fabric as it extends around, without being overwhelmed by the immense weight of glory. Hence, the author of the Epistle to the Hebrews elegantly describes the visible worlds as images of the invisible (Heb. 11:3), the elegant structure of the world serving us as a kind of mirror, in which we may behold God, though otherwise invisible. For the same reason, the Psalmist attributes language to celestial objects, a language which all nations understand (Ps. 19:1), the manifestation of the Godhead being too clear to escape the notice of any people, however obtuse. The apostle Paul, stating this still more clearly, says, 'That which may be known of God is manifest in them, for God has showed it unto them.

For the invisible things of him from the creation of the world are clearly seen, being understood by the things that are made, even his eternal power and Godhead' (Rom. 1:20).

2. In attestation of his wondrous wisdom, both the heavens and the earth present us with innumerable proofs, not only those more recondite proofs which astronomy, medicine, and all the natural sciences, are designed to illustrate, but proofs which force themselves on the notice of the most illiterate peasant, who cannot open his eyes without beholding them. It is true, indeed, that those who are more or less intimately acquainted with those liberal studies are thereby assisted and enabled to obtain a deeper insight into the secret workings of divine wisdom. No man, however, though he be ignorant of these, is incapacitated for discerning such proofs of creative wisdom as may well cause him to break forth in admiration of the Creator. To investigate the motions of the heavenly bodies, to determine their positions, measure their distances, and ascertain their properties, demands skill, and a more careful examination; and where these are so employed, as the Providence of God is thereby more fully unfolded, so it is reasonable to suppose that the mind takes a loftier flight, and obtains brighter views of his glory. Still, none who have the use of their eyes can be ignorant of the divine skill manifested so conspicuously in the endless variety, yet distinct and well-ordered array, of the heavenly host; and, therefore, it is plain that the Lord has furnished every man with abundant proofs of his wisdom. The same is true in regard to the structure of the human frame. To determine the connection of its parts, its symmetry and beauty, with the skill of a Galen (*De Usu Partium*), requires singular acuteness; and yet all men acknowledge that the human body bears on its face such proofs of ingenious contrivance as are sufficient to proclaim the admirable wisdom of its Maker.

11. Bright, however, as is the manifestation which God gives both of himself and his immortal kingdom in the mirror of his works, so great is our stupidity, so dull are we in regard to these bright manifestations, that we derive no benefit from them. For in regard to the fabric and admirable arrangement of the universe, how few of us are there who, in lifting our eyes to the heavens, or looking abroad on the various regions of the earth, ever think of the Creator? Do we not rather overlook Him, and sluggishly content ourselves with a view of his works? And then in regard to supernatural events, though these are occurring every day, how few are there who ascribe them to the ruling providence of God – how many who imagine that they are casual results produced by the blind evolutions of the wheel of chance? Even when under the guidance and direction of these events, we are in a manner forced to the contemplation of God (a circumstance which all must occasionally experience), and are thus led to form some impressions of Deity, we immediately fly off to carnal dreams and depraved fictions, and so by our vanity corrupt heavenly truth. This far, indeed, we differ from each other, in that every one appropriates to himself some peculiar error; but we are all alike in this, that we substitute monstrous fictions for the one living and true God – a disease not confined to obtuse and vulgar minds, but affecting the noblest, and those who, in other respects, are singularly acute. How lavishly in this respect have the whole body of philosophers betrayed their stupidity and want of sense? To say nothing of the others whose absurdities are of a still grosser description, how completely does Plato, the soberest and most religious of them all, lose himself in his round globe? What must be the case with the rest, when the leaders, who ought to have set them an example, commit such blunders, and labour under such hallucinations? In like manner, while the government of the world places the doctrine of providence beyond dispute, the practical result is the same as if it were believed that all things were carried hither and thither at the caprice of chance; so prone are we to vanity and error. I am still referring to the most distinguished of the philosophers, and not to the common herd, whose madness in profaning the truth of God exceeds all bounds.

14. In vain for us, therefore, does Creation exhibit so many bright lamps lighted up to show forth the glory of its Author. Though they beam upon us from every quarter, they are altogether insufficient of themselves to lead us into the right path. Some sparks, undoubtedly, they do throw out; but these are quenched before they can give forth a brighter effulgence. Wherefore, the apostle, in the very place where he says that the worlds are images of invisible things, adds that it is by *faith* we understand that they were framed by the word of God (Heb. 11:3); thereby intimating that the invisible Godhead is indeed represented by such displays, but that we have no eyes to perceive it until they are enlightened through faith by internal revelation from God. When Paul says that that which may be known of God is manifested by the creation of the world, he does not mean such a manifestation as may be comprehended by the wit of man (Rom. 1:19); on the contrary, he shows that it has no further effect than to render us inexcusable (Acts 17:27). And though he says, elsewhere, that we have not far to seek for God, inasmuch as he dwells within us, he shows, in another passage, to what extent this nearness to God is availing. God, says he, 'in times past, suffered all nations to walk in their own ways. Nevertheless, he left not himself without witness, in that he did good, and gave us rain from heaven, and fruitful seasons, filling our hearts with food and gladness' (Acts 14:16, 17). But though God is not left without a witness, while, with numberless varied acts of kindness, he woos men to the knowledge of himself, yet they cease not to follow their own ways, in other words, deadly errors.

15. But though we are deficient in natural powers which might enable us to rise to a pure and clear knowledge of God, still, as the dullness which prevents us is within, there is no room for excuse. We cannot plead ignorance, without being at the same time convicted by our own consciences both of sloth and ingratitude. It were, indeed, a strange defence for man to pretend that he has no ears to hear the truth, while dumb creatures have voices loud enough to declare it; to allege that he is unable to see that which creatures without eyes demonstrate, to excuse himself on the ground of weakness of mind, while all creatures without reason are able to teach. Wherefore, when we wander and go astray, we are justly shut out from every species of excuse, because all things point to the right path. But while man must bear the guilt of corrupting the seed of divine knowledge so wondrously deposited in his mind, and preventing it from bearing good and genuine fruit, it is still most true that we are not sufficiently instructed by that bare and simple, but magnificent testimony which the creatures bear to the glory of their Creator. For no sooner do we, from a survey of the world, obtain some slight knowledge of Deity, than we pass by the true God, and set up in his stead the dream and phantom of our own brain, drawing away the praise of justice, wisdom, and goodness, from the fountain-head, and transferring it to some other quarter. Moreover, by the erroneous estimate we form, we either so obscure or pervert his daily works, as at once to rob them of their glory and the author of them of his just praise.

PART II

GOD'S WORD AND GOD'S SPIRIT

✝ CHAPTER 6 ✝

The need of Scripture, as a guide and teacher,
in coming to God as a creator.

Sections

1. God gives his elect a better help to the knowledge of himself – the Holy Scriptures. This he did from the very first.
3. This view confirmed (1) by the depravity of our nature making it necessary in every one who would know God to have recourse to the word; (2) from those passages of the Psalms in which God is introduced as reigning.

    1. Therefore, though the effulgence which is presented to every eye, both in the heavens and on the earth, leaves the ingratitude of man without excuse, since God, in order to bring the whole human race under the same condemnation, holds forth to all, without exception, a mirror of his Deity in his works, another and better help must be given to guide us properly to God as a Creator. Not in vain, therefore, has he added the light of his Word in order that he might make himself known unto salvation, and bestowed the privilege on those whom he was pleased to bring into nearer and more familiar relation to himself. For, seeing how the minds of men were carried to and fro, and found no certain resting-place, he chose the Jews for a peculiar people, and then hedged them in that they might not, like others, go astray. And not in vain does he, by the same means, retain us in his knowledge, since but for this, even those who, in comparison of others, seem to stand strong, would quickly fall away. For as the aged, or those whose sight is defective, when any book however fair, is set before them, though they perceive that there is something written are scarcely able to make out two consecutive words, but, when aided by glasses, begin to read distinctly, so Scripture, gathering together the impressions of Deity, which, till then, lay confused in our minds, dissipates the darkness, and shows us the true God clearly. God therefore bestows a gift of singular value, when, for the instruction of the Church, he employs not dumb teachers merely, but opens his own sacred mouth; when he not only proclaims that some God must be worshipped, but at the same time declares that He is the God to whom worship is due; when he not only teaches his elect to have respect to God, but manifests himself as the God to whom this respect should be paid...

    3. For if we reflect how prone the human mind is to lapse into forgetfulness of God, how readily inclined to every kind of error, how bent every now and then on devising new and ficti-tious religions, it will be easy to understand how necessary it was to make such a depository of doctrine as would secure it from either perishing by the neglect, vanishing away amid the errors, or being corrupted by the presumptuous audacity of men. It being thus manifest that God, foreseeing the inefficiency of his image imprinted on the fair form of the universe, has given the assistance of his Word to all whom he has ever been pleased to instruct effectually, we, too, must pursue this straight path, if we aspire in earnest to a genuine contemplation of God; we must go, I say, to the Word, where the character of God, drawn from his works is described accurately and to the life; these works being estimated, not by our depraved judgment, but by the standard of eternal truth. If, as I lately said, we turn aside from it, how great soever the speed with which we move, we shall never reach the goal, because we are off the course. We should consider that the brightness of the Divine countenance, which even an apostle declares to be inaccessible (1 Tim. 6:16), is a kind of labyrinth – a labyrinth to us inextricable, if the Word do not serve us as a thread to guide our path; and that it is better to limp in the way, than run with the greatest swiftness out of it. Hence the Psalmist, after repeatedly declaring (Pss. 93; 96; 97; 99; etc.) that superstition should be banished from the world in order that pure religion may flourish, introduces God as *reigning*; meaning by the term, not the power which he possesses and which he exerts in the government of universal nature, but the doctrine by which he maintains his due supremacy: because error never can be eradicated from the heart of man until the true knowledge of God has been implanted in it.

✛ CHAPTER 7 ✛

The testimony of the spirit necessary to give full authority to Scripture. The impiety of pretending that the credibility of Scripture depends on the judgment of the Church.

Sections
4. The authority of Scripture is founded on its being spoken by God. This confirmed by the conscience of the godly, and the consent of all men of the least candour.
5. The authority of Scripture is sealed on the hearts of believers by the testimony of the Holy Spirit. The certainty of this testimony.

4.   ...Our faith in doctrine is not established until we have a perfect conviction that God is its author. Hence, the highest proof of Scripture is uniformly taken from the character of him whose Word it is. The prophets and apostles boast not their own acuteness or any qualities which win credit to speakers, nor do they dwell on reasons; but they appeal to the sacred name of God, in order that the whole world may be compelled to submission. The next thing to be considered is, how it appears not probable merely, but certain, that the name of God is neither rashly nor cunningly pretended. If, then, we would consult most effectually for our consciences, and save them from being driven about in a whirl of uncertainty, from wavering, and even stumbling at the smallest obstacle, our conviction of the truth of Scripture must be derived from a higher source than human conjectures, judgments, or reasons; namely, the secret testimony of the Spirit. It is true, indeed, that if we choose to proceed in the way of arguments it is easy to establish, by evidence of various kinds, that if there is a God in heaven, the Law, the Prophecies, and the Gospel, proceeded from him. Nay, although learned men, and

men of the greatest talent, should take the opposite side, summoning and ostentatiously displaying all the powers of their genius in the discussion; if they are not possessed of shameless effrontery, they will be compelled to confess that the Scripture exhibits clear evidence of its being spoken by God, and, consequently, of its containing his heavenly doctrine. We shall see a little farther on, that the volume of sacred Scripture very far surpasses all other writings. Nay, if we look at it with clear eyes, and unblessed judgment, it will forthwith present itself with a divine majesty which will subdue our presumptuous opposition, and force us to do it homage.

Still, however, it is preposterous to attempt, by discussion, to rear up a full faith in Scripture. True, were I called to contend with the craftiest despisers of God, I trust, though I am not possessed of the highest ability or eloquence, I should not find it difficult to stop their obstreperous mouths; I could, without much ado, put down the boastings which they mutter in corners, were anything to be gained by refuting their cavils. But although we may maintain the sacred Word of God against gainsayers, it does not follow that we shall forthwith implant the certainty which faith requires in their hearts. Profane men think that religion rests only on opinion, and, therefore, that they may not believe foolishly, or on slight grounds, desire and insist to have it proved by reason that Moses and the prophets were divinely inspired. But I answer, that the testimony of the Spirit is superior to reason. For as God alone can properly bear witness to his own words, so these words will not obtain full credit in the hearts of men, until they are sealed by the inward testimony of the Spirit. The same Spirit, therefore, who spoke by the mouth of the prophets, must penetrate our hearts, in order to convince us that they faithfully delivered the message with which they were divinely entrusted. This connection is most aptly expressed by Isaiah in these words, 'My Spirit that is upon thee, and my words which I have put in thy mouth, shall not depart out of thy mouth, nor out of the mouth of thy seed, nor out of the mouth of thy seed's seed, saith the Lord, from henceforth and for ever' (Isa. 59:21). Some worthy persons feel disconcerted, because, while the wicked murmur with impunity at the Word of God, they have not a clear proof at hand to silence them, forgetting that the Spirit is called an earnest and seal to confirm the faith of the godly, for this very reason, that, until he enlightens their minds, they are tossed to and fro in a sea of doubts.

5. Let it therefore be held as fixed, that those who are inwardly taught by the Holy Spirit acquiesce implicitly in Scripture; that Scripture, carrying its own evidence along with it, deigns not to submit to proofs and arguments, but owes the full conviction with which we ought to receive it to the testimony of the Spirit. Enlightened by him, we no longer believe, either on our own judgment or that of others, that the Scriptures are from God; but, in a way superior to human judgment, feel perfectly assured – as much so as if we beheld the divine image visibly impressed on it – that it came to us, by the instrumentality of men, from the very mouth of God. We ask not for proofs or probabilities on which to rest our judgment, but we subject our intellect and judgment to it as too transcendent for us to estimate. This, however, we do, not in the manner in which some are wont to fasten on an unknown object, which, as soon as known, displeases, but because we have a thorough conviction that, in holding it, we hold unassailable truth; not like miserable men, whose minds are enslaved by superstition, but because we feel a divine energy living and breathing in it – an energy by which we are drawn and animated to obey it, willingly indeed, and knowingly, but more vividly and effectually than could be done by human will or knowledge. Hence, God most justly exclaims by the mouth of Isaiah, 'Ye are my witnesses, saith the Lord, and my servant whom I have chosen, that ye may know and believe me, and understand that I am he' (Isa. 43:10).

Such, then, is a conviction which asks not for reasons; such, a knowledge which accords with the highest reason, namely, knowledge in which the mind rests more firmly and securely than in any reasons; such in fine, the conviction which revelation from heaven alone can produce. I say nothing more than every believer experiences in himself, though my words fall far short of the reality. I do not dwell on this subject at present, because we will return to it again: only let us now understand that the only true faith is that which the Spirit of God seals on our hearts. Nay, the modest and teachable reader will find a sufficient reason in the promise contained in Isaiah, that all the children of the renovated Church 'shall be taught of the Lord' (Isa. 54:13)...

✝ CHAPTER 9 ✝

All the principles of piety subverted by fanatics, who substitute revelations for Scripture.

Sections

2.   The impositions of Satan cannot be detected without the aid of the written Word.
3.   How the Spirit and the written Word are indissolubly connected.

2.   ...It is easy to understand that we must give diligent heed both to the reading and hearing of Scripture, if we would obtain any benefit from the Spirit of God (just as Peter praises those who attentively study the doctrine of the prophets (2 Pet. 1:19), though it might have been thought to be superseded after the gospel light arose), and, on the contrary, that any spirit which passes by the wisdom of God's Word, and suggests any other doctrine, is deservedly suspected of vanity and falsehood. Since Satan transforms himself into an angel of light, what authority can the Spirit have with us if he be not ascertained by an infallible mark? And assuredly he is pointed out to us by the Lord with sufficient clearness; but these miserable men err as if bent on their own destruction, while they seek the Spirit from themselves rather than from Him. But they say that it is insulting to subject the Spirit, to whom all things are to be subject, to the Scripture: as if it were disgraceful to the Holy Spirit to maintain a perfect resemblance throughout, and be in all respects without variation consistent with himself. True, if he were subjected to a human, an angelical, or to any foreign standard, it might be thought that he was rendered subordinate, or, if you will, brought into bondage, but so long as he is compared with himself, and considered in himself, how can it be said that he is thereby injured? I admit that he is brought to a test, but the very test by which it has pleased him that his majesty should be confirmed. It ought to be enough for us when once we hear his voice; but lest Satan should insinuate himself under his name, he wishes us to recognise him by the image which he has stamped on the Scriptures. The author of the Scriptures cannot vary, and change his likeness. Such as he there appeared at first, such he will perpetually remain. There is nothing contumelious to him in this, unless we are to think it would be honourable for him to degenerate, and revolt against himself.

3. Their cavil about our cleaving to the dead letter carries with it the punishment which they deserve for despising Scripture. It is clear that Paul is there arguing against false apostles (2 Cor. 3:6), who, by recommending the law without Christ, deprived the people of the benefit of the New Covenant, by which the Lord engages that he will write his law on the hearts of believers, and engrave it on their inward parts. The letter therefore is dead, and the law of the Lord kills its readers when it is dissevered from the grace of Christ, and only sounds in the ear without touching the heart. But if it is effectually impressed on the heart by the Spirit; if it exhibits Christ, it is the word of life converting the soul, and making wise the simple. Nay, in the very same passage, the apostle calls his own preaching the ministration of the Spirit (2 Cor. 3:8), intimating that the Holy Spirit so cleaves to his own truth, as he has expressed it in Scripture, that he then only exerts and puts forth his strength when the word is received with due honour and respect.

There is nothing repugnant here to what was lately said (Chap. 7) that we have no great certainty of the word itself, until it be confirmed by the testimony of the Spirit. For the Lord has so knit together the certainty of his word and his Spirit, that our minds are duly imbued with reverence for the word when the Spirit shining upon it enables us there to behold the face of God; and, on the other hand, we embrace the Spirit with no danger of delusion when we recognise him in his image, that is, in his word. Thus, indeed, it is. God did not produce his word before men for the sake of sudden display, intending to abolish it the moment the Spirit should arrive; but he employed the same Spirit, by whose agency he had administered the word, to complete his work by the efficacious confirmation of the word. In this way Christ explained to the two disciples (Lk. 24:27), not that they were to reject the Scriptures and trust to their own wisdom, but that they were to understand the Scriptures. In like manner, when Paul says to the Thessalonians, 'Quench not the Spirit', he does not carry them aloft to empty speculation apart from the word; he immediately adds, 'Despise not prophesying' (1 Thess. 5:19, 20). By this, doubtless, he intimates that the light of the Spirit is quenched the moment prophesying falls into contempt. How is this answered by those swelling enthusiasts, in whose idea the only true illumination consists, in carelessly laying aside, and bidding adieu to the Word of God, while, with no less confidence than folly, they fasten upon any dreaming notion which may have casually sprung up in their minds? Surely a very different sobriety becomes the children of God. As they feel that without the Spirit of God they are utterly devoid of the light of truth, so they are not ignorant that the word is the instrument by which the illumination of the Spirit is dispensed. They know of no other Spirit than the one who dwelt and spake in the apostles – the Spirit by whose oracles they are daily invited to the hearing of the word.

PART III

GOD THE TRINITY AND HIS CREATION

✝ CHAPTER 13 ✝

The unity of the divine essence in three persons taught,
in Scripture, from the foundation of the world.

Sections

7.   Proofs of the eternal Deity of the Son. The Son of the Word of the Eternal Father, and, therefore, the Son Eternal God. Objection. Reply.

16. What view to be taken of the Trinity. The form of Christian baptism proves that they are in one essence. The Arian and Macedonian heresies.

17. Of the distinction of Persons. They are distinct, but not divided. This proved.

18. Analogies taken from human affairs to be cautiously used. Due regard to be paid to those mentioned by Scripture.

19. How the Three Persons not only do not destroy, but constitute the most perfect unity

20. Conclusion of this part of the chapter, and summary of the true doctrine concerning the unity of Essence and the Three Persons.

7.   Before proceeding farther, it will be necessary to prove the divinity of the Son and the Holy Spirit. Thereafter, we shall see how they differ from each other. When the Word of God is set before us in the Scriptures, it were certainly most absurd to imagine that it is only a fleeting and evanescent voice, which is sent out into the air, and comes forth beyond God himself, as was the case with the communications made to the patriarchs, and all the prophecies. The reference is rather to the wisdom ever dwelling with God, and by which all oracles and prophecies were inspired. For, as Peter testifies (1 Pet. 1:11), the ancient prophets spake by the Spirit of Christ just as did the apostles, and all who after them were ministers of the heavenly doctrine. But as Christ was not yet manifested, we necessarily understand that the Word was begotten of the Father before all ages. But if that Spirit, whose organs the prophets were, belonged to the Word, the inference is irresistible, that the Word was truly God. And this is clearly enough shown by Moses in his account of the creation, where he places the Word as intermediate. For why does he distinctly narrate that God, in creating each of his works, said, Let there be this – let there be that, unless that the unsearchable glory of God might shine forth in his image? I know prattlers would easily evade this, by saying that 'Word' is used for 'order' or 'command'; but the apostles are better expositors, when they tell us that the worlds were created by the Son, and that he sustains all things by his mighty word (Heb. 1:2). For we here see that *word* is used for the nod or command of the Son, who is himself the eternal and essential Word of the

Father. And no man of sane mind can have any doubt as to Solomon's meaning, when he introduces Wisdom as begotten by God, and presiding at the creation of the world, and all other divine operations (Prov. 8:22). For it were trifling and foolish to imagine any temporary command at a time when God was pleased to execute his fixed and eternal counsel, and something more still mysterious. To this our Saviour's words refer, 'My Father worketh hitherto, and I work' (Jn 5:17). In thus affirming, that from the foundation of the world he constantly worked with the Father, he gives a clearer explanation of what Moses simply touched. The meaning therefore is, that God spoke in such a manner as left the Word his peculiar part in the work, and thus made the operation common to both. But the clearest explanation is given by John, when he states that the Word – which was from the beginning, God and with God, was, together with God the Father, the maker of all things. For he both attributes a substantial and permanent essence to the Word, assigning to it a certain peculiarity, and distinctly showing how God spoke the world into being. Therefore, as all revelations from heaven are duly designated by the title of the Word of God, so the highest place must be assigned to that substantial Word, the source of all inspiration, which, as being liable to no variation, remains for ever one and the same with God, and is God.

16. But as God has manifested himself more clearly by the advent of Christ, so he has made himself more familiarly known in three persons. Of many proofs let this one suffice. Paul connects together these three, God, Faith, and Baptism, and reasons from the one to the other – because there is one faith he infers that there is one God; and because there is one baptism he infers that there is one faith. Therefore, if by baptism we are initiated into the faith and worship of one God, we must of necessity believe that he into whose name we are baptised is the true God. And there cannot be a doubt that our Saviour wished to testify, by a solemn rehearsal, that the perfect light of faith is now exhibited, when he said, 'Go and teach all nations, baptising them in the name of the Father, and of the Son, and of the Holy Spirit' (Mt. 28:19), since this is the same thing as to be baptised into the name of the one God, who has been fully manifested in the Father, the Son, and the Spirit. Hence it plainly appears, that the three persons, in whom alone God is known, subsist in the Divine essence. And since faith certainly ought not to look hither and thither, or run up and down after various objects, but to look, refer, and cleave to God alone, it is obvious that were there various kinds of faith, there behaved also to be various gods. Then, as the baptism of faith is a sacrament, its unity assures us of the unity of God. Hence also it is proved that it is lawful only to be baptised into one God, because we make a profession of faith in him in whose name we are baptised. What, then, is our Saviour's meaning in commanding baptism to be administered in the name of the Father, and the Son, and the Holy Spirit, if it be not that we are to believe with one faith in the name of the Father, and the Son, and the Holy Spirit? But is this any thing else than to declare that the Father, Son, and Spirit, are one God? Wherefore, since it must be held certain that there is one God, not more than one, we conclude that the Word and Spirit are of the very essence of God. Nothing could be more stupid than the trifling of the Arians, who, while acknowledging the divinity of the Son, denied his divine essence. Equally extravagant were the ravings of the Macedonians, who insisted that by the Spirit were only meant the gifts of grace poured out upon men. For as wisdom understanding, prudence, fortitude, and the fear of the Lord, proceed from the Spirit, so he is the one Spirit of wisdom, prudence, fortitude, and piety. He is not divided according to the distribution of his gifts, but, as the apostle assures us (1 Cor. 12:11), however they be divided, he remains one and the same.

17. On the other hand, the Scriptures demonstrate that there is some distinction between the Father and the Word, the Word and the Spirit; but the magnitude of the mystery reminds us of the great reverence and soberness which ought to be employed in discussing it. It seems to me, that nothing can be more admirable than the words of Gregory Nanzianzen: 'I cannot think of the unity without being irradiated by the Trinity: I cannot distinguish between the Trinity without being carried up to the unity.' Therefore, let us beware of imagining such a Trinity of persons as will distract our thoughts, instead of bringing them instantly back to the unity. The words Father, Son, and Holy Spirit, certainly indicate a real distinction, not allowing us to suppose that they are merely epithets by which God is variously designated from his works. Still they indicate distinction only, not division. The passages we have already quoted show that the Son has a distinct subsistence from the Father, because the Word could not have been with God unless he were distinct from the Father; nor but for this could he have had his glory with the Father. In like manner, Christ distinguishes the Father from himself when he says that there is another who bears witness of him (Jn 5:32; 8:16). To the same effect is it elsewhere said, that the Father made all things by the Word. This could not be, if he were not in some respect distinct from him. Besides, it was not the Father that descended to the earth, but he who came forth from the Father; nor was it the Father that died and rose again, but he whom the Father had sent. This distinction did not take its beginning at the incarnation: for it is clear that the only begotten Son previously existed in the bosom of the Father (Jn 1:18). For who will dare to affirm that the Son entered his Father's bosom for the first time, when he came down from heaven to assume human nature? Therefore, he was previously in the bosom of the Father, and had his glory with the Father. Christ intimates the distinction between the Holy Spirit and the Father, when he says that the Spirit proceedeth from the Father, and between the Holy Spirit and himself, when he speaks of him as another as he does when he declares that he will send another Comforter; and in many other passages besides (Jn 14:6; 15:26; 14:16).

18. I am not sure whether it is expedient to borrow analogies from human affairs to express the nature of this distinction. The ancient Fathers sometimes do so, but they at the same time admit that what they bring forward as analogous is very widely different. And hence it is that I have a great dread of any thing like presumption here, lest some rash saying may furnish an occasion of calumny to the malicious, or of delusion to the unlearned. It were unbecoming, however, to say nothing of a distinction which we observe that the Scriptures have pointed out. This distinction is, that to the Father is attributed the beginning of action, the fountain and source of all things; to the Son, wisdom, counsel, and arrangement in action, while the energy and efficacy of action is assigned to the Spirit. Moreover, though the eternity of the Father is also the eternity of the Son and Spirit, since God never could be without his own wisdom and energy; and though in eternity there can be no room for first or last, still the distinction of order is not unmeaning or superfluous, the Father being considered first, next the Son from him, and then the Spirit from both. For the mind of every man naturally inclines to consider, first, God, secondly, the wisdom emerging from him, and, lastly, the energy by which he executes the purposes of his counsel. For this reason, the Son is said to be of the

Father only; the Spirit of both the Father and the Son. This is done in many passages, but in none more clearly than in the eighth chapter to the Romans, where the same Spirit is called indiscriminately the Spirit of Christ, and the Spirit of him who raised up Christ from the dead. And not improperly. For Peter also testifies (1 Pet. 1:21), that it was the Spirit of Christ which inspired the prophets, though the Scriptures so often say that it was the Spirit of God the Father.

19. Moreover, this distinction is so far from interfering with the most perfect unity of God, that the Son may thereby be proved to be one God with the Father, inasmuch as he constitutes one Spirit with him, and that the Spirit is not different from the Father and the Son, inasmuch as he is the Spirit of the Father and the Son. In each hypostasis the whole nature is understood, the only difference being that each has his own peculiar subsistence. The whole Father is in the Son, and the whole Son in the Father, as the Son himself also declares (Jn 14:10), 'I am in the Father, and the Father in me'; nor do ecclesiastical writers admit that the one is separated from the other by any difference of essence. 'By those names which denote distinctions,' says Augustine, 'is meant the relation which they mutually bear to each other, not the very substance by which they are one.' In this way, the sentiments of the Fathers, which might sometimes appear to be at variance with each other, are to be reconciled. At one time they teach that the Father is the beginning of the Son, at another they assert that the Son has both divinity and essence from himself, and therefore is one beginning with the Father. The cause of this discrepancy is well and clearly explained by Augustine, when he says, 'Christ, as to himself, is called God, as to the Father he is called Son.' And again, 'The Father, as to himself, is called God, as to the Son he is called Father. He who, as to the Son, is called Father, is not Son; and he who, as to himself, is called Father, and he who, as to himself, is called Son, is the same God.' Therefore, when we speak of the Son simply, without reference to the Father, we truly and properly affirm that he is of himself, and, accordingly, call him the only beginning; but when we denote the relation which he bears to the Father, we correctly make the Father the beginning of the Son. Augustine's fifth book on the Trinity is wholly devoted to the explanation of this subject. But it is far safer to rest contented with the relation as taught by him, than get bewildered in vain speculation by subtle prying into a sublime mystery.

20. Let those, then, who love soberness, and are contented with the measure of faith, briefly receive what is useful to be known. It is as follows: When we profess to believe in one God, by the name God is understood the one simple essence, comprehending three persons or hypostases; and, accordingly, whenever the name of God is used indefinitely, the Son and Spirit, not less than the Father, is meant. But when the Son is joined with the Father, relation comes into view, and so we distinguish between the Persons. But as the Personal subsistence carry an order with them, the principle and origin being in the Father, whenever mention is made of the Father and Son, or of the Father and Spirit together, the name of God is specially given to the Father. In this way the unity of essence is retained, and respect is had to the order, which, however derogates in no respect from the divinity of the Son and Spirit. And surely since we have already seen how the apostles declare the Son of God to have been He whom Moses and the prophets declared to be Jehovah, we must always arrive at a unity of essence. We, therefore, hold it detestable blasphemy to call the Son a different God from the Father, because the simple name God admits not of relation, nor can God, considered in himself, be said to be this or that. Then, that the name Jehovah, taken indefinitely, may be applied to Christ, is clear from the words of Paul, 'For this thing I besought the Lord thrice.' After giving the answer, 'My grace is sufficient for thee,' he subjoins, 'that the power of Christ may rest upon me' (2 Cor. 12:8, 9). For it is certain that the name of Lord is there put for Jehovah, and, therefore, to restrict it to the person of the Mediator were puerile and frivolous, the words being used absolutely, and not with the view of comparing the Father and the Son. And we know that, in accordance with the received usage of the Greeks, the apostles uniformly substitute the word *Kurion* for Jehovah. Not to go far for an example, Paul besought the Lord in the same sense in which Peter quotes the passage of Joel, 'Whosoever shall call upon the name of the Lord shall be saved' (Acts 2:21; Joel 2:28). Where this name is specially applied to the Son, there is a different ground for it, as will be seen in its own place; at present it is sufficient to remember, that Paul, after praying to God absolutely, immediately subjoins the name of Christ. Thus, too, the Spirit is called God absolutely by Christ himself. For nothing prevents us from holding that he is the entire spiritual essence of God, in which are comprehended Father, Son, and Spirit. This is plain from Scripture. For as God is there called a Spirit, so the Holy Spirit also, in so far as he is a hypostasis of the whole essence, is said to be both of God and from God.

✝ CHAPTER 14 ✝

In the creation of the world, and all things in it, the true God distinguished by certain marks from fictitious gods.

Sections

20. The latter part of the chapter briefly embracing the history of creation, and showing what it is of importance for us to know concerning God.
21. The special object of this knowledge is to prevent us, through ingratitude or thoughtlessness, from overlooking the perfections of God. Example of this primary knowledge.
22. Another object of this knowledge – that perceiving how these things were created for our use, we may be excited to trust in God, pray to him, and love him.

20.   Since we are placed in this most beautiful theatre, let us not decline to take a pious delight in the clear and manifest works of God. For, as we have elsewhere observed, though not the chief, it is, in point of order, the first evidence of faiths to remember to which side soever we turn, that all which meets the eye is the work of God, and at the same time to meditate with pious care on the end which God had in view in creating it. Wherefore, in order that we may apprehend with true faith what it is necessary to know concerning God, it is of importance to attend to the history of the creation, as briefly recorded by Moses and afterwards more copiously illustrated by pious writers, more especially by Basil and Ambrose. From this history we learn that God, by the power of his Word and his Spirit, created the heavens and the earth out of nothing; that thereafter he produced things inanimate and animate of every kind, arranging an innumerable variety of objects in admirable order, giving each kind its proper nature, office, place, and station; at the same time, as all things were liable to corruption, providing for

the perpetuation of each single species, cherishing some by secret methods, and, as it were, from time to time instilling new vigour into them, and bestowing on others a power of continuing their race, so preventing it from perishing at their own death. Heaven and earth being thus most richly adorned, and copiously supplied with all things, like a large and splendid mansion gorgeously constructed and exquisitely furnished, at length man was made – man, by the beauty of his person and his many noble endowments, the most glorious specimen of the works of God. But, as I have no intention to give the history of creation in detail, it is sufficient to have again thus briefly touched on it in passing. I have already reminded my reader, that the best course for him is to derive his knowledge of the subject from Moses and others who have carefully and faithfully transmitted an account of the creation.

21. It is unnecessary to dwell at length on the end that should be aimed at in considering the works of God. The subject has been in a great measure explained elsewhere, and in so far as required by our present work, may now be disposed of in a few words. Undoubtedly were one to attempt to speak in due terms of the inestimable wisdom, power, justice, and goodness of God, in the formation of the world, no grace or splendour of diction could equal the greatness of the subject. Still there can be no doubt that the Lord would have us constantly occupied with such holy meditation, in order that, while we contemplate the immense treasures of wisdom and goodness exhibited in the creatures as in so many mirrors, we may not only run our eye over them with a hasty, and, as it were, evanescent glance, but dwell long upon them, seriously and faithfully turn them in our minds, and every now and then bring them to recollection. But as the present work is of a didactic nature, we cannot fittingly enter on topics which require lengthened discourse. Therefore, in order to be compendious, let the reader understand that he has a genuine apprehension of the character of God as the Creator of the world; first, if he attends to the general rule, never thoughtlessly or obliviously to overlook the glorious perfections which God displays in his creatures; and, secondly, if he makes a self-application of what he sees, so as to fix it deeply on his heart. The former is exemplified when we consider how great the Architect must be who framed and ordered the multitude of the starry host so admirably, that it is impossible to imagine a more glorious sight, so stationing some, and fixing them to particular spots that they cannot move; giving a freer course to others yet setting limits to their wanderings; so tempering the movement of the whole as to measure out day and night, months, years, and seasons, and at the same time so regulating the inequality of days as to prevent every thing like confusion. The former course is, moreover, exemplified when we attend to his power in sustaining the vast mass, and guiding the swift revolutions of the heavenly bodies, etc. These few examples sufficiently explain what is meant by recognising the divine perfections in the creation of the world. Were we to attempt to go over the whole subject we should never come to a conclusion, there being as many miracles of divine power, as many striking evidences of wisdom and goodness, as there are classes of objects, nay, as there are individual objects, great or small, throughout the universe.

22. The other course which has a closer relation to faith remains to be considered – that while we observe how God has destined all things for our good and salvation, we at the same time feel his power and grace, both in ourselves and in the great blessings which he has bestowed upon us; thence stirring up ourselves to confidence in him, to invocation, praise, and love. Moreover, as I lately observed, the Lord himself, by the very order of creation, has demonstrated that he created all things for the sake of man. Nor is it unimportant to observe, that he divided the formation of the world into six days, though it had been in no respect more difficult to complete the whole work, in all its parts, in one moment than by a gradual progression. But he was pleased to display his providence and paternal care towards us in this, that before he formed man, he provided whatever he foresaw would be useful and salutary to him. How ungrateful, then, were it to doubt whether we are cared for by this most excellent Parent, who we see cared for us even before we were born! How impious were it to tremble in distrust, lest we should one day be abandoned in our necessity by that kindness which, antecedent to our existence, displayed itself in a complete supply of all good things! Moreover, Moses tells us that everything which the world contains is liberally placed at our disposal. This God certainly did not that he might delude us with an empty form of donation. Nothing, therefore, which concerns our safety will ever be wanting. To conclude, in one word; as often as we call God the Creator of heaven and earth, let us remember that the distribution of all the things which he created are in his hand and power, but that we are his sons, whom he has undertaken to nourish and bring up in allegiance to him, that we may expect the substance of all good from him alone, and have full hope that he will never suffer us to be in want of things necessary to salvation, so as to leave us dependent on some other source; that in everything we desire we may address our prayers to him, and, in every benefit we receive, acknowledge his hand, and give him thanks; that thus allured by his great goodness and beneficence, we may study with our whole heart to love and serve him.

✝ CHAPTER 15 ✝
State in which man was created. The faculties of the soul – the image of God – free will – original righteousness.

Sections

1. A twofold knowledge of God – before the fall and after it. The former here considered. Particular rules or precautions to be observed in this discussion. What we are taught by a body formed out of the dust, and tenanted by a spirit.
2. The immortality of the soul proved from (1) the testimony of conscience, (2) the knowledge of God, (3) the noble faculties with which it is endued, (4) its activity and wondrous fancies in sleep, (5) innumerable passages of Scripture.
4. The image of God is in the soul. Its nature may be learnt from its renewal by Christ. What comprehended under this renewal. What the image of God in man before the fall. In what things it now appears. When and where it will be seen in perfection.
8. The power and office of the intellect and will in man before the fall. Man's free will. This freedom lost by the fall – a fact unknown to philosophers. The delusion of Pelagians and Papists. Objection as to the fall of man when free, refuted.

1. We have now to speak of the creation of man, not only because of all the works of God it is the noblest, and most admirable specimen of his justice, wisdom, and goodness, but, as we observed at the outset, we cannot clearly and properly know God unless the knowledge of

ourselves be added. This knowledge is twofold – relating, first, to the condition in which we were at first created; and, secondly to our condition such as it began to be immediately after Adam's fall. For it would little avail us to know how we were created if we remained ignorant of the corruption and degradation of our nature in consequence of the fall. At present, however, we confine ourselves to a consideration of our nature in its original integrity. And, certainly, before we descend to the miserable condition into which man has fallen, it is of importance to consider what he was at first. For there is need of caution, lest we attend only to the natural ills of man, and thereby seem to ascribe them to the Author of nature; impiety deeming it a sufficient defence if it can pretend that everything vicious in it proceeded in some sense from God, and not hesitating, when accused, to plead against God, and throw the blame of its guilt upon Him. Those who would be thought to speak more reverently of the Deity catch at an excuse for their depravity from nature, not considering that they also, though more obscurely, bring a charge against God, on whom the dishonour would fall if anything vicious were proved to exist in nature. Seeing, therefore, that the flesh is continually on the alert for subterfuges, by which it imagines it can remove the blame of its own wickedness from itself to some other quarter, we must diligently guard against this depraved procedure, and accordingly treat of the calamity of the human race in such a way as may cut off every evasion, and vindicate the justice of God against all who would impugn it. We shall afterwards see, in its own place (Book 2 Chap. 1 sect. 3), how far mankind now are from the purity originally conferred on Adam. And, first, it is to be observed, that when he was formed out of the dust of the ground a curb was laid on his pride – nothing being more absurd than that those should glory in their excellence who not only dwell in tabernacles of clay, but are themselves in part dust and ashes. But God having not only deigned to animate a vessel of clay, but to make it the habitation of an immortal spirit, Adam might well glory in the great liberality of his Maker.

2.   Moreover, there can be no question that man consists of a body and a soul; meaning by soul, an immortal though created essence, which is his nobler part. Sometimes he is called a spirit. But though the two terms, while they are used together differ in their meaning, still, when spirit is used by itself it is equivalent to soul, as when Solomon speaking of death says, that the spirit returns to God who gave it (Eccles. 12:7). And Christ, in commending his spirit to the Father, and Stephen his to Christ, simply mean, that when the soul is freed from the prison-house of the body, God becomes its perpetual keeper. Those who imagine that the soul is called a spirit because it is a breath or energy divinely infused into bodies, but devoid of essence, err too grossly, as is shown both by the nature of the thing, and the whole tenor of Scripture. It is true, indeed, that men cleaving too much to the earth are dull of apprehension, nay, being alienated from the Father of Light, are so immersed in darkness as to imagine that they will not survive the grave; still the light is not so completely quenched in darkness that all sense of immortality is lost. Conscience, which, distinguishing, between good and evil, responds to the judgment of God, is an undoubted sign of an immortal spirit. How could motion devoid of essence penetrate to the judgment-seat of God, and under a sense of guilt strike itself with terror? The body cannot be affected by any fear of spiritual punishment. This is competent only to the soul, which must therefore be endued with essence. Then the mere knowledge of a God sufficiently proves that souls which rise higher than the world must be immortal, it being impossible that any evanescent vigour could reach the very fountain of life.

In fine, while the many noble faculties with which the human mind is endued proclaim that something divine is engraven on it, they are so many evidences of an immortal essence. For such sense as the lower animals possess goes not beyond the body, or at least not beyond the objects actually presented to it. But the swiftness with which the human mind glances from heaven to earth, scans the secrets of nature, and, after it has embraced all ages, with intellect and memory digests each in its proper order, and reads the future in the past, clearly demonstrates that there lurks in man a something separated from the body. We have intellect by which we are able to conceive of the invisible God and angels – a thing of which body is altogether incapable. We have ideas of rectitude, justice, and honesty – ideas which the bodily senses cannot reach. The seat of these ideas must therefore be a spirit. Nay, sleep itself, which stupefying the man, seems even to deprive him of life, is no obscure evidence of immortality; not only suggesting thoughts of things which never existed, but foreboding future events. I briefly touch on topics which even profane writers describe with a more splendid eloquence. For pious readers, a simple reference is sufficient. Were not the soul some kind of essence separated from the body, Scripture would not teach that we dwell in houses of clay, and at death remove from a tabernacle of flesh; that we put off that which is corruptible, in order that, at the last day, we may finally receive according to the deeds done in the body. These, and similar passages which everywhere occur, not only clearly distinguish the soul from the body, but by giving it the name of man, intimate that it is his principal part. Again, when Paul exhorts believers to cleanse themselves from all filthiness of the flesh and the spirit, he shows that there are two parts in which the taint of sin resides. Peter, also, in calling Christ the Shepherd and Bishop of souls, would have spoken absurdly if there were no souls towards which he might discharge such an office. Nor would there be any ground for what he says concerning the eternal salvation of souls, or for his injunction to purify our souls, or for his assertion that fleshly lusts war against the soul; neither could the author of the Epistle to the Hebrews say, that pastors watch as those who must give an account for our souls, if souls were devoid of essence. To the same effect Paul calls God to witness upon his soul, which could not be brought to trial before God if incapable of suffering punishment. This is still more clearly expressed by our Saviour, when he bids us fear him who, after he has killed the body, is able also to cast into hell fire. Again when the author of the Epistle to the Hebrews distinguishes the fathers of our flesh from God, who alone is the Father of our spirits, he could not have asserted the essence of the soul in clearer terms. Moreover, did not the soul, when freed from the fetters of the body, continue to exist, our Saviour would not have represented the soul of Lazarus as enjoying blessedness in Abraham's bosom, while, on the contrary, that of Dives was suffering dreadful torments. Paul assures us of the same thing when he says, that so long as we are present in the body, we are absent from the Lord. Not to dwell on a matter as to which there is little obscurity, I will only add, that Luke mentions among the errors of the Sadducees that they believed in neither angel nor spirit.

4. But our definition of the image seems not to be complete until it appears more clearly what the faculties are in which man excels, and in which he is to be regarded as a mirror of the divine glory. This, however, cannot be better known than from the remedy provided for the corruption of nature. It cannot be doubted that when Adam lost his first estate he became alienated from God. Wherefore, although we grant that the image of God was not utterly effaced and destroyed in him, it was, however, so corrupted, that any thing which remains is fearful deformity; and, therefore, our deliverance begins with that renovation which we obtain from Christ, who is, therefore, called the second Adam, because he restores us to true and substantial integrity. For although Paul, contrasting the quickening Spirit which believers receive from Christ, with the living soul which Adam was created (1 Cor. 15:45), commends the richer measure of grace bestowed in regeneration, he does not, however, contradict the statement, that the end of regeneration is to form us anew in the image of God. Accordingly, he elsewhere shows that the new man is renewed after the image of him that created him (Col. 3:19). To this corresponds another passage, 'Put ye on the new man, who after God is created' (Eph. 4:24). We must now see what particulars Paul comprehends under this renovation. In the first place, he mentions knowledge, and in the second, true righteousness and holiness. Hence we infer, that at the beginning the image of God was manifested by light of intellect, rectitude of heart, and the soundness of every part. For though I admit that the forms of expression are elliptical, this principle cannot be overthrown – that the leading feature in the renovation of the divine image must also have held the highest place in its creation. To the same effect Paul elsewhere says, that beholding the glory of Christ with unveiled face, we are transformed into the same image. We now see how Christ is the most perfect image of God, into which we are so renewed as to bear the image of God in knowledge, purity, righteousness, and true holiness. This being established, the imagination of Osiander, as to bodily form, vanishes of its own accord. As to that passage of St Paul (1 Cor. 11:7), in which the man alone to the express exclusion of the woman, is called the image and glory of God, it is evident from the context, that it merely refers to civil order. I presume it has already been sufficiently proved, that the image comprehends everything which has any relation to the spiritual and eternal life. The same thing, in different terms, is declared by St John when he says, that the light which was from the beginning, in the eternal Word of God, was the light of man (Jn 1:4). His object being to extol the singular grace of God in making man excel the other animals, he at the same time shows how he was formed in the image of God, that he may separate him from the common herd, as possessing not ordinary animal existence, but one which combines with it the light of intelligence. Therefore, as the image of God constitutes the entire excellence of human nature, as it shone in Adam before his fall, but was afterwards vitiated and almost destroyed, nothing remaining but a ruin, confused, mutilated, and tainted with impurity, so it is now partly seen in the elect, in so far as they are regenerated by the Spirit. Its full lustre, however, will be displayed in heaven. But in order to know the particular properties in which it consists, it will be proper to treat of the faculties of the soul. For there is no solidity in Augustine's speculation, that the soul is a mirror of the Trinity, inasmuch as it comprehends within itself, intellect, will, and memory. Nor is there probability in the opinion of those who place likeness to God in the dominion bestowed upon man, as if he only resembled God in this, that he is appointed lord and master of all things. The likeness must be within, in himself. It must be something which is not external to him but is properly the internal good of the soul.

8. Therefore, God has provided the soul of man with intellect, by which he might discern good from evil, just from unjust, and might know what to follow or to shun, reason going before with her lamp. To this he has joined will, to which choice belongs. Man excelled in these noble endowments in his primitive condition, when reason, intelligence, prudence, and judgment, not only sufficed for the government of his earthly life, but also enabled him to rise up to God and eternal happiness. Thereafter choice was added to direct the appetites, and temper all the organic motions; the will being thus perfectly submissive to the authority of reason. In this upright state, man possessed freedom of will, by which, if he chose, he was able to obtain eternal life. It were here unseasonable to introduce the question concerning the secret predestination of God, because we are not considering what might or might not happen, but what the nature of man truly was. Adam, therefore, might have stood if he chose, since it was only by his own will that he fell; but it was because his will was pliable in either direction and he had not received constancy to persevere, that he so easily fell. Still he had a free choice of good and evil; and not only so, but in the mind and will there was the highest rectitude, and all the organic parts were duly framed to obedience, until man corrupted its good properties, and destroyed himself. Hence the great darkness of philosophers who have looked for a complete building in a ruin, and fit arrangement in disorder. The principle they set out with was, that man could not be a rational animal unless he had a free choice of good and evil. They also imagined that the distinction between virtue and vice was destroyed, if man did not of his own counsel arrange his life. So far well, had there been no change in man. This being unknown to them, it is not surprising that they throw every thing into confusion. But those who, while they profess to be the disciples of Christ, still seek for free-will in man, notwithstanding of his being lost and drowned in spiritual destruction, labour under manifold delusion, making a heterogeneous mixture of inspired doctrine and philosophical opinions, and so erring as to both. At present it is necessary only to remember, that man, at his first creation, was very different from all his posterity; who, deriving their origin from him after he was corrupted, received a hereditary taint. At first every part of the soul was formed to rectitude. There was soundness of mind and freedom of will to choose the good. If any one objects that it was placed, as it were, in a slippery position, because its power was weak, I answer, that the degree conferred was sufficient to take away every excuse. For surely the Deity could not be tied down to this condition – to make man such, that he either could not or would not sin. Such a nature might have been more excellent; but to expostulate with God as if he had been bound to confer this nature on man, is more than unjust, seeing he had full right to determine how much or how little He would give. Why He did not sustain him by the virtue of perseverance is hidden in his counsel; it is ours to keep within the bounds of soberness. Man had received the power, if he had the will, but he had not the will which would have given the power; for this will would have been followed by perseverance. Still, after he had received so much, there is no excuse for his having spontaneously brought death upon himself. No necessity was laid upon God to give him more than that intermediate and even transient will, that out of man's fall he might extract materials for his own glory.

PART IV

GOD'S PROVIDENCE

✝ CHAPTER 16 ✝

The world, created by God, still cherished and protected by Him.
Each and all of its parts governed by his providence.

Sections

1. Even the wicked, under the guidance of carnal sense, acknowledge that God is the Creator. The godly acknowledge not this only, but that he is a most wise and powerful governor and preserver of all created objects. In so doing, they lean on the Word of God, some passages from which are produced.
3. Figment of the Sophists as to an indolent Providence refuted. Consideration of the Omnipotence as combined with the Providence of God. Double benefit resulting from a proper acknowledgement of the Divine Omnipotence. Cavils of Infidelity.
5. Special Providence of God asserted and proved by arguments founded on a consideration of the Divine Justice and Mercy. Proved also by passages of Scripture, relating to the sky, the earth, and animals.

1. It were cold and lifeless to represent God as a momentary Creator, who completed his work once for all, and then left it. Here, especially, we must dissent from the profane, and maintain that the presence of the divine power is conspicuous, not less in the perpetual condition of the world than in its first creation. For, although even wicked men are forced, by the mere view of the earth and sky, to rise to the Creator, yet faith has a method of its own in assigning the whole praise of creation to God. To this effect is the passage of the apostle already quoted that by faith we understand that the worlds were framed by the Word of God (Heb. 11:3); because, without proceeding to his Providence, we cannot understand the full force of what is meant by God being the Creator, how much soever we may seem to comprehend it with our mind, and confess it with our tongue. The carnal mind, when once it has perceived the power of God in the creation, stops there, and, at the farthest, thinks and ponders on nothing else than the wisdom, power, and goodness displayed by the Author of such a work (matters which rise spontaneously, and force themselves on the notice even of the unwilling), or on some general agency on which the power of motion depends, exercised in preserving and governing it. In short, it imagines that all things are sufficiently sustained by the energy divinely infused into them at first. But faith must penetrate deeper. After learning that there is a Creator, it must forthwith infer that he is also a Governor and Preserver, and that, not by producing a kind of general motion in the machine of the globe as well as in each of its parts, but by a special providence sustaining, cherishing, superintending, all the things which he has made, to the very

minutest, even to a sparrow. Thus David, after briefly premising that the world was created by God, immediately descends to the continual course of Providence, 'By the word of the Lord were the heavens framed, and all the host of them by the breath of his mouth,' immediately adding, 'The Lord looketh from heaven, he beholdeth the children of men' (Ps. 33:6, 13, etc.). He subjoins other things to the same effect. For although all do not reason so accurately, yet because it would not be credible that human affairs were superintended by God, unless he were the maker of the world, and no one could seriously believe that he is its Creator without feeling convinced that he takes care of his works; David with good reason, and in admirable order, leads us from the one to the other. In general, indeed, philosophers teach, and the human mind conceives, that all the parts of the world are invigorated by the secret inspiration of God. They do not, however reach the height to which David rises taking all the pious along with him, when he says, 'These wait all upon thee, that thou mayest give them their meat in due season. That thou givest them they gather: thou openest thine hand, they are filled with good. Thou hidest thy face, they are troubled: thou takest away their breath, they die, and return to their dust. Thou sendest forth thy Spirit, they are created, and thou renewest the face of the earth' (Ps. 104:27–30). Nay, though they subscribe to the sentiment of Paul, that in God 'we live, and move, and have our being' (Acts 17:28), yet they are far from having a serious apprehension of the grace which he commends, because they have not the least relish for that special care in which alone the paternal favour of God is discerned.

3. And truly God claims omnipotence to himself, and would have us to acknowledge it; not the vain, indolent, slumbering omnipotence which sophists feign, but vigilant, efficacious, energetic, and ever active; not an omnipotence which may only act as a general principle of confused motion, as in ordering a stream to keep within the channel once prescribed to it, but one which is intent on individual and special movements. God is deemed omnipotent, not because he can act though he may cease or be idle, or because by a general instinct he continues the order of nature previously appointed; but because, governing heaven and earth by his providence, he so overrules all things that nothing happens without his counsel. For when it is said in the Psalms, 'He has done whatsoever he has pleased' (Ps. 115:3), the thing meant is his sure and deliberate purpose. It were insipid to interpret the Psalmist's words in philosophic fashion, to mean that God is the primary agent, because the beginning and cause of all motion. This rather is the solace of the faithful, in their adversity, that every thing which they endure is by the ordination and command of God, that they are under his hand. But if the government of God thus extends to all his works, it is a childish cavil to confine it to natural influx. Those moreover who confine the providence of God within narrow limits, as if he allowed all things to be borne along freely according to a perpetual law of nature, do not more defraud God of his glory than themselves of a most useful doctrine; for nothing were more wretched than man if he were exposed to all possible movements of the sky, the air, the earth, and the water. We may add, that by this view the singular goodness of God towards each individual is unbecomingly impaired. David exclaims (Ps. 8:3), that infants hanging at their mothers' breasts are eloquent enough to celebrate the glory of God, because, from the very moment of their births they find an aliment prepared for them by heavenly care. Indeed, if we do not shut our eyes and senses to the fact, we must see that some mothers have full provision for their infants, and others almost none, according as it is the pleasure of God to nourish one child more liberally, and another more sparingly. Those who attribute due praise to the omnipotence of God thereby derive a double benefit. He to whom heaven and earth belong, and whose nod all creatures must obey, is fully able to reward the homage which they pay to him, and they can rest secure in the protection of Him to whose control everything that could do them harm is subject, by whose authority, Satan, with all his furies and engines, is curbed as with a bridle, and on whose will everything adverse to our safety depends. In this way, and in no other, can the immoderate and superstitious fears, excited by the dangers to which we are exposed, be calmed or subdued. I say superstitious fears. For such they are, as often as the dangers threatened by any created objects inspire us with such terror, that we tremble as if they had in themselves a power to hurt us, or could hurt at random or by chance; or as if we had not in God a sufficient protection against them. For example, Jeremiah forbids the children of God 'to be dismayed at the signs of heaven, as the heathen are dismayed at them' (Jer. 10:2). He does not, indeed, condemn every kind of fear. But as unbelievers transfer the government of the world from God to the stars, imagining that happiness or misery depends on their decrees or presages, and not on the Divine will, the consequence is, that their fear, which ought to have reference to him only, is diverted to stars and comets. Let him, therefore, who would beware of such unbelief, always bear in mind, that there is no random power, or agency, or motion in the creatures, who are so governed by the secret counsel of God, that nothing happens but what he has knowingly and willingly decreed.

5.   Assuming that the beginning of motion belongs to God, but that all things move spontaneously or casually, according to the impulse which nature gives, the vicissitudes of day and nights, summer and winter, will be the work of God; inasmuch as he, in assigning the office of each, appointed a certain law, namely, that they should always with uniform tenor observe the same course, day succeeding night, month succeeding month, and year succeeding year. But, as at one time, excessive heat, combined with drought, burns up the fields; at another time excessive rains rot the crops, while sudden devastation is produced by tempests and storms of hail, these will not be the works of God, unless in so far as rainy or fair weather, heat or cold, are produced by the concourse of the stars, and other natural causes. According to this view, there is no place left either for the paternal favour, or the judgments of God. If it is said that God fully manifests his beneficence to the human race, by furnishing heaven and earth with the ordinary power of producing food, the explanation is meagre and heathenish: as if the fertility of one year were not a special blessing, the penury and dearth of another a special punishment and curse from God. But as it would occupy too much time to enumerate all the arguments, let the authority of God himself suffice. In the Law and the Prophets he repeatedly declares, that as often as he waters the earth with dew and rain, he manifests his favour, that by his command the heaven becomes hard as iron, the crops are destroyed by mildew and other evils, that storms and hail, in devastating the fields, are signs of sure and special vengeance. This being admitted, it is certain that not a drop of rain falls without the express command of God. David, indeed (Ps. 146:9), extols the general providence of God in supplying food to the young ravens that cry to him but when God himself threatens living creatures with famine, does he not plainly declare that they are all nourished by him, at one time with scanty, at another with more ample measure? It is childish, as I have already said, to confine this to particular acts, when Christ says, without reservation, that not a sparrow falls to the ground without the will of

his Father (Mt. 10:29). Surely, if the flight of birds is regulated by the counsel of God, we must acknowledge with the prophet, that while he 'dwelleth on high' he 'humbleth himself to behold the things that are in heaven and in the earth' (Ps. 113:5, 6).

✛ CHAPTER 17 ✛

Use to be made of the doctrine of providence.

Sections

1. Summary of the doctrine of Divine Providence: (1) It embraces the future and the past; (2) it works by means, without means, and against means; (3) mankind, and particularly the Church, the object of special care; 4. the mode of administration usually secret, but always just. This last point more fully considered.
9. A holy meditation on Divine Providence.
10. Meditation continued.
11. The use of the foregoing meditation.

1. Moreover, such is the proneness of the human mind to indulge in vain subtleties, that it becomes almost impossible for those who do not see the sound and proper use of this doctrine, to avoid entangling themselves in perplexing difficulties. It will, therefore, be proper here to advert to the end which Scripture has in view in teaching that all things are divinely ordained. And it is to be observed, first, that the Providence of God is to be considered with reference both to the past and the future; and, secondly, that in overruling all things, it works at one time with means, at another without means, and at another against means. Lastly, the design of God is to show that He takes care of the whole human race, but is especially vigilant in governing the Church, which he favours with a closer inspection. Moreover, we must add, that although the paternal favour and beneficence, as well as the judicial severity of God, is often conspicuous in the whole course of his Providence, yet occasionally as the causes of events are concealed, the thought is apt to rise, that human affairs are whirled about by the blind impulse of Fortune, or our carnal nature inclines us to speak as if God were amusing himself by tossing men up and down like balls. It is true, indeed, that if with sedate and quiet minds we were disposed to learn, the issue would at length make it manifest, that the counsel of God was in accordance with the highest reason, that his purpose was either to train his people to patience, correct their depraved affections, tame their wantonness, inure them to self-denial, and arouse them from torpor; or, on the other hand, to cast down the proud, defeat the craftiness of the ungodly, and frustrate all their schemes. How much soever causes may escape our notice, we must feel assured that they are deposited with him, and accordingly exclaim with David, 'Many, O Lord my God, are thy wonderful works which thou hast done, and thy thoughts which are to us-ward: if I would declare and speak of them, they are more than can be numbered' (Ps. 40:5). For while our adversities ought always to remind us of our sins, that the punishment may incline us to repentance, we see, moreover, how Christ declares there is something more in the secret counsel of his Father than to chastise every one as he deserves. For he says of the man who was born blind, 'Neither has this man sinned, nor his parents: but

that the works of God should be made manifest in him' (Jn 9:3). Here, where calamity takes precedence even of birth, our carnal sense murmurs as if God were unmerciful in thus afflicting those who have not offended. But Christ declares that, provided we had eyes clear enough, we should perceive that in this spectacle the glory of his Father is brightly displayed. We must use modesty, not as it were compelling God to render an account, but so revering his hidden judgments as to account his will the best of all reasons. When the sky is overcast with dense clouds, and a violent tempest arises, the darkness which is presented to our eye, and the thunder which strikes our ears, and stupefies all our senses with terror, make us imagine that every thing is thrown into confusion, though in the firmament itself all continues quiet and serene. In the same way, when the tumultuous aspect of human affairs unfits us for judging, we should still hold, that God, in the pure light of his justice and wisdom, keeps all these commotions in due subordination, and conducts them to their proper end. And certainly in this matter many display monstrous infatuation, presuming to subject the works of God to their calculation, and discuss his secret counsels, as well as to pass a precipitate judgment on things unknown, and that with greater license than on the doings of mortal men. What can be more preposterous than to show modesty toward our equals, and choose rather to suspend our judgment than incur the blame of rashness, while we petulantly insult the hidden judgments of God, judgments which it becomes us to look up to and revere.

9.   At the same time, the Christian will not overlook inferior causes. For, while he regards those by whom he is benefited as ministers of the divine goodness, he will not, therefore, pass them by, as if their kindness deserved no gratitude, but feeling sincerely obliged to them, will willingly confess the obligation, and endeavour, according to his ability, to return it. In fine, in the blessings which he receives, he will revere and extol God as the principal author, but will also honour men as his ministers, and perceive, as is the truth, that by the will of God he is under obligation to those, by whose hand God has been pleased to show him kindness. If he sustains any loss through negligence or imprudence, he will, indeed, believe that it was the Lord's will it should so be, but, at the same time, he will impute it to himself. If one for whom it was his duty to care, but whom he has treated with neglect, is carried off by disease, although aware that the person had reached a limit beyond which it was impossible to pass, he will not, therefore, extenuate his fault, but, as he had neglected to do his duty faithfully towards him, will feel as if he had perished by his guilty negligence. Far less where, in the case of theft or murder, fraud and preconceived malice have existed, will he palliate it under the pretext of Divine Providence, but in the same crime will distinctly recognise the justice of God, and the iniquity of man, as each is separately manifested. But in future events, especially, will he take account of such inferior causes. If he is not left destitute of human aid, which he can employ for his safety, he will set it down as a divine blessing; but he will not, therefore, be remiss in taking measures, or slow in employing the help of those whom he sees possessed of the means of assisting him. Regarding all the aids which the creatures can lend him, as hands offered him by the Lord, he will avail himself of them as the legitimate instruments of Divine Providence. And as he is uncertain what the result of any business in which he engages is to be (save that he knows, that in all things the Lord will provide for his good), he will zealously aim at what he deems for the best, so far as his abilities enable him. In adopting his measures, he will not be carried away by his own impressions, but will commit and resign himself to the wisdom of

God, that under his guidance he may be led into the right path. However, his confidence in external aid will not be such that the presence of it will make him feel secure, the absence of it fill him with dismay, as if he were destitute. His mind will always be fixed on the Providence of God alone, and no consideration of present circumstances will be allowed to withdraw him from the steady contemplation of it. Thus Joab, while he acknowledges that the issue of the battle is entirely in the hand of God, does not therefore become inactive, but strenuously proceeds with what belongs to his proper calling, 'Be of good courage,' says he, 'and let us play the men for our people, and for the cities of our God; and the Lord do that which seemeth him good' (2 Sam. 10:12). The same conviction keeping us free from rashness and false confidence, will stimulate us to constant prayer, while at the same time filling our minds with good hope, it will enable us to feel secure, and bid defiance to all the dangers by which we are surrounded.

10. Here we are forcibly reminded of the inestimable felicity of a pious mind. Innumerable are the ills which beset human life, and present death in as many different forms. Not to go beyond ourselves, since the body is a receptacle, nay the nurse, of a thousand diseases, a man cannot move without carrying along with him many forms of destruction. His life is in a manner interwoven with death. For what else can be said where heat and cold bring equal danger? Then, in what direction soever you turn, all surrounding objects not only may do harm, but almost openly threaten and seem to present immediate death. Go on board a ship, you are but a plank's breadth from death. Mount a horse, the stumbling of a foot endangers your life. Walk along the streets, every tile upon the roofs is a source of danger. If a sharp instrument is in your own hand, or that of a friend, the possible harm is manifest. All the savage beasts you see are so many beings armed for your destruction. Even within a high walled garden, where everything ministers to delight, a serpent will sometimes lurk. Your house, constantly exposed to fire, threatens you with poverty by day, with destruction by night. Your fields, subject to hail, mildew, drought, and other injuries, denounce barrenness, and thereby famine. I say nothing of poison, treachery, robbery, some of which beset us at home, others follow us abroad. Amid these perils, must not man be very miserable, as one who, more dead than alive, with difficulty draws an anxious and feeble breath, just as if a drawn sword were constantly suspended over his neck? It may be said that these things happen seldom, at least not always, or to all, certainly never all at once. I admit it; but since we are reminded by the example of others, that they may also happen to us, and that our life is not an exception any more than theirs, it is impossible not to fear and dread as if they were to befall us. What can you imagine more grievous than such trepidation? Add that there is something like an insult to God when it is said, that man, the noblest of the creatures, stands exposed to every blind and random stroke of fortune. Here, however, we were only referring to the misery which man should feel, were he placed under the dominion of chance.

11. But when once the light of Divine Providence has illumined the believer's soul, he is relieved and set free, not only from the extreme fear and anxiety which formerly oppressed him, but from all care. For as he justly shudders at the idea of chance, so he can confidently commit himself to God. This, I say, is his comfort, that his heavenly Father so embraces all things under his power, so governs them at will by his nod, so regulates them by his wisdom, that nothing takes place save according to his appointment; that received into his favour, and entrusted to the care of his angels neither fire, nor water, nor sword, can do him harm, except in so far as God their master is pleased to permit. For thus sings the Psalm, 'Surely he shall deliver thee from the snare of the fowler, and from the noisome pestilence. He shall cover thee with his feathers, and under his wings shalt thou trust; his truth shall be thy shield and buckler. Thou shalt not be afraid for the terror by night; nor for the arrow that flieth by day; nor for the pestilence that walketh in darkness; nor for the destruction that wasteth at noonday', etc. (Ps. 91:2–6). Hence the exulting confidence of the saints, 'The Lord is on my side; I will not fear: what can man do unto me? The Lord taketh my part with them that help me.' 'Though an host should encamp against me, my heart shall not fear.' 'Yea, though I walk through the valley of the shadow of death, I will fear no evil' (Pss. 118:6; 27:3; 23:4).

How comes it, I ask, that their confidence never fails, but just that while the world apparently revolves at random, they know that God is every where at work, and feel assured that his work will be their safety? When assailed by the devil and wicked men, were they not confirmed by remembering and meditating on Providence, they should, of necessity, forthwith despond. But when they call to mind that the devil, and the whole train of the ungodly, are, in all directions, held in by the hand of God as with a bridle, so that they can neither conceive any mischief, nor plan what they have conceived, nor how much soever they may have planned, move a single finger to perpetrate, unless in so far as he permits, nay, unless in so far as he commands; that they are not only bound by his fetters, but are even forced to do him service – when the godly think of all these things they have ample sources of consolation. For, as it belongs to the Lord to arm the fury of such foes and turn and destine it at pleasure, so it is his also to determine the measure and the end, so as to prevent them from breaking loose and wantoning as they list. Supported by this conviction, Paul, who had said in one place that his journey was hindered by Satan (1 Thess. 2:18), in another resolves, with the permission of God, to undertake it (1 Cor. 16:7). If he had only said that Satan was the obstacle, he might have seemed to give him too much power, as if he were able even to overturn the counsels of God; but now, when he makes God the disposer, on whose permission all journeys depend, he shows, that however Satan may contrive, he can accomplish nothing except in so far as He pleases to give the word. For the same reason, David, considering the various turns which human life undergoes as it rolls, and in a manner whirls around, betakes himself to this asylum, 'My times are in thy hand' (Ps. 31:15). He might have said the course of life or 'time' in the singular number, but by 'times' he meant to express, that how unstable soever the condition of man may be, the vicissitudes which are ever and anon taking place are under divine regulation. Hence Resin and the king of Israel, after they had joined their forces for the destruction of Israel, and seemed torches which had been kindled to destroy and consume the land, are termed by the prophet 'smoking fire brands'. They could only emit a little smoke (Isa. 7:4). So Pharaoh, when he was an object of dread to all by his wealth and strength, and the multitude of his troops, is compared to the largest of beasts, while his troops are compared to fishes; and God declares that he will take both leader and army with his hooks, and drag them whither he pleases (Ezek. 29:4). In one word, not to dwell longer on this, give heed, and you will at once perceive that ignorance of Providence is the greatest of all miseries, and the knowledge of it the highest happiness.

✢ PART V ✢

MAN'S SIN AND GOD'S REMEDY

✢ BOOK TWO ✢

THE KNOWLEDGE OF GOD THE REDEEMER, IN CHRIST, AS FIRST MANIFESTED TO THE FATHERS, UNDER THE LAW, AND THEREAFTER TO US UNDER THE GOSPEL.

✢ CHAPTER 1 ✢

Through the fall and revolt of Adam the whole human race
made accursed and degenerate of original sin.

Sections

1. The knowledge of ourselves most necessary. To use it properly we must be divested of pride, and clothed with true humility, which will dispose us to consider our fall, and embrace the mercy of God in Christ.

2. Though there is plausibility in the sentiment which stimulates us to self-admiration, the only sound sentiment is that which inclines us to true humility of mind. Pretexts for pride. The miserable vanity of sinful man.

3. Different views taken by carnal wisdom and by conscience, which appeals to divine justice as its standard. The knowledge of ourselves, consisting of two parts, the former of which having already been discussed, the latter is here considered.

6. Depravation communicated not merely by imitation, but by propagation. This proved (1) from the contrast drawn between Adam and Christ. Confirmation from passages of Scripture; (2) from the general declaration that we are the children of wrath.

8. Definition of original sin. Two parts in the definition. Exposition of the latter part. Original sin exposes us to the wrath of God. It also produces in us the works of the flesh. Other definitions considered.

1. It was not without reason that the ancient proverb so strongly recommended to man the knowledge of himself. For if it is deemed disgraceful to be ignorant of things pertaining to the business of life, much more disgraceful is self-ignorance, in consequence of which we miserably deceive ourselves in matters of the highest moment, and so walk blindfold. But the more useful the precept is, the more careful we must be not to use it preposterously, as we see certain philosophers have done. For they, when exhorting man to know himself, state the motive to be,

that he may not be ignorant of his own excellence and dignity. They wish him to see nothing in himself but what will fill him with vain confidence, and inflate him with pride. But self-knowledge consists in this, first, When reflecting on what God gave us at our creation, and still continues graciously to give, we perceive how great the excellence of our nature would have been had its integrity remained, and, at the same time, remember that we have nothing of our own, but depend entirely on God, from whom we hold at pleasure whatever he has seen it meet to bestow; secondly, When viewing our miserable condition since Adam's fall, all confidence and boasting are overthrown, we blush for shame, and feel truly humble. For as God at first formed us in his own image, that he might elevate our minds to the pursuit of virtue, and the contemplation of eternal life, so to prevent us from heartlessly burying those noble qualities which distinguish us from the lower animals, it is of importance to know that we were endued with reason and intelligence, in order that we might cultivate a holy and honourable life, and regard a blessed immortality as our destined aim. At the same time, it is impossible to think of our primeval dignity without being immediately reminded of the sad spectacle of our ignominy and corruption, ever since we fell from our original in the person of our first parent. In this way, we feel dissatisfied with ourselves, and become truly humble, while we are inflamed with new desires to seek after God, in whom each may regain those good qualities of which all are found to be utterly destitute.

2.   In examining ourselves, the search which divine truth enjoins, and the knowledge which it demands, are such as may indispose us to every thing like confidence in our own powers, leave us devoid of all means of boasting, and so incline us to submission. This is the course which we must follow, if we would attain to the true goal, both in speculation and practice. I am not unaware how much more plausible the view is, which invites us rather to ponder on our good qualities, than to contemplate what must overwhelm us with shame – our miserable destitution and ignominy. There is nothing more acceptable to the human mind than flattery, and, accordingly, when told that its endowments are of a high order, it is apt to be excessively credulous. Hence it is not strange that the greater part of mankind have erred so egregiously in this matter. Owing to the innate self-love by which all are blinded, we most willingly persuade ourselves that we do not possess a single quality which is deserving of hatred; and hence, independent of any countenance from without, general credit is given to the very foolish idea, that man is perfectly sufficient of himself for all the purposes of a good and happy life. If any are disposed to think more modestly, and concede somewhat to God, that they may not seem to arrogate every thing as their own, still, in making the division, they apportion matters so, that the chief ground of confidence and boasting always remains with themselves. Then, if a discourse is pronounced which flatters the pride spontaneously springing up in man's inmost heart, nothing seems more delightful. Accordingly, in every age, he who is most forward in extolling the excellence of human nature, is received with the loudest applause. But be this heralding of human excellence what it may, by teaching man to rest in himself, it does nothing more than fascinate by its sweetness, and, at the same time, so delude as to drown in perdition all who assent to it. For what avails it to proceed in vain confidence, to deliberate, resolve, plan, and attempt what we deem pertinent to the purpose, and, at the very outset, prove deficient and destitute both of sound intelligence and true virtue, though we still confidently persist till we rush headlong on destruction? But this is the best that can happen to those who put confidence

in their own powers. Whosoever, therefore, gives heed to those teachers, who merely employ us in contemplating our good qualities, so far from making progress in self-knowledge, will be plunged into the most pernicious ignorance.

3. While revealed truth concurs with the general consent of mankind in teaching that the second part of wisdom consists in self-knowledge, they differ greatly as to the method by which this knowledge is to be acquired. In the judgment of the flesh man deems his self-knowledge complete, when, with overweening confidence in his own intelligence and integrity, he takes courage, and spurs himself on to virtuous deeds, and when, declaring war upon vice, he uses his utmost endeavour to attain to the honourable and the fair. But he who tries himself by the standard of divine justice, finds nothing to inspire him with confidence; and hence, the more thorough his self-examination, the greater his despondency. Abandoning all dependence on himself, he feels that he is utterly incapable of duly regulating his conduct. It is not the will of God, however, that we should forget the primeval dignity which he bestowed on our first parents – a dignity which may well stimulate us to the pursuit of goodness and justice. It is impossible for us to think of our first original, or the end for which we were created, without being urged to meditate on immortality, and to seek the kingdom of God. But such meditation, so far from raising our spirits, rather casts them down, and makes us humble. For what is our original? One from which we have fallen. What the end of our creation? One from which we have altogether strayed, so that, weary of our miserable lot, we groan, and groaning sigh for a dignity now lost. When we say that man should see nothing in himself which can raise his spirits, our meaning is, that he possesses nothing on which he can proudly plume himself. Hence, in considering the knowledge which man ought to have of himself, it seems proper to divide it thus, first, to consider the end for which he was created, and the qualities – by no means contemptible qualities – with which he was endued, thus urging him to meditate on divine worship and the future life; and, secondly, to consider his faculties, or rather want of faculties – a want which, when perceived, will annihilate all his confidence, and cover him with confusion. The tendency of the former view is to teach him what his duty is, of the latter, to make him aware how far he is able to perform it. We shall treat of both in their proper order.

6. We thus see that the impurity of parents is transmitted to their children, so that all, without exception, are originally depraved. The commencement of this depravity will not be found until we ascend to the first parent of all as the fountain-head. We must, therefore, hold it for certain, that, in regard to human nature, Adam was not merely a progenitor, but, as it were, a root, and that, accordingly, by his corruption, the whole human race was deservedly vitiated. This is plain from the contrast which the apostle draws between Adam and Christ, 'Wherefore, as by one man sin entered into the world, and death by sin; and so death passed upon all men, for that all have sinned; even so might grace reign through righteousness unto eternal life by Jesus Christ our Lord' (Rom. 5:19–21). To what quibble will the Pelagians here recur? That the sin of Adam was propagated by imitation! Is the righteousness of Christ then available to us only in so far as it is an example held forth for our imitation? Can any man tolerate such blasphemy? But if, out of all controversy, the righteousness of Christ, and thereby life, is ours by communication, it follows that both of these were lost in Adam that they might be recovered in Christ, whereas sin and death were brought in by Adam, that they might be abolished in Christ. There is no obscurity in the words 'As by one man's disobedience many were made sinners, so by the obedience of one shall many be made righteous.' Accordingly, the relation subsisting between the two is this, As Adam, by his ruin, involved and ruined us, so Christ, by his grace, restored us to salvation. In this clear light of truth I cannot see any need of a longer or more labourious proof. Thus, too, in the First Epistle to the Corinthians, when Paul would confirm believers in the confident hope of the resurrection, he shows that the life is recovered in Christ which was lost in Adam (1 Cor. 15:22). Having already declared that all died in Adam, he now also openly testifies, that all are imbued with the taint of sin. Condemnation, indeed, could not reach those who are altogether free from blame. But his meaning cannot be made clearer than from the other member of the sentence, in which he shows that the hope of life is restored in Christ. Every one knows that the only mode in which this is done is, when by a wondrous communication Christ transfuses into us the power of his own righteousness, as it is elsewhere said, 'The Spirit is life because of righteousness' (1 Cor. 15:22). Therefore, the only explanation which can be given of the expression 'in Adam all died', is, that he by sinning not only brought disaster and ruin upon himself, but also plunged our nature into like destruction; and that not only in one fault, in a matter not pertaining to us, but by the corruption into which he himself fell, he infected his whole seed. Paul never could have said that all are 'by nature the children of wrath' (Eph. 2:3), if they had not been cursed from the womb. And it is obvious that the nature there referred to is not nature such as God created, but as vitiated in Adam; for it would have been most incongruous to make God the author of death. Adam, therefore, when he corrupted himself, transmitted the contagion to all his posterity. For a heavenly Judge, even our Saviour himself, declares that all are by birth vicious and depraved, when he says that 'that which is born of the flesh is fleshy' (Jn 3:6), and that therefore the gate of life is closed against all until they have been regenerated.

8. But lest the thing itself of which we speak be unknown or doubtful, it will be proper to define original sin. I have no intention, however, to discuss all the definitions which different writers have adopted, but only to adduce the one which seems to me most accordant with truth. Original sin, then, may be defined a hereditary corruption and depravity of our nature, extending to all the parts of the soul, which first makes us obnoxious to the wrath of God, and then produces in us works which in Scripture are termed 'works of the flesh'. This corruption is repeatedly designated by Paul by the term 'sin' (Gal. 5:19); while the works which proceed from it, such as adultery, fornication, theft, hatred, murder, revellings, he terms, in the same way, the 'fruits of sin', though in various passages of Scripture, and even by Paul himself, they are also termed 'sins'. The two things, therefore, are to be distinctly observed – that being thus perverted and corrupted in all the parts of our nature, we are, merely on account of such corruption, deservedly condemned by God, to whom nothing is acceptable but righteousness, innocence, and purity. This is not liability for another's fault. For when it is said, that the sin of Adam has made us obnoxious to the justice of God, the meaning is not, that we, who are in ourselves inno- cent and blameless, are bearing his guilt, but that since by his transgression we are all placed under the curse, he is said to have brought us under obligation. Through him, however, not only has punishment been derived, but pollution instilled, for which punishment is justly due. Hence Augustine, though he often terms it 'another's sin' (that he may more clearly show how it comes to us by descent), at the same time asserts that it is each individual's own sin. And the apostle most distinctly testifies, that 'death passed upon all men, for that all have sinned' (Rom.

5:12); that is, are involved in original sin, and polluted by its stain. Hence, even infants bringing their condemnation with them from their mother's womb, suffer not for another's, but for their own defect. For although they have not yet produced the fruits of their own unrighteousness, they have the seed implanted in them. Nay, their whole nature is, as it were, a seed-bed of sin, and therefore cannot but be odious and abominable to God. Hence it follows, that it is properly deemed sinful in the sight of God; for there could be no condemnation without guilt. Next comes the other point – that this perversity in us never ceases, but constantly produces new fruits, in other words, those works of the flesh which we formerly described; just as a lighted furnace sends forth sparks and flames, or a fountain without ceasing pours out water. Hence, those who have defined original sin as the want of the original righteousness which we ought to have had, though they substantially comprehend the whole case, do not significantly enough express its power and energy. For our nature is not only utterly devoid of goodness, but so prolific in all kinds of evil, that it can never be idle. Those who term it 'concupiscence' use a word not very inappropriate, provided it were added (this, however, many will by no means concede), that everything which is in man, from the intellect to the will, from the soul even to the flesh, is defiled and pervaded with this concupiscence; or, to express it more briefly, that the whole man is in himself nothing else than concupiscence.

✛ CHAPTER 2 ✛

Man now deprived of freedom of will, and miserably enslaved.

Sections

12. To show how far the power both of the intellect and will now extends, it is maintained in general, and in conformity with the views of Augustine and the Schoolmen, that the natural endowments of man are corrupted, and the supernatural almost entirely lost. A separate consideration of the powers of the Intellect and the Will. Some general considerations: The intellect possesses some powers of perception. Still it labours under a twofold defect.

18. The power of the human intellect in regard to things celestial. These reducible to three heads, namely, divine knowledge, adoption, and will. The blindness of man in regard to these proved and thus tested by a simile.

12. I feel pleased with the well-known saying which has been borrowed from the writings of Augustine, that man's natural gifts were corrupted by sin, and his supernatural gifts withdrawn; meaning by supernatural gifts the light of faith and righteousness, which would have been sufficient for the attainment of heavenly life and everlasting felicity. Man, when he withdrew his allegiance to God, was deprived of the spiritual gifts by which he had been raised to the hope of eternal salvation. Hence it follows, that he is now an exile from the kingdom of God, so that all things which pertain to the blessed life of the soul are extinguished in him until he recover them by the grace of regeneration. Among these are faith, love to God, charity towards our neighbour, the study of righteousness and holiness. All these, when restored to us by Christ, are to be regarded as adventitious and above nature. If so, we infer that they were previously abolished. On the other hand, soundness of mind and integrity of heart were, at the same time, withdrawn, and it is this which constitutes the corruption of natural gifts. For although there is still some residue of intelligence and judgment as well as will, we cannot call a mind sound and entire which is both weak and immersed in darkness. As to the will, its depravity is but too well known. Therefore, since reason, by which man discerns between good and evil, and by which he understands and judges, is a natural gift, it could not be entirely destroyed; but being partly weakened and partly corrupted, a shapeless ruin is all that remains. In this sense it is said (Jn 1:5), that 'the light shineth in darkness, and the darkness comprehended it not', these words clearly expressing both points – that in the perverted and degenerate nature of man there are still some sparks which show that he is a rational animal, and differs from the brutes, inasmuch as he is endued with intelligence, and yet, that this light is so smothered by clouds of darkness that it cannot shine forth to any good effect. In like manner, the will, because inseparable from the nature of man, did not perish, but was so enslaved by depraved lusts as to be incapable of one righteous desire. The definition now given is complete, but there are several points which require to be explained. Therefore, proceeding agreeably to that primary distinction, by which we divided the soul into intellect and will, we will now inquire into the power of the intellect.

To charge the intellect with perpetual blindness, so as to leave it no intelligence of any description whatever, is repugnant not only to the Word of God, but to common experience. We see that there has been implanted in the human mind a certain desire of investigating truth, to which it never would aspire unless some relish for truth antecedently existed. There is, therefore, now, in the human mind, discernment to this extent, that it is naturally influenced by the love of truth, the neglect of which in the lower animals is a proof of their gross and irrational nature. Still it is true that this love of truth fails before it reaches the goal, forthwith falling away into vanity. As the human mind is unable, from dullness, to pursue the right path of investigation, and, after various wanderings, stumbling every now and then like one groping in darkness, at length gets completely bewildered, so its whole procedure proves how unfit it is to search the truth and find it. Then it labours under another grievous defect, in that it frequently fails to discern what the knowledge is which it should study to acquire. Hence, under the influence of a vain curiosity, it torments itself with superfluous and useless discussions, either not adverting at all to the things necessary to be known, or casting only a cursory and contemptuous glance at them. At all events, it scarcely ever studies them in sober earnest. Profane writers are constantly complaining of this perverse procedure, and yet almost all of them are found pursuing it. Hence Solomon, throughout the Book of Ecclesiastes, after enumerating all the studies in which men think they attain the highest wisdom, pronounces them vain and frivolous.

18. We must now explain what the power of human reason is, in regard to the kingdom of God, and spiritual discernments which consists chiefly of three things – the knowledge of God, the knowledge of his paternal favour towards us, which constitutes our salvation, and the method of regulating of our conduct in accordance with the Divine Law. With regard to the former two, but more properly the second, men otherwise the most ingenious are blinder than moles. I deny not, indeed, that in the writings of philosophers we meet occasionally with shrewd and apposite remarks on the nature of God, though they invariably savour somewhat of giddy imagination. As observed above, the Lord has bestowed on them some slight perception of his Godhead that they might not plead ignorance as an excuse for their impiety, and has, at times, instigated them to deliver some truths, the confession of which should be their own condemnation. Still, though seeing, they saw not. Their discernment was not such as to direct them to the truth, far less to enable them to attain it, but resembled that of the bewildered traveller, who sees the flash of lightning glance far and wide for a moment, and then vanish into the darkness of the night, before he can advance a single step. So far is such assistance from enabling him to find the right path. Besides, how many monstrous falsehoods intermingle with those minute particles of truth scattered up and down in their writings as if by chance. In short, not one of them even made the least approach to that assurance of the divine favour, without which the mind of man must ever remain a mere chaos of confusion. To the great truths, what God is in himself, and what he is in relation to us, human reason makes not the least approach (see Book 3 Chap. 2 sects. 14, 15, 16).

✠ CHAPTER 3 ✠

Every thing proceeding from the corrupt nature of man damnable.

Sections

3. Some of the heathen were possessed of admirable endowments, and, therefore, some argue that the nature of man is not entirely corrupt. Answer, Corruption is not entirely removed, but only inwardly restrained. Explanation of this answer.

3. Here, again we are met with a question very much the same as that which was previously solved. In every age there have been some who, under the guidance of nature, were all their lives devoted to virtue. It is of no consequence, that many blots may be detected in their conduct; by the mere study of virtue, they evinced that there was somewhat of purity in their nature. The value which virtues of this kind have in the sight of God will be considered more fully when we treat of the merit of works. Meanwhile, however, it will be proper to consider it in this place also, in so far as necessary for the exposition of the subject in hand. Such examples, then, seem to warn us against supposing that the nature of man is utterly vicious, since, under its guidance, some have not only excelled in illustrious deeds, but conducted themselves most honourably through the whole course of their lives. But we ought to consider, that, notwithstanding of the corruption of our nature, there is some room for divine grace, such grace as, without purifying it, may lay it under internal restraint. For, did the Lord let every mind loose to wanton in its lusts, doubtless there is not a man who would not show that his nature is capable of all the crimes with which Paul charges it (Rom. 3 compared with Ps. 14:3, etc.). What? Can you exempt yourself from the number of those whose feet are swift to shed blood; whose hands are foul with rapine and murder; whose throats are like open sepulchres; whose tongues are deceitful; whose lips are venomous; whose actions are useless, unjust, rotten, deadly; whose soul is without God; whose inward parts are full of wickedness; whose eyes are on the watch for deception; whose minds are prepared for insult; whose every part, in short, is framed for endless deeds of wickedness? If every soul is capable of such abominations (and the apostle declares this boldly), it is surely easy to see what the result would be, if the Lord were to permit human

passion to follow its bent. No ravenous beast would rush so furiously, no stream, however rapid and violent, so impetuously burst its banks. In the elect, God cures these diseases in the mode which will shortly be explained; in others, he only lays them under such restraint as may prevent them from breaking forth to a degree incompatible with the preservation of the established order of things. Hence, how much soever men may disguise their impurity, some are restrained only by shame, others by a fear of the laws, from breaking out into many kinds of wickedness. Some aspire to an honest life, as deeming it most conducive to their interest, while others are raised above the vulgar lot, that, by the dignity of their station, they may keep inferiors to their duty. Thus God, by his providence, curbs the perverseness of nature, preventing it from breaking forth into action, yet without rendering it inwardly pure.

PART VI

GOD'S LAW

✢ CHAPTER 6 ✢
Redemption for man lost to be sought in Christ.

Sections

1. The knowledge of God the Creator of no avail without faith in Christ the Redeemer. First reason. Second reason strengthened by the testimony of an apostle. Conclusion. This doctrine entertained by the children of God in all ages from the beginning of the world. Error of throwing open heaven to the heathen, who know nothing of Christ. The pretexts for this refuted by passages of Scripture.

1. The whole human race having been undone in the person of Adam, the excellence and dignity of our origin, as already described, is so far from availing us, that it rather turns to our greater disgrace, until God, who does not acknowledge man when defiled and corrupted by sin as his own work, appear as a Redeemer in the person of his only begotten Son. Since our fall from life unto death, all that knowledge of God the Creator, of which we have discoursed, would be useless, were it not followed up by faith, holding forth God to us as a Father in Christ. The natural course undoubtedly was, that the fabric of the world should be a school in which we might learn piety, and from it pass to eternal life and perfect felicity. But after looking at the perfection beheld wherever we turn our eye, above and below, we are met by the divine malediction, which, while it involves innocent creatures in our fault, of necessity fills our own souls with despair. For although God is still pleased in many ways to manifest his paternal favour towards us, we cannot, from a mere survey of the world, infer that he is a Father. Conscience urging us within, and showing that sin is a just ground for our being forsaken, will not allow us to think that God accounts or treats us as sons. In addition to this are our sloth and ingratitude. Our minds are so blinded that they cannot perceive the truth, and all our senses are so corrupt that we wickedly rob God of his glory. Wherefore, we must conclude with Paul, 'After that in the wisdom of God the world by wisdom knew not God, it pleased God by the foolishness of preaching to save them that believe' (1 Cor. 1:21). By the 'wisdom of God' he designates this magnificent theatre of heaven and earth replenished with numberless wonders, the wise contemplation of which should have enabled us to know God. But this we do with little profit; and, therefore, he invites us to faith in Christ – faith which, by a semblance of foolishness, disgusts the unbeliever. Therefore, although the preaching of the cross is not in accordance with human wisdom, we must, however, humbly embrace it if we would return to God our Maker, from whom we are estranged, that he may again become our Father. It is certain that after the fall of our first parent, no knowledge of God without a Mediator was effectual to

salvation. Christ speaks not of his own age merely, but embraces all ages, when he says, 'This is life eternal that they might know thee the only true God, and Jesus Christ, whom thou hast sent' (Jn 17:3). The more shameful therefore is the presumption of those who throw heaven open to the unbelieving and profane, in the absence of that grace which Scripture uniformly describes as the only door by which we enter into life. Should any confine our Saviour's words to the period subsequent to the promulgation of the Gospel, the refutation is at hand; since on a ground common to all ages and nations, it is declared, that those who are estranged from God, and as such, are under the curse, the children of wrath, cannot be pleasing to God until they are reconciled.

To this we may add the answer which our Saviour gave to the Samaritan woman, 'Ye worship ye know not what; we know what we worship: for salvation is of the Jews' (Jn 4:22). By these words, he both charges every Gentile religion with falsehood, and assigns the reason – that under the Law the Redeemer was promised to the chosen people only, and that, consequently, no worship was ever pleasing to God in which respect was not had to Christ. Hence also Paul affirms, that all the Gentiles were 'without God' and deprived of the hope of life. Now, since John teaches that there was life in Christ from the beginning, and that the whole world had lost it (Jn 1:4), it is necessary to return to that fountain. And, accordingly, Christ declares that inasmuch as he is a propitiator, he is life. And, indeed, the inheritance of heaven belongs to none but the sons of God (Jn 15:6). Now, it were most incongruous to give the place and rank of sons to any who have not been engrafted into the body of the only begotten Son. And John distinctly testifies that those become the sons of God who believe in his name. But as it is not my intention at present formally to discuss the subject of faith in Christ, it is enough to have thus touched on it in passing.

✝ CHAPTER 7 ✝

The Law given, not to retain a people for itself, but to keep alive the hope of salvation in Christ until his advent.

Sections

3. The Moral Law leads believers to Christ. Showing the perfect righteousness required by God, it convinces us of our inability to fulfil it. It thus denies us life, adjudges us to death, and so urges us to seek deliverance in Christ.

6. A consideration of the office and use of the Moral Law shows that it leads to Christ. The Law, while it describes the righteousness which is acceptable to God, proves that every man is unrighteous.

7. The Law fitly compared to a mirror, which shows us our wretchedness. This derogates not in any degree from its excellence.

10. A second use of the Law is to curb sinners. This most necessary for the good of the community at large; and this in respect not only of the reprobate, but also of the elect, previous to regeneration. This confirmed by the authority of an apostle.

12. The third and most appropriate use of the Law respects the elect: (1) It instructs and teaches them to make daily progress in doing the will of God, and (2) urges them by exhortation to obedience. Testimony of David. How he is to be reconciled with the apostle.

3. But in order that a sense of guilt may urge us to seek for pardon, it is of importance to know how our being instructed in the Moral Law renders us more inexcusable. If it is true, that a perfect righteousness is set before us in the Law, it follows, that the complete observance of it is perfect righteousness in the sight of God; that is, a righteousness by which a man may be deemed and pronounced righteous at the divine tribunal. Wherefore Moses, after promulgating the Law, hesitates not to call heaven and earth to witness, that he had set life and death, good and evil, before the people. Nor can it be denied, that the reward of eternal salvation, as promised by the Lord, awaits the perfect obedience of the Law (Deut. 30:19). Again, however, it is of importance to understand in what way we perform that obedience for which we justly entertain the hope of that reward. For of what use is it to see that the reward of eternal life depends on the observance of the Law, unless it moreover appears whether it be in our power in that way to attain to eternal life? Herein, then, the weakness of the Law is manifested; for, in none of us is that righteousness of the Law manifested, and, therefore, being excluded from the promises of life, we again fall under the curse. I state not only what happens, but what must necessarily happen. The doctrine of the Law transcending our capacity, a man may indeed look from a distance at the promises held forth, but he cannot derive any benefit from them. The only thing, therefore, remaining for him is, from their excellence to form a better estimate of his own misery, while he considers that the hope of salvation is cut off, and he is threatened with certain death. On the other hand, those fearful denunciations which strike not at a few individuals, but at every individual without exceptions rise up; rise up, I say, and, with inexorable severity, pursue us; so that nothing but instant death is presented by the Law.

6. That the whole matter may be made clearer, let us take a succinct view of the office and use of the Moral Law. Now this office and use seems to me to consist of three parts. First, by exhibiting the righteousness of God – in other words, the righteousness which alone is acceptable to God – it admonishes every one of his own unrighteousness, convicts, and finally condemns him. This is necessary, in order that man, who is blind and intoxicated with self-love, may be brought at once to know and to confess his weakness and impurity. For until his vanity is made perfectly manifest, he is puffed up with infatuated confidence in his own powers, and never can be brought to feel their feebleness so long as he measures them by a standard of his own choice. So soon, however, as he begins to compare them with the requirements of the Law, he has something to tame his presumption. How high soever his opinion of his own powers may be, he immediately feels that they pant under the heavy load, then totter and stumble, and finally fall and give way. He, then, who is schooled by the Law, lays aside the arrogance which formerly blinded him. In like manner must he be cured of pride, the other disease under which we have said that he labours. So long as he is permitted to appeal to his own judgment, he substitutes a hypocritical for a real righteousness, and, contented with this, sets up certain factitious observances in opposition to the grace of God. But after he is forced to weigh his conduct in the balance of the Law, renouncing all dependence on this fancied righteousness, he sees that he is at an infinite distance from holiness, and, on the other hand, that he teems with innumerable vices of which he formerly seemed free. The recesses in which concupiscence lies hid are so deep and tortuous that they easily elude our view; and hence the apostle had good reason for saying, 'I had not known lust, except the law had said, Thou shalt not covet.' For, if it be not brought forth from its lurking places, it miserably destroys in secret before its fatal sting is discerned.

7. Thus the Law is a kind of mirror. As in a mirror we discover any stains upon our face, so in the Law we behold, first, our impotence; then, in consequence of it, our iniquity; and, finally, the curse, as the consequence of both. He who has no power of following righteousness is necessarily plunged in the mire of iniquity, and this iniquity is immediately followed by the curse. Accordingly, the greater the transgression of which the Law convicts us, the severer the judgment to which we are exposed. To this effect is the apostle's declaration, that 'by the law is the knowledge of sin' (Rom. 3:20). By these words, he only points out the first office of the Law as experienced by sinners not yet regenerated. In conformity to this, it is said, 'the law entered that the offence might abound'; and, accordingly, that it is 'the ministration of death'; that it 'worketh wrath' and kills (Rom. 5:20; 2 Cor. 3:7; Rom. 4:15). For there cannot be a doubt that the clearer the consciousness of guilt, the greater the increase of sin; because then to transgression a rebellious feeling against the Lawgiver is added. All that remains for the Law, is to arm the wrath of God for the destruction of the sinner; for by itself it can do nothing but accuse, condemn, and destroy him. Thus Augustine says, 'If the Spirit of grace be absent, the law is present only to convict and slay us.' But to say this neither insults the Law, nor derogates in any degree from its excellence. Assuredly, if our whole will were formed and disposed to obedience, the mere knowledge of the Law would be sufficient for salvation; but since our carnal and corrupt nature is at enmity with the Divine Law, and is in no degree amended by its discipline, the consequence is, that the Law which, if it had been properly attended to, would have given life, becomes the occasion of sin and death. When all are convicted of transgression, the more it declares the righteousness of God, the more, on the other hand, it discloses our iniquity; the more certainly it assures us that life and salvation are treasured up as the reward of righteousness, the more certainly it assures us that the unrighteous will perish. So far, however, are these qualities from throwing disgrace on the Law, that their chief tendency is to give a brighter display of the divine goodness. For they show that it is only our weakness and depravity that prevents us from enjoying the blessedness which the Law openly sets before us. Hence additional sweetness is given to divine grace, which comes to our aid without the Law, and additional loveliness to the mercy which confers it, because they proclaim that God is never weary in doing good, and in loading us with new gifts.

10. The second office of the Law is, by means of its fearful denunciations and the consequent dread of punishment, to curb those who, unless forced, have no regard for rectitude and justice. Such persons are curbed not because their mind is inwardly moved and affected, but because, as if a bridle were laid upon them, they refrain their hands from external acts, and internally check the depravity which would otherwise petulantly burst forth. It is true, they are not on this account either better or more righteous in the sight of God. For although restrained by terror or shame, they dare not proceed to what their mind has conceived, nor give full license to their raging lust, their heart is by no means trained to fear and obedience. Nay, the more they restrain themselves, the more they are inflamed, the more they rage and boil, prepared for any act or outbreak whatsoever were it not for the terror of the Law. And not only so, but they thoroughly detest the Law itself, and execrate the Lawgiver; so that if they could, they would most willingly annihilate him, because they cannot bear either his ordering what is right, or his avenging the despisers of his Majesty. The feeling of all who are not yet regenerate, though in some more, in others less lively, is, that in regard to the observance of the Law, they are not led by voluntary submission, but dragged by the force of fear. Nevertheless, this forced and extorted righteousness is necessary for the good of society, its peace being secured by a provision but for which all things would be thrown into tumult and confusion. Nay, this tuition is not without its use, even to the children of God, who, previous to their effectual calling, being destitute of the Spirit of holiness, freely indulge the lusts of the flesh. When, by the fear of Divine vengeance, they are deterred from open outbreakings, though, from not being subdued in mind, they profit little at present, still they are in some measure trained to bear the yoke of righteousness, so that when they are called, they are not like mere novices, studying a discipline of which previously they had no knowledge. This office seems to be especially in the view of the apostle, when he says, 'That the law is not made for a righteous man, but for the lawless and disobedient, for the ungodly and for sinners, for unholy and profane, for murderers of fathers and murderers of mothers, for manslayers, for whoremongers, for them that defile themselves with mankind, for men-stealers, for liars, for perjured persons, and if there be any other thing that is contrary to sound doctrine' (1 Tim. 1:9, 10). He thus indicates that it is a restraint on unruly lusts that would otherwise burst all bonds.

12. The third use of the Law (being also the principal use, and more closely connected with its proper end) has respect to believers in whose hearts the Spirit of God already flourishes and reigns. For although the Law is written and engraven on their hearts by the finger of God, that is, although they are so influenced and actuated by the Spirit, that they desire to obey God, there are two ways in which they still profit in the Law. For it is the best instrument for enabling them daily to learn with greater truth and certainty what that will of the Lord is which they aspire to follow, and to confirm them in this knowledge; just as a servant who desires with all his soul to approve himself to his master, must still observe, and be careful to ascertain his master's dispositions, that he may comport himself in accommodation to them. Let none of us deem ourselves exempt from this necessity, for none have as yet attained to such a degree of wisdom, as that they may not, by the daily instruction of the Law, advance to a purer knowledge of the Divine will. Then, because we need not doctrine merely, but exhortation also, the servant of God will derive this further advantage from the Law: by frequently meditating upon it, he will be excited to obedience, and confirmed in it, and so drawn away from the slippery paths of sin. In this way must the saints press onward, since, however great the alacrity with which, under the Spirit, they hasten toward righteousness, they are retarded by the sluggishness of the flesh, and make less progress than they ought. The Law acts like a whip to the flesh, urging it on as men do a lazy sluggish ass. Even in the case of a spiritual man, inasmuch as he is still burdened with the weight of the flesh, the Law is a constant stimulus, pricking him forward when he would indulge in sloth. David had this use in view when he pronounced this high eulogium on the Law, 'The law of the Lord is perfect, converting the soul: the testimony of the Lord is sure, making wise the simple. The statutes of the Lord are right, rejoicing the heart: the commandment of the Lord is pure, enlightening the eyes' (Ps. 19:7, 8). Again, 'Thy word is a lamp unto my feet, and a light unto my path' (Ps. 119:105). The whole psalm abounds in passages to the same effect. Such passages are not inconsistent with those of Paul, which show not the utility of the Law to the regenerate, but what it is able of itself to bestow. The object of the Psalmist is to celebrate the advantages which the Lord, by means of his Law, bestows on those whom he inwardly inspires with a love of obedience. And he adverts not to the mere precepts, but also to the promise annexed to them, which alone makes that sweet which in itself is bitter. For what is less attractive than the Law, when, by its demands and threatening, it overawes the soul, and fills it with terror? David specially shows that in the Law he saw the Mediator, without whom it gives no pleasure or delight.

✝ CHAPTER 8 ✝

Exposition of the moral law.

Sections

1. The Law was committed to writing, in order that it might teach more fully and perfectly that knowledge, both of God and of ourselves, which the law of nature teaches meagrely and obscurely. Proof of this, from an enumeration of the principal parts of the Moral Law; and also from the dictate of natural law, written on the hearts of all, and, in a manner, effaced by sin.

2. Certain general maxims: From the knowledge of God, furnished by the Law, we learn that God is our Father and Ruler. Righteousness is pleasing, iniquity is an abomination in his sight. Hence, how weak soever we may be, our duty is to cultivate the one, and shun the other.

3. From the knowledge of ourselves, furnished by the Law, we learn to discern our own utter powerlessness, and are ashamed; and seeing it is in vain to seek for righteousness in ourselves, are induced to seek it elsewhere.

4. Hence, God has annexed promises and threatening to his promises. These not limited to the present life, but embrace things heavenly and eternal. They, moreover, attest the spotless purity of God, his love of righteousness, and also his kindness towards us.

51. The end of the Law. Proof. A summary of the Ten Commandments. The Law delivers not merely rudiments and first principles, but a perfect standard of righteousness, modelled on the divine purity.

54. A conduct duly regulated by the divine Law, characterised by charity toward our neighbour. This subverted by those who give the first place to self-love. Refutation of their opinion.

55. Who our neighbour is. Double error of the Schoolmen on this point.

1. I believe it will not be out of place here to introduce the Ten Commandments of the Law, and give a brief exposition of them. In this way it will be made more clear, that the worship which God originally prescribed is still in force (a point to which I have already adverted); and then a second point will be confirmed – that the Jews not only learned from the Law wherein true piety consisted, but from feeling their inability to observe it were overawed by the fear of judgments and so drawn, even against their will, towards the Mediator. In giving a summary of what constitutes the true knowledge of God we showed that we cannot form any just conception of the character of God, without feeling overawed by his majesty, and bound to do him service. In regard to the knowledge of ourselves, we showed that it principally consists in renouncing all idea of our own strength, and divesting ourselves of all confidence in our own

righteousness, while, on the other hand, under a full consciousness of our wants, we learn true humility and self-abasement. Both of these the Lord accomplishes by his Law, first, when, in assertion of the right which he has to our obedience, he calls us to reverence his majesty, and prescribes the conduct by which this reverence is manifested; and, secondly, when, by promulgating the rule of his justice (a rule, to the rectitude of which our nature, from being depraved and perverted, is continually opposed, and to the perfection of which our ability, from its infirmity and nervelessness for good, is far from being able to attain), he charges us both with impotence and unrighteousness. Moreover, the very things contained in the two tables are, in a manner, dictated to us by that internal law, which, as has been already said, is in a manner written and stamped on every heart. For conscience, instead of allowing us to stifle our perceptions, and sleep on without interruption, acts as an inward witness and monitor, reminds us of what we owe to God, points out the distinction between good and evil, and thereby convicts us of departure from duty. But man, being immured in the darkness of error, is scarcely able, by means of that natural law, to form any tolerable idea of the worship which is acceptable to God. At all events, he is very far from forming any correct knowledge of it. In addition to this, he is so swollen with arrogance and ambition, and so blinded with self-love, that he is unable to survey, and, as it were, descend into himself, that he may so learn to humble and abase himself, and confess his misery. Therefore, as a necessary remedy, both for our dullness and our contumacy, the Lord has given us his written Law, which, by its sure attestations, removes the obscurity of the law of nature, and also, by shaking off our lethargy, makes a more lively and permanent impression on our minds.

2. It is now easy to understand the doctrine of the Law –that God, as our Creator, is entitled to be regarded by us as a Father and Master, and should, accordingly, receive from us fear, love, reverence, and glory; nay, that we are not our own, to follow whatever course passion dictates, but are bound to obey him implicitly, and to acquiesce entirely in his good pleasure. Again, the Law teaches, that justice and rectitude are a delight, injustice an abomination to him, and, therefore, as we would not with impious ingratitude revolt from our Maker, our whole life must be spent in the cultivation of righteousness. For if we manifest becoming reverence only when we prefer his will to our own, it follows, that the only legitimate service to him is the practice of justice, purity, and holiness. Nor can we plead as an excuse, that we want the power, and, like debtors, whose means are exhausted, are unable to pay. We cannot be permitted to measure the glory of God by our ability; whatever we may be, he ever remains like himself, the friend of righteousness, the enemy of unrighteousness, and whatever his demands from us may be, as he can only require what is right, we are necessarily under a natural obligation to obey. Our inability to do so is our own fault. If lust, in which sin has its dominion, so enthrals us, that we are not free to obey our Father, there is no ground for pleading necessity as a defence, since this evil necessity is within, and must be imputed to ourselves.

3. When, under the guidance of the Law, we have advanced thus far, we must, under the same guidance, proceed to descend into ourselves. In this way, we at length arrive at two results: First, contrasting our conduct with the righteousness of the Law, we see how very far it is from being in accordance with the will of God, and, therefore, how unworthy we are of holding our place among his creatures, far less of being accounted his sons; and, secondly, taking a survey of our powers, we see that they are not only unequal to fulfil the Law, but are altogether null. The necessary consequence must be, to produce distrust of our own ability, and also anxiety and trepidation of mind. Conscience cannot feel the burden of its guilt, without forthwith turning to the judgment of God, while the view of this judgment cannot fail to excite a dread of death. In like manner, the proofs of our utter powerlessness must instantly beget despair of our own strength. Both feelings are productive of humility and abasement, and hence the sinner, terrified at the prospect of eternal death (which he sees justly impending over him for his iniquities), turns to the mercy of God as the only haven of safety. Feeling his utter inability to pay what he owes to the Law, and thus despairing of himself, he rethinks him of applying and looking to some other quarter for help.

4. But the Lord does not count it enough to inspire a reverence for his justice. To imbue our hearts with love to himself, and, at the same time, with hatred to iniquity, he has added promises and threatening. The eye of our mind being too dim to be attracted by the mere beauty of goodness, our most merciful Father has been pleased, in his great indulgence, to allure us to love and long after it by the hope of reward. He accordingly declares that rewards for virtue are treasured up with him, that none who yield obedience to his commands will labour in vain. On the other hand, he proclaims not only that iniquity is hateful in his sight, but that it will not escape with impunity, because he will be the avenger of his insulted majesty. That he may encourage us in every way, he promises present blessings, as well as eternal felicity, to the obedience of those who shall have kept his commands, while he threatens transgressors with present suffering, as well as the punishment of eternal death. The promise 'Ye shall therefore keep my statutes, and my judgments; which if a man do, he shall live in them' (Lev. 18:5), and corresponding to this the threatening 'The soul that sinneth, it shall die' (Ezek. 18:4, 20), doubtless point to a future life and death, both without end. But though in every passage where the favour or anger of God is mentioned, the former comprehends eternity of life and the latter eternal destruction, the Law, at the same time, enumerates a long catalogue of present blessings and curses (Lev. 26:4; Deut. 28:1). The threatenings attest the spotless purity of God, which cannot bear iniquity, while the promises attest at once his infinite love of righteousness (which he cannot leave unrewarded), and his wondrous kindness. Being bound to do him homage with all that we have, he is perfectly entitled to demand everything which he requires of us as a debt; and as a debt, the payment is unworthy of reward. He therefore foregoes his right, when he holds forth reward for services which are not offered spontaneously, as if they were not due. The amount of these services, in themselves, has been partly described and will appear more clearly in its own place. For the present, it is enough to remember that the promises of the Law are no mean commendation of righteousness as they show how much God is pleased with the observance of them, while the threatening denounced are intended to produce a greater abhorrence of unrighteousness, lest the sinner should indulge in the blandishments of vice, and forget the judgment which the divine Lawgiver has prepared for him.

51. It will not now be difficult to ascertain the general end contemplated by the whole Law – the fulfilment of righteousness, that man may form his life on the model of the divine purity. For therein God has so delineated his own character, that any one exhibiting in action what is commanded, would in some measure exhibit a living image of God. Wherefore Moses, when he wished to fix a summary of the whole in the memory of the Israelites, thus addressed them, 'And now, Israel, what does the Lord thy God require of thee, but to fear the Lord thy God, to walk in all his ways, and to love him, and to serve the Lord thy God with all thy heart, and with all thy soul, to keep the commandments of the Lord and his statutes which I command thee this day for thy good?' (Deut. 10:12, 13). And he ceased not to reiterate the same thing, whenever he had occasion to mention the end of the Law. To this the doctrine of the Law pays so much regard, that it connects man, by holiness of life, with his God; and, as Moses elsewhere expresses it (Deut. 6:5; 11:13), and makes him cleave to him. Moreover, this holiness of life is comprehended under the two heads above mentioned. 'Thou shalt love the Lord thy God with all thy heart, and with all thy soul, and with all thy mind, and with all thy strength, and thy neighbour as thyself.' First, our mind must be completely filled with love to God, and then this love must forthwith flow out toward our neighbour. This the apostle shows when he says, 'The end of the commandment is charity out of a pure heart, and a good conscience, and of faith unfeigned' (1 Tim. 1:5). You see that conscience and faith unfeigned are placed at the head, in other words, true piety; and that from this charity is derived. It is a mistake then to suppose, that merely the rudiments and first principles of righteousness are delivered in the Law, to form, as it were, a kind of introduction to good works, and not to guide to the perfect performance of them. For complete perfection, nothing more can be required than is expressed in these passages of Moses and Paul. How far, pray, would he wish to go, who is not satisfied with the instruction which directs man to the fear of God, to spiritual worship, practical obedience; in fine, purity of conscience, faith unfeigned, and charity? This confirms that interpretation of the Law which searches out, and finds in its precepts, all the duties of piety and charity. Those who merely search for dry and meagre elements, as if it taught the will of God only by halves, by no means understand its end, the apostle being witness.

54. Let us therefore hold, that our life will be framed in best accordance with the will of God, and the requirements of his Law, when it is, in every respect, most advantageous to our brethren. But in the whole Law, there is not one syllable which lays down a rule as to what man is to do or avoid for the advantage of his own carnal nature. And, indeed, since men are naturally prone to excessive self-love, which they always retain, how great soever their departure from the truth may be, there was no need of a law to inflame a love already existing in excess. Hence it is perfectly plain, that the observance of the Commandments consists not in the love of ourselves, but in the love of God and our neighbour; and that he leads the best and holiest life who as little as may be studies and lives for himself; and that none lives worse and more unrighteously than he who studies and lives only for himself, and seeks and thinks only of his own. Nay, the better to express how strongly we should be inclined to love our neighbour, the Lord has made self-love as it were the standard, there being no feeling in our nature of greater strength and vehemence. The force of the expression ought to be carefully weighed. For he does not (as some sophists have stupidly dreamed) assign the first place to self-love, and the second to charity. He rather transfers to others the love which we naturally feel for ourselves. Hence the apostle declares, that charity 'seeketh not her own' (1 Cor. 13:5). Nor is the argument worth a straw, That the thing regulated must always be inferior to the rule. The Lord did not make self-love the rule, as if love towards others were subordinate to it; but whereas, through natural gravity, the feeling of love usually rests on ourselves, he shows that it ought to diffuse itself in another direction – that we should be prepared to do good to our neighbour with no less alacrity, ardour, and solicitude, than to ourselves.

55. Our Saviour having shown, in the parable of the Samaritan (Lk 10:36), that the term 'neighbour' comprehends the most remote stranger, there is no reason for limiting the precept of love to our own connections. I deny not that the closer the relation the more frequent our offices of kindness should be. For the condition of humanity requires that there be more duties in common between those who are more nearly connected by the ties of relationship, or friendship, or neighbourhood. And this is done without any offence to God, by whose providence we are in a manner impelled to do it. But I say that the whole human race, without exception, are to be embraced with one feeling of charity: that here there is no distinction of Greek or Barbarian, worthy or unworthy, friend or foe, since all are to be viewed not in themselves, but in God. If we turn aside from this view, there is no wonder that we entangle ourselves in error. Wherefore, if we would hold the true course in love, our first step must be to turn our eyes not to man, the sight of whom might oftener produce hatred than love, but to God, who requires that the love which we bear to him be diffused among all mankind, so that our fundamental principle must ever be, Let a man be what he may, he is still to be loved, because God is loved.

✝ CHAPTER 9 ✝

Christ, though known to the Jews under the Law, yet only manifested under the Gospel.

Sections

4. Refutation of those who do not properly compare the Law and the Gospel. Answer to certain questions here occurring. The Law and the Gospel briefly compared.

4. We see the error of those who, in comparing the Law with the Gospel, represent it merely as a comparison between the merit of works, and the gratuitous imputation of righteousness. The contrast thus made is by no means to be rejected, because, by the term 'Law' Paul frequently understands that rule of holy living in which God exacts what is his due, giving no hope of life unless we obey in every respect; and, on the other hand, denouncing a curse for the slightest failure. This Paul does when showing that we are freely accepted of God, and accounted righteous by being pardoned, because that obedience of the Law to which the reward is promised is nowhere to be found. Hence he appropriately represents the righteousness of the Law and the Gospel as opposed to each other. But the Gospel has not succeeded the whole Law in such a sense as to introduce a different method of salvation. It rather confirms the Law, and proves that every thing which it promised is fulfilled. What was shadow, it has made substance. When Christ says that the Law and the Prophets were until John, he does not consign the fathers to the curse, which, as the slaves of the Law, they could not escape. He intimates that they were only imbued with the rudiments, and remained far beneath the height of the Gospel doctrine. Accordingly Paul, after calling the Gospel 'the power of God unto salvation to every one that believeth', shortly after adds, that it was 'witnessed by the Law and the Prophets' (Rom. 1:16; 3:21). And in the end of the same Epistle, though he describes 'the preaching of Jesus Christ' as 'the revelation of the mystery which was kept secret since the world began', he modifies the expression by adding, that it is 'now made manifest' 'by the scriptures of the prophets' (Rom. 16:25, 26). Hence we infer, that when the whole Law is spoken of, the Gospel differs from it only in respect of clearness of manifestation. Still, on account of the inestimable riches of grace set before us in Christ, there is good reason for saying, that by his advent the kingdom of heaven was erected on the earth (Mt. 12:28).

PART VII

THE PERSON OF JESUS CHRIST AND HIS WORK OF REDEMPTION

✛

✝ CHAPTER 12 ✝

Christ, to perform the office of mediator, behoved to become man.

Sections

  2. Why the Mediator behoved to be God and man – that he had to convert those who were heirs of hell into children of God.

2. This will become still clearer if we reflect, that the work to be performed by the Mediator was of no common description: being to restore us to the divine favour, so as to make us, instead of sons of men, sons of God; instead of heirs of hell, heirs of a heavenly kingdom. Who could do this unless the Son of God should also become the Son of man, and so receive what is ours as to transfer to us what is his, making that which is his by nature to become ours by grace? Relying on this earnest, we trust that we are the sons of God, because the natural Son of God assumed to himself a body of our body, flesh of our flesh, bones of our bones, that he might be one with us; he declined not to take what was peculiar to us, that he might in his turn extend to us what was peculiarly his own, and thus might be in common with us both Son of God and Son of man. Hence that holy brotherhood which he commends with his own lips, when he says, 'I ascend to my Father, and your Father, to my God, and your God' (Jn 20:17). In this way, we have a sure inheritance in the heavenly kingdom, because the only Son of God, to whom it entirely belonged, has adopted us as his brethren; and if brethren, then partners with him in the inheritance (Rom. 8:17). Moreover, it was especially necessary for this cause also that he who was to be our Redeemer should be truly God and man. It was his to swallow up death: who but Life could do so? It was his to conquer sin: who could do so save Righteousness itself? It was his to put to flight the powers of the air and the world: who could do so but the mighty power superior to both? But who possesses life and righteousness, and the dominion and government of heaven, but God alone? Therefore, God, in his infinite mercy, having determined to redeem us, became himself our Redeemer in the person of his only begotten Son.

✝ CHAPTER 14 ✝

How two natures constitute the person of the Mediator.

Sections

1. Proof of two natures in Christ – a human and a divine. Illustrated by analogy, from the union of body and soul. Illustration applied.

1. When it is said that the Word was made flesh, we must not understand it as if he were either changed into flesh, or confusedly intermingled with flesh, but that he made choice of the Virgin's womb as a temple in which he might dwell. He who was the Son of God became the Son of man, not by confusion of substance, but by unity of person. For we maintain, that the divinity was so conjoined and united with the humanity, that the entire properties of each nature remain entire, and yet the two natures constitute only one Christ. If, in human affairs, any thing analogous to this great mystery can be found, the most apposite similitude seems to be that of man, who obviously consists of two substances, neither of which however is so inter-mingled with the other as that both do not retain their own properties. For neither is soul body, nor is body soul. Wherefore that is said separately of the soul which cannot in any way apply to the body; and that, on the other hand, of the body which is altogether inapplicable to the soul; and that, again, of the whole man, which cannot be affirmed without absurdity either of the body or of the soul separately. Lastly, the properties of the soul are transferred to the body, and the properties of the body to the soul, and yet these form only one man, not more than one. Such modes of expression intimate both that there is in man one person formed of two compounds, and that these two different natures constitute one person. Thus the Scriptures speak of Christ. They sometimes attribute to him qualities which should be referred specially to his humanity and sometimes qualities applicable peculiarly to his divinity, and sometimes qualities which embrace both natures, and do not apply specially to either. This combination of a twofold nature in Christ they express so carefully, that they some-times communicate them with each other, a figure of speech which the ancients termed a communication of properties.

✝ CHAPTER 15 ✝

Three things briefly to be regarded in Christ –
his offices of Prophet, King, and Priest.

Sections

1. Among heretics and false Christians, Christ is found in name only; but by those who are truly and effectually called of God, he is acknowledged as a Prophet, King, and Priest.

1. Though heretics pretend the name of Christ, truly does Augustine affirm, that the foun-dation is not common to them with the godly, but belongs exclusively to the Church: for if those things which pertain to Christ be diligently considered, it will be found that Christ is with them in name only, not in reality. Thus in the present day, though the Papists have the words 'Son of God, Redeemer of the world' sounding in their mouths, yet, because contented

with an empty name, they deprive him of his virtue and dignity; what Paul says of 'not holding the head' is truly applicable to them (Col. 2:19). Therefore, that faith may find in Christ a solid ground of salvation, and so rest in him, we must set out with this principle, that the office which he received from the Father consists of three parts. For he was appointed both Prophet, King, and Priest...

✝ CHAPTER 16 ✝

How Christ performed the office of redeemer in procuring our salvation. The death, resurrection, and ascension of Christ.

Sections

3. Not used improperly; for God finds in us ground both of hatred and love.
6. Why Christ was crucified. This hidden doctrine typified in the Law, and completed by the apostles and prophets. In what sense Christ was made a curse for us. The cross of Christ connected with the shedding of his blood.
7. Of the death of Christ. Why he died. Advantages from his death. Of the burial of Christ. Advantages.
10. The article of the descent to hell more accurately expounded. A great ground of comfort.
13. Of the resurrection of Christ. The many advantages from it: (1) Our righteousness in the sight of God renewed and restored; (2) his life the basis of our life and hope, also the efficacious cause of new life in us; (3) the pledge of our future resurrection.
14. Of the ascension of Christ. Why he ascended. Advantages derived from it.
15. Of Christ's seat at the Father's right hand. What meant by it.
16. Many advantages from the ascension of Christ: (1) He gives access to the kingdom which Adam had shut up; (2) he intercedes for us with the Father; (3) his virtue being thence transfused into us, he works effectually in us for salvation.
17. Of the return of Christ to judgment. Its nature. The quick and dead who are to be judged. Passages apparently contradictory reconciled. Mode of judgment.
18. Advantages of the doctrine of Christ's return to judgment. Third part of the chapter, explaining the view to be taken of the Apostles' Creed. Summary of the Apostles' Creed.
19. Conclusion of the whole chapter, showing that in Christ the salvation of the elect in all its parts is comprehended.

3. Though this is said in accommodation to the weakness of our capacity, it is not said falsely. For God, who is perfect righteousness, cannot love the iniquity which he sees in all. All of us, therefore, have that within which deserves the hatred of God. Hence, in respect, first, of our corrupt nature; and, secondly, of the depraved conduct following upon it, we are all offensive to God, guilty in his sight, and by nature the children of hell. But as the Lord wills not to destroy in us that which is his own, he still finds something in us which in kindness he can love. For though it is by our own fault that we are sinners, we are still his creatures; though we have brought death upon ourselves he had created us for life. Thus, mere gratuitous love

prompts him to receive us into favour. But if there is a perpetual and irreconcilable repugnance between righteousness and iniquity, so long as we remain sinners we cannot be completely received. Therefore, in order that all ground of offence may be removed, and he may completely reconcile us to himself, he, by means of the expiation set forth in the death of Christ, abolishes all the evil that is in us, so that we, formerly impure and unclean, now appear in his sight just and holy. Accordingly, God the Father, by his love, prevents and anticipates our reconciliation in Christ. Nay, it is because he first loves us, that he afterwards reconciles us to himself. But because the iniquity, which deserves the indignation of God, remains in us until the death of Christ comes to our aid, and that iniquity is in his sight accursed and condemned, we are not admitted to full and sure communion with God, unless, in so far as Christ unites us. And, therefore, if we would indulge the hope of having God placable and propitious to us, we must fix our eyes and minds on Christ alone, as it is to him alone it is owing that our sins, which necessarily provoked the wrath of God, are not imputed to us.

6. The very form of the death embodies a striking truth. The cross was cursed not only in the opinion of men, but by the enactment of the Divine Law. Hence Christ, while suspended on it, subjects himself to the curse. And thus it behoved to be done, in order that the whole curse, which on account of our iniquities awaited us, or rather lay upon us, might be taken from us by being transferred to him. This was also shadowed in the Law, since the word by which sin itself is properly designated, was applied to the sacrifices and expiations offered for sin. By this application of the term, the Spirit intended to intimate, that they were a kind of purification, bearing, by substitutions the curse due to sin. But that which was represented figuratively in the Mosaic sacrifices is exhibited in Christ the archetype. Wherefore, in order to accomplish a full expiation, he made his soul to a propitiatory victim for sin (as the prophet says, Isa. 53:5, 10), on which the guilt and penalty being in a manner laid, ceases to be imputed to us. The apostle declares this more plainly when he says, that 'he made him to be sin for us, who knew no sin; that we might be made the righteousness of God in him' (2 Cor. 5:21). For the Son of God, though spotlessly pure, took upon him the disgrace and ignominy of our iniquities, and in return clothed us with his purity. To the same thing he seems to refer, when he says, that he 'condemned sin in the flesh' (Rom. 8:3), the Father having destroyed the power of sin when it was transferred to the flesh of Christ. This term, therefore, indicates that Christ, in his death, was offered to the Father as a propitiatory victim; that, expiation being made by his sacrifice, we might cease to tremble at the divine wrath. It is now clear what the prophet means when he says, that 'the Lord has laid upon him the iniquity of us all' (Isa. 53:6); namely, that as he was to wash away the pollution of sins, they were transferred to him by imputation. Of this the cross to which he was nailed was a symbol, as the apostle declares, 'Christ has redeemed us from the curse of the law, being made a curse for us: for it is written, Cursed is every one that hangeth on a tree: that the blessing of Abraham might come on the Gentiles through Jesus Christ' (Gal. 3:13, 14). In the same way Peter says, that he 'bare our sins in his own body on the tree' (1 Pet. 2:24), inasmuch as from the very symbol of the curse, we perceive more clearly that the burden with which we were oppressed was laid upon him. Nor are we to understand that by the curse which he endured he was himself overwhelmed, but rather that by enduring it he repressed, broke, annihilated all its force. Accordingly, faith apprehends acquittal in the condemnation of Christ, and blessing in his curse. Hence it is not without cause that Paul magnificently celebrates the triumph which Christ obtained upon the cross, as if the cross, the symbol of ignominy, had been converted into a triumphal chariot. For he says, that he blotted out the handwriting of ordinances that was against us, which was contrary to us, and took it out of the way, nailing it to his cross: that 'having spoiled principalities and powers he made a show of them openly, triumphing over them in it' (Col. 2:14, 15). Nor is this to be wondered at; for, as another apostle declares, Christ, 'through the eternal Spirit, offered himself without spot to God,' (Heb. 9:14), and hence that transformation of the cross which were otherwise against its nature. But that these things may take deep root and have their seat in our inmost hearts, we must never lose sight of sacrifice and ablution. For, were not Christ a victim, we could have no sure conviction of his being our substitute-ransom and propitiation. And hence mention is always made of blood whenever Scripture explains the mode of redemption: although the shedding of Christ's blood was available not only for propitiation, but also acted as a laver to purge our defilements.

7. The Creed next mentions that he 'was dead and buried'. Here again it is necessary to consider how he substituted himself in order to pay the price of our redemption. Death held us under its yoke, but he in our place delivered himself into its power, that he might exempt us from it. This the apostle means when he says, 'that he tasted death for every man' (Heb. 2:9). By dying he prevented us from dying; or (which is the same thing) he by his death purchased life for us (see Calvin in Psychopann). But in this he differed from us, that in permitting himself to be overcome of death, it was not so as to be engulfed in its abyss but rather to annihilate it, as it must otherwise have annihilated us; he did not allow himself to be so subdued by it as to be crushed by its power; he rather laid it prostrate, when it was impending over us, and exulting over us as already overcome. In fine, his object was 'that through death he might destroy him that had the power of death, that is, the devil, and deliver them who through fear of death were all their lifetime subject to bondage' (Heb. 2:14, 15). This is the first-fruit which his death produced to us. Another is, that by fellowship with him he mortifies our earthly members that they may not afterwards exert themselves in action, and kill the old man, that he may not hereafter be in vigour and bring forth fruit. An effect of his burials moreover is that we as his fellows are buried to sin. For when the apostle says, that we are ingrafted into the likeness of Christ's death and that we are buried with him unto sin, that by his cross the world is crucified unto us and we unto the world, and that we are dead with him, he not only exhorts us to manifest an example of his death, but declares that there is an efficacy in it which should appear in all Christians, if they would not render his death unfruitful and useless. Accordingly in the death and burial of Christ a twofold blessing is set before us – deliverance from death, to which we were enslaved, and the mortification of our flesh (Rom. 6:5; Gal. 2:19; 6:14; Col. 3:3).

10. But, apart from the Creed, we must seek for a surer exposition of Christ's descent to hell: and the word of God furnishes us with one not only pious and holy, but replete with excellent consolation. Nothing had been done if Christ had only endured corporeal death. In order to interpose between us and God's anger, and satisfy his righteous judgment, it was necessary that he should feel the weight of divine vengeance. Whence also it was necessary that he should engage, as it were, at close quarters with the powers of hell and the horrors of eternal death. We lately quoted from the prophet, that the 'chastisement of our peace was laid upon him' that he 'was bruised for our iniquities' that he 'bore our infirmities'; expressions which intimate, that, like a sponsor and surety for the guilty, and, as it were, subjected to condemnation, he undertook and paid all the penalties which must have been exacted from them, the only exception being, that the pains of death could not hold him. Hence there is nothing strange in its being said that he descended to hell, seeing he endured the death which is inflicted on the wicked by an angry God. It is frivolous and ridiculous to object that in this way the order is perverted, it being absurd that an event which preceded burial should be placed after it. But after explaining what Christ endured in the sight of man, the Creed appropriately adds the invisible and incomprehensible judgment which he endured before God, to teach us that not only was the body of Christ given up as the price of redemption, but that there was a greater and more excellent price – that he bore in his soul the tortures of condemned and ruined man.

13. Next follows the resurrection from the dead, without which all that has hitherto been said would be defective. For seeing that in the cross, death, and burial of Christ, nothing but weakness appears, faith must go beyond all these, in order that it may be provided with full strength. Hence, although in his death we have an effectual completion of salvation, because by it we are reconciled to God, satisfaction is given to his justice, the curse is removed, and the penalty paid; still it is not by his death, but by his resurrection, that we are said to be begotten again to a living hope (1 Pet. 1:3); because, as he, by rising again, became victorious over death, so the victory of our faith consists only in his resurrection. The nature of it is better expressed in the words of Paul, 'Who [Christ] was delivered for our offences, and was raised again for our justification' (Rom. 4:25); as if he had said, By his death sin was taken away, by his resurrection righteousness was renewed and restored. For how could he by dying have freed us from death, if he had yielded to its power? How could he have obtained the victory for us, if he had fallen in the contest?

Our salvation may be thus divided between the death and the resurrection of Christ: by the former sin was abolished and death annihilated; by the latter righteousness was restored and life revived, the power and efficacy of the former being still bestowed upon us by means of the latter. Paul accordingly affirms, that he was declared to be the Son of God by his resurrection (Rom. 1:4), because he then fully displayed that heavenly power which is both a bright mirror of his divinity, and a sure support of our faith; as he also elsewhere teaches, that 'though he was crucified through weakness, yet he liveth by the power of God' (2 Cor. 13:4). In the same sense, in another passage, treating of perfection, he says, 'That I may know him and the power of his resurrection' (Phil. 3:10). Immediately after he adds, 'being made conformable unto his death'. In perfect accordance with this is the passage in Peter, that God 'raised him up from the dead, and gave him glory, that your faith and hope might be in God' (1 Pet. 1:21). Not that faith founded merely on his death is vacillating, but that the divine power by which he maintains our faith is most conspicuous in his resurrection. Let us remember, therefore, that when death only is mentioned, everything peculiar to the resurrection is at the same time included, and that there is a like synecdoche in the term 'resurrection', as often as it is used apart from death, everything peculiar to death being included. But as, by rising again, he obtained the victory, and became the resurrection and the life, Paul justly argues, 'If Christ be not raised, your faith is vain; ye are yet in your sins' (1 Cor. 15:17). Accordingly, in another passage, after exulting in the death of Christ in opposition to the terrors of condemnation, he thus enlarges, 'Christ that died, yea rather, that is risen again, who is even at the right hand of God, who also maketh intercession for us' (Rom. 8:34). Then, as we have already explained that the mortification of our flesh depends on communion with the cross, so we must also understand, that a corresponding benefit is derived from his resurrection. For as the apostle says, 'Like as Christ was raised up from the dead by the glory of the Father, even so we also should walk in newness of life' (Rom. 6:4). Accordingly, as in another passage, from our being dead with Christ, he inculcates, 'Mortify therefore your members which are upon the earth' (Col. 3:5); so from our being risen with Christ he infers, 'seek those things which are above, where Christ sitteth at the right hand of God' (Col. 3:1). In these words we are not only urged by the example of a risen Saviour to follow newness of life, but are taught that by his power we are renewed unto righteousness. A third benefit derived from it is, that, like an earnest, it assures us of our own resurrection, of which it is certain that his is the surest representation. This subject is discussed at length (1 Cor. 15). But it is to be observed, in passing, that when he is said to have 'risen from the dead', these terms express the reality both of his death and resurrection, as if it had been said, that he died the same death as other men naturally die, and received immortality in the same mortal flesh which he had assumed.

14. The resurrection is naturally followed by the ascension into heaven. For although Christ, by rising again, began fully to display his glory and virtue, having laid aside the abject and ignoble condition of a mortal life, and the ignominy of the cross, yet it was only by his ascension to heaven that his reign truly commenced. This the apostle shows, when he says he ascended 'that he might fill all things' (Eph. 4:10); thus reminding us, that under the appearance of contradiction, there is a beautiful harmony, inasmuch as though he departed from us, it was that his departure might be more useful to us than that presence which was confined in a humble tabernacle of flesh during his abode on the earth. Hence John, after repeating the celebrated invitation 'If any man thirst, let him come unto me and drink' immediately adds, 'the Holy Ghost was not yet given; because that Jesus was not yet glorified' (Jn 7:37, 39). This our Lord himself also declared to his disciples, 'It is expedient for you that I go away: for if I go not away the Comforter will not come unto you' (Jn 16:7). To console them for his bodily absence, he tells them that he will not leave them comfortless, but will come again to them in a manner invisible indeed, but more to be desired, because they were then taught by a surer experience that the government which he had obtained, and the power which he exercises would enable his faithful followers not only to live well, but also to die happily. And, indeed we see how much more abundantly his Spirit was poured out, how much more gloriously his kingdom was advanced, how much greater power was employed in aiding his followers and discomfiting his enemies. Being raised to heaven, he withdrew his bodily presence from our sight, not that he might cease to be with his followers, who are still pilgrims on the earth, but that he might rule both heaven and earth more immediately by his power; or rather, the promise which he made to be with us even to the end of the world, he fulfilled by this ascension, by which, as his body has been raised above all heavens, so his power and efficacy have been propagated and diffused beyond all the bounds of heaven and earth. This I prefer to explain in the words of Augustine rather than my own: 'Through death Christ was to go to the right hand of the Father, whence he is to come to judge the quick and the dead, and that in corporal presence, according to the sound doctrine and rule of faith. For, in spiritual presence, he was to be with them after his ascension' (August. Tract. in Joann. 109). In another passage he is more full and explicit: 'In regard to ineffable and invisible grace, is fulfilled what he said, Lo, I am with you alway, even to the end of the world (Mt. 28:20); but in regard to the flesh which the Word assumed in regard to his being born of a Virgin, in regard to his being apprehended by the Jews, nailed to the tree, taken down from the cross, wrapt in linen clothes, laid in the sepulchre, and manifested on his resurrection, it may be said, Me ye have not always with you. Why? because, in bodily presence, he conversed with his disciples forty days, and leading them out where they saw, but followed not, he ascended into heaven, and is not here: for there he sits at the right hand of the Father: and yet he is here, for the presence of his Godhead was not withdrawn. Therefore, as regards his divine presence, we have Christ always: as regards his bodily presence, it was truly said to the disciples, Me ye have not always. For a few days the Church had him bodily present. Now, she apprehends him by faith, but sees him not by the eye' (August. Tract. 51).

15. Hence it is immediately added, that he 'sitteth at the right hand of God the Father', a similitude borrowed from princes, who have their assessors to whom they commit the office of ruling and issuing commands. Thus Christ, in whom the Father is pleased to be exalted, and by whose hand he is pleased to reign, is said to have been received up, and seated on his right hand (Mk 16:19); as if it had been said, that he was installed in the government of heaven and earth, and formally admitted to possession of the administration committed to him, and not only admitted for once, but to continue until he descend to judgment. For so the apostle interprets, when he says, that the Father 'set him at his own right hand in the heavenly places, far above all principality, and power, and might, and dominion, and every name that is named not only in this world, but also in that which is to come; and has put all things under his feet, and given him to be the head over all things to the Church.' You see to what end he is so seated, namely, that all creatures both in heaven and earth should reverence his majesty, be ruled by his hand, do him implicit homage, and submit to his power. All that the apostles intend when they so often mention his seat at the Father's hand, is to teach, that every thing is placed at his disposal. Those, therefore, are in error, who suppose that his blessedness merely is indicated. We may observe, that there is nothing contrary to this doctrine in the testimony of Stephen, that he saw him standing (Acts 7:56), the subject here considered being not the position of his body, but the majesty of his empire, sitting meaning nothing more than presiding on the judgment-seat of heaven.

16. From this doctrine faith derives manifold advantages. First, it perceives that the Lord, by his ascension to heaven, has opened up the access to the heavenly kingdom, which Adam had shut. For having entered it in our flesh, as it were in our name, it follows, as the apostle says, that we are in a manner now seated in heavenly places, not entertaining a mere hope of heaven, but possessing it in our head. Secondly, faith perceives that his seat beside the Father is not without great advantage to us. Having entered the temple not made with hands, he constantly appears as our advocate and intercessor in the presence of the Father; directs attention to his own righteousness, so as to turn it away from our sins; so reconciles him to us, as by his intercession to pave for us a way of access to his throne, presenting it to miserable sinners, to whom it would otherwise be an object of dread, as replete with grace and mercy. Thirdly, it discerns his power, on which depend our strength, might, resources, and triumph over hell,

'When he ascended up on high, he led captivity captive' (Eph. 4:8). Spoiling his foes, he gave gifts to his people, and daily loads them with spiritual riches. He thus occupies his exalted seat, that thence transferring his virtue unto us, he may quicken us to spiritual life, sanctify us by his Spirit, and adorn his Church with various graces, by his protection preserve it safe from all harm, and by the strength of his hand curb the enemies raging against his cross and our salvation; in fine, that he may possess all power in heaven and earth, until he have utterly routed all his foes, who are also ours, and completed the structure of his Church. Such is the true nature of the kingdom, such the power which the Father has conferred upon him, until he arrive to complete the last act by judging the quick and the dead.

17.   Christ, indeed, gives his followers no dubious proofs of present power, but as his kingdom in the world is in a manner veiled by the humiliation of a carnal condition, faith is most properly invited to meditate on the visible presence which he will exhibit on the last day. For he will descend from heaven in visible form, in like manner as he was seen to ascend, and appear to all, with the ineffable majesty of his kingdom, the splendour of immortality, the boundless power of divinity, and an attending company of angels. Hence we are told to wait for the Redeemer against that day on which he will separate the sheep from the goats and the elect from the reprobate, and when not one individual either of the living or the dead shall escape his judgment. From the extremities of the universe shall be heard the clang of the trumpet summoning all to his tribunal; both those whom that day shall find alive, and those whom death shall previously have removed from the society of the living. There are some who take the words, quick and dead, in a different sense; and, indeed, some ancient writers appear to have hesitated as to the exposition of them; but our meaning being plain and clear, is much more accordant with the Creed which was certainly written for popular use. There is nothing contrary to it in the apostle's declaration, that it is appointed unto all men once to die. For though those who are surviving at the last day shall not die after a natural manner, yet the change which they are to undergo, as it shall resemble, is not improperly called, death (Heb. 9:27). 'We shall not all sleep, but we shall all be changed' (1 Cor. 15:51). What does this mean? Their mortal life shall perish and be swallowed up in one moment, and be transformed into an entirely new nature. Though no one can deny that that destruction of the flesh will be death, it still remains true that the quick and the dead shall be summoned to judgment (1 Thess. 4:16); for 'the dead in Christ shall rise first; then we which are alive and remain shall be caught up together with them in the clouds to meet the lord in the air'. Indeed, it is probable, that these words in the Creed were taken from Peter's sermon as related by Luke (Acts 10:42), and from the solemn charge of Paul to Timothy (2 Tim. 4:1).

18.   It is most consolatory to think, that judgment is vested in him who has already destined us to share with him in the honour of judgment (Mt. 19:28); so far is it from being true, that he will ascend the judgment-seat for our condemnation. How could a most merciful prince destroy his own people? how could the head disperse its own members? how could the advocate condemn his clients? For if the apostle, when contemplating the interposition of Christ, is bold to exclaim, 'Who is he that condemneth?' (Rom. 8:33), much more certain is it that Christ, the intercessor, will not condemn those whom he has admitted to his protection. It certainly gives no small security, that we shall be seated at no other tribunal than that of our Redeemer, from whom salvation is to be expected; and that he who in the Gospel now promises eternal

blessedness, will then as judge ratify his promise. The end for which the Father has honoured the Son by committing all judgment to him (Jn 5:22), was to pacify the consciences of his people when alarmed at the thought of judgment. Hitherto I have followed the order of the Apostles' Creed, because it states the leading articles of redemption in a few words, and may thus serve as a tablet in which the points of Christian doctrine, most deserving of attention, are brought separately and distinctly before us. I call it the Apostles' Creed, though I am by no means solicitous as to its authorship. The general consent of ancient writers certainly does ascribe it to the apostles, either because they imagined it was written and published by them for common use, or because they thought it right to give the sanction of such authority to a compendium faithfully drawn up from the doctrine delivered by their hands. I have no doubt, that, from the very commencement of the Church, and, therefore, in the very days of the apostles, it held the place of a public and universally received confession, whatever be the quarter from which it originally proceeded. It is not probable that it was written by some private individual, since it is certain that, from time immemorial, it was deemed of sacred authority by all Christians. The only point of consequence we hold to be incontrovertible – that it gives, in clear and succinct order, a full statement of our faith, and in every thing which it contains is sanctioned by the sure testimony of Scripture. This being understood, it were to no purpose to labour anxiously, or quarrel with any one as to the authorship, unless, indeed, we think it not enough to possess the sure truth of the Holy Spirit, without, at the same time, knowing by whose mouth it was pronounced, or by whose hand it was written.

19. When we see that the whole sum of our salvation, and every single part of it, are comprehended in Christ, we must beware of deriving even the minutest portion of it from any other quarter. If we seek salvation, we are taught by the very name of Jesus that he possesses it; if we seek any other gifts of the Spirit, we shall find them in his unction; strength in his government; purity in his conception; indulgence in his nativity, in which he was made like us in all respects, in order that he might learn to sympathise with us: if we seek redemption, we shall find it in his passion; acquittal in his condemnation; remission of the curse in his cross; satisfaction in his sacrifice; purification in his blood; reconciliation in his descent to hell; mortification of the flesh in his sepulchre; newness of life in his resurrection; immortality also in his resurrection; the inheritance of a celestial kingdom in his entrance into heaven; protection, security, and the abundant supply of all blessings, in his kingdom; secure anticipation of judgment in the power of judging committed to him. In fine, since in him all kinds of blessings are treasured up, let us draw a full supply from him, and none from any other quarter. Those who, not satisfied with him alone, entertain various hopes from others, though they may continue to look to him chiefly, deviate from the right path by the simple fact, that some portion of their thought takes a different direction. No distrust of this description can arise when once the abundance of his blessings is properly known.

✝ PART VIII ✝

FAITH AND REPENTANCE

✝ BOOK THREE ✝

THE MODE OF OBTAINING THE GRACE OF CHRIST. THE BENEFITS IT CONFERS, AND THE EFFECTS RESULTING FROM IT

✝ CHAPTER 1 ✝

The benefits of Christ made available to us by the secret operation of the spirit.

Sections

1. The Holy Spirit the bond which unites us with Christ. This the result of faith produced by the secret operation of the Holy Spirit. This obvious from Scripture.

1.   We must now see in what way we become possessed of the blessings which God has bestowed on his only begotten Son, not for private use, but to enrich the poor and needy. And the first thing to be attended to is, that so long as we are without Christ and separated from him, nothing which he suffered and did for the salvation of the human race is of the least benefit to us. To communicate to us the blessings which he received from the Father, he must become ours and dwell in us. Accordingly, he is called our Head, and the first-born among many brethren, while, on the other hand, we are said to be ingrafted into him and clothed with him, all which he possesses being, as I have said, nothing to us until we become one with him. And although it is true that we obtain this by faith, yet since we see that all do not indiscriminately embrace the offer of Christ which is made by the gospel, the very nature of the case teaches us to ascend higher, and inquire into the secret efficacy of the Spirit, to which it is owing that we enjoy Christ and all his blessings. I have already treated of the eternal essence and divinity of the Spirit; let us at present attend to the special point, that Christ came by water and blood, as the Spirit testifies concerning him, that we might not lose the benefits of the salvation which he has purchased. For as there are said to be three witnesses in heaven, the Father, the Word, and the Spirit, so there are also three on the earth, namely, water, blood, and Spirit. It is not without cause that the testimony of the Spirit is twice mentioned, a testimony which is engraven on our hearts by way of seal, and thus seals the cleansing and sacrifice of Christ. For which reason, also, Peter says, that believers are 'elect' 'through sanctification of the

Spirit, unto obedience and sprinkling of the blood of Jesus Christ' (1 Pet. 1:2). By these words he reminds us, that if the shedding of his sacred blood is not to be in vain, our souls must be washed in it by the secret cleansing of the Holy Spirit. For which reason, also, Paul, speaking of cleansing and purification, says, 'but ye are washed, but ye are sanctified, but ye are justified in the name of the Lord Jesus and by the Spirit of our God' (1 Cor. 6:11). The whole comes to this that the Holy Spirit is the bond by which Christ effectually binds us to himself. Here we may refer to what was said in the last Book concerning his anointing.

✢ CHAPTER 2 ✢
Of faith. The definition of it. Its peculiar properties.

Sections

14. Definition of faith explained under six principal heads. What meant by 'Knowledge' in the definition.
15. Why this knowledge must be sure and firm. Reason drawn from the consideration of our weakness. Another reason from the certainty of the promises of God.
16. The leading point in this certainty. Its fruits. A description of the true believer.
17. An objection to this certainty. Answer. Confirmation of the answer from the example of David. This enlarged upon from the opposite example of Ahab. Also from the uniform experience and the prayers of believers.
18. For this reason the conflict between the flesh and the Spirit in the soul of the believer described. The issue of this conflict, the victory of faith.
19. On the whole, the faith of the elect certain and indubitable. Conformation from analogy.

14. Let us now again go over the parts of the definition separately: I should think that, after a careful examination of them, no doubt will remain. By knowledge we do not mean comprehension, such as that which we have of things falling under human sense. For that knowledge is so much superior, that the human mind must far surpass and go beyond itself in order to reach it. Nor even when it has reached it does it comprehend what it feels, but persuaded of what it comprehends not, it understands more from mere certainty of persuasion than it could discern of any human matter by its own capacity. Hence it is elegantly described by Paul as ability 'to comprehend with all saints what is the breadth, and length, and depth, and height; and to know the love of Christ, which passeth knowledge' (Eph. 3:18, 19). His object was to intimate, that what our mind embraces by faith is every way infinite, that this kind of knowledge far surpasses all understanding. But because the 'mystery which has been hid from ages and from generations' is now 'made manifest to the saints' (Col. 1:26), faith is, for good reason, occasionally termed in Scripture 'understanding' (Col. 2:2); and 'knowledge', as by John (1 Jn 3:2), when he declares that believers know themselves to be the sons of God. And certainly they do know, but rather as confirmed by a belief of the divine veracity than taught by any demonstration of reason. This is also indicated by Paul when he says, that 'whilst we are at home in the body, we are absent from the Lord: (For we walk by faith, not by sight)' (2 Cor. 5:6, 7), thus showing, that

what we understand by faith is yet distant from us and escapes our view. Hence we conclude that the knowledge of faith consists more of certainty than discernment.

15. We add, that it is sure and firm, the better to express strength and constancy of persuasion. For as faith is not contented with a dubious and fickle opinion, so neither is it contented with an obscure and ill-defined conception. The certainty which it requires must be full and decisive, as is usual in regard to matters ascertained and proved. So deeply rooted in our hearts is unbelief, so prone are we to it, that while all confess with the lips that God is faithful, no man ever believes it without an arduous struggle. Especially when brought to the test, we by our wavering betray the vice which lurked within. Nor is it without cause that the Holy Spirit bears such distinguished testimony to the authority of God, in order that it may cure the disease of which I have spoken, and induce us to give full credit to the divine promises: 'The words of the Lord' (says David, Ps. 12:6) 'are pure words, as silver tried in a furnace of earth purified seven times': 'The word of the Lord is tried: he is a buckler to all those that trust in him' (Ps. 18:30). And Solomon declares the same thing almost in the same words, 'Every word of God is pure' (Prov. 30:5). But further quotation is superfluous, as the 119th Psalm is almost wholly occupied with this subject. Certainly, whenever God thus recommends his word, he indirectly rebukes our unbelief, the purport of all that is said being to eradicate perverse doubt from our hearts. There are very many also who form such an idea of the divine mercy as yields them very little comfort. For they are harassed by miserable anxiety while they doubt whether God will be merciful to them. They think, indeed, that they are most fully persuaded of the divine mercy, but they confine it within too narrow limits. The idea they entertain is, that this mercy is great and abundant, is shed upon many, is offered and ready to be bestowed upon all; but that it is uncertain whether it will reach to them individually, or rather whether they can reach to it. Thus their knowledge stopping short leaves them only midway; not so much confirming and tranquillising the mind as harassing it with doubt and disquietude. Very different is that feeling of full assurance which the Scriptures uniformly attribute to faith – an assurance which leaves no doubt that the goodness of God is clearly offered to us. This assurance we cannot have without truly perceiving its sweetness, and experiencing it in ourselves. Hence from faith the apostle deduces confidence, and from confidence boldness. His words are, 'In whom [Christ] we have boldness and access with confidence by the faith of him' (Eph. 3:12), thus undoubtedly showing that our faith is not true unless it enables us to appear calmly in the presence of God. Such boldness springs only from confidence in the divine favour and salvation. So true is this, that the term 'faith' is often used as equivalent to 'confidence'.

16. The principal hinge on which faith turns is this: We must not suppose that any promises of mercy which the Lord offers are only true out of us, and not at all in us: we should rather make them ours by inwardly embracing them. In this way only is engendered that confidence which he elsewhere terms 'peace' (Rom. 5:1); though perhaps he rather means to make peace follow from it. This is the security which quiets and calms the conscience in the view of the judgment of God, and without which it is necessarily vexed and almost torn with tumultuous dread, unless when it happens to slumber for a moment, forgetful both of God and of itself. And verily it is but for a moment. It never long enjoys that miserable obliviousness, for the memory of the divine judgment, ever and anon recurring, stings it to the quick. In one word, he only is a true believer who, firmly persuaded that God is reconciled, and is a kind

Father to him, hopes everything from his kindness, who, trusting to the promises of the divine favour, with undoubting confidence anticipates salvation; as the apostle shows in these words, 'We are made partakers of Christ, if we hold the beginning of our confidence steadfast unto the end' (Heb. 3:14). He thus holds, that none hope well in the Lord save those who confidently glory in being the heirs of the heavenly kingdom. No man, I say, is a believer but he who, trusting to the security of his salvation, confidently triumphs over the devil and death, as we are taught by the noble exclamation of Paul, 'I am persuaded, that neither death, nor life, nor angels, nor principalities, nor powers, nor things present, nor things to come, nor height, nor depth, nor any other creature, shall be able to separate us from the love of God, which is in Christ Jesus our Lord' (Rom. 8:38). In like manner, the same apostle does not consider that the eyes of our understanding are enlightened unless we know what is the hope of the eternal inheritance to which we are called (Eph. 1:18). Thus he uniformly intimates throughout his writings, that the goodness of God is not properly comprehended when security does not follow as its fruit.

17.   But it will be said that this differs widely from the experience of believers, who, in recognising the grace of God toward them, not only feel disquietude (this often happens), but sometimes tremble, overcome with terror, so violent are the temptations which assail their minds. This scarcely seems consistent with certainty of faith. It is necessary to solve this difficulty, in order to maintain the doctrine above laid down. When we say that faith must be certain and secure, we certainly speak not of an assurance which is never affected by doubt, nor a security which anxiety never assails; we rather maintain that believers have a perpetual struggle with their own distrust, and are thus far from thinking that their consciences possess a placid quiet, uninterrupted by perturbation. On the other hand, whatever be the mode in which they are assailed, we deny that they fall off and abandon that sure confidence which they have formed in the mercy of God. Scripture does not set before us a brighter or more memorable example of faith than in David, especially if regard be had to the constant tenor of his life. And yet how far his mind was from being always at peace is declared by innumerable complaints, of which it will be sufficient to select a few. When he rebukes the turbulent movements of his soul, what else is it but a censure of his unbelief? 'Why art thou cast down, my soul? and why art thou disquieted in me? hope thou in God' (Ps. 42:6). His alarm was undoubtedly a manifest sign of distrust, as if he thought that the Lord had forsaken him. In another passage we have a fuller confession: 'I said in my haste, I am cut off from before thine eyes' (Ps. 31:22). In another passage, in anxious and wretched perplexity, he debates with himself, nay, raises a question as to the nature of God: 'Has God forgotten to be gracious? has he in anger shut up his tender mercies?' (Ps. 77:9). What follows is still harsher: 'I said this is my infirmity; but I will remember the years of the right hand of the Most High. As if desperate, he adjudges himself to destruction. He not only confesses that he is agitated by doubt, but as if he had fallen in the contest, leaves himself nothing in reserve – God having deserted him, and made the hand which was wont to help him the instrument of his destruction. Wherefore, after having been tossed among tumultuous waves, it is not without reason he exhorts his soul to return to her quiet rest (Ps. 116:7). And yet (what is strange) amid those commotions, faith sustains the believer's heart, and truly acts the part of the palm tree, which supports any weights laid upon it, and rises above them; thus David, when he seemed to be overwhelmed, ceased not by urging himself forward to ascend to God. But he who anxiously contending with his own infirmity has recourse to faith, is already in a great measure victorious. This we may infer from the following passage, and others similar to it: 'Wait on the Lord: be of good courage, and he shall strengthen thine heart: wait, I say, on the Lord' (Ps. 27:14). He accuses himself of timidity, and repeating the same thing twice, confesses that he is ever and anon exposed to agitation. Still he is not only dissatisfied with himself for so feeling, but earnestly labours to correct it. Were we to take a nearer view of his case, and compare it with that of Ahaz, we should find a great difference between them. Isaiah is sent to relieve the anxiety of an impious and hypocritical king, and addresses him in these terms: 'Take heed, and be quiet; fear not', etc. (Isa. 7:4). How did Ahab act? As has already been said, his heart was shaken as a tree is shaken by the wind: though he heard the promise, he ceased not to tremble. This, therefore, is the proper hire and punishment of unbelief, so to tremble as in the day of trial to turn away from God, who gives access to himself only by faith. On the other hand, believers, though weighed down and almost overwhelmed with the burden of temptation, constantly rise up, though not without toil and difficulty; hence, feeling conscious of their own weakness, they pray with the prophet, 'Take not the word of truth utterly out of my mouth' (Ps. 119:43). By these words, we are taught that they at times become dumb, as if their faith were overthrown, and yet that they do not withdraw or turn their backs, but persevere in the contest, and by prayer stimulate their sluggishness, so as not to fall into stupor by giving way to it.

18.　To make this intelligible, we must return to the distinction between flesh and spirit, to which we have already adverted, and which here becomes most apparent. The believer finds within himself two principles: the one filling him with delight in recognising the divine goodness, the other filling him with bitterness under a sense of his fallen state; the one leading him to recline on the promise of the Gospel, the other alarming him by the conviction of his iniquity; the one making him exult with the anticipation of life, the other making him tremble with the fear of death. This diversity is owing to imperfection of faith, since we are never so well in the course of the present life as to be entirely cured of the disease of distrust, and completely replenished and engrossed by faith. Hence those conflicts: the distrust cleaving to the remains of the flesh rising up to assail the faith enlisting in our hearts. But if in the believer's mind certainty is mingled with doubt, must we not always be carried back to the conclusion, that faith consists not of a sure and clear, but only of an obscure and confused, understanding of the divine will in regard to us? By no means. Though we are distracted by various thoughts, it does not follow that we are immediately divested of faith. Though we are agitated and carried to and fro by distrust, we are not immediately plunged into the abyss; though we are shaken, we are not therefore driven from our place. The invariable issue of the contest is, that faith in the long run surmounts the difficulties by which it was beset and seemed to be endangered.

19.　The whole, then, comes to this: As soon as the minutest particle of faith is instilled into our minds, we begin to behold the face of God placid, serene, and propitious; far off, indeed, but still so distinctly as to assure us that there is no delusion in it. In proportion to the progress we afterwards make (and the progress ought to be uninterrupted), we obtain a nearer and surer view, the very continuance making it more familiar to us. Thus we see that a mind illumined with the knowledge of God is at first involved in much ignorance – ignorance, however, which is gradually removed. Still this partial ignorance or obscure discernment does not prevent that clear knowledge of the divine favour which holds the first and principal part in faith. For as one shut up in a prison, where from a narrow opening he receives the rays of the sun indirectly and in a manner divided, though deprived of a full view of the sun, has no doubt of the source from which the light comes, and is benefited by it; so believers, while bound with the fetters of an earthly body, though surrounded on all sides with much obscurity, are so far illumined by any slender light which beams upon them and displays the divine mercy as to feel secure.

20. The apostle elegantly adverts to both in different passages. When he says, 'We know in part, and we prophesy in part', and 'Now we see through a glass darkly' (1 Cor. 13:9, 12), he intimates how very minute a portion of divine wisdom is given to us in the present life. For although those expressions do not simply indicate that faith is imperfect so long as we groan under a height of flesh, but that the necessity of being constantly engaged in learning is owing to our imperfection, he at the same time reminds us, that a subject which is of boundless extent cannot be comprehended by our feeble and narrow capacities. This Paul affirms of the whole Church, each individual being retarded and impeded by his own ignorance from making so near an approach as were to be wished. But that the foretaste which we obtain from any minute portion of faith is certain, and by no means fallacious, he elsewhere shows, when he affirms that 'We all, with open face beholding as in a glass the glory of the Lord, are changed into the same image, from glory to glory, even as by the Spirit of the Lord' (2 Cor. 3:18). In such degrees of ignorance much doubt and trembling is necessarily implied, especially seeing that our heart is by its own natural bias prone to unbelief. To this we must add the temptations which, various in kind and infinite in number, are ever and anon violently assailing us. In particular, conscience itself, burdened with an incumbent load of sins, at one time complains and groans, at another accuses itself; at one time murmurs in secret, at another openly rebels. Therefore, whether adverse circumstances betoken the wrath of God, or conscience finds the subject and matter within itself, unbelief thence draws weapons and engines to put faith to flight, the aim of all its efforts being to make us think that God is adverse and hostile to us, and thus, instead of hoping for any assistance from him, to make us dread him as a deadly foe.

✝ CHAPTER 3 ✝
Regeneration by faith. Of repentance.

Sections

7.   (2) Repentance produced by fear of God. Hence the mention of divine judgment by the prophets and apostles. Example. Exposition of the second branch of the definition from a passage in Paul. Why the fear of God is the first part of Repentance.

8.   3. Repentance consists in the mortification of the flesh and the quickening of the Spirit. These required by the prophets. They are explained separately.

1.   Although we have already in some measure shown how faith possesses Christ, and gives us the enjoyment of his benefits, the subject would still be obscure were we not to add an exposition of the effects resulting from it. The sum of the Gospel is, not without good reason, made to consist in repentance and forgiveness of sins; and, therefore, where these two heads are omitted, any discussion concerning faith will be meagre and defective, and indeed almost useless. Now, since Christ confers upon us, and we obtain by faith, both free reconciliation and newness of life, reason and order require that I should here begin to treat of both. The shortest transition, however, will be from faith to repentance; for repentance being properly understood it will better appear how a man is justified freely by faith alone, and yet that holiness of life, *real* holiness, as it is called, is inseparable from the free imputation of righteousness. That repentance not only always follows faith, but is produced by it, ought to be without controversy (see Calvin in Joann. 1:13). For since pardon and forgiveness are offered by the preaching of the Gospel, in order that the sinner, delivered from the tyranny of Satan, the yoke of sin, and the miserable bondage of iniquity, may pass into the kingdom of God, it is certain that no man can embrace the grace of the Gospel without retaking himself from the errors of his former life into the right path, and making it his whole study to practise repentance. Those who think that repentance precedes faith instead of flowing from, or being produced by it, as the fruit by the tree, have never understood its nature, and are moved to adopt that view on very insufficient grounds.

5.   Though all this is true, yet the term 'repentance' (in so far as I can ascertain from Scripture) must be differently taken. For in comprehending faith under repentance, they are at variance with what Paul says in the Acts, as to his 'testifying both to the Jews and also to the Greeks, repentance toward God, and faith toward our Lord Jesus Christ' (Acts 20:21). Here he mentions faith and repentance as two different things. What then? Can true repentance exist without faith? By no means. But although they cannot be separated, they ought to be distinguished. As there is no faith without hope, and yet faith and hope are different, so repentance and faith, though constantly linked together, are only to be united, not confounded. I am not unaware that under the term 'repentance' is comprehended the whole work of turning to God, of which not the least important part is faith; but in what sense this is done will be perfectly obvious, when its nature and power shall have been explained. The term 'repentance' is derived in the Hebrew from 'conversion', or 'turning again'; and in the Greek from a 'change of mind and purpose'; nor is the thing meant inappropriate to both derivations, for it is substantially this, that withdrawing from ourselves we turn to God, and laying aside the old, put on a new mind. Wherefore, it seems to me, that repentance may be not inappropriately defined thus: A real conversion of our life unto God, proceeding from sincere and serious fear of God; and consisting in the mortification of our flesh and the old man, and the quickening of the Spirit. In this sense are to be understood all those addresses in which the prophets first, and the apostles afterwards, exhorted the people of their time to repentance. The great object for which they laboured was, to fill them with confusion for their sins and dread of the divine judgment, that they might fall down and humble themselves before him whom they had offended, and, with true repentance, retake themselves to the right path. Accordingly, they use indiscriminately in the same sense, the expressions 'turning', or 'returning' to the Lord; 'repenting', 'doing repentance'. Whence, also, the sacred history describes it as repentance towards God, when men who disregarded him and wantoned in their lusts begin to obey his word, and are prepared to go whithersoever he may call them. And John Baptist and Paul, under the expression 'bringing forth fruits meet for repentance' described a course of life exhibiting and bearing testimony, in all its actions, to such a repentance.

6. But before proceeding farther, it will be proper to give a clearer exposition of the definition which we have adopted. There are three things, then, principally to be considered in it. First, in the conversion of the life to God, we require a transformation not only in external works, but in the soul itself, which is able only after it has put off its old habits to bring forth fruits conformable to its renovation. The prophet, intending to express this, enjoins those whom he calls to repentance to make them 'a new heart and a new spirit' (Ezek. 18:31). Hence Moses, on several occasions, when he would show how the Israelites were to repent and turn to the Lord, tells them that it must be done with the whole heart, and the whole soul (a mode of expression of frequent recurrence in the prophets), and by terming it the circumcision of the heart, points to the internal affections. But there is no passage better fitted to teach us the genuine nature of repentance than the following: 'If thou wilt return, O Israel, saith the Lord, return unto me.' 'Break up your fallow ground, and sow not among thorns. Circumcise yourselves to the Lord, and take away the foreskins of your heart' (Jer. 4:1–4). See how he declares to them that it will be of no avail to commence the study of righteousness unless impiety shall first have been eradicated from their inmost heart. And to malice the deeper impression, he reminds them that they have to do with God, and can gain nothing by deceit, because he hates a double heart. For this reason Isaiah derides the preposterous attempts of hypocrites, who zealously aimed at an external repentance by the observance of ceremonies, but in the meanwhile cared not 'to loose the bands of wickedness, to undo the heavy burdens, and to let the oppressed go free' (Isa. 58:6). In these words he admirably shows wherein the acts of unfeigned repentance consist.

7. The second part of our definition is, that repentance proceeds from a sincere fear of God. Before the mind of the sinner can be inclined to repentance, he must be aroused by the thought of divine judgment; but when once the thought that God will one day ascend his tribunal to take an account of all words and actions has taken possession of his mind, it will not allow him to rest, or have one moment's peace, but will perpetually urge him to adopt a different plan of life, that he may be able to stand securely at that judgment-seat. Hence the Scripture, when exhorting to repentance, often introduces the subject of judgment, as in Jeremiah, 'Lest my fury come forth like fire, and burn that none can quench it, because of the evil of your doings' (Jer. 4:4). Paul, in his discourse to the Athenians says, 'The times of this ignorance God winked at; but now commandeth all men every where to repent: because he has appointed a day in the which he will judge the world in righteousness' (Acts 17:30, 31). The same thing is repeated in several other passages. Sometimes God is declared to be a judge, from the punishments already inflicted, thus leading sinners to reflect that worse awaits them if they do not quickly repent. There is an example of this in the 29th chapter of Deuteronomy. As repentance begins with dread and hatred of sin, the apostle sets down godly sorrow as one of its causes (2 Cor. 7:10). By godly sorrow he means when we not only tremble at the punishment, but hate and abhor the sin, because we know it is displeasing to God. It is not strange that this should be, for unless we are stung to the quick, the sluggishness of our carnal nature cannot be corrected; nay, no degree of pungency would suffice for our stupor and sloth, did not God lift the rod and strike deeper. There is, moreover, a rebellious spirit which must be broken as with hammers. The stern threatening which God employs are extorted from him by our depraved dispositions. For while we are asleep it were in vain to allure us by soothing measures. Passages to this effect are everywhere to be met with, and I need not quote them. But there is another reason why the fear of God lies at the root of repentance – that though the life of man were possessed of all kinds of virtue, still if they do not bear reference to God, how much soever they may be lauded in the world, they are mere abomination in heaven, inasmuch as it is the principal part of righteousness to render to God that service and honour of which he is impiously defrauded, whenever it is not our express purpose to submit to his authority.

8. We must now explain the third part of the definition, and show what is meant when we say that repentance consists of two parts – the mortification of the flesh, and the quickening of the spirit. The prophets, in accommodation to a carnal people, express this in simple and homely terms, but clearly, when they say, 'Depart from evil, and do good' (Ps. 34:14). 'Wash you, make you clean, put away the evil of your doings from before mine eyes; cease to do evil; learn to do well; seek judgment; relieve the oppressed,' etc. (Isa. 1:16, 17). In dissuading us from wickedness they demand the entire destruction of the flesh, which is full of perverseness and malice. It is a most difficult and arduous achievement to renounce ourselves, and lay aside our natural disposition. For the flesh must not be thought to be destroyed unless every thing that we have of our own is abolished. But seeing that all the desires of the flesh are enmity against God (Rom. 8:7), the first step to the obedience of his law is the renouncement of our own nature. Renovation is afterwards manifested by the fruits produced by it – justice, judgment, and mercy. Since it were not sufficient duly to perform such acts, were not the mind and heart previously endued with sentiments of justice, judgment, and mercy this is done when the Holy Spirit, instilling his holiness into our souls, so inspired them with new thoughts and affections, that they may justly be regarded as new. And, indeed, as we are naturally averse to God, unless self-denial precede, we shall never tend to that which is right. Hence we are so often enjoined to put off the old man, to renounce the world and the flesh, to forsake our lusts, and be renewed in the spirit of our mind. Moreover, the very name 'mortification' reminds us how difficult it is to forget our former nature, because we hence infer that we cannot be trained to the fear of God, and learn the first principles of piety, unless we are violently smitten with the sword of the Spirit and annihilated, as if God were declaring, that to be ranked among his sons there must be a destruction of our ordinary nature.

✝ PART IX ✝

THE CHRISTIAN LIFE

✝ CHAPTER 6 ✝

The life of a Christian man. Scriptural arguments exhorting to it.

Sections

4. False Christians who are opposed to this life censured: (1) They have not truly learned Christ, (2) the Gospel not the guide of their words or actions, (3) they do not imitate Christ the Master, (4) they would separate the Spirit from his word.

5. Christians ought not to despond: Provided (1) they take the word of God for their guide, (2) sincerely cultivate righteousness, (3) walk, according to their capacity, in the ways of the Lord, (4) make some progress, (5) persevere.

4.   This is the place to address those who, having nothing of Christ but the name and sign, would yet be called Christians. How dare they boast of this sacred name? None have intercourse with Christ but those who have acquired the true knowledge of him from the Gospel. The apostle denies that any man truly has learned Christ who has not learned to put off 'the old man, which is corrupt according to the deceitful lusts, and put on Christ' (Eph. 4:22). They are convicted, therefore, of falsely and unjustly pretending a knowledge of Christ, whatever be the volubility and eloquence with which they can talk of the Gospel. Doctrine is not an affair of the tongue, but of the life; is not apprehended by the intellect and memory merely, like other branches of learning; but is received only when it possesses the whole soul, and finds its seat and habitation in the inmost recesses of the heart. Let them, therefore, either cease to insult God, by boasting that they are what they are not, or let them show themselves not unworthy disciples of their divine Master. To doctrine in which our religion is contained we have given the first place, since by it our salvation commences; but it must be transfused into the breast, and pass into the conduct, and so transform us into itself, as not to prove unfruitful. If philosophers are justly offended, and banish from their company with disgrace those who, while professing an art which ought to be the mistress of their conduct, convert it into mere loquacious sophistry, with how much better reason shall we detest those flimsy sophists who are contented to let the Gospel play upon their lips, when, from its efficacy, it ought to penetrate the inmost affections of the heart, fix its seat in the soul, and pervade the whole man a hundred times more than the frigid discourses of philosophers?

5.   I insist not that the life of the Christian shall breathe nothing but the perfect Gospel, though this is to be desired, and ought to be attempted. I insist not so strictly on evangelical perfection, as to refuse to acknowledge as a Christian any man who has not attained it. In this way all would be excluded from the Church, since there is no man who is not far removed from this perfection, while many, who have made but little progress, would be undeservedly

rejected. What then? Let us set this before our eye as the end at which we ought constantly to aim. Let it be regarded as the goal towards which we are to run. For you cannot divide the matter with God, undertaking part of what his word enjoins, and omitting part at pleasure. For, in the first place, God uniformly recommends integrity as the principal part of his worship, meaning by integrity real singleness of mind, devoid of gloss and fiction, and to this is opposed a double mind; as if it had been said, that the spiritual commencement of a good life is when the internal affections are sincerely devoted to God, in the cultivation of holiness and justice. But seeing that, in this earthly prison of the body, no man is supplied with strength sufficient to hasten in his course with due alacrity, while the greater number are so oppressed with weakness, that hesitating, and halting, and even crawling on the ground, they make little progress, let every one of us go as far as his humble ability enables him, and prosecute the journey once begun. No one will travel so badly as not daily to make some degree of progress. This, therefore, let us never cease to do, that we may daily advance in the way of the Lord; and let us not despair because of the slender measure of success. How little soever the success may correspond with our wish, our labour is not lost when to-day is better than yesterday, provided with true singleness of mind we keep our aim, and aspire to the goal, not speaking flattering things to ourselves, nor indulging our vices, but making it our constant endeavour to become better, until we attain to goodness itself. If during the whole course of our life we seek and follow, we shall at length attain it, when relieved from the infirmity of flesh we are admitted to full fellowship with God.

✝ CHAPTER 7 ✝
A summary of the Christian life of self-denial.

Sections

1. Consideration of the second general division in regard to the Christian life. Its beginning and sum. A twofold respect. We are not our own. Respect to both the fruit and the use. Unknown to philosophers, who have placed reason on the throne of the Holy Spirit.

5. The advantage of our neighbour to be promoted. Here self-denial most necessary, and yet most difficult. Here a double remedy: (1) The benefits bestowed upon us are for the common benefit of the Church, (2) we ought to do all we can for our neighbour. This illustrated by analogy from the members of the human body. This duty of charity founded on the divine command.

6. Charity ought to have for its attendants patience and kindness. We should consider the image of God in our neighbours, and especially in those who are of the household of faith. Hence a fourfold consideration which refutes all objections. A common objection refuted.

7. Christian life cannot exist without charity. Remedies for the vices opposed to charity: (1) mercy, (2) humility, (3) modesty, (4) diligence, (5) perseverance.

1. Although the Law of God contains a perfect rule of conduct admirably arranged, it has seemed proper to our divine Master to train his people by a more accurate method, to the rule

which is enjoined in the Law; and the leading principle in the method is, that it is the duty of believers to present their 'bodies a living sacrifice, holy and acceptable unto God, which is their reasonable service' (Rom. 12:1). Hence he draws the exhortation: 'Be not conformed to this world: but be ye transformed by the renewing of your mind, that ye may prove what is that good, and acceptable, and perfect will of God.' The great point, then, is, that we are consecrated and dedicated to God, and, therefore, should not henceforth think, speak, design, or act, without a view to his glory. What he hath made sacred cannot, without signal insult to him, be applied to profane use. But if we are not our own, but the Lord's, it is plain both what error is to be shunned, and to what end the actions of our lives ought to be directed. We are not our own; therefore, neither is our own reason or will to rule our acts and counsels. We are not our own; therefore, let us not make it our end to seek what may be agreeable to our carnal nature. We are not our own; therefore, as far as possible, let us forget ourselves and the things that are ours. On the other hand, we are God's; let us, therefore, live and die to him (Rom. 14:8). We are God's; therefore, let his wisdom and will preside over all our actions. We are God's; to him, then, as the only legitimate end, let every part of our life be directed. O how great the proficiency of him who, taught that he is not his own, has withdrawn the dominion and government of himself from his own reason that he may give them to God! For as the surest source of destruction to men is to obey themselves, so the only haven of safety is to have no other will, no other wisdom, than to follow the Lord wherever he leads. Let this, then be the first step, to abandon ourselves, and devote the whole energy of our minds to the service of God. By service, I mean not only that which consists in verbal obedience, but that by which the mind, divested of its own carnal feelings, implicitly obeys the call of the Spirit of God. This transformation (which Paul calls 'the renewing of the mind', Rom. 12:2; Eph. 4:23), though it is the first entrance to life, was unknown to all the philosophers. They give the government of man to reason alone, thinking that she alone is to be listened to; in short, they assign to her the sole direction of the conduct. But Christian philosophy bids her give place, and yield complete submission to the Holy Spirit, so that the man himself no longer lives, but Christ lives and reigns in him (Gal. 2:20).

5. How difficult it is to perform the duty of seeking the good of our neighbour! Unless you leave off all thought of yourself and in a manner cease to be yourself, you will never accomplish it. How can you exhibit those works of charity which Paul describes unless you renounce yourself, and become wholly devoted to others? 'Charity (says he, 1 Cor. 13:4) suffereth long, and is kind; charity envieth not; charity vaunteth not itself, is not puffed up, doth not behave itself unseemly, seeketh not her own, is not easily provoked', etc. Were it the only thing required of us to seek not our own, nature would not have the least power to comply: she so inclines us to love ourselves only, that she will not easily allow us carelessly to pass by ourselves and our own interests that we may watch over the interests of others, nay, spontaneously to yield our own rights and resign it to another. But Scripture, to conduct us to this, reminds us, that whatever we obtain from the Lord is granted on the condition of our employing it for the common good of the Church, and that, therefore, the legitimate use of all our gifts is a kind and liberal communication of them with others. There cannot be a surer rule, nor a stronger exhortation to the observance of it, than when we are taught that all the endowments which we possess are divine deposits entrusted to us for the very purpose of being distributed for the good of our neighbour. But Scripture proceeds still farther when it likens these endowments to the different members of the body (1 Cor. 12:12). No member has its function for itself, or applies it for its own private use, but transfers it to its fellow-members; nor does it derive any other advantage from it than that which it receives in common with the whole body. Thus, whatever the pious man can do, he is bound to do for his brethren, not consulting his own interest in any other way than by striving earnestly for the common edification of the Church. Let this, then, be our method of showing good-will and kindness, considering that, in regard to everything which God has bestowed upon us, and by which we can aid our neighbour, we are his stewards, and are bound to give account of our stewardship; moreover, that the only right mode of administration is that which is regulated by love. In this way, we shall not only unite the study of our neighbour's advantage with a regard to our own, but make the latter subordinate to the former. And lest we should have omitted to perceive that this is the law for duly administering every gift which we receive from God, he of old applied that law to the minutest expressions of his own kindness. He commanded the first-fruits to be offered to him as an attestation by the people that it was impious to reap any advantage from goods not previously consecrated to him (Exod. 22:29; 23:19). But if the gifts of God are not sanctified to us until we have with our own hand dedicated them to the Giver, it must be a gross abuse that does not give signs of such dedication. It is in vain to contend that you cannot enrich the Lord by your offerings. Though, as the Psalmist says 'Thou art my Lord: my goodness extendeth not unto thee,' yet you can extend it 'to the saints that are in the earth' (Ps. 16:2, 3); and therefore a comparison is drawn between sacred oblations and alms as now corresponding to the offerings under the Law.

6. Moreover, that we may not weary in well-doing (as would otherwise forthwith and infallibly be the case), we must add the other quality in the apostle's enumeration, 'Charity suffereth long, and is kind, is not easily provoked' (1 Cor. 13:4). The Lord enjoins us to do good to all without exception, though the greater part, if estimated by their own merit, are most unworthy of it. But Scripture subjoins a most excellent reason, when it tells us that we are not to look to what men in themselves deserve, but to attend to the image of God, which exists in all, and to which we owe all honour and love. But in those who are of the household of faith, the same rule is to be more carefully observed, inasmuch as that image is renewed and restored in them by the Spirit of Christ. Therefore, whoever be the man that is presented to you as needing your assistance, you have no ground for declining to give it to him. Say he is a stranger. The Lord has given him a mark which ought to be familiar to you: for which reason he forbids you to despise your own flesh (Gal. 6:10). Say he is mean and of no consideration. The Lord points him out as one whom he has distinguished by the lustre of his own image (Isa. 58:7). Say that you are bound to him by no ties of duty. The Lord has substituted him as it were into his own place, that in him you may recognise the many great obligations under which the Lord has laid you to himself. Say that he is unworthy of your least exertion on his account; but the image of God, by which he is recommended to you, is worthy of yourself and all your exertions. But if he not only merits no good, but has provoked you by injury and mischief, still this is no good reason why you should not embrace him in love, and visit him with offices of love. He has deserved very differently from me, you will say. But what has the Lord deserved? Whatever injury he has done you, when he enjoins you to forgive him, he certainly means that it should be imputed to himself. In this way only we attain to what is not to say difficult but altogether against nature, to love those that hate us, render good for evil, and blessing for cursing, remembering that we are not to reflect on the wickedness of men, but look to the image of God in them, an image which, covering and obliterating their faults, should by its beauty and dignity allure us to love and embrace them.

7. We shall thus succeed in mortifying ourselves if we fulfil all the duties of charity. Those duties, however, are not fulfilled by the mere discharge of them, though none be omitted, unless it is done from a pure feeling of love. For it may happen that one may perform every one of these offices, in so far as the external act is concerned, and be far from performing them aright. For you see some who would be thought very liberal, and yet accompany every thing they give with insult, by the haughtiness of their looks, or the violence of their words. And to such a calamitous condition have we come in this unhappy age, that the greater part of men never almost give alms without contumely. Such conduct ought not to have been tolerated even among the heathen; but from Christians something more is required than to carry cheerfulness in their looks, and give attractiveness to the discharge of their duties by courteous language. First, they should put themselves in the place of him whom they see in need of their assistance, and pity his misfortune as if they felt and bore it, so that a feeling of pity and humanity should incline them to assist him just as they would themselves. He who is thus minded will go and give assistance to his brethren, and not only not taint his acts with arrogance or upbraiding but will neither look down upon the brother to whom he does a kindness, as one who needed his help, or keep him in subjection as under obligation to him, just as we do not insult a diseased member when the rest of the body labours for its recovery, nor think it under special obligation to the other members, because it has required more exertion than it has returned. A communication of offices between members is not regarded as at all gratuitous, but rather as the payment of that which being due by the law of nature it were monstrous to deny. For this reason, he who has performed one kind of duty will not think himself thereby discharged, as is usually the case when a rich man, after contributing somewhat of his substance, delegates remaining burdens to others as if he had nothing to do with them. Every one should rather consider, that however great he is, he owes himself to his neighbours, and that the only limit to his beneficence is the failure of his means. The extent of these should regulate that of his charity.

✝ CHAPTER 8 ✝

Of bearing the cross – one branch of self-denial.

Sections
1. What the cross is. By whom, and on whom, and for what cause imposed. Its necessity and dignity.
2. The cross necessary (1) to humble our pride, (2) to make us apply to God for aid. Example of David, (3) to give us experience of God's presence.
3. Manifold uses of the cross: (1) Produces patience, hope, and firm confidence in God, gives us victory and perseverance. Faith invincible.

4. (2) Frames us to obedience. Example of Abraham. This training how useful.

5. The cross necessary to subdue the wantonness of the flesh. This portrayed by an apposite simile. Various forms of the cross.

1. The pious mind must ascend still higher, namely, whither Christ calls his disciples when he says, that every one of them must 'take up his cross' (Mt. 16:24). Those whom the Lord has chosen and honoured with his intercourse must prepare for a hard, labourious, troubled life, a life full of many and various kinds of evils; it being the will of our heavenly Father to exercise his people in this way while putting them to the proof. Having begun this course with Christ the first-born, he continues it towards all his children. For though that Son was dear to him above others, the Son in whom he was 'well pleased', yet we see, that far from being treated gently and indulgently, we may say, that not only was he subjected to a perpetual cross while he dwelt on earth, but his whole life was nothing else than a kind of perpetual cross. The apostle assigns the reason, 'Though he was a Son, yet learned he obedience by the things which he suffered' (Heb. 5:8). Why then should we exempt ourselves from that condition to which Christ our Head behoved to submit; especially since he submitted on our account, that he might in his own person exhibit a model of patience? Wherefore, the apostle declares, that all the children of God are destined to be conformed to him. Hence it affords us great consolation in hard and difficult circumstances, which men deem evil and adverse, to think that we are holding fellowship with the sufferings of Christ; that as he passed to celestial glory through a labyrinth of many woes, so we too are conducted thither through various tribulations. For, in another passage, Paul himself thus speaks, 'we must through much tribulation enter the kingdom of God' (Acts 14:22); and again, 'that I may know him, and the power of his resurrection, and the fellowship of his sufferings, being made conformable unto his death' (Rom 8:29). How powerfully should it soften the bitterness of the cross, to think that the more we are afflicted with adversity, the surer we are made of our fellowship with Christ; by communion with whom our sufferings are not only blessed to us, but tend greatly to the furtherance of our salvation.

2. We may add, that the only thing which made it necessary for our Lord to undertake to bear the cross, was to testify and prove his obedience to the Father; whereas there are many reasons which make it necessary for us to live constantly under the cross. Feeble as we are by nature, and prone to ascribe all perfection to our flesh, unless we receive as it were ocular demonstration of our weakness, we readily estimate our virtue above its proper worth, and doubt not that, whatever happens, it will stand unimpaired and invincible against all difficulties. Hence we indulge a stupid and empty confidence in the flesh, and then trusting to it wax proud against the Lord himself; as if our own faculties were sufficient without his grace. This arrogance cannot be better repressed than when He proves to us by experience, not only how great our weakness, but also our frailty is. Therefore, he visits us with disgrace, or poverty, or bereavement, or disease, or other afflictions. Feeling altogether unable to support them, we forthwith, in so far as regards ourselves, give way, and thus humbled learn to invoke his strength, which alone can enable us to bear up under a weight of affliction. Nay, even the holiest of men, however well aware that they stand not in their own strength, but by the grace of God, would feel too secure in their own fortitude and constancy, were they not brought to a more thorough knowledge of themselves by the trial of the cross. This feeling gained even

upon David, 'In my prosperity I Said, I shall never be moved. Lord, by thy favour thou hast made my mountain to stand strong: thou didst hide thy face, and I was troubled' (Ps. 30:6, 7). He confesses that in prosperity his feelings were dulled and blunted, so that, neglecting the grace of God, on which alone he ought to have depended, he leant to himself, and promised himself perpetuity. If it so happened to this great prophet, who of us should not fear and study caution? Though in tranquillity they flatter themselves with the idea of greater constancy and patience, yet, humbled by adversity, they learn the deception. Believers, I say, warned by such proofs of their diseases, make progress in humility, and, divesting themselves of a depraved confidence in the flesh, betake themselves to the grace of God, and, when they have so betaken themselves, experience the presence of the divine power, in which is ample protection.

3. This Paul teaches when he says that tribulation worketh patience, and patience experience. God having promised that he will be with believers in tribulation, they feel the truth of the promise; while supported by his hand, they endure patiently. This they could never do by their own strength. Patience, therefore, gives the saints an experimental proof that God in reality furnishes the aid which he has promised whenever there is need. Hence also their faith is confirmed, for it were very ungrateful not to expect that in future the truth of God will be, as they have already found it, firm and constant. We now see how many advantages are at once produced by the cross. Overturning the overweening opinion we form of our own virtue, and detecting the hypocrisy in which we delight, it removes our pernicious carnal confidence, teaching us, when thus humbled, to recline on God alone, so that we neither are oppressed nor despond. Then victory is followed by hope, inasmuch as the Lord, by performing what he has promised, establishes his truth in regard to the future. Were these the only reasons, it is surely plain how necessary it is for us to bear the cross. It is of no little importance to be rid of your self-love, and made fully conscious of your weakness; so impressed with a sense of your weakness as to learn to distrust yourself – to distrust yourself so as to transfer your confidence to God, reclining on him with such heartfelt confidence as to trust in his aid, and continue invincible to the end, standing by his grace so as to perceive that he is true to his promises, and so assured of the certainty of his promises as to be strong in hope.

4. Another end which the Lord has in afflicting his people is to try their patience, and train them to obedience – not that they can yield obedience to him except in so far as he enables them; but he is pleased thus to attest and display striking proofs of the graces which he has conferred upon his saints, lest they should remain within unseen and unemployed. Accordingly, by bringing forward openly the strength and constancy of endurance with which he has provided his servants, he is said to try their patience. Hence the expressions that God tempted Abraham (Gen. 21:1, 12), and made proof of his piety by not declining to sacrifice his only son. Hence, too, Peter tells us that our faith is proved by tribulation, just as gold is tried in a furnace of fire. But who will say it is not expedient that the most excellent gift of patience which the believer has received from his God should be applied to uses by being made sure and manifest? Otherwise men would never value it according to its worth. But if God himself, to prevent the virtues which he has conferred upon believers from lurking in obscurity, nay, lying useless and perishing, does aright in supplying materials for calling them forth, there is the best reason for the afflictions of the saints, since without them their patience could not exist. I say, that by the cross they are also trained to obedience, because they are thus taught to live not according to their own wish, but at the disposal of God. Indeed, did all things proceed as they wish, they would not know what it is to follow God. Seneca mentions that there was an old proverb when any one was exhorted to endure adversity, 'Follow God;' thereby intimating, that men truly submitted to the yoke of God only when they gave their back and hand to his rod. But if it is most right that we should in all things prove our obedience to our heavenly Father, certainly we ought not to decline any method by which he trains us to obedience.

5. Still, however, we see not how necessary that obedience is, unless we at the same time consider how prone our carnal nature is to shake off the yoke of God whenever it has been treated with some degree of gentleness and indulgence. It just happens to it as with refractory horses, which, if kept idle for a few days at hack and manger, become ungovernable, and no longer recognise the rider, whose command before they implicitly obeyed. And we invariably become what God complains of in the people of Israel – waxing gross and fat, we kick against him who reared and nursed us (Deut. 32:15). The kindness of God should allure us to ponder and love his goodness; but since such is our malignity, that we are invariably corrupted by his indulgence, it is more than necessary for us to be restrained by discipline from breaking forth into such petulance. Thus, lest we become emboldened by an over-abundance of wealth; lest elated with honour, we grow proud; lest inflated with other advantages of body, or mind, or fortune, we grow insolent, the Lord himself interferes as he sees to be expedient by means of the cross, subduing and curbing the arrogance of our flesh, and that in various ways, as the advantage of each requires. For as we do not all equally labour under the same disease, so we do not all need the same difficult cure. Hence we see that all are not exercised with the same kind of cross. While the heavenly Physician treats some more gently, in the case of others he employs harsher remedies, his purpose being to provide a cure for all. Still none is left free and untouched, because he knows that all, without a single exception, are diseased.

✝ CHAPTER 9 ✝

Of meditating on the future life.

Sections

1. The design of God in afflicting his people: (1) To accustom us to despise the present life. Our infatuated love of it. Afflictions employed as the cure. (2) To lead us to aspire to heaven.

2. Excessive love of the present life prevents us from duly aspiring to the other. Hence the disadvantages of prosperity. Blindness of the human judgment. Our philosophising on the vanity of life only of momentary influence. The necessity of the cross.

3. The present life an evidence of the divine favour to his people; and therefore, not to be detested. On the contrary, should call forth thanksgiving. The crown of victory in heaven after the contest on earth.

1. Whatever be the kind of tribulation with which we are afflicted, we should always consider the end of it to be, that we may be trained to despise the present, and thereby stimulated to aspire to the future life. For since God well knows how strongly we are inclined by nature to a slavish love of this world, in order to prevent us from clinging too strongly to it, he employs the fittest reason for calling us back, and shaking off our lethargy. Every one of us, indeed, would be thought to aspire and aim at heavenly immortality during the whole course of his life. For we would be ashamed in no respect to excel the lower animals; whose condition would not be at all inferior to ours, had we not a hope of immortality beyond the grave. But when you attend to the plans, wishes, and actions of each, you see nothing in them but the earth. Hence our stupidity; our minds being dazzled with the glare of wealth, power, and honours, that they can see no farther. The heart also, engrossed with avarice, ambition, and lust, is weighed down and cannot rise above them. In short, the whole soul, ensnared by the allurements of the flesh, seeks its happiness on the earth. To meet this disease, the Lord makes his people sensible of the vanity of the present life, by a constant proof of its miseries. Thus, that they may not promise themselves deep and lasting peace in it, he often allows them to be assailed by war, tumult, or rapine, or to be disturbed by other injuries. That they may not long with too much eagerness after fleeting and fading riches, or rest in those which they already possess, he reduces them to want, or, at least, restricts them to a moderate allowance, at one time by exile, at another by sterility, at another by fire, or by other means. That they may not indulge too complacently in the advantages of married life, he either vexes them by the misconduct of their partners, or humbles them by the wickedness of their children, or afflicts them by bereavement. But if in all these he is indulgent to them, lest they should either swell with vain-glory, or be elated with confidence, by diseases and dangers he sets palpably before them how unstable and evanescent are all the advantages competent to mortals. We duly profit by the discipline of the cross, when we learn that this life, estimated in itself, is restless, troubled, in numberless ways wretched, and plainly in no respect happy; that what are estimated its blessings are uncertain, fleeting, vain, and vitiated by a great admixture of evil. From this we conclude, that all we have to seek or hope for here is contest; that when we think of the crown we must raise our eyes to heaven. For we must hold, that our mind never rises seriously to desire and aspire after the future, until it has learned to despise the present life.

2. For there is no medium between the two things: the earth must either be worthless in our estimation, or keep us enslaved by an intemperate love of it. Therefore, if we have any regard to eternity, we must carefully strive to disencumber ourselves of these fetters. Moreover, since the present life has many enticements to allure us, and great semblance of delight, grace, and sweetness to soothe us, it is of great consequence to us to be now and then called off from its fascinations. For what, pray, would happen, if we here enjoyed an uninterrupted course of honour and felicity, when even the constant stimulus of affliction cannot arouse us to a due sense of our misery? That human life is like smoke or a shadow, is not only known to the learned; there is not a more trite proverb among the vulgar. Considering it a fact most useful to be known, they have recommended it in many well-known expressions. Still there is no fact which we ponder less carefully, or less frequently remember. For we form all our plans just as if we had fixed our immortality on the earth. If we see a funeral, or walk among graves, as the image of death is then present to the eye, I admit we philosophise admirably on the vanity of life. We do not indeed always do so, for those things often have no effect upon us at all. But, at the best, our philosophy is momentary. It vanishes as soon as we turn our back, and leaves not the vestige of remembrance behind; in short, it passes away, just like the applause of a theatre at some pleasant spectacle. Forgetful not only of death, but also of mortality itself, as if no rumour of it had ever reached us, we indulge in supine security as expecting a terrestrial immortality. Meanwhile, if any one breaks in with the proverb, that man is the creature of a day, we indeed acknowledge its truth, but, so far from giving heed to it, the thought of perpetuity still keeps hold of our minds. Who then can deny that it is of the highest importance to us all, I say not, to be admonished by words, but convinced by all possible experience of the miserable condition of our earthly life; since even when convinced we scarcely cease to gaze upon it with vicious, stupid admiration, as if it contained within itself the sum of all that is good? But if God finds it necessary so to train us, it must be our duty to listen to him when he calls, and shakes us from our torpor, that we may hasten to despise the world, and aspire with our whole heart to the future life.

3. Still the contempt which believers should train themselves to feel for the present life, must not be of a kind to beget hatred of it or ingratitude to God. This life, though abounding in all kinds of wretchedness, is justly classed among divine blessings which are not to be despised. Wherefore, if we do not recognise the kindness of God in it, we are chargeable with no little ingratitude towards him. To believers, especially, it ought to be a proof of divine benevolence, since it is wholly destined to promote their salvation. Before openly exhibiting the inheritance of eternal glory, God is pleased to manifest himself to us as a Father by minor proofs – the blessings which he daily bestows upon us. Therefore, while this life serves to acquaint us with the goodness of God, shall we disdain it as if it did not contain one particle of good? We ought, therefore, to feel and be affected towards it in such a manner as to place it among those gifts of the divine benignity which are by no means to be despised. Were there no proofs in Scripture (they are most numerous and clear), yet nature herself exhorts us to return thanks to God for having brought us forth into light, granted us the use of it, and bestowed upon us all the means necessary for its preservation. And there is a much higher reason when we reflect that here we are in a manner prepared for the glory of the heavenly kingdom. For the Lord hath ordained, that those who are ultimately to be crowned in heaven must maintain a previous warfare on the earth, that they may not triumph before they have overcome the difficulties of war, and obtained the victory. Another reason is, that we here begin to experience in various ways a foretaste of the divine benignity, in order that our hope and desire may be whetted for its full manifestation. When once we have concluded that our earthly life is a gift of the divine mercy, of which, agreeably to our obligation, it behoves us to have a grateful remembrance, we shall then properly descend to consider its most wretched condition, and thus escape from that excessive fondness for it, to which, as I have said, we are naturally prone.

✝ CHAPTER 10 ✝
How to use the present life, and the comforts of it.

Sections

1. Necessity of this doctrine. Use of the goods of the present life. Extremes to be avoided: (1) Excessive austerity, (2) carnal intemperance and lasciviousness.

2. God, by creating so many mercies, consulted not only for our necessities, but also for our comfort and delight. Confirmation from a passage in the Psalms, and from experience.
3. Excessive austerity, therefore, to be avoided. So also must the wantonness of the flesh. (1) The creatures invite us to know, love, and honour the Creator. (2) This not done by the wicked, who only abuse these temporal mercies.
4. All earthly blessings to be despised in comparison of the heavenly life. Aspiration after this life destroyed by an excessive love of created objects. First, Intemperance.

1. By such rudiments we are at the same time well instructed by Scripture in the proper use of earthly blessings, a subject which, in forming a scheme of life, is by no means to be neglected. For if we are to live, we must use the necessary supports of life; nor can we even shun those things which seem more subservient to delight than to necessity. We must therefore observe a mean, that we may use them with a pure conscience, whether for necessity or for pleasure. This the Lord prescribes by his word, when he tells us that to his people the present life is a kind of pilgrimage by which they hasten to the heavenly kingdom. If we are only to pass through the earth, there can be no doubt that we are to use its blessings only in so far as they assist our progress, rather than retard it. Accordingly, Paul, not without cause, admonishes us to use this world without abusing it, and to buy possessions as if we were selling them (1 Cor. 7:30, 31). But as this is a slippery place, and there is great danger of falling on either side, let us fix our feet where we can stand safely. There have been some good and holy men who, when they saw intemperance and luxury perpetually carried to excess, if not strictly curbed, and were desirous to correct so pernicious an evil, imagined that there was no other method than to allow man to use corporeal goods only in so far as they were necessaries: a counsel pious indeed, but unnecessarily austere; for it does the very dangerous thing of binding consciences in closer fetters than those in which they are bound by the word of God. Moreover, necessity, according to them, was abstinence from every thing which could be wanted, so that they held it scarcely lawful to make any addition to bread and water. Others were still more austere, as is related of Cratetes the Theban, who threw his riches into the sea, because he thought, that unless he destroyed them they would destroy him. Many also in the present day, while they seek a pretext for carnal intemperance in the use of external things, and at the same time would pave the way for licentiousness, assume for granted, what I by no means concede, that this liberty is not to be restrained by any modification, but that it is to be left to every man's conscience to use them as far as he thinks lawful. I indeed confess that here consciences neither can nor ought to be bound by fixed and definite laws; but that Scripture having laid down general rules for the legitimate uses we should keep within the limits which they prescribe.

2. Let this be our principle, that we err not in the use of the gifts of Providence when we refer them to the end for which their author made and destined them, since he created them for our good, and not for our destruction. No man will keep the true path better than he who shall have this end carefully in view. Now then, if we consider for what end he created food, we shall find that he consulted not only for our necessity, but also for our enjoyment and delight. Thus, in clothing, the end was, in addition to necessity, comeliness and honour; and in herbs,

✝ PART X ✝

JUSTIFICATION BY FAITH

✝ CHAPTER 11 ✝

Of justification by faith. Both the name and the reality defined.

Sections

1. Connection between the doctrine of Justification and that of Regeneration. The knowledge of this doctrine very necessary for two reasons.
2. For the purpose of facilitating the exposition of it, the terms are explained: (1) What it is to be justified in the sight of God, (2) to be justified by works, (3) to be justified by faith. Definition.
21. The accuracy of the definition of Justification by Faith established.
22. Definition confirmed (1) by passages of Scripture, (2) by the writings of the ancient Fathers.
23. Man justified by faith, not because by it he obtains the Spirit, and is thus made righteous, but because by faith he lays hold of the righteousness of Christ. An objection removed. An example of the doctrine of Justification by Faith from the works of Ambrose.

1.   I trust I have now sufficiently shown how man's only resource for escaping from the curse of the Law, and recovering salvation, lies in faith; and also what the nature of faith is, what the benefits which it confers, and the fruits which it produces. The whole may be thus summed up: Christ given to us by the kindness of God is apprehended and possessed by faith, by means of which we obtain in particular a twofold benefit; first, being reconciled by the righteousness of Christ, God becomes, instead of a judge, an indulgent Father; and, secondly, being sanctified by his Spirit, we aspire to integrity and purity of life. This second benefit, regeneration, appears to have been already sufficiently discussed. On the other hand, the subject of justification was discussed more cursorily, because it seemed of more consequence first to explain that the faith by which alone, through the mercy of God, we obtain free justification, is not destitute of good works; and also to show the true nature of these good works on which this question partly turns. The doctrine of Justification is now to be fully discussed, and discussed under the conviction, that as it is the principal ground on which religion must be supported, so it requires greater care and attention. For unless you understand first of all what your position is before God, and what the judgment which he passes upon you, you have no foundation on which your salvation can be laid, or on which piety towards God can be reared. The necessity of thoroughly understanding this subject will become more apparent as we proceed with it.

2.   Lest we should stumble at the very threshold (this we should do were we to begin the discussion without knowing what the subject is), let us first explain the meaning of the expressions 'To be justified in the sight of God, to be Justified by faith or by works'. A man is said to be justified in the sight of God when in the judgment of God he is deemed righteous, and is accepted on account of his righteousness; for as iniquity is abominable to God, so neither can the sinner find grace in his sight, so far as he is and so long as he is regarded as a sinner. Hence, wherever sin is, there also are the wrath and vengeance of God. He, on the other hand, is justified who is regarded not as a sinner, but as righteous, and as such stands acquitted at the judgment-seat of God, where all sinners are condemned. As an innocent man, when charged before an impartial judge, who decides according to his innocence, is said to be justified by the judge, as a man is said to be justified by God when, removed from the catalogue of sinners, he has God as the witness and assertor of his righteousness. In the same manner, a man will be said to be 'justified by works' if in his life there can be found a purity and holiness which merits an attestation of righteousness at the throne of God, or if by the perfection of his works he can answer and satisfy the divine justice. On the contrary, a man will be 'justified by faith' when, excluded from the righteousness of works, he by faith lays hold of the righteousness of Christ, and clothed in it appears in the sight of God not as a sinner, but as righteous. Thus we simply interpret justification, as the acceptance with which God receives us into his favour as if we were righteous; and we say that this justification consists in the forgiveness of sins and the imputation of the righteousness of Christ.

21.   Let us now consider the truth of what was said in the definition – that justification by faith is reconciliation with God, and that this consists solely in the remission of sins. We must always return to the axioms that the wrath of God lies upon all men so long as they continue sinners. This is elegantly expressed by Isaiah in these words: 'Behold, the Lord's hand is not shortened, that it cannot save; neither his ear heavy, that it cannot hear: but your iniquities have separated between you and your God, and your sins have hid his face from you, that he will not hear' (Isa. 59:1, 2). We are here told that sin is a separation between God and man; that His countenance is turned away from the sinner; and that it cannot be otherwise, since, to have any intercourse with sin is repugnant to his righteousness. Hence the apostle shows that man is at enmity with God until he is restored to favour by Christ (Rom. 5:8–10). When the Lord, therefore, admits him to union, he is said to justify him, because he can neither receive him into favour, nor unite him to himself, without changing his condition from that of a sinner into that of a righteous man. We add that this is done by remission of sins. For if those whom the Lord has reconciled to himself are estimated by works, they will still prove to be in reality sinners, while they ought to be pure and free from sin. It is evident therefore, that the only way in which those whom God embraces are made righteous, is by having their pollutions wiped away by the remission of sins, so that this justification may be termed in one word the 'remission of sins'.

22.   Both of these become perfectly clear from the words of Paul: 'God was in Christ reconciling the world unto himself, not imputing their trespasses unto them; and has committed unto us the word of reconciliation.' He then subjoins the sum of his embassy: 'He has made him to be sin for us who knew no sin; that we might be made the righteousness of God in him' (2 Cor. 5:19-21). He here uses righteousness and reconciliation indiscriminately, to make us understand that the one includes the other. The mode of obtaining this righteousness he explains to be, that our sins are not imputed to us. Wherefore, you cannot henceforth doubt how God justifies us when you hear that he reconciles us to himself by not imputing our faults. In the same manner, in the Epistle to the Romans, he proves, by the testimony of David, that righteousness is imputed without works, because he declares the man to be blessed 'whose transgression is forgiven, whose sin is covered', and 'unto whom the Lord imputeth not iniquity' (Rom. 4:6; Ps. 32:1, 2). There he undoubtedly uses blessedness for righteousness; and as he declares that it consists in forgiveness of sins, there is no reason why we should define it otherwise. Accordingly, Zacharias, the father of John the Baptist, sings that the knowledge of salvation consists in the forgiveness of sins (Lk. 1:77). The same course was followed by Paul when, in addressing the people of Antioch, he gave them a summary of salvation. Luke states that he concluded in this way: 'Through this man is preached unto you the forgiveness of sins, and by him all that believe are justified from all things from which ye could not be justified by the law of Moses' (Acts 13:38, 39). Thus the apostle connects forgiveness of sins with justification in such a way as to show that they are altogether the same; and hence he properly argues that justification, which we owe to the indulgence of God, is gratuitous. Nor should it seem an unusual mode of expression to say that believers are justified before God not by works, but by gratuitous acceptance, seeing it is frequently used in Scripture, and sometimes also by ancient writers. Thus Augustine says: 'The righteousness of the saints in this world consists more in the forgiveness of sins than the perfection of virtue.' To this corresponds the well-known sentiment of Bernard: 'Not to sin is the righteousness of God, but the righteousness of man is the indulgence of God.' He previously asserts that Christ is our righteousness in absolution, and, therefore, that those only are just who have obtained pardon through mercy.

23.   Hence also it is proved, that it is entirely by the intervention of Christ's righteousness that we obtain justification before God. This is equivalent to saying that man is not just in himself, but that the righteousness of Christ is communicated to him by imputation, while he is strictly deserving of punishment. Thus vanishes the absurd dogma, that man is justified by faith, inasmuch as it brings him under the influence of the Spirit of God by whom he is rendered righteous. This is so repugnant to the above doctrine that it never can be reconciled with it. There can be no doubt that he who is taught to seek righteousness out of himself does not previously possess it in himself. This is most clearly declared by the apostle, when he says, that he who knew no sin was made an expiatory victim for sin, that we might be made the righteousness of God in him (2 Cor. 5:21). You see that our righteousness is not in ourselves, but in Christ; that the only way in which we become possessed of it is by being made partakers with Christ, since with him we possess all riches. There is nothing repugnant to this in what he elsewhere says: 'God sending his own Son in the likeness of sinful flesh, and for sin condemned sin in the flesh: that the righteousness of the law might be fulfilled in us' (Rom. 8:3, 4). Here the only fulfilment to which he refers is that which we obtain by imputation. Our Lord Jesus Christ communicates his righteousness to us, and so by some wondrous ways in so far as pertains to the justice of God transfuses its power into us. That this was the apostle's view is abundantly clear from another sentiment which he had expressed a little before: 'As by one man's disobedience many were made sinners, so by the obedience of one shall many be made righteous' (Rom. 5:19). To declare that we are deemed righteous, solely because the obedience of Christ is

imputed to us as if it where our own, is just to place our righteousness in the obedience of Christ. Wherefore, Ambrose appears to me to have most elegantly adverted to the blessing of Jacob as an illustration of this righteousness, when he says that as he who did not merit the birthright in himself personated his brother, put on his garments which gave forth a most pleasant odour, and thus introduced himself to his father that he might receive a blessing to his own advantage, though under the person of another, so we conceal ourselves under the precious purity of Christ, our first-born brother, that we may obtain an attestation of righteousness from the presence of God. The words of Ambrose are, 'Isaac's smelling the odour of his garments, perhaps means that we are justified not by works, but by faith, since carnal infirmity is an impediment to works, but errors of conduct are covered by the brightness of faith, which merits the pardon of faults'. And so indeed it is; for in order to appear in the presence of God for salvation, we must send forth that fragrant odour, having our vices covered and buried by his perfection.

✝ CHAPTER 12 ✝
Necessity of contemplating the judgment-seat of God, in order to be seriously convinced of the doctrine of gratuitous justification.

Sections
1. Source of error on the subject of Justification. Sophists speak as if the question were to be discussed before some human tribunal. It relates to the majesty and justice of God. Hence nothing accepted without absolute perfection. Passages confirming this doctrine. If we descend to the righteousness of the Law, the curse immediately appears.
2. Source of hypocritical confidence. Illustrated by a simile. Exhortation. Testimony of Job, David, and Paul.

1.   Although the perfect truth of the above doctrine is proved by clear passages of Scripture, yet we cannot clearly see how necessary it is, before we bring distinctly into view the foundations on which the whole discussion ought to rest. First, then, let us remember that the righteousness which we are considering is not that of a human, but of a heavenly tribunal; and so beware of employing our own little standard to measure the perfection which is to satisfy the justice of God. It is strange with what rashness and presumption this is commonly defined. Nay, we see that none talk more confidently, or, so to speak, more blusteringly, of the righteousness of works than those whose diseases are most palpable, and blemishes most apparent. This they do because they reflect not on the righteousness of Christ, which, if they had the slightest perception of it, they would never treat with so much insult. It is certainly undervalued, if not recognised to be so perfect that nothing can be accepted that is not in every respect entire and absolute, and tainted by no impurity; such indeed as never has been, and never will be, found in man. It is easy for any man, within the precincts of the schools, to talk of the sufficiency of works for justification; but when we come into the presence of God there must be a truce to such talk. The matter is there discussed in earnest, and is no longer a theatrical logomachy. Hither must we turn our minds if we would inquire to any purpose

concerning true righteousness; the question must be: How shall we answer the heavenly Judge when he calls us to account? Let us contemplate that Judge, not as our own unaided intellect conceives of him, but as he is portrayed to us in Scripture (see especially the book of Job), with a brightness which obscures the stars, a strength which melts the mountains, an anger which shakes the earth, a wisdom which takes the wise in their own craftiness, a purity before which all things become impure, a righteousness to which not even angels are equal (so far is it from making the guilty innocent), a vengeance which once kindled burns to the lowest hell (Exod. 34:7; Nah. 1:3; Deut. 32:22). Let him, I say, sit in judgment on the actions of men, and who will feel secure in sitting himself before his throne? 'Who among us,' says the prophets 'shall dwell with the devouring fire? who among us shall dwell with everlasting burnings? He that walketh righteously, and speaketh uprightly,' etc. (Isa. 33:14, 15). Let whoso will come forth. Nay, the answer shows that no man can. For, on the other hand, we hear the dreadful voice: 'If thou, Lord, shouldst mark our iniquities, O Lord, who shall stand?' (Ps. 130:3). All must immediately perish, as Job declares, 'Shall mortal man be more just than God? shall a man be more pure than his Maker? Behold, he put no trust in his servants; and his angels he charged with folly: How much less in them that dwell in houses of clay, whose foundation is in the dust, which are crushed before the moth? They are destroyed from morning to evening' (Job 4:17–20). Again, 'Behold, he putteth no trust in his saints; yea, the heavens are not clean in his sight. How much more abominable and filthy is man, which drinketh iniquity like water?' (Job 15:15, 16). I confess, indeed, that in the book of Job reference is made to a righteousness of a more exalted description than the observance of the Law. It is of importance to attend to this distinction; for even could a man satisfy the Law, he could not stand the scrutiny of that righteousness which transcends all our thoughts. Hence, although Job was not conscious of offending, he is still dumb with astonishment, because he sees that God could not be appeased even by the sanctity of angels, were their works weighed in that supreme balance. But to advert no farther to this righteousness, which is incomprehensible, I only say, that if our life is brought to the standard of the written Law, we are lethargic indeed if we are not filled with dread at the many maledictions which God has employed for the purpose of arousing us, and among others, the following general one: 'Cursed be he that confirmeth not all the words of this law to do them' (Deut. 27:26). In short, the whole discussion of this subject will be insipid and frivolous, unless we seat ourselves before the heavenly Judge, and anxious for our acquittal, voluntarily humble ourselves, confessing our nothingness.

2. Thus then must we raise our eyes that we may learn to tremble instead of vainly exulting. It is easy, indeed, when the comparison is made among men, for every one to plume himself on some quality which others ought not to despise; but when we rise to God, that confidence instantly falls and dies away. The case of the soul with regard to God is very analogous to that of the body in regard to the visible firmament. The bodily eye, while employed in surveying adjacent objects, is pleased with its own perspicacity; but when directed to the sun, being dazzled and overwhelmed by the refulgence, it becomes no less convinced of its weakness than it formerly was of its power in viewing inferior objects. Therefore, lest we deceive ourselves by vain confidence, let us recollect that even though we deem ourselves equal or superior to other men, this is nothing to God, by whose judgment the decision must be given. But if our presumption cannot be tamed by these considerations, he will answer us as he did

the Pharisees, 'Ye are they which justify yourselves before men; but God knoweth your hearts: for that which is highly esteemed among men is abomination in the sight of God' (Lk. 16:15). Go now and make a proud boast of your righteousness among men, while God in heaven abhors it. But what are the feelings of the servants of God, of those who are truly taught by his Spirit? 'Enter not into judgment with thy servant; for in thy sight shall no man living be justified' (Ps. 143:2). Another, though in a sense somewhat different, says, 'How should man be just with God? If he will contend with him he cannot answer him one of a thousand' (Job 9:2, 3). Here we are plainly told what the righteousness of God is, namely, a righteousness which no human works can satisfy which charges us with a thousand sins, while not one sin can be excused. Of this righteousness Paul, that chosen vessel of God, had formed a just idea, when he declared, 'I know nothing by myself, yet am I not hereby justified' (1 Cor. 4:4).

✝ CHAPTER 13 ✝

Two things to be observed in gratuitous justification.

Sections

3.   Peace of conscience obtained by free justification only. Testimony of Solomon, of conscience itself, and the apostle Paul, who contends that faith is made vain if righteousness come by the law.

3.   If we now inquire in what way the conscience can be quieted as in the view of God, we shall find that the only way is by having righteousness bestowed upon us freely by the gift of God. Let us always remember the words of Solomon, 'Who can say I have made my heart clean, I am free from my sin?' (Prov. 20:9). Undoubtedly there is not one man who is not covered with infinite pollutions. Let the most perfect man descend into his own conscience, and bring his actions to account, and what will the result be? Will he feel calm and quiescent, as if all matters were well arranged between himself and God; or will he not rather be stung with dire torment, when he sees that the ground of condemnation is within him if he be estimated by his works? Conscience, when it beholds God, must either have sure peace with his justice, or be beset by the terrors of hell. We gain nothing, therefore, by discoursing of righteousness, unless we hold it to be a righteousness stable enough to support our souls before the tribunal of God. When the soul is able to appear intrepidly in the presence of God, and receive his sentence without dismay, then only let us know that we have found a righteousness that is not fictitious. It is not, therefore, without cause, that the apostle insists on this matter. I prefer giving it in his words rather than my own: 'If they which are of the law be heirs, faith is made void, and the promise made of no effect' (Rom. 4:14). He first infers that faith is made void if the promise of righteousness has respect to the merit of our works, or depends on the observance of the Law. Never could any one rest securely in it, for never could he feel fully assured that he had fully satisfied the Law; and it is certain that no man ever fully satisfied it by works. Not to go far for proof of this, every one who will use his eyes aright may be his own witness. Hence it appears how deep and dark the abyss is into which hypocrisy plunges the minds of men, when they indulge so securely as, without hesitations to oppose their flattery to the judgment of God, as if

they were relieving him from his office as judge. Very different is the anxiety which fills the breasts of believers, who sincerely examine themselves. Every mind, therefore, would first begin to hesitate, and at length to despair, while each determined for itself with how great a load of debt it was still oppressed, and how far it was from coming up to the enjoined condition. Thus, then, faith would be oppressed and extinguished. To have faith is not to fluctuate, to vary, to be carried up and down, to hesitate, remain in suspense, vacillate, in fine, to despair; it is to possess sure certainty and complete security of mind, to have whereon to rest and fix your foot.

✝ CHAPTER 14 ✝

The beginning of justification. In what sense progressive.

Sections

1. Men either idolatrous, profane, hypocritical, or regenerate. Idolaters void of righteousness, full of unrighteousness, and hence in the sight of God altogether wretched and undone.
2. Still a great difference in the characters of men. This difference manifested (1) in the gifts of God, (2) in the distinction between honourable and base, (3) in the blessings of the present life.
3. All human virtue, how praiseworthy soever it may appear, is corrupted (1) by impurity of heart, (2) by the absence of a proper nature.

1. In farther illustration of the subject, let us consider what kind of righteousness man can have, during the whole course of his life, and for this purpose let us make a fourfold division. Mankind, either endued with no knowledge of God, are sunk in idolatry; or, initiated in the sacraments, but by the impurity of their lives denying him whom they confess with their mouths, are Christians in name only; or they are hypocrites, who with empty glosses hide the iniquity of the heart; or they are regenerated by the Spirit of God, and aspire to true holiness. In the first place, when men are judged by their natural endowments, not an iota of good will be found from the crown of the head to the sole of the foot, unless we are to charge Scripture with falsehood, when it describes all the sons of Adam by such terms as these: 'The heart is deceitful above all things, and desperately wicked'; 'The imagination of man's heart is evil from his youth'; 'The Lord knoweth the thoughts of man that they are vanity'; 'They are all gone aside: they are altogether become filthy; there is none that does good, no, not one.' In short, that they are *flesh*, under which name are comprehended all those works which are enumerated by Paul: adultery, fornication, uncleanness, lasciviousness idolatry witchcraft, hatred, variance, emulation, wrath, strife, seditions, heresies, envyings, murders, drunkenness, revellings, and all kinds of pollution and abomination which it is possible to imagine. Such, then, is the worth on which men are to plume themselves. But if any among them possess an integrity of manners which presents some semblance of sanctity among men, yet because we know that God regards not the outward appearance, we must penetrate to the very source of action, if we would see how far works avail for righteousness. We must, I say, look

within, and see from what affection of the heart these works proceed. This is a very wide field of discussion, but as the matter may be explained in few words, I will use as much brevity as I can.

2. First, then, I deny not, that whatever excellent endowments appear in unbelievers are divine gifts. Nor do I set myself so much in opposition to common sense, as to contend that there was no difference between the justice, moderation, and equity of Titus and Trojan, and the rage, intemperance, and cruelty of Caligula, Nero, and Domitian; between the continence of Vespasian, and the obscene lusts of Tiberius; and (not to dwell on single virtues and vices) between the observance of law and justice, and the contempt of them. So great is the difference between justice and injustice, that it may be seen even where the former is only a lifeless image. For what order would remain in the world if we were to confound them? Hence this distinction between honourable and base actions God has not only engraven on the minds of each, but also often confirms in the administration of his providence. For we see how he visits those who cultivate virtue with many temporal blessings. Not that that external image of virtue in the least degree merits his favour, but he is pleased thus to show how much he delights in true righteousness, since he does not leave even the outward semblance of it to go unrewarded. Hence it follows, as we lately observed, that those virtues, or rather images of virtues, of whatever kind, are divine gifts, since there is nothing in any degree praiseworthy which proceeds not from him.

3. Still the observation of Augustine is true, that all who are strangers to the true God, however excellent they may be deemed on account of their virtues are more deserving of punishment than of reward, because, by the pollution of their heart, they contaminate the pure gifts of God (August. contra Julia. Lib. 4). For though they are instruments of God to preserve human society by justice, continence, friendship, temperance, fortitude, and prudence, yet they execute these good works of God in the worst manner, because they are kept from acting ill, not by a sincere love of goodness, but merely by ambition or self-love, or some other sinister affection. Seeing then that these actions are polluted as in their very source, by impurity of heart, they have no better title to be classed among virtues than vices, which impose upon us by their affinity or resemblance to virtue. In short, when we remember that the object at which righteousness always aims is the service of God, whatever is of a different tendency deservedly forfeits the name. Hence, as they have no regard to the end which the divine wisdom prescribes, although from the performance the act seems good, yet from the perverse motive it is sin. Augustine, therefore, concludes that all the Fabriciuses, the Scipios, and Catos, in their illustrious deeds, sinned in this, that, wanting the light of faith, they did not refer them to the proper end, and that, therefore, there was no true righteousness in them, because duties are estimated not by acts but by motives.

✝ CHAPTER 19 ✝

Of Christian liberty.

Sections

2. This liberty consists of three parts. First, Believers renouncing the righteousness of the Law, look only to Christ. Objection. Answer, distinguishing between Legal and Evangelical righteousness.

4. The second part of Christian liberty – that the conscience, freed from the yoke of the Law, voluntarily obeys the will of God. This cannot be done so long as we are under the Law. Reason.

7. Third part of liberty – the free rise of things indifferent. The knowledge of this part necessary to remove despair and superstition. Superstition described.

8. Proof of this third part from the Epistle to the Romans. Those who observe it not only use evasion. (1) Despisers of God, (2) the desperate, (3) the ungrateful. The end and scope of this third part.

9. Second part of the chapter, showing the nature and efficacy of Christian liberty, in opposition to the Epicureans. Their character described. Pretext and allegation. Use of things indifferent. Abuse detected. Mode of correcting it.

2. Christian liberty seems to me to consist of three parts. First, the consciences of believers, while seeking the assurance of their justification before God, must rise above the Law, and think no more of obtaining justification by it. For while the Law, as has already been demonstrated, leaves not one man righteous, we are either excluded from all hope of justification, or we must be loosed from the Law, and so loosed as that no account at all shall be taken of works. For he who imagines that in order to obtain justification he must bring any degree of works whatever, cannot fix any mode or limit, but makes himself debtor to the whole Law. Therefore, laying aside all mention of the Law, and all idea of works, we must in the matter of justification have recourse to the mercy of God only; turning away our regard from ourselves, we must look only to Christ. For the question is, not how we may be righteous, but how, though unworthy and unrighteous, we may be regarded as righteous. If consciences would obtain any assurance of this, they must give no place to the Law. Still it cannot be rightly inferred from this that believers have no need of the Law. It ceases not to teach, exhort, and urge them to good, although it is not recognised by their consciences before the judgment-seat of God. The two things are very different, and should be well and carefully distinguished. The whole lives of Christians ought to be a kind of aspiration after piety, seeing they are called unto holiness (Eph. 1:4; 1 Thess. 4:5). The office of the Law is to excite them to the study of purity and holiness, by reminding them of their duty. For when the conscience feels anxious as to how it may have the favour of God, as to the answer it could give, and the confidence it would feel, if brought to his judgment-seat, in such a case the requirements of the Law are not to be brought forward, but Christ, who surpasses all the perfection of the Law, is alone to be held forth for righteousness.

4. Another point which depends on the former is, that consciences obey the Law, not as if compelled by legal necessity; but being free from the yoke of the Law itself, voluntarily obey the will of God. Being constantly in terror so long as they are under the dominion of the Law,

they are never disposed promptly to obey God, unless they have previously obtained this liberty. Our meaning shall be explained more briefly and clearly by an example. The command of the Law is, 'Thou shalt love the Lord thy God with all thine heart, and with all thy soul, and with all thy might' (Deut. 6:5). To accomplish this, the soul must previously be divested of every other thought and feeling, the heart purified from all its desires, all its powers collected and united on this one object. Those who, in comparison of others, have made much progress in the way of the Lord, are still very far from this goal. For although they love God in their mind, and with a sincere affection of heart, yet both are still in a great measure occupied with the lusts of the flesh, by which they are retarded and prevented from proceeding with quickened pace towards God. They indeed make many efforts, but the flesh partly enfeebles their strength, and partly binds them to itself. What can they do while they thus feel that there is nothing of which they are less capable than to fulfill the Law? They wish, aspire, endeavour; but do nothing with the requisite perfection. If they look to the Law, they see that every work which they attempt or design is accursed. Nor can any one deceive himself by inferring that the work is not altogether bad, merely because it is imperfect, and, therefore, that any good which is in it is still accepted of God. For the Law demanding perfect love condemns all imperfection, unless its rigour is mitigated. Let any man therefore consider his work which he wishes to be thought partly good, and he will find that it is a transgression of the Law by the very circumstance of its being imperfect.

7.   The third part of this liberty is that we are not bound before God to any observance of external things which are in themselves indifferent (ajdiavfora), but that we are now at full liberty either to use or omit them. The knowledge of this liberty is very necessary to us; where it is wanting our consciences will have no rest, there will be no end of superstition. In the present day many think us absurd in raising a question as to the free eating of flesh, the free use of dress and holidays, and similar frivolous trifles, as they think them; but they are of more importance than is commonly supposed. For when once the conscience is entangled in the net, it enters a long and inextricable labyrinth, from which it is afterwards most difficult to escape. When a man begins to doubt whether it is lawful for him to use linen for sheets, shirts, napkins, and handkerchiefs, he will not long be secure as to hemp, and will at last have doubts as to tow; for he will revolve in his mind whether he cannot sup without napkins, or dispense with handkerchiefs. Should he deem a daintier food unlawful, he will afterwards feel uneasy for using loafbread and common eatables, because he will think that his body might possibly be supported on a still meaner food. If he hesitates as to a more genial wine, he will scarcely drink the worst with a good conscience; at last he will not dare to touch water if more than usually sweet and pure. In fine, he will come to this, that he will deem it criminal to trample on a straw lying in his way. For it is no trivial dispute that is here commenced, the point in debate being, whether the use of this thing or that is in accordance with the divine will, which ought to take precedence of all our acts and counsels. Here some must by despair be hurried into an abyss, while others, despising God and casting off his fear, will not be able to make a way for themselves without ruin. When men are involved in such doubts whatever be the direction in which they turn, every thing they see must offend their conscience.

8.   'I know,' says Paul, 'that there is nothing unclean of itself' (by unclean meaning unholy), 'but to him that esteemeth any thing to be unclean, to him it is unclean' (Rom. 14:14). By these

words he makes all external things subject to our liberty, provided the nature of that liberty approves itself to our minds as before God. But if any superstitious idea suggests scruples, those things which in their own nature were pure are to us contaminated. Wherefore the apostle adds, 'Happy is he that condemneth not himself in that which he alloweth. And he that doubteth is damned if he eat, because he eateth not of faith: for whatsoever is not of faith is sin' (Rom. 14:22, 23). When men, amid such difficulties, proceed with greater confidence, securely doing whatever pleases them, do they not in so far revolt from God? Those who are thoroughly impressed with some fear of God, if forced to do many things repugnant to their consciences are discouraged and filled with dread. All such persons receive none of the gifts of God with thanksgiving, by which alone Paul declares that all things are sanctified for our use (1 Tim. 4:5). By thanksgiving I understand that which proceeds from a mind recognising the kindness and goodness of God in his gifts. For many, indeed, understand that the blessings which they enjoy are the gifts of God, and praise God in their words; but not being persuaded shalt these have been given to them, how can they give thanks to God as the giver? In one word, we see whither this liberty tends – that we are to use the gifts of God without any scruple of conscience, without any perturbation of mind, for the purpose for which he gave them: in this way our souls may both have peace with him, and recognise his liberality towards us. For here are comprehended all ceremonies of free observance, so that while our consciences are not to be laid under the necessity of observing them, we are also to remember that, by the kindness of God, the use of them is made subservient to edification.

9.　It is, however, to be carefully observed, that Christian liberty is in all its parts a spiritual matter, the whole force of which consists in giving peace to trembling consciences, whether they are anxious and disquieted as to the forgiveness of sins, or as to whether their imperfect works, polluted by the infirmities of the flesh, are pleasing to God, or are perplexed as to the use of things indifferent. It is, therefore, perversely interpreted by those who use it as a cloak for their lusts, that they may licentiously abuse the good gifts of God, or who think there is no liberty unless it is used in the presence of men, and, accordingly, in using it pay no regard to their weak brethren. Under this head, the sins of the present age are more numerous. For there is scarcely any one whose means allow him to live sumptuously, who does not delight in feasting, and dress, and the luxurious grandeur of his house, who wishes not to surpass his neighbours in every kind of delicacy, and does not plume himself amazingly on his splendour. And all these things are defended under the pretext of Christian liberty. They say they are things indifferent: I admit it, provided they are used indifferently. But when they are too eagerly longed for, when they are proudly boasted of, when they are indulged in luxurious profusion, things which otherwise were in themselves lawful are certainly defiled by these vices. Paul makes an admirable distinction in regard to things indifferent: 'Unto the pure all things are pure: but unto them that are defiled and unbelieving is nothing pure; but even their mind and conscience is defiled' (Tit. 1:15). For why is a woe pronounced upon the rich who have received their consolation? (Lk. 6:24), who are full, who laugh now, who 'lie upon beds of ivory and stretch themselves upon their couches', 'join house to house', 'lay field to field', 'and the harp and the viol, the tablet and pipe, and wine, are in their feasts' (Amos 6:6; Isa. 5:8, 10). Certainly ivory and gold, and riches, are the good creatures of God, permitted, nay destined, by divine providence for the use of man; nor was it ever forbidden to laugh, or to be full, or to add new to old and hereditary possessions, or to be delighted with music, or to drink wine. This is true, but when the means are supplied to roll and wallow in luxury, to intoxicate the mind and soul with present and be always hunting after new pleasures, is very far from a legitimate use of the gifts of God. Let them, therefore, suppress immoderate desire, immoderate profusion, vanity, and arrogance, that they may use the gifts of God purely with a pure conscience. When their mind is brought to this state of soberness, they will be able to regulate the legitimate use. On the other hand, when this moderation is wanting, even plebeian and ordinary delicacies are excessive. For it is a true saying, that a haughty mind often dwells in a coarse and homely garb, while true humility lurks under fine linen and purple. Let every one then live in his own station, poorly or moderately, or in splendour; but let all remember that the nourishment which God gives is for life, not luxury, and let them regard it as the law of Christian liberty, to learn with Paul in whatever state they are, 'therewith to be content', to know 'both how to be abased' and 'how to abound', 'to be full and to be hungry, both to abound and to suffer need' (Phil. 4:11).

✛ PART XI ✛

PRAYER

✛ CHAPTER 20 ✛

Of prayer – a perpetual exercise of faith.
The daily benefits derived from it.

Sections

1. A general summary of what is contained in the previous part of the work. A transition to the doctrine of prayer. Its connection with the subject of faith.

2. Prayer defined. Its necessity and use.

3. Objection, that prayer seems useless, because God already knows our wants. Answer, from the institution and end of prayer. Confirmation by example. Its necessity and propriety. Perpetually reminds us of our duty, and leads to meditation on divine providence. Conclusion. Prayer a most useful exercise. This proved by three passages of Scripture.

4. Rules to be observed in prayer. First, reverence to God. How the mind ought to be composed.

5. All giddiness of mind must be excluded, and all our feelings seriously engaged. This confirmed by the form of lifting the hand in prayer. We must ask only in so far as God permits. To help our weakness, God gives the Spirit to be our guide in prayer. What the office of the Spirit in this respect. We must still pray both with the heart and the lips.

6. Second rule of prayer, a sense of our want. This rule violated (1) by perfunctory and formal prayer, (2) by hypocrites who have no sense of their sins, (3) by giddiness in prayer. Remedies.

1. From the previous part of the work we clearly see how completely destitute man is of all good, how devoid of every means of procuring his own salvation. Hence, if he would obtain succour in his necessity, he must go beyond himself, and procure it in some other quarter. It has farther been shown that the Lord kindly and spontaneously manifests himself in Christ, in whom he offers all happiness for our misery, all abundance for our want, opening up the treasures of heaven to us, so that we may turn with full faith to his beloved Son, depend upon him with full expectation, rest in him, and cleave to him with full hope. This, indeed, is that secret and hidden philosophy which cannot be learned by syllogisms: a philosophy thoroughly understood by those whose eyes God has so opened as to see light in his light (Ps. 36:9). But after we have learned by faith to know that whatever is necessary for us or defective in us is supplied in God and in our Lord Jesus Christ, in whom it hath pleased the Father that all fulness should dwell, that we may thence draw as from an inexhaustible fountain, it remains for us to seek and in prayer implore of him what we have learned to be in him. To know God as

the sovereign disposer of all good, inviting us to present our requests, and yet not to approach or ask of him, were so far from availing us, that it were just as if one told of a treasure were to allow it to remain buried in the ground. Hence the apostle, to show that a faith unaccompanied with prayer to God cannot be genuine, states this to be the order: As faith springs from the Gospel, so by faith our hearts are framed to call upon the name of God (Rom. 10:14). And this is the very thing which he had expressed some time before – that the *Spirit of adoption*, which seals the testimony of the Gospel on our hearts, gives us courage to make our requests known unto God, calls forth groanings which cannot be uttered, and enables us to cry, *Abba*, Father (Rom. 8:26). This last point, as we have hitherto only touched upon it slightly in passing, must now be treated more fully.

2.   To *prayer*, then, are we indebted for penetrating to those riches which are treasured up for us with our heavenly Father. For there is a kind of intercourse between God and men, by which, having entered the upper sanctuary, they appear before him and appeal to his promises, that when necessity requires they may learn by experiences that what they believed merely on the authority of his word was not in vain. Accordingly, we see that nothing is set before us as an object of expectation from the Lord which we are not enjoined to ask of Him in prayer, so true it is that prayer digs up those treasures which the Gospel of our Lord discovers to the eye of faith. The necessity and utility of this exercise of prayer no words can sufficiently express. Assuredly it is not without cause our heavenly Father declares that our only safety is in calling upon his name, since by it we invoke the presence of his providence to watch over our interests, of his power to sustain us when weak and almost fainting, of his goodness to receive us into favour, though miserably loaded with sin; in fine, call upon him to manifest himself to us in all his perfections. Hence, admirable peace and tranquillity are given to our consciences; for the straits by which we were pressed being laid before the Lord, we rest fully satisfied with the assurance that none of our evils are unknown to him, and that he is both able and willing to make the best provision for us.

3.   But some one will say, Does he not know without a monitor both what our difficulties are, and what is meet for our interest, so that it seems in some measure superfluous to solicit him by our prayers, as if he were winking, or even sleeping, until aroused by the sound of our voice? Those who argue thus attend not to the end for which the Lord taught us to pray. It was not so much for his sake as for ours. He wills indeed, as is just, that due honour be paid him by acknowledging that all which men desire or feel to be useful, and pray to obtain, is derived from him. But even the benefit of the homage which we thus pay him redounds to ourselves. Hence the holy patriarchs, the more confidently they proclaimed the mercies of God to themselves and others felt the stronger incitement to prayer. It will be sufficient to refer to the example of Elijah, who being assured of the purpose of God had good ground for the promise of rain which he gives to Ahab, and yet prays anxiously upon his knees, and sends his servant seven times to inquire (1 Kgs 18:42); not that he discredits the oracle, but because he knows it to be his duty to lay his desires before God, lest his faith should become drowsy or torpid. Wherefore, although it is true that while we are listless or insensible to our wretchedness, he wakes and watches for us and sometimes even assists us unasked; it is very much for our interest to be constantly supplicating him; first, that our heart may always be inflamed with a serious and ardent desire of seeking, loving and serving him, while we accustom ourselves to

have recourse to him as a sacred anchor in every necessity; secondly, that no desires, no longing whatever, of which we are ashamed to make him the witness, may enter our minds, while we learn to place all our wishes in his sight, and thus pour out our heart before him; and, lastly, that we may be prepared to receive all his benefits with true gratitude and thanksgiving, while our prayers remind us that they proceed from his hand. Moreover, having obtained what we asked, being persuaded that he has answered our prayers, we are led to long more earnestly for his favour, and at the same time have greater pleasure in welcoming the blessings which we perceive to have been obtained by our prayers. Lastly, use and experience confirm the thought of his providence in our minds in a manner adapted to our weakness, when we understand that he not only promises that he will never fail us, and spontaneously gives us access to approach him in every time of need, but has his hand always stretched out to assist his people, not amusing them with words, but proving himself to be a present aid. For these reasons, though our most merciful Father never slumbers nor sleeps, he very often seems to do so, that thus he may exercise us, when we might otherwise be listless and slothful, in asking, entreating, and earnestly beseeching him to our great good. It is very absurd, therefore, to dissuade men from prayer, by pretending that Divine Providence, which is always watching over the government of the universe is in vain importuned by our supplications, when, on the contrary, the Lord himself declares, that he is 'nigh unto all that call upon him, to all that call upon him in truth' (Ps. 145:18). No better is the frivolous allegation of others, that it is super-fluous to pray for things which the Lord is ready of his own accord to bestow; since it is his pleasure that those very things which flow from his spontaneous liberality should be acknowl-edged as conceded to our prayers. This is testified by that memorable sentence in the psalms to which many others corresponds: 'The eyes of the Lord are upon the righteous, and his ears are open unto their cry' (Ps. 34:15). This passage, while extolling the care which Divine Providence spontaneously exercises over the safety of believers, omits not the exercise of faith by which the mind is aroused from sloth. The eyes of God are awake to assist the blind in their necessity, but he is likewise pleased to listen to our groans, that he may give us the better proof of his love. And thus both things are true, 'He that keepeth Israel shall neither slumber nor sleep' (Ps. 121:4); and yet whenever he sees us dumb and torpid, he withdraws as if he had forgotten us.

4.   Let the first rule of right prayer then be, to have our heart and mind framed as becomes those who are entering into converse with God. This we shall accomplish in regard to the mind, if, laying aside carnal thoughts and cares which might interfere with the direct and pure contemplation of God, it not only be wholly intent on prayer, but also, as far as possible, be borne and raised above itself. I do not here insist on a mind so disengaged as to feel none of the gnaw-ings of anxiety; on the contrary, it is by much anxiety that the fervour of prayer is inflamed. Thus we see that the holy servants of God betray great anguish, not to say solicitude, when they cause the voice of complaint to ascend to the Lord from the deep abyss and the jaws of death. What I say is, that all foreign and extraneous cares must be dispelled by which the mind might be driven to and fro in vague suspense, be drawn down from heaven, and kept grovelling on the earth. When I say it must be raised above itself, I mean that it must not bring into the presence of God any of those things which our blind and stupid reason is wont to devise, nor keep itself confined within the little measure of its own vanity, but rise to a purity worthy of God.

5. Both things are specially worthy of notice. First, let every one in professing to pray turn thither all his thoughts and feelings, and be not (as is usual) distracted by wandering thoughts; because nothing is more contrary to the reverence due to God than that levity which bespeaks a mind too much given to license and devoid of fear. In this matter we ought to labour the more earnestly the more difficult we experience it to be; for no man is so intent on prayer as not to feel many thoughts creeping in, and either breaking off the tenor of his prayer, or retarding it by some turning or digression. Here let us consider how unbecoming it is when God admits us to familiar intercourse to abuse his great condescension by mingling things sacred and profane, reverence for him not keeping our minds under restraint; but just as if in prayer we were conversing with one like ourselves forgetting him, and allowing our thoughts to run to and fro. Let us know, then, that none duly prepare themselves for prayer but those who are so impressed with the majesty of God that they engage in it free from all earthly cares and affections. The ceremony of lifting up our hands in prayer is designed to remind us that we are far removed from God, unless our thoughts rise upward: as it is said in the psalm, 'Unto thee, O Lord, do I lift up my soul' (Ps. 25:1). And Scripture repeatedly uses the expression to 'raise our prayer', meaning that those who would be heard by God must not grovel in the mire. The sum is, that the more liberally God deals with us, condescendingly inviting us to disburden our cares into his bosom, the less excusable we are if this admirable and incomparable blessing does not in our estimation outweigh all other things, and win our affection, that prayer may seriously engage our every thought and feeling. This cannot be unless our mind, strenuously exerting itself against all impediments, rise upward. Our second proposition was, that we are to ask only in so far as God permits. For though he bids us pour out our hearts (Ps. 62:8) he does not indiscriminately give loose reins to foolish and depraved affections; and when he promises that he will grant believers their wish, his indulgence does not proceed so far as to submit to their caprice. In both matters grievous delinquencies are everywhere committed. For not only do many without modesty, without reverence, presume to invoke God concerning their frivolities, but impudently bring forward their dreams, whatever they may be, before the tribunal of God. Such is the folly or stupidity under which they labour, that they have the hardihood to obtrude upon God desires so vile, that they would blush exceedingly to impart them to their fellow men. Profane writers have derided and even expressed their detestation of this presumption, and yet the vice has always prevailed. Hence, as the ambitious adopted Jupiter as their patron; the avaricious, Mercury; the literary aspirants, Apollo and Minerva; the warlike, Mars; the licentious, Venus: so in the present day, as I lately observed, men in prayer give greater license to their unlawful desires than if they were telling jocular tales among their equals. God does not suffer his condescension to be thus mocked, but vindicating his own light, places our wishes under the restraint of his authority. We must, therefore, attend to the observation of John, 'This is the confidence that we have in him, that if we ask any thing according to his will, he heareth us' (1 Jn 5:14). But as our faculties are far from being able to attain to such high perfection, we must seek for some means to assist them. As the eye of our mind should be intent upon God, so the affection of our heart ought to follow in the same course. But both fall far beneath this, or rather, they faint and fail, and are carried in a contrary direction. To assist this weakness, God gives us the guidance of the Spirit in our prayers to dictate what is right, and regulate our affections. For seeing 'we know not what we should pray for as we ought', 'the Spirit itself maketh intercession for us with groanings which cannot be uttered' (Rom. 8:26) not that he actually prays or groans, but he excites in us sighs, and wishes, and confidence, which our natural powers are not at all able to conceive. Nor is it without cause Paul gives the name of 'groanings which cannot be uttered' to the prayers which believers send forth under the guidance of the Spirit. For those who are truly exercised in prayer are not unaware that blind anxieties so restrain and perplex them, that they can scarcely find what it becomes them to utter; nay, in attempting to lisp they halt and hesitate. Hence it appears that to pray aright is a special gift. We do not speak thus in indulgence to our sloth, as if we were to leave the office of prayer to the Holy Spirit, and give way to that carelessness to which we are too prone. Thus we sometimes hear the impious expression, that we are to wait in suspense until he take possession of our minds while otherwise occupied. Our meaning is, that, weary of our own heartlessness and sloth, we are to long for the aid of the Spirit. Nor, indeed, does Paul, when he enjoins us to pray 'in the Spirit' (1 Cor. 14:15), cease to exhort us to vigilance, intimating, that while the inspiration of the Spirit is effectual to the formation of prayer, it by no means impedes or retards our own endeavours; since in this matter God is pleased to try how efficiently faith influences our hearts.

6.   Another rule of prayer is, that in asking we must always truly feel our wants, and seriously considering that we need all the things which we ask, accompany the prayer with a sincere, nay, ardent desire of obtaining them. Many repeat prayers in a perfunctory manner from a set form, as if they were performing a task to God, and though they confess that this is a necessary remedy for the evils of their condition, because it were fatal to be left without the divine aid which they implore, it still appears that they perform the duty from custom, because their minds are meanwhile cold, and they ponder not what they ask. A general and confused feeling of their necessity leads them to pray, but it does not make them solicitous as in a matter of present consequence, that they may obtain the supply of their need. Moreover, can we suppose anything more hateful or even more execrable to God than this fiction of asking the pardon of sins, while he who asks at the very time either thinks that he is not a sinner, or, at least, is not thinking that he is a sinner; in other words, a fiction by which God is plainly held in derision? But mankind, as I have lately said, are full of depravity, so that in the way of perfunctory service they often ask many things of God which they think come to them without his beneficence, or from some other quarter, or are already certainly in their possession. There is another fault which seems less heinous, but is not to be tolerated. Some murmur out prayers without meditation, their only principle being that God is to be propitiated by prayer. Believers ought to be specially on their guard never to appear in the presence of God with the intention of presenting a request unless they are under some serious impression, and are, at the same time, desirous to obtain it. Nay, although in these things which we ask only for the glory of God, we seem not at first sight to consult for our necessity, yet we ought not to ask with less fervour and vehemence of desire. For instance, when we pray that his name be hallowed – that hallowing must, so to speak, be earnestly hungered and thirsted after.

✝ PART XII ✝

GOD'S ELECTION AND MAN'S DESTINY

✝ CHAPTER 21 ✝

Of the eternal election, by which God has predestinated
some to salvation, and others to destruction.

Sections

1. The doctrine of Election and Predestination. It is useful, necessary, and most sweet. Ignorance of it impairs the glory of God, plucks up humility by the roots, begets and fosters pride. The doctrine establishes the certainty of salvation, peace of conscience, and the true origin of the Church. Answer to two classes of men: (1) The curious.

2. A sentiment of Augustine confirmed by an admonition of our Saviour and a passage of Solomon.

3. An answer to a second class: (2) Those who are unwilling that the doctrine should be adverted to. An objection founded on a passage of Solomon, solved by the words of Moses.

7. The apostle shows that the same thing has been done in regard to individuals under the Christian dispensation.

1. The covenant of life is not preached equally to all, and among those to whom it is preached, does not always meet with the same reception. This diversity displays the unsearchable depth of the divine judgment, and is without doubt subordinate to God's purpose of eternal election. But if it is plainly owing to the mere pleasure of God that salvation is spontaneously offered to some, while others have no access to it, great and difficult questions immediately arise, questions which are inexplicable, when just views are not entertained concerning election and predestination. To many this seems a perplexing subject, because they deem it most incongruous that of the great body of mankind some should be predestinated to salvation, and others to destruction. How ceaselessly they entangle themselves will appear as we proceed. We may add, that in the very obscurity which deters them, we may see not only the utility of this doctrine, but also its most pleasant fruits. We shall never feel persuaded as we ought that our salvation flows from the free mercy of God as its fountain, until we are made acquainted with his eternal election, the grace of God being illustrated by the contrast – that he does not adopt all promiscuously to the hope of salvation, but gives to some what he denies to others. It is plain how greatly ignorance of this principle detracts from the glory of God, and impairs true humility. But though thus necessary to be known, Paul declares that it cannot be known unless God, throwing works entirely out of view, elect those whom he has predestined. His words are, 'Even so then at this present time also, there is a remnant according to the election of grace. And if by grace, then it is no more of works: otherwise grace is no more grace. But

if it be of works, then it is no more grace: otherwise work is no more work' (Rom. 11:6). If to make it appear that our salvation flows entirely from the good mercy of God, we must be carried back to the origin of election, then those who would extinguish it, wickedly do as much as in them lies to obscure what they ought most loudly to extol, and pluck up humility by the very roots. Paul clearly declares that it is only when the salvation of a remnant is ascribed to gratuitous election, we arrive at the knowledge that God saves whom he wills of his mere good pleasure, and does not pay a debt, a debt which never can be due. Those who preclude access, and would not have any one to obtain a taste of this doctrine, are equally unjust to God and men, there being no other means of humbling us as we ought, or making us feel how much we are bound to him. Nor, indeed, have we elsewhere any sure ground of confidence. This we say on the authority of Christ, who, to deliver us from all fear, and render us invincible amid our many dangers, snares and mortal conflicts, promises safety to all that the Father has taken under his protection (Jn 10:26). From this we infer, that all who know not that they are the peculiar people of God, must be wretched from perpetual trepidation, and that those therefore, who, by overlooking the three advantages which we have noted, would destroy the very foundation of our safety, consult ill for themselves and for all the faithful. What? Do we not here find the very origin of the Church, which, as Bernard rightly teaches (Serm. in Cantic.) could not be found or recognised among the creatures, because it lies hid (in both cases wondrously) within the lap of blessed predestination, and the mass of wretched condemnation?

But before I enter on the subject, I have some remarks to address to two classes of men. The subject of predestination, which in itself is attended with considerable difficulty is rendered very perplexed and hence perilous by human curiosity, which cannot be restrained from wandering into forbidden paths and climbing to the clouds determined if it can that none of the secret things of God shall remain unexplored. When we see many, some of them in other respects not bad men, every where rushing into this audacity and wickedness, it is necessary to remind them of the course of duty in this matter. First, then, when they inquire into predestination, let them remember that they are penetrating into the recesses of the divine wisdom, where he who rushes forward securely and confidently, instead of satisfying his curiosity will enter an inextricable labyrinth. For it is not right that man should with impunity pry into things which the Lord has been pleased to conceal within himself, and scan that sublime eternal wisdom which it is his pleasure that we should not apprehend but adore, that therein also his perfections may appear. Those secrets of his will, which he has seen it meet to manifest, are revealed in his word – revealed in so far as he knew to be conducive to our interest and welfare.

2. 'We have come into the way of faith,' says Augustine: 'let us constantly adhere to it. It leads to the chambers of the king, in which are hidden all the treasures of wisdom and knowledge. For our Lord Jesus Christ did not speak invidiously to his great and most select disciples when he said, "I have yet many things to say unto you, but ye cannot bear them now" (John 16:12). We must walk, advance, increase, that our hearts may be able to comprehend those things which they cannot now comprehend. But if the last day shall find us making progress, we shall there learn what here we could not' (August. Hom. in Joann). If we give due weight to the consideration, that the word of the Lord is the only way which can conduct us to the investigation of whatever it is lawful for us to hold with regard to him – is the only light which can enable us to discern what we ought to see with regard to him, it will curb and restrain all presumption. For it will show us that the moment we go beyond the bounds of the word we are out of the course, in darkness, and must every now and then stumble, go astray, and fall. Let it, therefore, be our first principle that to desire any other knowledge of predestination than that which is expounded by the word of God, is no less infatuated than to walk where there is no path, or to seek light in darkness. Let us not be ashamed to be ignorant in a matter in which ignorance is learning. Rather let us willingly abstain from the search after knowledge, to which it is both foolish as well as perilous, and even fatal to aspire. If an unrestrained imagination urges us, our proper course is to oppose it with these words, 'It is not good to eat much honey: so for men to search their own glory is not glory' (Prov. 25:27). There is good reason to dread a presumption which can only plunge us headlong into ruin.

3. There are others who, when they would cure this disease, recommend that the subject of predestination should scarcely if ever be mentioned, and tell us to shun every question concerning it as we would a rock. Although their moderation is justly commendable in thinking that such mysteries should be treated with moderation, yet because they keep too far within the proper measure, they have little influence over the human mind, which does not readily allow itself to be curbed. Therefore, in order to keep the legitimate course in this matter, we must return to the word of God, in which we are furnished with the right rule of understanding. For Scripture is the school of the Holy Spirit, in which as nothing useful and necessary to be known has been omitted, so nothing is taught but what it is of importance to know. Every thing, therefore delivered in Scripture on the subject of predestination, we must beware of keeping from the faithful, lest we seem either maliciously to deprive them of the blessing of God, or to accuse and scoff at the Spirit, as having divulged what ought on any account to be suppressed. Let us, I say, allow the Christian to unlock his mind and ears to all the words of God which are addressed to him, provided he do it with this moderation – that whenever the Lord shuts his sacred mouth, he also desists from inquiry. The best rule of sobriety is, not only in learning to follow wherever God leads, but also when he makes an end of teaching, to cease also from wishing to be wise. The danger which they dread is not so great that we ought on account of it to turn away our minds from the oracles of God. There is a celebrated saying of Solomon, 'It is the glory of God to conceal a thing' (Prov. 25:2). But since both piety and common sense dictate that this is not to be understood of every thing, we must look for a distinction, lest under the pretence of modesty and sobriety we be satisfied with a brutish ignorance. This is clearly expressed by Moses in a few words, 'The secret things belong unto the Lord our God: but those things which are revealed belong unto us, and to our children for ever' (Deut. 29:29). We see how he exhorts the people to study the doctrine of the Law in accordance with a heavenly decree, because God has been pleased to promulgate it, while he at the same time confines them within these boundaries, for the simple reason that it is not lawful for men to pry into the secret things of God.

7. Although it is now sufficiently plain that God by his secret counsel chooses whom he will while he rejects others, his gratuitous election has only been partially explained until we come to the case of single individuals, to whom God not only offers salvation, but so assigns it, that the certainty of the result remains not dubious or suspended. These are considered as belonging to that one seed of which Paul makes mention (Rom. 9:8; Gal. 3:16, etc.). For although adoption was deposited in the hand of Abraham, yet as many of his posterity were cut off as rotten members, in order that election may stand and be effectual, it is necessary to ascend to the head in whom the heavenly Father has connected his elect with each other, and bound them to himself by an indissoluble tie. Thus in the adoption of the family of Abraham, God gave them a liberal display of favour which he has denied to others; but in the members of Christ there is a far more excellent display of grace, because those ingrafted into him as their head never fail to obtain salvation. Hence Paul skilfully argues from the passage of Malachi which I quoted (Rom. 9:13; Mal. 1:2), that when God, after making a covenant of eternal life, invites any people to himself, a special mode of election is in part understood, so that he does not with promiscuous grace effectually elect all of them. The words 'Jacob have I loved' refer to the whole progeny of the patriarch, which the prophet there opposes to the posterity of Esau. But there is nothing in this repugnant to the fact, that in the person of one man is set before us a specimen of election, which cannot fail of accomplishing its object. It is not without cause Paul observes, that these are called 'a remnant' (Rom. 9:27; 11:5); because experience shows that of the general body many fall away and are lost, so that often a small portion only remains. The reason why the general election of the people is not always firmly ratified, readily presents itself – that on those with whom God makes the covenant, he does not immediately bestow the Spirit of regeneration, by whose power they persevere in the covenant even to the end. The external invitation, without the internal efficacy of grace which would have the effect of retaining them, holds a kind of middle place between the rejection of the human race and the election of a small number of believers. The whole people of Israel are called the Lord's inheritance, and yet there were many foreigners among them. Still, because the covenant which God had made to be their Father and Redeemer was not altogether null, he has respect to that free favour rather than to the perfidious defection of many; even by them his truth was not abolished, since by preserving some residue to himself, it appeared that his calling was without repentance. When God ever and anon gathered his Church from among the sons of Abraham rather than from profane nations, he had respect to his covenant, which, when violated by the great body, he restricted to a few, that it might not entirely fail. In short, that common adoption of the seed of Abraham was a kind of visible image of a greater benefit which God deigned to bestow on some out of many. This is the reason why Paul so carefully distinguishes between the sons of Abraham according to the flesh and the spiritual sons who are called after the example of Isaac. Not that simply to be a son of Abraham was a vain or useless privilege (this could not be said without insult to the covenant), but that the immutable counsel of God, by which he predestinated to himself whomsoever he would, was alone effectual for their salvation. But until the proper view is made clear by the production of passages of Scripture, I advise my readers not to prejudge the question. We say, then, that Scripture clearly proves this much, that God by his eternal and immutable counsel determined once for all those whom it was his pleasure one day to admit to salvation, and those whom, on the other hand, it was his pleasure to doom to destruction. We maintain that this counsel, as regards the elect, is founded on his free mercy, without any respect to human worth, while those whom he dooms to destruction are excluded from access to life by a just and blameless, but at the same time incomprehensible judgment. In regard to the elect, we regard calling as the evidence of election, and justification as another symbol of its manifestation, until it is fully accomplished by the attainment of glory. But as the Lord seals his elect by calling and justification, so by excluding the reprobate either from the knowledge of his name or the sanctification of his Spirit, he by these marks in a manner discloses the judgment which awaits them. I will here omit many of the fictions which foolish men have devised to overthrow predestination. There is no need of refuting objections which the moment they are produced abundantly betray their hollowness. I will dwell only on those points which either form the subject of dispute among the learned, or may occasion any difficulty to the simple, or may be employed by impiety as specious pretexts for assailing the justice of God.

✛ CHAPTER 22 ✛
This doctrine confirmed by proofs from scripture.

Sections
1. Some imagine that God elects or reprobates according to a foreknowledge of merit. Others make it a charge against God that he elects some and passes by others. Both refuted (1) by invincible arguments, (2) by the testimony of Augustine.
3. The reason is the good pleasure of God, which so reigns in election that no works, either past or future, are taken into consideration. This proved by notable declarations of one Saviour and passages of Paul.

1. Many controvert all the positions which we have laid down, especially the gratuitous election of believers, which, however, cannot be overthrown. For they commonly imagine that God distinguishes between men according to the merits which he foresees that each individual is to have, giving the adoption of sons to those whom he foreknows will not be unworthy of his grace, and dooming those to destruction whose dispositions he perceives will be prone to mischief and wickedness. Thus by interposing foreknowledge as a veil, they not only obscure election, but pretend to give it a different origin. Nor is this the commonly received opinion of the vulgar merely, for it has in all ages had great supporters. This I candidly confess, lest any one should expect greatly to prejudice our cause by opposing it with their names. The truth of God is here too certain to be shaken, too clear to be overborne by human authority. Others who are neither versed in Scripture, nor entitled to any weight, assail sound doctrine with a petulance which it is impossible to tolerate. Because God of his mere good pleasure electing some passes by others, they raise a plea against him. But if the fact is certain, what can they gain by quarrelling with God? We teach nothing but what experience proves to be true – that God has always been at liberty to bestow his grace on whom he would. Not to ask in what respect the posterity of Abraham excelled others if it be not in a worth, the cause of which has no existence out of God, let them tell why men are better than oxen or asses. God might have made them dogs when he formed them in his own image. Will they allow the lower animals to expostulate with God, as if the inferiority of their condition were unjust? It is certainly not more equitable that men should enjoy the privilege which they have not acquired by any merit, than that he should variously distribute favours as seems to him meet. If they pass to the case of individuals where inequality is more offensive to them, they ought at least,

in regard to the example of our Saviour, to be restrained by feelings of awe from talking so confidently of this sublime mystery. He is conceived a mortal man of the seed of David; what, I would ask them, are the virtues by which he deserved to become in the very womb, the head of angels the only begotten Son of God, the image and glory of the Father, the light, righteousness, and salvation of the world? It is wisely observed by Augustine, that in the very head of the Church we have a bright mirror of free election, lest it should give any trouble to us the members – that he did not become the Son of God by living righteously, but was freely presented with this great honour, that he might afterwards make others partakers of his gifts. Should any one here ask, why others are not what he was, or why we are all at so great a distance from him, why we are all corrupt while he is purity, he would not only betray his madness, but his effrontery also. But if they are bent on depriving God of the free right of electing and reprobating, let them at the same time take away what has been given to Christ. It will now be proper to attend to what Scripture declares concerning each. When Paul declares that we were chosen in Christ before the foundation of the world (Eph. 1:4), he certainly shows that no regard is had to our own worth; for it is just as if he had said, Since in the whole seed of Adam our heavenly Father found nothing worthy of his election, he turned his eye upon his own Anointed, that he might select as members of his body those whom he was to assume into the fellowship of life. Let believers, then, give full effect to this reason – that we were in Christ adopted unto the heavenly inheritance, because in ourselves we were incapable of such excellence. This he elsewhere observes in another passage, in which he exhorts the Colossians to give thanks that they had been made meet to be partakers of the inheritance of the saints (Col. 1:12). If election precedes that divine grace by which we are made fit to obtain immortal life, what can God find in us to induce him to elect us? What I mean is still more clearly explained in another passage: God, says he 'has chosen us in him before the foundation of the world, that we might be holy and without blame before him in love: having predestinated us unto the adoption of children by Jesus Christ to himself, according to the good pleasure of his will' (Eph. 1:4, 5). Here he opposes the good pleasure of God to our merits of every description.

3.   Wherever this good pleasure of God reigns, no good works are taken into account. The apostle, indeed, does not follow out the antithesis, but it is to be understood, as he himself explains it in another passage, 'Who has called us with a holy calling, not according to our works, but according to his own purpose and grace, which was given us in Christ Jesus before the world began' (1 Tim. 2:9). We have already shown that the additional words 'that we might be holy' remove every doubt. If you say that he foresaw they would be holy, and therefore elected them, you invert the order of Paul. You may, therefore, safely infer, If he elected us that we might be holy, he did not elect us because he foresaw that we would be holy. The two things are evidently inconsistent – that the pious owe it to election that they are holy, and yet attain to election by means of works. There is no force in the cavil to which they are ever recurring, that the Lord does not bestow election in recompense of preceding, but bestows it in consideration of future merits. For when it is said that believers were elected that they might be holy, it is at the same time intimated that the holiness which was to be in them has its origin in election. And how can it be consistently said, that things derived from election are the cause of election? The very thing which the apostle had said, he seems afterwards to confirm by adding, 'According to his good pleasure which he has purposed in himself' (Eph. 1:9); for the

expression that God 'purposed in himself' is the same as if it had been said, that in forming his decree he considered nothing external to himself; and, accordingly, it is immediately subjoined, that the whole object contemplated in our election is, that 'we should be to the praise of his glory'. Assuredly divine grace would not deserve all the praise of election, were not election gratuitous; and it would not be gratuitous did God in electing any individual pay regard to his future works. Hence, what Christ said to his disciples is found to be universally applicable to all believers, 'Ye have not chosen me, but I have chosen you' (Jn 15:16). Here he not only excludes past merits, but declares that they had nothing in themselves for which they could be chosen except in so far as his mercy anticipated. And how are we to understand the words of Paul, 'Who has first given to him, and it shall be recompensed unto him again?' (Rom. 11:35). His meaning obviously is, that men are altogether indebted to the preventing goodness of God, there being nothing in them, either past or future, to conciliate his favour.

✦ CHAPTER 24 ✦

Election confirmed by the calling of God. The reprobate bring upon themselves the righteous destruction to which they are doomed.

Sections

1. In this and the five following sections the certainty of election vindicated from the assaults of Satan. The leading arguments are: (1) effectual calling, (2) Christ apprehended by faith, (3) The protection of Christ, the guardian of the elect. We must not attempt to penetrate to the hidden recesses of the divine wisdom, in order to learn what is decreed with regard to us at the judgment-seat. We must begin and end with the call of God. This confirmed by an apposite saying of Bernard.

5. Christ the foundation of this calling and election. He who does not lean on him alone cannot be certain of his election. He is the faithful interpreter of the eternal counsel in regard to our salvation.

6. Another security of our election is the protection of Christ our Shepherd. How it is manifested to us. Objections: (1) as to the future state, (2) as to perseverance. Both objections refuted.

7. Objection, that those who seem elected sometimes fall away. Answer. A passage of Paul dissuading us from security explained. The kind of fear required in the elect.

4. Therefore as those are in error who make the power of election dependent on the faith by which we perceive that we are elected, so we shall follow the best order, if, in seeking the certainty of our election, we cleave to those posterior signs which are sure attestations to it. Among the temptations with which Satan assaults believers, none is greater or more perilous, than when disquieting them with doubts as to their election, he at the same time stimulates them with a depraved desire of inquiring after it out of the proper way (see Luther in Genes. cap. 26). By inquiring out of the proper way, I mean when puny man endeavours to penetrate to the hidden recesses of the divine wisdom, and goes back even to the remotest eternity, in order that he may understand what final determination God has made with regard to him.

In this way he plunges headlong into an immense abyss, involves himself in numberless inextricable snares, and buries himself in the thickest darkness. For it is right that the stupidity of the human mind should be punished with fearful destruction, whenever it attempts to rise in its own strength to the height of divine wisdom. And this temptation is the more fatal, that it is the temptation to which of all others almost all of us are most prone. For there is scarcely a mind in which the thought does not sometimes rise, Whence your salvation but from the election of God? But what proof have you of your election? When once this thought has taken possession of any individual, it keeps him perpetually miserable, subjects him to dire torment, or throws him into a state of complete stupor. I cannot wish a stronger proof of the depraved ideas, which men of this description form of predestination, than experience itself furnishes, since the mind cannot be infected by a more pestilential error than that which disturbs the conscience, and deprives it of peace and tranquillity in regard to God. Therefore, as we dread shipwreck, we must avoid this rock, which is fatal to every one who strikes upon it. And though the discussion of predestination is regarded as a perilous sea, yet in sailing over it the navigation is calm and safe, nay pleasant, provided we do not voluntarily court danger. For as a fatal abyss engulfs those who, to be assured of their election, pry into the eternal counsel of God without the word, yet those who investigate it rightly, and in the order in which it is exhibited in the word, reap from it rich fruits of consolation.

Let our method of inquiry then be, to begin with the calling of God and to end with it. Although there is nothing in this to prevent believers from feeling that the blessings which they daily receive from the hand of God originate in that secret adoption, as they themselves express it in Isaiah, 'Thou hast done wonderful things; thy counsels of old are faithfulness and truth' (Isa. 25:1). For with this as a pledge, God is pleased to assure us of as much of his counsel as can be lawfully known. But lest any should think that testimony weak, let us consider what clearness and certainty it gives us. On this subject there is an apposite passage in Bernard. After speaking of the reprobate, he says, 'The purpose of God stands, the sentence of peace on those that fear him also stands, a sentence concealing their bad and recompensing their good qualities; so that, in a wondrous manner, not only their good but their bad qualities work together for good. Who will lay any thing to the charge of God's elect? It is completely sufficient for my justification to have him propitious against whom only I have sinned. Every thing which he has decreed not to impute to me, is as if it had never been.' A little after he says, 'O the place of true rest, a place which I consider not unworthy of the name of inner-chamber, where God is seen, not as if disturbed with anger, or distracted by care, but where his will is proved to be good, and acceptable, and perfect. That vision does not terrify but soothe, does not excite restless curiosity but calms it, does not fatigue but tranquillises the senses. Here is true rest. A tranquil God tranquillises all things; and to see him at rest, is to be at rest' (Bernard, super Cantic. Serm. 14).

5. First, if we seek for the paternal mercy and favour of God, we must turn our eyes to Christ, in whom alone the Father is well pleased (Mt. 3:17). When we seek for salvation, life, and a blessed immortality, to him also must we retake ourselves, since he alone is the fountain of life and the anchor of salvation, and the heir of the kingdom of heaven. Then what is the end of election, but just that, being adopted as sons by the heavenly Father, we may by his favour obtain salvation and immortality? How much soever you may speculate and discuss you will perceive that in its ultimate object it goes no farther. Hence, those whom God has adopted as sons, he is said to have elected, not in themselves, but in Christ Jesus (Eph. 1:4); because he could love them only in him, and only as being previously made partakers with him, honour them with the inheritance of his kingdom. But if we are elected in him, we cannot find the certainty of our election in ourselves; and not even in God the Father, if we look at him apart from the Son. Christ, then, is the mirror in which we ought, and in which, without deception, we may contemplate our election. For since it is into his body that the Father has decreed to ingraft those whom from eternity he wished to be his, that he may regard as sons all whom he acknowledges to be his members, if we are in communion with Christ, we have proof sufficiently clear and strong that we are written in the Book of Life. Moreover, he admitted us to sure communion with himself, when, by the preaching of the Gospel, he declared that he was given us by the Father, to be ours with all his blessings (Rom. 8:32). We are said to be clothed with him, to be one with him, that we may live, because he himself lives. The doctrine is often repeated, 'God so loved the world, that he gave his only begotten Son, that whosoever believeth in him should not perish, but have everlasting life' (Jn 3:16). He who believes in him is said to have passed from death unto life (Jn 5:24). In this sense he calls himself the 'bread of life', of which if a man eat, he shall never die (Jn 6:35). He, I say, was our witness, that all by whom he is received in faith will be regarded by our heavenly Father as sons. If we long for more than to be regarded as sons of God and heirs, we must ascend above Christ. But if this is our final goal, how infatuated is it to seek out of him what we have already obtained in him, and can only find in him? Besides, as he is the Eternal Wisdom, the Immutable Truth, the Determinate Counsel of the Father, there is no room for fear that any thing which he tells us will vary in the minutest degree from that will of the Father after which we inquire. Nay, rather he faithfully discloses it to us as it was from the beginning, and always will be. The practical influence of this doctrine ought also to be exhibited in our prayers. For though a belief of our election animates us to involve God, yet when we frame our prayers, it were preposterous to obtrude it upon God, or to stipulate in this way, 'O Lord, if I am elected, hear me.' He would have us to rest satisfied with his promises, and not to inquire elsewhere whether or not he is disposed to hear us. We shall thus be disentangled from many snares, if we know how to make a right use of what is rightly written; but let us not inconsiderately wrest it to purposes different from that to which it ought to be confined.

6.   Another confirmation tending to establish our confidence is, that our election is connected with our calling. For those whom Christ enlightens with the knowledge of his name, and admits into the bosom of his Church, he is said to take under his guardianship and protection. All whom he thus receives are said to be committed and entrusted to him by the Father, that they may be kept unto life eternal. What would we have? Christ proclaims aloud that all whom the Father is pleased to save he has delivered into his protection (Jn 6:37–39; 17:6, 12). Therefore, if we would know whether God cares for our salvation, let us ask whether he has committed us to Christ, whom he has appointed to be the only Saviour of all his people. Then, if we doubt whether we are received into the protection of Christ, he obviates the doubt when he spontaneously offers himself as our Shepherd, and declares that we are of the number of his sheep if we hear his voice (Jn 10:3, 16). Let us, therefore, embrace Christ, who is kindly offered to us, and comes forth to meet us: he will number us among his flock, and keep us within his fold. But anxiety arises as to our future state. For as Paul teaches, that those are called who were previously elected, so our Saviour shows that many are called, but few chosen (Mt. 22:14). Nay, even Paul himself dissuades us from security, when he says, 'Let him that thinketh he standeth take heed lest he fall' (1 Cor. 10:12). And again, 'Well, because of unbelief they were broken off, and thou standest by faith. Be not high-minded, but fear: for if God spared not the natural branches, take heed lest he also spare not thee' (Rom. 11:20, 21). In fine, we are sufficiently taught by experience itself, that calling and faith are of little value without perseverance, which, however, is not the gift of all. But Christ has freed us from anxiety on this head; for the following promises undoubtedly have respect to the future: 'All that the Father giveth me shall come to me, and him that comes to me I will in no wise cast out.' Again, 'This is the will of him that sent me, that of all which he has given me I should lose nothing; but should raise it up at the last day' (Jn 6:37, 39). Again, 'My sheep hear my voice, and I know them, and they follow me: and I give unto them eternal life, and they shall never perish, neither shall any man pluck them out of my hand. My Father which gave them me is greater than all: and no man is able to pluck them out of my Father's hand' (Jn 10:27, 28). Again, when he declares, 'Every plant which my heavenly Father has not planted shall be rooted up' (Mt. 15:13), he intimates conversely that those who have their root in God can never be deprived of their salvation. Agreeable to this are the words of John, 'If they had been of us, they would no doubt have continued with us' (1 Jn 2:19). Hence, also, the magnificent triumph of Paul over life and death, things present, and things to come (Rom. 8:38). This must be founded on the gift of perseverance. There is no doubt that he employs the sentiment as applicable to all the elect. Paul elsewhere says, 'Being confident of this very thing, that he who has begun a good work in you will perform it until the day of Jesus Christ' (Phil. 1:6). David, also, when his faith threatened to fail, leant on this support, 'Forsake not the works of thy hands.' Moreover, it cannot be doubted, that since Christ prays for all the elect, he asks the same thing for them as he asked for Peter – that their faith fail not (Lk. 22:32). Hence we infer, that there is no danger of their falling away, since the Son of God, who asks that their piety may prove constant, never meets with a refusal. What then did our Saviour intend to teach us by this prayer, but just to confide, that whenever we are his our eternal salvation is secure?

7. But it daily happens that those who seemed to belong to Christ revolt from him and fall away: Nay, in the very passage where he declares that none of those whom the Father has given to him have perished, he excepts the son of perdition. This, indeed, is true; but it is equally true that such persons never adhered to Christ with that heartfelt confidence by which I say that the certainty of our election is established: 'They went out from us,' says John, 'but they were not of us; for if they had been of us, they would, no doubt, have continued with us' (1 Jn 2:19). I deny not that they have signs of calling similar to those given to the elect; but I do not at all admit that they have that sure confirmation of election which I desire believers to seek from the word of the Gospel. Wherefore, let not examples of this kind move us away from tranquil confidence in the promise of the Lord, when he declares that all by whom he is received in true faith have been given him by the Father, and that none of them, while he is their Guardian and Shepherd, will perish (Jn 3:16; 6:39). Of Judas we shall shortly speak. Paul does not dissuade Christians from security simply, but from careless, carnal security, which is accompanied with pride, arrogance, and contempt of others, which extinguishes humility and reverence for God, and

produces a forgetfulness of grace received (Rom. 11:20). For he is addressing the Gentiles, and showing them that they ought not to exult proudly and cruelly over the Jews, in consequence of whose rejection they had been substituted in their stead. He also enjoins fear, not a fear under which they may waver in alarm, but a fear which, teaching us to receive the grace of God in humility, does not impair our confidence in it, as has elsewhere been said. We may add, that he is not speaking to individuals, but to sects in general (see 1 Cor. 10:12). The Church having been divided into two parties, and rivalship producing dissension, Paul reminds the Gentiles that their having been substituted in the place of a peculiar and holy people was a reason for modesty and fear. For there were many vain-glorious persons among them, whose empty boasting it was expedient to repress. But we have elsewhere seen, that our hope extends into the future, even beyond death, and that nothing is more contrary to its nature than to be in doubt as to our future destiny.

✝ CHAPTER 25 ✝

Of the last resurrection.

Sections

1. For invincible perseverance in our calling, it is necessary to be animated with the blessed hope of our Saviour's final advent.
2. The perfect happiness reserved for the elect at the final resurrection unknown to philosophers.
3. The truth and necessity of this doctrine of a final resurrection. To confirm our belief in it we have (1) the example of Christ, and (2) the omnipotence of God. There is an insep-arable connection between us and our risen Saviour. The bodies of the elect must be conformed to the body of their Head. It is now in heaven. Therefore, our bodies also must rise, and, reanimated by their souls, reign with Christ in heaven. The resurrection of Christ a pledge of ours.

1. Although Christ, the Sun of righteousness, shining upon us through the gospel, has, as Paul declares, after conquering death, given us the light of life; and hence on believing we are said to have passed from 'death unto life', being no longer strangers and pilgrims, but fellow-citizens with the saints, and of the household of God, who has made us sit with his only begotten Son in heavenly places, so that nothing is wanting to our complete felicity; yet, lest we should feel it grievous to be exercised under a hard warfare, as if the victory obtained by Christ had produced no fruit, we must attend to what is elsewhere taught concerning the nature of hope. For since we hope for what we see not, and faith, as is said in another passage, is 'the evidence of things not seen', so long as we are imprisoned in the body we are absent from the Lord. For which reason Paul says, 'Ye are dead, and your life is hid with Christ in God. When Christ, who is our life, shall appear, then shall ye also appear with him in glory.' Our present condition, therefore, requires us to 'live soberly, righteously, and godly', 'looking for that blessed hope, and the glorious appearing of the great God and our Saviour Jesus Christ'. Here there is need of no ordinary patience, lest, worn out with fatigue, we either turn backwards or

abandon our post. Wherefore, all that has hitherto been said of our salvation calls upon us to raise our minds towards heaven, that, as Peter exhorts, though we now see not Christ, 'yet believing', we may 'rejoice with joy unspeakable and full of glory', receiving the end of our faith, even the salvation of our souls. For this reason Paul says, that the faith and charity of the saints have respect to the faith and hope which is laid up for them in heaven (Col. 1:5). When we thus keep our eyes fixed upon Christ in heaven, and nothing on earth prevents us from directing them to the promised blessedness, there is a true fulfilment of the saying 'where your treasure is, there will your heart be also' (Mt. 6:21). Hence the reason why faith is so rare in the world, nothing being more difficult for our sluggishness than to surmount innumerable obstacles in striving for the prize of our high calling. To the immense load of miseries which almost overwhelm us, are added the jeers of profane men, who assail us for our simplicity, when spontaneously renouncing the allurements of the present life we seem, in seeking a happiness which lies hid from us, to catch at a fleeting shadow. In short, we are beset above and below, behind and before, with violent temptations, which our minds would be altogether unable to withstand, were they not set free from earthly objects and devoted to the heavenly life, though apparently remote from us. Wherefore, he alone has made solid progress in the Gospel who has acquired the habit of meditating continually on a blessed resurrection.

2. In ancient times philosophers discoursed, and even debated with each other, concerning the chief good: none, however, except Plato acknowledged that it consisted in union with God. He could not, however, form even an imperfect idea of its true nature; nor is this strange, as he had learned nothing of the sacred bond of that union. We even in this our earthly pilgrimage know wherein our perfect and only felicity consists – a felicity which, while we long for it, daily inflames our hearts more and more, until we attain to full fruition. Therefore I said, that none participate in the benefits of Christ save those who raise their minds to the resurrection. This, accordingly, is the mark which Paul sets before believers, and at which he says they are to aim, forgetting every thing until they reach it (Phil. 3:8). The more strenuously, therefore, must we contend for it, lest if the world engross us we be severely punished for our sloth. Accordingly, he in another passage distinguishes believers by this mark, that their conversation is in heaven, from whence they look for the Saviour (Phil. 3:20). And that they may not faint in their course, he associates all the other creatures with them. As shapeless ruins are everywhere seen, he says, that all things in heaven and earth struggle for renovation. For since Adam by his fall destroyed the proper order of nature, the creatures groan under the servitude to which they have been subjected through his sin; not that they are at all endued with sense, but that they naturally long for the state of perfection from which they have fallen. Paul therefore describes them as groaning and travailing in pain (Rom. 8:19); so that we who have received the first-fruits of the Spirit may be ashamed to grovel in our corruption, instead of at least imitating the inanimate elements which are bearing the punishment of another's sin. And in order that he may stimulate us the more powerfully, he terms the final advent of Christ our 'redemption'. It is true, indeed, that all the parts of our redemption are already accomplished; but as Christ was once offered for sins (Heb. 9:28), so he shall again appear without sin unto salvation. Whatever, then, be the afflictions by which we are pressed, let this redemption sustain us until its final accomplishment.

3. The very importance of the subject ought to increase our ardour. Paul justly contends, that if Christ rise not the whole gospel is delusive and vain (1 Cor. 15:13–17); for our condition would be more miserable than that of other mortals, because we are exposed to much hatred and insult, and incur danger every hour; nay, are like sheep destined for slaughter; and hence the authority of the Gospel would fail, not in one part merely, but in its very essence, including both our adoption and the accomplishment of our salvation. Let us, therefore, give heed to a matter of all others the most serious, so that no length of time may produce weariness. I have deferred the brief consideration to be given of it to this place, that my readers may learn, when they have received Christ, the author of perfect salvation, to rise higher, and know that he is clothed with heavenly immortality and glory in order that the whole body may be rendered conformable to the Head. For thus the Holy Spirit is ever setting before us in his person an example of the resurrection. It is difficult to believe that after our bodies have been consumed with rottenness, they will rise again at their appointed time. And hence, while many of the philosophers maintained the immortality of the soul, few of them assented to the resurrection of the body. Although in this they were inexcusable, we are thereby reminded that the subject is too difficult for human apprehension to reach it. To enable faith to surmount the great difficulty, Scripture furnishes two auxiliary proofs, the one the likeness of Christ's resurrection, and the other the omnipotence of God. Therefore, whenever the subject of the resurrection is considered, let us think of the case of our Saviour, who, having completed his mortal course in our nature which he had assumed, obtained immortality, and is now the pledge of our future resurrection. For in the miseries by which we are beset, we always bear 'about in the body the dying of the Lord Jesus, that the life also of Jesus might be made manifest in our mortal flesh' (2 Cor. 4:10). It is not lawful, it is not even possible, to separate him from us, without dividing him. Hence Paul's argument, 'If there be no resurrection of the dead, then is Christ not risen' (1 Cor. 15:13); for he assumes it as an acknowledged principle, that when Christ was subjected to death, and by rising gained a victory over death, it was not on his own account, but in the Head was begun what must necessarily be fulfilled in all the members, according to the degree and order of each. For it would not be proper to be made equal to him in all respects. It is said in the psalm, 'Neither wilt thou suffer thine Holy One to see corruption' (Ps. 16:10). Although a portion of this confidence appertain to us according to the measure bestowed on us, yet the full effect appeared only in Christ, who, free from all corruption, resumed a spotless body. Then, that there may be no doubt as to our fellowship with Christ in a blessed resurrection, and that we may be contented with this pledge, Paul distinctly affirms that he sits in the heavens, and will come as a judge on the last day for the express purpose of changing our vile body, 'that it may be fashioned like unto his glorious body' (Phil. 3:21). For he elsewhere says that God did not raise up his Son from death to give an isolated specimen of his mighty power, but that the Spirit exerts the same efficacy in regard to them that believe; and accordingly he says, that the Spirit when he dwells in us is life, because the end for which he was given is to quicken our mortal body (Rom. 8:10, 11; Col. 3:4). I briefly glance at subjects which might be treated more copiously, and deserve to be adorned more splendidly, and yet in the little I have said I trust pious readers will find sufficient materials for building up their faith. Christ rose again that he might have us as partakers with him of future life. He was raised up by the Father, inasmuch as he was the Head of the Church, from which he cannot possibly be dissevered.

He was raised up by the power of the Spirit, who also in us performs the office of quickening. In fine, he was raised up to be the resurrection and the life. But as we have said, that in this mirror we behold a living image of the resurrection, so it furnishes a sure evidence to support our minds, provided we faint not, nor grow weary at the long delay, because it is not ours to measure the periods of time at our own pleasure; but to rest patiently till God in his own time renew his kingdom. To this Paul refers when he says, 'But every man in his own order: Christ the first-fruits; afterward they that are Christ's at his coming' (1 Cor. 15:23).

But lest any question should be raised as to the resurrection of Christ on which ours is founded, we see how often and in what various ways he has borne testimony to it. Scoffing men will deride the narrative which is given by the Evangelist as a childish fable. For what importance will they attach to a message which timid women bring and the disciples almost dead with fear, afterwards confirm? Why does not Christ rather place the illustrious trophies of his victory in the midst of the temple and the forum? Why does he not come forth, and in the presence of Pilate strike terror? Why does he not show himself alive again to the priests and all Jerusalem? Profane men will scarcely admit that the witnesses whom he selects are well qualified. I answer, that though at the commencement their infirmity was contemptible, yet the whole was directed by the admirable providence of God, so that partly from love to Christ and religious zeal, partly from incredulity, those who were lately overcome with fear now hurry to the sepulchre, not only that they might be eye-witnesses of the fact, but that they might hear angels announce what they actually saw. How can we question the veracity of those who regarded what the women told them as a fable, until they saw the reality? It is not strange that the whole people and also the governor, after they were furnished with sufficient evidence for conviction, were not allowed to see Christ or the other signs (Mt. 27:66; 28:11). The sepulchre is sealed, sentinels keep watch, on the third day the body is not found. The soldiers are bribed to spread the report that his disciples had stolen the body. As if they had had the means of deforming a band of soldiers, or been supplied with weapons, or been trained so as to make such a daring attempt. But if the soldiers had not courage enough to repel them, why did they not follow and apprehend some of them by the aid of the populace? Pilate, therefore, in fact, put his signet to the resurrection of Christ, and the guards who were placed at the sepulchre by their silence or falsehood also became heralds of his resurrection. Meanwhile, the voice of angels was heard, 'He is not here, but is risen' (Lk. 24:6). The celestial splendour plainly shows that they were not men but angels. Afterwards, if any doubt still remained, Christ himself removed it. The disciples saw him frequently; they even touched his hands and his feet, and their unbelief is of no little avail in confirming our faith. He discoursed to them of the mysteries of the kingdom of God, and at length, while they beheld, ascended to heaven. This spectacle was exhibited not to eleven apostles only, but was seen by more than five hundred brethren at once (1 Cor. 15:6). Then by sending the Holy Spirit he gave a proof not only of life but also of supreme power, as he had foretold, 'It is expedient for you that I go away: for if I go not away, the Comforter will not come unto you' (Jn 16:7). Paul was not thrown down on the way by the power of a dead man, but felt that he whom he was opposing was possessed of sovereign authority. To Stephen he appeared for another purpose – that he might overcome the fear of death by the certainty of life. To refuse assent to these numerous and authentic proofs is not diffidence, but depraved and therefore infatuated obstinacy.

✝ PART XIII ✝

THE CHURCH

✝ BOOK FOUR ✝

OF THE HOLY CATHOLIC CHURCH
OF THE EXTERNAL MEANS OR HELPS BY WHICH GOD
ALLURES US INTO FELLOWSHIP WITH CHRIST
AND KEEPS US IN IT

✝ CHAPTER 1 ✝

Of the true church. Duty of cultivating unity with her,
as mother of all the godly.

Sections

1. The church now to be considered. With her God has deposited whatever is necessary to faith and good order. A summary of what is contained in this Book. Why it begins with the Church.

4. The name of Mother given to the Church shows how necessary it is to know her. No salvation out of the Church.

7. Second part of the Chapter. Concerning the marks of the Church. In what respect the Church is invisible. In what respect she is visible.

8. God alone knoweth them that are his. Still he has given marks to discern his children.

9. These marks are the ministry of the word, and administration of the sacraments instituted by Christ. The same rule not to be followed in judging of individuals and of churches.

10. We must on no account forsake the Church distinguished by such marks. Those who act otherwise are apostates, deserters of the truth and of the household of God, deniers of God and Christ, violators of the mystical marriage.

11. These marks to be the more carefully observed, because Satan strives to efface them, or to make us revolt from the Church. The twofold error of despising the true, and submitting to a false Church.

12. Though the common profession should contain some corruption, this is not a sufficient reason for forsaking the visible Church. Some of these corruptions specified. Caution necessary. The duty of the members.

13. The immoral lives of certain professors no ground for abandoning the Church. Error on this head of the ancient and modern Cathari. Their first objection. Answer to it from three of our Saviour's parables.

1. In the last Book, it has been shown, that by the faith of the Gospel Christ becomes ours, and we are made partakers of the salvation and eternal blessedness procured by him. But as our ignorance and sloth (I may add, the vanity of our mind) stand in need of external helps, by which faith may be begotten in us, and may increase and make progress until its consummation, God, in accommodation to our infirmity, has added such helps, and secured the effectual preaching of the Gospel, by depositing this treasure with the Church. He has appointed pastors and teachers, by whose lips he might edify his people (Eph. 4:11); he has invested them with authority, and, in short, omitted nothing that might conduce to holy consent in the faith, and to right order. In particular, he has instituted sacraments, which we feel by experience to be most useful helps in fostering and confirming our faith. For seeing we are shut up in the prison of the body, and have not yet attained to the rank of angels, God, in accommodation to our capacity, has in his admirable providence provided a method by which, though widely separated, we might still draw near to him. Wherefore, due order requires that we first treat of the Church, of its Government, Orders, and Power; next, of the Sacraments; and, lastly, of Civil Government – at the same time guarding pious readers against the corruptions of the Papacy, by which Satan has adulterated all that God had appointed for our salvation. I will begin with the Church, into whose bosom God is pleased to collect his children, not only that by her aid and ministry they may be nourished so long as they are babes and children, but may also be guided by her maternal care until they grow up to manhood, and, finally, attain to the perfection of faith. What God has thus joined, let not man put asunder (Mk 10:9): to those to whom he is a Father, the Church must also be a mother. This was true not merely under the Law, but even now after the advent of Christ; since Paul declares that we are the children of a new, even a heavenly Jerusalem (Gal. 4:26).

4. But as it is now our purpose to discourse of the visible Church, let us learn, from her single title of Mother, how useful, nay, how necessary the knowledge of her is, since there is no other means of entering into life unless she conceive us in the womb and give us birth, unless she nourish us at her breasts, and, in short, keep us under her charge and government, until, divested of mortal flesh, we become like the angels (Mt. 22:30). For our weakness does not permit us to leave the school until we have spent our whole lives as scholars. Moreover, beyond the pale of the Church no forgiveness of sins, no salvation, can be hoped for, as Isaiah and Joel testify (Isa. 37:32; Joel 2:32). To their testimony Ezekiel subscribes, when he declares, 'They shall not be in the assembly of my people, neither shall they be written in the writing of the house of Israel' (Ezek. 3:9); as, on the other hand, those who turn to the cultivation of true piety are said to inscribe their names among the citizens of Jerusalem. For which reason it is said in the psalm, 'Remember me, O Lord, with the favour that thou bearest unto thy people: O visit me with thy salvation; that I may see the good of thy chosen, that I may rejoice in the gladness of thy nation, that I may glory with thine inheritance' (Ps. 106:4, 5). By these words the paternal favour of God and the special evidence of spiritual life are confined to his peculiar people, and hence the abandonment of the Church is always fatal.

7. The judgment which ought to be formed concerning the visible Church which comes under our observation, must, I think, be sufficiently clear from what has been said. I have observed that the Scriptures speak of the Church in two ways. Sometimes when they speak of the Church they mean the Church as it really is before God – the Church into which none are admitted but those who by the gift of adoption are sons of God, and by the sanctification of the Spirit true members of Christ. In this case it not only comprehends the saints who dwell on the earth, but all the elect who have existed from the beginning of the world. Often, too, by the name of Church is designated the whole body of mankind scattered throughout the world, who profess to worship one God and Christ, who by baptism are initiated into the faith; by partaking of the Lord's Supper profess unity in true doctrine and charity, agree in holding the word of the Lord, and observe the ministry which Christ has appointed for the preaching of it. In this Church there is a very large mixture of hypocrites, who have nothing of Christ but the name and outward appearance: of ambitious, avaricious, envious, evil-speaking men, some also of impurer lives, who are tolerated for a time, either because their guilt cannot be legally established, or because due strictness of discipline is not always observed. Hence, as it is necessary to believe the invisible Church, which is manifest to the eye of God only, so we are also enjoined to regard this Church which is so called with reference to man, and to cultivate its communion.

8. Accordingly, inasmuch as it was of importance to us to recognise it, the Lord has distinguished it by certain marks, and as it were symbols. It is, indeed, the special prerogative of God to know those who are his, as Paul declares in the passage already quoted (2 Tim. 2:19). And doubtless it has been so provided as a check on human rashness, the experience of every day reminding us how far his secret judgments surpass our apprehension. For even those who seemed most abandoned, and who had been completely despaired of, are by his goodness recalled to life, while those who seemed most stable often fall. Hence, as Augustine says, 'In regard to the secret predestination of God, there are very many sheep without, and very many wolves within' (August. Hom. in Joann. 45). For he knows, and has his mark on those who know neither him nor themselves. Of those again who openly bear his badge, his eyes alone see who of them are unfeignedly holy, and will persevere even to the end, which alone is the completion of salvation. On the other hand, foreseeing that it was in some degree expedient for us to know who are to be regarded by us as his sons, he has in this matter accommodated himself to our capacity. But as here full certainty was not necessary, he has in its place substituted the judgment of charity, by which we acknowledge all as members of the Church who by confession of faith, regularity of conduct, and participation in the sacraments, unite with us in acknowledging the same God and Christ. The knowledge of his body, inasmuch as he knew it to be more necessary for our salvation, he has made known to us by surer marks.

9. Hence the form of the Church appears and stands forth conspicuous to our view. Wherever we see the word of God sincerely preached and heard, wherever we see the sacraments administered according to the institution of Christ, there we cannot have any doubt that the Church of God has some existence, since his promise cannot fail, 'Where two or three are gathered together in my name, there am I in the midst of them' (Mt. 18:20). But that we may have a clear summary of this subject, we must proceed by the following steps: The Church universal is the multitude collected out of all nations, who, though dispersed and far distant from each other, agree in one truth of divine doctrine, and are bound together by the tie of a common religion. In this way it comprehends single churches, which exist in different towns and villages, according to the wants of human society, so that each of them justly obtains the name and authority of the Church; and also comprehends single individuals, who by a religious profession are accounted to belong to such churches, although they are in fact aliens from the Church, but have not been cut off by a public decision. There is, however, a slight difference in the mode of judging of individuals and of churches. For it may happen in practice that those whom we deem not altogether worthy of the fellowship of believers, we yet ought to treat as brethren, and regard as believers, on account of the common consent of the Church in tolerating and bearing with them in the body of Christ. Such persons we do not approve by our suffrage as members of the Church, but we leave them the place which they hold among the people of God, until they are legitimately deprived of it. With regard to the general body we must feel differently; if they have the ministry of the word, and honour the administration of the sacraments, they are undoubtedly entitled to be ranked with the Church, because it is certain that these things are not without a beneficial result. Thus we both maintain the Church universal in its unity, which malignant minds have always been eager to dissever, and deny not due authority to lawful assemblies distributed as circumstances require.

10. We have said that the symbols by which the Church is discerned are the preaching of the word and the observance of the sacraments, for these cannot anywhere exist without producing fruit and prospering by the blessing of God. I say not that wherever the word is preached fruit immediately appears; but that in every place where it is received, and has a fixed abode, it uniformly displays its efficacy. Be this as it may, when the preaching of the Gospel is reverently heard, and the sacraments are not neglected, there for the time the face of the Church appears without deception or ambiguity and no man may with impunity spurn her authority, or reject her admonitions, or resist her counsels, or make sport of her censures, far less revolt from her, and violate her unity. For such is the value which the Lord sets on the communion of his Church, that all who contumaciously alienate themselves from any Christian society, in which the true ministry of his word and sacraments is maintained, he regards as deserters of religion. So highly does he recommend her authority, that when it is violated he considers that his own authority is impaired. For there is no small weight in the designation given to her 'the house of God', 'the pillar and ground of the truth' (1 Tim. 3:15). By these words Paul intimates, that to prevent the truth from perishing in the world, the Church is its faithful guardian, because God has been pleased to preserve the pure preaching of his word by her instrumentality, and to exhibit himself to us as a parent while he feeds us with spiritual nourishment, and provides whatever is conducive to our salvation. Moreover, no mean praise is conferred on the Church when she is said to have been chosen and set apart by Christ as his spouse, 'not having spot or wrinkle, or any such thing' (Eph. 5:27), as 'his body, the fulness of him that filleth all in all' (Eph. 1:23). Whence it follows, that revolt from the Church is denial of God and Christ. Wherefore there is the more necessity to beware of a dissent so iniquitous; for seeing by it we aim as far as in us lies at the destruction of God's truth, we deserve to be crushed by the full thunder of his anger. No crime can be imagined more atrocious than that of sacrilegiously and perfidiously violating the sacred marriage which the only begotten Son of God has condescended to contract with us.

11.   Wherefore let these marks be carefully impressed upon our minds, and let us estimate them as in the sight of the Lord. There is nothing on which Satan is more intent than to destroy and efface one or both of them – at one time to delete and abolish these marks, and thereby destroy the true and genuine distinction of the Church; at another, to bring them into contempt, and so hurry us into open revolt from the Church. To his wiles it was owing that for several ages the pure preaching of the word disappeared, and now, with the same dishonest aim, he labours to overthrow the ministry, which, however, Christ has so ordered in his Church, that if it is removed the whole edifice must fall. How perilous, then, nay, how fatal the temptation, when we even entertain a thought of separating ourselves from that assembly in which are beheld the signs and badges which the Lord has deemed sufficient to characterise his Church! We see how great caution should be employed in both respects. That we may not be imposed upon by the name of Church, every congregation which claims the name must be brought to that test as to a Lydian stone. If it holds the order instituted by the Lord in word and sacraments there will be no deception; we may safely pay it the honour due to a church: on the other hand, if it exhibit itself without word and sacraments, we must in this case be no less careful to avoid the imposture than we were to shun pride and presumption in the other.

12.   When we say that the pure ministry of the word and pure celebration of the sacraments is a fit pledge and earnest, so that we may safely recognise a church in every society in which both exist, our meaning is, that we are never to discard it so long as these remain, though it may otherwise teem with numerous faults. Nay, even in the administration of word and sacraments defects may creep in which ought not to alienate us from its communion. For all the heads of true doctrine are not in the same position. Some are so necessary to be known, that all must hold them to be fixed and undoubted as the proper essentials of religion: for instance, that God is one, that Christ is God, and the Son of God, that our salvation depends on the mercy of God, and the like. Others, again, which are the subject of controversy among the churches, do not destroy the unity of the faith; for why should it be regarded as a ground of dissension between churches, if one, without any spirit of contention or perverseness in dogmatising, hold that the soul on quitting the body flies to heaven, and another, without venturing to speak positively as to the abode, holds it for certain that it lives with the Lord? The words of the apostle are, 'Let us therefore, as many as be perfect, be thus minded: and if in anything ye be otherwise minded, God shall reveal even this unto you' (Phil. 3:15). Does he not sufficiently intimate that a difference of opinion as to these matters which are not absolutely necessary, ought not to be a ground of dissension among Christians? The best thing, indeed, is to be perfectly agreed, but seeing there is no man who is not involved in some mist of ignorance, we must either have no church at all, or pardon delusion in those things of which one may be ignorant, without violating the substance of religion and forfeiting salvation. Here, however, I have no wish to patronise even the minutest errors, as if I thought it right to foster them by flattery or connivance; what I say is, that we are not on account of every minute difference to abandon a church, provided it retain sound and unimpaired that doctrine in which the safety of piety consists, and keep the use of the sacraments instituted by the Lord. Meanwhile, if we strive to reform what is offensive, we act in the discharge of duty. To this effect are the words of Paul, 'If anything be revealed to another that sitteth by, let the first hold his peace' (1 Cor. 14:30). From this it is evident that to each member of the Church, according to his measure of grace, the study of public edification has been assigned, provided it be done decently and in order. In other words, we must neither renounce the communion of the Church, nor, continuing in it, disturb peace and discipline when duly arranged.

13. Our indulgence ought to extend much farther in tolerating imperfection of conduct. Here there is great danger of falling, and Satan employs all his machinations to ensnare us. For there always have been persons who, imbued with a false persuasion of absolute holiness, as if they had already become a kind of spirit, spurn the society of all in whom they see that something human still remains. Such of old were the Cathari and the Donatists, who were similarly infatuated. Such in the present day are some of the Anabaptists, who would be thought to have made superior progress. Others, again, sin in this respect, not so much from that insane pride as from inconsiderate zeal. Seeing that among those to whom the Gospel is preached, the fruit produced is not in accordance with the doctrine, they forthwith conclude that there no church exists. The offence is indeed well founded, and it is one to which in this most unhappy age we give far too much occasion. It is impossible to excuse our accursed sluggishness, which the Lord will not leave unpunished, as he is already beginning sharply to chastise us. Woe then to us who, by our dissolute licence of wickedness, cause weak consciences to be wounded! Still those of whom we have spoken sin in their turn, by not knowing how to set bounds to their offence. For where the Lord requires mercy they omit it, and give themselves up to immoderate severity. Thinking there is no church where there is not complete purity and integrity of conduct, they, through hatred of wickedness, withdraw from a genuine church, while they think they are shunning the company of the ungodly. They allege that the Church of God is holy. But that they may at the same time understand that it contains a mixture of good and bad, let them hear from the lips of our Saviour that parable in which he compares the Church to a net in which all kinds of fishes are taken, but not separated until they are brought ashore. Let them hear it compared to a field which, planted with good seed, is by the fraud of an enemy mingled with tares, and is not freed of them until the harvest is brought into the barn. Let them hear, in fine, that it is a thrashing-floor in which the collected wheat lies concealed under the chaff, until, cleansed by the fanners and the sieve, it is at length laid up in the granary. If the Lord declares that the Church will labour under the defect of being burdened with a multitude of wicked until the day of judgment, it is in vain to look for a church altogether free from blemish (Mt. 13).

✝ CHAPTER 3 ✝
Of the teachers and ministers of the church.
Their election and office.

Sections

1. Summary of the chapter. Reasons why God, in governing the Church, uses the ministry of men: (1) To declare his condescension, (2) to train us to humility and obedience, (3) to bind us to each other in mutual charity. These reasons confirmed by Scripture.
2. This ministry of men most useful to the whole Church. Its advantages enumerated.
3. The honourable terms in which the ministry is spoken of. Its necessity established by numerous examples.

4.   Second part of the chapter, treating of Ecclesiastical office-bearers in particular. Some of them, as Apostles, Prophets, and Evangelists, temporary. Others, as Pastors and Teachers, perpetual and indispensable.

1.   We are now to speak of the order in which the Lord has been pleased that his Church should be governed. For though it is right that he alone should rule and reign in the Church, that he should preside and be conspicuous in it, and that its government should be exercised and administered solely by his word; yet as he does not dwell among us in visible presence, so as to declare his will to us by his own lips, he in this (as we have said) uses the ministry of men, by making them, as it were, his substitutes, not by transferring his right and honour to them, but only doing his own work by their lips, just as an artificer uses a tool for any purpose. What I have previously expounded I am again forced to repeat. God might have acted, in this respect, by himself, without any aid or instrument, or might even have done it by angels; but there are several reasons why he rather chooses to employ men. First, in this way he declares his conde-scension towards us, employing men to perform the function of his ambassadors in the world, to be the interpreters of his secret will; in short, to represent his own person. Thus he shows by experience that it is not to no purpose he calls us his temples, since by man's mouth he gives responses to men as from a sanctuary. Secondly, it forms a most excellent and useful training to humility, when he accustoms us to obey his word though preached by men like ourselves, or, it may be, our inferiors in worth. Did he himself speak from heaven, it were no wonder if his sacred oracles were received by all ears and minds reverently and without delay. For who would not dread his present power? Who would not fall prostrate at the first view of his great majesty? Who would not be overpowered by that immeasurable splendour? But when a feeble man, sprung from the dust, speaks in the name of God, we give the best proof of our piety and obedience, by listening with docility to his servant, though not in any respect our superior. Accordingly, he hides the treasure of his heavenly wisdom in frail earthen vessels (2 Cor. 4:7), that he may have a more certain proof of the estimation in which it is held by us. Moreover, nothing was fitter to cherish mutual charity than to bind men together by this tie, appointing one of them as a pastor to teach the others who are enjoined to be disciples, and receive the common doctrine from a single mouth. For did every man suffice for himself, and stand in no need of another's aid (such is the pride of the human intellect), each would despise all others, and be in his turn despised. The Lord, therefore, has astricted his Church to what he foresaw would be the strongest bond of unity when he deposited the doctrine of eternal life and salva-tion with men, that by their hands he might communicate it to others. To this Paul had respect when he wrote to the Ephesians, 'There is one body, and one Spirit, even as ye are called in one hope of your calling; one Lord, one faith, one baptism, one God and Father of all, who is above all, and through all, and in you all. But unto every one of us is given grace according to the measure of the gift of Christ. Wherefore he saith, When he ascended up on high, he led captivity captive, and gave gifts unto men. (Now that he ascended, what is it but that he also descended first into the lower parts of the earth? He that descended is the same also that ascended up far above all heavens, that he might fill all things.) And he gave some, apostles; and some, prophets; and some, evangelists; and some, pastors and teachers; for the perfecting of the saints, for the work of the ministry, for the edifying of the body of Christ: till we all come in the unity of the faith, and of the knowledge of the Son of God, unto a perfect man, unto the measure of the stature of the fulness of Christ: that we henceforth be no more children, tossed to and fro, and carried about with every wind of doctrine, by the sleight of men, and cunning craftiness, whereby they lie in wait to deceive; but speaking the truth in love, may grow up into him in all things, which is the head, even Christ: from whom the whole body fitly joined together and compacted by that which every joint supplieth, according to the effectual working in the measure of every part, maketh increase of the body unto the edifying of itself in love' (Eph. 4:4–16).

2. By these words he shows that the ministry of men, which God employs in governing the Church, is a principal bond by which believers are kept together in one body. He also intimates, that the Church cannot be kept safe, unless supported by those guards to which the Lord has been pleased to commit its safety. Christ 'ascended up far above all heavens, that he might fill all things' (Eph. 4:10). The mode of filling is this: By the ministers to whom he has committed this office, and given grace to discharge it, he dispenses and distributes his gifts to the Church, and thus exhibits himself as in a manner actually present by exerting the energy of his Spirit in this his institution, so as to prevent it from being vain or fruitless. In this way, the renewal of the saints is accomplished, and the body of Christ is edified; in this way we grow up in all things unto Him who is the Head, and unite with one another; in this way we are all brought into the unity of Christ, provided prophecy flourishes among us, provided we receive his apostles, and despise not the doctrine which is administered to us. Whoever, therefore, studies to abolish this order and kind of government of which we speak, or disparages it as of minor importance, plots the devastation, or rather the ruin and destruction, of the Church. For neither are the light and heat of the sun, nor meat and drink, so necessary to sustain and cherish the present life, as is the apostolical and pastoral office to preserve a Church in the earth.

3. Accordingly, I have observed above, that God has repeatedly commended its dignity by the titles which he has bestowed upon it, in order that we might hold it in the highest estimation, as among the most excellent of our blessings. He declares, that in raising up teachers, he confers a special benefit on men, when he bids his prophet exclaim, 'How beautiful upon the mountains are the feet of him that bringeth good tidings, that publisheth peace' (Isa. 52:7); when he calls the apostles the light of the world and the salt of the earth (Mt. 5:13, 14). Nor could the office be more highly eulogised than when he said, 'He that heareth you heareth me; and he that despiseth you despiseth me' (Lk. 10:16). But the most striking passage of all is that in the Second Epistle to the Corinthians, where Paul treats as it were professedly of this question. He contends, that there is nothing in the Church more noble and glorious than the ministry of the Gospel, seeing it is the administration of the Spirit of righteousness and eternal life. These and similar passages should have the effect of preventing that method of governing and maintaining the Church by ministers, a method which the Lord has ratified for ever, from seeming worthless in our eyes, and at length becoming obsolete by contempt. How very necessary it is, he has declared not only by words but also by examples. When he was pleased to shed the light of his truth in greater effulgence on Cornelius, he sent an angel from heaven to despatch Peter to him (Acts 10:3). When he was pleased to call Paul to the knowledge of himself, and ingraft him into the Church, he does not address him with his own voice, but sends him to a man from whom he may both obtain the doctrine of salvation and the sanctification of baptism (Acts 9:6–20). If it was not by mere accident that the angel, who is the interpreter of God, abstains from declaring the will of God, and orders a man to be called to declare it; that Christ, the only Master of believers, commits Paul to the teaching of a man, that Paul whom he had determined to carry into the third heaven, and honour with a wondrous revelation of things that could not be spoken (2 Cor. 12:2), who will presume to despise or disregard as superfluous that ministry, whose utility God has been pleased to attest by such evidence?

4. Those who preside over the government of the Church, according to the institution of Christ, are named by Paul, first, 'Apostles'; secondly, 'Prophets'; thirdly, 'Evangelists'; fourthly, 'Pastors'; and, lastly, 'Teachers' (Eph. 4:11). Of these, only the two last have an ordinary office in the Church. The Lord raised up the other three at the beginning of his kingdom, and still occasionally raises them up when the necessity of the times requires. The nature of the apostolic function is clear from the command, 'Go ye into all the world, and preach the Gospel to every creature' (Mk 16:15). No fixed limits are given them, but the whole world is assigned to be reduced under the obedience of Christ, that by spreading the Gospel as widely as they could, they might everywhere erect his kingdom. Accordingly, Paul, when he would approve his apostleship, does not say that he had acquired some one city for Christ, but had propagated the Gospel far and wide – had not built on another man's foundation, but planted churches where the name of his Lord was unheard. The apostles, therefore, were sent forth to bring back the world from its revolt to the true obedience of God, and everywhere establish his kingdom by the preaching of the Gospel; or, if you choose, they were like the first architects of the Church, to lay its foundations throughout the world. By 'Prophets', he means not all interpreters of the divine will, but those who excelled by special revelation; none such now exist, or they are less manifest. By 'Evangelists', I mean those who, while inferior in rank to the apostles, were next them in office, and even acted as their substitutes. Such were Luke, Timothy, Titus, and the like; perhaps, also, the seventy disciples whom our Saviour appointed in the second place to the apostles (Lk. 10:1). According to this interpretation, which appears to me consonant both to the words and the meaning of Paul, those three functions were not instituted in the Church to be perpetual, but only to endure so long as churches were to be formed where none previously existed, or at least where churches were to be transferred from Moses to Christ; although I deny not, that afterward God occasionally raised up Apostles, or at least Evangelists, in their stead, as has been done in our time. For such were needed to bring back the Church from the revolt of Antichrist. The office I nevertheless call extraordinary, because it has no place in churches duly constituted. Next come 'Pastors' and 'Teachers', with whom the Church never can dispense, and between whom, I think, there is this difference, that teachers preside not over discipline, or the administration of the sacraments, or admonitions, or exhortations, but the interpretation of Scripture only, in order that pure and sound doctrine may be maintained among believers. But all these are embraced in the pastoral office.

✝ CHAPTER 12 ✝

Of the discipline of the church, and its principal use in censures and excommunication.

Sections

1. Of the power of the keys, or the common discipline of the Church. Necessity and very great utility of this discipline.
2. Its various degrees: (1) Private admonition, (2) rebukes before witnesses, (3) excommunication.
3. Different degrees of delinquency. Modes of procedure in both kinds of chastisement.
4. Delicts to be distinguished from flagitious wickedness. The last to be more severely punished.
5. Ends of this discipline: (1) That the wicked may not, by being admitted to the Lord's Table, put insult on Christ, (2) that they may not corrupt others, (3) that they themselves may repent.

1. The discipline of the Church, the consideration of which has been deferred till now, must be briefly explained, that we may be able to pass to other matters. Now discipline depends in a very great measure on the power of the keys and on spiritual jurisdiction. That this may be more easily understood, let us divide the Church into two principal classes – clergy and people. The term 'clergy' I use in the common acceptation for those who perform a public ministry in the Church. We shall speak first of the common discipline to which all ought to be subject, and then proceed to the clergy, who have besides that common discipline one peculiar to themselves. But as some, from hatred of discipline, are averse to the very name, for their sake we observe, if no society, nay, no house with even a moderate family, can be kept in a right state without discipline, much more necessary is it in the Church, whose state ought to be the best ordered possible. Hence as the saving doctrine of Christ is the life of the Church, so discipline is, as it were, its sinews; for to it it is owing that the members of the body adhere together, each in its own place. Wherefore, all who either wish that discipline were abolished, or who impede the restoration of it, whether they do this of design or through thoughtlessness, certainly aim at the complete devastation of the Church. For what will be the result if every one is allowed to do as he pleases? But this must happen if to the preaching of the Gospel are not added private admonition, correction, and similar methods of maintaining doctrine, and not allowing it to become lethargic. Discipline, therefore, is a kind of curb to restrain and tame those who war against the doctrine of Christ, or it is a kind of stimulus by which the indifferent are aroused; sometimes, also, it is a kind of fatherly rod, by which those who have made some more grievous lapse are chastised in mercy with the meekness of the spirit of Christ. Since, then, we already see some beginnings of a fearful devastation in the Church from the total want of care and method in managing the people, necessity itself cries aloud that there is need of a remedy. Now the only remedy is this which Christ enjoins, and the pious have always had in use.

2. The first foundation of discipline is to provide for private admonition; that is, if any one does not do his duty spontaneously, or behaves insolently, or lives not quite honestly, or

commits something worthy of blame, he must allow himself to be admonished; and every one must study to admonish his brother when the case requires. Here especially is there occasion for the vigilance of pastors and presbyters, whose duty is not only to preach to the people, but to exhort and admonish from house to house, whenever their hearers have not profited sufficiently by general teaching; as Paul shows, when he relates that he taught 'publicly, and from house to house', and testifies that he is 'pure from the blood of all men', because he had not shunned to declare 'all the counsel of God' (Acts 20:20, 26, 27) Then does doctrine obtain force and authority, not only when the minister publicly expounds to all what they owe to Christ, but has the right and means of exacting this from those whom he may observe to be sluggish or disobedient to his doctrine. Should any one either perversely reject such admonitions, or by persisting in his faults, show that he contemns them, the injunction of Christ is, that after he has been a second time admonished before witnesses, he is to be summoned to the bar of the Church, which is the consistory of elders, and there admonished more sharply, as by public authority, that if he reverence the Church he may submit and obey (Mt. 18:15, 17). If even in this way he is not subdued, but persists in his iniquity, he is then, as a despiser of the Church, to be debarred from the society of believers.

3. Put as our Saviour is not there speaking of secret faults merely, we must attend to the distinction that some sins are private, others public or openly manifest. Of the former, Christ says to every private individual, 'go and tell him his fault between thee and him alone' (Mt. 18:15). Of open sins Paul says to Timothy, 'Those that sin rebuke before all, that others also may fear' (1 Tim. 5:20). Our Saviour had previously used the words, 'If thy brother shall trespass against thee'. This clause, unless you would be captious, you cannot understand otherwise than, If this happens *in a manner known to yourself*, others not being privy to it. The injunction which Paul gave to Timothy to rebuke those openly who sin openly, he himself followed with Peter (Gal. 2:14). For when Peter sinned so as to give public offence, he did not admonish him apart, but brought him forward in face of the Church. The legitimate course, therefore, will be to proceed in correcting secret faults by the steps mentioned by Christ, and in open sins, accompanied with public scandal, to proceed at once to solemn correction by the Church.

4. Another distinction to be attended to is, that some sins are mere delinquencies, others crimes and flagrant iniquities. In correcting the latter, it is necessary to employ not only admonition or rebuke, but a sharper remedy, as Paul shows when he not only verbally rebukes the incestuous Corinthian, but punishes him with excommunication, as soon as he was informed of his crime (1 Cor. 5:4). Now then we begin better to perceive how the spiritual jurisdiction of the Church, which animadverts on sins according to the word of the Lord, is at once the best help to sound doctrine, the best foundation of order, and the best bond of unity. Therefore, when the Church banishes from its fellowship open adulterers, fornicators, thieves, robbers, the seditious, the perjured, false witnesses, and others of that description; likewise the contumacious, who, when duly admonished for lighter faults, hold God and his tribunal in derision, instead of arrogating to itself anything that is unreasonable, it exercises a jurisdiction which it has received from the Lord. Moreover, lest any one should despise the judgment of the Church, or count it a small matter to be condemned by the suffrages of the faithful, the Lord has declared that it is nothing else than the promulgation of his own sentence, and that

that which they do on earth is ratified in heaven. For they act by the word of the Lord in condemning the perverse, and by the word of the Lord in taking the penitent back into favour (Jn 20:23). Those, I say, who trust that churches can long stand without this bond of discipline are mistaken, unless, indeed, we can with impunity dispense with a help which the Lord foresaw would be necessary. And, indeed, the greatness of the necessity will be better perceived by its manifold uses.

5.   There are three ends to which the Church has respect in thus correcting and excommunicating. The first is, that God may not be insulted by the name of Christians being given to those who lead shameful and flagitious lives, as if his holy Church were a combination of the wicked and abandoned. For seeing that the Church is the body of Christ, she cannot be defiled by such fetid and putrid members, without bringing some disgrace on her Head. Therefore that there may be nothing in the Church to bring disgrace on his sacred name, those whose turpitude might throw infamy on the name must be expelled from his family. And here, also, regard must be had to the Lord's Supper, which might he profaned by a promiscuous admission. For it is most true, that he who is intrusted with the dispensation of it, if he knowingly and willingly admits any unworthy person whom he ought and is able to repel, is as guilty of sacrilege as if he had cast the Lord's body to dogs. Wherefore, Chrysostom bitterly inveighs against priests, who, from fear of the great, dare not keep any one back. 'Blood [says he, Hom. 83, in Mt.] will be required at your hands. If you fear man, he will mock you, but if you fear God, you will be respected also by men. Let us not tremble at fasces, purple, or diadems; our power here is greater. Assuredly I will sooner give up my body to death, and allow my blood to be shed, than be a partaker of that pollution.' Therefore, lest this most sacred mystery should be exposed to ignominy, great selection is required in dispensing it, and this cannot be except by the jurisdiction of the Church. A second end of discipline is, that the good may not, as usually happens, be corrupted by constant communication with the wicked. For such is our proneness to go astray, that nothing is easier than to seduce us from the right course by bad example. To this use of discipline the apostle referred when he commanded the Corinthians to discard the incestuous man from their society. 'A little leaven leaveneth the whole lump' (1 Cor. 5:6) And so much danger did he foresee here, that he prohibited them from keeping company with such persons. 'If any man that is called a brother be a fornicator, or covetous, or an idolater, or a railer, or a drunkard, or an extortioner; with such an one, no not to eat' (1 Cor. 5:11). A third end of discipline is, that the sinner may be ashamed, and begin to repent of his turpitude. Hence it is for their interest also that their iniquity should be chastised, that whereas they would have become more obstinate by indulgence, they may be aroused by the rod. This the apostle intimates when he thus writes, 'If any man obey not our word by this epistle, note that man, and have no company with him, that he may be ashamed' (2 Thess. 3:14). Again, when he says that he had delivered the Corinthian to Satan, 'that the spirit may be saved in the day of the Lord Jesus' (1 Cor. 5:5); that is, as I interpret it, he gave him over to temporal condemnation, that he might be made safe for eternity. And he says that he gave him over to Satan because the devil is without the Church, as Christ is in the Church. Some interpret this of a certain infliction on the flesh, but this interpretation seems to me most improbable.

✝ PART XIV ✝

THE SACRAMENTS

✝ CHAPTER 14 ✝

Of the sacraments.

Sections

1. Of the sacraments in general. A sacrament defined.
3. Definition explained. Why God seals his promises to us by sacraments.
5. Error of those who attempt to separate the word, or promise of God, from the element.
6. Why sacraments are called Signs of the Covenant.
7. They are such signs, though the wicked should receive them, but are signs of grace only to believers.
17. The matter of the sacrament always present when the sacrament is duly administered.

1. Akin to the preaching of the Gospel, we have another help to our faith in the sacraments, in regard to which, it greatly concerns us that some sure doctrine should be delivered, informing us both of the end for which they were instituted, and of their present use. First, we must attend to what a sacrament is. It seems to me, then, a simple and appropriate definition to say, that it is an external sign, by which the Lord seals on our consciences his promises of good-will toward us, in order to sustain the weakness of our faith, and we in our turn testify our piety towards him, both before himself, and before angels as well as men. We may also define more briefly by calling it a testimony of the divine favour toward us, confirmed by an external sign, with a corresponding attestation of our faith towards Him. You may make your choice of these definitions, which in meaning differ not from that of Augustine, which defines a sacrament to be a visible sign of a sacred thing, or a visible form of an invisible grace, but does not contain a better or surer explanation. As its brevity makes it somewhat obscure, and thereby misleads the more illiterate, I wished to remove all doubt, and make the definition fuller by stating it at greater length.

3. From the definition which we have given, we perceive that there never is a sacrament without an antecedent promise, the sacrament being added as a kind of appendix, with the view of confirming and sealing the promise, and giving a better attestation, or rather, in a manner, confirming it. In this way God provides first for our ignorance and sluggishness, and, secondly, for our infirmity; and yet, properly speaking, it does not so much confirm his word as establish us in the faith of it. For the truth of God is in itself sufficiently stable and certain, and cannot receive a better confirmation from any other quarter than from itself. But as our faith is slender and weak, so if it be not propped up on every side, and supported by all kinds of means, it is forthwith shaken and tossed to and fro, wavers, and even falls. And here, indeed,

155

our merciful Lord, with boundless condescension, so accommodates himself to our capacity, that seeing how from our animal nature we are always creeping on the ground, and cleaving to the flesh, having no thought of what is spiritual, and not even forming an idea of it, he declines not by means of these earthly elements to lead us to himself, and even in the flesh to exhibit a mirror of spiritual blessings. For, as Chrysostom says (Hom. 60, ad Popul.): 'Were we incorporeal, he would give us these things in a naked and incorporeal form. Now because our souls are implanted in bodies, he delivers spiritual things under things visible. Not that the qualities which are set before us in the sacraments are inherent in the nature of the things, but God gives them this signification.'

5. Nor are those to be listened to who oppose this view with a more subtle than solid dilemma. They argue thus: We either know that the word of God which precedes the sacrament is the true will of God, or we do not know it. If we know it, we learn nothing new from the sacrament which succeeds. If we do not know it, we cannot learn it from the sacrament, whose whole efficacy depends on the word. Our brief reply is: The seals which are affixed to diplomas, and other public deeds, are nothing considered in themselves, and would be affixed to no purpose if nothing was written on the parchment, and yet this does not prevent them from sealing and confirming when they are appended to writings. It cannot be alleged that this comparison is a recent fiction of our own, since Paul himself used it, terming circumcision a 'seal' (Rom. 4:11), where he expressly maintains that the circumcision of Abraham was not for justification, but was an attestation to the covenant, by the faith of which he had been previously justified. And how, pray, can any one be greatly offended when we teach that the promise is sealed by the sacrament, since it is plain, from the promises themselves, that one promise confirms another? The clearer any evidence is, the fitter is it to support our faith. But sacraments bring with them the clearest promises, and, when compared with the word, have this peculiarity, that they represent promises to the life, as if painted in a picture. Nor ought we to be moved by an objection founded on the distinction between sacraments and the seals of documents – that since both consist of the carnal elements of this world, the former cannot be sufficient or adequate to seal the promises of God, which are spiritual and eternal, though the latter may be employed to seal the edicts of princes concerning fleeting and fading things. But the believer, when the sacraments are presented to his eye, does not stop short at the carnal spectacle, but by the steps of analogy which I have indicated, rises with pious consideration to the sublime mysteries which lie hidden in the sacraments.

6. As the Lord calls his promises covenants (Gen. 6:18; 9:9; 17:2), and sacraments signs of the covenants, so something similar may be inferred from human covenants. What could the slaughter of a hog effect, unless words were interposed or rather preceded? Swine are often killed without any interior or occult mystery. What could be gained by pledging the right hand, since hands are not unfrequently joined in giving battle? But when words have preceded, then by such symbols of covenant sanction is given to laws, though previously conceived, digested, and enacted by words. Sacraments, therefore, are exercises which confirm our faith in the word of God; and because we are carnal, they are exhibited under carnal objects, that thus they may train us in accommodation to our sluggish capacity, just as nurses lead children by the hand. And hence Augustine calls a sacrament a 'visible word' (August. in Joann. Hom. 89), because it represents the promises of God as in a picture, and places them in our view in a

graphic bodily form (August. contra Faust. Lib. 19). We might refer to other similitudes, by which sacraments are more plainly designated, as when they are called the pillars of our faith. For just as a building stands and leans on its foundation, and yet is rendered more stable when supported by pillars, so faith leans on the word of God as its proper foundation, and yet when sacraments are added leans more firmly, as if resting on pillars. Or we may call them mirrors, in which we may contemplate the riches of the grace which God bestows upon us. For then, as has been said, he manifests himself to us in as far as our dulness can enable us to recognise him, and testifies his love and kindness to us more expressly than by word.

7.   It is irrational to contend that sacraments are not manifestations of divine grace toward us, because they are held forth to the ungodly also, who, however, so far from experiencing God to be more propitious to them, only incur greater condemnation. By the same reasoning, the Gospel will be no manifestation of the grace of God, because it is spurned by many who hear it; nor will Christ himself be a manifestation of grace, because of the many by whom he was seen and known, very few received him. Something similar may be seen in public enactments. A great part of the body of the people deride and evade the authenticating seal, though they know it was employed by their sovereign to confirm his will; others trample it under foot, as a matter by no means appertaining to them; while others even execrate it: so that, seeing the condition of the two things to be alike, the appropriateness of the comparison which I made above ought to be more readily allowed. It is certain, therefore, that the Lord offers us his mercy, and a pledge of his grace, both in his sacred word and in the sacraments; but it is not apprehended save by those who receive the word and sacraments with firm faith: in like manner as Christ, though offered and held forth for salvation to all, is not, however, acknowledged and received by all. Augustine, when intending to intimate this, said that the efficacy of the word is produced in the sacrament, *not because it is spoken, but because it is believed*. Hence Paul, addressing believers, includes communion with Christ, in the sacraments, as when he says, 'As many of you as have been baptised into Christ have put on Christ' (Gal. 3:27). Again, 'For by one Spirit we are all baptised into one body' (1 Cor. 12:13). But when he speaks of a preposterous use of the sacraments, he attributes nothing more to them than to frigid, empty figures; thereby intimating, that however the ungodly and hypocrites may, by their perverseness, either suppress, or obscure, or impede the effect of divine grace in the sacraments, that does not prevent them, where and whenever God is so pleased, from giving a true evidence of communion with Christ, or prevent them from exhibiting, and the Spirit of God from performing, the very thing which they promise. We conclude, therefore, that the sacraments are truly termed evidences of divine grace, and, as it were, seals of the good-will which he entertains toward us. They, by sealing it to us, sustain, nourish, confirm, and increase our faith. The objections usually urged against this view are frivolous and weak. They say that our faith, if it is good, cannot be made better; for there is no faith save that which leans unshakingly, firmly, and undividedly, on the mercy of God. It had been better for the objectors to pray, with the apostles, 'Lord, increase our faith' (Lk. 17:5), than confidently to maintain a perfection of faith which none of the sons of men ever attained, none ever shall attain, in this life. Let them explain what kind of faith his was who said, 'Lord, I believe; help thou mine unbelief' (Mk 9:24). That faith, though only commenced, was good, and might, by the removal of the unbelief, be made better. But there is no better argument to refute them than their own

consciousness. For if they confess themselves sinners (this, whether they will or not, they cannot deny), then they must of necessity impute this very quality to the imperfection of their faith.

17. Wherefore, let it be a fixed point, that the office of the sacraments differs not from the word of God; and this is to hold forth and offer Christ to us, and, in him, the treasures of heavenly grace. They confer nothing, and avail nothing, if not received in faith, just as wine and oil, or any other liquor, however large the quantity which you pour out, will run away and perish unless there be an open vessel to receive it. When the vessel is not open, though it may be sprinkled all over, it will nevertheless remain entirely empty. We must be aware of being led into a kindred error by the terms, somewhat too extravagant, which ancient Christian writers have employed in extolling the dignity of the sacraments. We must not suppose that there is some latent virtue inherent in the sacraments by which they, in themselves, confer the gifts of the Holy Spirit upon us, in the same way in which wine is drunk out of a cup, since the only office divinely assigned them is to attest and ratify the benevolence of the Lord towards us; and they avail no farther than accompanied by the Holy Spirit to open our minds and hearts, and make us capable of receiving this testimony, in which various distinguished graces are clearly manifested. For the sacraments, as we lately observed, are to us what messengers of good news are to men, or earnests in ratifying pactions. They do not of themselves bestow any grace, but they announce and manifest it, and, like earnests and badges, give a ratification of the gifts which the divine liberality has bestowed upon us. The Holy Spirit, whom the sacraments do not bring promiscuously to all, but whom the Lord specially confers on his people, brings the gifts of God along with him, makes way for the sacraments, and causes them to bear fruit. But though we deny not that God, by the immediate agency of his Spirit, countenances his own ordinance, preventing the administration of the sacraments which he has instituted from being fruitless and vain, still we maintain that the internal grace of the Spirit, as it is distinct from the external ministration, ought to be viewed and considered separately. God, therefore, truly performs whatever he promises and figures by signs; nor are the signs without effect, for they prove that he is their true and faithful author. The only question here is, whether the Lord works by proper and intrinsic virtue (as it is called), or resigns his office to external symbols? We maintain, that whatever organs he employs detract nothing from his primary operation. In this doctrine of the sacraments, their dignity is highly extolled, their use plainly shown, their utility sufficiently proclaimed, and moderation in all things duly maintained; so that nothing is attributed to them which ought not to be attributed, and nothing denied them which they ought to possess. Meanwhile, we get rid of that fiction by which the cause of justification and the power of the Holy Spirit are included in elements as vessels and vehicles, and the special power which was overlooked is distinctly explained. Here, also, we ought to observe, that what the minister figures and attests by outward action, God performs inwardly, lest that which God claims for himself alone should be ascribed to mortal man. This Augustine is careful to observe: 'How does both God and Moses sanctify? Not Moses for God, but Moses by visible sacraments through his ministry, God by invisible grace through the Holy Spirit. Herein is the whole fruit of visible sacraments; for what do these visible sacraments avail without that sanctification of invisible grace?'

✛ CHAPTER 15 ✛

Of baptism.

Sections

1. Baptism defined. Its primary object. This consists of three things. First, to attest the forgiveness of sins.
2. Passages of Scripture proving the forgiveness of sins.
3. Forgiveness not only of past but also of future sins. This no encouragement to license in sin.
4. Refutation of those who share forgiveness between Baptism and Repentance.
5. Second thing in Baptism – to teach that we are ingrafted into Christ for mortification and newness of life.
6. Third thing in Baptism – to teach us that we are united to Christ so as to be partakers of all his blessings. Second and third things conspicuous in the baptism both of John and the apostles.
14. Second part of the chapter. Of baptism as a confirmation of our faith.

1.   Baptism is the initiatory sign by which we are admitted to the fellowship of the Church, that being ingrafted into Christ we may be accounted children of God. Moreover, the end for which God has given it (this I have shown to be common to all mysteries) is, first, that it may be conducive to our faith in him; and, secondly, that it may serve the purpose of a confession among men. The nature of both institutions we shall explain in order. Baptism contributes to our faith three things, which require to be treated separately. The first object, therefore, for which it is appointed by the Lord, is to be a sign and evidence of our purification, or (better to explain my meaning) it is a kind of sealed instrument by which he assures us that all our sins are so deleted, covered, and effaced, that they will never come into his sight, never be mentioned, never imputed. For it is his will that all who have believed, be baptised for the remission of sins. Hence those who have thought that baptism is nothing else than the badge and mark by which we profess our religion before men, in the same way as soldiers attest their profession by bearing the insignia of their commander, having not attended to what was the principal thing in baptism; and this is, that we are to receive it in connection with the promise, 'He that believeth and is baptised shall be saved' (Mark 16:16).

2.   In this sense is to be understood the statement of Paul, that 'Christ loved the Church, and gave himself for it, that he might sanctify and cleanse it with the washing of water by the word' (Eph. 5:25, 26); and again, 'not by works of righteousness which we have done, but according to his mercy he saved us, by the washing of regeneration and renewing of the Holy Ghost' (Tit. 3:5). Peter also says that 'baptism also doth now save us' (1 Pet. 3:21). For he did not mean to intimate that our ablution and salvation are perfected by water, or that water possesses in itself the virtue of purifying, regenerating, and renewing; nor does he mean that it is the cause of salvation, but only that the knowledge and certainty of such gifts are perceived in this sacrament. This the words themselves evidently show. For Paul connects together the word of life and baptism of water, as if he had said, by the Gospel the message of our ablution and sanctification is announced; by baptism this message is sealed. And Peter immediately subjoins, that that baptism is 'not the putting away of the filth of the flesh, but the

answer of a good conscience toward God, which is of faith'. Nay, the only purification which baptism promises is by means of the sprinkling of the blood of Christ, who is figured by water from the resemblance to cleansing and washing. Who, then, can say that we are cleansed by that water which certainly attests that the blood of Christ is our true and only laver? So that we cannot have a better argument to refute the hallucination of those who ascribe the whole to the virtue of water than we derive from the very meaning of baptism, which leads us away as well from the visible element which is presented to our eye, as from all other means, that it may fix our minds on Christ alone.

3.   Nor is it to be supposed that baptism is bestowed only with reference to the past, so that, in regard to new lapses into which we fall after baptism, we must seek new remedies of expiation in other so-called sacraments, just as if the power of baptism had become obsolete. To this error, in ancient times, it was owing that some refused to be initiated by baptism until their life was in extreme danger, and they were drawing their last breath, that they might thus obtain pardon for all the past. Against this preposterous precaution ancient bishops frequently inveigh in their writings. We ought to consider that at whatever time we are baptised, we are washed and purified once for the whole of life. Wherefore, as often as we fall, we must recall the remembrance of our baptism, and thus fortify our minds, so as to feel certain and secure of the remission of sins. For though, when once administered, it seems to have passed, it is not abolished by subsequent sins. For the purity of Christ was therein offered to us, always is in force, and is not destroyed by any stain: it wipes and washes away all our defilements. Nor must we hence assume a licence of sinning for the future (there is certainly nothing in it to countenance such audacity), but this doctrine is intended only for those who, when they have sinned, groan under their sins burdened and oppressed, that they may have wherewith to support and console themselves, and not rush headlong into despair. Thus Paul says that Christ was made a propitiation for us for the remission of sins that are past (Rom. 3:25). By this he denies not that constant and perpetual forgiveness of sins is thereby obtained even till death: he only intimates that it is designed by the Father for those poor sinners who, wounded by remorse of conscience, sigh for the physician. To these the mercy of God is offered. Those who, from hopes of impunity, seek a licence for sin, only provoke the wrath and justice of God.

4.   I know it is a common belief that forgiveness, which at our first regeneration we receive by baptism alone, is after baptism procured by means of penitence and the keys. But those who entertain this fiction err from not considering that the power of the keys, of which they speak, so depends on baptism, that it ought not on any account to be separated from it. The sinner receives forgiveness by the ministry of the Church; in other words, not without the preaching of the Gospel. And of what nature is this preaching? That we are washed from our sins by the blood of Christ. And what is the sign and evidence of that washing if it be not baptism? We see, then, that that forgiveness has reference to baptism. This error had its origin in the fictitious sacrament of penance, on which I have already touched. What remains will be said at the proper place. There is no wonder if men who, from the grossness of their minds, are excessively attached to external things, have here also betrayed the defect, if not contented with the pure institution of God, they have introduced new helps devised by themselves, as if baptism were not itself a sacrament of penance. But if repentance is recommended during the whole of life, the power of baptism ought to have the same extent. Wherefore, there can be no doubt that

all the godly may, during the whole course of their lives, whenever they are vexed by a consciousness of their sins, recall the remembrance of their baptism, that they may thereby assure themselves of that sole and perpetual ablution which we have in the blood of Christ.

5.   Another benefit of baptism is, that it shows us our mortification in Christ and new life in him. 'Know ye not', says the apostle, 'that as many of us as were baptised into Jesus Christ, were baptised into his death? Therefore we are buried with him by baptism into death,' that we 'should walk in newness of life' (Rom. 6:3, 4). By these words, he not only exhorts us to imitation of Christ, as if he had said, that we are admonished by baptism, in like manner as Christ died, to die to our lusts, and as he rose, to rise to righteousness; but he traces the matter much higher, that Christ by baptism has made us partakers of his death, ingrafting us into it. And as the twig derives substance and nourishment from the root to which it is attached, so those who receive baptism with true faith truly feel the efficacy of Christ's death in the mortification of their flesh, and the efficacy of his resurrection in the quickening of the Spirit. On this he founds his exhortation, that if we are Christians we should be dead unto sin, and alive unto righteousness. He elsewhere uses the same argument – that we are circumcised, and put off the old man, after we are buried in Christ by baptism (Col. 2:12). And in this sense, in the passage which we formerly quoted, he calls it 'the washing of regeneration, and renewing of the Holy Ghost' (Tit. 3:5). We are promised, first, the free pardon of sins and imputation of righteousness; and, secondly, the grace of the Holy Spirit, to form us again to newness of life.

6.   The last advantage which our faith receives from baptism is its assuring us not only that we are ingrafted into the death and life of Christ, but so united to Christ himself as to be partakers of all his blessings. For he consecrated and sanctified baptism in his own body, that he might have it in common with us as the firmest bond of union and fellowship which he deigned to form with us; and hence Paul proves us to be the sons of God, from the fact that we put on Christ in baptism (Gal. 3:27). Thus we see the fulfilment of our baptism in Christ, whom for this reason we call the proper object of baptism. Hence it is not strange that the apostles are said to have baptised in the name of Christ, though they were enjoined to baptise in the name of the Father and Spirit also (Acts 8:16; 19:5; Mt. 28:19). For all the divine gifts held forth in baptism are found in Christ alone. And yet he who baptises into Christ cannot but at the same time invoke the name of the Father and the Spirit. For we are cleansed by his blood, just because our gracious Father, of his incomparable mercy, willing to receive us into favour, appointed him Mediator to effect our reconciliation with himself. Regeneration we obtain from his death and resurrection only, when sanctified by his Spirit we are imbued with a new and spiritual nature. Wherefore we obtain, and in a manner distinctly perceive, in the Father the cause, in the Son the matter, and in the Spirit the effect of our purification and regeneration. Thus first John baptised, and thus afterwards the apostles by the baptism of repentance for the remission of sins, understanding by the term 'repentance', regeneration, and by the 'remission' of sins, ablution.

14.   Now that the end to which the Lord had regard in the institution of baptism has been explained, it is easy to judge in what way we ought to use and receive it. For inasmuch as it is appointed to elevate, nourish, and confirm our faith, we are to receive it as from the hand of its author, being firmly persuaded that it is himself who speaks to us by means of the sign; that it is himself who washes and purifies us, and effaces the remembrance of our faults; that it is himself who makes us the partakers of his death, destroys the kingdom of Satan, subdues the power of concupiscence, nay, makes us one with himself, that being clothed with him we may be accounted the children of God. These things, I say, we ought to feel as truly and certainly in our mind as we see our body washed, immersed, and surrounded with water. For this analogy or similitude furnishes the surest rule in the sacraments – that in corporeal things we are to see spiritual, just as if they were actually exhibited to our eye, since the Lord has been pleased to represent them by such figures; not that such graces are included and bound in the sacrament, so as to be conferred by its efficacy, but only that by this badge the Lord declares to us that he is pleased to bestow all these things upon us. Nor does he merely feed our eyes with bare show; he leads us to the actual object, and effectually performs what he figures.

✝ CHAPTER 16 ✝

Infant baptism. Its accordance with the institution of Christ, and the nature of the sign.

Sections

2. This demonstrated from a consideration of the promises. These explain the nature and validity of infant baptism.
3. Promises annexed to the symbol of water cannot be better seen than in the institution of circumcision.
4. The promise and thing figured in circumcision and baptism one and the same. The only difference in the external ceremony.
5. Hence the baptism of the children of Christian parents as competent as the circumcision of Jewish children. An objection founded on a stated day for circumcision refuted.
6. An argument for infant baptism founded on the covenant which God made with Abraham. An objection disposed of. The grace of God not diminished by the advent of Christ.
9. Twofold use and benefit of infant baptism. In respect (1) of parents, (2) of children baptised.

2. In the first place, then, it is a well-known doctrine, and one as to which all the pious are agreed, that the right consideration of signs does not lie merely in the outward ceremonies, but depends chiefly on the promise and the spiritual mysteries, to typify which the ceremonies themselves are appointed. He, therefore, who would thoroughly understand the effect of baptism – its object and true character – must not stop short at the element and corporeal object, but look forward to the divine promises which are therein offered to us, and rise to the internal secrets which are therein represented. He who understands these has reached the solid truth, and, so to speak, the whole substance of baptism, and will thence perceive the nature and use of outward sprinkling. On the other hand, he who passes them by in contempt, and keeps his thoughts entirely fixed on the visible ceremony, will neither understand the force, nor the proper nature of baptism, nor comprehend what is meant, or what end is gained by the use of water. This is confirmed by passages of Scripture too numerous and too

clear to make it necessary here to discuss them more at length. It remains, therefore, to inquire into the nature and efficacy of baptism, as evinced by the promises therein given. Scripture shows, *first*, that it points to that cleansing from sin which we obtain by the blood of Christ; and, *secondly*, to the mortification of the flesh which consists in participation in his death, by which believers are regenerated to newness of life, and thereby to the fellowship of Christ. To these general heads may be referred all that the Scriptures teach concerning baptism, with this addition, that it is also a symbol to testify our religion to men.

3.   Now, since prior to the institution of baptism, the people of God had circumcision in its stead, let us see how far these two signs differ, and how far they resemble each other. In this way it will appear what analogy there is between them. When the Lord enjoins Abraham to observe circumcision (Gen. 17:10), he premises that he would be a God unto him and to his seed, adding, that in himself was a perfect sufficiency of all things, and that Abraham might reckon on his hand as a fountain of every blessing. These words include the promise of eternal life, as our Saviour interprets when he employs it to prove the immortality and resurrection of believers: 'God', says he, 'is not the God of the dead, but of the living' (Mt. 22:32). Hence, too, Paul, when showing to the Ephesians how great the destruction was from which the Lord had delivered them, seeing that they had not been admitted to the covenant of circumcision, infers that at that time they were aliens from the covenant of promise, without God, and without hope (Eph. 2:12), all these being comprehended in the covenant. Now, the first access to God, the first entrance to immortal life, is the remission of sins. Hence it follows, that this corresponds to the promise of our cleansing in baptism. The Lord afterwards covenants with Abraham, that he is to walk before him in sincerity and innocence of heart: this applies to mortification or regeneration. And lest any should doubt whether circumcision were the sign of mortification, Moses explains more clearly elsewhere when he exhorts the people of Israel to circumcise the foreskin of their heart, because the Lord had chosen them for his own people, out of all the nations of the earth. As the Lord, in choosing the posterity of Abraham for his people, commands them to be circumcised, so Moses declares that they are to be circumcised in heart, thus explaining what is typified by that carnal circumcision. Then, lest any one should attempt this in his own strength, he shows that it is the work of divine grace. All this is so often inculcated by the prophets, that there is no occasion here to collect the passages which everywhere occur. We have, therefore, a spiritual promise given to the fathers in circumcision, similar to that which is given to us in baptism, since it figured to them both the forgiveness of sins and the mortification of the flesh. Besides, as we have shown that Christ, in whom both of these reside, is the foundation of baptism, so must he also be the foundation of circumcision. For he is promised to Abraham, and in him all nations are blessed. To seal this grace, the sign of circumcision is added.

4.   There is now no difficulty in seeing wherein the two signs agree, and wherein they differ. The promise, in which we have shown that the power of the signs consists, is one in both – the promise of the paternal favour of God, of forgiveness of sins, and eternal life. And the thing figured is one and the same – regeneration. The foundation on which the completion of these things depends is one in both. Wherefore, there is no difference in the internal meaning, from which the whole power and peculiar nature of the sacrament is to be estimated. The only difference which remains is in the external ceremony, which is the least part of it, the chief part consisting in the promise and the thing signified. Hence we may conclude, that everything applicable to circumcision applies also to baptism, excepting always the difference in the visible ceremony. To this analogy and comparison we are led by that rule of the apostle, in which he enjoins us to bring every interpretation of Scripture to the analogy of faith (Rom. 12:3, 6). And certainly in this matter the truth may almost be felt. For just as circumcision, which was a kind of badge to the Jews, assuring them that they were adopted as the people and family of God, was their first entrance into the Church, while they, in their turn, professed their allegiance to God, so now we are initiated by baptism, so as to be enrolled among his people, and at the same time swear unto his name. Hence it is incontrovertible, that baptism has been substituted for circumcision, and performs the same office.

5. Now, if we are to investigate whether or not baptism is justly given to infants, will we not say that the man trifles, or rather is delirious, who would stop short at the element of water, and the external observance, and not allow his mind to rise to the spiritual mystery? If reason is listened to, it will undoubtedly appear that baptism is properly administered to infants as a thing due to them. The Lord did not anciently bestow circumcision upon them without making them partakers of all the things signified by circumcision. He would have deluded his people with mere imposture, had he quieted them with fallacious symbols: the very idea is shocking. He distinctly declares, that the circumcision of the infant will be instead of a seal of the promise of the covenant. But if the covenant remains firm and fixed, it is no less applicable to the children of Christians in the present day, than to the children of the Jews under the Old Testament. Now, if they are partakers of the thing signified, how can they be denied the sign? If they obtain the reality, how can they be refused the figure? The external sign is so united in the sacrament with the word, that it cannot be separated from it: but if they can be separated, to which of the two shall we attach the greater value? Surely, when we see that the sign is subservient to the word, we shall say that it is subordinate, and assign it the inferior place. Since, then, the word of baptism is destined for infants, why should we deny them the sign, which is an appendage of the word? This one reason, could no other be furnished, would be amply sufficient to refute all gainsayers. The objection, that there was a fixed day for circumcision, is a mere quibble. We admit that we are not now, like the Jews, tied down to certain days; but when the Lord declares, that though he prescribes no day, yet he is pleased that infants shall be formally admitted to his covenant, what more do we ask?

6. Scripture gives us a still clearer knowledge of the truth. For it is most evident that the covenant, which the Lord once made with Abraham, is not less applicable to Christians now than it was anciently to the Jewish people, and therefore that word has no less reference to Christians than to Jews. Unless, indeed, we imagine that Christ, by his advent, diminished, or curtailed the grace of the Father – an idea not free from execrable blasphemy. Wherefore, both the children of the Jews, because, when made heirs of that covenant, they were separated from the heathen, were called a holy seed, and for the same reason the children of Christians, or those who have only one believing parent, are called holy, and, by the testimony of the apostle, differ from the impure seed of idolaters. Then, since the Lord, immediately after the covenant was made with Abraham, ordered it to be sealed in infants by an outward sacrament, how can it be said that Christians are not to attest it in the present day, and seal it in their children? Let it not be objected, that the only symbol by which the Lord ordered his covenant to be confirmed was that of circumcision, which was long ago abrogated. It is easy to answer, that, in accordance with the form of the old dispensation, he appointed circumcision to confirm his covenant, but that it being abrogated, the same reason for confirmation still continues, a reason which we have in common with the Jews. Hence it is always necessary carefully to consider what is common to both, and wherein they differed from us. The covenant is common, and the reason for confirming it is common. The mode of confirming it is so far different, that they had circumcision, instead of which we now have baptism. Otherwise, if the testimony by which the Jews were assured of the salvation of their seed is taken from us, the consequence will be, that, by the advent of Christ, the grace of God, which was formerly given to the Jews, is more obscure and less perfectly attested to us. If this cannot be said without extreme insult to Christ, by whom the infinite goodness of the Father has been more brightly and benignly than ever shed upon the earth, and declared to men, it must be confessed that it cannot be more confined, and less clearly manifested, than under the obscure shadows of the Law.

9. It remains briefly to indicate what benefit redounds from the observance, both to believers who bring their children to the church to be baptised, and to the infants themselves, to whom the sacred water is applied, that no one may despise the ordinance as useless or superfluous: though any one who would think of ridiculing baptism under this pretence, would also ridicule the divine ordinance of circumcision: for what can they adduce to impugn the one, that may not be retorted against the other? Thus the Lord punishes the arrogance of those who forthwith condemn whatever their carnal sense cannot comprehend. But God furnishes us with other weapons to repress their stupidity. His holy institution, from which we feel that our faith derives admirable consolation, deserves not to be called superfluous. For the divine symbol communicated to the child, as with the impress of a seal, confirms the promise given to the godly parent, and declares that the Lord will be a God not to him only, but to his seed; not merely visiting him with his grace and goodness, but his posterity also to the thousandth generation. When the infinite goodness of God is thus displayed, it, in the first place, furnishes most ample materials for proclaiming his glory, and fills pious breasts with no ordinary joy, urging them more strongly to love their affectionate Parent, when they see that, on their account, he extends his care to their posterity. I am not moved by the objection, that the promise ought to be sufficient to confirm the salvation of our children. It has seemed otherwise to God, who, seeing our weakness, has herein been pleased to condescend to it. Let those, then, who embrace the promise of mercy to their children, consider it as their duty to offer them to the Church, to be sealed with the symbol of mercy, and animate themselves to surer confidence, on seeing with the bodily eye the covenant of the Lord engraven on the bodies of their children. On the other hand, children derive some benefit from their baptism, when, being ingrafted into the body of the Church, they are made an object of greater interest to the other members. Then when they have grown up, they are thereby strongly urged to an earnest desire of serving God, who has received them as sons by the formal symbol of adoption, before, from nonage, they were able to recognise him as their Father. In fine, we ought to stand greatly in awe of the denunciation, that God will take vengeance on every one who despises to impress the symbol of the covenant on his child (Gen. 17:15), such contempt being a rejection, and, as it were, abjuration of the offered grace.

✝ CHAPTER 17 ✝

Of the Lord's Supper, and the benefits conferred by it.

Sections

1. Why the Holy Supper was instituted by Christ. The knowledge of the sacrament, how necessary. The signs used. Why there are no others appointed.

2. The manifold uses and advantages of this sacrament to the pious.

3. The Lord's Supper exhibits the great blessings of redemption, and even Christ himself. This even evident from the words of the institution. The thing specially to be considered in them. Congruity of the signs and the things signified.

4. The chief parts of this sacrament.

5. How Christ, the Bread of Life, is to be received by us. Two faults to be avoided. The receiving of it must bear reference both to faith and the effect of faith. What meant by eating Christ. In what sense Christ the bread of life.

10. No distance of place can impede it. In the Supper it is not presented as an empty symbol, but, as the apostle testifies, we receive the reality. Objection, that the expression is figurative. Answer. A sure rule with regard to the sacraments.

11. Conclusion of the first part of the chapter. The sacrament of the Supper consists of two parts – corporeal signs, and spiritual truth. These comprehend the meaning, matter, and effect. Christ truly exhibited to us by symbols.

1. After God has once received us into his family, it is not that he may regard us in the light of servants, but of sons, performing the part of a kind and anxious parent, and providing for our maintenance during the whole course of our lives. And, not contented with this, he has been pleased by a pledge to assure us of his continued liberality. To this end, he has given another sacrament to his Church by the hand of his only begotten Son – a spiritual feast, at which Christ testifies that he himself is living bread (Jn 6:51), on which our souls feed, for a true and blessed immortality. Now, as the knowledge of this great mystery is most necessary, and, in proportion to its importance, demands an accurate exposition, and Satan, in order to deprive the Church of this inestimable treasure, long ago introduced, first, mists, and then darkness, to obscure its light, and stirred up strife and contention to alienate the minds of the simple from a relish for this sacred food, and in our age, also, has tried the same artifice, I will proceed, after giving a simple summary adapted to the capacity of the ignorant, to explain those difficulties by which Satan has tried to ensnare the world. First, then, the signs are bread and wine, which represent the invisible food which we receive from the body and blood of Christ. For as God, regenerating us in baptism, ingrafts us into the fellowship of his Church, and makes us his by adoption, so we have said that he performs the office of a provident parent, in continually supplying the food by which he may sustain and preserve us in the life to which he has begotten us by his word. Moreover, Christ is the only food of our soul, and, therefore, our heavenly Father invites us to him, that, refreshed by communion with him, we may ever and anon gather new vigour until we reach the heavenly immortality. But as this mystery of the secret union of Christ with believers is incomprehensible by nature, he exhibits its figure and image in visible signs adapted to our capacity, nay, by giving, as it were, earnests and

badges, he makes it as certain to us as if it were seen by the eye; the familiarity of the similitude giving it access to minds however dull, and showing that souls are fed by Christ just as the corporeal life is sustained by bread and wine. We now, therefore, understand the end which this mystical benediction has in view – to assure us that the body of Christ was once sacrificed for us, so that we may now eat it, and, eating, feel within ourselves the efficacy of that one sacrifice, that his blood was once shed for us so as to be our perpetual drink. This is the force of the promise which is added, 'Take, eat; this is my body, which is broken for you' (Mt. 26:26, etc.). The body which was once offered for our salvation we are enjoined to take and eat, that, while we see ourselves made partakers of it, we may safely conclude that the virtue of that death will be efficacious in us. Hence he terms the cup the covenant in his blood. For the covenant which he once sanctioned by his blood he in a manner renews, or rather continues, in so far as regards the confirmation of our faith, as often as he stretches forth his sacred blood as drink to us.

2. Pious souls can derive great confidence and delight from this sacrament, as being a testimony that they form one body with Christ, so that everything which is his they may call their own. Hence it follows, that we can confidently assure ourselves, that eternal life, of which he himself is the heir, is ours, and that the kingdom of heaven, into which he has entered, can no more be taken from us than from him; on the other hand, that we cannot be condemned for our sins, from the guilt of which he absolves us, seeing he has been pleased that these should be imputed to himself as if they were his own. This is the wondrous exchange made by his boundless goodness. Having become with us the Son of Man, he has made us with himself sons of God. By his own descent to the earth he has prepared our ascent to heaven. Having received our mortality, he has bestowed on us his immortality. Having undertaken our weakness, he has made us strong in his strength. Having submitted to our poverty, he has transferred to us his riches. Having taken upon himself the burden of unrighteousness with which we were oppressed, he has clothed us with his righteousness.

3. To all these things we have a complete attestation in this sacrament, enabling us certainly to conclude that they are as truly exhibited to us as if Christ were placed in bodily presence before our view, or handled by our hands. For these are words which can never lie nor deceive – Take, eat, drink. This is my body, which is broken for you: this is my blood, which is shed for the remission of sins. In bidding us take, he intimates that it is ours: in bidding us eat, he intimates that it becomes one substance with us: in affirming of his body that it was broken, and of his blood that it was shed for us, he shows that both were not so much his own as ours, because he took and laid down both, not for his own advantage, but for our salvation. And we ought carefully to observe, that the chief, and almost the whole energy of the sacrament, consists in these words, It is broken for you: it is shed for you. It would not be of much importance to us that the body and blood of the Lord are now distributed, had they not once been set forth for our redemption and salvation. Wherefore they are represented under bread and wine, that we may learn that they are not only ours, but intended to nourish our spiritual life; that is, as we formerly observed, by the corporeal things which are produced in the sacrament, we are by a kind of analogy conducted to spiritual things. Thus when bread is given as a symbol of the body of Christ, we must immediately think of this similitude. As bread nourishes, sustains, and protects our bodily life, so the body of Christ is the only food to invigorate and keep alive the soul. When we behold wine set forth as a symbol of blood, we must think that such use as wine serves to the body, the same is spiritually bestowed by the blood of Christ; and the use is to foster, refresh, strengthen, and exhilarate. For if we duly consider what profit we have gained by the breaking of his sacred body, and the shedding of his blood, we shall clearly perceive that these properties of bread and wine, agreeably to this analogy, most appropriately represent it when they are communicated to us.

4.   Therefore, it is not the principal part of a sacrament simply to hold forth the body of Christ to us without any higher consideration, but rather to seal and confirm that promise by which he testifies that his flesh is meat indeed, and his blood drink indeed, nourishing us unto life eternal, and by which he affirms that he is the bread of life, of which, whosoever shall eat, shall live for ever – I say, to seal and confirm that promise, and in order to do so, it sends us to the cross of Christ, where that promise was performed and fulfilled in all its parts. For we do not eat Christ duly and savingly unless as crucified, while with lively apprehension we perceive the efficacy of his death. When he called himself the bread of life, he did not take that appellation from the sacrament, as some perversely interpret; but such as he was given to us by the Father, such he exhibited himself when becoming partaker of our human mortality, he made us partakers of his divine immortality; when offering himself in sacrifice, he took our curse upon himself, that he might cover us with his blessing, when by his death he devoured and swallowed up death, when in his resurrection he raised our corruptible flesh, which he had put on, to glory and incorruption.

5.   It only remains that the whole become ours by application. This is done by means of the Gospel, and more clearly by the sacred Supper, where Christ offers himself to us with all his blessings, and we receive him in faith. The sacrament, therefore, does not make Christ become for the first time the bread of life; but, while it calls to remembrance that Christ was made the bread of life that we may constantly eat him, it gives us a taste and relish for that bread, and makes us feel its efficacy. For it assures us, first, that whatever Christ did or suffered was done to give us life; and, secondly, that this quickening is eternal; by it we are ceaselessly nourished, sustained, and preserved in life. For as Christ would not have not been the bread of life to us if he had not been born, if he had not died and risen again; so he could not now be the bread of life, were not the efficacy and fruit of his nativity, death, and resurrection, eternal. All this Christ has elegantly expressed in these words, 'The bread that I will give is my flesh, which I will give for the life of the world' (Jn 6:51); doubtless intimating, that his body will be as bread in regard to the spiritual life of the soul, because it was to be delivered to death for our salvation, and that he extends it to us for food when he makes us partakers of it by faith. Wherefore he once gave himself that he might become bread, when he gave himself to be crucified for the redemption of the world; and he gives himself daily, when in the word of the Gospel he offers himself to be partaken by us, inasmuch as he was crucified, when he seals that offer by the sacred mystery of the Supper, and when he accomplishes inwardly what he externally designates. Moreover, two faults are here to be avoided. We must neither, by setting too little value on the signs, dissever them from their meanings to which they are in some degree annexed, nor by immoderately extolling them, seem somewhat to obscure the mysteries themselves. That Christ is the bread of life by which believers are nourished unto eternal life, no man is so utterly devoid of religion as not to acknowledge. But all are not agreed as to the mode of partaking of him. For there are some who define the eating of the flesh of Christ, and the drinking of his blood, to be, in one word, nothing more than believing in Christ himself. But Christ seems to me to have intended to teach something more express and more sublime in that noble discourse, in which he recommends the eating of his flesh – that we are quickened by the true partaking of him, which he designated by the terms eating and drinking, lest any one should suppose that the life which we obtain from him is obtained by simple knowledge. For as it is not the sight but the eating of bread that gives nourishment to the body, so the soul must partake of Christ truly and thoroughly, that by his energy it may grow up into spiritual life. Meanwhile, we admit that this is nothing else than the eating of faith, and that no other eating can be imagined. But there is this difference between their mode of speaking and mine. According to them, to eat is merely to believe; while I maintain that the flesh of Christ is eaten by believing, because it is made ours by faith, and that that eating is the effect and fruit of faith; or, if you will have it more clearly, according to them, eating is faith, whereas it rather seems to me to be a consequence of faith. The difference is little in words, but not little in reality. For, although the apostle teaches that Christ dwells in our hearts by faith (Eph. 3:17), no one will interpret that dwelling to be faith All see that it explains the admirable effect of faith, because to it it is owing that believers have Christ dwelling in them. In this way, the Lord was pleased, by calling himself the bread of life, not only to teach that our salvation is treasured up in the faith of his death and resurrection, but also, by virtue of true communication with him, his life passes into us and becomes ours, just as bread when taken for food gives vigour to the body.

10. The sum is, that the flesh and blood of Christ feed our souls just as bread and wine maintain and support our corporeal life. For there would be no aptitude in the sign, did not our souls find their nourishment in Christ. This could not be, did not Christ truly form one with us, and refresh us by the eating of his flesh, and the drinking of his blood. But though it seems an incredible thing that the flesh of Christ, while at such a distance from us in respect of place, should be food to us, let us remember how far the secret virtue of the Holy Spirit surpasses all our conceptions, and how foolish it is to wish to measure its immensity by our feeble capacity. Therefore, what our mind does not comprehend let faith conceive – that the Spirit truly unites things separated by space. That sacred communion of flesh and blood by which Christ transfuses his life into us, just as if it penetrated our bones and marrow, he testifies and seals in the Supper, and that not by presenting a vain or empty sign, but by there exerting an efficacy of the Spirit by which he fulfils what he promises. And truly the thing there signified he exhibits and offers to all who sit down at that spiritual feast, although it is beneficially received by believers only who receive this great benefit with true faith and heartfelt gratitude. For this reason the apostle said, 'The cup of blessing which we bless, is it not the communion of the blood of Christ? The bread which we break, is it not the communion of the body of Christ?' (1 Cor. 10:16.) There is no ground to object that the expression is figurative, and gives the sign the name of the thing signified. I admit, indeed, that the breaking of bread is a symbol, not the reality. But this being admitted, we duly infer from the exhibition of the symbol that the thing itself is exhibited. For unless we would charge God with deceit, we will never presume to say that he holds forth an empty symbol. Therefore, if by the breaking of bread the Lord truly represents the partaking of his body, there ought to be no doubt whatever that he truly exhibits and performs it. The rule which the pious ought always to observe is, whenever they see the symbols instituted by the Lord, to think and feel surely persuaded that the truth of the thing signified is also present. For why does the Lord put the symbol of his body into your hands, but just to assure you that you truly partake of him? If this is true let us feel as much assured that the visible sign is given us in seal of an invisible gift as that his body itself is given to us.

11.   I hold then (as has always been received in the Church, and is still taught by those who feel aright), that the sacred mystery of the Supper consists of two things – the corporeal signs, which, presented to the eye, represent invisible things in a manner adapted to our weak capacity, and the spiritual truth, which is at once figured and exhibited by the signs. When attempting familiarly to explain its nature, I am accustomed to set down three things – the thing meant, the matter which depends on it, and the virtue or efficacy consequent upon both. The thing meant consists in the promises which are in a manner included in the sign. By the matter, or substance, I mean Christ, with his death and resurrection. By the effect, I understand redemption, justification, sanctification, eternal life, and all other benefits which Christ bestows upon us. Moreover, though all these things have respect to faith, I leave no room for the cavil, that when I say Christ is conceived by faith, I mean that he is only conceived by the intellect and imagination. He is offered by the promises, not that we may stop short at the sight or mere knowledge of him, but that we may enjoy true communion with him. And, indeed, I see not how any one can expect to have redemption and righteousness in the cross of Christ, and life in his death, without trusting first of all to true communion with Christ himself. Those blessings could not reach us, did not Christ previously make himself ours. I say then, that in the mystery of the Supper, by the symbols of bread and wine, Christ, his body and his blood, are truly exhibited to us, that in them he fulfilled all obedience, in order to procure righteousness for us – first that we might become one body with him; and, secondly, that being made partakers of his substance, we might feel the result of this fact in the participation of all his blessings.

THE BOOK OF MARTYRS

by

✠ JOHN FOXE ✠

An edited edition based on an 1869 publication revised by W. Bramley-Moore

A history of the lives, sufferings and triumphant deaths of the
early Christians and the protestant martyrs

CONTENTS

CHAPTER 1

History of Christian Martyrs to the First General Persecutions

Introduction

Christ our Saviour, in the Gospel of St Matthew, hearing the confession of Simon Peter, who, first of all other, openly acknowledged Him to be the Son of God, and perceiving the secret hand of His Father therein, called him (alluding to his name) a rock, upon which rock He would build His Church so strong that the gates of hell should not prevail against it. In which words three things are to be noted: First, that Christ will have a Church in this world. Secondly, that the same Church should mightily be impugned, not only by the world, but also by the uttermost strength and powers of all hell. And, thirdly, that the same Church, notwithstanding the uttermost of the devil and all his malice, should continue.

Which prophecy of Christ we see wonderfully to be verified, insomuch that the whole course of the Church to this day may seem nothing else but a verifying of the said prophecy. First, that Christ hath set up a Church, needeth no declaration. Secondly, what force of princes, kings, monarchs, governors, and rulers of this world, with their subjects, publicly and privately, with all their strength and cunning, have bent themselves against this Church! And, thirdly, how the said Church, all this notwithstanding, hath yet endured and holden its own! What storms and tempests it hath overpast, wondrous it is to behold: for the more evident declaration whereof, I have addressed this present history, to the end, first, that the wonderful works of God in His Church might appear to His glory; also that, the continuance and proceedings of the Church, from time to time, being set forth, more knowledge and experience may redound thereby, to the profit of the reader and edification of Christian faith.

As it is not our business to enlarge upon our Saviour's history, either before or after His crucifixion, we shall only find it necessary to remind our readers of the discomfiture of the Jews by His subsequent resurrection. Although one apostle had betrayed Him; although another had denied Him, under the solemn sanction of an oath; and although the rest had forsaken Him, unless we may except 'the disciple who was known unto the high-priest'; the history of His resurrection gave a new direction to all their hearts, and, after the mission of the Holy Spirit, imparted new confidence to their minds. The powers with which they were endued emboldened them to proclaim His name, to the confusion of the Jewish rulers, and the astonishment of Gentile proselytes.

St Stephen

St Stephen suffered the next in order. His death was occasioned by the faithful manner in which he preached the Gospel to the betrayers and murderers of Christ. To such a degree of madness were they excited, that they cast him out of the city and stoned him to death. The time when he suffered is generally supposed to have been at the Passover which succeeded to that of our Lord's crucifixion, and to the era of his ascension, in the following spring.

Upon this a great persecution was raised against all who professed their belief in Christ as the Messiah, or as a prophet. We are immediately told by St Luke, that 'there was a great persecution against the church which was at Jerusalem' and that 'they were all scattered abroad throughout the regions of Judaea and Samaria, except the apostles.'

About two thousand Christians, with Nicanor, one of the seven deacons, suffered martyrdom during the 'persecution that arose about Stephen.'

James the Great

The next martyr we meet with, according to St Luke, in the History of the Apostles' Acts, was James the son of Zebedee, the elder brother of John, and a relative of our Lord; for his mother Salome was cousin-german to the Virgin Mary. It was not until ten years after the death of Stephen that the second martyrdom took place; for no sooner had Herod Agrippa been appointed governor of Judea, than, with a view to ingratiate himself with them, he raised a sharp persecution against the Christians, and determined to make an effectual blow, by striking at their leaders. The account given us by an eminent primitive writer, Clemens Alexandrinus, ought not to be overlooked; that, as James was led to the place of martyrdom, his accuser was brought to repent of his conduct by the apostle's extraordinary courage and undauntedness, and fell down at his feet to request his pardon, professing himself a Christian, and resolving that James should not receive the crown of martyrdom alone. Hence they were both beheaded at the same time. Thus did the first apostolic martyr cheerfully and resolutely receive that cup, which he had told our Saviour he was ready to drink. Timon and Parmenas suffered martyrdom about the same time; the one at Philippi, and the other in Macedonia. These events took place AD 44.

Philip

Was born at Bethsaida, in Galilee and was first called by the name of 'disciple.' He laboured diligently in Upper Asia, and suffered martyrdom at Heliopolis, in Phrygia. He was scourged, thrown into prison, and afterwards crucified, AD 54.

Matthew

Whose occupation was that of a toll-gatherer, was born at Nazareth. He wrote his Gospel in Hebrew, which was afterwards translated into Greek by James the Less. The scene of his labours was Parthia, and Ethiopia, in which latter country he suffered martyrdom, being slain with a halberd in the city of Nadabah, AD 60.

James the Less

Is supposed by some to have been the brother of our Lord, by a former wife of Joseph. This is very doubtful, and accords too much with the Catholic superstition, that Mary never had any other children except our Saviour. He was elected to the oversight of the churches of Jerusalem; and was the author of the Epistle ascribed to James in the sacred canon. At the age of ninety-four he was beaten and stoned by the Jews; and finally had his brains dashed out with a fuller's club.

Matthias

Of whom less is known than of most of the other disciples, was elected to fill the vacant place of Judas. He was stoned at Jerusalem and then beheaded.

Andrew

Was the brother of Peter. He preached the gospel to many Asiatic nations; but on his arrival at Edessa he was taken and crucified on a cross, the two ends of which were fixed transversely in the ground. Hence the derivation of the term St Andrew's Cross.

St Mark

Was born of Jewish parents of the tribe of Levi. He is supposed to have been converted to Christianity by Peter, whom he served as an amanuensis, and under whose inspection he wrote his Gospel in the Greek language. Mark was dragged to pieces by the people of Alexandria, at the great solemnity of Serapis their idol, ending his life under their merciless hands.

Peter

Among many other saints, the blessed apostle Peter was condemned to death, and crucified, as some do write, at Rome; albeit some others, and not without cause, do doubt thereof. Hegesippus saith that Nero sought matter against Peter to put him to death; which, when the people perceived, they entreated Peter with much ado that he would fly the city. Peter, through their importunity at length persuaded, prepared himself to avoid. But, coming to the gate, he saw the Lord Christ come to meet him, to whom he, worshipping, said, 'Lord, whither dost Thou go?' To whom He answered and said, 'I am come again to be crucified.' By this, Peter, perceiving his suffering to be understood, returned into the city. Jerome saith that he was crucified, his head being down and his feet upward, himself so requiring, because he was (he said) unworthy to be crucified after the same form and manner as the Lord was.

Paul

Paul, the apostle, who before was called Saul, after his great travail and unspeakable labours in promoting the Gospel of Christ, suffered also in this first persecution under Nero. Abdias, declareth that under his execution Nero sent two of his esquires, Ferega and Parthemius, to bring him word of his death. They, coming to Paul instructing the people, desired him to pray for them, that they might believe; who told them that shortly after they should believe and be baptised at His sepulcher. This done, the soldiers came and led him out of the city to the place of execution, where he, after his prayers made, gave his neck to the sword.

Jude

The brother of James, was commonly called Thaddeus. He was crucified at Edessa, AD 72.

Bartholomew

Preached in several countries, and having translated the Gospel of Matthew into the language of India, he propagated it in that country. He was at length cruelly beaten and then crucified by the impatient idolaters.

Thomas

Called Didymus, preached the Gospel in Parthia and India, where exciting the rage of the pagan priests, he was martyred by being thrust through with a spear.

Luke

The evangelist, was the author of the Gospel which goes under his name. He travelled with Paul through various countries, and is supposed to have been hanged on an olive tree, by the idolatrous priests of Greece.

Simon

Surnamed Zelotes, preached the Gospel in Mauritania, Africa, and even in Britain, in which latter country he was crucified, AD 74.

John

The 'beloved disciple' was brother to James the Great. The churches of Smyrna, Pergamos, Sardis, Philadelphia, Laodicea, and Thyatira, were founded by him. From Ephesus he was ordered to be sent to Rome, where it is affirmed he was cast into a cauldron of boiling oil. He escaped by miracle, without injury. Domitian afterwards banished him to the Isle of Patmos, where he wrote the Book of Revelation. Nerva, the successor of Domitian, recalled him. He was the only apostle who escaped a violent death.

Barnabas

Was of Cyprus, but of Jewish descent, his death is supposed to have taken place about AD 73.

And yet, notwithstanding all these continual persecutions and horrible punishments, the Church daily increased, deeply rooted in the doctrine of the apostles and of men apostolical, and watered plenteously with the blood of saints.

✝ CHAPTER 2 ✝
The Ten Primitive Persecutions

The First Persecution, Under Nero, AD 67

The first persecution of the Church took place in the year 67, under Nero, the sixth emperor of Rome. This monarch reigned for the space of five years, with tolerable credit to himself, but then gave way to the greatest extravagancy of temper, and to the most atrocious barbarities. Among other diabolical whims, he ordered that the city of Rome should be set on fire, which order was executed by his officers, guards, and servants. While the imperial city was in flames, he went up to the tower of Macaenas, played upon his harp, sung the song of the burning of Troy, and openly declared that he wished the ruin of all things before his death. Besides the noble pile, called the Circus, many other palaces and houses were consumed; several thousands perished in the flames, were smothered in the smoke, or buried beneath the ruins.

This dreadful conflagration continued nine days; when Nero, finding that his conduct was greatly blamed, and a severe odium cast upon him, determined to lay the whole upon the Christians, at once to excuse himself, and have an opportunity of glutting his sight with new cruelties. This was the occasion of the first persecution; and the barbarities exercised on the Christians were such as even excited the commiseration of the Romans themselves. Nero even refined upon cruelty, and contrived all manner of punishments for the Christians that the most infernal imagination could design. In particular, he had some sewed up in skins of wild beasts, and then worried by dogs until they expired; and others dressed in shirts made stiff with wax, fixed to axletrees, and set on fire in his gardens, in order to illuminate them. This persecution was general throughout the whole Roman Empire; but it rather increased than diminished the spirit of Christianity. In the course of it, St Paul and St Peter were martyred.

To their names may be added Erastus, chamberlain of Corinth; Aristarchus, the Macedonian, and Trophimus, an Ephesian, converted by St Paul, and fellow-labourer with him; Joseph, commonly called Barsabas, and Ananias, bishop of Damascus; each of the Seventy.

The Second Persecution, Under Domitian, AD 81

The emperor Domitian, who was naturally inclined to cruelty, first slew his brother, and then raised the second persecution against the Christians. In his rage he put to death some of the Roman senators, some through malice; and others to confiscate their estates. He then commanded all the lineage of David be put to death.

Among the numerous martyrs that suffered during this persecution was Simeon, bishop of Jerusalem, who was crucified; and St John, who was boiled in oil, and afterward banished to Patmos. Flavia, the daughter of a Roman senator, was likewise banished to Pontus; and a law was made, 'That no Christian, once brought before the tribunal, should be exempted from punishment without renouncing his religion.'

A variety of fabricated tales were, during this reign, composed in order to injure the Christians. Such was the infatuation of the pagans, that, if famine, pestilence, or earthquakes afflicted any of the Roman provinces, it was laid upon the Christians. These persecutions among the Christians increased the number of informers and many, for the sake of gain, swore away the lives of the innocent.

Another hardship was, that, when any Christians were brought before the magistrates, a test oath was proposed, when, if they refused to take it, death was pronounced against them; and if they confessed themselves Christians, the sentence was the same.

The following were the most remarkable among the numerous martyrs who suffered during this persecution.

Dionysius, the Areopagite, was an Athenian by birth, and educated in all the useful and ornamental literature of Greece. He then travelled to Egypt to study astronomy, and made very particular observations on the great and supernatural eclipse, which happened at the time of our Saviour's crucifixion. The sanctity of his conversation and the purity of his manners recommended him so strongly to the Christians in general, that he was appointed bishop of Athens.

Nicodemus, a benevolent Christian of some distinction, suffered at Rome during the rage of Domitian's persecution.

Protasius and Gervasius were martyred at Milan.

Timothy was the celebrated disciple of St Paul, and bishop of Ephesus, where he zealously governed the Church until AD 97. At this period, as the pagans were about to celebrate a feast called Catagogion, Timothy, meeting the procession, severely reproved them for their ridiculous idolatry, which so exasperated the people that they fell upon him with their clubs, and beat him in so dreadful a manner that he expired of the bruises two days later.

The Third Persecution, Under Trajan, AD 108

In the third persecution Pliny the Second, a man learned and famous, seeing the lamentable slaughter of Christians, and moved therewith to pity, wrote to Trajan, certifying him that there were many thousands of them daily put to death, of which none did any thing contrary to the Roman laws worthy of persecution. 'The whole account they gave of their crime or error (whichever it is to be called) amounted only to this – that they were accustomed on a stated day to meet before daylight, and to repeat together a set form of prayer to Christ as a God, and to bind themselves by an obligation not indeed to commit wickedness; but, on the contrary, never to commit theft, robbery, or adultery, never to falsify their word, never to defraud any man: after which it was their custom to separate, and reassemble to partake in common of a harmless meal.'

In this persecution suffered the blessed martyr, Ignatius, who is held in famous reverence among very many. This Ignatius was appointed to the bishopric of Antioch next after Peter in succession. Some do say, that he, being sent from Syria to Rome, because he professed Christ, was given to the wild beasts to be devoured. It is also said of him, that when he passed through Asia, being under the most strict custody of his keepers, he strengthened and confirmed the churches through all the cities as he went, both with his exhortations and preaching of the Word of God. Accordingly, having come to Smyrna, he wrote to the Church at Rome, exhorting them not to use means for his deliverance from martyrdom, lest they should deprive him of that which he most longed and hoped for. 'Now I begin to be a disciple. I care for nothing, of visible or invisible things, so that I may but win Christ. Let fire and the cross, let the companies of wild beasts, let breaking of bones and tearing of limbs, let the grinding of the whole body, and all the malice of the devil, come upon me; be it so, only may I win Christ Jesus!' And even when he was sentenced to be thrown to the beasts, such as the burning desire that he had to suffer, that he spake, what time he heard the lions roaring, saying: 'I am the wheat of Christ: I am going to be ground with the teeth of wild beasts, that I may be found pure bread.'

Trajan being succeeded by Adrian, the latter continued this third persecution with as much severity as his predecessor. About this time Alexander, bishop of Rome, with his two deacons, were martyred; as were Quirinus and Hernes, with their families;

Zenon, a Roman nobleman, and about ten thousand other Christians.

In Mount Ararat many were crucified, crowned with thorns, and spears run into their sides, in imitation of Christ's passion. Eustachius, a brave and successful Roman commander, was by the emperor ordered to join in an idolatrous sacrifice to celebrate some of his own victories; but his faith (being a Christian in his heart) was so much greater than his vanity, that he nobly refused it. Enraged at the denial, the ungrateful emperor forgot the service of this skilful commander, and ordered him and his whole family to be martyred.

At the martyrdom of Faustines and Jovita, brothers and citizens of Brescia, their torments were so many, and their patience so great, that Calocerius, a pagan, beholding them, was struck with admiration, and exclaimed in a kind of ecstasy, 'Great is the God of the Christians!' for which he was apprehended, and suffered a similar fate.

Many other similar cruelties and rigours were exercised against the Christians, until Quadratus, bishop of Athens, made a learned apology in their favour before the emperor, who happened to be there and Aristides, a philosopher of the same city, wrote an elegant epistle, which caused Adrian to relax in his severities, and relent in their favour.

Adrian dying AD 138, was succeeded by Antoninus Pius, one of the most amiable monarchs that ever reigned, and who stayed the persecutions against the Christians.

The Fourth Persecution, Under Marcus Aurelius Antoninus, AD 162

Marcus Aurelius, followed about the year of our Lord 161, a man of nature more stern and severe; and, although in study of philosophy and in civil government no less commendable, yet, toward the Christians sharp and fierce; by whom was moved the fourth persecution.

The cruelties used in this persecution were such that many of the spectators shuddered with horror at the sight, and were astonished at the intrepidity of the sufferers. Some of the martyrs were obliged to pass, with their already wounded feet, over thorns, nails, sharp shells, etc. upon their points, others were scourged until their sinews and veins lay bare, and after suffering the most excruciating tortures that could be devised, they were destroyed by the most terrible deaths.

Germanicus, a young man, but a true Christian, being delivered to the wild beasts on account of his faith, behaved with such astonishing courage that several pagans became converts to a faith which inspired such fortitude.

Polycarp, the venerable bishop of Smyrna, hearing that persons were seeking for him, escaped, but was discovered by a child. After feasting the guards who apprehended him, he desired an hour in prayer, which being allowed, he prayed with such fervency, that his guards repented that they had been instrumental in taking him. He was, however, carried before the proconsul, condemned, and burnt in the market-place.

The proconsul then urged him, saying, 'Swear, and I will release thee; reproach Christ.'

Polycarp answered, 'Eighty and six years have I served him, and he never once wronged me; how then shall I blaspheme my King, Who hath saved me?' At the stake to which he was only tied, but not nailed as usual, as he assured them he should stand immovable, the flames, on their kindling the fagots, encircled his body, like an arch, without touching him; and the executioner, on seeing this, was ordered to pierce him with a sword, when so great a quantity of blood flowed out as extinguished the fire. But his body, at the instigation of the enemies of the Gospel, especially Jews, was ordered to be consumed in the pile, and the request of his friends, who wished to give it Christian burial, rejected. They nevertheless collected his bones and as much of his remains as possible, and caused them to be decently interred.

Metrodorus, a minister, who preached boldly, and Pionius, who made some excellent apologies for the Christian faith, were likewise burnt. Carpus and Papilus, two worthy Christians, and Agatonica, a pious woman, suffered martyrdom at Pergamopolis, in Asia.

Felicitatis, an illustrious Roman lady, of a considerable family, and the most shining virtues, was a devout Christian. She had seven sons, whom she had educated with the most exemplary piety.

Januarius, the eldest, was scourged, and pressed to death with weights; Felix and Philip, the two next had their brains dashed out with clubs; Silvanus, the fourth, was murdered by being thrown from a precipice; and the three younger sons, Alexander, Vitalis, and Martial, were beheaded. The mother was beheaded with the same sword as the three latter.

Justin, the celebrated philosopher, fell a martyr in this persecution. He was a native of Neapolis, in Samaria, and was born AD 103. Justin was a great lover of truth, and a universal scholar; he investigated the Stoic and Peripatetic philosophy, and attempted the Pythagorean; but the behaviour of one of its professors disgusting him, he applied himself to the Platonic, in which he took great delight. About the year 133, when he was thirty years of age, he became a convert to Christianity, and then, for the first time, perceived the real nature of truth.

He wrote an elegant epistle to the Gentiles, and employed his talents in convincing the Jews of the truth of the Christian rites; spending a great deal of time in travelling, until he took up his abode in Rome, and fixed his habitation upon the Viminal mount.

He kept a public school, taught many who afterward became great men, and wrote a treatise to confuse heresies of all kinds. As the pagans began to treat the Christians with great severity, Justin wrote his first apology in their favour. This piece displays great learning and genius, and occasioned the emperor to publish an edict in favour of the Christians.

Soon after, he entered into frequent contests with Crescens, a person of a vicious life and conversation, but a celebrated cynic philosopher; and his arguments appeared so powerful, yet disgusting to the cynic, that he resolved on, and in the sequel accomplished, his destruction.

The second apology of Justin, upon certain severities, gave Crescens the cynic an opportunity of prejudicing the emperor against the writer of it; upon which Justin, and six of his companions, were apprehended. Being commanded to sacrifice to the pagan idols, they refused, and were condemned to be scourged, and then beheaded; which sentence was executed with all imaginable severity. Several were beheaded for refusing to sacrifice to the image of Jupiter; in particular Concordus, a deacon of the city of Spolito.

Some of the restless northern nations having risen in arms against Rome, the emperor marched to encounter them. He was, however, drawn into an ambuscade, and dreaded the loss of his whole army. Enveloped with mountains, surrounded by enemies, and perishing with thirst, the pagan deities were invoked in vain; when the men belonging to the militine, or thundering legion, who were all Christians, were commanded to call upon their God for succour. A miraculous deliverance immediately ensued; a prodigious quantity of rain fell, which, being caught by the men, and filling their dykes, afforded a sudden and astonishing relief. It appears that the storm which miraculously flashed in the face of the enemy so intimidated them, that part deserted to the Roman army; the rest were defeated, and the revolted provinces entirely recovered.

This affair occasioned the persecution to subside for some time, at least in those parts immediately under the inspection of the emperor; but we find that it soon after raged in France, particularly at Lyons, where the tortures to which many of the Christians were put, almost exceed the powers of description.

The principal of these martyrs were Vetius Agathus, a young man; Blandina, a Christian lady, of a weak constitution; Sanctus, a deacon of Vienna; red-hot plates of brass were placed upon the tenderest parts of his body; Biblias, a weak woman, once an apostate. Attalus, of Pergamus; and Pothinus, the venerable bishop of Lyons, who was ninety years of age. Blandina, on the day when she and the three other champions were first brought into the amphitheater, she was suspended on a piece of wood fixed in the ground, and exposed as food for the wild beasts; at which time, by her earnest prayers, she encouraged others. But none of the wild beasts would touch her, so that she was remanded to prison. When she was again produced for the third and last time, she was accompanied by Ponticus, a youth of fifteen, and the constancy of their faith so enraged the multitude that neither the sex of the one nor the youth of the other were respected, being exposed to all manner of punishments and tortures. Being strengthened by Blandina, he persevered unto death; and she, after enduring all the torments heretofore mentioned, was at length slain with the sword.

When the Christians, upon these occasions, received martyrdom, they were ornamented, and crowned with garlands of flowers; for which they, in heaven, received eternal crowns of glory.

It has been said that the lives of the early Christians consisted of 'persecution above ground and prayer below ground'. Their lives are expressed by the Coliseum and the catacombs. Beneath Rome are the excavations which we call the catacombs, which were at once temples and tombs. The early Church of Rome might well be called the Church of the Catacombs. There are some sixty catacombs near Rome, in which some six hundred miles of galleries have been traced, and these are not all. These galleries are about eight feet high and from three to five feet wide, containing on either side several rows of long, low, horizontal recesses, one above another like berths in a ship. In these the dead bodies were placed and the front closed, either by a single marble slab or several great tiles laid in mortar. On these slabs or tiles, epitaphs or symbols are graved or painted. Both pagans and Christians buried their dead in these catacombs. When the Christian graves have been opened the skeletons tell their own terrible tale. Heads are found severed from the body, ribs and shoulder blades are broken, bones are often calcined from fire. But despite the awful story of persecution that we may read here, the inscriptions breathe forth peace and joy and triumph. Here are a few: 'Here lies Marcia, put to rest in a dream of peace'; 'Lawrence to his sweetest son, borne away of angels'; 'Victorious in peace and in Christ'; 'Being called away, he went in peace.'

Remember when reading these inscriptions the story the skeletons tell of persecution, of torture, and of fire. But the full force of these epitaphs is seen when we contrast them with the pagan epitaphs, such as: 'Live for the present hour, since we are sure of nothing else'; 'I lift my hands against the gods who took me away at the age of twenty though I had done no harm'; 'Once I was not. Now I am not. I know nothing about it, and it is no concern of mine'; 'Traveller, curse me not as you pass, for I am in darkness and cannot answer.'

The most frequent Christian symbols on the walls of the catacombs, are, the good shepherd with the lamb on his shoulder, a ship under full sail, harps, anchors, crowns, vines, and above all the fish.

The Fifth Persecution, Commencing with Severus, AD 192

Severus, having been recovered from a severe fit of sickness by a Christian, became a great favourer of the Christians in general; but the prejudice and fury of the ignorant multitude prevailing, obsolete laws were put in execution against the Christians. The progress of Christianity alarmed the pagans, and they revived the stale calumny of placing accidental misfortunes to the account of its professors, AD 192.

But, though persecuting malice raged, yet the Gospel shone with resplendent brightness; and, firm as an impregnable rock, withstood the attacks of its boisterous enemies with success. Tertullian, who lived in this age, informs us that if the Christians had collectively withdrawn themselves from the Roman territories, the empire would have been greatly depopulated.

Victor, bishop of Rome, suffered martyrdom in the first year of the third century, AD 201. Leonidus, the father of the celebrated Origen, was beheaded for being a Christian. Many of Origen's hearers likewise suffered martyrdom; particularly two brothers, named Plutarchus and Serenus; another Serenus, Heron, and Heraclides, were beheaded. Rhais had boiled pitch poured upon her head, and was then burnt, as was Marcella her mother. Potainiena, the sister of Rhais, was executed in the same manner as Rhais had been; but Basilides, an officer belonging to the army, and ordered to attend her execution, became her convert.

Basilides being, as an officer, required to take a certain oath, refused, saying, that he could not swear by the Roman idols, as he was a Christian. Struck with surprise, the people could not, at first, believe what they heard; but he had no sooner confirmed the same, than he was dragged before the judge, committed to prison, and speedily afterward beheaded.

Irenaeus, bishop of Lyons, was born in Greece, and received both a polite and a Christian education. It is generally supposed that the account of the persecutions at Lyons was written by himself. He succeeded the martyr Pothinus as bishop of Lyons, and ruled his diocese with great propriety; he was a zealous opposer of heresies in general, and, about AD 187, he wrote a celebrated tract against heresy. Victor, the bishop of Rome, wanting to impose the keeping of Easter there, in preference to other places, it occasioned some disorders among the Christians. In particular, Irenaeus wrote him a synodical epistle, in the name of the Gallic churches. This zeal, in favour of Christianity, pointed him out as an object of resentment to the emperor; and in AD 202, he was beheaded.

The persecutions now extending to Africa, many were martyred in that quarter of the globe; the most particular of whom we shall mention.

Perpetua, a married lady, of about twenty-two years. Those who suffered with her were, Felicitas, a married lady, big with child at the time of her being apprehended, and Revocatus, catechumen of Carthage, and a slave. The names of the other prisoners, destined to suffer upon this occasion, were Saturninus, Secundulus, and Satur. On the day appointed for their execution, they were led to the amphitheatre. Satur, Saturninus, and Revocatus were ordered to run the gauntlet between the hunters, or such as had the care of the wild beasts. The hunters being drawn up in two ranks, they ran between, and were severely lashed as they passed. Felicitas and Perpetua were stripped, in order to be thrown to a mad bull, which made his first attack upon Perpetua, and stunned her; he then darted at Felicitas, and gored her dreadfully; but not killing them, the executioner did that office with a sword. Revocatus and Satur were destroyed by wild beasts; Saturninus was beheaded; and Secundulus died in prison. These executions were in 205, on the eighth day of March.

Speratus and twelve others were likewise beheaded; as was Androcles in France. Asclepiades, bishop of Antioch, suffered many tortures, but his life was spared.

Cecilia, a young lady of good family in Rome, was married to a gentleman named Valerian. She converted her husband and brother, who were beheaded; and the maximus, or officer, who led them to execution, becoming their convert, suffered the same fate. The lady was placed naked in a scalding bath, and having continued there a considerable time, her head was struck off with a sword, AD 222.

Calistus, bishop of Rome, was martyred, AD 224; but the manner of his death is not recorded; and Urban, bishop of Rome, met the same fate AD 232.

The Sixth Persecution, Under Maximus, AD 235

In Cappadocia, the president, Seremianus, did all he could to exterminate the Christians from that province.

The principal persons who perished under this reign were Pontianus, bishop of Rome; Anteros, a Grecian, his successor, who gave offence to the government by collecting the acts of the martyrs, Pammachius and Quiritus, Roman senators, with all their families, and many other Christians; Simplicius, senator; Calepodius, a Christian minister, thrown into the Tyber; Martina, a noble and beautiful virgin; and Hippolitus, a Christian prelate, tied to a wild horse, and dragged until he expired.

During this persecution, raised by Maximus, numberless Christians were slain without trial, and buried indiscriminately in heaps, sometimes fifty or sixty being cast into a pit together, without the least decency.

The tyrant Maximus dying, AD 238, was succeeded by Gordian, during whose reign, and that of his successor Philip, the Church was free from persecution for the space of more than ten years; but in AD 249, a violent persecution broke out in Alexandria, at the instigation of a pagan priest, without the knowledge of the emperor.

The Seventh Persecution, Under Decius, AD 249

This was occasioned partly by the hatred he bore to his predecessor Philip, who was deemed a Christian and was partly by his jealousy concerning the amazing increase of Christianity; for the heathen temples began to be forsaken, and the Christian churches thronged.

These reasons stimulated Decius to attempt the very extirpation of the name of Christian; and it was unfortunate for the Gospel, that many errors had, about this time, crept into the Church: the Christians were at variance with each other; self-interest divided those whom social love ought to have united; and the virulence of pride occasioned a variety of factions.

The heathens in general were ambitious to enforce the imperial decrees upon this occasion, and looked upon the murder of a Christian as a merit to themselves. The martyrs, upon this occasion, were innumerable; but the principal we shall give some account of.

Fabian, the bishop of Rome, was the first person of eminence who felt the severity of this persecution. The deceased emperor, Philip, had, on account of his integrity, committed his treasure to the care of this good man. But Decius, not finding as much as his avarice made him expect, determined to wreak his vengeance on the good prelate. He was accordingly seized; and on January 20, AD 250, he suffered decapitation.

Julian, a native of Cilicia, as we are informed by St Chrysostom, was seized upon for being a Christian. He was put into a leather bag, together with a number of serpents and scorpions, and in that condition thrown into the sea.

Peter, a young man, amiable for the superior qualities of his body and mind, was beheaded for refusing to sacrifice to Venus. He said, 'I am astonished you should sacrifice to an infamous woman, whose debaucheries even your own historians record, and whose life consisted of such actions as your laws would punish. No, I shall offer the true God the acceptable sacrifice of praises and prayers.' Optimus, the proconsul of Asia, on hearing this, ordered the prisoner to be stretched upon a wheel, by which all his bones were broken, and then he was sent to be beheaded.

Nichomachus, being brought before the proconsul as a Christian, was ordered to sacrifice to the pagan idols. Nichomachus replied, 'I cannot pay that respect to devils, which is only due to the Almighty.' This speech so much enraged the proconsul that Nichomachus was put to the rack. After enduring the torments for a time, he recanted; but scarcely had he given this proof of his frailty, than he fell into the greatest agonies, dropped down on the ground, and expired immediately.

Denisa, a young woman of only sixteen years of age, who beheld this terrible judgment, suddenly exclaimed, 'O unhappy wretch, why would you buy a moment's ease at the expense of a miserable eternity!' Optimus, hearing this, called to her, and Denisa avowing herself to be a Christian, she was beheaded, by his order, soon after.

Andrew and Paul, two companions of Nichomachus, the martyr, AD 251, suffered martyrdom by stoning, and expired, calling on their blessed Redeemer.

Alexander and Epimachus, of Alexandria, were apprehended for being Christians: and, confessing the accusation, were beat with staves, torn with hooks, and at length burnt in the fire; and we are informed, in a fragment preserved by Eusebius, that four female martyrs suffered on the same day, and at the same place, but not in the same manner; for these were beheaded.

Lucian and Marcian, two wicked pagans, though skilful magicians, becoming converts to Christianity, to make amends for their former errors, lived the lives of hermits, and subsisted upon bread and water only. After some time spent in this manner, they became zealous preachers, and made many converts. The persecution, however, raging at this time, they were seized upon, and carried before Sabinus, the governor of Bithynia. On being asked by what authority they took upon themselves to preach, Lucian answered, 'That the laws of charity and humanity obliged all men to endeavour the conversion of their neighbours, and to do everything in their power to rescue them from the snares of the devil.'

Lucian having answered in this manner, Marcian said, 'Their conversion was by the same grace which was given to St Paul, who, from a zealous persecutor of the Church, became a preacher of the Gospel.'

The proconsul, finding that he could not prevail with them to renounce their faith, condemned them to be burnt alive, which sentence was soon after executed.

Trypho and Respicius, two eminent men, were seized as Christians, and imprisoned at Nice. Their feet were pierced with nails; they were dragged through the streets, scourged, torn with iron hooks, scorched with lighted torches, and at length beheaded, February 1, AD 251.

Agatha, a Sicilian lady, was not more remarkable for her personal and acquired endowments, than her piety; her beauty was such, that Quintian, governor of Sicily, became enamoured of her, and made many attempts upon her chastity without success. In order to gratify his passions with the greater conveniency, he put the virtuous lady into the hands of Aphrodica, a very infamous and licentious woman. This wretch tried every artifice to win her to the desired prostitution; but found all her efforts were vain; for her chastity was impregnable, and she well knew that virtue alone could procure true happiness. Aphrodica acquainted Quintian with the inefficacy of her endeavors, who, enraged to be foiled in his designs, changed his lust into resentment. On her confessing that she was a Christian, he determined to gratify his revenge, as he could not his passion. Pursuant to his orders, she was scourged, burnt with red-hot irons, and torn with sharp hooks. Having borne these torments with admirable fortitude, she was next laid naked upon live coals, intermingled with glass, and then being carried back to prison, she there expired on February 5, AD 251.

Cyril, bishop of Gortyna, was seized by order of Lucius, the governor of that place, who, nevertheless, exhorted him to obey the imperial mandate, perform the sacrifices, and save his venerable person from destruction; for he was now eighty-four years of age. The good prelate replied that as he had long taught others to save their souls, he should only think now of his own salvation. The worthy prelate heard his fiery sentence without emotion, walked cheerfully to the place of execution, and underwent his martyrdom with great fortitude.

The persecution raged in no place more than the island of Crete; for the governor, being exceedingly active in executing the imperial decrees, that place streamed with pious blood.

Babylas, a Christian of a liberal education, became bishop of Antioch, AD 237, on the demise of Zebinus. He acted with inimitable zeal, and governed the Church with admirable prudence during the most tempestuous times.

The first misfortune that happened to Antioch during his mission, was the siege of it by Sapor, king of Persia; who, having overrun all Syria, took and plundered this city among others, and used the Christian inhabitants with greater severity than the rest, but was soon totally defeated by Gordian.

After Gordian's death, in the reign of Decius, that emperor came to Antioch, where, having a desire to visit an assembly of Christians, Babylas opposed him, and absolutely refused to let him come in. The emperor dissembled his anger at that time; but soon sending for the bishop, he sharply reproved him for his insolence, and then ordered him to sacrifice to the pagan deities as an expiation for his offence. This being refused, he was committed to prison, loaded with chains, treated with great severities, and then beheaded, together with three young men who had been his pupils. AD 251.

Alexander, bishop of Jerusalem, about this time was cast into prison on account of his religion, where he died through the severity of his confinement.

Julianus, an old man, lame with the gout, and Cronion, another Christian, were bound on the backs of camels, severely scourged, and then thrown into a fire and consumed. Also forty virgins, at Antioch, after being imprisoned, and scourged, were burnt.

In the year of our Lord 251, the emperor Decius having erected a pagan temple at Ephesus, he commanded all who were in that city to sacrifice to the idols. This order was nobly refused by seven of his own soldiers, namely, Maximianus, Martianus, Joannes, Malchus, Dionysius, Seraion, and Constantinus. The emperor wishing to win these soldiers to renounce their faith by his entreaties and lenity, gave them a considerable respite until he returned from an expedition. During the emperor's absence, they escaped, and hid themselves in a cavern; which the emperor being informed of at his return, the mouth of the cave was closed up, and they all perished with hunger.

Theodora, a beautiful young lady of Antioch, on refusing to sacrifice to the Roman idols, was condemned to the stews, that her virtue might be sacrificed to the brutality of lust. Didymus, a Christian, disguised himself in the habit of a Roman soldier, went to the house, informed Theodora who he was, and advised her to make her escape in his clothes. This being effected, and a man found in the brothel instead of a beautiful lady, Didymus was taken before the president, to whom confessing the truth, and owning that he was a Christian the sentence of death was immediately pronounced against him. Theodora, hearing that her deliverer was likely to suffer, came to the judge, threw herself at his feet, and begged that the sentence might fall on her as the guilty person; but, deaf to the cries of the innocent, and insensible to the calls of justice, the inflexible judge condemned both; when they were executed accordingly, being first beheaded, and their bodies afterward burnt.

Secundianus, having been accused as a Christian, was conveyed to prison by some soldiers. On the way, Verianus and Marcellinus said, 'Where are you carrying the innocent?' This interrogatory occasioned them to be seized, and all three, after having been tortured, were hanged and decapitated.

Origen, the celebrated presbyter and catechist of Alexandria, at the age of sixty-four, was seized, thrown into a loathsome prison, laden with fetters, his feet placed in the stocks, and his legs extended to the utmost for several successive days. He was threatened with fire, and tormented by every lingering means the most infernal imaginations could suggest. During this cruel temporising, the emperor Decius died, and Gallus, who succeeded him, engaging in a war with the Goths, the Christians met with a respite. In this interim, Origen obtained his enlargement, and, retiring to Tyre, he there remained until his death, which happened when he was in the sixty-ninth year of his age.

Gallus, the emperor, having concluded his wars, a plague broke out in the empire: sacrifices to the pagan deities were ordered by the emperor, and persecutions spread from the interior to the extreme parts of the empire, and many fell martyrs to the impetuosity of the rabble, as well as the prejudice of the magistrates. Among these were Cornelius, the Christian bishop of Rome, and Lucius, his successor, in 253.

Most of the errors which crept into the Church at this time arose from placing human reason in competition with revelation; but the fallacy of such arguments being proved by the most able divines, the opinions they had created vanished away like the stars before the sun.

The Eighth Persecution, Under Valerian, AD 257

Began under Valerian, in the month of April, 257, and continued for three years and six months. The martyrs that fell in this persecution were innumerable, and their tortures and deaths as various and painful. The most eminent martyrs were the following, though neither rank, sex, nor age were regarded.

Rufina and Secunda were two beautiful and accomplished ladies, daughters of Asterius, a gentleman of eminence in Rome. Rufina, the elder, was designed in marriage for Armentarius, a young nobleman; Secunda, the younger, for Verinus, a person of rank and opulence. The suitors, at the time of the persecution's commencing, were both Christians; but when danger appeared, to save their fortunes, they renounced their faith. They took great pains to persuade the ladies to do the same, but, disappointed in their purpose, the lovers were base enough to inform against the ladies, who, being apprehended as Christians, were brought before Junius Donatus, governor of Rome, where, AD 257, they sealed their martyrdom with their blood.

Stephen, bishop of Rome, was beheaded in the same year, and about that time Saturninus, the pious orthodox bishop of Toulouse, refusing to sacrifice to idols, was treated with all the barbarous indignities imaginable, and fastened by the feet to the tail of a bull. Upon a signal given, the enraged animal was driven down the steps of the temple, by which the worthy martyr's brains were dashed out.

Sextus succeeded Stephen as bishop of Rome. He is supposed to have been a Greek by birth or by extraction, and had for some time served in the capacity of a deacon under Stephen. His great fidelity, singular wisdom, and uncommon courage distinguished him upon many occasions; and the happy conclusion of a controversy with some heretics is generally ascribed to his piety and prudence. In the year 258, Marcianus, who had the management of the Roman government, procured an order from the emperor Valerian, to put to death all the Christian clergy in Rome, and hence the bishop with six of his deacons, suffered martyrdom in 258.

Let us draw near to the fire of martyred Lawrence, that our cold hearts may be warmed thereby. The merciless tyrant, understanding him to be not only a minister of the sacraments, but a distributor also of the Church riches, promised to himself a double prey, by the apprehension of one soul. First, with the rake of avarice to scrape to himself the treasure of poor Christians; then with the fiery fork of tyranny, so to toss and turmoil them, that they should wax weary of their profession. With furious face and cruel countenance, the greedy wolf demanded where this Lawrence had bestowed the substance of the Church: who, craving three days' respite, promised to declare where the treasure might be had. In the meantime, he caused a good number of poor Christians to be congregated. So, when the day of his answer was come, the persecutor strictly charged him to stand to his promise. Then valiant Lawrence, stretching out his arms over the poor, said: 'These are the precious treasure of the Church; these are the treasure indeed, in whom the faith of Christ reigneth, in whom Jesus Christ hath His mansion-place. What more precious jewels can Christ have, than those in whom He hath promised to dwell? For so it is written, "I was an hungered, and ye gave me meat: I was thirsty, and ye gave me drink: I was a stranger, and ye took me in." And again, "Inasmuch as ye have done it unto one of the least of these my brethren, ye have done it unto me." What greater riches can Christ our Master possess, than the poor people in whom He loveth to be seen?'

O, what tongue is able to express the fury and madness of the tyrant's heart! Now he stamped, he stared, he ramped, he fared as one out of his wits: his eyes like fire glowed, his mouth like a boar formed, his teeth like a hellhound grinned. Now, not a reasonable man, but a roaring lion, he might be called.

'Kindle the fire (he cried) – of wood make no spare. Hath this villain deluded the emperor? Away with him, away with him: whip him with scourges, jerk him with rods, buffet him with fists, brain him with clubs. Jesteth the traitor with the emperor? Pinch him with fiery tongs, gird him with burning plates, bring out the strongest chains, and the fire-forks, and the grated bed of iron: on the fire with it; bind the rebel hand and foot; and when the bed is fire-hot, on with him: roast him, broil him, toss him, turn him: on pain of our high displeasure do every man his office, O ye tormentors.'

The word was no sooner spoken, but all was done. After many cruel handlings, this meek lamb was laid, I will not say on his fiery bed of iron, but on his soft bed of down. So mightily God wrought with his martyr Lawrence, so miraculously God tempered His element the fire; that it became not a bed of consuming pain, but a pallet of nourishing rest.

In Africa the persecution raged with peculiar violence; many thousands received the crown of martyrdom, among whom the following were the most distinguished characters.

Cyprian, bishop of Carthage, an eminent prelate, and a pious ornament of the Church. The brightness of his genius was tempered by the solidity of his judgment; and with all the accomplishments of the gentleman, he blended the virtues of a Christian. His doctrines were orthodox and pure; his language easy and elegant; and his manners graceful and winning: in fine, he was both the pious and polite preacher. In his youth he was educated in the principles of Gentilism, and having a considerable fortune, he lived in the very extravagance of splendour, and all the dignity of pomp.

About the year 246, Coecilius, a Christian minister of Carthage, became the happy instrument of Cyprian's conversion: on which account, and for the great love that he always afterward bore for the author of his conversion, he was termed Coecilius Cyprian. Previous to his baptism, he studied the Scriptures with care and being struck with the beauties of the truths they contained, he determined to practise the virtues therein recommended. Subsequent to his baptism, he sold his estate, distributed the money among the poor, dressed himself in plain attire, and commenced a life of austerity. He was soon after made a presbyter; and, being greatly admired for his virtues and works, on the death of Donatus, in AD 248, he was almost unanimously elected bishop of Carthage.

Cyprian's care not only extended over Carthage, but to Numidia and Mauritania. In all his transactions he took great care to ask the advice of his clergy, knowing that unanimity alone could be of service to the Church, this being one of his maxims, 'That the bishop was in the church, and the church in the bishop; so that unity can only be preserved by a close connexion between the pastor and his flock.'

In AD 250, Cyprian was publicly proscribed by the emperor Decius, under the appellation of Coecilius Cyprian, bishop of the Christians; and the universal cry of the pagans was, 'Cyprian to the lions, Cyprian to the beasts!' The bishop, however, withdrew from the rage of the populace, and his effects were immediately confiscated. During his retirement, he wrote thirty pious and elegant letters to his flock; but several schisms that then crept into the Church, gave him great uneasiness. The rigour of the persecution abating, he returned to Carthage, and did everything in his power to expunge erroneous opinions. A terrible plague breaking out in Carthage, it was, as usual, laid to the charge of the Christians; and the magistrates began to persecute accordingly, which occasioned an epistle from them to Cyprian, in answer to which he vindicates the cause of Christianity. AD 257, Cyprian was brought before the proconsul Aspasius Paturnus, who exiled him to a little city on the Lybian sea. On the death of this proconsul, he returned to Carthage, but was soon after seized, and carried before the new governor, who condemned him to be beheaded; which sentence was executed on the fourteenth of September, AD 258.

The disciples of Cyprian, martyred in this persecution, were Lucius, Flavian, Victoricus, Remus, Montanus, Julian, Primelus, and Donatian.

At Utica, a most terrible tragedy was exhibited: three hundred Christians were, by the orders of the proconsul, placed round a burning limekiln. A pan of coals and incense being prepared, they were commanded either to sacrifice to Jupiter, or to be thrown into the kiln. Unanimously refusing, they bravely jumped into the pit, and were immediately suffocated.

Fructuosus, bishop of Tarragon, in Spain, and his two deacons, Augurius and Eulogius, were burnt for being Christians.

Alexander, Malchus, and Priscus, three Christians of Palestine, with a woman of the same place, voluntarily accused themselves of being Christians; on which account they were sentenced to be devoured by tigers, which sentence was executed accordingly.

Maxima, Donatilla, and Secunda, three virgins of Tuburga, had gall and vinegar given them to drink, were then severely scourged, tormented on a gibbet, rubbed with lime, scorched on a gridiron, worried by wild beasts, and at length beheaded.

It is here proper to take notice of the singular but miserable fate of the emperor Valerian, who had so long and so terribly persecuted the Christians. This tyrant, by a stratagem, was taken prisoner by Sapor, emperor of Persia, who carried him into his own country, and there treated him with the most unexampled indignity, making him kneel down as the meanest slave, and treading upon him as a footstool when he mounted his horse. After having kept him for the space of seven years in this abject state of slavery, he caused his eyes to be put out, though he was then eighty-three years of age. This not satiating his desire of revenge, he soon after ordered his body to be flayed alive, and rubbed with salt, under which torments he expired; and thus fell one of the most tyrannical emperors of Rome, and one of the greatest persecutors of the Christians.

AD 260, Gallienus, the son of Valerian, succeeded him, and during his reign (a few martyrs excepted) the Church enjoyed peace for some years.

The Ninth Persecution Under Aurelian, AD 274

The principal sufferers were: Felix, bishop of Rome. This prelate was advanced to the Roman see in 274. He was the first martyr to Aurelian's petulance, being beheaded on the twenty-second of December, in the same year. Agapetus, a young gentleman, who sold his estate, and gave the money to the poor, was seized as a Christian, tortured, and then beheaded at Praeneste, a city within a day's journey of Rome. These are the only martyrs left upon record during this reign, as it was soon put to a stop by the emperor's being murdered by his own domestics, at Byzantium.

Aurelian was succeeded by Tacitus, who was followed by Probus, as the latter was by Carus: this emperor being killed by a thunder storm, his sons, Carnious and Numerian, succeeded him, and during all these reigns the Church had peace.

Diocletian mounted the imperial throne, AD 284; at first he showed great favour to the Christians. In the year 286, he associated Maximian with him in the empire; and some Christians were put to death before any general persecution broke out. Among these were Felician and Primus, two brothers.

Marcus and Marcellianus were twins, natives of Rome, and of noble descent. Their parents were heathens, but the tutors, to whom the education of the children was intrusted, brought them up as Christians. Their constancy at length subdued those who wished them to become pagans, and their parents and whole family became converts to a faith they had before reprobated. They were martyred by being tied to posts, and having their feet pierced with nails. After remaining in this situation for a day and a night, their sufferings were put an end to by thrusting lances through their bodies.

Zoe, the wife of the jailer, who had the care of the before-mentioned martyrs, was also converted by them, and hung upon a tree, with a fire of straw lighted under her. When her body was taken down, it was thrown into a river, with a large stone tied to it, in order to sink it.

In the year of Christ 286, a most remarkable affair occurred; a legion of soldiers, consisting of six thousand six hundred and sixty-six men, contained none but Christians. This legion was called the Theban Legion, because the men had been raised in Thebias: they were quartered in the east until the emperor Maximian ordered them to march to Gaul, to assist him against the rebels of Burgundy. They passed the Alps into Gaul, under the command of Mauritius, Candidus, and Exupernis, their worthy commanders, and at length joined the emperor. Maximian, about this time, ordered a general sacrifice, at which the whole army was to assist;

and likewise he commanded that they should take the oath of allegiance and swear, at the same time, to assist in the extirpation of Christianity in Gaul. Alarmed at these orders, each individual of the Theban Legion absolutely refused either to sacrifice or take the oaths prescribed. This so greatly enraged Maximian, that he ordered the legion to be decimated, that is, every tenth man to be selected from the rest, and put to the sword. This bloody order having been put in execution, those who remained alive were still inflexible, when a second decimation took place, and every tenth man of those living was put to death. This second severity made no more impression than the first had done; the soldiers preserved their fortitude and their principles, but by the advice of their officers they drew up a loyal remonstrance to the emperor. This, it might have been presumed, would have softened the emperor, but it had a contrary effect: for, enraged at their perseverance and unanimity, he commanded that the whole legion should be put to death, which was accordingly executed by the other troops, who cut them to pieces with their swords, September 22, AD 286.

Alban, from whom St Alban's, in Hertfordshire, received its name, was the first British martyr. Great Britain had received the Gospel of Christ from Lucius, the first Christian king, but did not suffer from the rage of persecution for many years after. He was originally a pagan, but converted by a Christian ecclesiastic, named Amphibalus, whom he sheltered on account of his religion. The enemies of Amphibalus, having intelligence of the place where he was secreted, came to the house of Alban; in order to facilitate his escape, when the soldiers came, he offered himself up as the person they were seeking for. The deceit being detected, the governor ordered him to be scourged, and then he was sentenced to be beheaded.

The venerable Bede assures us, that, upon this occasion, the executioner suddenly became a convert to Christianity, and entreated permission to die for Alban, or with him. Obtaining the latter request, they were beheaded by a soldier, who voluntarily undertook the task of executioner. This happened on June 22, AD 287, at Verulam, now St Alban's, in Hertfordshire, where a magnificent church was erected to his memory about the time of Constantine the Great. The edifice, being destroyed in the Saxon wars, was rebuilt by Offa, king of Mercia, and a monastery erected adjoining to it, some remains of which are still visible, and the church is a noble Gothic structure.

Faith, a Christian female, of Acquitain, in France, was ordered to be broiled upon a gridiron, and then beheaded, AD 287.

Quintin was a Christian, and a native of Rome, but determined to attempt the propagation of the Gospel in Gaul, with one Lucian, they preached together in Amiens; after which Lucian went to Beaumaris, where he was martyred. Quintin remained in Picardy, and was very zealous in his ministry. Being seized upon as a Christian, he was stretched with pullies until his joints were dislocated; his body was then torn with wire scourges, and boiling oil and pitch poured on his naked flesh; lighted torches were applied to his sides and armpits; and after he had been thus tortured, he was remanded back to prison, and died of the barbarities he had suffered, October 31, AD 287. His body was sunk in the Somme.

The Tenth Persecution, Under Diocletian, AD 303

Under the Roman emperors, commonly called the Era of the Martyrs, was occasioned partly by the increasing number and luxury of the Christians, and the hatred of Galerius, the adopted son of Diocletian, who, being stimulated by his mother, a bigoted pagan, never ceased persuading the emperor to enter upon the persecution, until he had accomplished his purpose.

The fatal day fixed upon to commence the bloody work, was February 23, AD 303, that being the day in which the Terminalia were celebrated, and on which, as the cruel pagans boasted, they hoped to put a termination to Christianity. On the appointed day, the persecution began in Nicomedia, on the morning of which the prefect of that city repaired, with a great number of officers and assistants, to the church of the Christians, where, having forced open the doors, they seized upon all the sacred books, and committed them to the flames.

The whole of this transaction was in the presence of Diocletian and Galerius, who, not contented with burning the books, had the church levelled with the ground. This was followed by a severe edict, commanding the destruction of all other Christian churches and books; and an order soon succeeded, to render Christians of all denomination outlaws.

The publication of this edict occasioned an immediate martyrdom, for a bold Christian not only tore it down from the place to which it was affixed, but execrated the name of the emperor for his injustice. A provocation like this was sufficient to call down pagan vengeance upon his head; he was accordingly seized, severely tortured, and then burned alive.

All the Christians were apprehended and imprisoned; and Galerius privately ordered the imperial palace to be set on fire, that the Christians might be charged as the incendiaries, and a plausible pretence given for carrying on the persecution with the greater severities. A general sacrifice was commenced, which occasioned various martyrdoms. No distinction was made of age or sex; the name of Christian was so obnoxious to the pagans that all indiscriminately fell sacrifices to their opinions. Many houses were set on fire, and whole Christian families perished in the flames; and others had stones fastened about their necks, and being tied together were driven into the sea. The persecution became general in all the Roman provinces, but more particularly in the east; and as it lasted ten years, it is impossible to ascertain the numbers martyred, or to enumerate the various modes of martyrdom.

Racks, scourges, swords, daggers, crosses, poison, and famine, were made use of in various parts to dispatch the Christians; and invention was exhausted to devise tortures against such as had no crime, but thinking differently from the votaries of superstition.

A city of Phrygia, consisting entirely of Christians, was burnt, and all the inhabitants perished in the flames.

Tired with slaughter, at length, several governors of provinces represented to the imperial court, the impropriety of such conduct. Hence many were respited from execution, but, though they were not put to death, as much as possible was done to render their lives miserable, many of them having their ears cut off, their noses slit, their right eyes put out, their limbs rendered useless by dreadful dislocations, and their flesh seared in conspicuous places with red-hot irons.

It is necessary now to particularise the most conspicuous persons who laid down their lives in martyrdom in this bloody persecution.

Sebastian, a celebrated martyr, was born at Narbonne, in Gaul, instructed in the principles of Christianity at Milan, and afterward became an officer of the emperor's guard at Rome. He remained a true Christian in the midst of idolatry; unallured by the splendours of a court, untainted by evil examples, and uncontaminated by the hopes of preferment. Refusing to be a pagan, the emperor ordered him to be taken to a field near the city, termed the Campus Martius, and there to be shot to death with arrows; which sentence was executed accordingly. Some pious Christians coming to the place of execution, in order to give his body burial, perceived signs of life in him, and immediately moving him to a place of security, they, in a short time effected his recovery, and prepared him for a second martyrdom; for, as soon as he was able to go out, he placed himself intentionally in the emperor's way as he was going to the temple, and reprehended him for his various cruelties and unreasonable prejudices against Christianity. As soon as Diocletian had overcome his surprise, he ordered Sebastian to be seized, and carried to a place near the palace, and beaten to death; and, that the Christians should not either use means again to recover or bury his body, he ordered that it should be thrown into the common sewer. Nevertheless, a Christian lady named Lucina, found means to remove it from the sewer, and bury it in the catacombs, or repositories of the dead.

The Christians, about this time, upon mature consideration, thought it unlawful to bear arms under a heathen emperor. Maximilian, the son of Fabius Victor, was the first beheaded under this regulation.

Vitus, a Sicilian of considerable family, was brought up a Christian; when his virtues increased with his years, his constancy supported him under all afflictions, and his faith was superior to the most dangerous perils. His father, Hylas, who was a pagan, finding that he had been instructed in the principles of Christianity by the nurse who brought him up, used all his endeavors to bring him back to paganism, and at length sacrificed his son to the idols, June 14, AD 303.

Victor was a Christian of a good family at Marseilles, in France; he spent a great part of the night in visiting the afflicted, and confirming the weak; which pious work he could not, consistently with his own safety, perform in the daytime; and his fortune he spent in relieving the distresses of poor Christians. He was at length, however, seized by the emperor Maximian's decree, who ordered him to be bound, and dragged through the streets. During the execution of this order, he was treated with all manner of cruelties and indignities by the enraged populace. Remaining still inflexible, his courage was deemed obstinacy. Being by order stretched upon the rack, he turned his eyes toward heaven, and prayed to God to endue him with patience, after which he underwent the tortures with most admirable fortitude. After the executioners were tired with inflicting torments on him, he was conveyed to a dungeon. In his confinement, he converted his jailers, named Alexander, Felician, and Longinus. This affair coming to the ears of the emperor, he ordered them immediately to be put to death, and the jailers were accordingly beheaded. Victor was then again put to the rack, unmercifully beaten with batons, and again sent to prison. Being a third time examined concerning his religion, he persevered in his principles; a small altar was then brought, and he was commanded to offer incense upon it immediately. Fired with indignation at the request, he boldly stepped forward, and with his foot overthrew both altar and idol. This so enraged the emperor Maximian, who was present, that he ordered the foot with which he had kicked the altar to be immediately cut off; and Victor was thrown into a mill, and crushed to pieces with the stones, AD 303.

Maximus, governor of Cilicia, being at Tarsus, three Christians were brought before him; their names were Tarachus, an aged man, Probus, and Andronicus. After repeated tortures and exhortations to recant, they, at length, were ordered for execution.

Being brought to the amphitheatre, several beasts were let loose upon them; but none of the animals, though hungry, would touch them. The keeper then brought out a large bear, that had that very day destroyed three men; but this voracious creature and a fierce lioness both refused to touch the prisoners. Finding the design of destroying them by the means of wild beasts ineffectual, Maximus ordered them to be slain by the sword, on October 11, AD 303.

Romanus, a native of Palestine, was deacon of the church of Caesarea at the time of the commencement of Diocletian's persecution. Being condemned for his faith at Antioch, he was scourged, put to the rack, his body torn with hooks, his flesh cut with knives, his face scarified, his teeth beaten from their sockets, and his hair plucked up by the roots. Soon after he was ordered to be strangled, November 17, AD 303.

Susanna, the niece of Caius, bishop of Rome, was pressed by the emperor Diocletian to marry a noble pagan, who was nearly related to him. Refusing the honour intended her, she was beheaded by the emperor's order.

Dorotheus, the high chamberlain of the household to Diocletian, was a Christian, and took great pains to make converts. In his religious labours, he was joined by Gorgonius, another Christian, and one belonging to the palace. They were first tortured and then strangled.

Peter, a eunuch belonging to the emperor, was a Christian of singular modesty and humility. He was laid on a gridiron, and broiled over a slow fire until he expired.

Cyprian, known by the title of the magician, to distinguish him from Cyprian, bishop of Carthage, was a native of Antioch. He received a liberal education in his youth, and particularly applied himself to astrology; after which he traveled for improvement through Greece, Egypt, India, etc. In the course of time he became acquainted with Justina, a young lady of Antioch, whose birth, beauty, and accomplishments, rendered her the admiration of all who knew her. A pagan gentleman applied to Cyprian, to promote his suit with the beautiful Justina; this he undertook, but soon himself became converted, burnt his books of astrology and magic, received baptism, and felt animated with a powerful spirit of grace. The conversion of Cyprian had a great effect on the pagan gentleman who paid his addresses to Justina, and he in a short time embraced Christianity. During the persecutions of Diocletian, Cyprian and Justina were seized upon as Christians, the former was torn with pincers, and the latter chastised; and, after suffering other torments, both were beheaded.

Eulalia, a Spanish lady of a Christian family, was remarkable in her youth for sweetness of temper, and solidity of understanding seldom found in the capriciousness of juvenile years. Being apprehended as a Christian, the magistrate attempted by the mildest means, to bring her over to paganism, but she ridiculed the pagan deities with such asperity, that the judge, incensed at her behaviour, ordered her to be tortured. Her sides were accordingly torn by hooks, and her breasts burnt in the most shocking manner, until she expired by the violence of the flames, December, AD 303.

In the year 304, when the persecution reached Spain, Dacian, the governor of Terragona, ordered Valerius the bishop, and Vincent the deacon, to be seized, loaded with irons, and imprisoned. The prisoners being firm in their resolution, Valerius was banished, and Vincent was racked, his limbs dislocated, his flesh torn with hooks, and he was laid on a gridiron, which had not only a fire placed under it, but spikes at the top, which ran into his flesh.

✝ CHAPTER 7 ✝

An account of the life and persecutions of John Wickliffe

It will not be inappropriate to devote a few pages of this work to a brief detail of the lives of some of those men who first stepped forward, regardless of the bigoted power which opposed all reformation, to stem the time of papal corruption, and to seal the pure doctrines of the Gospel with their blood.

Among these, Great Britain has the honour of taking the lead, and first maintaining that freedom in religious controversy which astonished Europe, and demonstrated that political and religious liberty are equally the growth of that favoured island. Among the earliest of these eminent persons was John Wickliffe.

This celebrated reformer, denominated the 'Morning Star of the Reformation,' was born about the year 1324, in the reign of Edward II. Of his extraction we have no certain account. His parents designing him for the Church, sent him to Queen's College, Oxford, about that period founded by Robert Eaglesfield, confessor to Queen Philippi. But not meeting with the advantages for study in that newly established house which he expected, he removed to Merton College, which was then esteemed one of the most learned societies in Europe.

The first thing which drew him into public notice, was his defence of the university against the begging friars, who about this time, from their settlement in Oxford in 1230, had been troublesome neighbours to the university. Feuds were continually fomented; the friars appealing to the pope, the scholars to the civil power; and sometimes one party, and sometimes, the other, prevailed. The friars became very fond of a notion that Christ was a common beggar; that his disciples were beggars also; and that begging was of Gospel institution. This doctrine they urged from the pulpit and wherever they had access.

Wickliffe had long held these religious friars in contempt for the laziness of their lives, and had now a fair opportunity of exposing them. He published a treatise against able beggary, in which he lashed the friars, and proved that they were not only a reproach to religion, but also to human society. The university began to consider him one of their first champions, and he was soon promoted to the mastership of Baliol College.

About this time, Archbishop Islip founded Canterbury Hall, in Oxford, where he established a warden and eleven scholars. To this wardenship Wickliffe was elected by the archbishop, but upon his demise, he was displaced by his successor, Stephen Langham, bishop of Ely. As there was a degree of flagrant injustice in the affair, Wickliffe appealed to the pope, who subsequently gave it against him from the following cause: Edward III, then king of England, had withdrawn the tribute, which from the time of King John had been paid to the pope. The pope menaced; Edward called a parliament. The parliament resolved that King John had done an illegal thing, and given up the rights of the nation, and advised the king not to submit, whatever consequences might follow.

The clergy now began to write in favour of the pope, and a learned monk published a spirited and plausible treatise, which had many advocates. Wickliffe, irritated at seeing so bad a cause so well defended, opposed the monk, and did it in so masterly a way that he was considered no longer as unanswerable. His suit at Rome was immediately determined against him; and nobody doubted but his opposition to the pope, at so critical a period, was the true cause of his being non-suited at Rome.

Wickliffe was afterward elected to the chair of the divinity professor: and now fully convinced of the errors of the Romish Church, and the vileness of its monastic agents, he determined to expose them. In public lectures he lashed their vices and opposed their follies. He unfolded a variety of abuses covered by the darkness of superstition. At first he began to loosen the prejudices of the vulgar, and proceeded by slow advances; with the metaphysical disquisitions of the age, he mingled opinions in divinity apparently novel. The usurpations of the court of Rome was a favourite topic. On these he expatiated with all the keenness of argument, joined to logical reasoning. This soon procured him the clamour of the clergy, who, with the archbishop of Canterbury, deprived him of his office.

At this time the administration of affairs was in the hands of the duke of Lancaster, well known by the name of John of Gaunt. This prince had very free notions of religion, and was at enmity with the clergy. The exactions of the court of Rome having become very burdensome, he determined to send the bishop of Bangor and Wickliffe to remonstrate against these abuses, and it was agreed that the pope should no longer dispose of any benefices belonging to the Church of England. In this embassy, Wickliffe's observant mind penetrated into the constitution and policy of Rome, and he returned more strongly than ever determined to expose its avarice and ambition.

Having recovered his former situation, he inveighed, in his lectures, against the pope – his usurpation, his infallibility, his pride, his avarice, and his tyranny. He was the first who termed the pope Antichrist. From the pope, he would turn to the pomp, the luxury, and trappings of the bishops, and compared them with the simplicity of primitive bishops. Their superstitions and deceptions were topics that he urged with energy of mind and logical precision.

From the patronage of the duke of Lancaster, Wickliffe received a good benefice; but he was no sooner settled in his parish, than his enemies and the bishops began to persecute him with renewed vigour. The duke of Lancaster was his friend in this persecution, and by his presence and that of Lord Percy, earl marshal of England, he so overawed the trial, that the whole ended in disorder.

After the death of Edward III his grandson Richard II succeeded, in the eleventh year of his age. The duke of Lancaster not obtaining to be the sole regent, as he expected, his power began to decline, and the enemies of Wickliffe, taking advantage of the circumstance, renewed their articles of accusation against him. Five bulls were despatched in consequence by the pope to the king and certain bishops, but the regency and the people manifested a spirit of contempt at the haughty proceedings of the pontiff, and the former at that time wanting money to oppose an expected invasion of the French, proposed to apply a large sum, collected for the use of the pope, to that purpose. The question was submitted to the decision of Wickliffe. The bishops, however, supported by the papal authority, insisted upon bringing Wickliffe to trial, and he was actually undergoing examination at Lambeth, when, from the riotous behaviour of the populace without, and awed by the command of Sir Lewis Clifford, a gentleman of the court, that they should not proceed to any definitive sentence, they terminated the whole affair in a prohibition to Wickliffe, not to preach those doctrines which were obnoxious to the pope; but this was laughed at by our reformer, who, going about barefoot, and in a long frieze gown, preached more vehemently than before.

In the year 1378, a contest arose between two popes, Urban VI and Clement VII which was the lawful pope, and true vice-regent of God. This was a favourable period for the exertion of Wickliffe's talents: he soon produced a tract against popery, which was eagerly read by all sorts of people.

About the end of the year, Wickliffe was seized with a violent disorder, which it was feared might prove fatal. The begging friars, accompanied by four of the most eminent citizens of Oxford, gained admittance to his bed chamber, and begged of him to retract, for his soul's sake, the unjust things he had asserted of their order. Wickliffe, surprised at the solemn message, raised himself in his bed, and with a stern countenance replied, 'I shall not die, but live to declare the evil deeds of the friars.'

When Wickliffe recovered, he set about a most important work, the translation of the Bible into English. Before this work appeared, he published a tract, wherein he showed the necessity of it. The zeal of the bishops to suppress the Scriptures greatly promoted its sale, and they who were not able to purchase copies, procured transcripts of particular Gospels or Epistles. Afterward, when Lollardy increased, and the flames kindled, it was a common practice to fasten about the neck of the condemned heretic such of these scraps of Scripture as were found in his possession, which generally shared his fate.

Immediately after this transaction, Wickliffe ventured a step further, and affected the doctrine of transubstantiation. This strange opinion was invented by Paschade Radbert, and asserted with amazing boldness. Wickliffe, in his lecture before the University of Oxford, 1381, attacked this doctrine, and published a treatise on the subject. Dr Barton, at this time vice-chancellor of Oxford, calling together the heads of the university, condemned Wickliffe's doctrines as heretical, and threatened their author with excommunication. Wickliffe could now derive no support from the duke of Lancaster, and being cited to appear before his former adversary, William Courteney, now made archbishop of Canterbury, he sheltered himself under the plea, that, as a member of the university, he was exempt from episcopal jurisdiction. This plea was admitted, as the university were determined to support their member.

The court met at the appointed time, determined, at least to sit in judgment upon his opinions, and some they condemned as erroneous, others as heretical. The publication on this subject was immediately answered by Wickliffe, who had become a subject of the archbishop's determined malice. The king, solicited by the archbishop, granted a license to imprison the teacher of heresy, but the commons made the king revoke this act as illegal. The primate, however, obtained letters from the king, directing the head of the University of Oxford to search for all heresies and books published by Wickliffe; in consequence of which order, the university became a scene of tumult. Wickliffe is supposed to have retired from the storm, into an obscure part of the kingdom. The seeds, however, were scattered, and Wickliffe's opinions were so prevalent that it was said if you met two persons upon the road, you might be sure that one was a Lollard. At this period, the disputes between the two popes continued. Urban published a bull, in which he earnestly called upon all who had any regard for religion, to exert themselves in its cause; and to take up arms against Clement and his adherents in defence of the holy see.

A war, in which the name of religion was so vilely prostituted, roused Wickliffe's inclination, even in his declining years. He took up his pen once more, and wrote against it with the greatest acrimony. He expostulated with the pope in a very free manner, and asks him boldly: 'How he durst make the token of Christ on the cross (which is the token of peace, mercy and charity) a banner to lead us to slay Christian men, for the love of two false priests, and to oppress Christendom worse than Christ and his apostles were oppressed by the Jews?' 'When,' said he, 'will the proud priest of Rome grant indulgences to mankind to live in peace and charity, as he now does to fight and slay one another?'

This severe piece drew upon him the resentment of Urban, and was likely to have involved him in greater troubles than he had before experienced, but providentially he was delivered out of their hands. He was struck with the palsy, and though he lived some time, yet it was in such a way that his enemies considered him as a person below their resentment.

Wickliffe returning within short space, either from his banishment, or from some other place where he was secretly kept, repaired to his parish of Lutterworth, where he was parson; and there, quietly departing this mortal life, slept in peace in the Lord, in the end of the year 1384, upon Silvester's day. It appeared that he was well aged before he departed, 'and that the same thing pleased him in his old age, which did please him being young'.

Wickliffe had some cause to give them thanks, that they would at least spare him until he was dead, and also give him so long respite after his death, forty-one years to rest in his sepulchre before they ungraved him, and turned him from earth to ashes; which ashes they also took and threw into the river. And so was he resolved into three elements, earth, fire, and water, thinking thereby utterly to extinguish and abolish both the name and doctrine of Wickliffe forever. Not much unlike the example of the old Pharisees and sepulchre knights, who, when they had brought the Lord unto the grave, thought to make him sure never to rise again. But these and all others must know that, as there is no counsel against the Lord, so there is no keeping down of verity, but it will spring up and come out of dust and ashes, as appeared right well in this man; for though they dug up his body, burned his bones, and drowned his ashes, yet the Word of God and the truth of his doctrine, with the fruit and success thereof, they could not burn.

✝ CHAPTER 12 ✝

The life and story of the true servant and martyr of God, William Tyndale

We have now to enter into the story of the good martyr of God, William Tyndale; which William Tyndale, as he was a special organ of the Lord appointed, and as God's mattock to shake the inward roots and foundation of the pope's proud prelacy, so the great prince of darkness, with his impious imps, having a special malice against him, left no way unsought how craftily to entrap him, and falsely to betray him, and maliciously to spill his life, as by the process of his story here following may appear.

William Tyndale, the faithful minister of Christ, was born about the borders of Wales, and brought up from a child in the University of Oxford, where he, by long continuance, increased as well in the knowledge of tongues, and other liberal arts, as especially in the knowledge of the Scriptures, whereunto his mind was singularly addicted; insomuch that he, lying then in Magdalen Hall, read privily to certain students and fellows of Magdalen College some parcel of divinity; instructing them in the knowledge and truth of the Scriptures. His manners and conversation being correspondent to the same, were such that all they that knew him reputed him to be a man of most virtuous disposition, and of life unspotted.

Thus he, in the University of Oxford, increasing more and more in learning, and proceeding in degrees of the schools, spying his time, removed from thence to the University of Cambridge, where he likewise made his abode a certain space. Being now further ripened in the knowledge of God's Word, leaving that university, he resorted to one Master Welch, a knight of Gloucestershire, and was there schoolmaster to his children, and in good favour with his master. As this gentleman kept a good ordinary commonly at his table, there resorted to him many times sundry abbots, deans, archdeacons, with divers other doctors, and great beneficed men; who there, together with Master Tyndale siting at the same table, did use many times to enter communication, and talk of learned men, as of Luther and of Erasmus; also of divers other controversies and questions upon the Scripture.

Then Master Tyndale, as he was learned and well practiced in God's matters, spared not to show unto them simply and plainly his judgment, and when they at any time did vary from Tyndale in opinions, he would show them in the Book, and lay plainly before them the open and manifest places of the Scriptures, to confute their errors, and confirm his sayings. And thus continued they for a certain season, reasoning and contending together divers times, until at length they waxed weary, and bare a secret grudge in their hearts against him.

As this grew on, the priests of the country, clustering together, began to grudge and storm against Tyndale, railing against him in alehouses and other places, affirming that his sayings were heresy; and accused him secretly to the chancellor, and others of the bishop's officers.

It followed not long after this that there was a sitting of the bishop's chancellor appointed, and warning was given to the priests to appear, amongst whom Master Tyndale was also warned to be there. And whether he had any misdoubt by their threatenings, or knowledge given him that they would lay some things to his charge, it is uncertain; but certain this is (as he himself declared), that he doubted their privy accusations; so that he by the way, in going thitherwards, cried in his mind heartily to God, to give him strength fast to stand in the truth of His Word.

When the time came for his appearance before the chancellor, he threatened him grievously, reviling and rating him as though he had been a dog, and laid to his charge many things whereof no accuser could be brought forth, notwithstanding that the priests of the country were there present. Thus Master Tyndale, escaping out of their hands, departed home, and returned to his master again.

There dwelt not far off a certain doctor, that had been chancellor to a bishop, who had been of old, familiar acquaintance with Master Tyndale, and favoured him well; unto whom Master Tyndale went and opened his mind upon divers questions of the Scripture: for to him he durst be bold to disclose his heart. Unto whom the doctor said, 'Do you not know that the pope is very Antichrist, whom the Scripture speaketh of? But beware what you say; for if you shall be perceived to be of that opinion, it will cost you your life.'

Not long after, Master Tyndale happened to be in the company of a certain divine, recounted for a learned man, and, in communing and disputing with him, he drove him to that issue, that the said great doctor burst out into these blasphemous words, 'We were better to be without God's laws than the pope's.' Master Tyndale, hearing this, full of godly zeal, and not bearing that blasphemous saying, replied, 'I defy the pope, and all his laws,' and added, If God spared him life, ere many years he would cause a boy that driveth the plough to know more of the Scripture than he did.

The grudge of the priests increasing still more and more against Tyndale, they never ceased barking and rating at him, and laid many things sorely to his charge, saying that he was a heretic. Being so molested and vexed, he was constrained to leave that country, and to seek another place; and so coming to Master Welch, he desired him, of his good will, that he might depart from him, saying: 'Sir, I perceive that I shall not be suffered to tarry long here in this country, neither shall you be able, though you would, to keep me out of the hands of the spirituality; what displeasure might grow to you by keeping me, God knoweth; for the which I should be right sorry.'

So that in fine, Master Tyndale, with the good will of his master, departed, and soon came up to London, and there preached a while, as he had done in the country.

Bethinking himself of Cuthbert Tonstal, then bishop of London, and especially of the great commendation of Erasmus, who, in his annotations, so extolleth the said Tonstal for his learning, Tyndale thus cast with himself, that if he might attain unto his service, he were a happy man. Coming to Sir Henry Guildford, the king's comptroller, and bringing with him an oration of Isocrates, which he had translated out of Greek into English, he desired him to speak to the said bishop of London for him; which he also did; and willed him moreover to write an epistle to the bishop, and to go himself with him. This he did, and delivered his epistle to a servant of his, named William Hebilthwait, a man of his old acquaintance. But God, who secretly disposeth the course of things, saw that was not best for Tyndale's purpose, nor for the profit of His Church, and therefore gave him to find little favour in the bishop's sight; the answer of whom was this: his house was full; he had more than he could well find: and he advised him to seek in London abroad, where, he said, he could lack no service.

Being refused of the bishop he came to Humphrey Mummuth, alderman of London, and besought him to help him: who the same time took him into his house, where the said Tyndale lived (as Mummuth said) like a good priest, studying both night and day. He would eat but sodden meat by his good will, nor drink but small single beer. He was never seen in the house to wear linen about him, all the space of his being there.

And so remained Master Tyndale in London almost a year, marking with himself the course of the world, and especially the demeanor of the preachers, how they boasted themselves, and set up their authority; beholding also the pomp of the prelates, with other things more, which greatly misliked him; insomuch that he understood not only that there was no room in the bishop's house for him to translate the New Testament, but also that there was no place to do it in all England.

Therefore, having by God's providence some aid ministered unto him by Humphrey Mummuth, and certain other good men, he took his leave of the realm, and departed into Germany, where the good man, being inflamed with a tender care and zeal of his country, refused no travail nor diligence, how, by all means possible, to reduce his brethren and countrymen of England to the same taste and understanding of God's holy Word and verity, which the Lord had endued him withal. Whereupon, considering in his mind, and conferring also with John Frith, Tyndale thought with himself no way more to conduce thereunto, than if the Scripture were turned into the vulgar speech, that the poor people might read and see the simple plain Word of God. He perceived that it was not possible to establish the lay people in any truth, except the Scriptures were so plainly laid before their eyes in their mother tongue that they might see the meaning of the text; for else, whatsoever truth should be taught them, the enemies of the truth would quench it, either with reasons of sophistry, and traditions of their own making, founded without all ground of Scripture; or else juggling with the text, expounding it in such a sense as it were impossible to gather of the text, if the right meaning thereof were seen.

Master Tyndale considered this only, or most chiefly, to be the cause of all mischief in the Church, that the Scriptures of God were hidden from the people's eyes; for so long the abominable doings and idolatries maintained by the pharisaical clergy could not be espied; and therefore all their labour was with might and main to keep it down, so that either it should not be read at all, or if it were, they would darken the right sense with the mist of their sophistry, and so entangle those who rebuked or despised their abominations; wresting the Scripture unto their own purpose, contrary unto the meaning of the text, they would so delude the unlearned lay people, that though thou felt in thy heart, and wert sure that all were false that they said, yet couldst thou not solve their subtle riddles.

For these and such other considerations this good man was stirred up of God to translate the Scripture into his mother tongue, for the profit of the simple people of his country; first setting in hand with the New Testament, which came forth in print about AD 1525. Cuthbert Tonstal, bishop of London, with Sir Thomas More, being sore aggrieved, despised how to destroy that false erroneous translation, as they called it.

It happened that one Augustine Packington, a mercer, was then at Antwerp, where the bishop was. This man favoured Tyndale, but showed the contrary unto the bishop. The bishop, being desirous to bring his purpose to pass, communed how that he would gladly buy the New Testaments. Packington hearing him say so, said, 'My lord! I can do more in this matter than most merchants that be here, if it be your pleasure; for I know the Dutchmen and strangers that have brought them of Tyndale, and have them here to sell; so that if it be your lordship's pleasure, I must disburse money to pay for them, or else I cannot have them: and so I will assure you to have every book of them that is printed and unsold.' The bishop, thinking he had God 'by the toe', said, 'Do your diligence, gentle Master Packington! get them for me, and I will pay whatsoever they cost; for I intend to burn and destroy them all at Paul's Cross.' This Augustine Packington went unto William Tyndale, and declared the whole matter, and so, upon compact made between them, the bishop of London had the books, Packington had the thanks, and Tyndale had the money.

After this, Tyndale corrected the same New Testaments again, and caused them to be newly imprinted, so that they came thick and threefold over into England. When the bishop perceived that, he sent for Packington, and said to him, 'How cometh this, that there are so many New Testaments abroad? You promised me that you would buy them all.' Then answered Packington, 'Surely, I bought all that were to be had, but I perceive they have printed more since. I see it will never be better so long as they have letters and stamps: wherefore you were best to buy the stamps too, and so you shall be sure,' at which answer the bishop smiled, and so the matter ended.

In short space after, it fortuned that George Constantine was apprehended by Sir Thomas More, who was then chancellor of England, as suspected of certain heresies. Master More asked of him, saying, 'Constantine! I would have thee be plain with me in one thing that I will ask; and I promise thee I will show thee favour in all other things whereof thou art accused. There is beyond the sea, Tyndale, Joye, and a great many of you: I know they cannot live without help. There are some that succour them with money; and thou, being one of them, hadst thy part thereof, and therefore knowest whence it came. I pray thee, tell me, who be they that help them thus?' 'My lord,' quoth Constantine, 'I will tell you truly: it is the bishop of London that hath holpen us, for he hath bestowed among us a great deal of money upon New Testaments to burn them; and that hath been, and yet is, our only succour and comfort.' 'Now by my troth,' quoth More, 'I think even the same; for so much I told the bishop before he went about it.'

After that, Master Tyndale took in hand to translate the Old Testament, finishing the five books of Moses, with sundry most learned and godly prologues most worthy to be read and read again by all good Christians. These books being sent over into England, it cannot be spoken what a door of light they opened to the eyes of the whole English nation, which before were shut up in darkness.

At his first departing out of the realm he took his journey into Germany, where he had conference with Luther and other learned men; after he had continued there a certain season he came down into the Netherlands, and had his most abiding in the town of Antwerp.

The godly books of Tyndale, and especially the New Testament of his translation, after that they began to come into men's hands, and to spread abroad, wrought great and singular profit to the godly; but the ungodly (envying and disdaining that the people should be anything wiser than they and, fearing lest by the shining beams of truth, their works of darkness should be discerned) began to stir with no small ado.

At what time Tyndale had translated Deuteronomy, minding to print the same at Hamburg, he sailed thitherward; upon the coast of Holland he suffered shipwreck, by which he lost all his books, writings, and copies, his money and his time, and so was compelled to begin all again. He came in another ship to Hamburg, where, at his appointment, Master Coverdale tarried for him, and helped him in the translating of the whole five books of Moses, from Easter until December, in the house of a worshipful widow, Mistress Margaret Van Emmerson, AD 1529, a great sweating sickness being at the same time in the town. So, having dispatched his business at Hamburg, he returned to Antwerp.

When God's will was, that the New Testament in the common tongue should come abroad, Tyndale, the translator thereof, added to the latter end a certain epistle, wherein he desired them that were learned to amend, if ought were found amiss. Wherefore if there had been any such default deserving correction, it had been the part of courtesy and gentleness, for men of knowledge and judgment to have showed their learning therein, and to have redressed what was to be amended. But the clergy, not willing to have that book prosper, cried out upon it, that there were a thousand heresies in it, and that it was not to be corrected, but utterly to be suppressed. Some said it was not possible to translate the Scriptures into English; some that it was not lawful for the lay people to have it in their mother tongue; some, that it would make them all heretics. And to the intent to induce the temporal rulers unto their purpose, they said it would make the people to rebel against the king.

All this Tyndale himself, in his prologue before the first book of Moses, declareth; showing further what great pains were taken in examining that translation, and comparing it with their own imaginations, that with less labour, he supposeth, they might have translated a great part of the Bible; showing moreover that they scanned and examined every tittle and point in such sort, and so narrowly, that there was not one therein, but if it lacked a prick over his head, they did note it, and numbered it unto the ignorant people for a heresy.

So great were then the froward devices of the English clergy (who should have been the guides of light unto the people), to drive the people from the knowledge of the Scripture, which neither they would translate themselves, nor yet abide it to be translated of others; to the intent (as Tyndale saith) that the world being kept still in darkness, they might sit in the consciences of the people through vain superstition and false doctrine, to satisfy their ambition, and insatiable covetousness, and to exalt their own honour above king and emperor.

The bishops and prelates never rested before they had brought the king to their consent; by reason whereof, a proclamation in all haste was devised and set forth under public authority, that the Testament of Tyndale's translation was inhibited – which was about AD 1537. And not content herewith, they proceeded further, how to entangle him in their nets, and to bereave him of his life; which how they brought to pass, now it remaineth to be declared.

In the registers of London it appeareth manifest how that the bishops and Sir Thomas More having before them such as had been at Antwerp, most studiously would search and examine all things belonging to Tyndale, where and with whom he hosted, whereabouts stood the house, what was his stature, in what apparel he went, what resort he had; all which things when they had diligently learned then began they to work their feats.

William Tyndale, being in the town of Antwerp, had been lodged about one whole year in the house of Thomas Pointz, an Englishman, who kept a house of English merchants. Came thither one out of England, whose name was Henry Philips, his father being customer of Poole, a comely fellow, like as he had been a gentleman having a servant with him: but wherefore he came, or for what purpose he was sent thither, no man could tell.

Master Tyndale divers times was desired forth to dinner and support amongst merchants; by means whereof this Henry Philips became acquainted with him, so that within short space Master Tyndale had a great confidence in him, and brought him to his lodging, to the house of Thomas Pointz; and had him also once or twice with him to dinner and supper, and further entered such friendship with him, that through his procurement he lay in the same house of the said Pointz; to whom he showed moreover his books, and other secrets of his study, so little did Tyndale then mistrust this traitor.

But Pointz, having no great confidence in the fellow, asked Master Tyndale how he came acquainted with this Philips. Master Tyndale answered, that he was an honest man, handsomely learned, and very conformable. Pointz, perceiving that he bare such favour to him, said no more, thinking that he was brought acquainted with him by some friend of his. The said Philips, being in the town three or four days, upon a time desired Pointz to walk with him forth of the town to show him the commodities thereof, and in walking together without the town, had communication of divers things, and some of the king's affairs; by which talk Pointz as yet suspected nothing. But after, when the time was past, Pointz perceived this to be the mind of Philips, to feel whether the said Pointz might, for lucre of money, help him to his purpose, for he perceived before that Philips was monied, and would that Pointz should think no less. For he had desired Pointz before to help him to divers things; and such things as he named, he required might be of the best, 'for,' said he, 'I have money enough'.

Philips went from Antwerp to the court of Brussels, which is from thence twenty-four English miles, whence he brought with him to Antwerp, the procurator-general, who is the emperor's attorney, with certain other officers.

Within three or four days, Pointz went forth to the town of Barois, being eighteen English miles from Antwerp, where he had business to do for the space of a month or six weeks; and in the time of his absence Henry Philips came again to Antwerp, to the house of Pointz, and coming in, spake with his wife, asking whether Master Tyndale were within. Then went he forth again and set the officers whom he had brought with him from Brussels, in the street, and about the door. About noon he came again, and went to Master Tyndale, and desired him to lend him forty shillings, 'for,' said he, 'I lost my purse this morning, coming over at the passage between this and Mechlin'. So Master Tyndale took him forty shillings, which was easy to be had of him, if he had it; for in the wily subtleties of this world he was simple and inexpert. Then said Philips, 'Master Tyndale! you shall be my guest here this day.' 'No,' said Master Tyndale, 'I go forth this day to dinner, and you shall go with me, and be my guest, where you shall be welcome.'

So when it was dinner time, Master Tyndale went forth with Philips, and at the going forth of Pointz's house, was a long narrow entry, so that two could not go in front. Master Tyndale would have put Philips before him, but Philips would in no wise, but put Master Tyndale before, for that he pretended to show great humanity. So Master Tyndale, being a man of no great stature, went before, and Philips, a tall, comely person, followed behind him; who had set officers on either side of the door upon two seats, who might see who came in the entry. Philips pointed with his finger over Master Tyndale's head down to him, that the officers might see that it was he whom they should take. The officers afterwards told Pointz, when they had laid him in prison, that they pitied to see his simplicity. They brought him to the emperor's attorney, where he dined. Then came the procurator-general to the house of Pointz, and sent away all that was there of Master Tyndale's, as well his books as other things; and from thence Tyndale was had to the castle of Vilvorde, eighteen English miles from Antwerp.

Master Tyndale, remaining in prison, was proffered an advocate and a procurator; the which he refused, saying that he would make answer for himself. He had so preached to them who had him in charge, and such as was there conversant with him in the Castle that they reported of him, that if he were not a good Christian man, they knew not whom they might take to be one.

At last, after much reasoning, when no reason would serve, although he deserved no death, he was condemned by virtue of the emperor's decree, made in the assembly at Augsburg. Brought forth to the place of execution, he was tied to the stake, strangled by the hangman, and afterwards consumed with fire, at the town of Vilvorde, AD 1536; crying at the stake with a fervent zeal, and a loud voice, 'Lord! open the king of England's eyes.'

Such was the power of his doctrine, and the sincerity of his life, that during the time of his imprisonment (which endured a year and a half), he converted, it is said, his keeper, the keeper's daughter, and others of his household.

As touching his translation of the New Testament, because his enemies did so much carp at it, pretending it to be full of heresies, he wrote to John Frith, as followeth, 'I call God to record against the day we shall appear before our Lord Jesus, that I never altered one syllable of God's Word against my conscience, nor would do this day, if all that is in earth, whether it be honour, pleasure, or riches, might be given me.'

✝ CHAPTER 16 ✝

Persecutions in England during the reign of Queen Mary

The premature death of that celebrated young monarch Edward VI occasioned the most extraordinary and wonderful occurrences, which had ever existed from the times of our blessed Lord and Saviour's incarnation in human shape. This melancholy event became speedily a subject of general regret. The succession to the British throne was soon made a matter of contention; and the scenes which ensued were a demonstration of the serious affliction in which the kingdom was involved. As his loss to the nation was more and more unfolded, the remembrance of his government was more and more the basis of grateful recollection. The very awful prospect, which was soon presented to the friends of Edward's administration, under the direction of his counsellors and servants, was a contemplation which the reflecting mind was compelled to regard with most alarming apprehensions. The rapid approaches which were made towards a total reversion of the proceedings of the young king's reign, denoted the advances which were thereby represented to an entire resolution in the management of public affairs both in Church and state.

Alarmed for the condition in which the kingdom was likely to be involved by the king's death, an endeavor to prevent the consequences, which were but too plainly foreseen, was productive of the most serious and fatal effects. The king, in his long and lingering affliction, was induced to make a will, by which he bequeathed the English crown to Lady Jane, the daughter of the duke of Suffolk, who had been married to Lord Guildford, the son of the duke of Northumberland, and was the granddaughter of the second sister of King Henry, by Charles, duke of Suffolk. By this will, the succession of Mary and Elizabeth, his two sisters, was entirely superseded, from an apprehension of the returning system of popery; and the king's council, with the chief of the nobility, the lord-mayor of the city of London, and almost all the judges and the principal lawyers of the realm, subscribed their names to this regulation, as a sanction to the measure. Lord Chief Justice Hale, though a true Protestant and an upright

judge, alone declined to unite his name in favour of Lady Jane, because he had already signified his opinion that Mary was entitled to assume the reins of government. Others objected to
Mary's being placed on the throne, on account of their fears that she might marry a foreigner,
and thereby bring the crown into considerable danger. Her partiality to popery also left little
doubt in the minds of any, that she would be induced to revive the dormant interests of the
pope, and change the religion which had been used both in the days of her father, King Henry,
and in those of her brother Edward: for in all his time she had manifested the greatest stubbornness and inflexibility of temper, as must be obvious from her letter to the lords of the
council, whereby she put in her claim to the crown, on her brother's decease.

When this happened, the nobles, who had associated to prevent Mary's succession, and
had been instrumental in promoting, and, perhaps, advising the measures of Edward, speedily
proceeded to proclaim Lady Jane Gray, to be queen of England, in the city of London and
various other populous cities of the realm. Though young, she possessed talents of a very
superior nature, and her improvements under a most excellent tutor had given her many
very great advantages.

Her reign was of only five days' continuance, for Mary, having succeeded by false promises
in obtaining the crown, speedily commenced the execution of her avowed intention of extir-
pating and burning every Protestant. She was crowned at Westminster in the usual form, and
her elevation was the signal for the commencement of the bloody persecution which followed.

Having obtained the sword of authority, she was not sparing in its exercise. The supporters
of Lady Jane Gray were destined to feel its force. The duke of Northumberland was the first
who experienced her savage resentment. Within a month after his confinement in the Tower,
he was condemned, and brought to the scaffold, to suffer as a traitor. From his varied crimes,
resulting out of a sordid and inordinate ambition, he died unpitied and unlamented.

The changes, which followed with rapidity, unequivocally declared that the queen was disaffected to the present state of religion. Dr Poynet was displaced to make room for Gardiner to be
bishop of Winchester, to whom she also gave the important office of lord-chancellor. Dr Ridley
was dismissed from the see of London, and Bonne introduced. J. Story was put out of the
bishopric of Chichester, to admit Dr Day. J. Hooper was sent prisoner to the Fleet, and Dr Heath
put into the see of Worcester. Miles Coverdale was also excluded from Exeter, and Dr Vesie
placed in that diocese. Dr Tonstall was also promoted to the see of Durham. These things being
marked and perceived, great heaviness and discomfort grew more and more to all good men's
hearts; but to the wicked great rejoicing. They that could dissemble took no great care how the
matter went; but such, whose consciences were joined with the truth, perceived already coals to
be kindled, which after should be the destruction of many a true Christian.

The Words and Behaviour of the Lady Jane upon the Scaffold

The next victim was the amiable Lady Jane Gray, who, by her acceptance of the crown at the
earnest solicitations of her friends, incurred the implacable resentment of the bloody Mary.
When she first mounted the scaffold, she spoke to the spectators in this manner: 'Good people,
I am come hither to die, and by a law I am condemned to the same. The fact against the queen's
highness was unlawful, and the consenting thereunto by me: but, touching the procurement

and desire thereof by me, or on my behalf, I do wash my hands thereof in innocency before God, and the face of you, good Christian people, this day,' and therewith she wrung her hands, wherein she had her book. Then said she, 'I pray you all, good Christian people, to bear me witness, that I die a good Christian woman, and that I do look to be saved by no other mean, but only by the mercy of God in the blood of His only Son Jesus Christ: and I confess that when I did know the Word of God, I neglected the same, loved myself and the world, and therefore this plague and punishment is happily and worthily happened unto me for my sins; and yet I thank God, that of His goodness He hath thus given me a time and a respite to repent. And now, good people, while I am alive, I pray you assist me with your prayers.' And then, kneeling down, she turned to Feckenham, saying, 'Shall I say this Psalm?' and he said, 'Yea.' Then she said the Psalm of *Miserere mei Deus*, in English, in a most devout manner throughout to the end; and then she stood up, and gave her maid, Mrs Ellen, her gloves and handkerchief, and her book to Mr Bruges; and then she untied her gown, and the executioner pressed upon her to help her off with it: but she, desiring him to let her alone, turned towards her two gentle-women, who helped her off therewith, giving to her a fair handkerchief to put about her eyes.

Then the executioner kneeled down, and asked her forgiveness, whom she forgave most willingly. Then he desired her to stand upon the straw, which doing, she saw the block. Then she said, 'I pray you, despatch me quickly.' Then she kneeled down, saying, 'Will you take it off before I lay me down?' And the executioner said, 'No, madam.' Then she tied a handkerchief about her eyes, and feeling for the block, she said, 'What shall I do? Where is it? Where is it?' One of the standers-by guiding her thereunto, she laid her head upon the block, and then stretched forth her body, and said, 'Lord, into Thy hands I commend my spirit'; and so finished her life, in the year of our Lord 1554, the twelfth day of February, about the seventeenth year of her age.

Thus died Lady Jane; and on the same day Lord Guildford, her husband, one of the duke of Northumberland's sons, was likewise beheaded, two innocents in comparison with them that sat upon them. For they were both very young, and ignorantly accepted that which others had contrived, and by open proclamation consented to take from others, and give to them.

Touching the condemnation of this pious lady, it is to be noted that Judge Morgan, who gave sentence against her, soon after he had condemned her, fell mad, and in his raving cried out continually to have the Lady Jane taken away from him, and so he ended his life.

On the twenty-first day of the same month, Henry, duke of Suffolk, was beheaded on Tower-hill, the fourth day after his condemnation: about which time many gentlemen and yeomen were condemned, whereof some were executed at London, and some in the country. In the number of whom was Lord Thomas Gray, brother to the said duke, being apprehended not long after in North Wales, and executed for the same. Sir Nicholas Throgmorton, also, very narrowly escaped.

John Rogers, Vicar of St Sepulchre's, and Reader of St Paul's, London

John Rogers was educated at Cambridge, and was afterward many years chaplain to the merchant adventurers at Antwerp in Brabant. Here he met with the celebrated martyr William Tyndale, and Miles Coverdale, both voluntary exiles from their country for their aversion to popish superstition and idolatry. They were the instruments of his conversion; and he united with them in that translation of the Bible into English, entitled 'The Translation of Thomas Matthew.' From the Scriptures he knew that unlawful vows may be lawfully broken; hence he married, and removed to Wittenberg in Saxony, for the improvement of learning; and he there learned the Dutch language, and received the charge of a congregation, which he faithfully executed for many years. On King Edward's accession, he left Saxony to promote the work of reformation in England; and, after some time, Nicholas Ridley, then bishop of London, gave him a prebend in St Paul's Cathedral, and the dean and chapter appointed him reader of the divinity lesson there. Here he continued until Queen Mary's succession to the throne, when the Gospel and true religion were banished, and the Antichrist of Rome, with his superstition and idolatry, introduced.

The circumstance of Mr Rogers having preached at Paul's cross, after Queen Mary arrived at the Tower, has been already stated. He confirmed in his sermon the true doctrine taught in King Edward's time, and exhorted the people to beware of the pestilence of popery, idolatry, and superstition. For this he was called to account, but so ably defended himself that, for that time, he was dismissed. The proclamation of the queen, however, to prohibit true preaching, gave his enemies a new handle against him. Hence he was again summoned before the council, and commanded to keep his house. He did so, though he might have escaped; and though he perceived the state of the true religion to be desperate. He knew he could not want a living in Germany; and he could not forget a wife and ten children, and to seek means to succour them. But all these things were insufficient to induce him to depart, and, when once called to answer in Christ's cause, he stoutly defended it, and hazarded his life for that purpose.

After long imprisonment in his own house, the restless Bonner, bishop of London, caused him to be committed to Newgate, there to be lodged among thieves and murderers.

After Mr Rogers had been long and straitly imprisoned, and lodged in Newgate among thieves, often examined, and very uncharitably entreated, and at length unjustly and most cruelly condemned by Stephen Gardiner, bishop of Winchester, the fourth day of February, in the year of our Lord 1555, being Monday in the morning, he was suddenly warned by the keeper of Newgate's wife, to prepare himself for the fire; who, being then sound asleep, could scarce be awaked. At length being raised and awaked, and bid to make haste, then said he, 'If it be so, I need not tie my points.' And so was had down, first to bishop Bonner to be degraded: which being done, he craved of Bonner but one petition; and Bonner asked what that should be. Mr Rogers replied that he might speak a few words with his wife before his burning, but that could not be obtained of him.

When the time came that he should be brought out of Newgate to Smithfield, the place of his execution, Mr Woodroofe, one of the sheriffs, first came to Mr Rogers, and asked him if he would revoke his abominable doctrine, and the evil opinion of the Sacrament of the altar. Mr Rogers answered, 'That which I have preached I will seal with my blood.' Then Mr Woodroofe said, 'Thou art an heretic.' 'That shall be known', quoth Mr Rogers, 'at the Day of Judgment.' 'Well,' said Mr Woodroofe, 'I will never pray for thee.' 'But I will pray for you,' said Mr Rogers; and so was brought the same day, the fourth of February, by the sheriffs, towards Smithfield, saying the Psalm *Miserere* by the way, all the people wonderfully rejoicing at his constancy; with great praises and thanks to God for the same. And there in the presence of Mr Rochester, comptroller of the queen's household, Sir Richard Southwell, both the sheriffs, and a great number of people, he was burnt to ashes, washing his hands in the flame as he was burning. A little before his burning, his pardon was brought, if he would have recanted; but he utterly refused it. He was the first martyr of all the blessed company that suffered in Queen Mary's time that gave the first adventure upon the fire. His wife and children, being eleven in number, ten able to go, and one sucking at her breast, met him by the way, as he went towards Smithfield. This sorrowful sight of his own flesh and blood could nothing move him, but that he constantly and cheerfully took his death with wonderful patience, in the defence and quarrel of the Gospel of Christ.

Rev Lawrence Saunders

Mr Saunders, after passing some time in the school of Eaton, was chosen to go to King's College in Cambridge, where he continued three years, and profited in knowledge and learning very much for that time. Shortly after he quitted the university, and went to his parents, but soon returned to Cambridge again to his study, where he began to add to the knowledge of Latin, the study of the Greek and Hebrew tongues, and gave himself up to the study of the Holy Scriptures, the better to qualify himself for the office of preacher.

In the beginning of King Edward's reign, when God's true religion was introduced, after licence obtained, he began to preach, and was so well liked of them who then had authority that they appointed him to read a divinity lecture in the College of Forthringham. The College of Forthringham being dissolved he was placed to be a reader in the minster at Litchfield. After a certain space, he departed from Litchfield to a benefice in Leicestershire, called Church-langton, where he held a residence, taught diligently, and kept a liberal house. Thence he was orderly called to take a benefice in the city of London, namely, All-hallows in Bread-street. After this he preached at Northampton, nothing meddling with the state, but boldly uttering his conscience against the popish doctrines which were likely to spring up again in England, as a just plague for the little love which the English nation then bore to the blessed Word of God, which had been so plentifully offered unto them.

The queen's party who were there, and heard him, were highly displeased with him for his sermon, and for it kept him among them as a prisoner. But partly for love of his brethren and friends, who were chief actors for the queen among them, and partly because there was no law broken by his preaching, they dismissed him.

Some of his friends, perceiving such fearful menacing, counselled him to fly out of the realm, which he refused to do. But seeing he was with violence kept from doing good in that place, he returned towards London, to visit his flock.

In the afternoon of Sunday, October 15, 1554, as he was reading in his church to exhort his people, the bishop of London interrupted him, by sending an officer for him.

His treason and sedition the bishop's charity was content to let slip until another time, but a heretic he meant to prove him, and all those, he said, who taught and believed that the administration of the Sacraments, and all orders of the Church, are the most pure, which come the nearest to the order of the primitive Church.

After much talk concerning this matter, the bishop desired him to write what he believed of transubstantiation. Lawrence Saunders did so, saying, 'My Lord, you seek my blood, and you shall have it: I pray God that you may be so baptised in it that you may ever after loathe blood-sucking, and become a better man.' Upon being closely charged with contumacy, the severe replies of Mr Saunders to the bishop (who had before, to get the favour of Henry VIII written and set forth in print, a book of true obedience, wherein he had openly declared Queen Mary to be a bastard) so irritated him that he exclaimed, 'Carry away this frenzied fool to prison.'

After this good and faithful martyr had been kept in prison one year and a quarter, the bishops at length called him, as they did his fellow-prisoners, openly to be examined before the queen's council.

His examination being ended, the officers led him out of the place, and stayed until the rest of his fellow-prisoners were likewise examined, that they might lead them all together to prison.

After his excommunication and delivery over to the secular power, he was brought by the sheriff of London to the Compter, a prison in his own parish of Bread-street, at which he rejoiced greatly, both because he found there a fellow-prisoner, Mr Cardmaker, with whom he had much Christian and comfortable discourse; and because out of prison, as before in his pulpit, he might have an opportunity of preaching to his parishioners. On the fourth of February, Bonner, bishop of London, came to the prison to degrade him; the day following, in the morning the sheriff of London delivered him to certain of the queen's guard, who were appointed to carry him to the city of Coventry, there to be burnt.

When they had arrived at Coventry, a poor shoemaker, who used to serve him with shoes, came to him, and said, 'O my good master, God strengthen and comfort you.' 'Good shoemaker,' Mr Saunders replied, 'I desire thee to pray for me, for I am the most unfit man for this high office, that ever was appointed to it; but my gracious God and dear Father is able to make me strong enough.' The next day, being the eighth of February, 1555, he was led to the place of execution, in the park, without the city. He went in an old gown and a shirt, barefooted, and oftentimes fell flat on the ground, and prayed. When he was come to nigh the place, the officer, appointed to see the execution done, said to Mr Saunders that he was one of them who marred the queen's realm, but if he would recant, there was pardon for him. 'Not I,' replied the holy martyr, 'but such as you have injured the realm. The blessed Gospel of Christ is what I hold; that do I believe, that have I taught, and that will I never revoke!' Mr Saunders then slowly moved towards the fire, sank to the earth and prayed; he then rose up, embraced the stake, and frequently said, 'Welcome, thou cross of Christ! Welcome everlasting life!' Fire was then put to the fagots, and, he was overwhelmed by the dreadful flames, and sweetly slept in the Lord Jesus.

The History, Imprisonment, and Examination of Mr John Hooper, Bishop of Worcester and Gloucester

John Hooper, student and graduate in the University of Oxford, was stirred with such fervent desire to the love and knowledge of the Scriptures that he was compelled to move from thence, and was retained in the house of Sir Thomas Arundel, as his steward, until Sir Thomas had intelligence of his opinions and religion, which he in no case did favour, though he exceedingly favoured his person and condition and wished to be his friend. Mr Hooper now prudently left

Sir Thomas' house and arrived at Paris, but in a short time returned to England, and was retained by Mr Sentlow, until the time that he was again molested and sought for, when he passed through France to the higher parts of Germany; where, commencing acquaintance with learned men, he was by them free and lovingly entertained, both at Basel, and especially at Zurich, by Mr Bullinger, who was his singular friend; here also he married his wife, who was a Burgonian, and applied very studiously to the Hebrew tongue.

At length, when God saw it good to stay the bloody time of the six articles, and to give us King Edward to reign over this realm, with some peace and rest unto the Church, amongst many other English exiles, who then repaired homeward, Mr Hooper also, moved in conscience, thought not to absent himself, but seeing such a time and occasion, offered to help forward the Lord's work, to the uttermost of his ability.

When Mr Hooper had taken his farewell of Mr Bullinger, and his friends in Zurich, he repaired again to England in the reign of King Edward VI, and coming to London, used continually to preach, most times twice, or at least once a day.

In his sermons, according to his accustomed manner, he corrected sin, and sharply inveighed against the iniquity of the world and the corrupt abuses of the Church. The people in great flocks and companies daily came to hear his voice, as the most melodious sound and tune of Orpheus' harp, insomuch, that oftentimes when he was preaching, the church would be so full that none could enter farther than the doors thereof. In his doctrine he was earnest, in tongue eloquent, in the Scriptures perfect, in pains indefatigable, in his life exemplary.

Having preached before the king's majesty, he was soon after made bishop of Gloucester. In that office he continued two years, and behaved himself so well that his very enemies could find no fault with him, and after that he was made bishop of Worcester.

Dr Hooper executed the office of a most careful and vigilant pastor, for the space of two years and more, as long as the state of religion in King Edward's time was sound and flourishing.

After he had been cited to appear before Bonner and Dr Heath, he was led to the Council, accused falsely of owing the queen money, and in the next year, 1554, he wrote an account of his severe treatment during near eighteen months' confinement in the Fleet, and after his third examination, January 28, 1555, at St Mary Overy's, he, with the Rev Mr Rogers, was conducted to the Compter in Southwark, there to remain until the next day at nine o'clock, to see whether they would recant. 'Come, Brother Rogers,' said Dr Hooper, 'must we two take this matter first in hand, and begin to fry in these fagots?' 'Yes, Doctor,' said Mr Rogers, 'by God's grace.' 'Doubt not,' said Dr Hooper, 'but God will give us strength'; and the people so applauded their constancy that they had much ado to pass.

January 29, Bishop Hooper was degraded and condemned, and the Rev Mr Rogers was treated in like manner. At dark, Dr Hooper was led through the city to Newgate; notwithstanding this secrecy, many people came forth to their doors with lights, and saluted him, praising God for his constancy.

During the few days he was in Newgate, he was frequently visited by Bonner and others, but without avail. As Christ was tempted, so they tempted him, and then maliciously reported that he had recanted. The place of his martyrdom being fixed at Gloucester, he rejoiced very much, lifting up his eyes and hands to heaven, and praising God that he saw it good to send him among the people over whom he was pastor, there to confirm with his death the truth which he had before taught them.

On February 7, he came to Gloucester, about five o'clock, and lodged at one Ingram's house. After his first sleep, he continued in prayer until morning; and all the day, except a little time at his meals, and when conversing such as the guard kindly permitted to speak to him, he spent in prayer.

Sir Anthony Kingston, at one time Dr Hooper's good friend, was appointed by the queen's letters to attend at his execution. As soon as he saw the bishop he burst into tears. With tender entreaties he exhorted him to live. 'True it is,' said the bishop, 'that death is bitter, and life is sweet; but alas! consider that the death to come is more bitter, and the life to come is more sweet.'

The same day a blind boy obtained leave to be brought into Dr Hooper's presence. The same boy, not long before, had suffered imprisonment at Gloucester for confessing the truth. 'Ah! poor boy,' said the bishop, 'though God hath taken from thee thy outward sight, for what reason He best knoweth, yet He hath endued thy soul with the eye of knowledge and of faith. God give thee grace continually to pray unto Him, that thou lose not that sight, for then wouldst thou indeed be blind both in body and soul.'

When the mayor waited upon him preparatory to his execution, he expressed his perfect obedience, and only requested that a quick fire might terminate his torments. After he had got up in the morning, he desired that no man should be suffered to come into the chamber, that he might be solitary until the hour of execution.

About eight o'clock, on February 9, 1555, he was led forth, and many thousand persons were collected, as it was market-day. All the way, being straitly charged not to speak, and beholding the people, who mourned bitterly for him, he would sometimes lift up his eyes towards heaven, and look very cheerfully upon such as he knew: and he was never known, during the time of his being among them, to look with so cheerful and ruddy a countenance as he did at that time. When he came to the place appointed where he should die, he smilingly beheld the stake and preparation made for him, which was near unto the great elm tree over against the college of priests, where he used to preach.

Now, after he had entered into prayer, a box was brought and laid before him upon a stool, with his pardon from the queen, if he would turn. At the sight whereof he cried, 'If you love my soul, away with it!' The box being taken away, Lord Chandois said, 'Seeing there is no remedy; despatch him quickly.'

Command was now given that the fire should be kindled. But because there were not more green fagots than two horses could carry, it kindled not speedily, and was a pretty while also before it took the reeds upon the fagots. At length it burned about him, but the wind having full strength at that place, and being a lowering cold morning, it blew the flame from him, so that he was in a manner little more than touched by the fire.

Within a space after, a few dry fagots were brought, and a new fire kindled with fagots (for there were no more reeds) and those burned at the nether parts, but had small power above, because of the wind, saving that it burnt his hair and scorched his skin a little. In the time of which fire, even as at the first flame, he prayed, saying mildly, and not very loud, but as one without pain, 'O Jesus, Son of David, have mercy upon me, and receive my soul!' After the second fire was spent, he wiped both his eyes with his hands, and beholding the people, he said with an indifferent, loud voice, 'For God's love, good people, let me have more fire!' and all this while his nether parts did burn; but the fagots were so few that the flame only singed his upper parts.

The third fire was kindled within a while after, which was more extreme than the other two. In this fire he prayed with a loud voice, 'Lord Jesus, have mercy upon me! Lord Jesus receive my spirit!' And these were the last words he was heard to utter. But when he was black in the mouth, and his tongue so swollen that he could not speak, yet his lips went until they were shrunk to the gums: and he knocked his breast with his hands until one of his arms fell off, and then knocked still with the other, while the fat, water, and blood dropped out at his fingers' ends, until by renewing the fire, his strength was gone, and his hand clave fast in knocking to the iron upon his breast. Then immediately bowing forwards, he yielded up his spirit.

Thus was he three-quarters of an hour or more in the fire.

Even as a lamb, patiently he abode the extremity thereof, neither moving forwards, backwards, nor to any side; but he died as quietly as a child in his bed. And he now reigneth, I doubt not, as a blessed martyr in the joys of heaven, prepared for the faithful in Christ before the foundations of the world; for whose constancy all Christians are bound to praise God.

The Life and Conduct of Dr Rowland Taylor of Hadley

Dr Rowland Taylor, vicar of Hadley, in Suffolk, was a man of eminent learning, and had been admitted to the degree of doctor of the civil and canon law.

His attachment to the pure and uncorrupted principles of Christianity recommended him to the favour and friendship of Dr Cranmer, archbishop of Canterbury, with whom he lived a considerable time, until through his interest he obtained the living at Hadley.

Not only was his word a preaching unto them, but all his life and conversation was an example of unfeigned Christian life and true holiness. He was void of all pride, humble and meek as any child; so that none were so poor but they might boldly, as unto their father, resort unto him; neither was his lowliness childish or fearful, but, as occasion, time, and place required, he would be stout in rebuking the sinful and evildoers; so that none was so rich but he would tell them plainly his fault, with such earnest and grave rebukes as became a good curate and pastor. He was a man very mild, void of all rancour, grudge or evil will; ready to do good to all men; readily forgiving his enemies; and never sought to do evil to any.

To the poor that were blind, lame, sick, bedrid, or that had many children, he was a very father, a careful patron, and diligent provider, insomuch that he caused the parishioners to make a general provision for them; and he himself (beside the continual relief that they always found at his house) gave an honest portion yearly to the common almsbox. His wife also was an honest, discreet, and sober matron, and his children well nurtured, brought up in the fear of God and good learning.

He was a good salt of the earth, silverly biting the corrupt manners of evil men; a light in God's house, set upon a candlestick for all good men to imitate and follow.

Thus continued this good shepherd among his flock, governing and leading them through the wilderness of this wicked world, all the days of the most innocent and holy king of blessed memory, Edward VI. But on his demise, and the succession of Queen Mary to the throne, he escaped not the cloud that burst on so many beside; for two of his parishioners, Foster, an attorney, and Clark, a tradesman, out of blind zeal, resolved that Mass should be celebrated, in all its superstitious forms, in the parish church of Hadley, on Monday before Easter. This Dr Taylor, entering the church, strictly forbade; but Clark forced the Doctor out of the church, celebrated Mass, and immediately informed the lord-chancellor, bishop of Winchester of his behaviour, who summoned him to appear, and answer the complaints that were alleged against him.

The doctor upon the receipt of the summons, cheerfully prepared to obey the same; and rejected the advice of his friends to fly beyond sea. When Gardiner saw Dr Taylor, he, according to his common custom, reviled him. Dr Taylor heard his abuse patiently, and when the bishop said, 'How darest thou look me in the face! knowest thou not who I am?' Dr Taylor replied, 'You are Dr Stephen Gardiner, bishop of Winchester, and lord-chancellor, and yet but a mortal man. But if I should be afraid of your lordly looks, why fear ye not God, the Lord of us all? With what countenance will you appear before the judgment seat of Christ, and answer to your oath made first unto King Henry VIII, and afterward unto King Edward VI, his son?'

A long conversation ensued, in which Dr Taylor was so piously collected and severe upon his antagonist, that he exclaimed: 'Thou art a blasphemous heretic! Thou indeed blasphemist the blessed Sacrament (here he put off his cap), and speakest against the holy Mass, which is made a sacrifice for the quick and the dead.' The bishop afterward committed him into the king's bench.

When Dr Taylor came there, he found the virtuous and vigilant preacher of God's Word, Mr Bradford; who equally thanked God that He had provided him with such a comfortable fellow-prisoner; and they both together praised God, and continued in prayer, reading and exhorting one another.

After Dr Taylor had lain some time in prison, he was cited to appear in the arches of Bow-church.

Dr Taylor being condemned, was committed to the Clink, and the keepers were charged to treat him roughly; at night he was removed to the Poultry Compter.

When Dr Taylor had lain in the Compter about a week on the fourth of February, Bonner came to degrade him, bringing with him such ornaments as appertained to the massing mummery; but the Doctor refused these trappings until they were forced upon him.

The night after he was degraded his wife came with John Hull, his servant, and his son Thomas, and were by the gentleness of the keepers permitted to sup with him.

After supper, walking up and down, he gave God thanks for His grace, that had given him strength to abide by His holy Word. With tears they prayed together, and kissed one another. Unto his son Thomas he gave a Latin book, containing the notable sayings of the old martyrs, and in the end of that he wrote his testament: 'I say to my wife, and to my children, The Lord gave you unto me, and the Lord hath taken me from you, and you from me: blessed be the name of the Lord! I believe that they are blessed which die in the Lord. God careth for sparrows, and for the hairs of our heads. I have ever found Him more faithful and favourable, than is any father or husband. Trust ye therefore in Him by the means of our dear Saviour Christ's merits: believe, love, fear, and obey Him: pray to Him, for He hath promised to help. Count me not dead, for I shall certainly live, and never die. I go before, and you shall follow after, to our long home.'

On the morrow the sheriff of London with his officers came to the Compter by two o'clock in the morning, and brought forth Dr Taylor; and without any light led him to the Woolsack, an inn without Aldgate. Dr Taylor's wife, suspecting that her husband should that night be carried away, watched all night in St Botolph's church-porch beside Aldgate, having her two children, the one named Elizabeth, of thirteen years of age (whom, being left without father or mother, Dr Taylor had brought up of alms from three years old), the other named Mary, Dr Taylor's own daughter.

Now, when the sheriff and his company came against St Botolph's church, Elizabeth cried, saying, 'O my dear father! Mother, mother, here is my father led away.' Then his wife cried, 'Rowland, Rowland, where art thou?' for it was a very dark morning, that the one could not well see the other. Dr Taylor answered, 'Dear wife, I am here'; and stayed. The sheriff's men would have led him forth, but the sheriff said, 'Stay a little, masters, I pray you; and let him speak to his wife'; and so they stayed.

Then came she to him, and he took his daughter Mary in his arms; and he, his wife, and Elizabeth kneeled down and said the Lord's Prayer, at which sight the sheriff wept apace, and so did divers others of the company. After they had prayed, he rose up and kissed his wife, and shook her by the hand, and said, 'Farewell, my dear wife; be of good comfort, for I am quiet in my conscience. God shall stir up a father for my children.'

All the way Dr Taylor was joyful and merry, as one that counted himself going to a most pleasant banquet or bridal. He spake many notable things to the sheriff and yeomen of the guard that conducted him, and often moved them to weep, through his much earnest calling upon them to repent, and to amend their evil and wicked living. Oftentimes also he caused them to wonder and rejoice, to see him so constant and steadfast, void of all fear, joyful in heart, and glad to die.

When Dr Taylor had arrived at Aldham Common, the place where he should suffer, seeing a great multitude of people, he asked, 'What place is this, and what meaneth it that so much people are gathered hither?' It was answered, 'It is Aldham Common, the place where you must suffer; and the people have come to look upon you.' Then he said, 'Thanked be God, I am even at home'; and he alighted from his horse and with both hands rent the hood from his head.

His head had been notched and clipped like as a man would clip a fool's; which cost the good bishop Bonner had bestowed upon him. But when the people saw his reverend and ancient face, with a long white beard, they burst out with weeping tears, and cried, saying: 'God save thee, good Dr Taylor! Jesus Christ strengthen thee, and help thee! the Holy Ghost comfort thee!' with such other like good wishes.

When he had prayed, he went to the stake and kissed it, and set himself into a pitch barrel, which they had put for him to stand in, and stood with his back upright against the stake, with his hands folded together, and his eyes towards heaven, and continually prayed.

They then bound him with the chains, and having set up the fagots, one Warwick cruelly cast a fagot at him, which struck him on his head, and cut his face, so that the blood ran down. Then said Dr Taylor, 'O friend, I have harm enough; what needed that?'

Sir John Shelton standing by, as Dr Taylor was speaking, and saying the Psalm *Miserere* in English, struck him on the lips:

'You knave,' he said, 'speak Latin: I will make thee.' At last they kindled the fire; and Dr Taylor holding up both his hands, calling upon God, and said, 'Merciful Father of heaven! for Jesus Christ, my Saviour's sake, receive my soul into Thy hands!' So he stood still without either crying or moving, with his hands folded together, until Soyce, with a halberd struck him on the head until his brains fell out, and the corpse fell down into the fire.

Thus rendered up this man of God his blessed soul into the hands of his merciful Father, and to his most dear Saviour Jesus Christ, whom he most entirely loved, faithfully and earnestly preached, obediently followed in living, and constantly glorified in death.

Martyrdom of William Hunter

William Hunter had been trained to the doctrines of the Reformation from his earliest youth, being descended from religious parents, who carefully instructed him in the principles of true religion.

Hunter, then nineteen years of age, refusing to receive the communion at Mass, was threatened to be brought before the bishop; to whom this valiant young martyr was conducted by a constable.

Bonner caused William to be brought into a chamber, where he began to reason with him, promising him security and pardon if he would recant. Nay, he would have been content if he would have gone only to receive and to confession, but William would not do so for all the world.

Upon this the bishop commanded his men to put William in the stocks in his gate house, where he sat two days and nights, with a crust of brown bread and a cup of water only, which he did not touch.

At the two days' end, the bishop came to him, and finding him steadfast in the faith, sent him to the convict prison, and commanded the keeper to lay irons upon him as many as he could bear. He continued in prison three-quarters of a year, during which time he had been before the bishop five times, besides the time when he was condemned in the consistory in St Paul's, February 9, at which time his brother, Robert Hunter, was present.

Then the bishop, calling William, asked him if he would recant, and finding he was unchangeable, pronounced sentence upon him, that he should go from that place to Newgate for a time, and thence to Brentwood, there to be burned.

About a month afterward, William was sent down to Brentwood, where he was to be executed. On coming to the stake, he knelt down and read the Fifty-first Psalm, until he came to these words, 'The sacrifices of God are a broken spirit; a broken and a contrite heart, O God, Thou wilt not despise.' Steadfast in refusing the queen's pardon, if he would become an apostate, at length one Richard Ponde, a bailiff, came, and made the chain fast about him.

William now cast his psalter into his brother's hand, who said, 'William, think on the holy passion of Christ, and be not afraid of death.' 'Behold,' answered William, 'I am not afraid.' Then he lifted up his hands to heaven, and said, 'Lord, Lord, Lord, receive my spirit;' and casting down the head again into the smothering smoke, he yielded up his life for the truth, sealing it with his blood to the praise of God.

Dr Robert Farrar

This worthy and learned prelate, the bishop of St David's in Wales, having in the former reign, as well as since the accession of Mary, been remarkably zealous in promoting the reformed doctrines, and exploding the errors of popish idolatry, was summoned, among others, before the persecuting bishop of Winchester, and other commissioners set apart for the abominable work of devastation and massacre.

His principal accusers and persecutors, on a charge of praemunire in the reign of Edward VI were George Constantine Walter, his servant; Thomas Young, chanter of the cathedral, afterward bishop of Bangor, etc. Dr Farrar ably replied to the copies of information laid against him, consisting of fifty-six articles. The whole process of this trial was long and tedious. Delay succeeded delay, and after that Dr Farrar had been long unjustly detained in custody under sureties, in the reign of King Edward, because he had been promoted by the duke of Somerset, whence after his fall he found fewer friends to support him against such as wanted his bishopric by the coming in of Queen Mary, he was accused and examined not for any matter of praemunire, but for his faith and doctrine; for which he was called before the bishop of Winchester with Bishop Hooper, Mr Rogers, Mr Bradford, Mr Saunders, and others, February 4, 1555; on which day he would also with them have been condemned, but his condemnation was deferred, and he sent to prison again, where he continued until February 14, and then was sent into Wales to receive sentence. He was six times brought up before Henry Morgan, bishop of St David's, who demanded if he would abjure; from which he zealously dissented, and appealed to Cardinal Pole; notwithstanding which, the bishop, proceeding in his rage, pronounced him a heretic excommunicate, and surrendered him to the secular power.

Dr Farrar, being condemned and degraded, was not long after brought to the place of execution in the town of Carmathen, in the market-place of which, on the south side of the market-cross, March 30, 1555, being Saturday next before Passion Sunday, he most constantly sustained the torments of the fire.

Concerning his constancy, it is said that one Richard Jones, a knight's son, coming to Dr Farrar a little before his death, seemed to lament the painfulness of the death he had to suffer; to whom the bishop answered that if he saw him once stir in the pains of his burning, he might then give no credit to his doctrine; and as he said, so did he maintain his promise, patiently standing without emotion, until one Richard Gravell with a staff struck him down.

Martyrdom of Rawlins White

Rawlins White was by his calling and occupation a fisherman, living and continuing in the said trade for the space of twenty years at least, in the town of Cardiff, where he bore a very good name amongst his neighbours.

Though the good man was altogether unlearned, and withal very simple, yet it pleased God to remove him from error and idolatry to a knowledge of the truth, through the blessed Reformation in Edward's reign. He had his son taught to read English, and after the little boy could read pretty well, his father every night after supper, summer and winter, made the boy read a portion of the Holy Scriptures, and now and then a part of some other good book.

When he had continued in his profession the space of five years, King Edward died, upon whose decease Queen Mary succeeded and with her all kinds of superstition crept in. White was taken by the officers of the town, as a man suspected of heresy, brought before the Bishop Llandaff, and committed to prison in Chepstow, and at last removed to the castle of Cardiff, where he continued for the space of one whole year. Being brought before the bishop in his chapel, he counselled him by threats and promises. But as Rawlins would in no wise recant his opinions, the bishop told him plainly that he must proceed against him by law, and condemn him as a heretic.

Before they proceeded to this extremity, the bishop proposed that prayer should be said for his conversion. 'This,' said White, 'is like a godly bishop, and if your request be godly and right, and you pray as you ought, no doubt God will hear you; pray you, therefore, to your God, and I will pray to my God.' After the bishop and his party had done praying, he asked Rawlins if he would now revoke. 'You find,' said the latter, 'your prayer is not granted, for I remain the same; and God will strengthen me in support of this truth.' After this, the bishop tried what saying Mass would do; but Rawlins called all the people to witness that he did not bow down to the host. Mass being ended, Rawlins was called for again; to whom the bishop used many persuasions; but the blessed man continued so steadfast in his former profession that the bishop's discourse was to no purpose. The bishop now caused the definitive sentence to be read, which being ended, Rawlins was carried again to Cardiff, to a loathsome prison in the town, called Cockmarel, where he passed his time in prayer, and in the singing of Psalms. In about three weeks the order came from town for his execution.

When he came to the place, where his poor wife and children stood weeping, the sudden sight of them so pierced his heart, that the tears trickled down his face. Being come to the altar of his sacrifice, in going toward the stake, he fell down upon his knees, and kissed the ground; and in rising again, a little earth sticking on his face, he said these words. 'Earth unto earth, and dust unto dust; thou art my mother, and unto thee I shall return.'

When all things were ready, directly over against the stake, in the face of Rawlins White, there was a stand erected, whereon stepped up a priest, addressing himself to the people, but, as he spoke of the Romish doctrines of the Sacraments, Rawlins cried out, 'Ah! Thou wicked hypocrite, dost thou presume to prove thy false doctrine by Scripture? Look in the text that followeth; did not Christ say, "Do this in remembrance of me?"'

Then some that stood by cried out, 'Put fire! Set on fire!' which being done, the straw and reeds cast up a great and sudden flame. In which flame this good man bathed his hands so long, until such time as the sinews shrank, and the fat dropped away, saving that once he did, as it were, wipe his face with one of them. All this while, which was somewhat long, he cried with a loud voice, 'O Lord, receive my spirit!' until he could not open his mouth. At last the extremity of the fire was so vehement against his legs that they were consumed almost before the rest of his body was hurt, which made the whole body fall over the chains into the fire sooner than it would have done. Thus died this good old man for his testimony of God's truth, and is now rewarded, no doubt, with the crown of eternal life.

Rev George Marsh

George Marsh, born in the parish of Deane, in the county of Lancaster, received a good education and trade from his parents; about his twenty-fifth year he married, and lived, blessed with several children, on his farm until his wife died. He then went to study at Cambridge, and became the curate of Rev Lawrence Saunders, in which duty he constantly and zealously set forth the truth of God's Word, and the false doctrines of the modern Antichrist.

Being confined by Dr Coles, the bishop of Chester, within the precincts of his own house, he was kept from any intercourse with his friends during four months; his friends and mother, earnestly wished him to have flown from 'the wrath to come,' but Mr Marsh thought that such a step would ill agree with that profession he had during nine years openly made. He, however, secreted himself, but he had much struggling, and in secret prayer begged that God would direct him, through the advice of his best friends, for his own glory and to what was best. At length, determined by a letter he received, boldly to confess the faith of Christ, he took leave of his mother-in-law and other friends, recommending his children to their care and departed for Smethehills, whence he was, with others, conducted to Lathum, to undergo examination before the earl of Derby, Sir William Nores, Mr Sherburn, the parson of Garpnal, and others. The various questions put to him he answered with a good conscience, but when Mr Sherburn interrogated him upon his belief of the Sacrament of the altar, Mr Marsh answered like a true Protestant that the essence of the bread and wine was not at all changed, hence, after receiving dreadful threats from some, and fair words from others, for his opinions, he was remanded to ward, where he lay two nights without any bed.

On Palm Sunday he underwent a second examination, and Mr Marsh much lamented that his fear should at all have induced him to prevaricate, and to seek his safety, as long as he did not openly deny Christ; and he again cried more earnestly to God for strength that he might not be overcome by the subtleties of those who strove to overrule the purity of his faith. He underwent three examinations before Dr Coles, who, finding him steadfast in the Protestant faith, began to read his sentence; but he was interrupted by the chancellor, who prayed the bishop to stay before it was too late. The priest then prayed for Mr Marsh, but the latter, upon being again solicited to recant, said he durst not deny his Saviour Christ, lest he lose His everlasting mercy, and so obtain eternal death. The bishop then proceeded in the sentence. He was committed to a dark dungeon, and lay deprived of the consolation of any one (for all were afraid to relieve or communicate with him) until the day appointed came that he should suffer. The sheriffs of the city, Amry and Couper, With their officers, went to the north gate, and took out Mr George Marsh, who walked all the way with the Book in his hand, looking upon the same, whence the people said, 'This man does not go to his death as a thief, nor as one that deserveth to die.'

When he came to the place of execution without the city, near Spittal-Boughton, Mr Cawdry, deputy chamberlain of Chester, showed Mr Marsh a writing under a great seal, saying that it was a pardon for him if he would recant. He answered that he would gladly accept the same did it not tend to pluck him from God.

After that, he began to speak to the people showing the cause of his death, and would have exhorted them to stick unto Christ, but one of the sheriffs prevented him. Kneeling down, he then said his prayers, put off his clothes unto his shirt, and was chained to the post, having a number of fagots under him, and a thing made like a firkin, with pitch and tar in it, over his head. The fire being unskilfully made, and the wind driving it in eddies, he suffered great extremity, which notwithstanding he bore with Christian fortitude.

When he had been a long time tormented in the fire without moving, having his flesh so broiled and puffed up that they who stood before him could not see the chain wherewith he was fastened, and therefore supposed that he had been dead, suddenly he spread abroad his arms, saying, 'Father of heaven have mercy upon me!' and so yielded his spirit into the hands of the Lord. Upon this, many of the people said he was a martyr, and died gloriously patient. This caused the bishop shortly after to make a sermon in the cathedral church, and therein he affirmed, that the said 'Marsh was a heretic, burnt as such, and is a firebrand in hell.' Mr Marsh suffered April 24, 1555.

William Flower

William Flower, otherwise Branch, was born at Snow-hill, in the county of Cambridge, where he went to school some years, and then came to the abby of Ely. After he had remained a while he became a professed monk, was made a priest in the same house, and there celebrated and sang Mass. After that, by reason of a visitation, and certain injunctions by the authority of Henry VIII he took upon him the habit of a secular priest, and returned to Snow-hill, where he was born, and taught children about half a year.

He then went to Ludgate, in Suffolk, and served as a secular priest about a quarter of a year; from thence to Stoniland; at length to Tewksbury, where he married a wife, with whom he ever after faithfully and honestly continued. After marriage he resided at Tewksbury about two years, and thence went to Brosley, where he practised physic and surgery; but departing from those parts he came to London, and finally settled at Lambeth, where he and his wife dwelt together. However, he was generally abroad, excepting once or twice in a month, to visit and see his wife. Being at home upon Easter Sunday morning, he came over the water from Lambeth into St Margaret's Church at Westminster; when seeing a priest, named John Celtham, administering and giving the Sacrament of the altar to the people, and being greatly offended in his conscience with the priest for the same, he struck and wounded him upon the head, and also upon the arm and hand, with his wood knife, the priest having at the same time in his hand a chalice with the consecrated host therein, which became sprinkled with blood.

Mr Flower, for this injudicious zeal, was heavily ironed, and put into the gatehouse at Westminster; and afterward summoned before bishop Bonner and his ordinary, where the bishop, after he had sworn him upon a Book, ministered articles and interrogatories to him.

After examination, the bishop began to exhort him again to return to the unity of his mother the Catholic Church, with many fair promises. These Mr Flower steadfastly rejecting, the bishop ordered him to appear in the same place in the afternoon, and in the meantime to consider well his former answer; but he, neither apologising for having struck the priest, nor swerving from his faith, the bishop assigned him the next day, April 20, to receive sentence if he would not recant. The next morning, the bishop accordingly proceeded to the sentence, condemning and excommunicating him for a heretic, and after pronouncing him to be degraded, committed him to the secular power.

On April 24, St Mark's eve, he was brought to the place of martyrdom, in St Margaret's churchyard, Westminster, where the fact was committed: and there coming to the stake, he prayed to Almighty God, made a confession of his faith, and forgave all the world.

This done, his hand was held up against the stake, and struck off, his left hand being fastened behind him. Fire was then set to him, and he burning therein, cried with a loud voice, 'O Thou Son of God receive my soul!' three times. His speech being now taken from him, he spoke no more, but notwithstanding he lifted up the stump with his other arm as long as he could.

Thus he endured the extremity of the fire, and was cruelly tortured, for the few fagots that were brought being insufficient to burn him they were compelled to strike him down into the fire, where lying along upon the ground, his lower part was consumed in the fire, whilst his upper part was little injured, his tongue moving in his mouth for a considerable time.

Rev John Cardmaker and John Warne

May 30, 1555, the Rev John Cardmaker, otherwise called Taylor, prebendary of the Church of Wells, and John Warne, upholsterer, of St John's, Walbrook, suffered together in Smithfield. Mr Cardmaker, who first was an observant friar before the dissolution of the abbeys, afterward was a married minister, and in King Edward's time appointed to be a reader in St Paul's; being apprehended in the beginning of Queen Mary's reign, with Dr Barlow, bishop of Bath, he was brought to London, and put in the Fleet prison, King Edward's laws being yet in force. In Mary's reign, when brought before the bishop of Winchester, the latter offered them the queen's mercy, if they would recant.

Articles having been preferred against Mr John Warne, he was examined upon them by Bonner, who earnestly exhorted him to recant his opinions, to whom he answered, 'I am persuaded that I am in the right opinion, and I see no cause to recant; for all the filthiness and idolatry lies in the Church of Rome.'

The bishop then, seeing that all his fair promises and terrible threatenings could not prevail, pronounced the definitive sentence of condemnation, and ordered May 30, 1555, for the execution of John Cardmaker and John Warne, who were brought by the sheriffs to Smithfield. Being come to the stake, the sheriffs called Mr Cardmaker aside, and talked with him secretly, during which Mr Warne prayed, was chained to the stake, and had wood and reeds set about him.

The people were greatly afflicted, thinking that Mr Cardmaker would recant at the burning of Mr Warne. At length Mr Cardmaker departed from the sheriffs, and came towards the stake, knelt down, and made a long prayer in silence to himself. He then rose up, put off his clothes to his shirt, and went with a bold courage unto the stake and kissed it; and taking Mr Warne by the hand, he heartily comforted him, and was bound to the stake, rejoicing. The people seeing this so suddenly done, contrary to their previous expectation, cried out, 'God be praised! the Lord strengthen thee, Cardmaker! the Lord Jesus receive thy spirit!' And this continued while the executioner put fire to them, and both had passed through the fire to the blessed rest and peace among God's holy saints and martyrs, to enjoy the crown of triumph and victory prepared for the elect soldiers and warriors of Christ Jesus in His blessed Kingdom, to whom be glory and majesty forever. Amen.

John Simpson and John Ardeley

John Simpson and John Ardeley were condemned on the same day with Mr Cardmaker and John Warne, which was the twenty-fifth of May. They were shortly after sent down from London to Essex, where they were burnt in one day, John Simpson at Rochford, and John Ardeley at Railey, glorifying God in His beloved Son, and rejoicing that they were accounted worthy to suffer.

Thomas Haukes, Thomas Watts, and Anne Askew

Thomas Haukes, with six others, was condemned on the ninth of February, 1555. In education he was erudite; in person, comely, and of good stature; in manners, a gentleman, and a sincere Christian. A little before death, several of Mr Hauke's friends, terrified by the sharpness of the punishment he was going to suffer, privately desired that in the midst of the flames he should show them some token, whether the pains of burning were so great that a man might not collectedly endure it. This he promised to do; and it was agreed that if the rage of the pain might be suffered, then he should lift up his hands above his head towards heaven, before he gave up the ghost.

Not long after, Mr Haukes was led away to the place appointed for slaughter by Lord Rich, and being come to the stake, mildly and patiently prepared himself for the fire, having a strong chain cast about his middle, with a multitude of people on every side compassing him about, unto whom after he had spoken many things, and poured out his soul unto God, the fire was kindled.

When he had continued long in it, and his speech was taken away by violence of the flame, his skin drawn together, and his fingers consumed with the fire, so that it was thought that he was gone, suddenly and contrary to all expectation, this good man being mindful of his promise, reached up his hands burning in flames over his head to the living God, and with great rejoicings as it seemed, struck or clapped them three times together. A great shout followed this wonderful circumstance, and then this blessed martyr of Christ, sinking down in the fire, gave up his spirit, June 10, 1555.

Thomas Watts, of Billericay, in Essex, of the diocese of London, was a linen draper. He had daily expected to be taken by God's adversaries, and this came to pass on the fifth of April, 1555, when he was brought before Lord Rich, and other commissioners at Chelmsford, and accused for not coming to the church. Being consigned over to the bloody bishop, who gave him several hearings, and, as usual, many arguments, with much entreaty, that he would be a disciple of Antichrist, but his preaching availed not, and he resorted to his last revenge – that of condemnation.

At the stake, after he had kissed it, he spake to Lord Rich, charging him to repent, for the Lord would revenge his death. Thus did this good martyr offer his body to the fire, in defence of the true Gospel of the Saviour.

Thomas Osmond, William Bamford, and Nicholas Chamberlain, all of the town of Coxhall, being sent up to be examined, Bonner, after several hearings, pronounced them obstinate heretics, and delivered them to the sheriffs, in whose custody they remained until they were delivered to the sheriff of Essex county, and by him were executed, Chamberlain at Colchester, the fourteenth of June; Thomas Osmond at Maningtree, and William Bamford, alias Butler, at Harwich, the fifteenth of June, 1555; all dying full of the glorious hope of immortality.

Then Wriotheseley, lord-chancellor, offered Anne Askew the king's pardon if she would recant; who made this answer, that she came not thither to deny her Lord and Master. And thus the good Anne Askew, being compassed in with flames of fire, as a blessed sacrifice unto God, slept in the Lord, AD 1546, leaving behind her a singular example of Christian constancy for all men to follow.

Rev John Bradford, and John Leaf, an Apprentice

Rev John Bradford was born at Manchester, in Lancashire; he was a good Latin scholar, and afterward became a servant of Sir John Harrington, knight.

He continued several years in an honest and thriving way; but the Lord had elected him to a better function. Hence he departed from his master, quitting the Temple, at London, for the University of Cambridge, to learn, by God's law, how to further the building of the Lord's temple. In a few years after, the university gave him the degree of master of arts, and he became a fellow of Pembroke Hall.

Martin Bucer first urged him to preach, and when he modestly doubted his ability, Bucer was wont to reply, 'If thou hast not fine wheat bread, yet give the poor people barley bread, or whatsoever else the Lord hath committed unto thee.' Dr Ridley, that worthy bishop of London, and glorious martyr of Christ, first called him to take the degree of a deacon and gave him a prebend in his cathedral Church of St Paul.

In this preaching office Mr Bradford diligently laboured for the space of three years. Sharply he reproved sin, sweetly he preached Christ crucified, ably he disproved heresies and errors, earnestly he persuaded to godly life. After the death of blessed King Edward VI Mr Bradford still continued diligent in preaching, until he was suppressed by Queen Mary.

An act now followed of the blackest ingratitude, and at which a pagan would blush. It has been recited, that a tumult was occasioned by Mr Bourne's (then bishop of Bath) preaching at St Paul's Cross; the indignation of the people placed his life in imminent danger; indeed a dagger was thrown at him. In this situation he entreated Mr Bradford, who stood behind him, to speak in his place, and assuage the tumult. The people welcomed Mr Bradford, and the latter afterward kept close to him, that his presence might prevent the populace from renewing their assaults.

The same Sunday in the afternoon, Mr Bradford preached at Bow-church in Cheapside, and reproved the people sharply for their seditious misdemeanour. Notwithstanding this conduct, within three days after, he was sent for to the Tower of London, where the queen then was, to appear before the Council. There he was charged with this act of saving Mr Bourne, which was called seditious, and they also objected against him for preaching. Thus he was committed, first to the Tower, then to other prisons, and, after his condemnation, to the Poultry Compter, where he preached twice a day continually, unless sickness hindered him. Such was his credit with the keeper of the king's Bench, that he permitted him in an evening to visit a poor, sick person near the steel-yard, upon his promise to return in time, and in this he never failed.

The night before he was sent to Newgate, he was troubled in his sleep by foreboding dreams, that on Monday after he should be burned in Smithfield. In the afternoon the keeper's wife came up and announced this dreadful news to him, but in him it excited only thankfulness to God. At night half a dozen friends came, with whom he spent all the evening in prayer and godly exercises.

When he was removed to Newgate, a weeping crowd accompanied him, and a rumour having been spread that he was to suffer at four the next morning, an immense multitude attended. At nine o'clock Mr Bradford was brought into Smithfield. The cruelty of the sheriff deserves notice; for his brother-in-law, Roger Beswick, having taken him by the hand as he passed, Mr Woodroffe, with his staff, cut his head open.

Mr Bradford, being come to the place, fell flat on the ground, and putting off his clothes unto the shirt, he went to the stake, and there suffered with a young man of twenty years of age, whose name was John Leaf, an apprentice to Mr Humphrey Gaudy, tallow-chandler, of Christchurch, London. Upon Friday before Palm Sunday, he was committed to the Compter in Breadstreet, and afterward examined and condemned by the bloody bishop.

It is reported of him, that, when the bill of his confession was read unto him, instead of pen, he took a pin, and pricking his hand, sprinkled the blood upon the said bill, desiring the reader thereof to show the bishop that he had sealed the same bill with his blood already.

They both ended this mortal life, July 12, 1555, like two lambs, without any alteration of their countenances, hoping to obtain that prize they had long run for; to which may Almighty God conduct us all, through the merits of Christ our Saviour!

We shall conclude this article with mentioning that Mr Sheriff Woodroffe, it is said, within half a year after, was struck on the right side with a palsy, and for the space of eight years after (until his dying day), he was unable to turn himself in his bed; thus he became at last a fearful object to behold.

The day after Mr Bradford and John Leaf suffered in Smithfield, William Minge, priest, died in prison at Maidstone. With as great constancy and boldness he yielded up his life in prison, as if it had pleased God to have called him to suffer by fire, as other godly men had done before at the stake, and as he himself was ready to do, had it pleased God to have called him to this trial.

Rev John Bland, Rev John Frankesh, Nicholas Shetterden, and Humphrey Middleton

These Christian persons were all burnt at Canterbury for the same cause. Frankesh and Bland were ministers and preachers of the Word of God, the one being parson of Adesham, and the other vicar of Rolvenden. Mr Bland was cited to answer for his opposition to antichristianism, and underwent several examinations before Dr Harpsfield, archdeacon of Canterbury, and finally on June 25, 1555, again withstanding the power of the pope, he was condemned, and delivered to the secular arm. On the same day were condemned John Frankesh, Nicholas Shetterden, Humphrey Middleton, Thacker, and Crocker, of whom Thacker only recanted.

Being delivered to the secular power, Mr Bland, with the three former, were all burnt together at Canterbury, July 12, 1555, at two several stakes, but in one fire, when they, in the sight of God and His angels, and before men, like true soldiers of Jesus Christ, gave a constant testimony to the truth of His holy Gospel.

Dirick Carver and John Launder

The twenty-second of July, 1555, Dirick Carver, brewer, of Brighthelmstone, aged forty, was burnt at Lewes. And the day following John Launder, husbandman, aged twenty-five, of Godstone, Surrey, was burnt at Stening.

Dirick Carver was a man whom the Lord had blessed as well with temporal riches as with his spiritual treasures. At his coming into the town of Lewes to be burnt, the people called to him, beseeching God to strengthen him in the faith of Jesus Christ; and, as he came to the stake, he knelt down, and prayed earnestly. Then his Book was thrown into a barrel, and when he had stripped himself, he too, went into the barrel. As soon as he was in, he took the Book, and threw it among the people, upon which the sheriff commanded, in the name of the king and queen, on pain of death, to throw in the Book again. And immediately the holy martyr began to address the people. After he had prayed a while, he said, 'O Lord my God, Thou hast written, he that will not forsake wife, children, house, and every thing that he hath, and take up Thy cross and follow Thee, is not worthy of Thee! But Thou, Lord, knowest that I have forsaken all to come unto Thee. Lord, have mercy upon me, for unto Thee I commend my spirit! and my soul doth rejoice in Thee!' These were the last words of this faithful servant of Christ before enduring the fire. And when the fire came to him, he cried, 'O Lord, have mercy upon me!' and sprang up in the fire, calling upon the name of Jesus, until he gave up the ghost.

James Abbes

This young man wandered about to escape apprehension, but was at last informed against, and brought before the bishop of Norwich, who influenced him to recant; to secure him further in apostasy, the bishop afterward gave him a piece of money; but the interference of Providence is here remarkable. This bribe lay so heavily upon his conscience, that he returned, threw back the money, and repented of his conduct. Like Peter, he was contrite, steadfast in the faith, and sealed it with his blood at Bury, August 2, 1555, praising and glorifying God.

John Denley, John Newman, and Patrick Packingham

Mr Denley and Mr Newman were returning one day to Maidstone, the place of their abode, when they were met by E. Tyrrel, Esq., a bigoted justice of the peace in Essex, and a cruel persecutor of the Protestants. He apprehended them merely on suspicion. On July 5, 1555, they were condemned, and consigned to the sheriffs, who sent Mr Denley to Uxbridge, where he perished, August 8, 1555. While suffering in agony, and singing a Psalm, Dr Story inhumanly ordered one of the tormentors to throw a fagot at him, which cut his face severely, caused him to cease singing, and to raise his hands to his face. Just as Dr Story was remarking in jest that he had spoiled a good song, the pious martyr again changed, spread his hands abroad in the flames, and through Christ Jesus resigned his soul into the hands of his Maker.

Mr Packingham suffered at the same town on the twenty-eight of the same month.

Mr Newman, pewterer, was burnt at Saffron Waldon, in Essex, August 31, for the same cause, and Richard Hook about the same time perished at Chichester.

W. Coker, W. Hooper, H. Laurence, R. Colliar, R. Wright and W. Stere, these persons all of Kent, were examined at the same time with Mr Bland and Mr Shetterden, by Thornton, bishop of Dover, Dr Harpsfield, and others. These six martyrs and witnesses of the truth were consigned to the flames in Canterbury, at the end of August, 1555.

Elizabeth Warne, widow of John Warne, upholsterer, martyr, was burnt at Stratford-le-Bow, near London, at the end of August, 1555.

George Tankerfield, of London, cook, born at York, aged twenty-seven, in the reign of Edward VI had been a papist; but the cruelty of bloody Mary made him suspect the truth of those doctrines which were enforced by fire and torture. Tankerfield was imprisoned in Newgate about the end of February, 1555, and on August 26, at St Alban's, he braved the excruciating fire, and joyfully died for the glory of his Redeemer.

Rev Robert Smith was first in the service of Sir T. Smith, provost of Eton; and was afterward removed to Windsor, where he had a clerkship of ten pounds a year.

He was condemned, July 12, 1555, and suffered August 8, at Uxbridge. He doubted not but that God would give the spectators some token in support of his own cause; this actually happened; for, when he was nearly half burnt, and supposed to be dead, he suddenly rose up, moved the remaining parts of his arms and praised God, then, hanging over the fire, he sweetly slept in the Lord Jesus.

Mr Stephen Harwood and Mr Thomas Fust suffered about the same time with Smith and Tankerfield, With whom they were condemned. Mr William Hale also, of Thorp, in Essex, was sent to Barnet, where about the same time he joined the ever-blessed company of martyrs.

George King, Thomas Leyes, and John Wade, falling sick in Lollard's Tower, were removed to different houses, and died. Their bodies were thrown out in the common fields as unworthy of burial, and lay until the faithful conveyed them away at night.

Mr William Andrew of Horseley, Essex, was imprisoned in Newgate for heresy; but God chose to call him to himself by the severe treatment he endured in Newgate, and thus to mock the sanguinary expectations of his Catholic persecutors. His body was thrown into the open air, but his soul was received into the everlasting mansions of his heavenly Creator.

Rev Robert Samuel

This gentleman was minister of Bradford, Suffolk, where he industriously taught the flock committed to his charge, while he was openly permitted to discharge his duty. He was first persecuted by Mr Foster, of Copdock, near Ipswich, a severe and bigoted persecutor of the followers of Christ, according to the truth in the Gospel. Notwithstanding Mr Samuel was ejected from his living, he continued to exhort and instruct privately; nor would he obey the order for putting away his wife, whom he had married in King Edward's reign; but kept her at Ipswich, where Foster, by warrant, surprised him by night with her. After being imprisoned in Ipswich jail, he was taken before Dr Hopton, bishop of Norwich, and Dr Dunnings, his chancellor, two of the most sanguinary among the bigots of those days. To intimidate the worthy pastor, he was in prison chained to a post in such a manner that the weight of his body was supported by the points of his toes: added to this his allowance of provision was reduced to a quantity so insufficient to sustain nature that he was almost ready to devour his own flesh.

From this dreadful extremity there was even a degree of mercy in ordering him to the fire. Mr Samuel suffered August 31, 1555.

Bishops Ridley and Latimer

These reverend prelates suffered October 17, 1555, at Oxford, on the same day Wolsey and Pygot perished at Ely. Pillars of the Church and accomplished ornaments of human nature, they were the admiration of the realm, amiably conspicuous in their lives, and glorious in their deaths.

Dr Ridley was born in Northumberland, was first taught grammar at Newcastle, and afterward removed to Cambridge, where his aptitude in education raised him gradually until he came to be the head of Pembroke College, where he received the title of Doctor of Divinity. Having returned from a trip to Paris, he was appointed chaplain by Henry VIII and bishop of Rochester, and was afterwards translated to the see of London in the time of Edward VI.

To his sermons the people resorted, swarming about him like bees, coveting the sweet flowers and wholesome juice of the fruitful doctrine, which he did not only preach, but showed the same by his life, as a glittering lanthorn to the eyes and senses of the blind, in such pure order that his very enemies could not reprove him in any one jot.

His tender treatment of Dr Heath, who was a prisoner with him during one year, in Edward's reign, evidently proves that he had no Catholic cruelty in his disposition. In person he was erect and well proportioned; in temper forgiving; in self-mortification severe. His first duty in the morning was private prayer: he remained in his study until ten o'clock, and then attended the daily prayer used in his house. Dinner being done, he sat about an hour, conversing pleasantly, or playing at chess. His study next engaged his attention, unless business or visits occurred; about five o'clock prayers followed; and after he would recreate himself at chess for about an hour, then retire to his study until eleven o'clock, and pray on his knees as in the morning. In brief, he was a pattern of godliness and virtue, and such he endeavoured to make men wherever he came.

His attentive kindness was displayed particularly to old Mrs Bonner, mother of Dr Bonner, the cruel bishop of London. Dr Ridley, when at his manor at Fulham, always invited her to his house, placed her at the head of his table, and treated her like his own mother; he did the same by Bonner's sister and other relatives; but when Dr Ridley was under persecution, Bonner pursued a conduct diametrically opposite, and would have sacrificed Dr Ridley's sister and her husband, Mr George Shipside, had not Providence delivered him by the means of Dr Heath, bishop of Worcester.

Dr Ridley was first in part converted by reading Bertram's book on the Sacrament, and by his conferences with archbishop Cranmer and Peter Martyr.

When Edward VI was removed from the throne, and the bloody Mary succeeded, Bishop Ridley was immediately marked as an object of slaughter. He was first sent to the Tower, and afterward, at Oxford, was consigned to the common prison of Bocardo, With archbishop Cranmer and Mr Latimer. Being separated from them, he was placed in the house of one Irish, where he remained until the day of his martyrdom, from 1554, until October 16, 1555.

It will easily be supposed that the conversations of these chiefs of the martyrs were elaborate, learned, and instructive. Such indeed they were, and equally beneficial to all their spiritual comforts. Bishop Ridley's letters to various Christian brethren in bonds in all parts, and his disputations with the mitred enemies of Christ, alike proved the clearness of his head and the integrity of his heart. In a letter to Mr Grindal (afterward archbishop of Canterbury) he mentions with affection those who had preceded him in dying for the faith, and those who were expected to suffer; he regrets that popery is re-established in its full abomination, which he attributes to the wrath of God, made manifest in return for the lukewarmness of the clergy and the people in justly appreciating the blessed light of the Reformation.

This old practised soldier of Christ, Master Hugh Latimer, was the son of one Hugh Latimer, of Thurkesson in the county of Leicester, a husbandman, of a good and wealthy estimation; where also he was born and brought up until he was four years of age, or thereabout: at which time his parents, having him as then left for their only son, with six daughters, seeing his ready, prompt, and sharp wit, purposed to train him up in erudition, and knowledge of good literature; wherein he so profited in his youth at the common schools of his own country, that at the age of fourteen years, he was sent to the University of Cambridge; where he entered into the study of the school divinity of that day, and was from principle a zealous observer of the Romish superstitions of the time. In his oration when he commenced Bachelor of Divinity, he inveighed against the reformer Melancthon, and openly declaimed against good Mr Stafford, divinity lecturer in Cambridge.

Mr Thomas Bilney, moved by a brotherly pity towards Mr Latimer, begged to wait upon him in his study, and to explain to him the groundwork of his (Mr Bilney's) faith. This blessed interview effected his conversion: the persecutor of Christ became his zealous advocate, and before Dr Stafford died he became reconciled to him.

Once converted, he became eager for the conversion of others, and commenced to be public preacher, and private instructor in the university. His sermons were so pointed against the absurdity of praying in the Latin tongue, and withholding the oracles of salvation from the people who were to be saved by belief in them, that he drew upon himself the pulpit animadversions of several of the resident friars and heads of houses, whom he subsequently silenced by his severe criticisms and eloquent arguments. This was at Christmas, 1529. At length Dr West preached against Mr Latimer at Barwell Abbey, and prohibited him from preaching again in the churches of the university, notwithstanding which, he continued during three years to advocate openly the cause of Christ, and even his enemies confessed the power of those talents he possessed. Mr Bilney remained here some time with Mr Latimer, and thus the place where they frequently walked together obtained the name of Heretics' Hill.

Mr Latimer at this time traced out the innocence of a poor woman, accused by her husband of the murder of her child. Having preached before King Henry VIII at Windsor, he obtained the unfortunate mother's pardon. This, with many other benevolent acts, served only to excite the spleen of his adversaries. He was summoned before Cardinal Wolsey for heresy, but being a strenuous supporter of the king's supremacy, in opposition to the pope's, by favour of Lord Cromwell and Dr Buts (the king's physician) he obtained the living of West Kingston, in Wiltshire. For his sermons here against purgatory, the immaculacy of the Virgin, and the worship of images, he was cited to appear before Warham, archbishop of Canterbury, and

John, bishop of London. He was required to subscribe certain articles, expressive of his conformity to the accustomed usages; and there is reason to think, after repeated weekly examinations, that he did subscribe, as they did not seem to involve any important article of belief.

Guided by Providence, he escaped the subtle nets of his persecutors, and at length, through the powerful friends before mentioned, became bishop of Worcester, in which function he qualified or explained away most of the papal ceremonies he was for form's sake under the necessity of complying with. He continued in this active and dignified employment some years.

Beginning afresh to set forth his plow he laboured in the Lord's harvest most fruitfully, discharging his talent as well in divers places of this realm, as before the king at the court. In the same place of the inward garden, which was before applied to lascivious and courtly pastimes, there he dispensed the fruitful Word of the glorious Gospel of Jesus Christ, preaching there before the king and his whole court, to the edification of many.

He remained a prisoner in the Tower until the coronation of Edward VI, when he was again called to the Lord's harvest in Stamford, and many other places: he also preached at London in the convocation house, and before the young king; indeed he lectured twice every Sunday, regardless of his great age (then above sixty-seven years) and his weakness through a bruise received from the fall of a tree. Indefatigable in his private studies, he rose to them in winter and in summer at two o'clock in the morning.

By the strength of his own mind, or of some inward light from above, he had a prophetic view of what was to happen to the Church in Mary's reign, asserting that he was doomed to suffer for the truth, and that Winchester, then in the Tower, was preserved for that purpose. Soon after Queen Mary was proclaimed, a messenger was sent to summon Mr Latimer to town, and there is reason to believe it was wished that he should make his escape.

Thus Master Latimer coming up to London, through Smithfield (where merrily he said that Smithfield had long groaned for him), was brought before the Council, where he patiently bore all the mocks and taunts given him by the scornful papists. He was cast into the Tower, where he, being assisted with the heavenly grace of Christ, sustained imprisonment a long time, notwithstanding the cruel and unmerciful handling of the lordly papists, which thought then their kingdom would never fall; he showed himself not only patient, but also cheerful in and above all that which they could or would work against him. Yea, such a valiant spirit the Lord gave him, that he was able not only to despise the terribleness of prisons and torments, but also to laugh to scorn the doings of his enemies.

Mr Latimer, after remaining a long time in the Tower, was transported to Oxford, with Cranmer and Ridley, the disputations at which place have been already mentioned in a former part of this work. He remained imprisoned until October, and the principal objects of all his prayers were three – that he might stand faithful to the doctrine he had professed, that God would restore his Gospel to England once again, and preserve the Lady Elizabeth to be queen; all of which happened. When he stood at the stake without the Bocardo gate, Oxford, with Dr Ridley, and fire was putting to the pile of fagots, he raised his eyes benignantly towards heaven, and said, 'God is faithful, who will not suffer you to be tempted above that ye are able.' His body was forcibly penetrated by the fire, and the blood flowed abundantly from the heart; as if to verify his constant desire that his heart's blood might be shed in defence of the Gospel. His polemical and friendly letters are lasting monuments of his integrity and talents. It has been before said, that public disputation took place in April, 1554, new examinations took place in October, 1555, previous to the degradation and condemnation of Cranmer, Ridley, and Latimer. We now draw to the conclusion of the lives of the two last.

Dr Ridley, the night before execution, was very facetious, had himself shaved, and called his supper a marriage feast; he remarked upon seeing Mrs Irish (the keeper's wife) weep, 'Though my breakfast will be somewhat sharp, my supper will be more pleasant and sweet.'

The place of death was on the north side of the town, opposite Baliol College. Dr Ridley was dressed in a black gown furred, and Mr Latimer had a long shroud on, hanging down to his feet. Dr Ridley, as he passed Bocardo, looked up to see Dr Cranmer, but the latter was then engaged in disputation with a friar. When they came to the stake, Dr Ridley embraced Latimer fervently, and bid him: 'Be of good heart, brother, for God will either assuage the fury of the flame, or else strengthen us to abide it.' He then knelt by the stake, and after earnestly praying together, they had a short private conversation. Dr Smith then preached a short sermon against the martyrs, who would have answered him, but were prevented by Dr Marshal, the vice-chancellor. Dr Ridley then took off his gown and tippet, and gave them to his brother-in-law, Mr Shipside. He gave away also many trifles to his weeping friends, and the populace were anxious to get even a fragment of his garments. Mr Latimer gave nothing, and from the poverty of his garb, was soon stripped to his shroud, and stood venerable and erect, fearless of death.

Dr Ridley being unclothed to his shirt, the smith placed an iron chain about their waists, and Dr Ridley bid him fasten it securely; his brother having tied a bag of gunpowder about his neck, gave some also to Mr Latimer.

Dr Ridley then requested of Lord Williams, of Fame, to advocate with the queen the cause of some poor men to whom he had, when bishop, granted leases, but which the present bishop refused to confirm. A lighted fagot was now laid at Dr Ridley's feet, which caused Mr Latimer to say: 'Be of good cheer, Ridley; and play the man. We shall this day, by God's grace, light up such a candle in England, as I trust, will never be put out.'

When Dr Ridley saw the fire flaming up towards him, he cried with a wonderful loud voice, 'Lord, Lord, receive my spirit.' Master Latimer, crying as vehemently on the other side, 'O Father of heaven, receive my soul!' received the flame as it were embracing of it. After that he had stroked his face with his hands, and as it were, bathed them a little in the fire, he soon died (as it appeareth) with very little pain or none.

Well! dead they are, and the reward of this world they have already. What reward remaineth for them in heaven, the day of the Lord's glory, when he cometh with His saints, shall declare.

In the following month died Stephen Gardiner, bishop of Winchester and lord-chancellor of England. This papistical monster was born at Bury, in Suffolk, and partly educated at Cambridge. Ambitious, cruel, and bigoted, he served any cause; he first espoused the king's part in the affair of Anne Boleyn: upon the establishment of the Reformation he declared the supremacy of the pope an execrable tenet; and when Queen Mary came to the crown, he entered into all her papistical bigoted views, and became a second time bishop of Winchester. It is conjectured it was his intention to have moved the sacrifice of Lady Elizabeth, but when he arrived at this point, it pleased God to remove him.

It was on the afternoon of the day when those faithful soldiers of Christ, Ridley and Latimer, perished, that Gardiner sat down with a joyful heart to dinner. Scarcely had he taken a few mouthfuls, when he was seized with illness, and carried to his bed, where he lingered fifteen days in great torment, unable in any wise to evacuate, and burnt with a devouring fever, that terminated in death. Execrated by all good Christians, we pray the Father of mercies, that he may receive that mercy above he never imparted below.

Mr John Philpot

This martyr was the son of a knight, born in Hampshire, and brought up at New College, Oxford, where for several years he studied the civil law, and became eminent in the Hebrew tongue. He was a scholar and a gentleman, zealous in religion, fearless in disposition, and a detester of flattery. After visiting Italy, he returned to England, affairs in King Edward's days wearing a more promising aspect. During this reign he continued to be archdeacon of Winchester under Dr Poinet, who succeeded Gardiner. Upon the accession of Mary, a convocation was summoned, in which Mr Philpot defended the Reformation against his ordinary, Gardiner, again made bishop of Winchester, and soon was conducted to Bonner and other commissioners for examination, October 2, 1555, after being eighteen months' imprisoned. Upon his demanding to see the commission, Dr Story cruelly observed, 'I will spend both my gown and my coat, but I will burn thee! Let him be in Lollard's Tower (a wretched prison), for I will sweep the king's Bench and all other prisons of these heretics!'

Upon Mr Philpot's second examination, it was intimated to him that Dr Story had said that the lord-chancellor had commanded that he should be made away with. It is easy to foretell the result of this inquiry. He was committed to Bonner's coal house, where he joined company with a zealous minister of Essex, who had been induced to sign a bill of recantation; but afterward, stung by his conscience, he asked the bishop to let him see the instrument again, when he tore it to pieces; which induced Bonner in a fury to strike him repeatedly, and tear away part of his beard. Mr Philpot had a private interview with Bonner the same night, and was then remanded to his bed of straw like other prisoners, in the coal house. After seven examinations, Bonner ordered him to be set in the stocks, and on the following Sunday separated him from his fellow-prisoners as a sower of heresy, and ordered him up to a room near the battlements of St Paul's, eight feet by thirteen, on the other side of Lollard's Tower, and which could be overlooked by any one in the bishop's outer gallery. Here Mr Philpot was searched, but happily he was successful in secreting some letters containing his examinations.

In the eleventh investigation before various bishops, and Mr Morgan, of Oxford, the latter was so driven into a corner by the close pressure of Mr Philpot's arguments, that he said to him, 'Instead of the spirit of the Gospel which you boast to possess, I think it is the spirit of the buttery, which your fellows have had, who were drunk before their death, and went, I believe, drunken to it.' To this unfounded and brutish remark, Mr Philpot indignantly replied, 'It appeareth by your communication that you are better acquainted with that spirit than the Spirit of God; wherefore I tell thee, thou painted wall and hypocrite, in the name of the living God, whose truth I have told thee, that God shall rain fire and brimstone upon such blasphemers as thou art!' He was then remanded by Bonner, with an order not to allow him his Bible nor candlelight.

On December 4, Mr Philpot had his next hearing, and this was followed by two more, making in all, fourteen conferences, previous to the final examination in which he was condemned, such were the perseverance and anxiety of the Catholics, aided by the argumentative abilities of the most distinguished of the papal bishops, to bring him into the pale of their Church. Those examinations, which were very long and learned, were all written down by Mr Philpot, and a stronger proof of the imbecility of the Catholic doctors, cannot, to an unbiased mind, be exhibited.

On December 16, in the consistory of St Paul's Bishop Bonner, after laying some trifling accusations to his charge, such as secreting powder to make ink, writing some private letters, etc., proceeded to pass the awful sentence upon him, after he and the other bishops had urged him by every inducement to recant. He was afterward conducted to Newgate, where the avaricious Catholic keeper loaded him with heavy irons, which by the humanity of Mr Macham were ordered to be taken off. On December 17, Mr Philpot received intimation that he was to die next day, and the next morning about eight o'clock, he joyfully met the sheriffs, who were to attend him to the place of execution.

Upon entering Smithfield, the ground was so muddy that two officers offered to carry him to the stake, but he replied: 'Would you make me a pope? I am content to finish my journey on foot.' Arriving at the stake, he said, 'Shall I disdain to suffer at the stake, when my Redeemer did not refuse to suffer the most vile death upon the cross for me?' He then meekly recited the One hundred and seventh and One hundred and eighth Psalms, and when he had finished his prayers, was bound to the post, and fire applied to the pile. On December 18, 1555, perished this illustrious martyr, reverenced by man, and glorified in heaven!

John Lomas, Agnes Snoth, Anne Wright, Joan Sole, and Joan Catmer

These five martyrs suffered together, January 31, 1556. John Lomas was a young man of Tenterden. He was cited to appear at Canterbury, and was examined January 17. His answers being adverse to the idolatrous doctrine of the papacy, he was condemned on the following day, and suffered January 31.

Agnes Snoth, widow, of Smarden Parish, was several times summoned before the Catholic Pharisees, and rejecting absolution, indulgences, transubstantiation, and auricular confession, she was adjudged worthy to suffer death, and endured martyrdom, January 31, with Anne Wright and Joan Sole, who were placed in similar circumstances, and perished at the same time, with equal resignation. Joan Catmer, the last of this heavenly company, of the parish Hithe, was the wife of the martyr George Catmer.

Seldom in any country, for political controversy, have four women been led to execution, whose lives were irreproachable, and whom the pity of savages would have spared. We cannot but remark here that, when the Protestant power first gained the ascendency over the Catholic superstition, and some degree of force in the laws was necessary to enforce uniformity, whence some bigoted people suffered privation in their person or goods, we read of few burnings, savage cruelties, or poor women brought to the stake, but it is the nature of error to resort to force instead of argument, and to silence truth by taking away existence, of which the Redeemer himself is an instance.

The above five persons were burnt at two stakes in one fire, singing hosannas to the glorified Saviour, until the breath of life was extinct. Sir John Norton, who was present, wept bitterly at their unmerited sufferings.

Archbishop Cranmer

Dr Thomas Cranmer was descended from an ancient family, and was born at the village of Arselacton, in the county of Northampton. After the usual school education he was sent to Cambridge, and was chosen fellow of Jesus College. Here he married a gentleman's daughter, by which he forfeited his fellowship, and became a reader in Buckingham College, placing his wife at the Dolphin Inn, the landlady of which was a relation of hers, whence arose the idle report that he was an ostler. His lady shortly after dying in childbed; to his credit he was re-chosen a fellow of the college before mentioned. In a few years after, he was promoted to be Divinity Lecturer, and appointed one of the examiners over those who were ripe to become Bachelors or Doctors in Divinity. It was his principle to judge of their qualifications by the knowledge they possessed of the Scriptures, rather than of the ancient fathers, and hence many popish priests were rejected, and others rendered much improved.

He was strongly solicited by Dr Capon to be one of the fellows on the foundation of Cardinal Wolsey's college, Oxford, of which he hazarded the refusal. While he continued in Cambridge, the question of Henry VIII's divorce with Catharine was agitated. At that time, on account of the plague, Dr Cranmer removed to the house of a Mr Cressy, at Waltham Abbey, whose two sons were then educating under him. The affair of divorce, contrary to the king's approbation, had remained undecided above two or three years, from the intrigues of the canonists and civilians, and though the cardinals Campeius and Wolsey were commissioned from Rome to decide the question, they purposely protracted the sentence.

It happened that Dr Gardiner (secretary) and Dr Fox, defenders of the king in the above suit, came to the house of Mr Cressy to lodge, while the king removed to Greenwich. At supper, a conversation ensued with Dr Cranmer, who suggested that the question whether a man may marry his brother's wife or not, could be easily and speedily decided by the Word of God, and this as well in the English courts as in those of any foreign nation. The king, uneasy at the delay, sent for Dr Gardiner and Dr Fox to consult them, regretting that a new commission must be sent to Rome, and the suit be endlessly protracted. Upon relating to the king the conversation which had passed on the previous evening with Dr Cranmer, his majesty sent for him, and opened the tenderness of conscience upon the near affinity of the queen. Dr Cranmer advised that the matter should be referred to the most learned divines of Cambridge and Oxford, as he was unwilling to meddle in an affair of such weight; but the king enjoined him to deliver his sentiments in writing, and to repair for that purpose to the earl of Wiltshire's, who would accommodate him with books, and everything requisite for the occasion.

This Dr Cranmer immediately did, and in his declaration not only quoted the authority of the Scriptures, of general councils, and the ancient writers, but maintained that the bishop of Rome had no authority whatever to dispense with the Word of God. The king asked him if he would stand by this bold declaration, to which replying in the affirmative, he was deputed ambassador to Rome, in conjunction with the earl of Wiltshire, Dr Stokesley, Dr Carne,

Dr Bennet, and others, previous to which, the marriage was discussed in most of the universities of Christendom and at home.

When the pope presented his toe to be kissed, as customary, the earl of Wiltshire and his party refused. Indeed, it is affirmed that a spaniel of the earl's attracted by the littler of the pope's toe, made a snap at it, whence his holiness drew in his sacred foot, and kicked at the offender with the other.

Upon the pope demanding the cause of their embassy, the earl presented Dr Cranmer's book, declaring that his learned friends had come to defend it. The pope treated the embassy honourably, and appointed a day for the discussion, which he delayed, as if afraid of the issue of the investigation. The earl returned, and Dr Cranmer, by the king's desire, visited the emperor, and was successful in bringing him over to his opinion. Upon the doctor's return to England, Dr Warham, archbishop of Canterbury, having quitted this transitory life, Dr Cranmer was deservedly, and by Dr Warham's desire, elevated to that eminent station.

In this function, it may be said that he followed closely the charge of St Paul. Diligent in duty, he rose at five in the morning, and continued in study and prayer until nine: between then and dinner, he devoted to temporal affairs. After dinner, if any suitors wanted hearing, he would determine their business with such an affability that even the defaulters were scarcely displeased. Then he would play at chess for an hour, or see others play, and at five o'clock he heard the Common Prayer read, and from this until supper he took the recreation of walking. At supper his conversation was lively and entertaining; again he walked or amused himself until nine o'clock, and then entered his study.

He ranked high in favour with King Henry, and even had the purity and the interest of the English Church deeply at heart. His mild and forgiving disposition is recorded in the following instance. An ignorant priest, in the country, had called Cranmer an ostler, and spoken very derogatory of his learning. Lord Cromwell receiving information of it, the man was sent to the Fleet, and his case was told to the archbishop by a Mr Chertsey, a grocer, and a relation of the priest's. His grace, having sent for the offender, reasoned with him, and solicited the priest to question him on any learned subject. This the man, overcome by the bishop's good nature, and knowing his own glaring incapacity, declined, and entreated his forgiveness, which was immediately granted, with a charge to employ his time better when he returned to his parish. Cromwell was much vexed at the lenity displayed, but the bishop was ever more ready to receive injury than to retaliate in any other manner than by good advice and good offices.

At the time that Cranmer was raised to be archbishop, he was king's chaplain, and archdeacon of Taunton; he was also constituted by the pope the penitentiary general of England. It was considered by the king that Cranmer would be obsequious; hence the latter married the king to Anne Boleyn, performed her coronation, stood godfather to Elizabeth, the first child, and divorced the king from Catharine. Though Cranmer received a confirmation of his dignity from the pope, he always protested against acknowledging any other authority than the king's, and he persisted in the same independent sentiments when before Mary's commissioners in 1555.

One of the first steps after the divorce was to prevent preaching throughout his diocese, but this narrow measure had rather a political view than a religious one, as there were many who inveighed against the king's conduct. In his new dignity Cranmer agitated the question of supremacy, and by his powerful and just arguments induced the parliament to 'render to Caesar the things that are Caesar's.' During Cranmer's residence in Germany, 1531, he became acquainted with Ossiander, at Nuremberg, and married his niece, but left her with him while on his return to England. After a season he sent for her privately, and she remained with him until the year 1539, when the Six Articles compelled him to return her to her friends for a time.

It should be remembered that Ossiander, having obtained the approbation of his friend Cranmer, published the laborious work of the Harmony of the Gospels in 1537. In 1534 the archbishop completed the dearest wish of his heart, the removal of every obstacle to the perfection of the Reformation, by the subscription of the nobles and bishops to the king's sole supremacy. Only Bishop Fisher and Sir Thomas More made objection; and their agreement not to oppose the succession Cranmer was willing to consider as sufficient, but the monarch would have no other than an entire concession.

Not long after, Gardiner, in a private interview with the king, spoke inimically of Cranmer (whom he maliciously hated) for assuming the title of primate of all England, as derogatory to the supremacy of the king. This created much jealousy against Cranmer, and his translation of the Bible was strongly opposed by Stokesley, bishop of London. It is said, upon the demise of Queen Catharine, that her successor Anne Boleyn rejoiced – a lesson this to show how shallow is the human judgment! since her own execution took place in the spring of the following year, and the king, on the day following the beheading of this sacrificed lady, married the beautiful Jane Seymour, a maid of honour to the late queen. Cranmer was ever the friend of Anne Boleyn, but it was dangerous to oppose the will of the carnal tyrannical monarch.

In 1538, the Holy Scriptures were openly exposed to sale; and the places of worship over-flowed everywhere to hear its holy doctrines expounded. Upon the king's passing into a law the famous Six Articles, which went nearly again to establish the essential tenets of the Romish creed, Cranmer shone forth with all the luster of a Christian patriot, in resisting the doctrines they contained, and in which he was supported by the bishops of Sarum, Worcester, Ely, and Rochester, the two former of whom resigned their bishoprics. The king, though now in opposition to Cranmer, still revered the sincerity that marked his conduct. The death of Lord Cromwell in the Tower, in 1540, the good friend of Cranmer, was a severe blow to the wavering Protestant cause, but even now Cranmer, when he saw the tide directly adverse to the truth, boldly waited on the king in person, and by his manly and heartfelt pleading, caused the Book of Articles to be passed on his side, to the great confusion of his enemies, who had contemplated his fall as inevitable.

Cranmer now lived in as secluded a manner as possible, until the rancour of Winchester preferred some articles against him, relative to the dangerous opinion he taught in his family, joined to other treasonable charges. These the king himself delivered to Cranmer, and believing firmly the fidelity and assertions of innocence of the accused prelate, he caused the matter to be deeply investigated, and Winchester and Dr Lenden, with Thornton and Barber, of the bishop's household, were found by the papers to be the real conspirators. The mild, forgiving Cranmer would have interceded for all remission of publishment, had not Henry, pleased with the subsidy voted by parliament, let them be discharged. These nefarious men, however, again renewing their plots against Cranmer, fell victims to Henry's resentment, and Gardiner forever lost his confidence. Sir G. Gostwick soon after laid charges against the archbishop, which Henry quashed, and the primate was willing to forgive.

In 1544, the archbishop's palace at Canterbury was burnt, and his brother-in-law with others perished in it. These various afflictions may serve to reconcile us to a humble state; for of what happiness could this great and good man boast, since his life was constantly harassed either by political, religious, or natural crosses? Again the inveterate Gardiner laid high charges against the meek archbishop and would have sent him to the Tower; but the king was his friend, gave him his signet that he might defend him, and in the Council not only declared the bishop one of the best affected men in his realm, but sharply rebuked his accusers for their calumny.

A peace having been made, Henry, and the French king, Henry the Great, were unanimous to have the Mass abolished in their kingdom, and Cranmer set about this great work; but the death of the English monarch, in 1546, suspended the procedure, and King Edward his successor continued Cranmer in the same functions, upon whose coronation he delivered a charge that will ever honour his memory, for its purity, freedom, and truth. During this reign he prosecuted the glorious Reformation with unabated zeal, even in the year 1552, when he was seized with a severe ague, from which it pleased God to restore him that he might testify by his death the truth of that seed he had diligently sown.

The death of Edward, in 1553, exposed Cranmer to all the rage of his enemies. Though the archbishop was among those who supported Mary's accession, he was attainted at the meeting of parliament, and in November adjudged guilty of high treason at Guildhall, and degraded from his dignities. He sent a humble letter to Mary, explaining the cause of his signing the will in favour of Edward, and in 1554 he wrote to the Council, whom he pressed to obtain a pardon from the queen, by a letter delivered to Dr Weston, but which the letter opened, and on seeing its contents, basely returned.

Treason was a charge quite inapplicable to Cranmer, who supported the queen's right; while others, who had favoured Lady Jane were dismissed upon paying a small fine. A calumny was now spread against Cranmer that he complied with some of the popish ceremonies to ingratiate himself with the queen, which he dared publicly to disavow, and justified his articles of faith. The active part which the prelate had taken in the divorce of Mary's mother had ever rankled deeply in the heart of the queen, and revenge formed a prominent feature in the death of Cranmer.

We have in this work noticed the public disputations at Oxford, in which the talents of Cranmer, Ridley, and Latimer shone so conspicuously, and tended to their condemnation. The first sentence was illegal, inasmuch as the usurped power of the pope had not yet been re-established by law.

Being kept in prison until this was effected, a commission was despatched from Rome, appointing Dr Brooks to sit as the representative of his holiness, and Drs. Story and Martin as those of the queen. Cranmer was willing to bow to the authority of Drs. Story and Martin, but against that of Dr Brooks he protested. Such were the remarks and replies of Cranmer, after a long examination, that Dr Brooks observed, 'We come to examine you, and methinks you examine us.'

Being sent back to confinement, he received a citation to appear at Rome within eighteen days, but this was impracticable, as he was imprisoned in England; and as he stated, even had he been at liberty, he was too poor to employ an advocate. Absurd as it must appear, Cranmer was condemned at Rome, and on February 14, 1556, a new commission was appointed, by which, Thirlby, bishop of Ely, and Bonner, of London, were deputed to sit in judgment at Christ-church, Oxford. By virtue of this instrument, Cranmer was gradually degraded, by putting mere rags on him to represent the dress of an archbishop; then stripping him of his attire, they took off his own gown, and put an old worn one upon him instead. This he bore unmoved, and his enemies, finding that severity only rendered him more determined, tried the opposite course, and placed him in the house of the dean of Christ-church, where he was treated with every indulgence.

This presented such a contrast to the three years' hard imprisonment he had received, that it threw him off his guard. His open, generous nature was more easily to be seduced by a liberal conduct than by threats and fetters. When Satan finds the Christian proof against one mode of attack, he tries another; and what form is so seductive as smiles, rewards, and power, after a long, painful imprisonment? Thus it was with Cranmer: his enemies promised him his former greatness if he would but recant, as well as the queen's favour, and this at the very time they knew that his death was determined in council. To soften the path to apostasy, the first paper brought for his signature was conceived in general terms; this once signed, five others were obtained as explanatory of the first, until finally he put his hand to the following detestable instrument: 'I, Thomas Cranmer, late archbishop of Canterbury, do renounce, abhor, and detest all manner of heresies and errors of Luther and Zuinglius, and all other teachings which are contrary to sound and true doctrine. And I believe most constantly in my heart, and with my mouth I confess one holy and Catholic Church visible, without which there is no salvation; and therefore I acknowledge the Bishop of Rome to be supreme head on earth, whom I acknowledge to be the highest bishop and pope, and Christ's vicar, unto whom all Christian people ought to be subject.

'And as concerning the sacraments, I believe and worship in the sacrament of the altar the body and blood of Christ, being contained most truly under the forms of bread and wine; the bread, through the mighty power of God being turned into the body of our Saviour Jesus Christ, and the wine into his blood.

'And in the other six sacraments, also (alike as in this) I believe and hold as the universal Church holdeth, and the Church of Rome judgeth and determineth.

'Furthermore, I believe that there is a place of purgatory, where souls departed be punished for a time, for whom the Church doth godily and wholesomely pray, like as it doth honour saints and make prayers to them.

'Finally, in all things I profess, that I do not otherwise believe than the Catholic Church and the Church of Rome holdeth and teacheth. I am sorry that I ever held or thought otherwise. And I beseech Almighty God, that of His mercy He will vouchsafe to forgive me whatsoever I have offended against God or His Church, and also I desire and beseech all Christian people to pray for me.

'And all such as have been deceived either by mine example or doctrine, I require them by the blood of Jesus Christ that they will return to the unity of the Church, that we may be all of one mind, without schism or division.

'And to conclude, as I submit myself to the Catholic Church of Christ, and to the supreme head thereof, so I submit myself unto the most excellent majesties of Philip and Mary, king and queen of this realm of England, etc., and to all other their laws and ordinances, being ready always as a faithful subject ever to obey them. And God is my witness, that I have not done this for favour or fear of any person, but willingly and of mine own conscience, as to the instruction of others.'

'Let him that standeth take heed lest he fall!' said the apostle, and here was a falling off indeed! The papists now triumphed in their turn: they had acquired all they wanted short of his life. His recantation was immediately printed and dispersed, that it might have its due effect upon the astonished Protestants. But God counter-worked all the designs of the Catholics by the extent to which they carried the implacable persecution of their prey. Doubtless, the love of life induced Cranmer to sign the above declaration: yet death may be said to have been preferable to life to him who lay under the stings of a goaded conscience and the contempt of every Gospel Christian; this principle he strongly felt in all its force and anguish.

The queen's revenge was only to be satiated by Cranmer's blood, and therefore she wrote an order to Dr Pole, to prepare a sermon to be preached March 21, directly before his martyrdom, at St Mary's, Oxford. Dr Pole visited him the day previous, and was induced to believe that he would publicly deliver his sentiments in confirmation of the articles to which he had subscribed. About nine in the morning of the day of sacrifice, the queen's commissioners, attended by the magistrates, conducted the amiable unfortunate to St Mary's Church. His torn, dirty garb, the same in which they habited him upon his degradation, excited the commiseration of the people. In the church he found a low mean stage, erected opposite to the pulpit, on which being placed, he turned his face, and fervently prayed to God.

The church was crowded with persons of both persuasions, expecting to hear the justification of the late apostasy: the Catholics rejoicing, and the Protestants deeply wounded in spirit at the deceit of the human heart. Dr Pole, in his sermon, represented Cranmer as having been guilty of the most atrocious crimes; encouraged the deluded sufferer not to fear death, not to doubt the support of God in his torments, nor that Masses would be said in all the churches of Oxford for the repose of his soul. The doctor then noticed his conversion, and which he ascribed to the evident working of Almighty power and in order that the people might be convinced of its reality, asked the prisoner to give them a sign. This Cranmer did, and begged the congregation to pray for him, for he had committed many and grievous sins; but, of all, there was one which awfully lay upon his mind, of which he would speak shortly.

During the sermon Cranmer wept bitter tears: lifting up his hands and eyes to heaven, and letting them fall, as if unworthy to live: his grief now found vent in words: before his confession he fell upon his knees, and, in the following words unveiled the deep contrition and agitation which harrowed up his soul.

'O Father of heaven! O Son of God, Redeemer of the world! O Holy Ghost, three persons all one God! have mercy on me, most wretched caitiff and miserable sinner. I have offended both against heaven and earth, more than my tongue can express. Whither then may I go, or whither may I flee? To heaven I may be ashamed to lift up mine eyes and in earth I find no place of refuge or succour. To Thee, therefore, O Lord, do I run; to Thee do I humble myself, saying, O Lord, my God, my sins be great, but yet have mercy upon me for Thy great mercy. The great mystery that God became man, was not wrought for little or few offences. Thou didst not give

Thy Son, O Heavenly Father, unto death for small sins only, but for all the greatest sins of the world, so that the sinner return to Thee with his whole heart, as I do at present. Wherefore, have mercy on me, O God, whose property is always to have mercy, have mercy upon me, O Lord, for Thy great mercy. I crave nothing for my own merits, but for Thy name's sake, that it may be hallowed thereby, and for Thy dear Son, Jesus Christ's sake. And now therefore, O Father of Heaven, hallowed be Thy name,' etc.

Then rising, he said he was desirous before his death to give them some pious exhortations by which God might be glorified and themselves edified. He then descanted upon the danger of a love for the world, the duty of obedience to their majesties, of love to one another and the necessity of the rich administering to the wants of the poor. He quoted the three verses of the fifth chapter of James, and then proceeded, 'Let them that be rich ponder well these three sentences: for if they ever had occasion to show their charity, they have it now at this present, the poor people being so many, and victual so dear.

'And now forasmuch as I am come to the last end of my life, whereupon hangeth all my life past, and all my life to come, either to live with my master Christ for ever in joy, or else to be in pain for ever with the wicked in hell, and I see before mine eyes presently, either heaven ready to receive me, or else hell ready to swallow me up; I shall therefore declare unto you my very faith how I believe, without any Collor of dissimulation: for now is no time to dissemble, whatsoever I have said or written in times past.

'First, I believe in God the Father Almighty, Maker of heaven and earth, etc. And I believe every article of the Catholic faith, every word and sentence taught by our Saviour Jesus Christ, His apostles and prophets, in the New and Old Testament.

'And now I come to the great thing which so much troubleth my conscience, more than any thing that ever I did or said in my whole life, and that is the setting abroad of a writing contrary to the truth, which now here I renounce and refuse, as things written with my hand contrary to the truth which I thought in my heart, and written for fear of death, and to save my life, if it might be; and that is, all such bills or papers which I have written or signed with my hand since my degradation, wherein I have written many things untrue. And forasmuch as my hand hath offended, writing contrary to my heart, therefore my hand shall first be punished; for when I come to the fire it shall first be burned.

'And as for the pope, I refuse him as Christ's enemy, and Antichrist, With all his false doctrine.'

Upon the conclusion of this unexpected declaration, amazement and indignation were conspicuous in every part of the church. The Catholics were completely foiled, their object being frustrated, Cranmer, like Samson, having completed a greater ruin upon his enemies in the hour of death, than he did in his life.

Cranmer would have proceeded in the exposure of the popish doctrines, but the murmurs of the idolaters drowned his voice, and the preacher gave an order to 'lead the heretic away!' The savage command was directly obeyed, and the lamb about to suffer was torn from his stand to the place of slaughter, insulted all the way by the revilings and taunts of the pestilent monks and friars.

With thoughts intent upon a far higher object than the empty threats of man, he reached the spot dyed with the blood of Ridley and Latimer. There he knelt for a short time in earnest devotion, and then arose, that he might undress and prepare for the fire. Two friars who had been parties in prevailing upon him to abjure, now endeavoured to draw him off again from the truth, but he was steadfast and immovable in what he had just professed, and publicly taught. A chain was provided to bind him to the stake, and after it had tightly encircled him, fire was put to the fuel, and the flames began soon to ascend.

Then were the glorious sentiments of the martyr made manifest; then it was, that stretching out his right hand, he held it unshrinkingly in the fire until it was burnt to a cinder, even before his body was injured, frequently exclaiming, 'This unworthy right hand.'

His body did abide the burning with such steadfastness that he seemed to have no more than the stake to which he was bound; his eyes were lifted up to heaven, and he repeated 'this unworthy right hand' as long as his voice would suffer him; and using often the words of Stephen, 'Lord Jesus, receive my spirit,' in the greatness of the flame, he gave up the ghost.

The Vision of Three Ladders

When Robert Samuel was brought forth to be burned, certain there were that heard him declare what strange things had happened unto him during the time of his imprisonment; to wit, that after he had famished or pined with hunger two or three days together, he then fell into a sleep, as it were one half in a slumber, at which time one clad all in white seemed to stand before him, who ministered comfort unto him by these words:

'Samuel, Samuel, be of good cheer, and take a good heart unto thee: for after this day shalt thou never be either hungry or thirsty.'

No less memorable it is, and worthy to be noted, concerning the three ladders which he told to divers he saw in his sleep, set up toward heaven; of the which there was one somewhat longer than the rest, but yet at length they became one, joining (as it were) all three together.

As this godly martyr was going to the fire, there came a certain maid to him, which took him about the neck, and kissed him, who, being marked by them that were present, was sought for the next day after, to be had to prison and burned, as the very party herself informed me: howbeit, as God of His goodness would have it, she escaped their fiery hands, keeping herself secret in the town a good while after.

But as this maid, called Rose Nottingham, was marvellously preserved by the providence of God, so there were other two honest women who did fall into the rage and fury of that time. The one was a brewer's wife, the other was a shoemaker's wife, but both together now espoused to a new husband, Christ.

With these two was this maid aforesaid very familiar and well acquainted, who, on a time giving counsel to the one of them, that she should convey herself away while she had time and space, had this answer at her hand again: 'I know well,' saith she, 'that it is lawful enough to fly away; which remedy you may use, if you list. But my case standeth otherwise. I am tied to a husband, and have besides young children at home; therefore I am minded, for the love of Christ and His truth, to stand to the extremity of the matter.'

And so the next day after Samuel suffered, these two godly wives, the one called Anne Potten, the other called Joan Trunchfield, the wife of Michael Trunchfield, shoemaker, of Ipswich, were apprehended, and had both into one prison together. As they were both by sex and nature somewhat tender, so were they at first less able to endure the straitness of the prison; and especially the brewer's wife was cast into marvellous great agonies and troubles of mind thereby. But Christ, beholding the weak infirmity of His servant, did not fail to help her when she was in this necessity; so at the length they both suffered after Samuel, in 1556, February 19. And these, no doubt, were those two ladders, which, being joined with the third, Samuel saw stretched up into heaven. This blessed Samuel, the servant of Christ, suffered the thirty-first of August, 1555.

The report goeth among some that were there present, and saw him burn, that his body in burning did shine in the eyes of them that stood by, as bright and white as new-tried silver.

When Agnes Bongeor saw herself separated from her prison-fellows, what piteous moan that good woman made, how bitterly she wept, what strange thoughts came into her mind, how naked and desolate she esteemed herself, and into what plunge of despair and care her poor soul was brought, it was piteous and wonderful to see; which all came because she went not with them to give her life in the defence of her Christ; for of all things in the world, life was least looked for at her hands.

For that morning in which she was kept back from burning, had she put on a smock, that she had prepared only for that purpose. And also having a child, a little young infant sucking on her, whom she kept with her tenderly all the time that she was in prison, against that day likewise did she send away to another nurse, and prepared herself presently to give herself for the testimony of the glorious Gospel of Jesus Christ. So little did she look for life, and so greatly did God's gifts work in her above nature, that death seemed a great deal better welcome than life. After which, she began a little to stay herself, and gave her whole exercise to reading and prayer, wherein she found no little comfort.

In a short time came a writ from London for the burning, which according to the effect thereof, was executed.

Hugh Laverick and John Aprice

Here we perceive that neither the impotence of age nor the affliction of blindness, could turn aside the murdering fangs of these Babylonish monsters. The first of these unfortunates was of the parish of Barking, aged sixty-eight, a painter and a cripple. The other was blind, dark indeed in his visual faculties, but intellectually illuminated with the radiance of the ever-lasting Gospel of truth. Inoffensive objects like these were informed against by some of the sons of bigotry, and dragged before the prelatical shark of London, where they underwent examination, and replied to the articles propounded to them, as other Christian martyrs had done before. On the ninth day of May, in the consistory of St Paul's, they were entreated to recant, and upon refusal, were sent to Fulham, where Bonner, by way of a dessert after dinner, condemned them to the agonies of the fire. Being consigned to the secular officers, May 15, 1556, they were taken in a cart from Newgate to Stratford-le-Bow, where they were fastened to the stake. When Hugh Laverick was secured by the chain, having no further occasion for his crutch, he threw it away saying to his fellow-martyr, while consoling him, 'Be of good cheer my brother; for my lord of London is our good physician; he will heal us both shortly – thee of thy blindness, and me of my lameness.' They sank down in the fire, to rise to immortality!

The day after the above martyrdoms, Catharine Hut, of Bocking, widow; Joan Horns, spinster, of Billerica; Elizabeth Thackwel, spinster, of Great Burstead, suffered death in Smithfield.

Thomas Dowry

We have again to record an act of unpitying cruelty, exercised on this lad, whom Bishop Hooper, had confirmed in the Lord and the knowledge of his Word.

How long this poor sufferer remained in prison is uncertain.

By the testimony of one John Paylor, register of Gloucester, we learn that when Dowry was brought before Dr Williams, then chancellor of Gloucester, the usual articles were presented him for subscription. From these he dissented; and, upon the doctor's demanding of whom and where he had learned his heresies, the youth replied, 'Indeed, Mr Chancellor, I learned from you in that very pulpit. On such a day (naming the day) you said, in preaching upon the Sacrament, that it was to be exercised spiritually by faith, and not carnally and really, as taught by the papists.' Dr Williams then bid him recant, as he had done; but Dowry had not so learned his duty. 'Though you,' said he, 'can so easily mock God, the world, and your own conscience, yet will I not do so.'

Preservation of George Crow and His Testament

This poor man, of Malden, May 26, 1556, put to sea, to lade in Lent with fuller's earth, but the boat, being driven on land, filled with water, and everything was washed out of her; Crow, however, saved his Testament, and coveted nothing else. With Crow was a man and a boy, whose awful situation became every minute more alarming, as the boat was useless, and they were ten miles from land, expecting the tide should in a few hours set in upon them. After prayer to God, they got upon the mast, and hung there for the space of ten hours, when the poor boy, overcome by cold and exhaustion, fell off, and was drowned. The tide having abated, Crow proposed to take down the masts, and float upon them, which they did; and at ten o'clock at night they were borne away at the mercy of the waves. On Wednesday, in the night, Crow's companion died through the fatigue and hunger, and he was left alone, calling upon God for succour. At length he was picked up by a Captain Morse, bound to Antwerp, who had nearly steered away, taking him for some fisherman's buoy floating in the sea. As soon as Crow was got on board, he put his hand in his bosom, and drew out his Testament, which indeed was wet, but not otherwise injured. At Antwerp he was well received, and the money he had lost was more than made good to him.

Executions at Stratford-le-Bow

At this sacrifice, which we are about to detail no less than thirteen were doomed to the fire. Each one refusing to subscribe contrary to conscience, they were condemned, and the twenty-seventh of June, 1556, was appointed for their execution at Stratford-le-Bow. Their constancy and faith glorified their Redeemer, equally in life and in death.

Rev Julius Palmer

This gentleman's life presents a singular instance of error and conversion. In the time of Edward, he was a rigid and obstinate papist, so adverse to godly and sincere preaching, that he was even despised by his own party; that this frame of mind should be changed, and he suffer persecution and death in Queen Mary's reign, are among those events of omnipotence at which we wonder and admire.

Mr Palmer was born at Coventry, where his father had been mayor. Being afterward removed to Oxford, he became, under Mr Harley, of Magdalen College, an elegant Latin and Greek scholar. He was fond of useful disputation, possessed of a lively wit, and a strong memory. Indefatigable in private study, he rose at four in the morning, and by this practice qualified himself to become reader in logic in Magdalen College. The times of Edward, however, favouring the Reformation, Mr Palmer became frequently punished for his contempt of prayer and orderly behaviour, and was at length expelled the house.

He afterwards embraced the doctrines of the Reformation, which occasioned his arrest and final condemnation.

A certain nobleman offered him his life if he would recant. 'If so,' said he, 'thou wilt dwell with me. And if thou wilt set thy mind to marriage, I will procure thee a wife and a farm, and help to stuff and fit thy farm for thee. How sayst thou?' Palmer thanked him very courteously, but very modestly and reverently concluded that as he had already in two places renounced his living for Christ's sake, so he would with God's grace be ready to surrender and yield up his life also for the same, when God should send time.

When Sir Richard perceived that he would by no means relent: 'Well, Palmer,' saith he, 'then I perceive one of us twain shall be damned: for we be of two faiths, and certain I am there is but one faith that leadeth to life and salvation.' Palmer: 'O sir, I hope that we both shall be saved.' Sir Richard: 'How may that be?' Palmer: 'Right well, sir. For as it hath pleased our merciful Saviour, according to the Gospel's parable, to call me at the third hour of the day, even in my flowers, at the age of four and twenty years, even so I trust He hath called, and will call you, at the eleventh hour of this your old age, and give you everlasting life for your portion.' Sir Richard: 'Sayest thou so? Well, Palmer, well, I would I might have thee but one month in my house: I doubt not but I would convert thee, or thou shouldst convert me.' Then said Master Winchcomb, 'Take pity on thy golden years, and pleasant flowers of lusty youth, before it be too late.' Palmer: 'Sir, I long for those springing flowers that shall never fade away.'

He was tried on the fifteenth of July, 1556, together with one Thomas Askin, fellow prisoner. Askin and one John Guin had been sentenced the day before, and Mr Palmer, on the fifteenth, was brought up for final judgment. Execution was ordered to follow the sentence, and at five o'clock in the same afternoon, at a place called the Sand-pits, these three martyrs were fastened to a stake. After devoutly praying together, they sung the Thirty-first Psalm.

When the fire was kindled, and it had seized their bodies, without an appearance of enduring pain, they continued to cry, 'Lord Jesus, strengthen us! Lord Jesus receive our souls!' until animation was suspended and human suffering was past. It is remarkable, that, when their heads had fallen together in a mass as it were by the force of the flames, and the spectators thought Palmer as lifeless, his tongue and lips again moved, and were heard to pronounce the name of Jesus, to whom be glory and honour forever!

Joan Waste and Others

This poor, honest woman, blind from her birth, and unmarried, aged twenty-two, was of the parish of Allhallows, Derby. Her father was a barber, and also made ropes for a living: in which she assisted him, and also learned to knit several articles of apparel. Refusing to communicate with those who maintained doctrines contrary to those she had learned in the days of the pious Edward, she was called before Dr Draicot, the chancellor of Bishop Blaine, and Peter Finch, official of Derby.

With sophistical arguments and threats they endeavoured to confound the poor girl; but she proffered to yield to the bishop's doctrine, if he would answer for her at the Day of Judgment (as pious Dr Taylor had done in his sermons) that his belief of the real presence of the Sacrament was true. The bishop at first answered that he would; but Dr Draicot reminding him that he might not in any way answer for a heretic, he withdrew his confirmation of his own tenets; and she replied that if their consciences would not permit them to answer at God's bar for that truth they wished her to subscribe to, she would answer no more questions. Sentence was then adjudged, and Dr Draicot appointed to preach her condemned sermon, which took place August 1, 1556, the day of her martyrdom. His fulminating discourse being finished, the poor, sightless object was taken to a place called Windmill Pit, near the town, where she for a time held her brother by the hand, and then prepared herself for the fire, calling upon the pitying multitude to pray with her, and upon Christ to have mercy upon her, until the glorious light of the everlasting Sun of righteousness beamed upon her departed spirit.

In November, fifteen martyrs were imprisoned in Canterbury Castle, of whom all were either burnt or famished. Among the latter were J. Clark, D. Chittenden, W. Foster of Stone, Alice Potkins, and J. Archer, of Cranbrooke, weaver. The two first of these had not received condemnation, but the others were sentenced to the fire. Foster, at his examination, observed upon the utility of carrying lighted candles about on Candlemas-day, that he might as well carry a pitchfork; and that a gibbet would have as good an effect as the cross.

We have now brought to a close the sanguinary proscriptions of the merciless Mary, in the year 1556, the number of which amounted to above *eighty-four*!

The beginning of the year 1557, was remarkable for the visit of Cardinal Pole to the University of Cambridge, which seemed to stand in need of much cleansing from heretical preachers and reformed doctrines. One object was also to play the popish farce of trying Martin Bucer and Paulus Phagius, who had been buried about three or four years; for which purpose the churches of St Mary and St Michael, where they lay, were interdicted as vile and unholy places, unfit to worship God in, until they were perfumed and washed with the pope's holy water, etc., etc. The trumpery act of citing these dead reformers to appear, not having had the least effect upon them, on January 26, sentence of condemnation was passed, part of which ran in this manner, and may serve as a specimen of proceedings of this nature: 'We therefore pronounce the said Martin Bucer and Paulus Phagius excommunicated and anathematised, as well by the common law, as by letters of process; and that their memory be condemned, we also condemn their bodies and bones (which in that wicked time of schism, and other heresies flourishing in this kingdom, were rashly buried in holy ground) to be dug up, and cast far from the bodies and bones of the faithful, according to the holy canons, and we command that they and their writings, if any be there found, be publicly burnt; and we interdict all persons what-soever of this university, town, or places adjacent, who shall read or conceal their heretical book, as well by the common law, as by our letters of process!'

After the sentence thus read, the bishop commanded their bodies to be dug out of their graves, and being degraded from holy orders, delivered them into the hands of the secular power; for it was not lawful for such innocent persons as they were, abhorring all bloodshed, and detesting all desire of murder, to put any man to death.

February 6, the bodies, enclosed as they were in chests, were carried into the midst of the market-place at Cambridge, accompanied by a vast concourse of people. A great post was set fast in the ground, to which the chests were affixed with a large iron chain, and bound round their centres, in the same manner as if the dead bodies had been alive. When the fire began to ascend, and caught the coffins, a number of condemned books were also launched into the flames, and burnt. Justice, however, was done to the memories of these pious and learned men in Queen Elizabeth's reign, when Mr Ackworth, orator of the university, and Mr J. Pilkington, pronounced orations in honour of their memory, and in reprobation of their Catholic persecutors.

Cardinal Pole also inflicted his harmless rage upon the dead body of Peter Martyr's wife, who, by his command, was dug out of her grave, and buried on a distant dunghill, partly because her bones lay near St Fridewide's relics, held once in great esteem in that college, and partly because he wished to purify Oxford of heretical remains as well as Cambridge. In the succeeding reign, however, her remains were restored to their former cemetery, and even intermingled with those of the Catholic saint, to the utter astonishment and mortification of the disciples of his holiness the pope.

Cardinal Pole published a list of fifty-four articles, containing instructions to the clergy of his diocese of Canterbury, some of which are too ludicrous and puerile to excite any other sentiment than laughter in these days.

Persecutions in the Diocese of Canterbury

In the month of February, the following persons were committed to prison: R. Coleman, of Waldon, labourer; Joan Winseley, of Horsley Magna, spinster; S. Glover, of Rayley; R. Clerk, of Much Holland, mariner; W. Munt, of Much Bentley, sawyer; Marg. Field, of Ramsey, spinster; R. Bongeor, currier; R. Jolley, mariner; Allen Simpson, Helen Ewire, C. Pepper, widow; Alice Walley (who recanted), W. Bongeor, glazier, all of Colchester; R. Atkin, of Halstead, weaver; R. Barcock, of Wilton, carpenter; R. George, of Westbarnholt, labourer; R. Debnam of Debenham, weaver; C. Warren, of Cocksall, spinster; Agnes Whitlock, of Dover-court, spinster; Rose Allen, spinster; and T. Feresannes, minor; both of Colchester.

These persons were brought before Bonner, who would have immediately sent them to execution, but Cardinal Pole was for more merciful measures, and Bonner, in a letter of his to the cardinal, seems to be sensible that he had displeased him, for he has this expression: 'I thought to have them all hither to Fulham, and to have given sentence against them; nevertheless, perceiving by my last doing that your grace was offended, I thought it my duty, before I proceeded further, to inform your grace.' This circumstance verifies the account that the cardinal was a humane man; and though a zealous Catholic, we, as Protestants, are willing to render him that honour which his merciful character deserves. Some of the bitter persecutors denounced him to the pope as a favourer of heretics, and he was summoned to Rome, but Queen Mary, by particular entreaty, procured his stay. However, before his latter end, and a little before his last journey from Rome to England, he was strongly suspected of favouring the doctrine of Luther.

As in the last sacrifice four women did honour to the truth, so in the following auto da fé we have the like number of females and males, who suffered June 30, 1557, at Canterbury, and were J. Fishcock, F. White, N. Pardue, Barbary Final, widow; Bardbridge's widow, Wilson's wife, and Benden's wife.

Of this group in the Canterbury diocese we shall more particularly notice Alice Benden, wife of Edward Benden, of Staplehurst, Kent. She had been taken up in October, 1556, for non-attendance, and released upon a strong injunction to mind her conduct. Her husband was a bigoted Catholic, and publicly speaking of his wife's contumacy, she was conveyed to Canterbury Castle, where knowing, when she should be removed to the bishop's prison, she should be almost starved upon three farthings a day, she endeavoured to prepare herself for this suffering by living upon twopence halfpenny per day.

On January 22, 1557, her husband wrote to the bishop that if his wife's brother, Roger Hall, were to be kept from consoling and relieving her, she might turn; on this account, she was moved to a prison called Monday's Hole. Her brother sought diligently for her, and at the end of five weeks providentially heard her voice in the dungeon, but could not otherwise relieve her, than by putting some money in a loaf, and sticking it on a long pole. Dreadful must have been the situation of this poor victim, lying on straw, between stone walls, without a change of apparel, or the meanest requisites of cleanliness, during a period of nine weeks!

On March 25 she was summoned before the bishop, who, with rewards, offered her liberty if she would go home and be comfortable; but Mrs Benden had been inured to suffering, and, showing him her contracted limbs and emaciated appearance, refused to swerve from the truth. She was however removed from this black hole to the West Gate, whence, about the end of April, she was taken out to be condemned, and then committed to the castle prison until the nineteenth of June, the day of her burning. At the stake, she gave her handkerchief to one John Banks, as a memorial; and from her waist she drew a white lace, desiring him to give it to her brother, and tell him that it was the last band that had bound her, except the chain; and to her father she returned a shilling he had sent her.

The whole of these seven martyrs undressed themselves with alacrity, and, being prepared, knelt down, and prayed with an earnestness and Christian spirit that even the enemies of the cross were affected. After invocation made together, they were secured to the stake, and, being encompassed with the unsparing flames, they yielded their souls into the hands of the living Lord.

Matthew Plaise, weaver, a sincere and shrewd Christian, of Stone, Kent, was brought before Thomas, bishop of Dover, and other inquisitors, whom he ingeniously teased by his indirect answers, of which the following is a specimen.

Dr Harpsfield: 'Christ called the bread His body; what dost thou say it is?' Plaise: 'I do believe it was that which He gave them.' Dr H: 'What was that?' P: 'That which He brake.' Dr H: 'What did He brake?' P: 'That which He took.' Dr H: 'What did He take?' P: 'I say, what He gave them, that did they eat indeed.' Dr H: 'Well, then, thou sayest it was but bread which the disciples did eat.' P: 'I say, what He gave them, that did they eat indeed.'

A very long disputation followed, in which Plaise was desired to humble himself to the bishop; but this he refused. Whether this zealous person died in prison, was executed, or delivered, history does not mention.

Rev John Hullier

Rev John Hullier was brought up at Eton College, and in process of time became curate of Babram, three miles from Cambridge, and went afterward to Lynn; where, opposing the superstition of the papists, he was carried before Dr Thirlby, bishop of Ely, and sent to Cambridge Castle: here he lay for a time, and was then sent to Tolbooth prison, where, after three months, he was brought to St Mary's Church, and condemned by Dr Fuller. On Maunday Thursday he was brought to the stake: while undressing, he told the people to bear witness that he was about to suffer in a just cause, and exhorted them to believe that there was no other rock than Jesus Christ to build upon. A priest named Boyes, then desired the mayor to silence him. After praying, he went meekly to the stake, and being bound with a chain, and placed in a pitch barrel, fire was applied to the reeds and wood; but the wind drove the fire directly to his back, which caused him under the severe agony to pray the more fervently. His friends directed the executioner to fire the pile to windward of his face, which was immediately done.

A quantity of books were now thrown into the fire, one of which (the Communion Service) he caught, opened it, and joyfully continued to read it, until the fire and smoke deprived him of sight; then even, in earnest prayer, he pressed the book to his heart, thanking God for bestowing on him in his last moments this precious gift.

The day being hot, the fire burnt fiercely; and at a time when the spectators supposed he was no more, he suddenly exclaimed, 'Lord Jesus, receive my spirit,' and meekly resigned his life. He was burnt on Jesus Green, not far from Jesus College. He had gunpowder given him, but he was dead before it became ignited. This pious sufferer afforded a singular spectacle; for his flesh was so burnt from the bones, which continued erect, that he presented the idea of a skeleton figure chained to the stake. His remains were eagerly seized by the multitude, and venerated by all who admired his piety or detested inhuman bigotry.

Simon Miller and Elizabeth Cooper

In the following month of July, received the crown of martyrdom. Miller dwelt at Lynn, and came to Norwich, where, planting himself at the door of one of the churches, as the people came out, he requested to know of them where he could go to receive the Communion. For this a priest brought him before Dr Dunning, who committed him to ward; but he was suffered to go home, and arrange his affairs; after which he returned to the bishop's house, and to his prison, where he remained until the thirteenth of July, the day of his burning.

Elizabeth Cooper, wife of a pewterer, of St Andrews, Norwich, had recanted; but tortured for what she had done by the worm which dieth not, she shortly after voluntarily entered her parish church during the time of the popish service, and standing up, audibly proclaimed that she revoked her former recantation, and cautioned the people to avoid her unworthy example. She was taken from her own house by Mr Sutton the sheriff, who very reluctantly complied with the letter of the law, as they had been servants and in friendship together. At the stake, the poor sufferer, feeling the fire, uttered the cry of 'Oh!' upon which Mr Miller, putting his hand behind him towards her, desired her to be of a good courage, 'for (said he) good sister, we shall have a joyful and a sweet supper.' Encouraged by this example and exhortation, she stood the fiery ordeal without flinching, and, with him, proved the power of faith over the flesh.

Executions at Colchester

It was before mentioned that twenty-two persons had been sent up from Colchester, who upon a slight submission, were afterward released. Of these, William Munt, of Much Bentley, husbandman, with Alice, his wife, and Rose Allin, her daughter, upon their return home, abstained from church, which induced the bigoted priest secretly to write to Bonner. For a short time they absconded, but returning again, March 7, one Edmund Tyrrel (a relation of the Tyrrel who murdered King Edward V and his brother) with the officers, entered the house while Munt and his wife were in bed, and informed them that they must go to Colchester Castle. Mrs Munt at that time being very ill, requested her daughter to get her some drink; leave being permitted, Rose took a candle and a mug; and in returning through the house was met by Tyrrel, who cautioned her to advise her parents to become good Catholics. Rose briefly informed him that they had the Holy Ghost for their adviser; and that she was ready to lay down her own life for the same cause. Turning to his company, he remarked that she was willing to burn; and one of them told him to prove her, and see what she would do by and by. The unfeeling wretch immediately executed this project; and, seizing the young woman by the wrist, he held the lighted candle under her hand, burning it crosswise on the back, until the tendons divided from the flesh, during which he loaded her with many opprobrious epithets. She endured his rage unmoved, and then, when he had ceased the torture, she asked him to begin at her feet or head, for he need not fear that his employer would one day repay him. After this she took the drink to her mother.

This cruel act of torture does not stand alone on record. Bonner had served a poor blind harper in nearly the same manner, who had steadily maintained a hope that if every joint of him were to be burnt, he should not fly from the faith. Bonner, upon this, privately made a signal to his men, to bring a burning coal, which they placed in the poor man's hand, and then by force held it closed, until it burnt into the flesh deeply.

George Eagles, tailor, was indicted for having prayed that 'God would turn Queen Mary's heart, or take her away'; the ostensible cause of his death was his religion, for treason could hardly be imagined in praying for the reformation of such an execrable soul as that of Mary. Being condemned for this crime, he was drawn to the place of execution upon a sledge, with two robbers, who were executed with him. After Eagles had mounted the ladder, and been turned off a short time, he was cut down before he was at all insensible; a bailiff, named

William Swallow, then dragged him to the sledge, and with a common blunt cleaver, hacked off the head; in a manner equally clumsy and cruel, he opened his body and tore out the heart.

In all this suffering the poor martyr repined not, but to the last called upon his Saviour. The fury of these bigots did not end here; the intestines were burnt, and the body was quartered, the four parts being sent to Colchester, Harwich, Chelmsford, and St Rouse's. Chelmsford had the honour of retaining his head, which was affixed to a long pole in the market place. In time it was blown down, and lay several days in the street, until it was buried at night in the church-yard. God's judgment not long after fell upon Swallow, who in his old age became a beggar, and who was affected with a leprosy that made him obnoxious even to the animal creation; nor did Richard Potts, who troubled Eagles in his dying moments, escape the visiting hand of God.

Mrs Joyce Lewes

This lady was the wife of Mr T. Lewes, of Manchester. She had received the Romish religion as true, until the burning of that pious martyr, Mr Saunders, at Coventry. Understanding that his death arose from a refusal to receive the Mass, she began to inquire into the ground of his refusal, and her conscience, as it began to be enlightened, became restless and alarmed. In this inqui-etude, she resorted to Mr John Glover, who lived near, and requested that he would unfold those rich sources of Gospel knowledge he possessed, particularly upon the subject of transubstantia-tion. He easily succeeded in convincing her that the mummery of popery and the Mass were at variance with God's most holy Word, and honestly reproved her for following too much the vani-ties of a wicked world. It was to her indeed a word in season, for she soon became weary of her former sinful life and resolved to abandon the Mass and dilatrous worship. Though compelled by her husband's violence to go to church, her contempt of the holy water and other ceremonies was so manifest, that she was accused before the bishop for despising the sacramentals.

A citation, addressed to her, immediately followed, which was given to Mr Lewes, who, in a fit of passion, held a dagger to the throat of the officer, and made him eat it, after which he caused him to drink it down, and then sent him away. But for this the bishop summoned Mr Lewes before him as well as his wife; the former readily submitted, but the latter resolutely affirmed, that, in refusing holy water, she neither offended God, nor any part of his laws. She was sent home for a month, her husband being bound for her appearance, during which time Mr Glover impressed upon her the necessity of doing what she did, not from self-vanity, but for the honour and glory of God.

Mr Glover and others earnestly exhorted Lewes to forfeit the money he was bound in, rather than subject his wife to certain death; but he was deaf to the voice of humanity, and delivered her over to the bishop, who soon found sufficient cause to consign her to a loathsome prison, whence she was several times brought for examination. At the last time the bishop reasoned with her upon the fitness of her coming to Mass, and receiving as sacred the Sacrament and sacramentals of the Holy Ghost. 'If these things were in the Word of God,' said Mrs Lewes, 'I would with all my heart receive, believe, and esteem them.' The bishop, with the most ignorant and impious effrontery, replied, 'If thou wilt believe no more than what is warranted by Scriptures, thou art in a state of damnation!' Astonished at such a declaration, this worthy sufferer ably rejoined that his words were as impure as they were profane.

After condemnation, she lay a twelvemonth in prison, the sheriff not being willing to put her to death in his time, though he had been but just chosen. When her death warrant came from London, she sent for some friends, whom she consulted in what manner her death might be more glorious to the name of God, and injurious to the cause of God's enemies. Smilingly, she said: 'As for death, I think but lightly of. When I know that I shall behold the amiable countenance of Christ my dear Saviour, the ugly face of death does not much trouble me.' The evening before she suffered, two priests were anxious to visit her, but she refused both their confession and absolution, when she could hold a better communication with the High Priest of souls. About three o'clock in the morning, Satan began to shoot his fiery darts, by putting into her mind to doubt whether she was chosen to eternal life, and Christ died for her. Her friends readily pointed out to her those consolatory passages of Scripture which comfort the fainting heart, and treat of the Redeemer who taketh away the sins of the world.

About eight o'clock the sheriff announced to her that she had but an hour to live; she was at first cast down, but this soon passed away, and she thanked God that her life was about to be devoted to His service. The sheriff granted permission for two friends to accompany her to the stake – an indulgence for which he was afterward severely handled. Mr Reniger and Mr Bernher led her to the place of execution; in going to which, from its distance, her great weakness, and the press of the people, she had nearly fainted. Three times she prayed fervently that God would deliver the land from popery and the idolatrous Mass; and the people for the most part, as well as the sheriff, said Amen.

When she had prayed, she took the cup (which had been filled with water to refresh her) and said, 'I drink to all them that unfeignedly love the Gospel of Christ, and wish for the abolition of popery.' Her friends, and a great many women of the place, drank with her, for which most of them afterward were enjoined penance.

When chained to the stake, her countenance was cheerful, and the roses of her cheeks were not abated. Her hands were extended towards heaven until the fire rendered them powerless, when her soul was received into the arms of the Creator. The duration of her agony was but short, as the under-sheriff, at the request of her friends, had prepared such excellent fuel that she was in a few minutes overwhelmed with smoke and flame. The case of this lady drew a tear of pity from everyone who had a heart not callous to humanity.

Executions at Islington

About the seventeenth of September, suffered at Islington the following four professors of Christ: Ralph Allerton, James Austoo, Margery Austoo, and Richard Roth.

James Austoo and his wife, of St Allhallows, Barking, London, were sentenced for not believing in the presence. Richard Roth rejected the seven Sacraments, and was accused of comforting the heretics by the following letter written in his own blood, and intended to have been sent to his friends at Colchester:

'O dear Brethren and Sisters,

'How much reason have you to rejoice in God, that He hath given you such faith to overcome this bloodthirsty tyrant thus far! And no doubt He that hath begun that good work in you, will fulfill it unto the end. O dear hearts in Christ, what a crown of glory shall ye receive with Christ in the kingdom of God! O that it had been the good will of God that I had been ready to have gone with you; for I lie in my lord's Little-ease by day, and in the night I lie in the Coalhouse, apart from Ralph Allerton, or any other; and we look every day when we shall be condemned; for he said that I should be burned within ten days before Easter; but I lie still at the pool's brink, and every man goeth in before me; but we abide patiently the Lord's leisure, with many bonds, in fetters and stocks, by which we have received great joy of God. And now fare you well, dear brethren and sisters, in this world, but I trust to see you in the heavens face to face.

'O brother Munt, with your wife and my sister Rose, how blessed are you in the Lord, that God hath found you worthy to suffer for His sake! with all the rest of my dear brethren and sisters known and unknown. O be joyful even unto death. Fear it not, saith Christ, for I have overcome death. O dear heart, seeing that Jesus Christ will be our help, O tarry you the Lord's leisure. Be strong, let your hearts be of good comfort, and wait you still for the Lord. He is at hand. Yea, the angel of the Lord pitcheth his tent round about them that fear him, and delivereth them which way he seeth best. For our lives are in the Lord's hands; and they can do nothing unto us before God suffer them. Therefore give all thanks to God.

'O dear hearts, you shall be clothed in long white garments upon the mount of Sion, with the multitude of saints, and with Jesus Christ our Saviour, who will never forsake us. O blessed virgins, ye have played the wise virgins' part, in that ye have taken oil in your lamps that ye may go in with the Bridegroom, when he cometh, into the everlasting joy with Him. But as for the foolish, they shall be shut out, because they made not themselves ready to suffer with Christ, neither go about to take up His cross. O dear hearts, how precious shall your death be in the sight of the Lord! for dear is the death of His saints. O fare you well, and pray. The grace of our Lord Jesus Christ be with you all. Amen, Amen. Pray, pray, pray!

'Written by me, with my own blood,

'RICHARD ROTH.'

This letter, so justly denominating Bonner the 'bloodthirsty tyrant,' was not likely to excite his compassion. Roth accused him of bringing them to secret examination by night, because he was afraid of the people by day. Resisting every temptation to recant, he was condemned, and on September 17, 1557, these four martyrs perished at Islington, for the testimony of the Lamb, who was slain that they might be of the redeemed of God.

John Noyes

John Noyes, a shoemaker, of Laxfield, Suffolk, was taken to Eye, and at midnight, September 21, 1557, he was brought from Eye to Laxfield to be burned. On the following morning he was led to the stake, prepared for the horrid sacrifice. Mr Noyes, on coming to the fatal spot, knelt down, prayed, and rehearsed the Fiftieth Psalm. When the chain enveloped him, he said, 'Fear not them that kill the body, but fear him that can kill both body and soul, and cast it into everlasting fire!' As one Cadman placed a fagot against him, he blessed the hour in which he was born to die for the truth; and while trusting only upon the all-sufficient merits of the

Redeemer, fire was set to the pile, and the blazing fagots in a short time stifled his last words, 'Lord, have mercy on me! Christ, have mercy upon me!' The ashes of the body were buried in a pit, and with them one of his feet, whole to the ankle, with the stocking on.

Mrs Cicely Ormes

This young martyr, aged twenty-two, was the wife of Mr Edmund Ormes, worsted weaver of St Lawrence, Norwich. At the death of Miller and Elizabeth Cooper, before mentioned, she had said that she would pledge them of the same cup they drank of. For these words she was brought to the chancellor, who would have discharged her upon promising to go to church, and to keep her belief to herself. As she would not consent to this, the chancellor urged that he had shown more lenity to her than any other person, and was unwilling to condemn her, because she was an ignorant foolish woman; to this she replied (perhaps with more shrewdness than he expected) that however great his desire might be to spare her sinful flesh, it could not equal her inclination to surrender it up in so great a quarrel. The chancellor then pronounced the fiery sentence, and September 23, 1557, she was brought to the stake, at eight o'clock in the morning.

After declaring her faith to the people, she laid her hand on the stake, and said, 'Welcome, thou cross of Christ.' Her hand was sooted in doing this (for it was the same stake at which Miller and Cooper were burnt) and she at first wiped it; but directly after again welcomed and embraced it as the 'sweet cross of Christ.' After the tormentors had kindled the fire, she said, 'My soul doth magnify the Lord, and my spirit doth rejoice in God my Saviour.' Then crossing her hands upon her breast, and looking upwards with the utmost serenity, she stood the fiery furnace. Her hands continued gradually to rise until the sinews were dried, and then they fell. She uttered no sigh of pain, but yielded her life, an emblem of that celestial paradise in which is the presence of God, blessed forever.

It might be contended that this martyr voluntarily sought her own death, as the chancellor scarcely exacted any other penance of her than to keep her belief to herself; yet it should seem in this instance as if God had chosen her to be a shining light, for a twelve-month before she was taken, she had recanted; but she was wretched until the chancellor was informed, by letter, that she repented of her recantation from the bottom of her heart. As if to compensate for her former apostasy, and to convince the Catholics that she meant no more to compromise for her personal security, she boldly refused his friendly offer of permitting her to temporise. Her courage in such a cause deserves commendation – the cause of Him who has said, 'Whoever is ashamed of me on earth, of such will I be ashamed in heaven.'

Rev John Rough

This pious martyr was a Scotchman. At the age of seventeen, he entered himself as one of the order of Black Friars, at Stirling, in Scotland. He had been kept out of an inheritance by his friends, and he took this step in revenge for their conduct to him. After being there sixteen years, Lord Hamilton, earl of Arran, taking a liking to him, the archbishop of St Andrew's induced the provincial of the house to dispense with his habit and order; and he thus became the earl's chaplain. He remained in this spiritual employment a year, and in that time God wrought in him a saving knowledge of the truth; for which reason the earl sent him to preach in the freedom of Ayr, where he remained four years; but finding danger there from the religious complexion of the times, and learning that there was much Gospel freedom in England, he travelled up to the duke of Somerset, then Lord Protector of England, who gave him a yearly salary of twenty pounds, and authorised him, to preach at Carlisle, Berwick, and Newcastle, where he married. He was afterward removed to a benefice at Hull, in which he remained until the death of Edward VI.

In consequence of the tide of persecution then setting in, he fled with his wife to Friesland, and at Nordon they followed the occupation of knitting hose, caps, etc., for subsistence. Impeded in his business by the want of yarn, he came over to England to procure a quantity, and on November 10, arrived in London, where he soon heard of a secret society of the faithful, to whom he joined himself, and was in a short time elected their minister, in which occupation he strengthened them in every good resolution.

On December 12, through the information of one Taylor, a member of the society, Mr Rough, with Cuthbert Symson and others, was taken up in the Saracen's Head, Islington, where, under the pretext of coming to see a play, their religious exercises were holden. The queen's vice-chamberlain conducted Rough and Symson before the Council, in whose presence they were charged with meeting to celebrate the Communion. The Council wrote to Bonner and he lost no time in this affair of blood. In three days he had him up, and on the next (the twentieth) resolved to condemn him. The charges laid against him were, that he, being a priest, was married, and that he had rejected the service in the Latin tongue. Rough wanted not arguments to reply to these flimsy tenets. In short, he was degraded and condemned.

Mr Rough, it should be noticed, when in the north, in Edward VI's reign, had saved Dr Watson's life, who afterward sat with Bishop Bonner on the bench. This ungrateful prelate, in return for the kind act he had received, boldly accused Mr Rough of being the most pernicious heretic in the country. The godly minister reproved him for his malicious spirit; he affirmed that, during the thirty years he had lived, he had never bowed the knee to Baal; and that twice at Rome he had seen the pope borne about on men's shoulders with the false-named Sacrament carried before him, presenting a true picture of the very Antichrist; yet was more reverence shown to him than to the wafer, which they accounted to be their God. 'Ah?' said Bonner, rising, and making towards him, as if he would have torn his garment, 'Hast thou been at Rome, and seen our holy father the pope, and dost thou blaspheme him after this sort?' This said, he fell upon him, tore off a piece of his beard, and that the day might begin to his own satisfaction, he ordered the object of his rage to be burnt by half-past five the following morning.

Cuthbert Symson

Few professors of Christ possessed more activity and zeal than this excellent person. He not only laboured to preserve his friends from the contagion of popery, but he laboured to guard them against the terrors of persecution. He was deacon of the little congregation over which Mr Rough presided as minister.

Mr Symson has written an account of his own sufferings, which he cannot detail better than in his own words:

'On the thirteenth of December, 1557, I was committed by the Council to the Tower of London. On the following Thursday, I was called into the ward-room, before the constable of the Tower, and the recorder of London, Mr Cholmly, who commanded me to inform them of the names of those who came to the English service. I answered that I would declare nothing; in consequence of my refusal, I was set upon a rack of iron, as I judge for the space of three hours!

'They then asked me if I would confess: I answered as before.

After being unbound, I was carried back to my lodging. The Sunday after I was brought to the same place again, before the lieutenant and recorder of London, and they examined me. As I had answered before, so I answered now. Then the lieutenant swore by God I should tell; after which my two forefingers were bound together, and a small arrow placed between them, they drew it through so fast that the blood followed, and the arrow brake.

'After enduring the rack twice again, I was retaken to my lodging, and ten days after the lieutenant asked me if I would not now confess that which they had before asked of me. I answered, that I had already said as much as I would. Three weeks after I was sent to the priest, where I was greatly assaulted, and at whose hand I received the pope's curse, for bearing witness of the resurrection of Christ. And thus I commend you to God, and to the Word of His grace, with all those who unfeignedly call upon the name of Jesus; desiring God of His endless mercy, through the merits of His dear Son Jesus Christ, to bring us all to His everlasting Kingdom, Amen. I praise God for His great mercy shown upon us. Sing Hosanna to the Highest with me, Cuthbert Symson. God forgive my sins! I ask forgiveness of all the world, and I forgive all the world, and thus I leave the world, in the hope of a joyful resurrection!'

If this account be duly considered, what a picture of repeated tortures does it present! But even the cruelty of the narration is exceeded by the patient meekness with which it was endured. Here are no expressions of malice, no invocations even of God's retributive justice, not a complaint of suffering wrongfully! On the contrary, praise to God, forgiveness of sin, and a forgiving all the world, concludes this unaffected interesting narrative.

Bonner's admiration was excited by the steadfast coolness of this martyr. Speaking of Mr Symson in the consistory, he said, 'You see what a personable man he is, and then of his patience, I affirm, that, if he were not a heretic, he is a man of the greatest patience that ever came before me. Thrice in one day has he been racked in the Tower; in my house also he has felt sorrow, and yet never have I seen his patience broken.'

The day before this pious deacon was to be condemned, while in the stocks in the bishop's coal-house, he had the vision of a glorified form, which much encouraged him. This he certainly attested to his wife, to Mr Austen, and others, before his death.

With this ornament of the Christian Reformation were apprehended Mr Hugh Foxe and John Devinish; the three were brought before Bonner, March 19, 1558, and the papistical articles tendered. They rejected them, and were all condemned. As they worshipped together in the same society, at Islington, so they suffered together in Smithfield, March 28; in whose death the God of Grace was glorified, and true believers confirmed!

Thomas Hudson, Thomas Carman, and William Seamen

Were condemned by a bigoted vicar of Aylesbury, named Berry.

The spot of execution was called Lollard's Pit, without Bishopsgate, at Norwich. After joining together in humble petition to the throne of grace, they rose, went to the stake, and were encircled with their chains. To the great surprise of the spectators, Hudson slipped from under his chains, and came forward. A great opinion prevailed that he was about to recant; others thought that he wanted further time. In the meantime, his companions at the stake urged every promise and exhortation to support him. The hopes of the enemies of the cross, however, were disappointed: the good man, far from fearing the smallest personal terror at the approaching pangs of death, was only alarmed that his Saviour's face seemed to be hidden from him. Falling upon his knees, his spirit wrestled with God, and God verified the words of His Son, 'Ask, and it shall be given.' The martyr rose in an ecstasy of joy, and exclaimed, 'Now, I thank God, I am strong! and care not what man can do to me!' With an unruffled countenance he replaced himself under the chain, joined his fellow-sufferers, and with them suffered death, to the comfort of the godly, and the confusion of Antichrist.

Berry, unsatiated with this demoniacal act, summoned up two hundred persons in the town of Aylesham, whom he compelled to kneel to the cross at Pentecost, and inflicted other punishments. He struck a poor man for a trifling word, with a flail, which proved fatal to the unoffending object. He also gave a woman named Alice Oxes, so heavy a blow with his fist, as she met him entering the hall when he was in an ill-humour, that she died with the violence. This priest was rich, and possessed great authority; he was a reprobate, and, like the priest-hood, he abstained from marriage, to enjoy the more a debauched and licentious life. The Sunday after the death of Queen Mary, he was revelling with one of his concubines, before vespers; he then went to church, administered baptism, and in his return to his lascivious pastime, he was smitten by the hand of God. Without a moment given for repentance, he fell to the ground, and a groan was the only articulation permitted him. In him we may behold the difference between the end of a martyr and a persecutor.

The Story of Roger Holland

In a retired close near a field, in Islington, a company of decent persons had assembled, to the number of forty. While they were religiously engaged in praying and expounding the Scripture, twenty-seven of them were carried before Sir Roger Cholmly. Some of the women made their escape, twenty-two were committed to Newgate, who continued in prison seven weeks. Previous to their examination, they were informed by the keeper, Alexander, that nothing more was requisite to procure their discharge, than to hear Mass. Easy as this condition may seem, these martyrs valued their purity of conscience more than loss of life or property; hence, thirteen were burnt, seven in Smithfield, and six at Brentford; two died in prison, and the other seven were providentially preserved. The names of the seven who suffered were, H. Pond, R. Estland, R. Southain, M. Ricarby, J. Floyd, J. Holiday, and Roger Holland. They were sent to Newgate, June 16, 1558, and executed on the twenty-seventh.

This Roger Holland, a merchant-tailor of London, was first an apprentice with one Master Kemption, at the Black Boy in Watling Street, giving himself to dancing, fencing, gaming, banqueting, and wanton company. He had received for his master certain money, to the sum of thirty pounds; and lost every groat at dice. Therefore he purposed to convey himself away beyond the seas, either into France or into Flanders.

With this resolution, he called early in the morning on a discreet servant in the house, named Elizabeth, who professed the Gospel, and lived a life that did honour to her profession. To her he revealed the loss his folly had occasioned, regretted that he had not followed her advice, and begged her to give his master a note of hand from him acknowledging the debt, which he would repay if ever it were in his power; he also entreated his disgraceful conduct might be kept secret, lest it would bring the gray hairs to his father with sorrow to a premature grave.

The maid, with a generosity and Christian principle rarely surpassed, conscious that his imprudence might be his ruin, brought him the thirty pounds, which was part of a sum of money recently left her by legacy. 'Here,' said she, 'is the sum requisite: you shall take the money, and I will keep the note; but expressly on this condition, that you abandon all lewd and vicious company; that you neither swear nor talk immodestly, and game no more; for, should I learn that you do, I will immediately show this note to your master. I also require, that you shall promise me to attend the daily lecture at Allhallows, and the sermon at St Paul's every Sunday; that you cast away all your books of popery, and in their place substitute the Testament and the Book of Service, and that you read the Scriptures with reverence and fear, calling upon God for his grace to direct you in his truth. Pray also fervently to God, to pardon your former offences, and not to remember the sins of your youth, and would you obtain his favour ever dread to break his laws or offend his majesty. So shall God have you in His keeping, and grant you your heart's desire.' We must honour the memory of this excellent domestic, whose pious endeavours were equally directed to benefit the thoughtless youth in this life and that which is to come. God did not suffer the wish of this excellent domestic to be thrown upon a barren soil; within half a year after the licentious Holland became a zealous professor of the Gospel, and was an instrument of conversion to his father and others whom he visited in Lancashire, to their spiritual comfort and reformation from popery.

His father, pleased with his change of conduct, gave him forty pounds to commence business with in London.

Then Roger repaired to London again, and came to the maid that lent him the money to pay his master withal, and said unto her, 'Elizabeth, here is thy money I borrowed of thee; and for the friendship, good will, and the good counsel I have received at thy hands, to recompense thee I am not able, otherwise than to make thee my wife.' And soon after they were married, which was in the first year of Queen Mary.

After this he remained in the congregations of the faithful, until, the last year of Queen Mary, he, with the six others aforesaid, were taken.

And after Roger Holland there was none suffered in Smithfield for the testimony of the Gospel, God be thanked.

Flagellations by Bonner

When this Catholic hyena found that neither persuasions, threats, nor imprisonment, could produce any alteration in the mind of a youth named Thomas Hinshaw, he sent him to Fulham, and during the first night set him in the stocks, with no other allowance than bread and water. The following morning he came to see if this punishment had worked any change in his mind, and finding none, he sent Dr Harpsfield, his archdeacon, to converse with him. The doctor was soon out of humour at his replies, called him peevish boy, and asked him if he thought he went about to damn his soul? 'I am persuaded,' said Thomas, 'that you labour to promote the dark kingdom of the devil, not for the love of the truth.' These words the doctor conveyed to the bishop, who, in a passion that almost prevented articulation, came to Thomas, and said, 'Dost thou answer my archdeacon thus, thou naughty boy? But I'll soon handle thee well enough for it, be assured!' Two willow twigs were then brought him, and causing the unresisting youth to kneel against a long bench, in an arbour in his garden, he scourged him until he was compelled to cease for want of breath and fatigue. One of the rods was worn quite away.

Many other conflicts did Hinsaw undergo from the bishop; who, at length, to remove him effectually, procured false witnesses to lay articles against him, all of which the young man denied, and, in short, refused to answer any interrogatories administered to him. A fortnight after this, the young man was attacked by a burning ague, and at the request of his master. Mr Pugson, of St Paul's church-yard, he was removed, the bishop not doubting that he had given him his death in the natural way; he however remained ill above a year, and in the mean time Queen Mary died, by which act of providence he escaped Bonner's rage.

John Willes was another faithful person, on whom the scourging hand of Bonner fell. He was the brother of Richard Willes, before mentioned, burnt at Brentford. Hinshaw and Willes were confined in Bonner's coal-house together, and afterward removed to Fulham, where he and Hinshaw remained during eight or ten days, in the stocks. Bonner's persecuting spirit betrayed itself in his treatment of Willes during his examinations, often striking him on the head with a stick, seizing him by the ears, and filliping him under the chin, saying he held down his head like a thief. This producing no signs of recantation, he took him into his orchard, and in a small arbour there he flogged him first with a willow rod, and then with birch, until he was exhausted. This cruel ferocity arose from the answer of the poor sufferer, who, upon being asked how long it was since he had crept to the cross, replied, 'Not since he had come to years of discretion, nor would he, though he should be torn to pieces by wild horses.' Bonner then bade him make the sign of the cross on his forehead, which he refused to do, and thus was led to the orchard.

One day, when in the stocks, Bonner asked him how he liked his lodging and fare. 'Well enough,' said Willes, 'might I have a little straw to sit or lie upon.' Just at this time came in Willes' wife, then largely pregnant, and entreated the bishop for her husband, boldly declaring that she would be delivered in the house, if he were not suffered to go with her. To get rid of the good wife's importunity, and the trouble of a lying-in woman in his palace, he bade Willes make the sign of the cross, and say, *In nomine Patris, et Filii, et Spiritus Sancti, Amen*. Willes omitted the sign, and repeated the words, 'in the name of the Father, and of the Son, and of the Holy Ghost, Amen'. Bonner would have the words repeated in Latin, to which Willes made no objection, knowing the meaning of the words. He was then permitted to go home with his wife, his kinsman Robert Rouze being charged to bring him to St Paul's the next day, whither he himself went, and subscribing to a Latin instrument of little importance, was liberated. This is the last of the twenty-two taken at Islington.

Rev Richard Yeoman

This devout aged person was curate to Dr Taylor, at Hadley, and eminently qualified for his sacred function. Dr Taylor left him the curacy at his departure, but no sooner had Mr Newall gotten the benefice, than he removed Mr Yeoman, and substituted a Romish priest. After this he wandered from place to place, exhorting all men to stand faithfully to God's Word, earnestly to give themselves unto prayer, with patience to bear the cross now laid upon them for their trial, with boldness to confess the truth before their adversaries, and with an undoubted hope to wait for the crown and reward of eternal felicity. But when he perceived his adversaries lay wait for him, he went into Kent, and with a little packet of laces, pins, points, etc., he travelled from village to village, selling such things, and in this manner subsisted himself, his wife, and children.

At last Justice Moile, of Kent, took Mr Yeoman, and set him in the stocks a day and a night; but, having no evident matter to charge him with, he let him go again. Coming secretly again to Hadley, he tarried with his poor wife, who kept him privately, in a chamber of the town house, commonly called the Guildhall, more than a year. During this time the good old father abode in a chamber locked up all the day, spending his time in devout prayer, in reading the Scriptures, and in carding the wool which his wife spun. His wife also begged bread for herself and her children, by which precarious means they supported themselves. Thus the saints of God sustained hunger and misery, while the prophets of Baal lived in festivity, and were pampered at Jezebel's table.

Information being at length given to Newall, that Yeoman was secreted by his wife, he came, attended by the constables, and broke into the room where the object of his search lay in bed with his wife. He reproached the poor woman with being a whore, and would have indecently pulled the clothes off, but Yeoman resisted both this act of violence and the attack upon his wife's character, adding that he defied the pope and popery. He was then taken out, and set in stocks until day.

In the cage also with him was an old man, named John Dale, who had sat there three or four days, for exhorting the people during the time service was performing by Newall and his curate. His words were, 'O miserable and blind guides, will ye ever be blind leaders of the blind? Will ye never amend? Will ye never see the truth of God's Word? Will neither God's threats nor promises enter into your hearts? Will the blood of the martyrs nothing mollify your stony stomachs? O obdurate, hard-hearted, perverse, and crooked generation! to whom nothing can do good.'

These words he spake in fervency of spirit against the superstitious religion of Rome; wherefore Newall caused him forthwith to be attached, and set in the stocks in a cage, where he was kept until Sir Henry Doile, a justice, came to Hadley.

When Yeoman was taken, the parson called earnestly upon Sir Henry Doile to send them both to prison. Sir Henry Doile as earnestly entreated the parson to consider the age of the men, and their mean condition; they were neither persons of note nor preachers; wherefore he proposed to let them be punished a day or two and to dismiss them, at least John Dale, who was no priest, and therefore, as he had so long sat in the cage, he thought it punishment enough for this time. When the parson heard this, he was exceedingly mad, and in a great rage called them pestilent heretics, unfit to live in the commonwealth of Christians.

Sir Henry, fearing to appear too merciful, Yeoman and Dale were pinioned, bound like thieves with their legs under the horses' bellies, and carried to Bury jail, where they were laid in irons; and because they continually rebuked popery, they were carried into the lowest dungeon, where John Dale, through the jail-sickness and evil-keeping, died soon after: his body was thrown out, and buried in the fields. He was a man of sixty-six years of age, a weaver by occupation, well learned in the holy Scriptures, steadfast in his confession of the true doctrines of Christ as set forth in King Edward's time; for which he joyfully suffered prison and chains, and from this worldly dungeon he departed in Christ to eternal glory, and the blessed paradise of everlasting felicity.

After Dale's death, Yeoman was removed to Norwich prison, where, after strait and evil keeping, he was examined upon his faith and religion, and required to submit himself to his holy father the pope. 'I defy him (quoth he), and all his detestable abomination: I will in no wise have to do with him.' The chief articles objected to him, were his marriage and the Mass sacrifice. Finding he continued steadfast in the truth, he was condemned, degraded, and not only burnt, but most cruelly tormented in the fire. Thus he ended this poor and miserable life, and entered into that blessed bosom of Abraham, enjoying with Lazarus that rest which God has prepared for His elect.

Thomas Benbridge

Mr Benbridge was a single gentleman, in the diocese of Winchester. He might have lived a gentleman's life, in the wealthy possessions of this world; but he chose rather to enter through the strait gate of persecution to the heavenly possession of life in the Lord's Kingdom, than to enjoy present pleasure with disquietude of conscience. Manfully standing against the papists for the defence of the sincere doctrine of Christ's Gospel, he was apprehended as an adversary to the Romish religion, and led for examination before the bishop of Winchester, where he underwent several conflicts for the truth against the bishop and his colleague; for which he was condemned, and some time after brought to the place of martyrdom by Sir Richard Pecksal, sheriff.

When standing at the stake he began to untie his points, and to prepare himself; then he gave his gown to the keeper, by way of fee. His jerkin was trimmed with gold lace, which he gave to Sir Richard Pecksal, the high sheriff. His cap of velvet he took from his head, and threw away. Then, lifting his mind to the Lord, he engaged in prayer.

When fastened to the stake, Dr Seaton begged him to recant, and he should have his pardon; but when he saw that nothing availed, he told the people not to pray for him unless he would recant, no more than they would pray for a dog.

Mr Benbridge, standing at the stake with his hands together in such a manner as the priest holds his hands in his Memento, Dr Seaton came to him again, and exhorted him to recant, to whom he said, 'Away, Babylon, away!' One that stood by said, 'Sir, cut his tongue out'; another, a temporal man, railed at him worse than Dr Seaton had done.

When they saw he would not yield, they bade the tormentors to light the pile, before he was in any way covered with fagots. The fire first took away a piece of his beard, at which he did not shrink. Then it came on the other side and took his legs, and the nether stockings of his hose being leather, they made the fire pierce the sharper, so that the intolerable heat made him exclaim, 'I recant!' and suddenly he thrust the fire from him. Two or three of his friends being by, wished to save him; they stepped to the fire to help remove it, for which kindness they were sent to jail. The sheriff also of his own authority took him from the stake, and remitted him to prison, for which he was sent to the Fleet, and lay there sometime. Before, however, he was taken from the stake, Dr Seaton wrote articles for him to subscribe to. To these Mr Benbridge made so many objections that Dr Seaton ordered them to set fire again to the pile. Then with much pain and grief of heart he subscribed to them upon a man's back.

This done, his gown was given him again, and he was led to prison. While there, he wrote a letter to Dr Seaton, recanting those words he had spoken at the stake, and the articles which he had subscribed, for he was grieved that he had ever signed them. The same day he was again brought to the stake, where the vile tormentors rather broiled than burnt him. The Lord give his enemies repentance!

Mrs Prest

From the number condemned in this fanatical reign, it is almost impossible to obtain the name of every martyr, or to embellish the history of all with anecdotes and exemplifications of Christian conduct. Thanks be to Providence, our cruel task begins to draw towards a conclusion, with the end of the reign of papal terror and bloodshed. Monarchs, who sit upon thrones possessed by hereditary right, should, of all others, consider that the laws of nature are the laws of God, and hence that the first law of nature is the preservation of their subjects. Maxims of persecutions, of torture, and of death, they should leave to those who have effected sovereignty by fraud or by sword; but where, except among a few miscreant emperors of Rome, and the Roman pontiffs, shall we find one whose memory is so 'damned to everlasting fame' as that of Queen Mary? Nations bewail the hour which separates them forever from a beloved governor, but, with respect to that of Mary, it was the most blessed time of her whole reign. Heaven has ordained three great scourges for national sins – plague, pestilence, and famine. It was the will of God in Mary's reign to bring a fourth upon this kingdom, under the form of papistical persecution. It was sharp, but glorious; the fire which consumed the martyrs has undermined the popedom; and the Catholic states, at present the most bigoted and unenlightened, are those which are sunk lowest in the scale of moral dignity and political consequence. May they remain so, until the pure light of the Gospel shall dissipate the darkness of fanaticism and superstition! But to return.

Mrs Prest for some time lived about Cornwall, where she had a husband and children, whose bigotry compelled her to frequent the abominations of the Church of Rome. Resolving to act as her conscience dictated, she quitted them, and made a living by spinning. After some time, returning home, she was accused by her neighbours, and brought to Exeter, to be examined before Dr Troubleville, and his chancellor Blackston. As this martyr was accounted of inferior intellect, we shall put her in competition with the bishop, and let the reader judge which had the most of that knowledge conducive to everlasting life.

The bishop bringing the question to issue, respecting the bread and wine being flesh and blood, Mrs Prest said, 'I will demand of you whether you can deny your creed, which says, that Christ doth perpetually sit at the right hand of His Father, both body and soul, until He come again; or whether He be there in heaven our Advocate, and to make prayer for us unto God His Father? If He be so, He is not here on earth in a piece of bread. If He be not here, and if He do not dwell in temples made with hands, but in heaven, what! shall we seek Him here? If He did not offer His body once for all, why make you a new offering? If with one offering He made all perfect, why do you with a false offering make all imperfect? If He be to be worshipped in spirit and in truth, why do you worship a piece of bread? If He be eaten and drunken in faith and truth, if His flesh be not profitable to be among us, why do you say you make His flesh and blood, and say it is profitable for body and soul? Alas! I am a poor woman, but rather than to do as you do, I would live no longer. I have said, Sir.' Bishop: I promise you, you are a jolly Protestant. I pray you in what school have you been brought up? Mrs Prest: I have upon the Sundays visited the sermons, and there have I learned such things as are so fixed in my breast, that death shall not separate them. B: O foolish woman, who will waste his breath upon thee, or such as thou art? But how chanceth it that thou wentest away from thy husband? If thou wert an honest woman, thou wouldst not have left thy husband and children, and run about the country like a fugitive. Mrs P: Sir, I laboured for my living; and as my Master Christ counselleth me, when I was persecuted in one city, I fled into another. B: Who persecuted thee? Mrs P: My husband and my children. For when I would have them to leave idolatry, and to worship God in heaven, he would not hear me, but he with his children rebuked me, and troubled me. I fled not for whoredom, nor for theft, but because I would be no partaker with him and his of that foul idol the Mass; and wheresoever I was, as oft as I could, upon Sundays and holydays. I made excuses not to go to the popish Church. B: Belike then you are a good housewife, to fly from your husband the Church. Mrs P: My housewifery is but small; but God gave me grace to go to the true Church. B: The true Church, what dost thou mean? Mrs P: Not your popish Church, full of idols and abominations, but where two or three are gathered together in the name of God, to that Church will I go as long as I live. B: Belike then you have a church of your own. Well, let this mad woman be put down to prison until we send for her husband. Mrs P: No, I have but one husband, who is here already in this city, and in prison with me, from whom I will never depart.

Some persons present endeavouring to convince the bishop she was not in her right senses, she was permitted to depart. The keeper of the bishop's prisons took her into his house, where she either spun or worked as a servant, or walked about the city, discoursing upon the Sacrament of the altar. Her husband was sent for to take her home, but this she refused while the cause of religion could be served. She was too active to be idle, and her conversation, simple as they affected to think her, excited the attention of several Catholic priests and friars. They teased her with questions, until she answered them angrily, and this excited a laugh at her warmth.

'Nay,' said she, 'you have more need to weep than to laugh, and to be sorry that ever you were born, to be the chaplains of that whore of Babylon. I defy him and all his falsehood; and get you away from me, you do but trouble my conscience. You would have me follow your doings; I will first lose my life. I pray you depart.' 'Why, thou foolish woman,' said they, 'we come to thee for thy profit and soul's health.' To which she replied, 'What profit ariseth by you, that teach nothing but lies for truth? how save you souls, when you preach nothing but lies, and destroy souls?' 'How provest thou that?' said they. 'Do you not destroy your souls, when you teach the people to worship idols, stocks, and stones, the works of men's hands? and to worship a false God of your own making of a piece of bread, and teach that the pope is God's vicar, and hath power to forgive sins? and that there is a purgatory, when God's Son hath by His passion purged all? and say you make God and sacrifice Him, when Christ's body was a sacrifice once for all? Do you not teach the people to number their sins in your ears, and say they will be damned if they confess not all; when God's Word saith, Who can number his sins? Do you not promise them trentals and dirges and Masses for souls, and sell your prayers for money, and make them buy pardons, and trust to such foolish inventions of your imaginations? Do you not altogether act against God? Do you not teach us to pray upon beads, and to pray unto saints, and say they can pray for us? Do you not make holy water and holy bread to fray devils? Do you not do a thousand more abominations? And yet you say, you come for my profit, and to save my soul. No, no, one hath saved me. Farewell, you with your salvation.'

During the liberty granted her by the bishop, before-mentioned, she went into St Peter's Church, and there found a skilful Dutchman, who was affixing new noses to certain fine images which had been disfigured in King Edward's time; to whom she said, 'What a madman art thou, to make them new noses, which within a few days shall all lose their heads?' The Dutchman accused her and laid it hard to her charge. And she said unto him, 'Thou art accursed, and so are thy images.' He called her a whore. 'Nay,' said she, 'thy images are whores, and thou art a whore-hunter; for doth not God say, You go a whoring after strange gods, figures of your own making? and thou art one of them.' After this she was ordered to be confined, and had no more liberty.

During the time of her imprisonment, many visited her, some sent by the bishop, and some of their own will, among these was one Daniel, a great preacher of the Gospel, in the days of King Edward, about Cornwall and Devonshire, but who, through the grievous persecution he had sustained, had fallen off. Earnestly did she exhort him to repent with Peter, and to be more constant in his profession.

Mrs Walter Rauley and Mr William and John Kede, persons of great respectability, bore ample testimony of her godly conversation, declaring, that unless God were with her, it were impossible she could have so ably defended the cause of Christ. Indeed, to sum up the character of this poor woman, she united the serpent and the dove, abounding in the highest wisdom joined to the greatest simplicity. She endured imprisonment, threatenings, taunts, and the vilest epithets, but nothing could induce her to swerve; her heart was fixed; she had cast anchor; nor could all the wounds of persecution remove her from the rock on which her hopes of felicity were built.

Such was her memory, that, without learning, she could tell in what chapter any text of Scripture was contained: on account of this singular property, one Gregory Basset, a rank papist, said she was deranged, and talked as a parrot, wild without meaning. At length, having tried every manner without effect to make her nominally a Catholic, they condemned her.

After this, one exhorted her to leave her opinions, and go home to her family, as she was poor and illiterate. 'True (said she) though I am not learned, I am content to be a witness of Christ's death, and I pray you make no longer delay with me; for my heart is fixed, and I will never say otherwise, nor turn to your superstitious doing.'

To the disgrace of Mr Blackston, treasurer of the church, he would often send for this poor martyr from prison, to make sport for him and a woman whom he kept; putting religious questions to her, and turning her answers into ridicule. This done, he sent her back to her wretched dungeon, while he battened upon the good things of this world.

There was perhaps something simply ludicrous in the form of Mrs Prest, as she was of a very short stature, thick set, and about fifty-four years of age; but her countenance was cheerful and lively, as if prepared for the day of her marriage with the Lamb. To mock at her form was an indirect accusation of her Creator, who framed her after the fashion He liked best, and gave her a mind that far excelled the transient endowments of perishable flesh. When she was offered money, she rejected it, 'because (said she) I am going to a city where money bears no mastery, and while I am here God has promised to feed me'.

When sentence was read, condemning her to the flames, she lifted up her voice and praised God, adding, 'This day have I found that which I have long sought.' When they tempted her to recant, 'That will I not (said she); God forbid that I should lose the life eternal, for this carnal and short life. I will never turn from my heavenly husband to my earthly husband; from the fellowship of angels to mortal children; and if my husband and children be faithful, then am I theirs. God is my father, God is my mother, God is my sister, my brother, my kinsman; God is my friend, most faithful.'

Being delivered to the sheriff, she was led by the officer to the place of execution, without the walls of Exeter, called Sothenhey, where again the superstitious priests assaulted her. While they were tying her to the stake, she continued earnestly to exclaim 'God be merciful to me, a sinner!' Patiently enduring the devouring conflagration, she was consumed to ashes, and thus ended a life which in unshaken fidelity to the cause of Christ, was not surpassed by that of any preceding martyr.

Richard Sharpe, Thomas Banion, and Thomas Hale

Mr Sharpe, weaver, of Bristol, was brought the ninth day of March, 1556, before Dr Dalby, chancellor of the city of Bristol, and after examination concerning the Sacrament of the altar, was persuaded to recant; and on the twenty-ninth, he was enjoined to make his recantation in the parish church. But, scarcely had he publicly avowed his backsliding, before he felt in his conscience such a tormenting fiend, that he was unable to work at his occupation; hence, shortly after, one Sunday, he came into the parish church, called Temple, and after high Mass, stood up in the choir door, and said with a loud voice, 'Neighbours, bear me record that yonder idol (pointing to the altar) is the greatest and most abominable that ever was; and I am sorry that ever I denied my Lord God!' Notwithstanding the constables were ordered to apprehend him, he was suffered to go out of the church; but at night he was apprehended and carried to Newgate. Shortly after, before the chancellor, denying the Sacrament of the altar to be the body and blood of Christ, he was condemned to be burned by Mr Dalby. He was burnt the seventh of

May, 1558, and died godly, patiently, and constantly, confessing the Protestant articles of faith. With him suffered Thomas Hale, shoemaker, of Bristol, who was condemned by Chancellor Dalby. These martyrs were bound back to back.

Thomas Banion, a weaver, was burnt on August 27, of the same year, and died for the sake of the evangelical cause of his Saviour.

J. Corneford, of Wortham; C. Browne, of Maidstone; J. Herst, of Ashford; Alice Snoth, and Catharine Knight, an Aged Woman

With pleasure we have to record that these five martyrs were the last who suffered in the reign of Mary for the sake of the Protestant cause; but the malice of the papists was conspicuous in hastening their martyrdom, which might have been delayed until the event of the queen's illness was decided. It is reported that the archdeacon of Canterbury, judging that the sudden death of the queen would suspend the execution, travelled post from London, to have the satisfaction of adding another page to the black list of papistical sacrifices.

The articles against them were, as usual, the Sacramental elements and the idolatry of bending to images. They quoted St John's words, 'Beware of images!' and respecting the real presence, they urged according to St Paul, 'the things which are seen are temporal.' When sentence was about to be read against them, and excommunication to take place in the regular form, John Corneford, illuminated by the Holy Spirit, awfully turned the latter proceeding against themselves, and in a solemn impressive manner, recriminated their excommunication in the following words: 'In the name of our Lord Jesus Christ, the Son of the most mighty God, and by the power of His Holy Spirit, and the authority of His holy Catholic and apostolic Church, we do here give into the hands of Satan to be destroyed, the bodies of all those blasphemers and heretics that maintain any error against His most holy Word, or do condemn His most holy truth for heresy, to the maintenance of any false church or foreign religion, so that by this Thy just judgment, O most mighty God, against Thy adversaries, Thy true religion may be known to Thy great glory and our comfort and to the edifying of all our nation. Good Lord, so be it. Amen.'

This sentence was openly pronounced and registered, and, as if Providence had awarded that it should not be delivered in vain, within six days after, Queen Mary died, detested by all good men and accursed of God!

Though acquainted with these circumstances, the archdeacon's implacability exceeded that of his great exemplary, Bonner, who, though he had several persons at that time under his fiery grasp, did not urge their deaths hastily, by which delay he certainly afforded them an opportunity of escape. At the queen's decease, many were in bonds: some just taken, some examined, and others condemned. The writs indeed were issued for several burnings, but by the death of the three instigators of Protestant murder – the chancellor, the bishop, and the queen, who fell nearly together, the condemned sheep were liberated, and lived many years to praise God for their happy deliverance.

These five martyrs, when at the stake, earnestly prayed that their blood might be the last shed, nor did they pray in vain. They died gloriously, and perfected the number God had selected to bear witness of the truth in this dreadful reign, whose names are recorded in the

Book of Life; though last, not least among the saints made meet for immortality through the redeeming blood of the Lamb!

Catharine Finlay, alias Knight, was first converted by her son's expounding the Scriptures to her, which wrought in her a perfect work that terminated in martyrdom. Alice Snoth at the stake sent for her grandmother and godfather, and rehearsed to them the articles of her faith, and the Commandments of God, thereby convincing the world that she knew her duty. She died calling upon the spectators to bear witness that she was a Christian woman, and suffered joyfully for the testimony of Christ's Gospel.

Among the numberless enormities committed by the merciless and unfeeling Bonner, the murder of this innocent and unoffending child may be ranged as the most horrid. His father, John Fetty, of the parish of Clerkenwell, by trade a tailor, and only twenty-four years of age, had made blessed election; he was fixed secure in eternal hope, and depended on Him who so builds His Church that the gates of hell shall not prevail against it. But alas! the very wife of his bosom, whose heart was hardened against the truth, and whose mind was influenced by the teachers of false doctrine, became his accuser. Brokenbery, a creature of the pope, and parson of the parish, received the information of this wedded Delilah, in consequence of which the poor man was apprehended. But here the awful judgment of an ever-righteous God, who is 'of purer eyes than to behold evil,' fell upon this stone-hearted and perfidious woman; for no sooner was the injured husband captured by her wicked contriving, than she also was suddenly seized with madness, and exhibited an awful and awakening instance of God's power to punish the evil-doer. This dreadful circumstance had some effect upon the hearts of the ungodly hunters who had eagerly grasped their prey; but, in a relenting moment, they suffered him to remain with his unworthy wife, to return her good for evil, and to comfort two children, who, on his being sent to prison, would have been left without a protector, or have become a burden to the parish. As bad men act from little motives, we may place the indulgence shown him to the latter account.

We have noticed in the former part of our narratives of the martyrs, some whose affection would have led them even to sacrifice their own lives, to preserve their husbands; but here, agreeable to Scripture language, a mother proves, indeed, a monster in nature! Neither conjugal nor maternal affection could impress the heart of this disgraceful woman.

Although our afflicted Christian had experienced so much cruelty and falsehood from the woman who was bound to him by every tie both human and divine, yet, with a mild and forbearing spirit, he overlooked her misdeeds, during her calamity endeavouring all he could to procure relief for her malady, and soothing her by every possible expression of tenderness: thus she became in a few weeks nearly restored to her senses. But, alas! she returned again to her sin, 'as a dog returneth to his vomit.' Malice against the saints of the Most High was seated in her heart too firmly to be removed; and as her strength returned, her inclination to work wickedness returned with it. Her heart was hardened by the prince of darkness; and to her may be applied these afflicting and soul-harrowing words, 'Can the Ethiopian change his skin, or the leopard his spots? then may ye also do good, that are accustomed to do evil.' Weighing this text duly with another, 'I will have mercy on whom I will have mercy,' how shall we presume to refine away the sovereignty of God by presenting Jehovah at the bar of human reason, which, in religious matters, is too often opposed by infinite wisdom? 'Broad is the way, that leadeth to destruction, and many there be which go in thereat. Narrow is the way, which leadeth unto life, and few there be that find it.' The ways of heaven are indeed inscrutable, and it is our bounden duty to walk ever dependent on God, looking up to Him with humble confidence, and hope in His goodness, and ever confess His justice; and where we 'cannot unravel, there learn to trust'. This wretched woman, pursuing the horrid dictates of a heart hardened and depraved, was scarcely confirmed in her recovery, when, stifling the dictates of honour, gratitude, and every natural affection, she again accused her husband, who was once more apprehended, and taken before Sir John Mordant, knight, and one of Queen Mary's commissioners.

Upon examination, his judge finding him fixed in opinions which militated against those nursed by superstition and maintained by cruelty, he was sentenced to confinement and torture in Lollard's Tower. Here he was put into the painful stocks, and had a dish of water set by him, with a stone put into it, to what purpose God knoweth, except it were to show that he should look for little other subsistence: which is credible enough, if we consider their like practices upon divers before mentioned in this history; as, among others, upon Richard Smith, who died through their cruel imprisonment touching whom, when a godly woman came to Dr Story to have leave she might bury him, he asked her if he had any straw or blood in his mouth; but what he means thereby, I leave to the judgment of the wise.

On the first day of the third week of our martyr's sufferings, an object presented itself to his view, which made him indeed feel his tortures with all their force, and to execrate, with bitterness only short of cursing, the author of his misery. To mark and punish the proceedings of his tormentors, remained with the Most High, who noteth even the fall of a sparrow, and in whose sacred Word it is written, 'Vengeance is mine; I will repay.' This object was his own son, a child of the tender age of eight years. For fifteen days, had its hapless father been suspended by his tormentor by the right arm and left leg, and sometimes by both, shifting his positions for the purpose of giving him strength to bear and to lengthen the date of his sufferings. When the unoffending innocent, desirous of seeing and speaking to its parent, applied to Bonner for permission to do so, the poor child being asked by the bishop's chaplain the purport of his errand, he replied he wished to see his father. 'Who is thy father?' said the chaplain. 'John Fetty,' returned the boy, at the same time pointing to the place where he was confined. The interrogating miscreant on this said, 'Why, thy father is a heretic!' The little champion again rejoined, with energy sufficient to raise admiration in any breast, except that of this unprincipled and unfeeling wretch – this miscreant, eager to execute the behests of a remorseless queen – 'My father is no heretic: for you have Balaam's mark.'

Irritated by reproach so aptly applied, the indignant and mortified priest concealed his resentment for a moment, and took the undaunted boy into the house, where having him secure, he presented him to others, whose baseness and cruelty being equal to his own, they stripped him to the skin, and applied their scourges to so violent a degree, that, fainting beneath the stripes inflicted on his tender frame, and covered with the blood that flowed from them, the victim of their ungodly wrath was ready to expire under his heavy and unmerited punishment.

In this bleeding and helpless state was the suffering infant, covered only with his shirt, taken to his father by one of the actors in the horrid tragedy, who, while he exhibited the heart-rending spectacle, made use of the vilest taunts, and exulted in what he had done. The dutiful child, as if recovering strength at the sight of his father, on his knees implored his blessing. 'Alas! Will,' said the afflicted parent, in trembling amazement, 'who hath done this to thee!' the artless innocent related the circumstances that led to the merciless correction which had been so basely inflicted on him; but when he repeated the reproof bestowed on the chaplain, and which was prompted by an undaunted spirit, he was torn from his weeping parent, and conveyed again to the house, where he remained a close prisoner.

Bonner, somewhat fearful that what had been done could not be justified even among the bloodhounds of his own voracious pack, concluded in his dark and wicked mind, to release John Fetty, for a time at least, from the severities he was enduring in the glorious cause of everlasting truth! whose bright rewards are fixed beyond the boundaries of time, within the confines of eternity; where the arrow of the wicked cannot wound, even 'where there shall be no more sorrowing for the blessed, who, in the mansion of eternal bliss shall glorify the Lamb forever and ever'. He was accordingly by order of Bonner (how disgraceful to all dignity, to say bishop!) liberated from the painful bonds, and led from Lollard's Tower, to the chamber of that ungodly and infamous butcher, where he found the bishop bathing himself before a great fire; and at his first entering the chamber, Fetty said, 'God be here and peace!' 'God be here and peace (said Bonner), that is neither God speed nor good morrow!' 'If ye kick against this peace (said Fetty), then this is not the place that I seek for.'

A chaplain of the bishop, standing by, turned the poor man about, and thinking to abash him, said, in mocking wise, 'What have we here – a player!' While Fetty was thus standing in the bishop's chamber, he espied, hanging about the bishop's bed, a pair of great black beads, whereupon he said, 'My Lord, I think the hangman is not far off: for the halter (pointing to the beads) is here already!' At which words the bishop was in a marvellous rage. Then he immediately after espied also, standing in the bishop's chamber, in the window, a little crucifix. Then he asked the bishop what it was, and he answered, that it was Christ. 'Was He handled as cruelly as He is here pictured!' said Fetty. 'Yea, that He was,' said the bishop. 'And even so cruelly will you handle such as come before you; for you are unto God's people as Caiaphas was unto Christ!' The bishop, being in a great fury, said, 'Thou art a vile heretic, and I will burn thee, or else I will spend all I have, unto my gown.' 'Nay, my Lord (said Fetty), you were better to give it to some poor body, that he may pray for you.' Bonner, notwithstanding his passion, which was raised to the utmost by the calm and pointed remarks of this observing Christian, thought it most prudent to dismiss the father, on account of the nearly murdered child. His coward soul trembled for the consequences which might ensue; fear is inseparable from little minds; and this dastardly pampered priest experienced its effects so far as to induce him to assume the appearance of that he was an utter stranger to, namely, *mercy*.

The father, on being dismissed, by the tyrant Bonner, went home with a heavy heart, with his dying child, who did not survive many days the cruelties which had been inflicted on him.

How contrary to the will of our great King and Prophet, who mildly taught His followers, was the conduct of this sanguinary and false teacher, this vile apostate from his God to Satan! But the archfiend had taken entire possession of his heart, and guided every action of the sinner he had hardened; who, given up to terrible destruction, was running the race of the wicked, marking his footsteps with the blood of the saints, as if eager to arrive at the goal of eternal death.

Deliverance of Dr Sands

This eminent prelate, vice-chancellor of Cambridge, at the request of the duke of Northumberland, when he came down to Cambridge in support of Lady Jane Grey's claim to the throne, undertook at a few hours' notice, to preach before the duke and the university. The text he took was such as presented itself in opening the Bible, and a more appropriate one he could not have chosen, namely, the three last verses of Joshua. As God gave him the text, so He gave him also such order and utterance that it excited the most lively emotions in his numerous auditors. The sermon was about to be sent to London to be printed, when news arrived that the duke had returned and Queen Mary was proclaimed.

The duke was immediately arrested, and Dr Sands was compelled by the university to give up his office. He was arrested by the queen's order, and when Mr Mildmay wondered that so learned a man could wilfully incur danger, and speak against so good a princess as Mary, the doctor replied, 'If I would do as Mr Mildmay has done, I need not fear bonds. He came down armed against Queen Mary; before a traitor – now a great friend. I cannot with one mouth blow hot and cold in this manner.' A general plunder of Dr Sands' property ensued, and he was brought to London upon a wretched horse. Various insults he met on the way from the bigoted Catholics, and as he passed through Bishopsgate-street, a stone struck him to the ground. He was the first prisoner that entered the Tower, in that day, on a religious account; his man was admitted with his Bible, but his shirts and other articles were taken from him.

On Mary's coronation day the doors of the dungeon were so laxly guarded that it was easy to escape. A Mr Mitchell, like a true friend, came to him, afforded him his own clothes as a disguise, and was willing to abide the consequence of being found in his place. This was a rare friendship: but he refused the offer; saying, 'I know no cause why I should be in prison. To do thus were to make myself guilty. I will expect God's good will, yet do I think myself much obliged to you'; and so Mr Mitchell departed.

With Doctor Sands was imprisoned Mr Bradford; they were kept close in prison twenty-nine weeks. John Fowler, their keeper, was a perverse papist, yet, by often persuading him, at length he began to favour the Gospel, and was so persuaded in the true religion, that on a Sunday, when they had Mass in the chapel, Dr Sands administered the Communion to Bradford and to Fowler. Thus Fowler was their son begotten in bonds. To make room for Wyat and his accomplices, Dr Sands and nine other preachers were sent to the Marshalsea.

The keeper of the Marshalsea appointed to every preacher a man to lead him in the street; he caused them to go on before, and he and Dr Sands followed conversing together. By this time popery began to be unsavoury. After they had passed the bridge, the keeper said to Dr Sands: 'I perceive the vain people would set you forward to the fire. You are as vain as they, if you, being a young man, will stand in your own conceit, and prefer your own judgment before that of so many worthy prelates, ancient, learned, and grave men as be in this realm. If you do so, you shall find me a severe keeper, and one that utterly dislikes your religion.' Dr Sands answered, 'I know my years to be young, and my learning but small; it is enough to know Christ crucified, and he hath learned nothing who seeth not the great blasphemy that is in popery. I will yield unto God, and not unto man; I have read in the Scriptures of many godly and cour-teous keepers: may God make you one! if not, I trust He will give me strength and patience to bear your hard usage.' Then said the keeper, 'Are you resolved to stand to your religion?' 'Yes,' quoth the doctor, 'by God's grace!' 'Truly,' said the keeper, 'I love you the better for it; I did but tempt you: what favour I can show you, you shall be assured of; and I shall think myself happy if I might die at the stake with you.'

He was as good as his word, for he trusted the doctor to walk in the fields alone, where he met with Mr Bradford, who was also a prisoner in the King's Bench, and had found the same favour from his keeper. At his request, he put Mr Saunders in along with him, to be his bedfellow, and the Communion was administered to a great number of communicants.

When Wyat with his army came to Southwark, he offered to liberate all the imprisoned Protestants, but Dr Sands and the rest of the preachers refused to accept freedom on such terms.

After Dr Sands had been nine weeks prisoner in the Marshalsea, by the mediation of Sir Thomas Holcroft, knight marshal, he was set at liberty. Though Mr Holcroft had the queen's warrant, the bishop commanded him not to set Dr Sands at liberty, until he had taken sureties of two gentlemen with him, each one bound in £500, that Dr Sands should not depart out of the realm without licence. Mr Holcroft immediately after met with two gentlemen of the north, friends and cousins to Dr Sands, who offered to be bound for him.

After dinner, the same day, Sir Thomas Holcroft sent for Dr Sands to his lodgings at Westminster, to communicate to him all he had done. Dr Sands answered: 'I give God thanks, who hath moved your heart to mind me so well, that I think myself most bound unto you. God shall requite you, nor shall I ever be found unthankful. But as you have dealt friendly with me, I will also deal plainly with you. I came a freeman into prison; I will not go forth a bondman. As I cannot benefit my friends, so will I not hurt them. And if I be set at liberty, I will not tarry six days in this realm, if I may get out. If therefore I may not get free forth, send me to the Marshalsea again, and there you shall be sure of me.'

This answer Mr Holcroft much disapproved of; but like a true friend he replied: 'Seeing you cannot be altered, I will change my purpose, and yield unto you. Come of it what will, I will set you at liberty; and seeing you have a mind to go over sea, get you gone as quick as you can. One thing I require of you, that, while you are there, you write nothing to me hither, for this may undo me.'

Dr Sands having taken an affectionate farewell of him and his other friends in bonds, departed. He went by Winchester house, and there took boat, and came to a friend's house in London, called William Banks, and tarried there one night. The next night he went to another friend's house, and there he heard that strict search was making for him, by Gardiner's express order.

Dr Sands now conveyed himself by night to one Mr Berty's house, a stranger who was in the Marshalsea prison with him a while; he was a good Protestant and dwelt in Mark-lane. There he was six days, and then removed to one of his acquaintances in Cornhill; he caused his man Quinton to provide two geldings for him, resolved on the morrow to ride into Essex, to Mr Sands, his father-in-law, where his wife was, which, after a narrow escape, he effected. He had not been there two hours, before Mr Sands was told that two of the guards would that night apprehend Dr Sands.

That night Dr Sands was guided to an honest farmer's near the sea, where he tarried two days and two nights in a chamber without company. After that he removed to one James

Mower's, a shipmaster, who dwelt at Milton-Shore, where he waited for a wind to Flanders. While he was there, James Mower brought to him forty or fifty mariners, to whom he gave an exhortation; they liked him so well that they promised to die rather than he should be apprehended.

The sixth of May, Sunday, the wind served. In taking leave of his hostess, who had been married eight years without having a child, he gave her a fine handkerchief and an old royal of gold, and said, 'Be of good comfort; before that one whole year be past, God shall give you a child, a boy.' This came to pass, for, that day twelve-month, wanting one day, God gave her a son.

Scarcely had he arrived at Antwerp, when he learned that King Philip had sent to apprehend him. He next flew to Augsburg, in Cleveland, where Dr Sands tarried fourteen days, and then travelled towards Strassburg, where, after he had lived one year, his wife came to him. He was sick of a flux nine months, and had a child which died of the plague. His amiable wife at length fell into a consumption, and died in his arms. When his wife was dead, he went to Zurich, and there was in Peter Martyr's house for the space of five weeks.

As they sat at dinner one day, word was suddenly brought that Queen Mary was dead, and Dr Sands was sent for by his friends at Strassburg, where he preached. Mr Grindal and he came over to England, and arrived in London the same day that Queen Elizabeth was crowned. This faithful servant of Christ, under Queen Elizabeth, rose to the highest distinction in the Church, being successively bishop of Worcester, bishop of London, and archbishop of York.

Queen Mary's Treatment of Her Sister, the Princess Elizabeth

The preservation of Princess Elizabeth may be reckoned a remarkable instance of the watchful eye which Christ had over His Church. The bigotry of Mary regarded not the ties of consanguinity, of natural affection, of national succession. Her mind, physically morose, was under the dominion of men who possessed not the milk of human kindness, and whose principles were sanctioned and enjoined by the idolatrous tenets of the Romish pontiff. Could they have foreseen the short date of Mary's reign, they would have imbrued their hands in the Protestant blood of Elizabeth, and, as a *sine qua non* of the queen's salvation, have compelled her to bequeath the kingdom to some Catholic prince. The contest might have been attended with the horrors incidental to a religious civil war, and calamities might have been felt in England similar to those under Henry the Great in France, whom Queen Elizabeth assisted in opposing his priest-ridden Catholic subjects. As if Providence had the perpetual establishment of the Protestant faith in view, the difference of the duration of the two reigns is worthy of notice. Mary might have reigned many years in the course of nature, but the course of grace willed it otherwise. Five years and four months was the time of persecution allotted to this weak, disgraceful reign, while that of Elizabeth reckoned a number of years among the highest of those who have sat on the English throne, almost nine times that of her merciless sister!

Before Mary attained the crown, she treated Elizabeth with a sisterly kindness, but from that period her conduct was altered, and the most imperious distance substituted. Though Elizabeth had no concern in the rebellion of Sir Thomas Wyat, yet she was apprehended, and treated as a culprit in that commotion. The manner too of her arrest was similar to the mind that dictated it: the three cabinet members, whom she deputed to see the arrest executed, rudely entered the chamber at ten o'clock at night, and, though she was extremely ill, they could scarcely be induced to let her remain until the following morning. Her enfeebled state permitted her to be moved only by short stages in a journey of such length to London; but the princess, though afflicted in person, had a consolation in mind which her sister never could purchase: the people, through whom she passed on her way pitied her, and put up their prayers for her preservation.

Arrived at court, she was made a close prisoner for a fortnight, without knowing who was her accuser, or seeing anyone who could console or advise her. The charge, however, was at length unmasked by Gardiner, who, with nineteen of the Council, accused her of abetting Wyat's conspiracy, which she religiously affirmed to be false. Failing in this, they placed against her the transactions of Sir Peter Carew in the west, in which they were as unsuccessful as in the former. The queen now signified that it was her pleasure she should be committed to the Tower, a step which overwhelmed the princess with the greatest alarm and uneasiness. In vain she hoped the queen's majesty would not commit her to such a place; but there was no lenity to be expected; her attendants were limited, and a hundred northern soldiers appointed to guard her day and night.

On Palm Sunday she was conducted to the Tower. When she came to the palace garden, she cast her eyes towards the windows, eagerly anxious to meet those of the queen, but she was disappointed. A strict order was given in London that every one should go to church, and carry palms, that she might be conveyed without clamour or commiseration to her prison.

At the time of passing under London Bridge the fall of the tide made it very dangerous, and the barge some time stuck fast against the starlings. To mortify her the more, she was landed at Traitors' Stairs. As it rained fast, and she was obliged to step in the water to land, she hesitated; but this excited no complaisance in the lord in waiting. When she set her foot on the steps, she exclaimed, 'Here lands as true a subject, being prisoner, as ever landed at these stairs; and before Thee, O God, I speak it, having no friend but Thee alone!'

A large number of the wardens and servants of the Tower were arranged in order between whom the princess had to pass. Upon inquiring the use of this parade, she was informed it was customary to do so. 'If,' said she, 'it is on account of me, I beseech you that they may be dismissed.' On this the poor men knelt down, and prayed that God would preserve her grace, for which they were the next day turned out of their employments. The tragic scene must have been deeply interesting, to see an amiable and irreproachable princess sent like a lamb to languish in expectation of cruelty and death; against whom there was no other charge than her superiority in Christian virtues and acquired endowments. Her attendants openly wept as she proceeded with a dignified step to the frowning battlements of her destination. 'Alas!' said Elizabeth, 'what do you mean? I took you to comfort, not to dismay me; for my truth is such that no one shall have cause to weep for me.'

The next step of her enemies was to procure evidence by means which, in the present day, are accounted detestable. Many poor prisoners were racked, to extract, if possible, any matters of accusation which might affect her life, and thereby gratify Gardiner's sanguinary disposition. He himself came to examine her, respecting her removal from her house at Ashbridge to

Dunnington Castle a long while before. The princess had quite forgotten this trivial circumstance, and Lord Arundel, after the investigation, kneeling down, apologised for having troubled her in such a frivolous matter. 'You sift me narrowly,' replied the princess, 'but of this I am assured, that God has appointed a limit to your proceedings; and so God forgive you all.'

Her own gentlemen, who ought to have been her purveyors, and served her provision, were compelled to give place to the common soldiers, at the command of the constable of the Tower, who was in every respect a servile tool of Gardiner; her grace's friends, however, procured an order of Council which regulated this petty tyranny more to her satisfaction.

After having been a whole month in close confinement, she sent for the lord-chamberlain and Lord Chandois, to whom she represented the ill state of her health from a want of proper air and exercise. Application being made to the Council, Elizabeth was with some difficulty admitted to walk in the queen's lodgings, and afterwards in the garden, at which time the prisoners on that side were attended by their keepers, and not suffered to look down upon her. Their jealousy was excited by a child of four years, who daily brought flowers to the princess. The child was threatened with a whipping, and the father ordered to keep him from the princess's chambers.

On the fifth of May the constable was discharged from his office, and Sir Henry Benifield appointed in his room, accompanied by a hundred ruffian-looking soldiers in blue. This measure created considerable alarm in the mind of the princess, who imagined it was preparatory to her undergoing the same fate as Lady Jane Grey, upon the same block. Assured that this project was not in agitation, she entertained an idea that the new keeper of the Tower was commissioned to make away with her privately, as his equivocal character was in conformity with the ferocious inclination of those by whom he was appointed.

A report now obtained that her Grace was to be taken away by the new constable and his soldiers, which in the sequel proved to be true. An order of Council was made for her removal to the manor Woodstock, which took place on Trinity Sunday, May 13, under the authority of Sir Henry Benifield and Lord Tame. The ostensible cause of her removal was to make room for other prisoners. Richmond was the first place they stopped at, and here the princess slept, not however without much alarm at first, as her own servants were superseded by the soldiers, who were placed as guards at her chamber door. Upon representation, Lord Tame overruled this indecent stretch of power, and granted her perfect safety while under his custody.

In passing through Windsor, she saw several of her poor dejected servants waiting to see her. 'Go to them,' said she, to one of her attendants, 'and say these words from me, *tanquim ovis*, that is, like a sheep to the slaughter.'

The next night her Grace lodged at the house of a Mr Dormer, in her way to which the people manifested such tokens of loyal affection that Sir Henry was indignant, and bestowed on them very liberally the names of rebels and traitors. In some villages they rang the bells for joy, imagining the princess's arrival among them was from a very different cause; but this harmless demonstration of gladness was sufficient with the persecuting Benifield to order his soldiers to seize and set these humble persons in the stocks.

The day following, her Grace arrived at Lord Tame's house, where she stayed all night, and was most nobly entertained. This excited Sir Henry's indignation, and made him caution Lord Tame to look well to his proceedings; but the humanity of Lord Tame was not to be frightened, and he returned a suitable reply. At another time, this official prodigal, to show his consequence and disregard of good manners, went up into a chamber, where was appointed for her Grace a chair, two cushions, and a foot carpet, wherein he presumptuously sat and called his man to pull off his boots. As soon as it was known to the ladies and gentlemen they laughed him to scorn. When supper was done, he called to his lordship, and directed that all gentlemen and ladies should withdraw home, marvelling much that he would permit such a large company, considering the great charge he had committed to him. 'Sir Henry,' said his lordship, 'content yourself; all shall be avoided, your men and all.' 'Nay, but my soldiers,' replied Sir Henry, 'shall watch all night.' Lord Tame answered, 'There is no need.' 'Well,' said he, 'need or need not, they shall so do.'

The next day her Grace took her journey from thence to Woodstock, where she was enclosed, as before in the Tower of London, the soldiers keeping guard within and without the walls, every day, to the number of sixty; and in the night, without the walls were forty during all the time of her imprisonment.

At length she was permitted to walk in the gardens, but under the most severe restrictions, Sir Henry keeping the keys himself, and placing her always under many bolts and locks, whence she was induced to call him her jailer, at which he felt offended, and begged her to substitute the word officer. After much earnest entreaty to the Council, she obtained permission to write to the queen; but the jailer who brought her pen, ink, and paper stood by her while she wrote, and, when she left off, he carried the things away until they were wanted again. He also insisted upon carrying it himself to the queen, but Elizabeth would not suffer him to be the bearer, and it was presented by one of her gentlemen.

After the letter, Doctors Owen and Wendy went to the princess, as the state of her health rendered medical assistance necessary. They stayed with her five or six days, in which time she grew much better; they then returned to the queen, and spoke flatteringly of the princess' submission and humility, at which the queen seemed moved; but the bishops wanted a concession that she had offended her majesty. Elizabeth spurned this indirect mode of acknowledging herself guilty. 'If I have offended,' said she, 'and am guilty, I crave no mercy but the law, which I am certain I should have had ere this, if anything could have been proved against me. I wish I were as clear from the peril of my enemies; then should I not be thus bolted and locked up within walls and doors.'

Much question arose at this time respecting the propriety of uniting the princess to some foreigner, that she might quit the realm with a suitable portion. One of the Council had the brutality to urge the necessity of beheading her, if the king (Philip) meant to keep the realm in peace; but the Spaniards, detesting such a base thought, replied, 'God forbid that our king and master should consent to such an infamous proceeding!' Stimulated by a noble principle, the Spaniards from this time repeatedly urged to the king that it would do him the highest honour to liberate the Lady Elizabeth, nor was the king impervious to their solicitation. He took her out of prison, and shortly after she was sent for to Hampton court. It may be remarked in this place, that the fallacy of human reasoning is shown in every moment. The barbarian who suggested the policy of beheading Elizabeth little contemplated the change of condition which his speech would bring about. In her journey from Woodstock, Benifield treated her with the same severity as before; removing her on a stormy day, and not suffering her old servant, who had come to Colnbrook, where she slept, to speak to her.

She remained a fortnight strictly guarded and watched, before anyone dared to speak with her; at length the vile Gardiner with three more of the Council, came with great submission. Elizabeth saluted them, remarked that she had been for a long time kept in solitary confinement, and begged they would intercede with the king and queen to deliver her from prison. Gardiner's visit was to draw from the princess a confession of her guilt; but she was guarded against his subtlety, adding, that, rather than admit she had done wrong, she would lie in prison all the rest of her life. The next day Gardiner came again, and kneeling down, declared that the queen was astonished she would persist in affirming that she was blameless – whence it would be inferred that the queen had unjustly imprisoned her grace. Gardiner further informed her that the queen had declared that she must tell another tale, before she could be set at liberty. 'Then,' replied the high-minded Elizabeth, 'I had rather be in prison with honesty and truth, than have my liberty, and be suspected by her majesty. What I have said, I will stand to; nor will I ever speak falsehood!' The bishop and his friends then departed, leaving her locked up as before.

Seven days after the queen sent for Elizabeth at ten o'clock at night; two years had elapsed since they had seen each other. It created terror in the mind of the princess, who, at setting out, desired her gentlemen and ladies to pray for her, as her return to them again was uncertain.

Being conducted to the queen's bedchamber, upon entering it the princess knelt down, and having begged of God to preserve her majesty, she humbly assured her that her majesty had not a more loyal subject in the realm, whatever reports might be circulated to the contrary. With a haughty ungraciousness, the imperious queen replied: 'You will not confess your offence, but stand stoutly to your truth. I pray God it may so fall out.' 'If it do not,' said Elizabeth, 'I request neither favour nor pardon at your majesty's hands.' 'Well,' said the queen, 'you stiffly still persevere in your truth. Besides, you will not confess that you have not been wrongfully punished.' 'I must not say so, if it please your majesty, to you.' 'Why, then,' said the queen, 'belike you will to others.' 'No, if it please your majesty: I have borne the burden, and must bear it. I humbly beseech your majesty to have a good opinion of me and to think me to be your subject, not only from the beginning hitherto, but for ever, as long as life lasteth.'

They departed without any heartfelt satisfaction on either side; nor can we think the conduct of Elizabeth displayed that independence and fortitude which accompanies perfect innocence. Elizabeth's admitting that she would not say, neither to the queen nor to others, that she had been unjustly punished, was in direct contradiction to what she had told Gardiner, and must have arisen from some motive at this time inexplicable. King Philip is supposed to have been secretly concealed during the interview, and to have been friendly to the princess.

In seven days from the time of her return to imprisonment, her severe jailer and his men were discharged, and she was set at liberty, under the constraint of being always attended and watched by some of the queen's Council. Four of her gentlemen were sent to the Tower without any other charge against them than being zealous servants of their mistress. This event was soon after followed by the happy news of Gardiner's death, for which all good and merciful men glorified God, inasmuch as it had taken the chief tiger from the den, and rendered the life of the Protestant successor of Mary more secure.

This miscreant, while the princess was in the Tower, sent a secret writ, signed by a few of the Council, for her private execution, and, had Mr Bridges, lieutenant of the Tower, been as little scrupulous of dark assassination as this pious prelate was, she must have perished. The warrant not having the queen's signature, Mr Bridges hastened to her majesty to give her information of it, and to know her mind. This was a plot of Winchester's, who, to convict her of treasonable practices, caused several prisoners to be racked; particularly Mr Edmund Tremaine and Smithwicke were offered considerable bribes to accuse the guiltless princess.

Her life was several times in danger. While at Woodstock, fire was apparently put between the boards and ceiling under which she lay. It was also reported strongly that one Paul Penny, the keeper of Woodstock, a notorious ruffian, was appointed to assassinate her, but, however this might be, God counteracted in this point the nefarious designs of the enemies of the Reformation. James Basset was another appointed to perform the same deed: he was a peculiar favourite of Gardiner, and had come within a mile of Woodstock, intending to speak with Benifield on the subject. The goodness of God however so ordered it that while Basset was travelling to Woodstock, Benifield, by an order of Council, was going to London: in consequence of which, he left a positive order with his brother, that no man should be admitted to the princess during his absence, not even with a note from the queen; his brother met the murderer, but the latter's intention was frustrated, as no admission could be obtained.

When Elizabeth quitted Woodstock, she left the following lines written with her diamond on the window:

'Much suspected by me,

Nothing proved can be. Quoth Elizabeth, prisoner.'

With the life of Winchester ceased the extreme danger of the princess, as many of her other secret enemies soon after followed him, and, last of all, her cruel sister, who outlived Gardiner but three years.

The death of Mary was ascribed to several causes. The Council endeavoured to console her in her last moments, imagining it was the absence of her husband that lay heavy at her heart, but though his treatment had some weight, the loss of Calais, the last fortress possessed by the English in France, was the true source of her sorrow. 'Open my heart,' said Mary, 'when I am dead, and you shall find Calais written there.' Religion caused her no alarm; the priests had lulled to rest every misgiving of conscience, which might have obtruded, on account of the accusing spirits of the murdered martyrs. Not the blood she had spilled, but the loss of a town excited her emotions in dying, and this last stroke seemed to be awarded, that her fanatical persecution might be parallelled by her political imbecility.

We earnestly pray that the annals of no country, Catholic or pagan, may ever be stained with such a repetition of human sacrifices to papal power, and that the detestation in which the character of Mary is holden, may be a beacon to succeeding monarchs to avoid the rocks of fanaticism!

God's Punishment upon Some of the Persecutors of His People in Mary's Reign

After that arch-persecutor, Gardiner, was dead, others followed, of whom Dr Morgan, bishop of St David's, who succeeded Bishop Farrar, is to be noticed. Not long after he was installed in his bishopric, he was stricken by the visitation of God; his food passed through the throat, but rose again with great violence. In this manner, almost literally starved to death, he terminated his existence.

Bishop Thornton, suffragan of Dover, was an indefatigable persecutor of the true Church. One day after he had exercised his cruel tyranny upon a number of pious persons at Canterbury, he came from the chapter-house to Borne, where as he stood on a Sunday looking at his men playing at bowls, he fell down in a fit of the palsy, and did not long survive.

After the latter, succeeded another bishop or suffragan, ordained by Gardiner, who not long after he had been raised to the see of Dover, fell down a pair of stairs in the cardinal's chamber at Greenwich, and broke his neck. He had just received the cardinal's blessing – he could receive nothing worse.

John Cooper, of Watsam, Suffolk, suffered by perjury; he was from private pique persecuted by one Fenning, who suborned two others to swear that they heard Cooper say, 'If God did not take away Queen Mary, the devil would.' Cooper denied all such words, but Cooper was a Protestant and a heretic, and therefore he was hung, drawn and quartered, his property confiscated, and his wife and nine children reduced to beggary. The following harvest, however, Grimwood of Hitcham, one of the witnesses before mentioned, was visited for his villainy: while at work, stacking up corn, his bowels suddenly burst out, and before relief could be obtained, he died. Thus was deliberate perjury rewarded by sudden death!

In the case of the martyr Mr Bradford, the severity of Mr Sheriff Woodroffe has been noticed – he rejoiced at the death of the saints, and at Mr Rogers' execution, he broke the carman's head, because he stopped the cart to let the martyr's children take a last farewell of him. Scarcely had Mr Woodroffe's sheriffalty expired a week, when he was struck with a paralytic affection, and languished a few days in the most pitiable and helpless condition, presenting a striking contrast to his former activity in the cause of blood.

Ralph Lardyn, who betrayed the martyr George Eagles, is believed to have been afterward arraigned and hanged in consequence of accusing himself. At the bar, he denounced himself in these words: 'This has most justly fallen upon me, for betraying the innocent blood of that just and good man George Eagles, who was here condemned in the time of Queen Mary by my procurement, when I sold his blood for a little money.'

As James Abbes was going to execution, and exhorting the pitying bystanders to adhere steadfastly to the truth, and like him to seal the cause of Christ with their blood, a servant of the sheriff's interrupted him, and blasphemously called his religion heresy, and the good man a lunatic. Scarcely however had the flames reached the martyr, before the fearful stroke of God fell on the hardened wretch, in the presence of him he had so cruelly ridiculed. The man was suddenly seized with lunacy, cast off his clothes and shoes before the people (as Abbes had done just before, to distribute among some poor persons) at the same time exclaiming, 'Thus did James Abbes, the true servant of God, who is saved by I am damned.' Repeating this often, the sheriff had him secured, and made him put his clothes on, but no sooner was he alone, than he tore them off, and exclaimed as before. Being tied in a cart, he was conveyed to his master's house, and in about half a year he died; just before which a priest came to attend him, with the crucifix, etc., but the wretched man bade him take away such trumpery, and said that he and other priests had been the cause of his damnation, but that Abbes was saved.

One Clark, an avowed enemy of the Protestants in King Edward's reign, hung himself in the Tower of London.

Froling, a priest of much celebrity, fell down in the street and died on the spot.

Dale, an indefatigable informer, was consumed by vermin, and died a miserable spectacle.

Alexander, the severe keeper of Newgate, died miserably, swelling to a prodigious size, and became so inwardly putrid, that none could come near him. This cruel minister of the law would go to Bonner, Story, and others, requesting them to rid his prison, he was so much pestered with heretics! The son of this keeper, in three years after his father's death, dissipated his great property, and died suddenly in Newgate market. 'The sins of the father,' says the decalogue, 'shall be visited on the children.' John Peter, son-in-law of Alexander, a horrid blasphemer and persecutor, died wretchedly. When he affirmed anything, he would say, 'If it be not true, I pray I may rot ere I die.' This awful state visited him in all its loathsomeness.

Sir Ralph Ellerker was eagerly desirous to see the heart taken out of Adam Damlip, who was wrongfully put to death. Shortly after Sir Ralph was slain by the French, who mangled him dreadfully, cut off his limbs, and tore his heart out.

When Gardiner heard of the miserable end of Judge Hales, he called the profession of the Gospel a doctrine of desperation; but he forgot that the judge's despondency arose after he had consented to the papistry. But with more reason may this be said of the Catholic tenets, if we consider the miserable end of Dr Pendleton, Gardiner, and most of the leading persecutors. Gardiner, upon his death bed, was reminded by a bishop of Peter denying his master, 'Ah,' said Gardiner, 'I have denied with Peter, but never repented with Peter.'

After the accession of Elizabeth, most of the Catholic prelates were imprisoned in the Tower or the Fleet; Bonner was put into the Marshalsea.

Of the revilers of God's Word, we detail, among many others, the following occurrence. One William Maldon, living at Greenwich in servitude, was instructing himself profitably in reading an English primer one winter's evening. A serving man, named John Powell, sat by, and ridiculed all that Maldon said, who cautioned him not to make a jest of the Word of God. Powell nevertheless continued, until Maldon came to certain English Prayers, and read aloud, 'Lord, have mercy upon us, Christ have mercy upon us,' etc. Suddenly the reviler started, and exclaimed, 'Lord, have mercy upon us!' He was struck with the utmost terror of mind, said the evil spirit could not abide that Christ should have any mercy upon him, and sunk into madness. He was remitted to Bedlam, and became an awful warning that God will not always be insulted with impunity.

Henry Smith, a student in the law, had a pious Protestant father, of Camben, in Gloucestershire, by whom he was virtuously educated. While studying law in the middle temple, he was induced to profess Catholicism, and, going to Louvain, in France, he returned with pardons, crucifixes, and a great freight of popish toys. Not content with these things, he openly reviled the Gospel religion he had been brought up in; but conscience one night reproached him so dreadfully, that in a fit of despair he hung himself in his garters. He was buried in a lane, without the Christian service being read over him.

Dr Story, whose name has been so often mentioned in the preceding pages, was reserved to be cut off by public execution, a practice in which he had taken great delight when in power. He is supposed to have had a hand in most of the conflagrations in Mary's time, and was even ingenious in his invention of new modes of inflicting torture. When Elizabeth came to the throne, he was committed to prison, but unaccountably effected his escape to the continent, to carry fire and sword there among the Protestant brethren. From the duke of Alva, at Antwerp, he received a special commission to search all ships for contraband goods, and particularly for English heretical books.

Dr Story gloried in a commission that was ordered by Providence to be his ruin, and to preserve the faithful from his sanguinary cruelty. It was contrived that one Parker, a merchant, should sail to Antwerp and information should be given to Dr Story that he had a quantity of heretical books on board. The latter no sooner heard this, than he hastened to the vessel, sought everywhere above, and then went under the hatches, which were fastened down upon him. A prosperous gale brought the ship to England, and this traitorous, persecuting rebel was committed to prison, where he remained a considerable time, obstinately objecting to recant his Antichristian spirit, or admit of Queen Elizabeth's supremacy. He alleged, though by birth and education an Englishman, that he was a sworn subject of the king of Spain, in whose service the famous duke of Alva was. The doctor being condemned, was laid upon a hurdle, and drawn from the Tower to Tyburn, where after being suspended about half an hour, he was cut down, stripped, and the executioner displayed the heart of a traitor.

Thus ended the existence of this Nimrod of England.

✝ CHAPTER 18 ✝

The Rise, Progress, Persecutions, and Sufferings of the Quakers

In treating of these people in a historical manner, we are obliged to have recourse to much tenderness. That they differ from the generality of Protestants in some of the capital points of religion cannot be denied, and yet, as Protestant dissenters they are included under the description of the toleration act. It is not our business to inquire whether people of similar sentiments had any existence in the primitive ages of Christianity: perhaps, in some respects, they had not, but we are to write of them not as what they were, but what they now are. That they have been treated by several writers in a very contemptuous manner is certain; that they did not deserve such treatment, is equally certain.

The appellation Quakers, was bestowed upon them as a term of reproach, in consequence of their apparent convulsions which they laboured under when they delivered their discourses, because they imagined they were the effect of divine inspiration.

It is not our business, at present, to inquire whether the sentiments of these people are agreeable to the Gospel, but this much is certain, that the first leader of them, as a separate body, was a man of obscure birth, who had his first existence in Leicestershire, about the year 1624. In speaking of this man we shall deliver our own sentiments in a historical manner, and joining these to what have been said by the Friends themselves, we shall endeavor to furnish out a complete narrative.

George Fox was descended of honest and respected parents, who brought him up in the national religion: but from a child he appeared religious, still, solid, and observing, beyond his years, and uncommonly knowing in divine things. He was brought up to husbandry, and other country business, and was particularly inclined to the solitary occupation of a shepherd; an employment, that very well suited his mind in several respects, both for its innocency and solitude; and was a just emblem of his after ministry and service. In the year 1646, he entirely forsook the national Church, in whose tenets he had been brought up, as before observed; and in 1647, he travelled into Derbyshire and Nottinghamshire, without any set purpose of visiting particular places, but in a solitary manner he walked through several towns and villages, which way soever his mind turned. 'He fasted much,' said Sewell, 'and walked often in retired places, with no other companion than his Bible.' 'He visited the most retired and religious people in those parts,' says Penn, 'and some there were, short of few, if any, in this nation, who waited for the consolation of Israel night and day; as Zacharias, Anna, and Simeon, did of old time. To these he was sent, and these he sought out in the neighbouring counties, and among them he sojourned until his more ample ministry came upon him. At this time he taught, and was an example of silence, endeavouring to bring them from self-performances; testifying of, and turning them to the light of Christ within them, and encouraging them to wait in patience, and to feel the power of it to stir in their hearts, that their knowledge and worship of God might stand in the power of an endless life, which was to be found in the light as it was obeyed in the manifestation of it in man: for in the Word was life, and that life is the light of men. Life in the Word, light in men; and life in men too, as the light is obeyed; the children of the light living by the life of the Word, by which the Word begets them again to God, which is the generation and new birth, without which there is no coming into the Kingdom of God, and to which whoever comes is greater than John: that is, than John's dispensation, which was not that of the Kingdom, but the consummation of the legal, and forerunning of the Gospel times, the time of the Kingdom. Accordingly several meetings were gathering in those parts; and thus his time was employed for some years.'

In the year 1652, 'he had a visitation of the great work of God in the earth, and of the way that he was to go forth, in a public ministry, to begin it.' He directed his course northward, 'and in every place where he came, if not before he came to it, he had his particular exercise and service shown to him, so that the Lord was his leader indeed.' He made great numbers of converts to his opinions, and many pious and good men joined him in his ministry. These were drawn forth especially to visit the public assemblies to reprove, reform, and exhort them; sometimes in markets, fairs, streets, and by the highway-side, 'calling people to repentance, and to return to the Lord, with their hearts as well as their mouths; directing them to the light of Christ within them, to see, examine, and to consider their ways by, and to eschew the evil, and to do the good and acceptable will of God.'

They were not without opposition in the work they imagined themselves called to, being often set in the stocks, stoned, beaten, whipped and imprisoned, though honest men of good report, that had left wives, children, houses, and lands, to visit them with a living call to repentance. But these coercive methods rather forwarded than abated their zeal, and in those parts they brought over many proselytes, and amongst them several magistrates, and others of the better sort. They apprehended the Lord had forbidden them to pull off their hats to anyone, high or low, and required them to speak to the people, without distinction, the language of thou and thee. They scrupled bidding people good-morrow, or good-night, nor might they bend the knee to anyone, even in supreme authority. Both men and women went in a plain and simple dress, different from the fashion of the times. They neither gave nor accepted any titles of respect or honour, nor would they call any man master on earth. Several texts of Scripture they quoted in defence of these singularities; such as, 'Swear not at all'; 'How can ye believe, which receive honour one of another, and seek not the honour that cometh from God only?' etc., etc. They placed the basis of religion in an inward light, and an extraordinary impulse of the Holy Spirit.

In 1654, their first separate meeting in London was held in the house of Robert Dring, in Watling-street, for by that time they spread themselves into all parts of the kingdom, and had in many places set up meetings or assemblies, particularly in Lancashire, and the adjacent parts, but they were still exposed to great persecutions and trials of every kind. One of them in a letter to the protector, Oliver Cromwell, represents, though there are no penal laws in force obliging men to comply with the established religion, yet the Quakers are exposed upon other accounts; they are fined and imprisoned for refusing to take an oath; for not paying their tithes; for disturbing the public assemblies, and meeting in the streets, and places of public resort; some of them have been whipped for vagabonds, and for their plain speeches to the magistrate.

Under favour of the then toleration, they opened their meetings at the Bull and Mouth, in Aldersgate-street, where women, as well as men, were moved to speak. Their zeal transported them to some extravagancies, which laid them still more open to the lash of their enemies, who exercised various severities on them throughout the next reign. Upon the suppression of Venner's mad insurrection, the government, having published a proclamation, forbidding the Anabaptists, Quakers, and Fifth Monarchy Men, to assemble or meet together under pretence of worshipping God, except it be in some parochial church, chapel, or in private houses, by consent of the persons there inhabiting, all meetings in other places being declared to be unlawful and riotous, etc., etc., the Quakers thought it expedient to address the king thereon, which they did in the following words:

'O King Charles! Our desire is, that thou mayest live forever in the fear of God, and thy council. We beseech thee and thy council to read these following lines in tender bowels, and compassion for our souls, and for your good.

'And this consider, we are about four hundred imprisoned, in and about this city, of men and women from their families, besides, in the county jails, about ten hundred; we desire that our meetings may not be broken up, but that all may come to a fair trial, that our innocency may be cleared up.'

'London, 16th day, eleventh month, 1660'

On the twenty-eighth of the same month, they published the declaration referred to in their address, entitled 'A declaration from the harmless and innocent people of God, called Quakers, against all sedition, plotters, and fighters in the world, for removing the ground of jealousy and suspicion, from both magistrates and people in the kingdom, concerning wars and fightings.' It was presented to the king the twenty-first day of the eleventh month, 1660, and he promised them upon his royal word, that they should not suffer for their opinions as long as they lived peaceably; but his promises were very little regarded afterward.

In 1661 they assumed courage to petition the House of Lords for a toleration of their religion, and for a dispensation from taking the oaths, which they held unlawful, not from any disaffection to the government, or a belief that they were less obliged by an affirmation, but from a persuasion that all oaths were unlawful; and that swearing upon the most solemn occasions was forbidden in the New Testament. Their petition was rejected, and instead of granting them relief, an act was passed against them, the preamble to which set forth, 'That whereas several persons have taken up an opinion that an oath, even before a magistrate, is unlawful, and contrary to the Word of God; and whereas, under pretence of religious worship, the said persons do assemble in great numbers in several parts of the kingdom, separating themselves from the rest of his majesty's subjects, and the public congregations and usual places of divine worship; be it therefore enacted, that if any such persons, after the twenty-fourth of March, 1661–2, shall refuse to take an oath when lawfully tendered, or persuade others to do it, or maintain in writing or otherwise, the unlawfulness of taking an oath; or if they shall assemble for religious worship, to the number of five or more, of the age of fifteen, they shall for the first offence forfeit five pounds; for the second, ten pounds; and for the third shall abjure the realm, or be transported to the plantations: and the justices of peace at their open sessions may hear and finally determine in the affair.'

This act had a most dreadful effect upon the Quakers, though it was well known and notorious that these conscientious persons were far from sedition or disaffection to the government. George Fox, in his address to the king, acquaints him that three thousand and sixty-eight of their friends had been imprisoned since his majesty's restoration; that their meetings were daily broken up by men with clubs and arms, and their friends thrown into the water, and trampled under foot until the blood gushed out, which gave rise to their meeting in the open streets. A relation was printed, signed by twelve witnesses, which says that more than four thousand two hundred Quakers were imprisoned; and of them five hundred were in and about London, and, the suburbs; several of whom were dead in the jails.

Six hundred of them, says an account published at that time, were in prison, merely for religion's sake, of whom several were banished to the plantations. In short, the Quakers gave such full employment to the informers, that they had less leisure to attend the meetings of other dissenters.

Yet, under all these calamities, they behaved with patience and modesty towards the government, and upon occasion of the Ryehouse plot in 1682, thought proper to declare their innocence of that sham plot, in an address to the king, wherein 'appealing to the Searcher of all hearts,' they say, 'their principles do not allow them to take up defensive arms, much less to avenge themselves for the injuries they received from others: that they continually pray for the king's safety and preservation; and therefore take this occasion humbly to beseech his majesty to compassionate their suffering friends, with whom the jails are so filled, that they want air, to the apparent hazard of their lives, and to the endangering an infection in divers places. Besides, many houses, shops, barns, and fields are ransacked, and the goods, corn, and cattle swept away, to the discouraging trade and husbandry, and impoverishing great numbers of quiet and industrious people; and this, for no other cause, but for the exercise of a tender conscience in the worship of Almighty God, who is sovereign Lord and King of men's consciences.'

On the accession of James II they addressed that monarch honestly and plainly, telling him: 'We are come to testify our sorrow for the death of our good friend Charles, and our joy for thy being made our governor. We are told thou art not of the persuasion of the Church of England, no more than we; therefore we hope thou wilt grant us the same liberty which thou allowest thyself, which doing, we wish thee all manner of happiness.'

When James, by his dispensing power, granted liberty to the dissenters, they began to enjoy some rest from their troubles; and indeed it was high time, for they were swelled to an enormous amount. They, the year before this, to them one of glad release, in a petition to James for a cessation of their sufferings, set forth, 'that of late above one thousand five hundred of their friends, both men and women, and that now there remain one thousand three hundred and eighty-three; of which two hundred are women, many under sentence of praemunire; and more than three hundred near it, for refusing the oath of allegiance, because they could not swear. Three hundred and fifty have died in prison since the year 1680; in London, the jail of Newgate has been crowded, within these two years sometimes with near twenty in a room, whereby several have been suffocated, and others, who have been taken out sick, have died of malignant fevers within a few days. Great violences, outrageous distresses, and woeful havoc and spoil, have been made upon people's goods and estates, by a company of idle, extravagant, and merciless informers, by persecutions on the conventicle-act, and others, also on qui tam writs, and on other processes, for twenty pounds a month, and two thirds of their estates seized for the king. Some had not a bed to rest on, others had no cattle to till the ground, nor corn for feed or bread, nor tools to work with; the said informers and bailiffs in some places breaking into houses, and making great waste and spoil, under pretence of serving the king and the Church. Our religious assemblies have been charged at common law with being rioters and disturbers of the public peace, whereby great numbers have been confined in prison without regard to age, and many confined to holes and dungeons. The seizing for 20 pounds a month has amounted to many thousands, and several who have employed some hundreds of poor people in manufactures, are disabled to do so any more, by reason of long imprisonment. They spare neither widow nor fatherless, nor have they so much as a bed to lie on. The informers are both witnesses and prosecutors, to the ruin of great numbers of sober families; and justices of the peace have been threatened with the forfeiture of one hundred pounds, if they do not issue out warrants upon their informations.' With this petition they presented a list of their friends in prison, in the several counties, amounting to four hundred and sixty.

During the reign of King James II these people were, through the intercession of their friend Mr Penn, treated with greater indulgence than ever they had been before. They were now become extremely numerous in many parts of the country, and the settlement of Pennsylvania taking place soon after, many of them went over to America. There they enjoyed the blessings of a peaceful government, and cultivated the arts of honest industry.

As the whole colony was the property of Mr Penn, so he invited people of all denominations to come and settle with him. A universal liberty of conscience took place; and in this new colony the natural rights of mankind were, for the first time, established.

These Friends are, in the present age, a very harmless, inoffensive body of people; but of that we shall take more notice hereafter. By their wise regulations, they not only do honour to themselves, but they are of vast service to the community.

It may be necessary here to observe, that as the Friends, commonly called Quakers, will not take an oath in a court of justice, so their affirmation is permitted in all civil affairs; but they cannot prosecute a criminal, because, in the English courts of justice, all evidence must be upon oath.

An Account of the Persecutions of Friends, Commonly called Quakers, in the United States

About the middle of the seventeenth century, much persecution and suffering were inflicted on a sect of Protestant dissenters, commonly called Quakers: a people which arose at that time in England some of whom sealed their testimony with their blood.

The principal points upon which their conscientious nonconformity rendered them obnoxious to the penalties of the law, were,

1. The Christian resolution of assembling publicly for the worship of God, in a manner most agreeable to their consciences.
2. Their refusal to pay tithes, which they esteemed a Jewish ceremony, abrogated by the coming of Christ.
3. Their testimony against wars and fighting, the practice of which they judged inconsistent with the command of Christ: 'Love your enemies,' Matt. 5:44.
4. Their constant obedience to the command of Christ: 'Swear not at all,' Matt. 5:34.
5. Their refusal to pay rates or assessments for building and repairing houses for a worship which they did not approve.
6. Their use of the proper and Scriptural language, 'thou,' and 'thee,' to a single person: and their disuse of the custom of uncovering their heads, or pulling off their hats, by way of homage to man.
7. The necessity many found themselves under, of publishing what they believed to be the doctrine of truth; and sometimes even in the places appointed for the public national worship.

Their conscientious noncompliance in the preceding particulars, exposed them to much persecution and suffering, which consisted in prosecutions, fines, cruel beatings, whippings, and other corporal punishments; imprisonment, banishment, and even death.

To relate a particular account of their persecutions and sufferings, would extend beyond the limits of this work: we shall therefore refer, for that information, to the histories already mentioned, and more particularly to Besse's Collection of their sufferings; and shall confine our account here mostly to those who sacrificed their lives, and evinced, by their disposition of mind, constancy, patience, and faithful perseverance, that they were influenced by a sense of religious duty.

Numerous and repeated were the persecutions against them; and sometimes for transgressions or offences which the law did not contemplate or embrace. Many of the fines and penalties exacted of them, were not only unreasonable and exorbitant, but as they could not consistently pay them, were sometimes distrained to several times the value of the demand; whereby many poor families were greatly distressed, and obliged to depend on the assistance of their friends. Numbers were not only cruelly beaten and whipped in a public manner, like criminals, but some were branded and others had their ears cut off. Great numbers were long confined in loathsome prisons; in which some ended their days in consequence thereof. Many were sentenced to banishment; and a considerable number were transported. Some were banished on pain of death; and four were actually executed by the hands of the hangman, as we shall here relate, after inserting copies of some of the laws of the country where they suffered.

'At a General Court Held at Boston, the Fourteenth of October, 1656'

'Whereas, there is a cursed sect of heretics, lately risen up in the world, which are commonly called Quakers, who take upon them to be immediately sent from God, and infallibly assisted by the Spirit, to speak and write blasphemous opinions, despising government, and the order of God, in the Church and commonwealth, speaking evil of dignities, reproaching and reviling magistrates and ministers, seeking to turn the people from the faith, and gain proselytes to their pernicious ways: this court taking into consideration the premises, and to prevent the like mischief, as by their means is wrought in our land, doth hereby order, and by authority of this court, be it ordered and enacted, that what master or commander of any ship, bark, pink, or ketch, shall henceforth bring into any harbour, creek, or cove, within this jurisdiction, any Quaker or Quakers, or other blasphemous heretics, shall pay, or cause to be paid, the fine of one hundred pounds to the treasurer of the country, except it appear he want true knowledge or information of their being such; and, in that case, he hath liberty to clear himself by his oath, when sufficient proof to the contrary is wanting: and, for default of good payment, or good security for it, shall be cast into prison, and there to continue until the said sum be satisfied to the treasurer as foresaid.

'And the commander of any ketch, ship, or vessel, being legally convicted, shall give in sufficient security to the governor, or any one or more of the magistrates, who have power to determine the same, to carry them back to the place whence he brought them; and, on his refusal so to do, the governor, or one or more of the magistrates, are hereby empowered to issue out his or their warrants to commit such master or commander to prison, there to continue, until he give in sufficient security to the content of the governor, or any of the magistrates, as aforesaid.

'And it is hereby further ordered and enacted, that what Quaker soever shall arrive in this country from foreign parts, or shall come into this jurisdiction from any parts adjacent, shall be forthwith committed to the House of Correction; and, at their entrance, to be severely whipped, and by the master thereof be kept constantly to work, and none suffered to converse or speak with them, during the time of their imprisonment, which shall be no longer than necessity requires.

'And it is ordered, if any person shall knowingly import into any harbour of this jurisdiction, any Quakers' books or writings, concerning their devilish opinions, shall pay for such book or writing, being legally proved against him or them the sum of five pounds; and whosoever shall disperse or conceal any such book or writing, and it be found with him or her, or in his or her house and shall not immediately deliver the same to the next magistrate, shall forfeit or pay five pounds, for the dispersing or concealing of any such book or writing.

'And it is hereby further enacted, that if any persons within this colony shall take upon them to defend the heretical opinions of the Quakers, or any of their books or papers, shall be fined for the first time forty shillings; if they shall persist in the same, and shall again defend it the second time, four pounds; if notwithstanding they again defend and maintain the said Quakers' heretical opinions, they shall be committed to the House of Correction until there be convenient passage to send them out of the land, being sentenced by the court of Assistants to banishment.

'Lastly, it is hereby ordered, that what person or persons soever, shall revile the persons of the magistrates or ministers, as is usual with the Quakers, such person or persons shall be severely whipped or pay the sum of five pounds.

'This is a true copy of the court's order, as attests 'EDWARD RAWSON, Sec.'

'At a General Court Held at Boston, the Fourteenth of October, 1657'

'As an addition to the late order, in reference to the coming or bringing of any of the cursed sect of the Quakers into this jurisdiction, it is ordered that whosoever shall from henceforth bring, or cause to be brought, directly, or indirectly, any known Quaker or Quakers, or other blasphemous heretics, into this jurisdiction, every such person shall forfeit the sum of one hundred pounds to the country, and shall by warrant from any magistrate be committed to prison, there to remain until the penalty be satisfied and paid; and if any person or persons within this jurisdiction, shall henceforth entertain and conceal any such Quaker or Quakers, or other blasphemous heretics, knowing them so to be, every such person shall forfeit to the country forty shillings for every hour's entertainment and concealment of any Quaker or Quaker, etc., as aforesaid, and shall be committed to prison as aforesaid, until the forfeiture be fully satisfied and paid.

'And it is further ordered, that if any Quaker or Quakers shall presume, after they have once suffered what the law requires, to come into this jurisdiction, every such male Quaker shall, for the first offence, have one of his ears cut off, and be kept at work in the House of Correction, until he can be sent away at his own charge; and for the second offence, shall have his other ear cut off; and every woman Quaker, that has suffered the law here, that shall presume to come into this jurisdiction, shall be severely whipped, and kept at the House of Correction at work, until she be sent away at her own charge, and so also for her coming again, she shall be alike used as aforesaid.

'And for every Quaker, he or she, that shall a third time herein again offend, they shall have their tongues bored through with a hot iron, and be kept at the House of Correction close to work, until they be sent away at their own charge.

'And it is further ordered, that all and every Quaker arising from among ourselves, shall be dealt with, and suffer the like punishment as the law provides against foreign Quakers.

'EDWARD RAWSON, Sec.'

'An Act Made at a General Court, Held at Boston, the Twentieth of October, 1658'

Whereas, there is a pernicious sect, commonly called Quakers, lately risen, who by word and writing have published and maintained many dangerous and horrid tenets, and do take upon them to change and alter the received laudable customs of our nation, in giving civil respects to equals, or reverence to superiors; whose actions tend to undermine the civil government, and also to destroy the order of the churches, by denying all established forms of worship, and by withdrawing from orderly Church fellowship, allowed and approved by all orthodox professors of truth, and instead thereof, and in opposition thereunto, frequently meeting by themselves, insinuating themselves into the minds of the simple, or such as are at least affected to the order and government of church and commonwealth, whereby divers of our inhabitants have been infected, notwithstanding all former laws, made upon the experience of their arrogant and bold obtrusions, to disseminate their principles amongst us, prohibiting their coming into this jurisdiction, they have not been deferred from their impious attempts to undermine our peace, and hazard our ruin.

'For prevention thereof, this court doth order and enact, that any person or persons, of the cursed sect of the Quakers, who is not an inhabitant of, but is found within this jurisdiction, shall be apprehended without warrant, where no magistrate is at hand, by any constable, commissioner, or selectman, and conveyed from constable to constable, to the next magistrate, who shall commit the said person to close prison, there to remain (without bail) until the next court of Assistants, where they shall have legal trial.

'And being convicted to be of the sect of the Quakers, shall be sentenced to banishment, on pain of death. And that every inhabitant of this jurisdiction, being convicted to be of the aforesaid sect, either by taking up, publishing, or defending the horrid opinions of the Quakers, or the stirring up mutiny, sedition, or rebellion against the government, or by taking up their abusive and destructive practices, viz. denying civil respect to equals and superiors, and withdrawing from the Church assemblies; and instead thereof, frequenting meetings of their own, in opposition to our Church order; adhering to, or approving of any known Quaker, and the tenets and practices of Quakers, that are opposite to the orthodox received opinions of the godly; and endeavouring to disaffect others to civil government and Church order, or condemning the practice and proceedings of this court against the Quakers, manifesting thereby their complying with those, whose design is to overthrow the order established in Church and state: every such person, upon conviction before the said court of Assistants, in manner aforesaid, shall be committed to close prison for one month, and then, unless they choose voluntarily to depart this jurisdiction, shall give bond for their good behaviour and appear at the next court, continuing obstinate, and refusing to retract and reform the aforesaid opinions, they shall be sentenced to banishment, upon pain of death. And any one magistrate, upon information given him of any such person, shall cause him to be apprehended, and shall commit any such person to prison, according to his discretion, until he come to trial as aforesaid.'

It appears there were also laws passed in both of the then colonies of New Plymouth and New Haven, and in the Dutch settlement at New Amsterdam, now New York, prohibiting the people called Quakers, from coming into those places, under severe penalties; in consequence of which, some underwent considerable suffering.

The two first who were executed were William Robinson, merchant, of London, and Marmaduke Stevenson, a countryman, of Yorkshire. These coming to Boston, in the beginning of September, were sent for by the court of Assistants, and there sentenced to banishment, on pain of death. This sentence was passed also on Mary Dyar, mentioned hereafter, and Nicholas Davis, who were both at Boston. But William Robinson, being looked upon as a teacher, was also condemned to be whipped severely; and the constable was commanded to get an able man to do it. Then Robinson was brought into the street, and there stripped; and having his

285

hands put through the holes of the carriage of a great gun, where the jailer held him, the executioner gave him twenty stripes, with a threefold cord whip. Then he and the other prisoners were shortly after released, and banished, as appears from the following warrant:

'You are required by these, presently to set at liberty William Robinson, Marmaduke Stevenson, Mary Dyar, and Nicholas Davis, who, by an order of the court and council, had been imprisoned, because it appeared by their own confession, words, and actions, that they are Quakers: wherefore, a sentence was pronounced against them, to depart this jurisdiction, on pain of death; and that they must answer it at their peril, if they or any of them, after the fourteenth of this present month, September, are found within this jurisdiction, or any part thereof.

'EDWARD RAWSON'

'Boston, September 12, 1659'
Though Mary Dyar and Nicholas Davis left that jurisdiction for that time, yet Robinson and Stevenson, though they departed the town of Boston, could not yet resolve (not being free in mind) to depart that jurisdiction, though their lives were at stake. And so they went to Salem, and some places thereabouts, to visit and build up their friends in the faith. But it was not long before they were taken and put again into prison at Boston, and chains locked to their legs. In the next month, Mary Dyar returned also. And as she stood before the prison, speaking with one Christopher Holden, who was come thither to inquire for a ship bound for England, whither he intended to go, she was also taken into custody.

Thus, they had now three persons, who, according to their law, had forfeited their lives. And, on the twentieth of October, these three were brought into court, where John Endicot and others were assembled. And being called to the bar, Endicot commanded the keeper to pull off their hats; and then said, that they had made several laws to keep the Quakers from amongst them, and neither whipping, nor imprisoning, nor cutting off ears, nor banishment upon pain of death, would keep them from amongst them. And further, he said, that he or they desired not the death of any of them. Yet, notwithstanding, his following words, without more ado were, 'Give ear, and hearken to your sentence of death.' Sentence of death was also passed upon Marmaduke Stevenson, Mary Dyar, and William Edrid. Several others were imprisoned, whipped, and fined.

We have no disposition to justify the Pilgrims for these proceedings, but we think, considering the circumstances of the age in which they lived, their conduct admits of much palliation.

The fathers of New England, endured incredible hardships in providing for themselves a home in the wilderness; and to protect themselves in the undisturbed enjoyment of rights, which they had purchased at so dear a rate, they sometimes adopted measures, which, if tried by the more enlightened and liberal views of the present day, must at once be pronounced altogether unjustifiable. But shall they be condemned without mercy for not acting up to principles which were unacknowledged and unknown throughout the whole of Christendom? Shall they alone be held responsible for opinions and conduct which had become sacred by antiquity, and which were common to Christians of all other denominations? Every government then in existence assumed to itself the right to legislate in matters of religion; and to restrain heresy by penal statutes. This right was claimed by rulers, admitted by subjects, and is sanctioned by the names of Lord Bacon and Montesquieu, and many others equally famed for their talents and learning. It is unjust, then, to 'press upon one poor persecuted sect, the sins of all Christendom.' The fault of our fathers was the fault of the age; and though this cannot justify, it certainly furnishes an extenuation of their conduct. As well might you condemn them for not understanding and acting up to the principles of religious toleration. At the same time, it is but just to say, that imperfect as were their views of the rights of conscience, they were nevertheless far in advance of the age to which they belonged; and it is to them more than to any other class of men on earth, the world is indebted for the more rational views that now prevail on the subject of civil and religious liberty.

THE PRACTICE OF
THE PRESENCE OF GOD

by

✛ BROTHER LAWRENCE ✛

Based on an authentic edition, published by the Epworth Press,
25–35 City Road, E.C.1., London, 1890

THE PRACTICE OF THE PRESENCE OF GOD
THE BEST RULE OF A HOLY LIFE
being Conversations and Letters of Brother Lawrence

CONVERSATIONS

✛ FIRST CONVERSATION ✛

Conversion and precious employment ✛ Satisfaction in God's Presence
Faith our duty ✛ Resignation the fruit of watchfulness

✛ SECOND CONVERSATION ✛

Love the motive of all ✛ Once in fear, now in joy ✛ Diligence and love
Simplicity the key to Divine assistance ✛ Business abroad as at home
Times of prayer and self-mortification not essential for the practice
All scruples brought to God

✛ THIRD CONVERSATION ✛

Faith working by love ✛ Outward business no detriment
Perfect resignation the sure way

✝ FOURTH CONVERSATION ✝

The manner of going to God ✝ Hearty renunciation
Prayer and praise prevent discouragement ✝ Sanctification in common business
Prayer and the Presence of God ✝ The whole substance of religion
Self-estimation ✝ Further personal experience

LETTERS

✝ FIRST LETTER ✝

How the habitual sense of God's Presence was found

✝ SECOND LETTER ✝

Difference between himself and others
Faith alone consistently and persistently
Deprecates this state being considered a delusion

✝ THIRD LETTER ✝

For a soldier friend whom he encourages to trust in God

✝ FOURTH LETTER ✝

Writes of himself as of a third person, and encourages his correspondent
to press on to fuller practising of the Presence of God

✝ FIFTH LETTER ✝

Prayer for a sister who is about to make a vow and profession
A fresh insisting upon the necessity and virtue of practising the Presence of God

✝ SIXTH LETTER ✝

To a member of the order who had received from him a book, and to whom
he again enlarges on his favourite topic ✝ Encouragement to persevere

✝ SEVENTH LETTER ✝

At the age of nearly fourscore exhorts his correspondent, who is sixty-four,
to live and die with God and promises and asks for prayer

✢ EIGHTH LETTER ✢

Concerning wandering thoughts in prayer

✢ NINTH LETTER ✢

Enclosing a letter to a corresponding sister, whom he regards with respect
tinged with fear ✢ His old theme concisely put

✢ TENTH LETTER ✢

Has difficulty, but sacrifices his will, to write as requested
The loss of a friend may lead to acquaintance with the Friend

✢ ELEVENTH LETTER ✢

To one who is in great pain ✢ God is the Physician of body and of soul
Feels that he would gladly suffer at His wish

✢ TWELFTH LETTER ✢

To the same correspondent probably, and expresses his own abiding
comfort through faith

✢ THIRTEENTH LETTER ✢

To the same he exhorts for fuller and entire confidence in God, for body and soul

✢ FOURTEENTH LETTER ✢

Gratitude, for mercies to his correspondent, and measure of relief while he has
himself been near death, but with consolation in his suffering

✢ FIFTEENTH LETTER ✢

From his death-bed
Repeats the same exhortation to knowledge, that we may love

✛

CONVERSATIONS

Conversion and precious employment ✛ Satisfaction in God's Presence
Faith our duty ✛ Resignation the fruit of watchfulness

THE first time I saw Brother Lawrence was upon the 3rd of August, 1666. He told me that GOD had done him a singular favour, in his conversion at the age of eighteen.

That in the winter, seeing a tree stripped of its leaves, and considering that within a little time, the leaves would be renewed, and after that the flowers and fruit appear, he received a high view of the Providence and Power of GOD, which has never since been effaced from his soul. That this view had perfectly set him loose from the world, and kindled in him such a love for GOD, that he could not tell whether it had increased in above forty years that he had lived since.

That he had been footman to M. Fieubert, the treasurer, and that he was a great awkward fellow who broke everything.

That he had desired to be received into a monastery, thinking that he would there be made to smart for his awkwardness and the faults he should commit, and so he should sacrifice to GOD his life, with its pleasures: but that GOD had disappointed him, he having met with nothing but satisfaction in that state.

That we should establish ourselves in a sense of GOD's Presence, by continually conversing with Him. That it was a shameful thing to quit His conversation, to think of trifles and fooleries.

That we should feed and nourish our souls with high notions of GOD; which would yield us great joy in being devoted to Him.

That we ought to quicken, i.e., to enliven, our faith. That it was lamentable we had so little; and that instead of taking faith for the rule of their conduct, men amused themselves with trivial devotions, which changed daily. That the way of Faith was the spirit of the Church, and that it was sufficient to bring us to a high degree of perfection.

That we ought to give ourselves up to GOD, with regard both to things temporal and spiritual, and seek our satisfaction only in the fulfilling His will, whether He lead us by suffering or by consolation, for all would be equal to a soul truly resigned. That there needed fidelity in those drynesses, or insensibilities and irksomenesses in prayer, by which GOD tries our love to Him; that then was the time for us to make good and effectual acts of resignation, whereof one alone would oftentimes very much promote our spiritual advancement.

That as for the miseries and sins he heard of daily in the world, he was so far from wondering at them, that, on the contrary, he was surprised there were not more, considering the malice sinners were capable of: that for his part, he prayed for them; but knowing that GOD could remedy the mischiefs they did, when He pleased, he gave himself no farther trouble.

That to arrive at such resignation as GOD requires, we should watch attentively over all the passions which mingle as well in spiritual things as those of a grosser nature: that GOD would give light concerning those passions to those who truly desire to serve Him. That if this was my design, viz., sincerely to serve GOD, I might come to him (Bro. Lawrence) as often as I pleased, without any fear of being troublesome; but if not, that I ought no more to visit him.

✝ SECOND CONVERSATION ✝

Love the motive of all ✝ Once in fear, now in joy ✝ Diligence and love
Simplicity the key to Divine assistance ✝ Business abroad as at home
Times of prayer and self-mortification not essential for the practice
All scruples brought to God

THAT he had always been governed by love, without selfish views; and that having resolved to make the love of GOD the end of all his actions, he had found reasons to be well satisfied with his method. That he was pleased when he could take up a straw from the ground for the love of GOD, seeking Him only, and nothing else, not even His gifts.

That he had been long troubled in mind from a certain belief that he should be damned; that all the men in the world could not have persuaded him to the contrary; but that he had thus reasoned with himself about it: I did not engage in a religious life but for the love of GOD, and I have endeavoured to act only for Him; whatever becomes of me, whether I be lost or saved, I will always continue to act purely for the love of GOD. I shall have this good at least, that till death I shall have done all that is in me to love Him. That this trouble of mind had lasted four years; during which time he had suffered much.

That since that time he had passed his life in perfect liberty and continual joy. That he placed his sins betwixt him and GOD, as it were, to tell Him that he did not deserve His favours, but that GOD still continued to bestow them in abundance.

That in order to form a habit of conversing with GOD continually, and referring all we do to Him; we must at first apply to Him with some diligence: but that after a little care we should find His love inwardly excite us to it without any difficulty.

That he expected after the pleasant days GOD had given him, he should have his turn of pain and suffering; but that he was not uneasy about it, knowing very well, that as he could do nothing of himself, GOD would not fail to give him the strength to bear them.

That when an occasion of practising some virtue offered, he addressed himself to GOD, saying, LORD, I cannot do this unless Thou enablest me; and that then he received strength more than sufficient.

That when he had failed in his duty, he only confessed his fault, saying to GOD, I shall never do otherwise, if You leave me to myself; 'tis You must hinder my falling, and mend what is amiss. That after this, he gave himself no further uneasiness about it.

That we ought to act with GOD in the greatest simplicity, speaking to Him frankly and plainly, and imploring His assistance in our affairs, just as they happen. That GOD never failed to grant it, as he had often experienced.

That he had been lately sent into Burgundy, to buy the provision of wine for the society, which was a very unwelcome task for him, because he had no turn for business and because he was lame, and could not go about the boat but by rolling himself over the casks. That however he gave himself no uneasiness about it, nor about the purchase of the wine. That he said to GOD, It was His business he was about, and that he afterwards found it very well performed. That he had been sent into Auvergne the year before upon the same account; that he could not tell how the matter passed, but that it proved very well.

So, likewise, in his business in the kitchen (to which he had naturally a great aversion), having accustomed himself to do everything there for the love of GOD, and with prayer, upon all occasions, for His grace to do his work well, he had found everything easy, during the fifteen years that he had been employed there.

That he was very well pleased with the post he was now in; but that he was as ready to quit that as the former, since he was always pleasing himself in every condition, by doing little things for the love of GOD.

That with him the set times of prayer were not different from other times: that he retired to pray, according to the directions of his Superior, but that he did not want such retirement, nor ask for it, because his greatest business did not divert him from GOD.

That as he knew his obligation to love GOD in all things, and as he endeavoured so to do, he had no need of a director to advise him, but that he needed much a confessor to absolve him. That he was very sensible of his faults, but not discouraged by them; that he confessed them to GOD, and did not plead against Him to excuse them. When he had so done, he peaceably resumed his usual practice of love and adoration.

That in his trouble of mind, he had consulted nobody, but knowing only by the light of faith that GOD was present, he contented himself with directing all his actions to Him, i.e., doing them with a desire to please Him, let what would come of it.

That useless thoughts spoil all: that the mischief began there; but that we ought to reject them, as soon as we perceived their impertinence to the matter in hand, or our salvation; and return to our communion with GOD.

That at the beginning he had often passed his time appointed for prayer, in rejecting wandering thoughts, and falling back into them. That he could never regulate his devotion by certain methods as some do. That nevertheless, at first he had meditated for some time, but afterwards that went off, in a manner that he could give no account of.

That all bodily mortifications and other exercises are useless, but as they serve to arrive at the union with GOD by love; that he had well considered this, and found it the shortest way to go straight to Him by a continual exercise of love, and doing all things for His sake.

That we ought to make a great difference between the acts of the understanding and those of the will; that the first were comparatively of little value, and the others all.

That our only business was to love and delight ourselves in GOD.

That all possible kinds of mortification, if they were void of the love of GOD, could not efface a single sin. That we ought, without anxiety, to expect the pardon of our sins from the Blood of JESUS CHRIST, only endeavouring to love Him with all our hearts. That GOD seemed to have granted the greatest favours to the greatest sinners, as more signal monuments of His mercy.

That the greatest pains or pleasures, of this world, were not to be compared with what he had experienced of both kinds in a spiritual state: so that he was careful for nothing and feared nothing, desiring but one only thing of GOD, viz., that he might not offend Him.

That he had no scruples; for, said he, when I fail in my duty, I readily acknowledge it, saying, I am used to do so: I shall never do otherwise, if I am left to myself. If I fail not, then I give GOD thanks, acknowledging that it comes from Him.

✝ THIRD CONVERSATION ✝

Faith working by love   ✝   Outward business no detriment
Perfect resignation the sure way

HE told me, that the foundation of the spiritual life in him had been a high notion and esteem of GOD in faith; which when he had once well conceived, he had no other care at first, but faithfully to reject every other thought, that he might perform all his actions for the love of GOD. That when sometimes he had not thought of GOD for a good while, he did not disquiet himself for it; but after having acknowledged his wretchedness to GOD, he returned to Him with so much the greater trust in Him, by how much he found himself more wretched to have forgot Him.

That the trust we put in GOD honours Him much, and draws down great graces.

That it was impossible, not only that GOD should deceive, but also that He should long let a soul suffer which is perfectly resigned to Him, and resolved to endure everything for His sake.

That he had so often experienced the ready succours of Divine Grace upon all occasions, that from the same experience, when he had business to do, he did not think of it beforehand; but when it was time to do it, he found in GOD, as in a clear mirror, all that was fit for him to do. That of late he had acted thus, without anticipating care; but before the experience above mentioned, he had used it in his affairs.

When outward business diverted him a little from the thought of GOD, a fresh remembrance coming from GOD invested his soul, and so inflamed and transported him that it was difficult for him to contain himself.

That he was more united to GOD in his outward employments, than when he left them for devotion in retirement.

That he expected hereafter some great pain of body or mind; that the worst that could happen to him was, to lose that sense of GOD, which he had enjoyed so long; but that the goodness of GOD assured him He would not forsake him utterly, and that He would give him strength to bear whatever evil He permitted to happen to him; and therefore that he feared nothing, and had no occasion to consult with anybody about his state. That when he had attempted to do it, he had always come away more perplexed; and that as he was conscious of his readiness to lay down his life for the love of GOD, he had no apprehension of danger. That perfect resignation to GOD was a sure way to heaven, a way in which we had always sufficient light for our conduct.

That in the beginning of the spiritual life, we ought to be faithful in doing our duty and denying ourselves; but after that unspeakable pleasures followed: that in difficulties we need only have recourse to JESUS CHRIST, and beg His grace, with which everything became easy.

That many do not advance in the Christian progress, because they stick in penances, and particular exercises, while they neglect the love of GOD, which is the end. That this appeared plainly by their works, and was the reason why we see so little solid virtue.

That there needed neither art nor science for going to GOD, but only a heart resolutely determined to apply itself to nothing but Him, or for His sake, and to love Him only.

✝ FOURTH CONVERSATION ✝

The manner of going to God ✝ Hearty renunciation
Prayer and praise prevent discouragement ✝ Sanctification in common business
Prayer and the Presence of God ✝ The whole substance of religion
Self-estimation ✝ Further personal experience

HE discoursed with me very frequently, and with great openness of heart, concerning his manner of going to GOD, whereof some part is related already.

He told me, that all consists in one hearty renunciation of everything which we are sensible does not lead to GOD; that we might accustom ourselves to a continual conversation with Him, with freedom and in simplicity. That we need only to recognize GOD intimately present with us, to address ourselves to Him every moment, that we may beg His assistance for knowing His will in things doubtful, and for rightly performing those which we plainly see He requires of us, offering them to Him before we do them, and giving Him thanks when we have done.

That in this conversation with GOD, we are also employed in praising, adoring, and loving him incessantly, for His infinite goodness and perfection.

That, without being discouraged on account of our sins, we should pray for His grace with a perfect confidence, as relying upon the infinite merits of our LORD. That GOD never failed offering us His grace at each action; that he distinctly perceived it, and never failed of it, unless when his thoughts had wandered from a sense of GOD's Presence, or he had forgot to ask His assistance.

That GOD always gave us light in our doubts, when we had no other design but to please Him.

That our sanctification did not depend upon changing our works, but in doing that for GOD's sake, which we commonly do for our own. That it was lamentable to see how many people mistook the means for the end, addicting themselves to certain works, which they performed very imperfectly, by reason of their human or selfish regards.

That the most excellent method he had found of going to GOD, was that of doing our common business without any view of pleasing men [Gal. i. 10; Eph. vi. 5, 6.], and (as far as we are capable) purely for the love of GOD.

That it was a great delusion to think that the times of prayer ought to differ from other times, that we are as strictly obliged to adhere to GOD by action in the time of action, as by prayer in its season.

That his prayer was nothing else but a sense of the Presence of GOD, his soul being at that time insensible to everything but Divine love: and that when the appointed times of prayer were past, he found no difference, because he still continued with GOD, praising and blessing Him with all his might, so that he passed his life in continual joy; yet hoped that GOD would give him somewhat to suffer, when he should grow stronger.

That we ought, once for all, heartily to put our whole trust in GOD, and make a total surrender of ourselves to Him, secure that He would not deceive us.

That we ought not to be weary of doing little things for the love of GOD, who regards not the greatness of the work, but the love with which it is performed. That we should not wonder if, in the beginning, we often failed in our endeavours, but that at last we should gain a habit, which will naturally produce its acts in us, without our care, and to our exceeding great delight.

That the whole substance of religion was faith, hope, and charity; by the practice of which we become united to the will of GOD: that all beside is indifferent and to be used as a means, that we may arrive at our end, and be swallowed up therein, by faith and charity.

That all things are possible to him who believes, that they are less difficult to him who hopes, they are more easy to him who loves, and still more easy to him who perseveres in the practice of these three virtues.

That the end we ought to propose to ourselves is to become, in this life, the most perfect worshippers of GOD we can possibly be, as we hope to be through all eternity.

That when we enter upon the spiritual we should consider, and examine to the bottom, what we are. And then we should find ourselves worthy of all contempt, and such as do not deserve the name of Christians, subject to all kinds of misery, and numberless accidents, which trouble us, and cause perpetual vicissitudes in our health, in our humours, in our internal and external dispositions: in fine, persons whom GOD would humble by many pains and labours, as well within as without. After this, we should not wonder that troubles, temptations, oppositions and contradictions, happen to us from men. We ought, on the contrary, to submit ourselves to them, and bear them as long as GOD pleases, as things highly advantageous to us.

That the greater perfection a soul aspires after, the more dependent it is upon Divine grace.

Being questioned by one of his own society (to whom he was obliged to open himself) by what means he had attained such an habitual sense of GOD he told him that, since his first coming to the monastery, he had considered GOD as the end of all his thoughts and desires, as the mark to which they should tend, and in which they should terminate.

That in the beginning of his novitiate he spent the hours appointed for private prayer in thinking of GOD, so as to convince his mind of, and to impress deeply upon his heart, the Divine existence, rather by devout sentiments, and submission to the lights of faith, than by studied reasonings and elaborate meditations. That by this short and sure method, he exercised himself in the knowledge and love of GOD, resolving to use his utmost endeavour to live in a continual sense of His Presence, and, if possible, never to forget Him more.

That when he had thus in prayer filled his mind with great sentiments of that infinite Being, he went to his work appointed in the kitchen (for he was cook to the society); there having first considered severally the things his office required, and when and how each thing was to be done, he spent all the intervals of his time, as well before as after his work, in prayer.

That, when he began his business, he said to GOD, with a filial trust in Him, 'O my GOD, since Thou art with me, and I must now, in obedience to Thy commands, apply my mind to these outward things, I beseech Thee to grant me the grace to continue in Thy Presence; and to this end do Thou prosper me with Thy assistance, receive all my works, and possess all my affections.'

As he proceeded in his work, he continued his familiar conversation with his Maker, imploring His grace, and offering to Him all his actions.

When he had finished, he examined himself how he had discharged his duty; if he found well, he returned thanks to GOD; if otherwise, he asked pardon; and without being discouraged, he set his mind right again, and continued his exercise of the Presence of GOD, as if he had never deviated from it. 'Thus,' said he, 'by rising after my falls, and by frequently renewed acts of faith and love, I am come to a state, wherein it would be as difficult for me not to think of GOD, as it was at first to accustom myself to it.'

As Bro. Lawrence had found such an advantage in walking in the Presence of GOD, it was natural for him to recommend it earnestly to others; but his example was a stronger inducement than any arguments he could propose. His very countenance was edifying; such a sweet and calm devotion appearing in it, as could not but affect the beholders. And it was observed, that in the greatest hurry of business in the kitchen, he still preserved his recollection and heavenly-mindedness. He was never hasty nor loitering, but did each thing in its season, with an even uninterrupted composure and tranquillity of spirit. 'The time of business,' said he, 'does not with me differ from the time of prayer; and in the noise and clutter of my kitchen, while several persons are at the same time calling for different things, I possess GOD in as great tranquillity as if I were upon my knees at the Blessed Sacrament.'

LETTERS

✝ FIRST LETTER ✝

How the habitual sense of God's Presence was found

SINCE you desire so earnestly that I should communicate to you the method by which I arrived at that habitual sense of GOD's Presence, which our LORD, of His mercy, has been pleased to vouchsafe to me; I must tell you, that it is with great difficulty that I am prevailed on by your importunities; and now I do it only upon the terms, that you show my letter to nobody. If I knew that you would let it be seen, all the desire that I have for your advancement would not be able to determine me to it. The account I can give you is: Having found in many books different methods of going to GOD, and divers practices of the spiritual life, I thought this would serve rather to puzzle me, than facilitate what I sought after, which was nothing but how to become wholly GOD's.

This made me resolve to give the all for the All: so after having given myself wholly to GOD, to make all the satisfaction I could for my sins, I renounced, for the love of Him, everything that was not He; and I began to live as if there was none but He and I in the world. Sometimes I considered myself before Him as a poor criminal at the feet of his judge; at other times I beheld Him in my heart as my FATHER, as my GOD: I worshipped Him the oftenest that I could, keeping my mind in His holy Presence, and recalling it as often as I found it wandered from Him. I found no small pain in this exercise, and yet I continued it, notwithstanding all the difficulties that occurred, without troubling or disquieting myself when my mind had wandered involuntarily. I made this my business, as much all the day long as at the appointed times of prayer; for at all times, every hour, every minute, even in the height of my business, I drove away from my mind everything that was capable of interrupting my thought of GOD.

Such has been my common practice ever since I entered into religion; and though I have done it very imperfectly, yet I have found great advantages by it. These, I well know, are to be imputed to the mere mercy and goodness of GOD, because we can do nothing without Him; and I still less than any. But when we are faithful to keep ourselves in His holy Presence, and set Him always before us, this not only hinders our offending Him, and doing anything that may displease Him, at least wilfully, but it also begets in us a holy freedom, and if I may so speak, a familiarity with GOD, wherewith we ask, and that successfully, the graces we stand in need of. In fine, by often repeating these acts, they become habitual, and the Presence of GOD is rendered as it were natural to us. Give Him thanks, if you please, with me, for His great goodness towards me, which I can never sufficiently admire, for the many favours He has done to so miserable a sinner as I am. May all things praise Him. Amen.

✛ SECOND LETTER ✛

Difference between himself and others
Faith alone consistently and persistently
Deprecates this state being considered a delusion

NOT finding my manner of life in books, although I have no difficulty about it, yet, for greater security, I shall be glad to know your thoughts concerning it.

In a conversation some days since with a person of piety, he told me the spiritual life was a life of grace, which begins with servile fear, which is increased by hope of eternal life, and which is consummated by pure love; that each of these states had its different stages, by which one arrives at last at that blessed consummation.

I have not followed all these methods. On the contrary, from I know not what instincts, I found they discouraged me. This was the reason why, at my entrance into religion, I took a resolution to give myself up to GOD, as the best satisfaction I could make for my sins; and, for the love of Him, to renounce all besides.

For the first years, I commonly employed myself during the time set apart for devotion, with the thoughts of death, judgement, hell, heaven, and my sins. Thus I continued some years applying my mind carefully the rest of the day, and even in the midst of my business, to the Presence of GOD, whom I considered always as with me, often as in me.

At length I came insensibly to do the same thing during my set time of prayer, which caused in me great delight and consolation. This practice produced in me so high an esteem for GOD, that faith alone was capable to satisfy me in that point. [I suppose he means that all distinct notions he could form of GOD were unsatisfactory, because he perceived them to be unworthy of GOD, and therefore his mind was not to be satisfied but by the views of faith, which apprehends GOD as infinite and incomprehensible, as He is in Himself, and not as He can be conceived by human ideas.]

Such was my beginning; and yet I must tell you, that for the first ten years I suffered much: the apprehension that I was not devoted to GOD, as I wished to be, my past sins always present to my mind, and the great unmerited favours which GOD did me, were he matter and source of my sufferings. During this time I fell often, and rose again presently. It seemed to me that the creatures, reason, and GOD Himself were against me; And faith alone for me. I was troubled sometimes with thoughts, that to believe I had received such favours was an effect of my presumption, which pretended to be at once where others arrive with difficulty; at other times that it was a wilful delusion, and that there was no salvation for me.

When I thought of nothing but to end my days in these troubles (which did not at all diminish the trust I had in GOD, and which served only to increase my faith), I found myself changed all at once; and my soul, which till that time was in trouble, felt a profound inward peace, as if she were in her centre and place of rest.

Ever since that time I walk before GOD simply, in faith, with humility and with love; and I apply myself diligently to do nothing and think nothing which may displease Him. I hope that when I have done what I can, He will do with me what He pleases.

As for what passes in me at present, I cannot express it. I have no pain or difficulty about my state, because I have no will but that of GOD, which I endeavour to accomplish in all things, and to which I am so resigned, that I would not take up a straw from the ground against His order, or from any other motive but purely that of love to Him.

I have quitted all forms of devotion and set prayers but those to which my state obliges me. And I make it my business only to persevere in His holy Presence, wherein I keep myself by a simple attention, and a general fond regard to GOD, which I may call an actual Presence of GOD; or, to speak better, an habitual, silent, and secret conversation of the soul with GOD, which often causes in me joys and raptures inwardly, and sometimes also outwardly, so great that I am forced to use means to moderate them, and prevent their appearance to others.

In short, I am assured beyond all doubt, that my soul has been with GOD above these thirty years. I pass over many things, that I may not be tedious to you, yet I think it proper to inform you after what manner I consider myself before GOD, whom I behold as my King.

I consider myself as the most wretched of men, full of sores and corruption, and who has committed all sorts of crimes against his King; touched with a sensible regret I confess to Him all my wickedness, I ask His forgiveness, I abandon myself in His hands, that He may do what He pleases with me. This King, full of mercy and goodness, very far from chastising me, embraces me with love, makes me eat at His table, serves me with His own hands, gives me the key of His treasures; He converses and delights Himself with me incessantly, in a thousand and a thousand ways, and treats me in all respects as His favourite. It is thus I consider myself from time to time in His holy Presence.

My most usual method is this simple attention, and such a general passionate regard to GOD; to whom I find myself often attached with greater sweetness and delight than that of an infant at the mother's breast: so that if I dare use the expression, I should choose to call this state the bosom of GOD, for the inexpressible sweetness which I taste and experience there. If sometimes my thoughts wander from it by necessity or infirmity, I am presently recalled by inward motions, so charming and delicious that I am ashamed to mention them.

I desire your reverence to reflect rather upon my great wretchedness, of which you are fully informed, than upon the great favours which GOD does me, all unworthy and ungrateful as I am.

As for my set hours of prayer, they are only a continuation of the same exercise. Sometimes I consider myself there, as a stone before a carver, whereof he is to make a statue: presenting myself thus before GOD, I desire Him to make His perfect image in my soul, and render me entirely like Himself.

At other times, when I apply myself to prayer, I feel all my spirit and all my soul lift itself up without any care or effort of mine; and it continues as it were suspended and firmly fixed in GOD, as in its centre and place of rest.

I know that some charge this state with inactivity, delusion, and self-love: I confess that it is a holy inactivity, and would be a happy self-love, if the soul in that state were capable of it; because in effect, while she is in this repose, she cannot be disturbed by such acts as she was formerly accustomed to, and which were then her support, but would now rather hinder than assist her.

Yet I cannot bear that this should be called delusion; because the soul which thus enjoys GOD desires herein nothing but Him. If this be delusion in me, it belongs to GOD to remedy it. Let Him do what He pleases with me: I desire only Him, and to be wholly devoted Him.

You will, however, oblige me in sending me your opinion, to which I always pay a great deference, for I have a singular esteem for your reverence, and am yours in our Lord.

✝ THIRD LETTER ✝

For a soldier friend whom he encourages to trust in God

WE have a GOD who is infinitely gracious, and knows all our wants. I always thought that He would reduce you to extremity. He will come in His own time, and when you least expect it. Hope in Him more than ever: thank Him with me for the favours He does you, particularly for the fortitude and patience which He gives you in your afflictions: it is a plain mark of the care He takes of you; comfort yourself then with Him, and give thanks for all.

I admire also the fortitude and bravery of M. GOD has given him a good disposition, and a good will; but there is in him still a little of the world, and a great deal of youth. I hope the affliction which GOD has sent him will prove a wholesome remedy to him, and make him enter into himself; it is an accident very proper to engage him to put all his trust in Him, who accompanies him everywhere: let him think of Him the oftenest he can, especially in the greatest dangers. A little lifting up the heart suffices; a little remembrance of GOD, one act of inward worship, though upon a march, and sword in hand, are prayers which, however short, are nevertheless very acceptable to GOD; and far from lessening a soldier's courage in occasions of danger, they best serve to fortify it.

Let him then think of GOD the most he can; let him accustom himself, by degrees, to this small but holy exercise; nobody perceives it, and nothing is easier than to repeat often in the day these little internal adorations. Recommend to him, if you please, that he think of GOD the most he can, in the manner here directed; it is very fit and most necessary for a soldier, who is daily exposed to dangers of life, and often of his salvation. I hope that GOD will assist him and all the family, to whom I present my service, being theirs and yours.

✝ FOURTH LETTER ✝

Writes of himself as of a third person, and encourages his correspondent to press on to fuller practising of the Presence of God

I HAVE taken this opportunity to communicate to you the sentiments of one of our society concerning the admirable effects and continual assistances which he receives from the Presence of GOD. Let you and me both profit by them.

You must know, his continual care has been, for above forty years past that he has spent in religion, to be always with GOD; and to do nothing, say nothing, and think nothing which may displease Him; and this without any other view than purely for the love of Him, and because He deserves infinitely more.

He is now so accustomed to that Divine Presence, that he receives from it continual succours upon all occasions. For about thirty years, his soul has been filled with joys so continual, and sometimes so great, that he is forced to use means to moderate them, and to hinder their appearing outwardly.

If sometimes he is a little too much absent from that Divine Presence, GOD presently makes Himself to be felt in his soul to recall him; which often happens when he is most engaged in his outward business: he answers with exact fidelity to these inward drawings, either by an elevation of his heart towards GOD, or by a meek and fond regard to Him, or by such words as love forms upon these occasions; as for instance, My GOD, here I am all devoted to Thee: LORD, make me according to Thy heart. And then it seems to him (as in effect he feels it) that this GOD of love, satisfied with such few words, reposes again, and rests in the depth and centre of his soul. The experience of these things gives him such an assurance that GOD is always in the depth or bottom of his soul, and renders him incapable of doubting it, upon any account whatever.

Judge by this what content and satisfaction he enjoys, while he continually finds in himself so great a treasure: he is no longer in an anxious search after it, but has it open before him, and may take what he pleases of it.

He complains much of our blindness; and cries often that we are to be pitied who content ourselves with so little. GOD, saith he, has infinite treasure to bestow, and we take up with a little sensible devotion which passes in a moment. Blind as we are, we hinder GOD, and stop the current of His graces. But when He finds a soul penetrated with a lively faith, He pours into it His graces and favours plentifully; there they flow like a torrent, which, after being forcibly stopped against its ordinary course, when it has found a passage, spreads itself with impetuosity and abundance.

Yes, we often stop this torrent, by the little value we set upon it. But let us stop it no more: let us enter into ourselves and break down the bank which hinders it. Let us make way for grace;

let us redeem the lost time, for perhaps we have but little left; death follows us close, let us be well prepared for it; for we die but once, and a miscarriage there is irretrievable.

I say again, let us enter into ourselves. The time presses: there is no room for delay; our souls are at stake. I believe you have taken such effectual measures, that you will not be surprised. I commend you for it, it is the one thing necessary: we must, nevertheless, always work at it, because not to advance, in the spiritual life, is to go back. But those who have the gale of the HOLY SPIRIT go forward even in sleep. If the vessel of our soul is still tossed with winds and storms, let us awake the LORD, who reposes in it, and He will quickly calm the sea.

I have taken the liberty to impart to you these good sentiments, that you may compare them with your own: they will serve again to kindle and inflame them, if by misfortune (which GOD forbid, for it would be indeed a great misfortune) they should be, though never so little, cooled. Let us then both recall our first fervours. Let us profit by the example and the sentiments of this brother, who is little known of the world, but known of GOD, and extremely caressed by Him. I will pray for you; do you pray instantly for me, who am yours in our LORD.

✛ FIFTH LETTER ✛

Prayer for a sister who is about to make a vow and profession
A fresh insisting upon the necessity and virtue of practising the Presence of God

I RECEIVED this day two books and a letter from Sister, who is preparing to make her profession, and upon that account desires the prayers of your holy society, and yours in particular. I perceive that she reckons much upon them; pray do not disappoint her. Beg of GOD that she may make her sacrifice in the view of His love alone, and with a firm resolution to be wholly devoted to Him.

I will send you one of those books which treat of the Presence of GOD; a subject which, in my opinion, contains the whole spiritual life; and it seems to me that whoever duly practises it will soon become spiritual.

I know that for the right practice of it, the heart must be empty of all other things; because GOD will possess the heart alone; and as He cannot possess it alone, without emptying it of all besides, so neither can He act there, and do in it what He pleases, unless it be left vacant to Him.

There is not in the world a kind of life more sweet and delightful, than that of a continual conversation with GOD: those only can comprehend it who practise and experience it; yet I do not advise you to do it from that motive; it is not pleasure which we ought to seek in this exercise; but let us do it from a principle of love, and because GOD would have us.

Were I a preacher, I should above all other things preach the practice of the Presence of GOD; and were I a director, I should advise all the world to do it: so necessary do I think it, and so easy too.

Ah! knew we but the want we have of the grace and assistance of GOD, we should never lose sight of Him, no, not for a moment. Believe me; make immediately a holy and firm resolution never more wilfully to forget Him, and to spend the rest of your days in His sacred Presence, deprived for the love of Him, if He thinks fit, of all consolations.

Set heartily about this work, and if you do it as you ought, be assured that you will soon find the effects of it. I will assist you with my prayers, poor as they are: I recommend myself earnestly to yours, and those of your holy society.

✝ SIXTH LETTER ✝

To a member of the order who had received from him a book, and to whom he again enlarges on his favourite topic ✝ Encouragement to persevere

I HAVE received from Mrs. — the things which you gave her for me. I wonder that you have not given me your thoughts of the little book I sent to you, and which you must have received. Pray set heartily about the practice of it in your old age; it is better late than never.

I cannot imagine how religious persons can live satisfied without the practice of the Presence of GOD. For my part I keep myself retired with Him in the depth of centre of my soul as much as I can; and while I am so with Him I fear nothing; but the least turning from Him is insupportable.

This exercise does not much fatigue the body: it is, however, proper to deprive it sometimes, nay often, of many little pleasures which are innocent and lawful: for GOD will not permit that a soul which desires to be devoted entirely to Him should take other pleasures than with Him; that is more than reasonable.

I do not say that therefore we must put any violent constraint upon ourselves. No, we must serve GOD in a holy freedom, we must do our business faithfully, without trouble or disquiet; recalling our mind to GOD mildly and with tranquillity, as often as we find it wandering from Him.

It is, however, necessary to put our whole trust in GOD, laying aside all other cares, and even some particular forms of devotion, though very good in themselves, yet such as one often engages in unreasonably: because those devotions are only means to attain to the end; so when by this exercise of the Presence of GOD we are with Him who is our end, it is then useless to return to the means; but we may continue with Him our commerce of love, persevering in His holy Presence: one while by an act of praise, of adoration, or of desire; one while by an act of resignation, or thanksgiving; and in all the manner which our spirit can invent.

Be not discouraged by the repugnance which you may find in it from nature; you must do yourself violence. At the first, one often thinks it lost time; but you must go on, and resolve to persevere in it to death, notwithstanding all the difficulties that may occur. I recommend myself to the prayers of your holy society, and yours in particular. I am yours in our LORD.

✝ SEVENTH LETTER ✝

At the age of nearly fourscore exhorts his correspondent, who is sixty-four, to live and die with God and promises and asks for prayer

I PITY you much. It will be of great importance if you can leave the care of your affairs to, and spend the remainder of your life only in worshipping GOD. He requires no great matters of us;

a little remembrance of Him from time to time, a little adoration: sometimes to pray for His grace, sometimes to offer Him your sufferings, and sometimes to return Him thanks for the favours He has given you, and still gives you, in the midst of your troubles, and to console yourself with Him the oftenest you can. Lift up your heart to Him, sometimes even at your meals, and when you are in company: the least little remembrance will always be acceptable to Him. You need not cry very loud; He is nearer to us than we are aware of.

It is not necessary for being with GOD to be always at church; we may make an oratory of our heart, wherein to retire from time to time, to converse with Him in meekness, humility, and love. Every one is capable of such familiar conversation with GOD, some more, some less: He knows what we can do. Let us begin then; perhaps He expects but one generous resolution on our part. Have courage. We have but little time to live; you are near sixty-four, and I am almost eighty. Let us live and die with GOD: sufferings will be sweet and pleasant to us, while we are with Him: and the greatest pleasures will be, without Him, a cruel punishment to us. May He be blessed for all. Amen.

Use yourself then by degrees thus to worship Him, to beg His grace, to offer Him your heart from time to time, in the midst of your business, even every moment if you can. Do not always scrupulously confine yourself to certain rules, or particular forms of devotion; but act with a general confidence in GOD, with love and humility. You may assure — of my poor prayers, and that I am their servant, and yours particularly.

✛ EIGHTH LETTER ✛

Concerning wandering thoughts in prayer

YOU tell me nothing new: you are not the only one that is troubled with wandering thoughts. Our mind is extremely roving; but as the will is mistress of all our faculties, she must recall them, and carry them to GOD, as their last end.

When the mind, for want of being sufficiently reduced by recollection, at our first engaging in devotion, has contracted certain bad habits of wandering and dissipation, they are difficult to overcome, and commonly draw us, even against our wills, to the things of the earth.

I believe one remedy for this is, to confess our faults, and to humble ourselves before GOD. I do not advise you to use multiplicity of words in prayer; many words and long discourses being often the occasions of wandering: hold yourself in prayer before GOD, like a dumb or paralytic beggar at a rich man's gate: let it be your business to keep your mind in the Presence of the LORD. If it sometimes wander, and withdraw itself from Him, do not much disquiet yourself for that; trouble and disquiet serve rather to distract the mind, than to re-collect it; the will must bring it back in tranquillity; if you persevere in this manner, GOD will have pity on you.

One way to re-collect the mind easily in the time of prayer, and preserve it more in tranquillity, is not to let it wander too far at other times: you should keep it strictly in the Presence of GOD; and being accustomed to think of Him often, you will find it easy to keep your mind calm in the time of prayer, or at least to recall it from its wanderings.

I have told you already at large, in my former letters, of the advantages we may draw from this practice of the Presence of GOD: let us set about it seriously and pray for one another.

✛ NINTH LETTER ✛

Enclosing a letter to a corresponding sister, whom he regards with respect
tinged with fear ✛ His old theme concisely put

THE enclosed is an answer to that which I received from —; pray deliver it to her. She seems to me full of good will, but she would go faster than grace. One does not become holy all at once. I recommend her to you: we ought to help one another by our advice, and yet more by our good examples. You will oblige me to let me hear of her from time to time, and whether she be very fervent and very obedient.

Let us thus think often that our only business in this life is to please GOD, that perhaps all besides is but folly and vanity. You and I have lived above forty years in religion [i.e., a monastic life]. Have we employed them in loving and serving GOD, who by His mercy has called us to this state and for that very end? I am filled with shame and confusion, when I reflect on the one hand upon the great favours which GOD has done, and incessantly continues to do, me; and on the other, upon the ill use I have made of them, and my small advancement in the way of perfection.

Since by His mercy He gives us still a little time, let us begin in earnest, let us repair the lost time, let us return with a full assurance to that FATHER of mercies, who is always ready to receive us affectionately. Let us renounce, let us generously renounce, for the love of Him, all that is not Himself; He deserves infinitely more. Let us think of Him perpetually. Let us put all our trust in Him: I doubt not but we shall soon find the effects of it, in receiving the abundance of His grace, with which we can do all things, and without which we can do nothing but sin.

We cannot escape the dangers which abound in life, without the actual and continual help of GOD; let us then pray to Him for it continually. How can we pray to Him without being with Him? How can we be with Him but in thinking of Him often? And how can we often think of Him, but by a holy habit which we should form of it? You will tell me that I am always saying the same thing: it is true, for this is the best and easiest method I know; and as I use no other, I advise all the world to it. We must know before we can love. In order to know GOD, we must often think of Him; and when we come to love Him, we shall then also think of Him often, for our heart will be with our treasure. This is an argument which well deserves your consideration.

✛ TENTH LETTER ✛

Has difficulty, but sacrifices his will, to write as requested
The loss of a friend may lead to acquaintance with the Friend

I HAVE had a good deal of difficulty to bring myself to write to M. —, and I do it now purely because you and Madam desire me. Pray write the directions and send it to him. I am very well pleased with the trust which you have in GOD: I wish that He may increase it in you more and more: we cannot have too much in so good and faithful a Friend, who will never fail us in this world nor in the next.

If M. — makes his advantage of the loss he has had, and puts all his confidence in GOD, He will soon give him another friend, more powerful and more inclined to serve him. He disposes of hearts as He pleases. Perhaps M. — was too much attached to him he has lost. We ought to love our friends, but without encroaching upon the love of GOD, which must be the principal.

Pray remember what I have recommended to you, which is, to think often on GOD, by day, by night, in your business, and even in your diversions. He is always near you and with you; leave Him not alone. You would think it rude to leave a friend alone, who came to visit you: why then must GOD be neglected? Do not then forget Him, but think on Him often, adore Him continually live and die with Him; this is the glorious employment of a Christian; in a word, this is our profession, if we do not know it we must learn it. I will endeavour to help you with my prayers, and am yours in our LORD.

✝ ELEVENTH LETTER ✝

To one who is in great pain. God is the Physician of body and of soul
Feels that he would gladly suffer at His wish

I DO not pray that you may be delivered from your pains; but I pray GOD earnestly that He would give you strength and patience to bear them as long as He pleases. Comfort yourself with Him who holds you fastened to the cross: He will loose you when He thinks fit. Happy those who suffer with Him: accustom yourself to suffer in that manner, and seek from Him the strength to endure as much, and as long, as He shall judge to be necessary for you. The men of the world do not comprehend these truths, nor is it to be wondered at, since they suffer like what they are, and not like Christians: they consider sickness as a pain to nature, and not as a favour from GOD; and seeing it only in that light, they find nothing in it but grief and distress. But those who consider sickness as coming from the hand of GOD, as the effects of His mercy, and the means which He employs for their salvation, commonly find in it great sweetness and sensible consolation.

I wish you could convince yourself that GOD is often (in some sense) nearer to us and more effectually present with us, in sickness than in health. Rely upon no other Physician, for, according to my apprehension, He reserves your cure to Himself. Put then all your trust in Him, and you will soon find the effects of it in your recovery, which we often retard, by putting greater confidence in physic than in GOD.

Whatever remedies you make use of, they will succeed only so far as He permits. When pains come from GOD, He only can cure them. He often sends diseases of the body, to cure those of the soul. Comfort yourself with the sovereign Physician both of soul and body.

I foresee that you will tell me that I am very much at my ease, that I eat and drink at the table of the LORD. YOU have reason: but think you that it would be a small pain to the greatest criminal in the world, to eat at the king's table, and be served by him, and notwithstanding such favours to be without assurance of pardon? I believe he would feel exceeding great uneasiness, and such as nothing could moderate, but only his trust in the goodness of his sovereign. So I assure you, that whatever pleasures I taste at the table of my King, yet my sins, ever present before my eyes, as well as the uncertainty of my pardon, torment me, though in truth that torment itself is pleasing.

Be satisfied with the condition in which GOD places you: however happy you may think me, I envy you. Pains and suffering would be a paradise to me, while I should suffer with my GOD; and the greatest pleasure would be hell to me, if I could relish them without Him; all my consolation would be to suffer something for His sake.

I must, in a little time, go to GOD. What comforts me in this life is, that I now see Him by faith; and I see Him in such a manner as might make me say sometimes, I believe no more, but I see. I feel what faith teaches us, and, in that assurance and that practice of faith, I will live and die with Him.

Continue then always with GOD: 'tis the only support and comfort for your affliction. I shall beseech Him to be with you. I present my service.

To the same correspondent probably, and expresses his own abiding comfort through faith

IF we were well accustomed to the exercise of the Presence of GOD, all bodily diseases would be much alleviated thereby. GOD often permits that we should suffer a little, to purify our souls, and oblige us to continue with Him.

Take courage, offer Him your pains incessantly, pray to Him for strength to endure them. Above all, get a habit of entertaining yourself often with GOD, and forget Him the least you can. Adore Him in your infirmities, offer yourself to Him from time to time; and, in the height of your sufferings, beseech Him humbly and affectionately (as a child his father) to make you conformable to His holy will. I shall endeavour to assist you with my poor prayers.

GOD has many ways of drawing us to Himself. He sometimes hides Himself from us: but faith alone, which will not fail us in time of need, ought to be our support, and the foundation of our confidence, which must be all in GOD.

I know not how GOD will dispose of me: I am always happy: all the world suffer; and I, who deserve the severest discipline, feel joys so continual, and so great, that I can scarce contain them.

I would willingly ask of GOD a part of your sufferings, but that I know my weakness, which is so great, that if He left me one moment to myself, I should be the most wretched man alive. And yet I know not how He can leave me alone, because faith gives me as strong a conviction as sense can do, that He never forsakes us, till we have first forsaken Him. Let us fear to leave Him. Let us be always with Him. Let us live and die in His Presence. Do you pray for me, as I for you.

To the same he exhorts for fuller and entire confidence in God, for body and soul

I AM in pain to see you suffer so long; what gives me some ease, and sweetens the feeling I have of your griefs, is that they are proofs of GOD's love towards you: see them in that view, and you will bear them more easily. As your case is, 'tis my opinion that you should leave off human remedies, and resign yourself entirely to the providence of GOD; perhaps He stays only for that resignation and a perfect trust in Him to cure you. Since notwithstanding all your cares, physic has hitherto proved unsuccessful, and your malady still increases, it will not be tempting GOD to abandon yourself in His hands, and expect all from Him.

I told you, in my last, that He sometimes permits bodily diseases to cure the distempers of the soul. Have courage then: make a virtue of necessity: ask of GOD, not deliverance from your pains, but strength to bear resolutely, for the love of Him, all that He should please, and as long as He shall please.

Such prayers, indeed, are a little hard to nature, but most acceptable to GOD, and sweet to those that love Him. Love sweetens pains; and when one loves GOD, one suffers for His sake with joy and courage. Do you so, I beseech you; comfort yourself with Him, who is the only Physician of all our maladies. He is the FATHER of the afflicted, always ready to help us. He loves us infinitely more than we imagine: love Him then, and seek not consolation elsewhere: I hope you will soon receive it. Adieu. I will help you with my prayers, poor as they are, and shall be, always, yours in our LORD.

✝ FOURTEENTH LETTER ✝

Gratitude, for mercies to his correspondent, and measure of relief while he has himself been near death, but with consolation in his suffering

I RENDER thanks to our LORD, for having relieved you a little, according to your desire. I have been often near expiring, though I was never so much satisfied as then. Accordingly I did not pray for any relief, but I prayed for strength to suffer with courage, humility, and love. Ah, how sweet is it to suffer with GOD! however great the sufferings may be, receive them with love. 'Tis paradise to suffer and be with Him; so that if in this life we would enjoy the peace of paradise, we must accustom ourselves to a familiar, humble, affectionate conversation with Him: we must hinder our spirits wandering from Him upon any occasion: we must make our heart a spiritual temple, wherein to adore Him incessantly: we must watch continually over ourselves, that we may not do, nor say, nor think anything that may displease Him. When our minds are thus employed about GOD, suffering will become full of unction and consolation.

I know that to arrive at this state, the beginning is very difficult; for we must act purely in faith. But though it is difficult, we know also that we can do all things with the grace of GOD, which He never refuses to them who ask it earnestly. Knock, persevere in knocking, and I answer for it that He will open to you in His due time, and grant you all at once what He has deferred during many years. Adieu. Pray to Him for me, as I pray to Him for you. I hope to see Him quickly.

✝ FIFTEENTH LETTER ✝

From his death-bed
Repeats the same exhortation to knowledge, that we may love

GOD knoweth best what is needful for us, and all that He does is for our good. If we knew how much He loves us, we should be always ready to receive equally and with indifference from His hand the sweet and the bitter; all would please that came from Him. The sorest afflictions never appear intolerable, but when we see them in the wrong light. When we see them in the hand of GOD, who dispenses them: when we know that it is our loving FATHER, who abases and distresses us: our sufferings will lose their bitterness, and become even matter of consolation.

Let all our employment be to know GOD: the more one knows Him, the more one desires to know Him. And as knowledge is commonly the measure of love, the deeper and more extensive our knowledge shall be, the greater will be our love: and if our love of GOD were great we should love Him equally in pains and pleasures.

Let us not amuse ourselves to seek or to love GOD for any sensible favours (how elevated soever) which He has or may do us. Such favours, though never so great, cannot bring us so near to GOD as faith does in one simple act. Let us seek Him often by faith: He is within us; seek Him not elsewhere. Are we not rude and deserve blame, if we leave Him alone, to busy ourselves about trifles, which do not please Him and perhaps offend Him? 'Tis to be feared these trifles will one day cost us dear.

Let us begin to be devoted to Him in good earnest. Let us cast everything besides out of our hearts; He would possess them alone. Beg this favour of Him. If we do what we can on our parts, we shall soon see that change wrought in us which we aspire after. I cannot thank Him sufficiently for the relaxation He has vouchsafed you. I hope from His mercy the favour to see Him within a few days. Let us pray for one another.

[He took to his bed two days after and died within the week.]

A TREATISE CONCERNING RELIGIOUS AFFECTIONS

by
✛ JONATHAN EDWARDS ✛

✛

CONTENTS

Introduction

✛ **PART I** ✛

CONCERNING THE NATURE OF THE AFFECTIONS AND THEIR IMPORTANCE IN RELIGION

✛ **PART II** ✛

SHOWING WHAT ARE NO CERTAIN SIGNS THAT RELIGIOUS AFFECTIONS ARE GRACIOUS, OR THAT THEY ARE NOT

8. That comforts and joys seem to follow awakenings and convictions of conscience, in a certain order, is no sign

9. That they dispose persons to spend much time in religion, and to be zealously engaged in the external duties of worship, is no sign

10. That they much dispose persons with their mouths to praise and glorify God, is no sign

11. That they make persons that have them exceeding confident that what they experience is divine, and that they are in a good estate, is no sign

12. That the outward manifestations of them, and the relation persons give of them, are very affecting and pleasing to the godly, is no sign

✛ PART III ✛

SHOWING WHAT ARE DISTINGUISHING SIGNS OF TRULY GRACIOUS AND HOLY AFFECTIONS

1. Truly gracious affections arise from divine influences and operations on the heart

INTRODUCTION

THERE is no question whatsoever, that is of greater importance to mankind, and what is more concerns every individual person to be well resolved in, than this: *What are the distinguishing qualifications of those that are in favor with God, and entitled to his eternal rewards?* Or, which comes to the same thing, *What is the nature of true religion? And wherein do lie the distinguishing notes of that virtue and holiness that is acceptable in the sight of God?* But though it be of such importance, and though we have clear and abundant light in the word of God to direct us in this matter, yet there is no one point, wherein professing Christians do more differ one from another. It would be endless to reckon up the variety of opinions in this point, that divide the Christian world; making manifest the truth of that declaration of our Savior, 'Strait is the gate and narrow is the way, that leads to life, and few there be that find it.'

The consideration of these things has long engaged me to attend to this matter, with the utmost diligence and care, and exactness of search and inquiry, that I have been capable of. It is a subject on which my mind has been peculiarly intent, ever since I first entered on the study of divinity. But as to the success of my inquiries it must be left to the judgment of the reader of the following treatise.

I am sensible it is much more difficult to judge impartially of that which is the subject of this discourse, in the midst of the dust and smoke of such a state of controversy, as this land is now in, about things of this nature. As it is more difficult to write impartially, so it is more difficult to read impartially. Many will probably be hurt in their spirits, to find so much that appertains to religious affection, here condemned: and perhaps indignation and contempt will be excited in others by finding so much here justified and approved. And it may be, some will be ready to charge me with inconsistency with myself, in so much approving some things, and so much condemning others; as I have found this has always been objected to by some, ever since the beginning of our late controversies about religion. It is a hard thing to be a hearty zealous friend of what has been good and glorious, in the late extraordinary appearances, and to rejoice much in it; and at the same time to see the evil and pernicious tendency of what has been bad, and earnestly to oppose that. But yet, I am humbly but fully persuaded, we shall never be in the way of truth, nor go on in a way acceptable to God, and tending to the advancement of Christ's kingdom till we do so. There is indeed something very mysterious in it, that so much good, and so much bad, should be mixed together in the church of God; as it is a mysterious thing, and what has puzzled and amazed many a good Christian, that there should be that which is so divine and precious, as the saving grace of God, and the new and divine nature dwelling in the same heart, with so much corruption, hypocrisy, and iniquity, in a particular saint. Yet neither of these is more mysterious than real. And neither of them is a new or rare thing. It is no new thing, that much false religion should prevail, at a time of great reviving of true religion, and that at such a time multitudes of hypocrites should spring up among true saints. It was so in that great reformation, and revival of religion, that was in Josiah's time; as appears by Jer. 3:10, and 4:3, 4, and also by the great apostasy that there was in the land, so soon after his reign. So it was in that great outpouring of the Spirit upon the Jews, that was in the days of John the Baptist; as appears by the great apostasy of that people so soon after so general an awakening, and the temporary religious comforts and joys of many: John 5:35, 'Ye were willing for a season to rejoice in his light.' So it was in those great commotions that were among the multitude, occasioned by the preaching of Jesus Christ; of the many that were then called, but few were chosen; of the multitude that were roused and affected by his preaching, and at one time or other appeared mightily engaged, full of admiration of Christ, and elevated with joy, but few were true disciples, that stood the shock of the great trials that came afterwards, and endured to the end. Many were like the stony ground, or thorny ground; and but few, comparatively, like the good ground. Of the whole heap that was gathered, great part was chaff; that the wind afterwards drove away; and the heap of wheat that was left, was comparatively small; as appears abundantly, by the history of the New Testament. So it was in that great outpouring of the Spirit that was in the apostles' days as appears by Matt. 24:10-13, Gal. 3:1, and 4:11, 15, Phil. 2:21, and 3:18, 19, and the two epistles to the Corinthians, and many other parts of the New Testament. And so it was in the great reformation from Popery. It appears plainly to have been in the visible church of God, in times of great reviving of religion, from time to time, as it is with the fruit trees in the spring; there are a multitude of blossoms, all of which appear fair and beautiful, and there is a promising appearance of young fruits; but many of them are but of short continuance; they soon fall off, and never come to maturity.

Not that it is to be supposed that it will always be so; for though there never will, in this world, be an entire purity, either in particular saints, in a perfect freedom from mixtures of corruption; or in the church of God, without any mixture of hypocrites with saints, and counterfeit religion, and false appearances of grace with true religion, and real holiness: yet it is evident, that there will come a time of much greater purity in the church of God, than has been in ages past; it is plain by these texts of Scripture, Isa. 52:1, Ezek. 44:6, 7, Joel 3:17, Zech. 14:21, Ps. 69:32, 35, 36, Isa 35:8, 10; 4:3, 4, Ezek. 20:38, Ps. 37:9, 10, 21, 29. And one great reason of it will be that at that time God will give much greater light to his people, to distinguish between true religion and its counterfeits. Mal. 3:3, 'And he shall sit as a refiner and purifier of silver: and he shall purify the sons of Levi, and purge them as gold and silver, that they may offer to the Lord an offering in righteousness.' With v. 18, which is a continuation of the prophecy of the same happy times, 'Then shall ye return, and discern between the righteous and the wicked, between him that serveth God, and him that serveth him not.'

It is by the mixture of counterfeit religion with true, not discerned and distinguished, that the devil has had his greatest advantage against the cause and kingdom of Christ, all along hitherto. It is by this means, principally, that he has prevailed against all revivings of religion, that ever have been since the first founding of the Christian church. By this, he hurt the cause of Christianity, in and after the apostolic age, much more than by all the persecutions of both Jews and Heathens. The apostles, in all their epistles, show themselves much more concerned at the former mischief, than the latter. By this, Satan prevailed against the reformation, began by Luther, Zwinglius, etc., to put a stop to its progress, and bring it into disgrace; ten times more, than by all those bloody, cruel, and before unheard of persecutions of the church of Rome. By this, principally, has he prevailed against revivals of religion, that have been in our nation since the reformation. By this he prevailed against New England, to quench the love and spoil the joy of her espousals, about a hundred years ago. And I think, I have had opportunity enough to see plainly that by this the devil has prevailed against the late great revival of religion in New England, so happy and promising in its beginning. Here, most evidently has been the main advantage Satan has had against us; by this he has foiled us. It is by this means, that the daughter of Zion in this land now lies on the ground, in such piteous circumstances as we now behold her; with her garments rent, her face disfigured, her nakedness exposed, her limbs broken, and weltering in the blood of her own wounds, and in no wise able to arise, and this, so quickly after her late great joys and hopes: Lam. 1:17, 'Zion spreadeth forth her hands, and there is none to comfort her: the Lord hath commanded concerning Jacob, that his adversaries shall be roundabout him: Jerusalem is as a menstruous woman among them.' I have seen the devil prevail the same way, against two great revivings of religion in this country. Satan goes on with mankind, as he began with them. He prevailed against our first parents, and cast them out of paradise, and suddenly brought all their happiness and glory to an end, by appearing to be a friend to their happy paradisaic state, and pretending to advance it to higher degrees. So the same cunning serpent, that beguiled Eve through his subtlety, by perverting us from the simplicity that is in Christ, hath suddenly prevailed to deprive us of that fair prospect, we had a little while ago, of a kind of paradisaic state of the church of God in New England.

After religion has revived in the church of God, and enemies appear, people that are engaged to defend its cause, are commonly most exposed, where they are sensible of danger. While they are wholly intent upon the opposition that appears openly before them, to make head against that, and do neglect carefully to look all around them, the devil comes behind them, and gives a fatal stab unseen; and has opportunity to give a more home stroke, and wound the deeper, because he strikes at his leisure, and according to his pleasure, being obstructed by no guard or resistance.

And so it is ever likely to be in the church, whenever religion revives remarkably, till we have learned well to distinguish between true and false religion, between saving affections and experiences, and those manifold fair shows, and glistering appearances, by which they are counterfeited; the consequences of which, when they are not distinguished, are often inexpressibly dreadful. By this means, the devil gratifies himself, by bringing it to pass, that that should be offered to God, by multitudes, under a notion of a pleasing acceptable service to him, that is indeed above all things abominable to him. By this means he deceives great multitudes about the state of their souls; making them think they are something, when they are nothing; and so eternally undoes them; and not only so, but establishes many in a strong confidence of their eminent holiness, who are in God's sight some of the vilest of hypocrites. By this means, he many ways damps and wounds religion in the hearts of the saints, obscures and deforms it by corrupt mixtures, causes their religious affections woefully to degenerate, and sometimes, for a considerable time, to be like the manna that bred worms and stank; and dreadfully ensnares and confounds the minds of others of the saints and brings them into great difficulties and temptation, and entangles them in a wilderness, out of which they can by no means extricate themselves. By this means, Satan mightily encourages the hearts of open enemies of religion, and strengthens their hands, and fills them with weapons, and makes strong their fortresses; when, at the same time, religion and the church of God lie exposed to them, as a city without walls. By this means, he brings it to pass, that men work wickedness under a notion of doing God service, and so sin without restraint, yea with earnest forwardness and zeal, any with all their might. By this means he brings in even the friends of religion, insensibly to themselves, to do the work of enemies, by destroying religion in a far more effectual manner than open enemies can do, under a notion of advancing it. By this means the devil scatters the flock of Christ, and sets them one against another, and that with great heat of spirit, under a nation of zeal for God; and religion, by degrees degenerates into vain jangling; and during the strife, Satan leads both parties far out of the right way, driving each to great extremes, one on the right hand, and the other on the left, according as he finds they are most inclined, or most easily moved and swayed, till the right path in the middle is almost wholly neglected. And in the midst of this confusion, the devil has great opportunity to advance his own interest, and make it strong in ways innumerable, and get the government of all into his own hands and work his own will. And by what is seen of the terrible consequences of this counterfeit religion, when not distinguished from true religion, God's people in general have their minds unhinged and unsettled in things of religion, and know not where to set their foot, or what to think or do; and many are brought into doubts, whether there be anything in religion; and heresy, and infidelity, and atheism greatly prevail.

Therefore it greatly concerns us to use our utmost endeavors clearly to discern, and have it well settled and established, wherein true religion does consist. Till this be done, it may be expected, that great revivings of religion will be but of short continuance; till this be done, there is but little good to be expected of all our warm debates in conversation and from the press, not knowing clearly and distinctly what we ought to contend for.

My design is to contribute my mite, and use my best (however feeble) endeavors to this end, in the ensuing treatise; wherein it must be noted, that my design is somewhat diverse from the design of what I have formerly published, which was to show *the distinguishing marks of a work of the Spirit of God*, including both his common and saving operations; but what I aim at now, is to show the nature and signs of the *gracious operations* of God's Spirit, by which they are to be distinguished from all things whatsoever, that the minds of men are the subjects of, which are not of a saving nature. If I have succeeded, in this my aim, in any tolerable measure, I hope it will tend to promote the interest of religion. And whether I have succeeded to bring any light to this subject or no, and however my attempts may be reproached in these captious and censorious times, I hope in the mercy of a gracious God, for the acceptance of the sincerity of my endeavors; and hope also for the candor and prayers of the true followers of the meek and charitable Lamb of God.

✝ PART I ✝

CONCERNING THE NATURE OF THE AFFECTIONS AND THEIR IMPORTANCE IN RELIGION

1 Peter 1:8: *Whom having not seen, ye love; in whom, though now ye see him not, yet believing, ye rejoice with joy unspeakable and full of glory.*

IN these words, the apostle represents the state of the minds of the Christians he wrote to, under the persecutions they were then the subjects of. These persecutions are what he has respect to, in the two preceding verses, when he speaks of *the trial of their faith, and of their being in heaviness through manifold temptations.*

Such trials are of threefold benefit to true religion. Hereby the truth of it is manifested, and it appears to be indeed true religion; they, above all other things, have a tendency to distinguish between true religion and false, and to cause the difference between them evidently to appear. Hence they are called by the name of *trials*, in the verse nextly preceding the text, and in innumerable other places; they try the faith and religion of professors, of what sort it is, as apparent gold is tried in the fire, and manifested, whether it be true gold or no. And the faith of true Christians being thus tried and proved to be true, is 'found to praise, and honor, and glory,' as in that preceding verse.

And then, these trials are of further benefit to true religion; they not only manifest the truth of it, but they make its genuine beauty and amiableness remarkably to appear. True virtue never appears so lovely, as when it is most oppressed; and the divine excellency of real Christianity, is never exhibited with such advantage, as when under the greatest trials: then it is that true faith appears much more precious than gold! And upon this account is 'found to praise, and honor, and glory.'

And again, another benefit that such trials are of to true religion, is, that they purify and increase it. They not only manifest it to be true, but also tend to refine it, and deliver it from those mixtures of that which is false, which encumber and impede it; that nothing may be left but that which is true. They tend to cause the amiableness of true religion to appear to the best advantage, as was before observed; and not only so, but they tend to increase its beauty, by establishing and confirming it, and making it more lively and vigorous, and purifying it from those things that obscured its luster and glory. As gold that is tried in the fire, is purged from its alloy, and all remainders of dross, and comes forth more solid and beautiful; so true faith being tried as gold is tried in the fire, becomes more precious, and thus also is 'found unto praise, and honor, and glory.' The apostle seems to have respect to each of these benefits, that persecutions are of to true religion, in the verse preceding the text.

And, in the text, the apostle observes how true religion operated in the Christians he wrote to, under their persecutions, whereby these benefits of persecution appeared in them; or what manner of operation of true religion, in them, it was, whereby their religion, under persecution, was manifested to be true religion, and eminently appeared in the genuine beauty and amiableness of true religion, and also appeared to be increased and purified, and so was like to be 'found unto praise, and honor, and glory, at the appearing of Jesus Christ.' And there were two kinds of operation, or exercise of true religion, in them, under their sufferings, that the apostle takes notice of in the text, wherein these benefits appeared.

1.   *Love to Christ.* 'Whom having not yet seen, ye love.' The world was ready to wonder, what strange principle it was, that influenced them to expose themselves to so great sufferings, to forsake the things that were seen, and renounce all that was dear and pleasant, which was the object of sense. They seemed to the men of the world about them, as though they were beside themselves, and to act as though they hated themselves; there was nothing in their view, that could induce them thus to suffer, and support them under, and carry them through such trials. But although there was nothing that was seen, nothing that the world saw, or that the Christians themselves ever saw with their bodily eyes, that thus influenced and supported them, yet they had a supernatural principle of love to something unseen; they loved Jesus Christ, for they saw him spiritually whom the world saw not, and whom they themselves had never seen with bodily eyes.

2.   *Joy in Christ.* Though their outward sufferings were very grievous, yet their inward spiritual joys were greater than their sufferings; and these supported them, and enabled them to suffer with cheerfulness.

There are two things which the apostle takes notice of in the text concerning this joy. 1. The manner in which it rises, the way in which Christ, though unseen, is the foundation of it, viz., by faith; which is the evidence of things not seen: 'In whom, though now ye see him not, yet believing, ye rejoice.' 2. The nature of this joy, 'unspeakable and full of glory.' Unspeakable in the kind of it; very different from worldly joys, and carnal delights; of a vastly more pure, sublime, and heavenly nature, being something supernatural, and truly divine, and so ineffably excellent; the sublimity and exquisite sweetness of which, there were no words to set forth. Unspeakable also in degree; it pleasing God to give them this holy joy, with a liberal hand, and in large measure, in their state of persecution.

Their joy was full of glory. Although the joy was unspeakable, and no words were sufficient to describe it, yet something might be said of it, and no words more fit to represent its excellency than these, that it was *full of glory*; or, as it is in the original, *glorified joy*. In rejoicing with this joy, their minds were filled, as it were, with a glorious brightness, and their natures exalted and perfected. It was a most worthy, noble rejoicing, that did not corrupt and debase the mind, as many carnal joys do; but did greatly beautify and dignify it; it was a prelibation of the joy of heaven, that raised their minds to a degree of heavenly blessedness; it filled their minds with the light of God's glory, and made themselves to shine with some communication of that glory.

Hence the proposition or doctrine, that I would raise from these words, is this:

DOCTRINE. *True religion, in great part, consists in holy affections.*

We see that the apostle, in observing and remarking the operations and exercises of religion in the Christians he wrote to, wherein their religion appeared to be true and of the right kind, when it had its greatest trial of what sort it was, being tried by persecution as gold is tried in the fire, and when their religion not only proved true, but was most pure, and cleansed from its dross and mixtures of that which was not true, and when religion appeared in them most in its genuine excellency and native beauty, and was found to praise, and honor, and glory; he singles out the religious affections of *love* and *joy*, that were then in exercise in them: these are the exercises of religion he takes notice of wherein their religion did thus appear true and pure, and in its proper glory. Here, I would,

1. Show what is intended by the affections.
2. Observe some things which make it evident, that a great part of true religion lies in the affections.

1. It may be inquired, what the affections of the mind are? I answer: The affections are no other than the more vigorous and sensible exercises of the inclination and will of the soul.

God has endued the soul with two faculties: one is that by which it is capable of perception and speculation, or by which it discerns, and views, and judges of things; which is called the understanding. The other faculty is that by which the soul does not merely perceive and view things, but is some way inclined with respect to the things it views or considers; either is inclined *to* them, or is disinclined and averse *from* them; or is the faculty by which the soul does not behold things, as an indifferent unaffected spectator, but either as liking or disliking, pleased or displeased, approving or rejecting. This faculty is called by various names; it is sometimes called the *inclination*: and, as it has respect to the actions that are determined and governed by it, is called the *will*: and the mind, with regard to the exercises of this faculty, is often called the *heart*.

The exercise of this faculty are of two sorts; either those by which the soul is carried out towards the things that are in view, in approving of them, being pleased with them, and inclined to them; or those in which the soul opposes the things that are in view, in disapproving of them, and in being displeased with them, averse from them, and rejecting them.

And as the exercises of the inclination and will of the soul are various in their kinds, so they are much more various in their degrees. There are some exercises of pleasedness or displeasedness, inclination or disinclination, wherein the soul is carried but a little beyond the state of indifference. And there are other degrees above this, wherein the approbation or dislike, pleasedness or aversion, are stronger, wherein we may rise higher and higher, till the soul comes to act vigorously and sensibly, and the actings of the soul are with that strength, that (through the laws of the union which the Creator has fixed between the soul and the body) the motion of the blood and animal spirits begins to be sensibly altered; whence oftentimes arises some bodily sensation, especially about the heart and vitals, that are the fountain of the fluids of the body: from whence it comes to pass, that the mind, with regard to the exercises of this faculty, perhaps in all nations and ages, is called the *heart*. And it is to be noted, that they are these more vigorous and sensible exercises of this faculty that are called the *affections*.

The will, and the affections of the soul, are not two faculties; the affections are not essentially distinct from the will, nor do they differ from the mere actings of the will, and inclination of the soul, but only in the liveliness and sensibleness of exercise.

It must be confessed, that language is here somewhat imperfect, and the meaning of words in a considerable measure loose and unfixed, and not precisely limited by custom, which governs the use of language. In some sense, the affection of the soul differs nothing at all from the will and inclination, and the will never is in any exercise any further than it is affected; it is not moved out of a state of perfect indifference, any otherwise than as it is affected one way or other, and acts nothing any further. But yet there are many actings of the will and inclination, that are not so commonly called *affections*: in everything we do, wherein we act voluntarily, there is an exercise of the will and inclination; it is our inclination that governs us in our actions; but all the actings of the inclination and will, in all our common actions of life, are not ordinarily called affections. Yet, what are commonly called affections are not essentially different from them, but only in the degree and manner of exercise. In every act of the will whatsoever, the soul either likes or dislikes, is either inclined or disinclined to what is in view: these are not essentially different from those affections of love and hatred: that liking or inclination of the soul to a thing, if it be in a high degree, and be vigorous and lively, is the very same thing with the affection of love; and that disliking and disinclining, if in a greater degree, is the very same with hatred. In every act of the will for, or towards something not present, the soul is in some degree inclined to that thing; and that inclination, if in a considerable degree, is the very same with the affection of desire. And in every degree of the act of the will, wherein the soul approves of something present, there is a degree of pleasedness; and that pleasedness, if it be in a considerable degree, is the very same with the affections of joy or delight. And if the will disapproves of what is present, the soul is in some degree displeased, and if that displeasedness be great, it is the very same with the affection of grief or sorrow.

Such seems to be our nature, and such the laws of the union of soul and body, that there never is in any case whatsoever, any lively and vigorous exercise of the will or inclination of the soul, without some effect upon the body, in some alteration of the motion of its fluids, and especially of the animal spirits. And, on the other hand, from the same laws of the union of the soul and body, the constitution of the body, and the motion of its fluids, may promote the exercise of the affections. But yet it is not the body, but the mind only, that is the proper seat of the affections. The body of man is no more capable of being really the subject of love or hatred, joy or sorrow, fear or hope, than the body of a tree, or than the same body of man is capable of thinking and understanding. As it is the soul only that has ideas, so it is the soul only that is pleased or displeased with its ideas. As it is the soul only that thinks, so it is the soul only that loves or hates, rejoices or is grieved at what it thinks of. Nor are these motions of the animal spirits, and fluids of the body, anything properly belonging to the nature of the affections, though they always accompany them, in the present state; but are only effects or concomitants of the affections that are entirely distinct from the affections themselves, and no way essential to them; so that an unbodied spirit may be as capable of love and hatred, joy or sorrow, hope or fear, or other affections, as one that is united to a body.

The affections and passions are frequently spoken of as the same; and yet in the more common use of speech, there is in some respect a difference; and affection is a word that in its ordinary signification, seems to be something more extensive than passion, being used for all vigorous lively actings of the will or inclination; but passion for those that are more sudden, and whose effects on the animal spirits are more violent, and the mind more overpowered, and less in its own command.

As all the exercises of the inclination and will, are either in approving and liking, or disapproving and rejecting; so the affections are of two sorts; they are those by which the soul is carried out to what is in view, cleaving to it, or seeking it; or those by which it is averse from it, and opposes it.

Of the former sort are love, desire, hope, joy, gratitude, complacence. Of the latter kind are hatred, fear, anger, grief, and such like; which it is needless now to stand particularly to define.

And there are some affections wherein there is a composition of each of the aforementioned kinds of actings of the will; as in the affection of *pity*, there is something of the former kind, towards the person suffering, and something of the latter towards what he suffers. And so in zeal, there is in it high approbation of some person or thing, together with vigorous opposition to what is conceived to be contrary to it.

There are other mixed affections that might be also mentioned, but I hasten to,

2. The second thing proposed, which was to observe some things that render it evident, that true religion, in great part consists in the affections. And here,

1. *What has been said of the nature of the affections makes this evident, and may be sufficient, without adding anything further, to put this matter out of doubt; for who will deny that true religion consists in a great measure, in vigorous and lively actings of the inclination and will of the soul, or the fervent exercises of the heart?*

That religion which God requires, and will accept, does not consist in weak, dull, and lifeless wishes, raising us but a little above a state of indifference: God, in his word, greatly insists upon it, that we be good in earnest, 'fervent in spirit,' and our hearts vigorously engaged in religion: Rom. 12:11, 'Be ye fervent in spirit, serving the Lord.' Deut. 10:12, 'And now, Israel, what doth the Lord thy God require of thee, but to fear the Lord the God, to walk in all his ways, and to love him, and to serve the Lord thy God with all thy heart, and with all thy soul?' and chap. 6:4, 6, 'Hear, O Israel, the Lord our God is one Lord: And thou shalt love the Lord thy God with all thy heart, and with all thy might.' It is such a fervent vigorous engagedness of the heart in religion, that is the fruit of a real circumcision of the heart, or true regeneration, and that has the promises of life; Deut. 30:6, 'And the Lord thy God will circumcise thine heart, and the heart of thy seed, to love the Lord thy God with all thy heart, and with all thy soul, that thou mayest live.'

If we be not in good earnest in religion, and our wills and inclinations be not strongly exercised, we are nothing. The things of religion are so great, that there can be no suitableness in the exercises of our hearts, to their nature and importance, unless they be lively and powerful. In nothing is vigor in the actings of our inclinations so requisite, as in religion; and in nothing is lukewarmness so odious. True religion is evermore a powerful thing; and the power of it appears, in the first place in the inward exercises of it in the heart, where is the principal and original seat of it. Hence true religion is called the *power of godliness*, in distinction from the external appearances of it, that are the *form* of it, 2 Tim. 3:5: 'Having a form of godliness, but denying the power of it.' The Spirit of God, in those that have sound and solid religion, is a spirit of powerful holy affection; and therefore, God is said 'to have given the Spirit of power, and of love, and of a sound mind,' 2 Tim. 1:7. And such, when they receive the Spirit of God, in his sanctifying and saving influences, are said to be 'baptized with the Holy Ghost, and with fire,' by reason of the power and fervor of those exercises the Spirit of God excites in their hearts, whereby their hearts, when grace is in exercise, may be said to 'burn within them,' as is said of the disciples, Luke 24:32.

The business of religion is from time to time compared to those exercises, wherein men are wont to have their hearts and strength greatly exercised and engaged, such as running, wrestling or agonizing for a great prize or crown, and fighting with strong enemies that seek our lives, and warring as those, that by violence take a city or kingdom.

And though true grace has various degrees, and there are some that are but babes in Christ, in whom the exercise of the inclination and will, towards divine and heavenly things, is comparatively weak; yet everyone that has the power of godliness in his heart, has his inclinations and heart exercised towards God and divine things, with such strength and vigor that these holy exercises do prevail in him above all carnal or natural affections, and are effectual to overcome them: for every true disciple of Christ 'loves him above father or mother, wife and children, brethren and sisters, houses and lands: yea, than his own life.' From hence it follows, that wherever true religion is, there are vigorous exercises of the inclination and will towards divine objects: but by what was said before, the vigorous, lively, and sensible exercises of the will, are no other than the affections of the soul.

2. *The Author of the human nature has not only given affections to men, but has made them very much the spring of men's actions.* As the affections do not only necessarily belong to the human nature, but are a very great part of it; so (inasmuch as by regeneration persons are renewed in the whole man, and sanctified throughout) holy affections do not only necessarily belong to true religion, but are a very great part of it. And as true religion is of a practical nature, and God hath so constituted the human nature, that the affections are very much the spring of men's actions, this also shows, that true religion must consist very much in the affections.

Such is man's nature, that he is very inactive, any otherwise than he is influenced by some affection, either love or hatred, desire, hope, fear, or some other. These affections we see to be the springs that set men agoing, in all the affairs of life, and engage them in all their pursuits: these are the things that put men forward, and carry them along, in all their worldly business; and especially are men excited and animated by these, in all affairs wherein they are earnestly engaged, and which they pursue with vigor. We see the world of mankind to be exceeding busy and active; and the affections of men are the springs of the motion: take away all love and hatred, all hope and fear, all anger, zeal, and affectionate desire, and the world would be, in a great measure motionless and dead; there would be no such thing as activity amongst mankind, or any earnest pursuit whatsoever. It is affection that engages the covetous man, and him that is greedy of worldly profits, in his pursuits; and it is by the affections, that the ambitious man is put forward in pursuit of worldly glory; and it is the affections also that actuate the voluptuous man, in his pursuit of pleasure and sensual delights: the world continues, from age to age, in a continual commotion and agitation, in a pursuit of these things, but take away all affection, and the spring of all this motion would be gone, and the motion itself would cease. And as in worldly things, worldly affections are very much the spring of men's motion and action; so in religious matters, the spring of their actions is very much religious affection: he that has doctrinal knowledge and speculation only, without affection, never is engaged in the business of religion.

3. *Nothing is more manifest in fact, than that the things of religion take hold of men's souls, no further than they affect them.* There are multitudes that often hear the word of God, and therein hear of those things that are infinitely great and important, and that most nearly concern them, and all that is heard seems to be wholly ineffectual upon them, and to make no alteration in their disposition or behavior; and the reason is, they are not affected with what they hear. There are many that often hear of the glorious perfections of God, his almighty power and boundless wisdom, his infinite majesty, and that holiness of God, by which he is of purer eyes than to behold evil, and cannot look on iniquity, and the heavens are not pure in his sight, and of God's infinite goodness and mercy, and hear of the great works of God's wisdom, power and goodness, wherein there appear the admirable manifestations of these perfections; they hear particularly of the unspeakable love of God and Christ, and of the great things that Christ has done and suffered, and of the great things of another world, of eternal misery in bearing the fierceness and wrath of Almighty God, and of endless blessedness and glory in the presence of God, and the enjoyment of his dear love; they also hear the peremptory commands of God, and his gracious counsels and warnings, and the sweet invitations of the gospel; I say, they often hear these things and yet remain as they were before, with no sensible alteration in them, either in heart or practice, because they are not affected with what they hear; and ever will be so till they are affected. I am bold to assert, that there never was any considerable change wrought in the mind or conversation of any person, by anything of a religious nature, that ever he read, heard or saw, that had not his affections moved. Never was a natural man engaged earnestly to seek his salvation; never were any such brought to cry after wisdom, and lift up their voice for understanding, and to wrestle with God in prayer for mercy; and never was one humbled, and brought to the foot of God, from anything that ever he heard or imagined of his own unworthiness and deserving of God's displeasure; nor was ever one induced to fly for refuge unto Christ, while his heart remained unaffected. Nor was there ever a saint awakened out of a cold, lifeless flame, or recovered from a declining state in religion, and brought back from a lamentable departure from God, without having his heart affected. And in a word, there never was anything considerable brought to pass in the heart or life of any man living, by the things of religion, that had not his heart deeply affected by those things.

4. *The holy Scriptures do everywhere place religion very much in the affection; such as fear, hope, love, hatred, desire, joy, sorrow, gratitude, compassion, and zeal.*

The Scriptures place much of religion in godly fear; insomuch, that it is often spoken of as the character of those that are truly religious persons, that they tremble at God's word, that they fear before him, that their flesh trembles for fear of him, and that they are afraid of his judgments, that his excellency makes them afraid, and his dread falls upon them, and the like: and a compellation commonly given the saints in Scripture, is 'fearers of God,' or, 'they that fear the Lord.' And because the fear of God is a great part of true godliness, hence true godliness in general, is very commonly called by the name of *the fear of God*, as everyone knows, that knows anything of the Bible.

So hope in God and in the promises of his word, is often spoken of in the Scripture, as a very considerable part of true religion. It is mentioned as one of the three great things of which religion consists, 1 Cor. 13:13. Hope in the Lord is also frequently mentioned as the character of the saints: Ps. 146:5, 'Happy is he that hath the God of Jacob for his help, whose hope is in the

Lord his God.' Jer. 17:7, 'Blessed is the man that trusteth in the Lord, and whose hope the Lord is.' Ps. 31:24, 'Be of good courage, and he shall strengthen your heart, all ye that hope in the Lord.' And the like in many other places. Religious fear and hope are, once and again, joined together, as jointly constituting the character of the true saints; Ps. 33:18, 'Behold, the eye of the Lord is upon them that fear him, upon them that hope in his mercy.' Ps. 147:11, 'The Lord taketh pleasure in them that fear him, in those that hope in his mercy.' Hope is so great a part of true religion, that the apostle says, 'we are saved by hope,' Rom. 8:24. And this is spoken of as the helmet of the Christian soldier. 1 Thess. 5:8, 'And for a helmet, the *hope* of salvation; and the sure and steadfast anchor of the soul, which preserves it from being cast away by the storms of this evil world.' Heb. 6:19, 'Which hope we have as an anchor of the soul, both sure and steadfast, and which entereth into that within the vail.' It is spoken of as a great fruit and benefit which true saints receive by Christ's resurrection: 1 Pet. 1:3, 'Blessed be the God and Father of our Lord Jesus Christ, which, according to his abundant mercy, hath begotten us again unto a lively hope, by the resurrection of Jesus Christ from the dead.'

The Scriptures place religion very much in the affection of love, in *love* to God, and the Lord Jesus Christ, and love to the people of God, and to mankind. The texts in which this is manifest, both in the Old Testament and New, are innumerable. But of this more afterwards.

The contrary affection of *hatred* also, as having sin for its object, is spoken of in Scripture as no inconsiderable part of true religion. It is spoken of as that by which true religion may be known and distinguished; Prov. 8:13, 'The fear of the Lord is to hate evil.' And accordingly the saints are called upon to give evidence of their sincerity by this; Ps. 97:10, 'Ye that love the Lord hate evil.' And the Psalmist often mentions it as an evidence of his sincerity; Ps. 2, 3, 'I will walk within my house with a perfect heart. I will set no wicked thing before mine eyes; I hate the work of them that turn aside.' Ps. 119:104, 'I hate every false way.' So v. 127. Again, Ps. 139:21, 'Do I not hate them, O Lord, that hate thee?'

So holy desire, exercised in longings, hungerings, and thirstings after God and holiness, is often mentioned in Scripture as an important part of true religion; Isa. 26:8, 'The desire of our soul is to thy name, and to the remembrance of thee.' Ps. 27:4, 'One thing have I desired of the Lord, and that will I seek after, that I may dwell in the house of the Lord all the days of my life, to behold the beauty of the Lord, and to inquire in his temple.' Ps. 42:1, 2, 'As the hart panteth after the water brooks, so panteth my soul after thee, O God; my soul thirsteth for God, for the living God: when shall I come and appear before God?' Ps. 63:1, 2, 'My soul thirsteth for thee, my flesh longeth for thee, in a dry and thirsty land, where no water is; to see thy power and thy glory, so as I have seen thee in the sanctuary.' Ps. 84:1, 2, 'How amiable are thy tabernacles, O Lord of hosts! My soul longeth, yea, even fainteth for the courts of the Lord: my heart and my flesh crieth out for the living God.' Ps. 119:20, 'My soul breaketh for the longing that it hath unto thy judgments at all times.' So Pss. 73:25, 143:6, 7, and 130:6. Cant. 3:1, 2, and 6:8. Such a holy desire and thirst of soul is mentioned, as one thing which renders or denotes a man truly blessed, in the beginning of Christ's sermon on the mount, Matt. 5:6: 'Blessed are they that do hunger and thirst after righteousness; for they shall be filled.' And this holy thirst is spoken of, as a great thing in the condition of a participation of the blessings of eternal life; Rev. 21:6, 'I will give unto him that is athirst, of the fountain of the water of life freely.'

The Scriptures speaks of holy joy, as a great part of true religion. So it is represented in the text. And as an important part of religion, it is often exhorted to, and pressed, with great earnestness; Ps. 37:4, 'Delight thyself in the Lord; and he shall give thee the desires of thine heart.' Ps. 97:12, 'Rejoice in the Lord, ye righteous.' So Ps. 33:1, 'Rejoice in the Lord, O ye righteous.' Matt. 5:12, 'Rejoice, and be exceeding glad.' Phil. 3:1, 'Finally, brethren, rejoice in the Lord.' And chap. 4:4, 'Rejoice in the Lord alway; and again I say, Rejoice.' 1 Thess. 5:16, 'Rejoice evermore.' Ps. 149:2, 'Let Israel rejoice in him that made him; let the children of Zion be joyful in their king.' This is mentioned among the principal fruits of the Spirit of grace; Gal. 5:21, 'The fruit of the Spirit is love,' etc. The Psalmist mentions his holy joy, as an evidence of his sincerity. Ps. 119:14, 'I have rejoiced in the way of thy testimonies, as much as in all riches.'

Religious sorrow, mourning, and brokenness of heart, are also frequently spoken of as a great part of true religion. These things are often mentioned as distinguishing qualities of the true saints, and a great part of their character; Matt. 5:4, 'Blessed are they that mourn; for they shall be comforted.' Ps. 34:18, 'The Lord is nigh unto them that are of a broken heart; and saveth such as be of a contrite spirit.' Isa. 61:1, 2, 'The Lord hath anointed me, to bind up the broken-hearted, to comfort all that mourn.' This godly sorrow and brokenness of heart is often spoken of, not only as a great thing in the distinguishing character of the saints, but that in them, which is peculiarly acceptable and pleasing to God; Ps. 51:17, 'The sacrifices of God are a broken spirit: a broken and a contrite heart, O God, thou wilt not despise.' Isa. 57:15, 'Thus saith the high and lofty One that inhabiteth eternity, whose name is holy, I dwell in the high and holy place; with him also that is of a contrite and humble spirit, to revive the spirit of the humble, and to revive the heart of the contrite ones.' Chap. 66:2, 'To this man will I look, even to him that is poor, and of a contrite spirit.'

Another affection often mentioned, as that in the exercise of which much of true religion appears, is *gratitude*, especially as exercised in thankfulness and praise to God. This being so much spoken of in the book of Psalms, and other parts of the holy Scriptures, I need not mention particular texts.

Again, the holy Scriptures do frequently speak of compassion or mercy, as a very great and essential thing in true religion, insomuch that good men are in Scripture denominated from hence; and a merciful man and a good man are equivalent terms in Scripture; Isa. 57:1, 'The righteous perisheth, and no man layeth it to heart; and merciful men are taken away.' And the Scripture chooses out this quality, as that by which, in a peculiar manner, a righteous man is deciphered; Ps. 37:21, 'The righteous showeth mercy, and giveth;' and v. 26, 'He is ever merciful, and lendeth.' And Prov. 14:21, 'He that honoreth the Lord, hath mercy on the poor.' And Col. 3:12, 'Put ye on, as the elect of God, holy and beloved, bowels of mercies,' etc. This is one of those great things by which those who are truly blessed are described by our Savior; Matt. 5:7, 'Blessed are the merciful, for they shall obtain mercy.' And this Christ also speaks of, as one of the weightier matters of the law; Matt. 23:23, 'Woe unto you, scribes and Pharisees, hypocrites, for ye pay tithe of mint, and anise, and cummin, and have omitted the weightier matters of the law, judgment, mercy, and faith.' To the like purpose is that, Mic. 6:8, 'He hath showed thee, O man, what is good: and what doth the Lord require of thee, but to do justice, and love mercy, and walk humbly with thy God?' And also that, Hos. 6:6 'For I desired mercy, and not sacrifice.' Which seems to have been a text much delighted in by our Savior, by his manner of citing it once and again, Matt. 9:13, and 12:7.

Zeal is also spoken of, as a very essential part of the religion of true saints. It is spoken of as a great thing Christ had in view, in giving himself for our redemption; Tit. 2:14, 'Who gave himself for us, that he might redeem us from all iniquity, and purify unto himself a peculiar people, zealous of good works.' And this is spoken of, as the great thing wanting in the lukewarm Laodiceans, Rev. 3:15, 16, 19.

I have mentioned but a few texts, out of an innumerable multitude, all over the Scripture, which place religion very much in the affections. But what has been observed, may be sufficient to show that they who would deny that much of true religion lies in the affections, and maintain the contrary, must throw away what we have been wont to own for our Bible, and get some other rule, by which to judge of the nature of religion.

5. *The Scriptures do represent true religion, as being summarily comprehended in love, the chief of the affections, and fountain of all other affections.*

So our blessed Savior represents the matter, in answer to the lawyer, who asked him, which was the great commandment of the law Matt. 22:37-40: 'Jesus said unto him, Thou shalt love the Lord thy God with all thy heart, and with all thy soul, and with all thy mind. This is the first and great commandment. And the second is like unto it, Thou shalt love thy neighbor as thyself. On these two commandments hang all the law and the prophets.' Which last words signify as much, as that these two commandments comprehend all the duty prescribed, and the religion taught in the law and the prophets. And the apostle Paul does from time to time make the same representation of the matter; as in Rom. 13:8, 'He that loveth another, hath fulfilled the law.' And v. 10, 'Love is the fulfilling of the law.' And Gal. 5:14, 'For all the law is fulfilled in one word, even in this, Thou shalt love thy neighbor as thyself.' So likewise in 1 Tim. 1:5, 'Now the end of the commandment is charity, out of a pure heart,' etc. So the same apostle speaks of love, as the greatest thing in religion, and as the vitals, essence and soul of it; without which, the greatest knowledge and gifts, and the most glaring profession, and everything else which appertains to religion, are vain and worthless; and represents it as the fountain from whence proceeds all that is good, in 1 Cor. 13 throughout; for that which is there rendered *charity*, in the original is *agape*, the proper English of which is *love*.

Now, although it be true, that the love thus spoken of includes the whole of a sincerely benevolent propensity of the soul towards God and man; yet it may be considered, that it is evident from what has been before observed, that this propensity or inclination of the soul, when in sensible and vigorous exercise, becomes affection, and is no other than affectionate love. And surely it is such vigorous and fervent love which Christ speaks of, as the sum of all religion, when he speaks of loving God with all our hearts, with all our souls, and with all our minds, and our neighbor as ourselves, as the sum of all that was taught and prescribed in the law and the prophets.

Indeed it cannot be supposed, when this affection of love is here, and in other Scriptures, spoken of as the sum of all religion, that hereby is meant the act, exclusive of the habit, or that the exercise of the understanding is excluded, which is implied in all reasonable affection. But it is doubtless true, and evident from these Scriptures, that the essence of all true religion lies in holy love; and that in this divine affection, and an habitual disposition to it, and that light which is the foundation of it, and those things which are the fruits of it, consists the whole of religion.

From hence it clearly and certainly appears, that great part of true religion consists in the affections. For love is not only one of the affections, but it is the first and chief of the affections, and the fountain of all the affections. From love arises hatred of those things which are contrary to what we love, or which oppose and thwart us in those things that we delight in: and from the various exercises of love and hatred, according to the circumstances of the objects of these affections, as present or absent, certain or uncertain, probable or improbable, arise all those other affections of desire, hope, fear, joy, grief, gratitude, anger, etc. From a vigorous, affectionate, and fervent love to God, will necessarily arise other religious affections; hence will arise an intense hatred and abhorrence of sin, fear of sin, and a dread of God's displeasure, gratitude to God for his goodness, complacence and joy in God, when God is graciously and sensibly present, and grief when he is absent, and a joyful hope when a future enjoyment of God is expected, and fervent zeal for the glory of God. And in like manner, from a fervent love to men, will arise all other virtuous affections towards men.

6. *The religion of the most eminent saints we have an account of in the Scripture, consisted much in holy affections.*

I shall take particular notice of three eminent saints, who have expressed the frame and sentiments of their own hearts, and so described their own religion, and the manner of their intercourse with God, in the writings which they have left us, that are a part of the sacred canon.

The first instance I shall take notice of, is David, that 'man after God's own heart,' who has given us a lively portraiture of his religion in the book of Psalms. Those holy songs of his he has there left us, are nothing else but the expressions and breathings of devout and holy affections; such as an humble and fervent love to God, admiration of his glorious perfections and wonderful works, earnest desires, thirstings, and pantings of soul after God, delight and joy in God, a sweet and melting gratitude to God, for his great goodness, a holy exultation and triumph of soul in the favor, sufficiency, and faithfulness of God, his love to, and delight in the saints, the excellent of the earth, his great delight in the word and ordinances of God, his grief for his own and others' sins, and his fervent zeal for God, and against the enemies of God and his church. And these expressions of holy affection, which the psalms of David are everywhere full of, are the more to our present purpose, because those psalms are not only the expressions of the religion of so eminent a saint, that God speaks of as so agreeable to his mind; but were also, by the direction of the Holy Ghost, penned for the use of the church of God in its public worship, not only in that age, but in after ages; as being fitted to express the religion of all saints, in all ages, as well as the religion of the Psalmist. And it is moreover to be observed, that David, in the book of Psalms, speaks not as a private person, but as the Psalmist of Israel, as the subordinate head of the church of God, and leader in their worship and praises; and in many of the psalms speaks in the name of Christ, as personating him in these breathings forth of holy affection; and in many other psalms he speaks in the name of the church.

Another instance I shall observe, is the apostle Paul; who was in many respects, the chief of all the ministers of the New Testament; being above all others, a chosen vessel unto Christ, to bear his name before the Gentiles, and made a chief instrument of propagating and establishing the Christian church in the world, and of distinctly revealing the glorious mysteries of the gospel, for the instruction of the church in all ages; and (as has not been improperly thought by some) the most eminent servant of Christ that ever lived, received to the highest rewards in the heavenly kingdom of his Master. By what is said of him in the Scripture, he appears to have been a person that was full of affection. And it is very manifest, that the religion he expresses in his epistles, consisted very much in holy affections. It appears by all his expressions of himself, that he was, in the course of his life, inflamed, actuated, and entirely swallowed up, by a most ardent love to his glorious Lord, esteeming all things as loss, for the excellency of the knowledge of him, and esteeming them but dung that he might win him. He represents himself, as overpowered by this holy affection, and as it were compelled by it to go forward in his service, through all difficulties and sufferings, 2 Cor. 5:14, 15. And his epistles are full of expressions of an overpowering affection towards the people of Christ. He speaks of his dear love to them, 2 Cor. 12:19, Phil. 4:1, 2 Tim. 1:2; of his 'abundant love,' 2 Cor. 2:4; and of his 'affectionate and tender love,' as of a nurse towards her children, 1 Thess. 2:7, 8: 'But we were gentle among you, even as a nurse cherisheth her children; so, being affectionately desirous of you we were willing to have imparted unto you, not the gospel of God only, but also our own souls, because ye were dear unto us.' So also he speaks of his 'bowels of love,' Phil. 1:8, Philem. 5, 12, and 20. So he speaks of his 'earnest care' for others, 2 Cor. 8:16, and of his 'bowels of pity, or mercy towards them,' Phil. 2:1; and of his 'concern for others, even to anguish of heart,' 2 Cor. 2:4: 'For out of much affliction and anguish of heart, I wrote unto you with many tears; not that you should be grieved, but that ye might know the love which I have more abundantly unto you.' He speaks of the great conflict of his soul for them, Col. 2:1. He speaks of great and continual grief that he had in his heart from compassion to the Jews, Rom. 9:2. He speaks of 'his mouth's being opened, and his heart enlarged' towards Christians, 2 Cor. 6:11: 'O ye Corinthians, our mouth is open unto you, our heart is enlarged.' He often speaks of his 'affectionate and longing desires,' 1 Thess. 2:8, Rom. 1:11, Phil. 1:8, and chap. 4:1, 2 Tim. 1:4. The same apostle is very often, in his epistles, expressing the affection of *joy*, 2 Cor. 1:12 and chap. 7:7, and vv. 9, 16. Phil. 1:4, and chap. 2:12, and chap 3:3. Col. 1:34, 1 Thess. 3:9. He speaks of his 'rejoicing with great joy,' Phil 4:10, Philem. 1:7; of his 'joying and rejoicing,' Phil. 2:1, 7, and 'of his rejoicing exceedingly,' 2 Cor. 7:13, and of his being 'filled with comfort, and being exceeding joyful,' 2 Cor. 7:4. He speaks of himself as 'always rejoicing,' 2 Cor. 6:10. So he speaks of the triumphs of his soul, 2 Cor. 2:14, and of his glorying in tribulation, 2 Thess. 1:4, and Rom. 5:3. He also expresses the affection of *hope*, in Phil. 1:20, he speaks of his 'earnest expectation, and his hope.' He likewise expresses an affection of *godly jealousy*, 2 Cor. 11:2, 3. And it appears by his whole history, after his conversion, in the Acts, and also by all his epistles, and the accounts he gives of himself there that the affection of *zeal*, as having the cause of his Master, and the interest and prosperity of his church, for its object, was mighty in him, continually inflaming his heart, strongly engaging to those great and constant labors he went through, in instructing, exhorting, warning, and reproving others, 'travailing in birth with them,' conflicting with those powerful and innumerable enemies who continually opposed him, wrestling with principalities and powers, not fighting as one who beats the air, running the race set before him, continually pressing forwards through all manner of difficulties and sufferings; so that others thought him quite beside himself. And how full he was of affection, does further appear by his being so full of tears: in 2 Cor. 2:4, he speaks of his a many tears; and so Acts 20:19; and of his 'tears that he shed continually night and day,' v. 31.

Now if anyone can consider these accounts given in the Scripture of this great apostle, and which he gives of himself, and yet not see that his religion consisted much in affection, must have a strange faculty of managing his eyes to shut out the light which shines most full in his face.

The other instance I shall mention, is of the apostle John, that beloved disciple, who was the nearest and dearest to his Master, of any of the twelve, and was by him admitted to the greatest privileges of any of them; being not only one of the three who were admitted to be present with him in the mount at his transfiguration, and at the raising of Jairus's daughter, and whom he took with him when he was in his agony, and one of the three spoken of by the apostle Paul, as the three main pillars of the Christian church; but was favored above all, in being admitted to lean on his Master's bosom at his last supper, and in being chosen by Christ, as the disciple to whom he would reveal his wonderful dispensations towards his church, to the end of time; as we have an account in the Book of Revelation; and to shut up the canon of the New Testament, and of the whole Scripture; being preserved much longer than all the rest of the apostles, to set all things in order in the Christian church, after their death.

It is evident by all his writings (as is generally observed by divines) that he was a person remarkably full of affection: his addresses to those whom he wrote to being inexpressibly tender and pathetical, breathing nothing but the most fervent love; as though he were all made up of sweet and holy affection. The proofs of which cannot be given without disadvantage, unless we should transcribe his whole writings.

7. *He whom God sent into the world to be the light of the world, and head of the whole church, and the perfect example of true religion and virtue, for the imitation of all, the Shepherd whom the whole flock should follow wherever he goes, even the Lord Jesus Christ, was a person who was remarkably of a tender and affectionate heart; and his virtue was expressed very much in the exercise of holy affections.* He was the greatest instance of ardency, vigor and strength of love, to both God and man, that ever was. It was these affections which got the victory, in that mighty struggle and conflict of his affections, in his agonies, when 'he prayed more earnestly, and offered strong crying and tears,' and wrestled in tears and in blood. Such was the power of the exercises of his holy love, that they were stronger than death, and in that great struggle, overcame those strong exercises of the natural affections of fear and grief, when he was sore amazed, and his soul was exceeding sorrowful, even unto death. And he also appeared to be full of affection in the course of his life. We read of his great zeal, fulfilling that in the 69th Psalm, 'The zeal of thine house hath eaten me up,' John 2:17. We read of his grief for the sins of men, Mark 3:5: 'He looked round about on them with anger, being grieved for the hardness of their hearts;' and his breaking forth in tears and exclamations, from the consideration of the sin and misery of ungodly men and on the sight of the city of Jerusalem, which was full of such inhabitants, Luke 19:41, 42: 'And, when he was come near, he beheld the city, and wept over it, saying, if thou hadst known, even thou, at least in this thy day, the things which belong unto thy peace! But now they are hid from thine eyes.' With chap. 13:34, 'O Jerusalem, Jerusalem, which killest the prophets, and stonest them that are sent unto thee; how often would I have gathered thy children together, as a hen doth gather her brood under her wings, and ye would not!' We read of Christ's earnest desire, Luke 22:15: 'With desire have I desired to eat this passover with you before I suffer.' We often read of the affection of pity or compassion in

Christ, Matt. 15:32, and 18:34. Luke 7:13, and of his 'being moved with compassion,' Matt. 9:36, and 14:14, and Mark 6:34. And how tender did his heart appear to be, on occasion of Mary's and Martha's mourning for their brother, and coming to him with their complaints and tears! Their tears soon drew tears from his eyes he was affected with their grief, and wept with them; though he knew their sorrow should so soon be turned into joy, by their brother's being raised from the dead; see John 11. And how ineffably affectionate was that last and dying discourse, which Jesus had with his eleven disciples the evening before he was crucified; when he told them he was going away, and foretold them the great difficulties and sufferings they should meet with in the world, when he was gone; and comforted and counseled them as his dear little children; and bequeathed to them his Holy Spirit, and therein his peace, and his comfort and joy, as it were in his last will and testament, in the 13th, 14th, 15th, and 16th chapters of John; and concluded the whole with that affectionate intercessory prayer for them, and his whole church, in chap. 17. Of all the discourses ever penned, or uttered by the mouth of any man, this seems to be the most affectionate and affecting.

   8.   *The religion of heaven consists very much in affection.*

   There is doubtless true religion in heaven, and true religion in its utmost purity and perfection. But according to the Scripture representation of the heavenly state, the religion of heaven consists chiefly in holy and mighty love and joy, and the expression of these in most fervent and exalted praises. So that the religion of the saints in heaven, consists in the same things with that religion of the saints on earth, which is spoken of in our text, viz., love, and 'joy unspeakable and full of glory.' Now it would be very foolish to pretend, that because the saints in heaven be not united to flesh and blood, and have no animal fluids to be moved (through the laws of union of soul and body) with those great emotions of their souls, that therefore their exceeding love and joy are no affections. We are not speaking of the affections of the body, but of the affections of the soul, the chief of which are *love* and *joy*. When these are in the soul, whether that be in the body or out of it, the soul is affected and moved. And when they are in the soul, in that strength in which they are in the saints in heaven, the soul is mightily affected and moved, or, which is the same thing, has great affections. It is true, we do not experimentally know what love and joy are in a soul out of a body, or in a glorified body; i.e., we have not had experience of love and joy in a soul in these circumstances; but the saints on earth do know what divine love and joy in the soul are, and they know that love and joy are of the same kind with the love and joy which are in heaven, in separate souls there. The love and joy of the saints on earth, is the beginning and dawning of the light, life, and blessedness of heaven, and is like their love and joy there; or rather, the same in nature, though not the same with it, or like to it, in degree and circumstances. This is evident by many Scriptures, as Prov. 4:18; John 4:14, and chap. 6:40, 47, 50, 51, 54, 58; 1 John 3:16; 1 Cor. 13:8-12. It is unreasonable therefore to suppose, that the love and joy of the saints in heaven, not only differ in degree and circumstances, from the holy love and joy of the saints on earth, but is so entirely different in nature, that they are no affections; and merely because they have no blood and animal spirits to be set in motion by them, which motion of the blood and animal spirits is not of the essence of these affections, in men on the earth, but the effect of them; although by their reaction they may make some circumstantial difference in the sensation of the mind. There is a sensation of the mind which loves and rejoices, that is antecedent to any effects on the fluids of the body; and this sensation of the mind, therefore, does not depend on these motions in the body, and so may be in the soul without the body. And wherever there are the exercises of love and joy, there is that sensation of the mind, whether it be in the body or out; and that inward sensation, or kind of spiritual sense, or feeling, and motion of the soul, is what is called affection: the soul when it thus feels (if I may say so), and is thus moved, is said to be affected, and especially when this inward sensation and motion are to a very high degree, as they are in the saints in heaven. If we can learn anything of the state of heaven from the Scripture, the love and joy that the saints have there, is exceeding great and vigorous; impressing the heart with the strongest and most lively sensation of inexpressible sweetness, mightily moving, animating and engaging them, making them like a flame of fire. And if such love and joy be not affections, then the word *affection* is of no use in language. Will any say, that the saints in heaven, in beholding the face of their Father, and the glory of their Redeemer, and contemplating his wonderful works, and particularly his laying down his life for them, have their hearts nothing moved and affected by all which they behold or consider?

Hence, therefore, the religion of heaven, consisting chiefly in holy love and joy, consists very much in affection; and therefore, undoubtedly, true religion consists very much in affection. The way to learn the true nature of anything, is to go where that thing is to be found in its purity and perfection. If we would know the nature of true gold we must view it, not in the ore, but when it is refined. If we would learn what true religion is, we must go where there is true religion, and nothing but true religion, and in its highest perfection, without any defect or mixture. All who are truly religious are not of this world, they are strangers here, and belong to heaven; they are born from above, heaven is their native country, and the nature which they receive by this heavenly birth, is a heavenly nature, they receive an anointing from above; that principle of true religion which is in them, is a communication of the religion of heaven; their grace is the dawn of glory; and God fits them for that world by conforming them to it.

9. *This appears from the nature and design of the ordinances and duties, which God hath appointed, as means and expressions of true religion.*

To instance in the duty of prayer: it is manifest, we are not appointed in this duty, to declare God's perfections, his majesty, holiness, goodness, and all-sufficiency, and our own meanness, emptiness, dependence, and unworthiness, and our wants and desires, to inform God of these things, or to incline his heart, and prevail with him to be willing to show us mercy; but suitably to affect our own hearts with the things we express, and so to prepare us to receive the blessings we ask. And such gestures and manner of external behavior in the worship of God, which custom has made to be significations of humility and reverence, can be of no further use than as they have some tendency to affect our own hearts, or the hearts of others.

And the duty of singing praises to God seems to be appointed wholly to excite and express religious affections. No other reason can be assigned why we should express ourselves to God in verse, rather than in prose, and do it with music but only, that such is our nature and frame, that these things have a tendency to move our affections.

The same thing appears in the nature and design of the sacraments, which God hath appointed. God, considering our frame, hath not only appointed that we should be told of the great things of the gospel, and of the redemption of Christ, and instructed in them by his word;

but also that they should be, as it were, exhibited to our view, in sensible representations, in the sacraments, the more to affect us with them.

And the impressing divine things on the hearts and affections of men, is evidently one great and main end for which God has ordained that his word delivered in the holy Scriptures, should be opened, applied, and set home upon men, in preaching. And therefore it does not answer the aim which God had in this institution, merely for men to have good commentaries and expositions on the Scripture, and other good books of divinity; because, although these may tend as well as preaching to give men a good doctrinal or speculative understanding of the things of the word of God, yet they have not an equal tendency to impress them on men's hearts and affections. God hath appointed a particular and lively application of his word to men in the preaching of it, as a fit means to affect sinners with the importance of the things of religion, and their own misery, and necessity of a remedy, and the glory and sufficiency of a remedy provided; and to stir up the pure minds of the saints, and quicken their affections, by often bringing the great things of religion to their remembrance, and setting them before them in their proper colors, though they know them, and have been fully instructed in them already, 2 Pet. 1:12, 13. And particularly, to promote those two affections in them, which are spoken of in the text, love and joy: 'Christ gave some, apostles; and some, prophets; and some, evangelists; and some, pastors and teachers; that the body of Christ might be edified in love,' Eph. 4:11, 12, 16. The apostle in instructing and counseling Timothy concerning the work of the ministry, informs him that the great end of that word which a minister is to preach, is love or charity, 1 Tim. 3, 4, 5. And another affection which God has appointed preaching as a means to promote in the saints, is joy; and therefore ministers are called 'helpers of their joy,' 2 Cor. 1:24.

10. *It is an evidence that true religion, or holiness of heart, lies very much in the affection of the heart, that the Scriptures place the sin of the heart very much in hardness of heart.* Thus the Scriptures do everywhere. It was hardness of heart which excited grief and displeasure in Christ towards the Jews, Mark 3:5: 'He looked round about on them, with anger, being grieved for the hardness of their hearts.' It is from men's having such a heart as this, that they treasure up wrath for themselves: Rom. 2:5, 'After thy hardness and impenitent heart, treasurest up unto thyself wrath against the day of wrath, and revelation of the righteous judgment of God.' The reason given why the house of Israel would not obey God, was, that they were hard-hearted: Ezek. 3:7, 'But the house of Israel will not hearken unto thee; for they will not hearken unto me: for all the house of Israel are impudent and hard-hearted.' The wickedness of that perverse rebellious generation in the wilderness, is ascribed to the hardness of their hearts: Ps. 95:7-10, 'To-day if ye will hear his voice, harden not your heart, as in the provocation, and as in the day of temptation in the wilderness; when your fathers tempted me, proved me, and saw my work: forty years long was I grieved with this generation, and said, It is a people that do err in their heart,' etc. This is spoken of as what prevented Zedekiah's turning to the Lord: 2 Chron. 36:13, 'He stiffened his neck, and hardened his heart from turning to the Lord God of Israel.' This principle is spoken of, as that from whence men are without the fear of God, and depart from God's ways: Isa. 63:17, 'O Lord, why hast thou made us to err from thy ways and hardened our heart from thy fear?' And men's rejecting Christ, and opposing Christianity, is laid to this principle: Acts 19:9, 'But when divers were hardened, and believed not, but spake evil of that way before the multitude.' God's leaving men to the power of the sin and corruption of the heart is often expressed by God's hardening their hearts: Rom. 9:18, 'Therefore hath he mercy on whom he will have mercy, and whom he will he hardeneth.' John 12:40, 'He hath blinded their minds, and hardened their hearts.' And the apostle seems to speak of 'an evil heart that departs from the living God, and a hard heart,' as the same thing: Heb. 3:8, 'Harden not your heart, as in the provocation,' etc.; vv. 12, 13, 'Take heed, brethren, lest there be in any of you an evil heart of unbelief, in departing from the living God: but exhort one another daily, while it is called to-day; lest any of you be hardened through the deceitfulness of sin.' And that great work of God in conversion, which consists in delivering a person from the power of sin, and mortifying corruption, is expressed, once and again, by God's 'taking away the heart of stone, and giving a heart of flesh,' Ezek. 11:19, and chap. 36:26.

Now by a hard heart, is plainly meant an unaffected heart, or a heart not easy to be moved with virtuous affections, like a stone, insensible, stupid, unmoved, and hard to be impressed. Hence the hard heart is called a *stony heart*, and is opposed to a heart of flesh, that has feeling, and is sensibly touched and moved. We read in Scripture of a hard heart, and a tender heart; and doubtless we are to understand these, as contrary the one to the other. But what is a tender heart, but a heart which is easily impressed with what ought to affect it? God commends Josiah, because his heart was tender; and it is evident by those things which are mentioned as expressions and evidences of this tenderness of heart, that by his heart being tender is meant, his heart being easily moved with religious and pious affection: 2 Kgs 22:19, 'Because thine heart was tender, and thou hast humbled thyself before the Lord, when thou heardest what I spake against this place, and against the inhabitants thereof, that they should become a desolation and a curse, and hast rent thy clothes, and wept before me, I also have heard thee, saith the Lord.' And this is one thing, wherein it is necessary we should 'become as little children, in order to our entering into the kingdom of God,' even that we should have our hearts tender, and easily affected and moved in spiritual and divine things, as little children have in other things.

It is very plain in some places, in the texts themselves, that by hardness of heart is meant a heart void of affection. So, to signify the ostrich's being without natural affection to her young, it is said, Job 39:16, 'She hardeneth her heart against her young ones, as though they were not hers.' So a person having a heart unaffected in time of danger, is expressed by his hardening his heart: Prov. 28:14, 'Happy is the man that feareth alway; but he that hardeneth his heart shall fall into mischief.'

Now, therefore, since it is so plain, that by a hard heart, in Scripture, is meant a heart destitute of pious affections, and since also the Scriptures do so frequently place the sin and corruption of the heart in hardness of heart; it is evident, that the grace and holiness of the heart, on the contrary, must, in a great measure, consist in its having pious affections, and being easily susceptive of such affection. Divines are generally agreed, that sin radically and fundamentally consist in what is negative, or privative, having its root and foundation in a privation or want of holiness. And therefore undoubtedly, if it be so that sin does very much consist in hardness of hearts and so in the want of pious affections of heart, holiness does consist very much in those pious affections.

I am far from supposing that all affections do show a tender heart: hatred, anger, vainglory, and other selfish and self-exalting affections, may greatly prevail in the hardest heart. But yet it is evident, that hardness of heart and tenderness of heart, are expressions that relate to the affection of the heart, and denote the heart's being susceptible of, or shut up against certain affections; of which I shall have occasion to speak more afterwards.

Upon the whole, I think it clearly and abundantly evident, that true religion lies very much in the affections. Not that I think these arguments prove, that religion in the hearts of the truly godly, is ever in exact proportion to the degree of affection, and present emotion of the mind: for undoubtedly, there is much affection in the true saints which is not spiritual; their religious affections are often mixed; all is not from grace, but much from nature. And though the affections have not their seat in the body; yet the constitution of the body may very much contribute to the present emotion of the mind. And the degree of religion is rather to be judged of by the fixedness and strength of the habit that is exercised in affection, whereby holy affection is habitual, than by the degree of the present exercise; and the strength of that habit is not always in proportion to outward effects and manifestations, or inward effects, in the hurry and vehemence, and sudden changes of the course of the thoughts of the mind. But yet it is evident, that religion consists so much in affection, as that without holy affection there is no true religion; and no light in the understanding is good, which does not produce holy affection in the heart: no habit or principle in the heart is good, which has no such exercise; and no external fruit is good, which does not proceed from such exercises.

Having thus considered the evidence of the proposition laid down, I proceed to some inferences.

1. *We may hence learn how great their error is, who are for discarding all religious affections, as having nothing solid or substantial in them.*

There seems to be too much of a disposition this way, prevailing in this land at this time. Because many who, in the late extraordinary season, appeared to have great religious affections, did not manifest a right temper of mind, and run into many errors, in the time of their affections, and the heat of their zeal; and because the high affections of many seem to be so soon come to nothing, and some who seemed to be mightily raised and swallowed up with joy and zeal, for a while, seem to have returned like the dog to his vomit; hence religious affections in general are grown out of credit with great numbers, as though true religion did not at all consist in them. Thus we easily and naturally run from one extreme to another. A little while ago we were in the other extreme; there was a prevalent disposition to look upon all high religious affections as eminent exercises of true grace, without much inquiring into the nature and source of those affections, and the manner in which they arose: if persons did but appear to be indeed very much moved and raised, so as to be full of religious talk, and express themselves with great warmth and earnestness, and to be filled, or to be very full, as the phrases were; it was too much the manner, without further examination, to conclude such persons were full of the Spirit of God, and had eminent experience of his gracious influences. This was the extreme which was prevailing three or four years ago. But of late, instead of esteeming and admiring all religious affections without distinction, it is a thing much more prevalent, to reject and discard all without distinction. Herein appears the subtlety of Satan. While he saw that affections were much in vogue, knowing the greater part of the land were not versed in such things, and had not had much experience of great religious affections to enable them to judge well of them, and distinguish between true and false: then he knew he could best play his game, by sowing tares amongst the wheat, and mingling false affections with the works of God's Spirit: he knew this to be a likely way to delude and eternally ruin many souls, and greatly to wound religion in the saints, and entangle them in a dreadful wilderness, and by and by, to bring all religion into disrepute.

But now, when the ill consequences of these false affections appear, and it is become very apparent, that some of those emotions which made a glaring show, and were by many greatly admired, were in reality nothing; the devil sees it to be for his interest to go another way to work, and to endeavor to his utmost to propagate and establish a persuasion, that all affections and sensible emotions of the mind, in things of religion, are nothing at all to be regarded, but are rather to be avoided, and carefully guarded against, as things of a pernicious tendency. This he knows is the way to bring all religion to a mere lifeless formality, and effectually shut out the power of godliness, and everything which is spiritual, and to have all true Christianity turned out of doors. For although to true religion there must indeed be something else besides affection; yet true religion consists so much in the affections, that there can be no true religion without them. He who has no religious affection, is in a state of spiritual death, and is wholly destitute of the powerful, quickening, saving influences of the Spirit of God upon his heart. As there is no true religion where there is nothing else but affection, so there is no true religion where there is no religious affection. As on the one hand, there must be light in the under-standing, as well as an affected fervent heart; where there is heat without light, there can be nothing divine or heavenly in that heart; so on the other hand, where there is a kind of light without heat, a head stored with notions and speculations, with a cold and unaffected heart, there can be nothing divine in that light, that knowledge is no true spiritual knowledge of divine things. If the great things of religion are rightly understood, they will affect the heart. The reason why men are not affected by such infinitely great, important, glorious, and wonderful things, as they often hear and read of, in the word of God, is undoubtedly because they are blind; if they were not so, it would be impossible, and utterly inconsistent with human nature, that their hearts should be otherwise than strongly impressed, and greatly moved by such things.

This manner of slighting all religious affections, is the way exceedingly to harden the hearts of men, and to encourage them in their stupidity and senselessness, and to keep them in a state of spiritual death as long as they live, and bring them at last to death eternal. The prevailing prejudice against religious affections at this day, in the land, is apparently of awful effect to harden the hearts of sinners, and damp the graces of many of the saints, and stun the life and power of religion, and preclude the effect of ordinances, and hold us down in a state of dullness and apathy, and undoubtedly causes many persons greatly to offend God, in entertaining mean and low thoughts of the extraordinary work he has lately wrought in this land.

And for persons to despise and cry down all religious affections, is the way to shut all religion out of their own hearts, and to make thorough work in ruining their souls.

They who condemn high affections in others, are certainly not likely to have high affections themselves. And let it be considered, that they who have but little religious affection, have certainly but little religion. And they who condemn others for their religious affections, and have none themselves, have no religion.

There are false affections, and there are true. A man's having much affection, does not prove that he has any true religion: but if he has no affection it proves that he has no true religion. The right way, is not to reject all affections, nor to approve all; but to distinguish between affections, approving some, and rejecting others; separating between the wheat and the chaff, the gold and the dross, the precious and the vile.

2. *If it be so, that true religion lies much in the affections, hence we may infer, that such means are to be desired, as have much of a tendency to move the affections.* Such books, and such a way of preaching the word, and administration of ordinances, and such a way of worshipping God in prayer, and singing praises, is much to be desired, as has a tendency deeply to affect the hearts of those who attend these means.

Such a kind of means would formerly have been highly approved of, and applauded by the generality of the people of the land, as the most excellent and profitable, and having the greatest tendency to promote the ends of the means of grace. But the prevailing taste seems of late strangely to be altered: that pathetical manner of praying and preaching, which would formerly have been admired and extolled, and that for this reason, because it had such a tendency to move the affections, now, in great multitudes, immediately excites disgust, and moves no other affections, that those of displeasure and contempt.

Perhaps, formerly the generality (at least of the common people) were in the extreme, of looking too much to an affectionate address, in public performances: but now, a very great part of the people seem to have gone far into a contrary extreme. Indeed there may be such means, as may have a great tendency to stir up the passions of weak and ignorant persons, and yet have no great tendency to benefit their souls: for though they may have a tendency to excite affections, they may have little or none to excite gracious affections, or any affections tending to grace. But undoubtedly, if the things of religion, in the means used, are treated according to their nature, and exhibited truly, so as tends to convey just apprehensions, and a right judgment of them; the more they have a tendency to move the affections the better.

3. *If true religion lies much in the affections, hence we may learn, what great cause we have to be ashamed and confounded before God, that we are no more affected with the great things of religion.* It appears from what has been said, that this arises from our having so little true religion.

God has given to mankind affections, for the same purpose which he has given all the faculties and principles of the human soul for, viz., that they might be subservient to man's chief end, and the great business for which God has created him, that is, the business of religion. And yet how common is it among mankind, that their affections are much more exercised and engaged in other matters, than in religion! In things which concern men's worldly interest, their outward delights, their honor and reputation, and their natural relations, they have their desires eager, their appetites vehement, their love warm and affectionate, their zeal ardent; in these things their hearts are tender and sensible, easily moved, deeply impressed, much concerned, very sensibly affected, and greatly engaged; much depressed with grief at worldly losses, and highly raised with joy at worldly successes and prosperity. But how insensible and unmoved are most men, about the great things of another world! How dull are their affections! How heavy and hard their hearts in these matters! Here their love is cold, their desires languid, their zeal low, and their gratitude small. How they can sit and hear of the infinite height, and depth, and length, and breadth of the love of God in Christ Jesus, of his giving his infinitely dear Son, to be offered up a sacrifice for the sins of men, and of the unparalleled love of the innocent, and holy, and tender Lamb of God, manifested in his dying agonies, his bloody sweat, his loud and bitter cries, and bleeding heart, and all this for enemies, to redeem them from deserved, eternal burnings, and to bring to unspeakable and everlasting joy and glory; and yet be cold, and heavy, insensible, and regardless! Where are the exercises of our affections proper, if not here? What is it that does more require them? And what can be a fit occasion of their lively and vigorous exercise, if not such a one as this? Can anything be set in our view, greater and more important? Any thing more wonderful and surprising? Or more nearly concerning our interest? Can we suppose the wise Creator implanted such principles in the human nature as the affections, to be of use to us, and to be exercised on certain proper occasions, but to lie still on such an occasion as this? Can any Christian who believes the truth of these things, entertain such thoughts?

If we ought ever to exercise our affections at all, and if the Creator has not unwisely constituted the human nature in making these principles a part of it, when they are vain and useless; then they ought to be exercised about those objects which are most worthy of them. But is there anything which Christians can find in heaven or earth, so worthy to be the objects of their admiration and love, their earnest and longing desires, their hope, and their rejoicing, and their fervent zeal, as those things that are held forth to us in the gospel of Jesus Christ? In which not only are things declared most worthy to affect us, but they are exhibited in the most affecting manner. The glory and beauty of the blessed Jehovah, which is most worthy in itself, to be the object of our admiration and love, is there exhibited in the most affecting manner that can be conceived of, as it appears, shining in all its luster, in the face of an incarnate, infinitely loving, meek, compassionate, dying Redeemer. All the virtues of the Lamb of God, his humility, patience, meekness, submission, obedience, love and compassion, are exhibited to our view, in a manner the most tending to move our affections, of any that can be imagined; as they all had their greatest trial, and their highest exercise, and so their brightest manifestation, when he was in the most affecting circumstances; even when he was under his last sufferings, those unutterable and unparalleled sufferings he endured, from his tender love and pity to us. There also the hateful nature of our sins is manifested in the most affecting manner possible: as we see the dreadful effects of them, in that our Redeemer, who undertook to answer for us, suffered for them. And there we have the most affecting manifestation of God's hatred of sin, and his wrath and justice in punishing it; as we see his justice in the strictness and inflexibleness of it; and his wrath in its terribleness, in so dreadfully punishing our sins, in one who was infinitely dear to him, and loving to us. So has God disposed things, in the affair of our redemption, and in his glorious dispensations, revealed to us in the gospel, as though everything were purposely contrived in such a manner, as to have the greatest possible tendency to reach our hearts in the most tender part, and move our affections most sensibly and strongly. How great cause have we therefore to be humbled to the dust, that we are no more affected!

✛ PART II ✛

SHOWING WHAT ARE NO CERTAIN SIGNS THAT RELIGIOUS AFFECTIONS ARE GRACIOUS, OR THAT THEY ARE NOT

IF anyone, on the reading of what has been just now said, is ready to acquit himself, and say, 'I am not one of those who have no religious affections; I am often greatly moved with the consideration of the great things of religion': let him not content himself with this, that he has religious affections: for as we observed before, as we ought not to reject and condemn all affections, as though true religion did not at all consist in affection; so on the other hand, we ought not to approve of all, as though everyone that was religiously affected had true grace, and was therein the subject of the saving influences of the Spirit of God; and that therefore the right way is to distinguish among religious affections, between one sort and another. Therefore let us now endeavor to do this; and in order to do it, I would do two things.

1. I would mention some things, which are no signs one way or the other, either that affections are such as true religion consists in, or that they are otherwise; that we may be guarded against judging of affections by false signs.
2. I would observe some things, wherein those affections which are spiritual and gracious, differ from those which are not so, and may be distinguished and known.

First, I would take notice of some things, which are no signs that affections are gracious, or that they are not. It is no sign one way or the other, that religious affections are very great, or raised very high.

Some are ready to condemn all high affections: if persons appear to have their religious affections raised to an extraordinary pitch, they are prejudiced against them, and determine that they are delusions, without further inquiry. But if it be, as has been proved, that true religion lies very much in religious affections, then it follows, that if there be a great deal of true religion, there will be great religious affections; if true religion in the hearts of men be raised to a great height, divine and holy affections will be raised to a great height.

Love is an affection, but will any Christian say, men ought not to love God and Jesus Christ in a high degree? And will any say, we ought not to have a very great hatred of sin, and a very deep sorrow for it? Or that we ought not to exercise a high degree of gratitude to God for the mercies we receive of him, and the great things he has done for the salvation of fallen men? Or that we should not have very great and strong desires after God and holiness? Is there any who will profess, that his affections in religion are great enough; and will say, 'I have no cause to be humbled, that I am no more affected with the things of religion than I am; I have no reason to be ashamed, that I have no greater exercises of love to God and sorrow for sin, and gratitude for the mercies which I have received?' Who is there that will bless God that he is affected enough with what he has read and heard of the wonderful love of God to worms and rebels, in giving his only begotten Son to die for them, and of the dying love of Christ; and will pray that he may not be affected with them in any higher degree, because high affections are improper and very unlovely in Christians, being enthusiastical, and ruinous to true religion?

Our text plainly speaks of great and high affections when it speaks of 'rejoicing with joy unspeakable, and full of glory:' here the most superlative expressions are used, which language will afford. And the Scriptures often require us to exercise very high affections: thus in the first and great commandment of the law, there is an accumulation of expressions, as though words were wanting to express the degree in which we ought to love God: 'Thou shalt love the Lord thy God with all thy heart, with all thy soul, with all thy mind, and with all thy strength.' So the saints are called upon to exercise high degrees of joy: 'Rejoice,' says Christ to his disciples, 'and be exceeding glad,' Matt. 5:12. So it is said, Ps. 68:3, 'Let the righteous be glad: let them rejoice before God: yea, let them exceedingly rejoice.' So in the book of Psalms, the saints are often called upon to shout for joy; and in Luke 6:23, to leap for joy. So they are abundantly called upon to exercise high degrees of gratitude for mercies, to 'praise God with all their hearts, with hearts lifted up in the ways of the Lord, and their souls magnifying the Lord, singing his praises, talking of his wondrous works, declaring his doings,' etc.

And we find the most eminent saints in Scripture often professing high affections. Thus the Psalmist speaks of his love, as if it were unspeakable; Ps. 119:97, 'O how love I thy law!' So he expresses a great degree of hatred of sin, Ps. 139:21, 29: 'Do not I hate them, O Lord, that hate thee? And am not I grieved with them that rise up against thee? I hate them with perfect hatred.' He also expresses a high degree of sorrow for sin: he speaks of his sins 'going over his head as a heavy burden that was too heavy for him: and of his roaring all the day, and his moisture being turned into the drought of summer,' and his bones being as it were broken with sorrow. So he often expresses great degrees of spiritual desires, in a multitude of the strongest expressions which can be conceived of; such as 'his longing, his soul's thirsting as a dry and thirsty land, where no water is, his panting, his flesh and heart crying out, his soul's breaking for the longing it hath,' etc. He expresses the exercises of great and extreme grief for the sins of others, Ps. 119:136, 'Rivers of water run down mine eyes, because they keep not thy law.' And v. 53, 'Horror hath taken hold upon me, because of the wicked that forsake thy law.' He expresses high exercises of joy, Ps. 21:1: 'The king shall joy in thy strength, and in thy salvation how greatly shall he rejoice.' Ps. 71:23 'My lips shall greatly rejoice when I sing unto thee.' Ps. 63:3, 4, 5, 6, 7, 'Because thy loving kindness is better than life; my lips shall praise thee, Thus will I bless thee, while I live: I will lift up my hands in thy name. My soul shall be satisfied as with marrow and fatness; and my mouth shall praise thee with joyful lips; when I remember thee upon my bed, and meditate on thee in the night watches. Because thou hast been my help; therefore in the shadow of thy wings will I rejoice.'

The Apostle Paul expresses high exercises of affection. Thus he expresses the exercises of pity and concern for others' good, even to anguish of heart; a great, fervent, and abundant love, and earnest and longing desires, and exceeding joy; and speaks of the exultation and triumphs of his soul, and his earnest expectation and hope, and his abundant tears, and the travails of his soul, in pity, grief, earnest desires, godly jealousy, and fervent zeal, in many places that have been cited already, and which therefore I need not repeat. John the Baptist expressed great joy, John 3:39. Those blessed women that anointed the body of Jesus, are represented as in a very high exercise of religious affection, on occasion of Christ's resurrection, Matt. 28:8: 'And they departed from the sepulcher with fear and great joy.'

It is often foretold of the church of God, in her future happy seasons here on earth, that they shall exceedingly rejoice: Ps. 89:15, 16, 'They shall walk, O Lord, in the light of thy countenance.

In thy name shall they rejoice all the day: and in thy righteousness shall they be exalted.' Zech. 9:9, 'Rejoice greatly, O daughter of Zion; shout, O daughter of Jerusalem: behold thy King cometh,' etc. The same is represented in innumerable other places. And because high degrees of joy are the proper and genuine fruits of the gospel of Christ, therefore the angel calls this gospel, 'good tidings of great joy, that should be to all people.'

The saints and angels in heaven, that have religion in its highest perfection, are exceedingly affected with what they behold and contemplate of God's perfections and works. They are all as a pure heavenly flame of fire in their love and in the greatness and strength of their joy and gratitude: their praises are represented, 'as the voice of many waters and as the voice of a great thunder.' Now the only reason why their affections are so much higher than the holy affections of saints on earth, is, they see the things they are affected by, more according to their truth, and have their affections more conformed to the nature of things. And therefore, if religious affections in men here below, are but of the same nature and kind with theirs, the higher they are, and the nearer they are to theirs in degree, the better, because therein they will be so much the more conformed to truth, as theirs are.

From these things it certainly appears, that religious affections being in a very high degree, is no evidence that they are not such as have the nature of true religion. Therefore they do greatly err, who condemn persons as enthusiasts merely because their affections are very high.

1. *And on the other hand, it is no evidence that religious affections are of a spiritual and gracious nature, because they are great.*

It is very manifest by the holy Scripture, our sure and infallible rule to judge of things of this nature, that there are religious affections which are very high, that are not spiritual and saving. The Apostle Paul speaks of affections in the Galatians, which had been exceedingly elevated, and which yet he manifestly speaks of, as fearing that they were vain, and had come to nothing: Gal. 4:15, 'Where is the blessedness you spoke of? For I bear you record, that if it had been possible, you would have plucked out your own eyes, and have given them to me.' And in the 11th verse, he tells them, 'he was afraid of them, lest he had bestowed upon them labor in vain.' So the children of Israel were greatly affected with God's mercy to them, when they had seen how wonderfully he wrought for them at the Red Sea, where they sang God's praise; though they soon forgot his works. So they were greatly affected again at mount Sinai, when they saw the marvelous manifestations God made of himself there; and seemed mightily engaged in their minds, and with great forwardness made answer, when God proposed his holy covenant to them, saying, 'All that the Lord hath spoken will we do, and be obedient.' But how soon was there an end to all this mighty forwardness and engagedness of affection! How quickly were they turned aside after other gods, rejoicing and shouting around their golden calf! So great multitudes who were affected with the miracle of raising Lazarus from the dead, were elevated to a high degree, and made a mighty ado, when Jesus presently after entered into Jerusalem, exceedingly magnifying Christ, as though the ground were not good enough for the ass he rode to tread upon; and therefore cut branches of palm trees, and strewed them in the way; yea, pulled off their garments, and spread them in the way; and cried with loud voices, 'Hosanna to the Son of David, blessed is he that cometh in the name of the Lord, hosanna in the highest;' so as to make the whole city ring again, and put all into an uproar. We learn by the evangelist John, that the reason why the people made this ado, was because they were affected with the miracle of raising Lazarus, John 12:18. Here was a vast multitude crying Hosanna on this occasion, so that it gave occasion to the Pharisees to say, 'Behold, the world has gone after him,' John 12:19, but Christ had at that time but few true disciples. And how quickly was this ado at an end! All of this nature is quelled and dead, when this Jesus stands bound, with a mock robe and a crown of thorns, to be derided, spit upon, scourged, condemned and executed. Indeed, there was a great and loud outcry concerning him among the multitude then, as well as before; but of a very different kind: it is not then, Hosanna, hosanna, but Crucify, crucify.

And it is the concurring voice of all orthodox divines, that there may be religious affections, which are raised to a very high degree, and yet there be nothing of true religion.

2. *It is no sign that affections have the nature of true religion, or that they have not, that they have great effects on the body.*

All affections whatsoever, have in some respect or degree, an effect on the body. As was observed before, such is our nature, and such are the laws of union of soul and body, that the mind can have no lively or vigorous exercise, without some effect upon the body. So subject is the body to the mind, and so much do its fluids, especially the animal spirits, attend the motions and exercises of the mind, that there cannot be so much as an intense thought, without an effect upon them. Yea, it is questionable whether an imbodied soul ever so much as thinks one thought, or has any exercise at all, but that there is some corresponding motion or alteration of motion, in some degree, of the fluids, in some part of the body. But universal experience shows, that the exercise of the affections have in a special manner a tendency to some sensible effect upon the body. And if this be so, that all affections have some effect upon the body, we may then well suppose, the greater those affections be, and the more vigorous their exercise (other circumstances being equal) the greater will be the effect on the body. Hence it is not to be wondered at, that very great and strong exercises of the affections should have great effects on the body. And therefore, seeing there are very great affections, both common and spiritual; hence it is not to be wondered at, that great effects on the body should arise from both these kinds of affections. And consequently these effects are no signs, that the affections they arise from, are of one kind or the other.

Great effects on the body certainly are no sure evidences that affections are spiritual; for we see that such effects oftentimes arise from great affections about temporal things, and when religion is no way concerned in them. And if great affections about secular things, that are purely natural, may have these effects, I know not by what rule we should determine that high affections about religious things, which arise in like manner from nature, cannot have the like effect.

Nor, on the other hand, do I know of any rule any have to determine, that gracious and holy affections, when raised as high as any natural affections, and have equally strong and vigorous exercises, cannot have a great effect on the body. No such rule can be drawn from reason: I know of no reason, why a being affected with a view of God's glory should not cause the body to faint, as well as being affected with a view of Solomon's glory. And no such rule has as yet been produced from the Scripture; none has ever been found in all the late controversies which have been about things of this nature. There is a great power in spiritual affections: we read of the power which worketh in Christians, and of the Spirit of God being in them as the Spirit of power, and of the effectual working of his power in them. But man's nature is weak: flesh and blood are represented in Scripture as exceeding weak; and particularly with respect to its unfitness for great spiritual and heavenly operations and exercises, Matt. 26:41, 1 Cor. 15:43, and 50. The text we are upon speaks of 'joy unspeakable, and full of glory.' And who that considers what man's nature is, and what the nature of the affections is, can reasonably doubt but that such unutterable and glorious joys, may be too great and mighty for weak dust and ashes, so as to be considerably overbearing to it? It is evident by the Scripture that true divine discoveries, or ideas of God's glory, when given in a great degree have a tendency, by affecting the mind, to overbear the body; because the Scripture teaches us often, that if these ideas or views should be given to such a degree as they are given in heaven, the weak frame of the body could not subsist under it, and that no man can, in that manner, see God and live. The knowledge which the saints have of God's beauty and glory in this world, and those holy affections that arise from it, are of the same nature and kind with what the saints are the subjects of in heaven, differing only in degree and circumstances: what God gives them here, is a foretaste of heavenly happiness, and an earnest of their future inheritance. And who shall limit God in his giving this earnest, or say he shall give so much of the inheritance, such a part of the future reward as an earnest of the whole, and no more? And seeing God has taught us in his word, that the whole reward is such, that it would at once destroy the body, is it not too bold a thing for us, so to set bounds to the sovereign God, as to say that in giving the earnest of this reward in this world, he shall never give so much of it, as in the least to diminish the strength of the body, when God has nowhere thus limited himself?

The Psalmist, speaking of the vehement religious affections he had, speaks of an effect in his flesh or body, besides what was in his soul, expressly distinguishing one from the other, once and again: Ps. 84:2, 'My soul longeth, yea, even fainteth for the courts of the Lord: my heart and my flesh crieth out for the living God.' Here is a plain distinction between the heart and the flesh, as being each affected. So Ps. 63:1, 'My soul thirsteth for thee, my flesh longeth for thee, in a dry and thirsty land, where no water is.' Here also is an evident designed distinction between the soul and the flesh.

The prophet Habakkuk speaks of his body being overborne by a sense of the majesty of God, Hab. 3:16: 'When I heard, my belly trembled: my lips quivered at the voice: rottenness enter into my bones, and I trembled in myself.' So the Psalmist speaks expressly of his flesh trembling, Ps. 119:120: 'My flesh trembleth for fear of thee.'

That such ideas of God's glory as are sometimes given in this world, have a tendency to overbear the body, is evident, because the Scripture gives us an account, that this has sometimes actually been the effect of those external manifestations God has made of himself to some of the saints which were made to that end, viz., to give them an idea of God's majesty and glory. Such instances we have in the prophet Daniel, and the apostle John. Daniel, giving an account of an external representation of the glory of Christ, says, Dan. 10:8, 'And there remained no strength in me; for my comeliness was turned into corruption, and I retained no strength.' And the apostle John, giving an account of the manifestation made to him, says, Rev. 1:17, 'And when I saw him, I fell at his feet as dead.' It is in vain to say here, these were only external manifestations or symbols of the glory of Christ, which these saints beheld: for though it be true, that they were outward representations of Christ's glory, which they beheld with their bodily eyes; yet the end and use of these external symbols are representations was to give to these prophets an idea of the thing represented, and that was the true divine glory and majesty of Christ, which is his spiritual glory; they were made use of only as significations of this spiritual glory, and thus undoubtedly they received them, and improved them, and were affected by them. According to the end for which God intended these outward signs, they received by them a great and lively apprehension of the real glory and majesty of God's nature, which they were signs of; and thus were greatly affected, their souls swallowed up, and their bodies overborne. And I think they are very bold and daring, who will say God cannot, or shall not give the like clear and affecting ideas and apprehensions of the same real glory and majesty of his nature, to any of his saints, without the intervention of any such external shadows of it.

Before I leave this head, I would farther observe, that it is plain the Scripture often makes use of bodily effects, to express the strength of holy and spiritual affections; such as trembling, groaning, being sick, crying out, panting, and fainting. Now if it be supposed, that these are only figurative expressions, to represent the degree of affection: yet I hope all will allow, that they are fit and suitable figures to represent the high degree of those spiritual affections, which the Spirit of God makes use of them to represent; which I do not see how they would be, if those spiritual affections, let them be in never too high a degree, have no tendency to any such things; but that on the contrary, they are the proper effects and sad tokens of false affections, and the delusion of the devil. I cannot think, God would commonly make use of things which are very alien from spiritual affections, and are shrewd marks of the hand of Satan, and smell strong of the bottomless pit, as beautiful figures, to represent the high degree of holy and heavenly affections.

3. *It is no sign that affections are truly gracious affections, or that they are not, that they cause those who have them to be fluent, fervent, and abundant, in talking of the things of religion.*

There are many persons, who, if they see this in others, are greatly prejudiced against them. Their being so full of talk, is with them a sufficient ground to condemn them, as Pharisees, and ostentatious hypocrites. On the other hand, there are many, who if they see this effect in any, are very ignorantly and imprudently forward, at once to determine that they are the true children of God, and are under the saving influences of his Spirit, and speak of it as a great evidence of a new creature; they say, 'such a one's mouth is now opened: he used to be slow to speak; but now he is full and free; he is free now to open his heart, and tell his experiences, and declare the praises of God; it comes from him, as free as water from a fountain;' and the like. And especially are they captivated into a confident and undoubting persuasion, that they are savingly wrought upon, if they are not only free and abundant, but very affectionate and earnest in their talk.

But this is the fruit of but little judgment, a scanty and short experience; as events do abundantly show: and is a mistake persons often run into, through their trusting to their own wisdom and discerning, and making their own notions their rule, instead of the holy Scripture. Though the Scripture be full of rules, both how we should judge of our own state, and also how we should be conducted in our opinion of others; yet we have nowhere any rule, by which to judge ourselves or others to be in a good estate, from any such effect: for this is but the religion of the mouth and of the tongue, and what is in the Scripture represented by the leaves of a tree, which, though the tree ought not to be without them, yet are nowhere given as an evidence of the goodness of the tree.

That persons are disposed to be abundant in talking of things of religion, may be from a good cause, and it may be from a bad one. It may be because their hearts are very full of holy affections; 'for out of the abundance of the heart the mouth speaketh:' and it may be because persons' hearts are very full of religious affection which is not holy; for still out of the abundance of the heart the mouth speaketh. It is very much the nature of the affections, of whatever kind they be, and whatever objects they are exercised about, if they are strong, to dispose persons to be very much in speaking of that which they are affected with: and not only to speak much, but to speak very earnestly and fervently. And therefore persons talking abundantly and very fervently about the things of religion, can be an evidence of no more than this, that they are very much affected with the things of religion; but this may be (as has been already shown) and there be no grace. That which men are greatly affected with, while the high affection lasts, they will be earnestly engaged about, and will be likely to show that earnestness in their talk and behavior; as the greater part of the Jews, in all Judah and Galilee, did for a while, about John the Baptist's preaching and baptism, when they were willing for a season to rejoice in his light; a mighty ado was made, all over the land, and among all sorts of persons, about this great prophet and his ministry. And so the multitude, in like manner, often manifested a great earnestness, a mighty engagedness of spirit in everything that was external, about Christ and his preaching and miracles, 'being astonished at his doctrine, anon with joy receiving the word,' following him sometimes night and day, leaving meat, drink, and sleep to hear him: once following him into the wilderness, fasting three days going to hear him; sometimes crying him up to the clouds, saying, 'Never man spake like this man!' being fervent and earnest in what they said. But what did these things come to, in the greater part of them?

A person may be over full of talk of his own experiences; commonly falling upon it, everywhere, and in all companies; and when it is so, it is rather a dark sign than a good one. As a tree that is over full of leaves seldom bears much fruit; and as a cloud, though to appearance very pregnant and full of water, if it brings with it overmuch wind, seldom affords much rain to the dry and thirsty earth; which very thing the Holy Spirit is pleased several times to make use of, to represent a great show of religion with the mouth, without answerable fruit in the life: Prov. 25:24, 'Whoso boasteth himself of a false gift, is like clouds and wind without rain.' And the apostle Jude, speaking of some in the primitive times, that crept in unawares among the saints, and having a great show of religion, were for a while not suspected, 'These are clouds (says he) without water, carried about of winds,' Jude vv. 4 and 12. And the apostle Peter, speaking of the same, says, 2 Pet. 2:17, 'These are clouds without water, carried with a tempest.'

False affections, if they are equally strong, are much more forward to declare themselves, than true: because it is the nature of false religion, to affect show and observation; as it was with the Pharisees.

4. *It is no sign that affections are gracious, or that they are otherwise, that persons did not make them themselves, or excite them of their own contrivance and by their own strength.*

There are many in these days, that condemn all affections which are excited in a way that the subjects of them can give no account of, as not seeming to be the fruit of any of their own endeavors, or the natural consequence of the faculties and principles of human nature, in such circumstances, and under such means; but to be from the influence of some extrinsic and supernatural power upon their minds. How greatly has the doctrine of the inward experience, or sensible perceiving of the immediate power and operation of the Spirit of God, been reproached and ridiculed by many of late! They say, the manner of the Spirit of God is to co-operate in a silent, secret, and undiscernable way with the use of means, and our own endeavors; so that there is no distinguishing by sense, between the influences of the Spirit of God, and the natural operations of the faculties of our own minds.

And it is true, that for any to expect to receive the saving influences of the Spirit of God, while they neglect a diligent improvement of the appointed means of grace, is unreasonable presumption. And to expect that the Spirit of God will savingly operate upon their minds, without the Spirit's making use of means, as subservient to the effect, is enthusiastical. It is also undoubtedly true, that the Spirit of God is very various in the manner and circumstances of his operations, and that sometimes he operates in a way more secret and gradual, and from smaller beginnings, than at others.

But if there be indeed a power, entirely different from, and beyond our power, or the power of all means and instruments, and above the power of nature, which is requisite in order to the production of saving grace in the heart, according to the general profession of the country; then, certainly it is in no wise unreasonable to suppose, that this effect should very frequently be produced after such a manner, as to make it very manifest, apparent, and sensible that it is so. If grace be indeed owing to the powerful and efficacious operation of an extrinsic agent, or divine efficient out of ourselves, why is it unreasonable to suppose it should seem to be so to them who are the subjects of it? Is it a strange thing, that it should seem to be as it is? When grace in the heart indeed is not produced by our strength, nor is the effect of the natural power of our own faculties, or any means or instruments, but is properly the workmanship and production of the Spirit of the Almighty, is it a strange and unaccountable thing, that it should seem to them who are subjects of it, agreeable to truth, and not right contrary to truth; so that if persons tell of effects that they are conscious to in their own minds, that seem to them not to be from the natural power or operation of their minds, but from the supernatural power of some other agent, it should at once be looked upon as a sure evidence of their being under a delusion, because things seem to them to be as they are? For this is the objection which is made: it is looked upon as a clear evidence, that the apprehensions and affections that many persons have, are not really from such a cause, because they seem to them to be from that cause: they declare that what they are conscious of, seems to them evidently not to be from themselves, but from the mighty power of the Spirit of God; and others from hence condemn them, and determine what they experience is not from the Spirit of God, but from themselves, or from the devil. Thus unreasonably are multitudes treated at this day by their neighbors.

If it be indeed so, as the Scripture abundantly teaches, that grace in the soul is so the effect of God's power, that it is fitly compared to those effects which are farthest from being owing to any strength in the subject, such as a generation, or a being begotten, and resurrection, or a being raised from the dead, and creation, or a being brought out of nothing into being, and that it is an effect wherein the mighty power of God is greatly glorified, and the exceeding greatness of his power is manifested; then what account can be given of it, that the Almighty, in so great a work of his power, should so carefully hide his power, that the subjects of it should be able to discern nothing of it? Or what reason or revelation have any to determine that he does so? If we may judge by the Scripture this is not agreeable to God's manner, in his operations and dispensations; but on the contrary, it is God's manner, in the great works of his power and mercy which he works for his people, to order things so as to make his hand visible, and his power conspicuous, and men's dependence on him most evident, that no flesh should glory in his presence, that God alone might be exalted, and that the excellency of the power might be of God and not of man, and that Christ's power might be manifested in our weakness, and none might say mine own hand hath saved me. So it was in most of those temporal salvations which God wrought for Israel of old, which were types of the salvation of God's people from their spiritual enemies. So it was in the redemption of Israel from their Egyptian bondage; he redeemed them with a strong hand, and an outstretched arm; and that his power might be the more conspicuous, he suffered Israel first to be brought into the most helpless and forlorn circumstances. So it was in the great redemption by Gideon; God would have his army diminished to a handful, and they without any other arms than trumpets and lamps, and earthen pitchers. So it was in the deliverance of Israel from Goliath, by a stripling with a sling and a stone. So it was in that great work of God, his calling the Gentiles, and converting the Heathen world, after Christ's ascension, after that the world by wisdom knew not God, and all the endeavors of philosophers had proved in vain, for many ages, to reform the world, and it was by everything become abundantly evident, that the world was utterly helpless, by anything else but the mighty power of God. And so it was in most of the conversions of particular persons, we have an account of in the history of the New Testament: they were not wrought on in that silent, secret, gradual, and insensible manner, which is now insisted on; but with those manifest evidences of a supernatural power, wonderfully and suddenly causing a great change, which in these days are looked upon as certain signs of delusion and enthusiasm.

The Apostle, in Eph. 1:18, 19, speaks of God's enlightening the minds of Christians, and so bringing them to believe in Christ, to the end that they might know the exceeding greatness of his power to them who believe. The words are, 'The eyes of our understanding being enlightened; that ye may know what is the hope of his calling, and what the riches of the glory of his inheritance in the saints, and what is the exceeding greatness of his power to usward who believe, according to the working of his mighty power,' etc. Now when the apostle speaks of their being thus the subjects of his power, in their enlightening and effectual calling, to the end that they might know what his mighty power was to them who believe, he can mean nothing else than, 'that they might know by experience.' But if the saints know this power by experience, then they feel it and discern it, and are conscious of it; as sensibly distinguishable from the natural operations of their own minds, which is not agreeable to a motion of God's operating so secretly, and undiscernably, that it cannot be known that they are the subjects of the influence of any extrinsic power at all, any otherwise than as they may argue it from Scripture assertions; which is a different; thing from knowing it by experience.

So that it is very unreasonable and unscriptural to determine that affections are not from the gracious operations of God's Spirit, because they are sensibly not from the persons themselves that are the subjects of them.

On the other hand, it is no evidence that affections are gracious, that they are not properly produced by those who are the subjects of them, or that they arise in their minds in a manner they cannot account for.

There are some who make this an argument in their own favor; when speaking of what they have experienced, they say, 'I am sure I did not make it myself; it was a fruit of no contrivance or endeavor of mine; it came when I thought nothing of it; if I might have the world for it, I cannot make it again when I please.' And hence they determine that what they have experienced, must be from the mighty influence of the Spirit of God, and is of a saving nature; but very ignorantly, and without grounds. What they have been the subjects of, may indeed not be from themselves directly, but may be from the operation of an invisible agent, some spirit besides their own: but it does not thence follow, that it was from the Spirit of God. There are other spirits who have influence on the minds of men, besides the Holy Ghost. We are directed not to believe every spirit, but to try the spirits, whether they be of God. There are many false spirits, exceeding busy with men, who often transform themselves into angels of light, and do in many wonderful ways, with great subtlety and power, mimic the operations of the Spirit of God. And there are many of Satan's operations which are very distinguishable from the voluntary exercises of men's own minds. They are so, in those dreadful and horrid suggestions, and blasphemous injections with which he follows many persons; and in vain and fruitless frights and terrors, which he is the author of. And the power of Satan may be as immediate, and as evident in false comforts and joys, as in terrors and horrid suggestions; and oftentimes is so in fact. It is not in men's power to put themselves in such raptures, as the Anabaptists in Germany, and many other raving enthusiasts like them, have been the subjects of.

And besides, it is to be considered that persons may have those impressions on their minds, which may not be of their own producing, nor from an evil spirit, but from the Spirit of God, and yet not be from any saving, but a common influence of the Spirit of God; and the subjects of such impressions may be of the number of those we read of, Heb. 6:4, 5, 'that are once enlightened, and taste of the heavenly gift, and are made partakers of the Holy Ghost, and taste the good word of God, and the power of the world to come;' and yet may be wholly unacquainted with those 'better things that accompany salvations' of spoken of v. 9.

And where neither a good nor evil spirit have any immediate hand, persons, especially such as are of a weak and vapory habit of body, and the brain weak and easily susceptive of impressions, may have strange apprehensions and imaginations, and strong affections attending them, unaccountably arising, which are not voluntarily produced by themselves. We see that such persons are liable to such impressions about temporal things; and there is equal reason, why they should about spiritual things. As a person who is asleep has dreams that he is not the voluntary author of; so may such persons, in like manner, be the subjects of involuntary impressions, when they are awake.

5. *It is no sign that religious affections are truly holy and spiritual, or that they are not, that they come with texts of Scripture, remarkably brought to the mind.*

It is no sign that affections are not gracious, that they are occasioned by Scriptures so coming to mind; provided it be the Scripture itself, or the truth which the Scripture so brought contains and teaches, that is the foundation of the affection, and not merely, or mainly, the sudden and unusual manner of its coming to the mind.

But on the other hand, neither is it any sign that affections are gracious, that they arise on occasion of Scriptures brought suddenly and wonderfully to the mind; whether those affections be fear or hope, joy or sorrow, or any other. Some seem to look upon this as a good evidence that their affections are saving, especially if the affections excited are hope or joy, or any other which are pleasing and delightful. They will mention it as an evidence that all is right, that their experience came with the word, and will say, 'There were such and such sweet promises brought to my mind: they came suddenly, as if they were spoken to me: I had no hand in bringing such a text to my own mind; I was not thinking of anything leading to it; it came all at once, so that I was surprised. I had not thought of it a long time before; I did not know at first that it was Scripture; I did not remember that ever I had read it.' And it may be, they will add, 'One Scripture came flowing in after another, and so texts all over the Bible, the most sweet and pleasant, and the most apt and suitable which could be devised; and filled me full as I could hold: I could not but stand and admire: the tears flowed; I was full of joy, and could not doubt any longer.' And thus they think they have undoubted evidence that their affections must be from God, and of the right kind, and their state good: but without any manner of grounds. How came they by any such rule, as that if any affections or experiences arise with promises, and comfortable texts of Scripture, unaccountably brought to mind, without their recollection, or if a great number of sweet texts follow one another in a chain, that this is a certain evidence their experiences are saving? Where is any such rule to be found in the Bible, the great and only sure directory in things of this nature?

What deceives many of the less understanding and considerate sort of people, in this matter, seems to be this; that the Scripture is the word of God, and has nothing in it which is wrong, but is pure and perfect; and therefore, those experiences which come from the Scripture must be right. But then it should be considered, affections may arise on occasion of the Scripture, and not properly come from the Scripture, as the genuine fruit of the Scripture, and by a right use of it; but from an abuse of it. All that can be argued from the purity and perfection of the word of God, with respect to experiences, is this, that those experiences which are agreeable to the word of God, are right, and cannot be otherwise; and not that those affections must be right, which arise on occasion of the word of God coming to the mind.

What evidence is there that the devil cannot bring texts of Scripture to the mind, and misapply them to deceive persons? There seems to be nothing in this which exceeds the power of Satan. It is no work of such mighty power, to bring sounds or letters to persons' minds, that we have any reason to suppose nothing short of Omnipotence can be sufficient for it. If Satan has power to bring any words or sounds at all to persons' minds, he may have power to bring words contained in the Bible. There is no higher sort of power required in men, to make the sounds which express the words of a text of Scripture, than to make the sounds which express the words of an idle story or song. And so the same power in Satan, which is sufficient to renew one of those kinds of sounds in the mind, is sufficient to renew the other: the different signification, which depends wholly on custom, alters not the case, as to ability to make or revive the sounds or letters. Or will any suppose, that texts or Scriptures are such sacred things, that the devil durst not abuse them, nor touch them? In this also they are mistaken. He who was bold enough to lay hold on Christ himself, and carry him hither and thither, into the wilderness, and into a high mountain, and to a pinnacle of the temple, is not afraid to touch the Scripture, and abuse that for his own purpose; as he showed at the same time that he was so bold with Christ, he then brought one Scripture and another, to deceive and tempt him. And if Satan did presume, and was permitted to put Christ himself in mind of texts of Scripture to tempt *him*, what reason have we determined that he dare not, or will not be permitted, to put wicked men in the mind of texts of Scripture, to tempt and deceive *them*? And if Satan may thus abuse one text of Scripture, so he may another. Its being a very excellent place of Scripture, a comfortable and precious promise, alters not the case, as to his courage or ability. And if he can bring one comfortable text to the mind, so he may a thousand; and may choose out such Scriptures as tend most to serve his purpose; and may heap up Scripture promises, tending, according to the perverse application he makes of them, wonderfully to remove the rising doubts, and to confirm the false joy and confidence of a poor deluded sinner.

We know the devil's instruments, corrupt and heretical teachers, can and do pervert the Scripture, to their own and others' damnation, 2 Pet. 3:16. We see they have the free use of Scripture, in every part of it: there is no text so precious and sacred, but they are permitted to abuse it, to the eternal ruin of multitudes of souls; and there are no weapons they make use of with which they do more execution. And there is no manner of reason to determine, that the devil is not permitted thus to use the Scripture, as well as his instruments. For when the latter do it, they do it as his instruments and servants, and through his instigation and influence: and doubtless he does the same he instigates others to do; the devil's servants do but follow their master, and do the same work that he does himself.

And as the devil can abuse the Scripture, to deceive and destroy men, so may men's own folly and corruptions as well. The sin which is in men, acts like its father. Men's own hearts are deceitful like the devil, and use the same means to deceive.

So that it is evident, that any person may have high affections of hope and joy, arising on occasion of texts of Scripture, yea, precious promises of Scripture coming suddenly and remarkably to their minds, as though they were spoken to them, yea, a great multitude of such texts, following one another in a wonderful manner; and yet all this be no argument that these affections are divine, or that they are any other than the effects of Satan's delusions.

And I would further observe, that persons may have raised and joyful affections, which may come with the word of God, and not only so, but from the word, and those affections not be from Satan, nor yet properly from the corruptions of their own hearts, but from some influence of the Spirit of God with the word and yet have nothing of the nature of true and saving religion in them. Thus the stony ground hearers had great joy from the word; yea, which is represented as arising from the word, as growth from a seed; and their affections had, in their appearance, a very great and exact resemblance with those represented by the growth on the good ground, the difference not appearing until it was discovered by the consequences in a time of trial: and yet there was no saving religion in these affections.

6. *It is no evidence that religious affections are saving, or that they are otherwise, that there is an appearance of love in them.*

There are no professing Christians who pretend, that this is an argument against the truth and saving nature of religious affections. But, on the other hand, there are some who suppose, it is a good evidence that affections are from the sanctifying and saving influences of the Holy

Ghost. Their argument is that Satan cannot love; this affection being directly contrary to the devil, whose very nature is enmity and malice. And it is true, that nothing is more excellent, heavenly, and divine, than a spirit of true Christian love to God and men: it is more excellent than knowledge, or prophecy, or miracles, or speaking with the tongue of men and angels. It is the chief of the graces of God's Spirit, and the life, essence and sum of all true religion; and that by which we are most conformed to heaven, and most contrary to hell and the devil. But yet it is in arguing from hence, that there are no counterfeits of it. It may be observed that the more excellent anything is, the more will be the counterfeits of it. Thus there are many more counterfeits of silver and gold, than of iron and copper: there are many false diamonds and rubies, but who goes about to counterfeit common stones? Though the more excellent things are, the more difficult it is to make anything that shall be like them, in their essential nature and internal virtues; yet the more manifold will the counterfeits be, and the more will art and subtlety be displayed, in an exact imitation of the outward appearance. Thus there is the greatest danger of being cheated in buying of medicines that are most excellent and sovereign, though it be most difficult to imitate them with anything of the like value and virtue, and their counterfeits are good for nothing when we have them. So it is with Christian virtues and graces; the subtlety of Satan, and men's deceitful hearts, are wont chiefly to be exercised in counterfeiting those that are in highest repute. So there are perhaps no graces that have more counterfeits than love and humility; these being virtues wherein the beauty of a true Christian does especially appear.

But with respect to love; it is plain by the Scripture, that persons may have a kind of religious love, and yet have no saving grace. Christ speaks of many professing Christians that have such love, whose love will not continue, and so shall fail of salvation, Matt. 24:12, 13: 'And because iniquity shall abound the love of many shall wax cold. But he that shall endure unto the end, the same shall be saved.' Which latter words plainly show, that those spoken of before, whose love shall not endure to the end, but wax cold, should not be saved.

Persons may seem to have love to God and Christ, yea, to have very strong and violent affections of this nature, and yet have no grace. For this was evidently the case with many graceless Jews, such as cried Jesus up so high, following him day and night, without meat, drink, or sleep; such as said, 'Lord, I will follow thee whithersoever thou goest,' and cried, 'Hosanna to the Son of David.'

The apostle seems to intimate, that there were many in his days who had a counterfeit love to Christ, in Eph. 6:24: 'Grace be with all them that love our Lord Jesus Christ in sincerity.' The last word, in the original, signifies incorruption, which shows, that the apostle was sensible that there were many who had a kind of love to Christ, whose love was not pure and spiritual.

So also Christian love to the people of God may be counterfeited. It is evident by the Scripture, that there may be strong affections of this kind, without saving grace; as there were in the Galatians towards the Apostle Paul, when they were ready to pluck out their eyes and give them to him; although the apostle expresses his fear that their affections were come to nothing, and that he had bestowed upon them labor in vain, Gal. 4:11, 15.

7. *Persons having religious affections of many kinds, accompanying one another, is not sufficient to determine whether they have any gracious affections or no.*

Though false religion is wont to be maimed and monstrous, and not to have that entireness and symmetry of parts, which is to be seen in true religion: yet there may be a great variety of false affections together, that may resemble gracious affections.

It is evident that there are counterfeits of all kinds of gracious affections; as of love to God, and love to the brethren, as has been just now observed; so of godly sorrow for sin, as in Pharaoh, Saul, and Ahab, and the children of Israel in the wilderness, Exod. 9:27, 1 Sam. 24:16, 17, and 31:21, 1 Kgs 21:27, Num. 14:39, 40; and of the fear of God, as in the Samaritans, 'who feared the Lord, and served their own gods at the same time,' 2 Kgs 17:32, 33; and those enemies of God we read of, Ps. 66:3, who, 'through the greatness of God's power, submit themselves to him,' or, as it is in the Hebrew, 'lie unto him,' i.e., yield a counterfeit reverence and submission. So of a gracious gratitude, as in the children of Israel, who sang God's praise at the Red Sea, Ps. 106:12; and Naaman the Syrian, after his miraculous cure of his leprosy, 2 Kgs 5:15, etc.

So of spiritual joy, as in the stony ground hearers, Matt. 13:20, and particularly many of John the Baptist's hearers, John 5:35. So of zeal, as in Jehu, 2 Kgs 10:16, and in Paul before his conversion, Gal. 1:14, Phil. 3:6, and the unbelieving Jews, Acts 22:3, Rom. 10:2. So graceless persons may have earnest religious desires, which may be like Baalam's desires, which he expresses under an extraordinary view that he had of the happy state of God's people, as distinguished from all the rest of the world, Num. 23:9, 10. They may also have a strong hope of eternal life, as the Pharisees had.

And as men, while in a state of nature, are capable of a resemblance of all kinds of religious affections, so nothing hinders but that they may have many of them together. And what appears in fact, does abundantly evince that it is very often so indeed. It seems commonly to be so, that when false affections are raised high, many false affections attend each other. The multitude that attended Christ into Jerusalem, after that great miracle of raising Lazarus, seem to have been moved with many religious affections at once, and all in a high degree. They seem to have been filled with admiration, and there was a show of a high affection of love, and also of a great degree of reverence, in their laying their garments on the ground for Christ to tread upon; and also of great gratitude to him, for the great and good works he had wrought, praising him with loud voices for his salvation; and earnest desires of the coming of God's kingdom, which they supposed Jesus was now about to set up, and showed great hopes and raised expectations of it, expecting it would immediately appear; and hence were filled with joy, by which they were so animated in their acclamations, as to make the whole city ring with the noise of them; and appeared great in their zeal and forwardness to attend Jesus, and assist him without further delay, now in the time of the great feast of the Passover, to set up his kingdom. And it is easy, from nature, and the nature of the affections, to give an account why, when one affection is raised very high, that it should excite others; especially if the affection which is raised high, be that of counterfeit love, as it was in the multitude who cried Hosanna. This will naturally draw many other affections after it. For, as was observed before, love is the chief of the affections, and as it were the fountain of them. Let us suppose a person who has been for some time in great exercise and terror through fear of hell, and his heart weakened with distress and dreadful apprehensions, and upon the brink of despair, and is all at once delivered, by being firmly made to believe, through some delusion of Satan, that God has pardoned him, and accepts him as the object of his dear love, and promises him eternal life; as suppose through some vision, or strong idea or imagination, suddenly excited in him, of a person with a beautiful countenance, smiling on him, and with arms open, and with blood dropping down, which the person conceives to be Christ, without any other enlightening of the understanding, to give a view of the spiritual divine excellency of Christ and his fullness; and of the way of salvation revealed in the gospel: or perhaps by some voice or words coming as if they were spoken to him, such as these, 'Son, be of good cheer, thy sins be forgiven thee,' or, 'Fear not, it is the Father's good pleasure to give you the kingdom,' which he takes to be immediately spoken by God to him, though there was no preceding acceptance of Christ, or closing of the heart with him: I say, if we should suppose such a case, what various passions would naturally crowd at once, or one after another, into such a person's mind! It is easy to be accounted for, from mere principles of nature, that a person's heart, on such an occasion, should be raised up to the skies with transports of joy; and be filled with fervent affection, to that imaginary God or Redeemer, who he supposes has thus rescued him from the jaws of such dreadful destruction, that his soul was so amazed with the fears of, and has received him with such endearment, as a peculiar favorite; and that now he should be filled with admiration and gratitude, and his mouth should be opened, and be full of talk about what he has experienced; and that, for a while he should think and speak of scarce anything else, and should seem to magnify that God who has done so much for him, and call upon others to rejoice with him, and appear with a cheerful countenance, and talk with a loud voice: and however, before his deliverance, he was full of quarreling against the justice of God, that now it should be easy for him to submit to God, and own his unworthiness, and cry out against himself, and appear to be very humble before God, and lie at his feet as tame as a lamb; and that he should now confess his unworthiness, and cry out, 'Why me? Why me?' (Like Saul, who when Samuel told him that God had appointed him to be king, makes answer, 'Am not I a Benjamite, of the smallest of the tribes of Israel, and my family the least of all the families of the tribe of Benjamin? Wherefore then speakest thou so to me?' Much in the language of David, the true saint, 2 Sam. 7:18, 'Who am I, and what is my father's house, that thou has brought me hitherto?') Nor is it to be wondered at, that now he should delight to be with them who acknowledge and applaud his happy circumstances, and should love all such as esteem and admire him and what he has experienced, and have violent zeal against all such as would make nothing of such things, and be disposed openly to separate, and as it were to proclaim war with all who be not of his party, and should now glory in his sufferings, and be very much for condemning and censuring all who seem to doubt, or make any difficulty of these things; and while the warmth of his affections lasts, should be mighty forward to take pains, and deny himself, to promote the interest of the party who he imagines favors such things, and seem earnestly desirous to increase the number of them, as the Pharisees compassed sea and land to make one proselyte. And so I might go on, and mention many other things, which will naturally arise in such circumstances. He must have but slightly considered human nature, who thinks such things as these cannot arise in this manner, without any supernatural interposition of divine power.

As from true divine love flow all Christian affections, so from a counterfeit love in like manner naturally flow other false affections. In both cases, love is the fountain, and the other affections are the streams. The various faculties, principles, and affections of the human nature, are as it were many channels from one fountain: if there be sweet water in the fountain, sweet water will from thence flow out into those various channels; but if the water in the fountain be poisonous, then poisonous streams will also flow out into all those channels. So that the channels and streams will be alike, corresponding one with another; but the great difference will lie in the nature of the water. Or, man's nature may be compared to a tree, with many branches, coming from one root: if the sap in the root be good, there will also be good sap distributed throughout the branches, and the fruit that is brought forth will be good and wholesome; but if the sap in the root and stock be poisonous, so it will be in many branches (as in the other case), and the fruit will be deadly. The tree in both cases may be alike; there may be an exact resemblance in shape; but the difference is found only in eating the fruit. It is thus (in some measure at least) oftentimes between saints and hypocrites. There is sometimes a very great similitude between true and false experiences, in their appearance, and in what is expressed and related by the subjects of them: and the difference between them is much like the difference between the dreams of Pharaoh's chief butler and baker; they seemed to be much alike, insomuch that when Joseph interpreted the chief butler's dream, that he should be delivered from his imprisonment, and restored to the king's favor, and his honorable office in the palace, the chief baker had raised hopes and expectations, and told his dream also; but he was woefully disappointed; and though his dream was so much like the happy and well boding dream of his companion, yet it was quite contrary in its issue.

9. *Nothing can certainly be determined concerning the nature of the affections, by this, that comforts and joys seem to follow awakenings and convictions of conscience, in a certain order.*

Many persons seem to be prejudiced against affections and experiences that come in such a method, as has been much insisted on by many divines; first, such awakenings, fears, and awful apprehensions, followed with such legal humblings, in a sense of total sinfulness and helplessness, and then, such and such light and comfort; they look upon all such schemes, laying down such methods and steps, to be of men's devising; and particularly if high affections of joy follow great distress and terror, it is made by many an argument against those affections. But such prejudices and objections are without reason or Scripture. Surely it cannot be unreasonable to suppose, that before God delivers persons from a state of sin and exposedness to eternal destruction, he should give them some considerable sense of the evil he delivers from; that they may be delivered sensibly, and understand their own salvation, and know something of what God does for them. As men that are saved are in two exceeding different states, first a state of condemnation, and then in a state of justification and blessedness: and as God, in the work of the salvation of mankind, deals with them suitably to their intelligent rational nature; so its seems reasonable, and agreeable to God's wisdom, that men who are saved should be in these two states sensibly; first, that they should, sensibly to themselves, be in a state of condemnation, and so in a state of woeful calamity and dreadful misery, and so afterwards in a state of deliverance and happiness; and that they should be first sensible of their absolute extreme necessity, and afterwards of Christ's sufficiency and God's mercy through him.

And that it is God's manner of dealing with men, to 'lead them into a wilderness, before he speaks comfortably to them,' and so to order it, that they shall be brought into distress, and made to see their own helplessness and absolute dependence on his power and grace, before he appears to work any great deliverance for them, is abundantly manifest by the Scripture. Then is God wont to 'repent himself for his professing people, when their strength is gone, and there is none shut up or left,' and when they are brought to see that their false gods cannot help them, and that the rock in whom they trusted is vain, Deut. 32:36, 37. Before God delivered the children of Israel out of Egypt, they were prepared for it, by being made to 'see that they were in an evil case,' and 'to cry unto God, because of their hard bondage,' Exod. 2:23, and 5:19. And before God wrought that great deliverance for them at the Red Sea, they were brought into great distress, the wilderness had shut them in, they could not turn to the right hand nor the left, and the Red Sea was before them, and the great Egyptian host behind, and they were brought to see that they could do nothing to help themselves, and that if God did not help them, they should be immediately swallowed up; and then God appeared, and turned their cries into songs. So before they were brought to their rest, and to enjoy the milk and honey of Canaan, God 'led them through a great and terrible wilderness, that he might humble them and teach them what was in their heart, and so do them good in their latter end,' Deut. 8:2, 16. The woman that had the issue of blood twelve years, was not delivered, until she had first 'spent all her living on earthly physicians, and could not be healed of any,' and so was left helpless, having no more money to spend; and then she came to the great Physician, without any money or price, and was healed by him, Luke 8:43, 44. Before Christ would answer the request of the woman of Canaan, he first seemed utterly to deny her, and humbled her, and brought her to own herself worthy to be called a dog; and then he showed her mercy, and received her as a dear child, Matt. 15:22, etc. The Apostle Paul, before a remarkable deliverance, was 'pressed out of measure, above strength, insomuch that he despaired even of life; but had the sentence of death in himself, that he might not trust in himself, but in God that raiseth the dead,' 2 Cor. 1:8, 9, 10. There was first a great tempest, and the ship was covered with the waves, and just ready to sink, we find the disciples were brought to cry to Jesus, 'Lord save us, we perish;' and then the winds and seas were rebuked, and there was a great calm, Matt. 8:24, 25, 26. The leper, before he is cleansed, must have his mouth stopped, by a covering on his upper lip, and was to acknowledge his great misery and utter uncleanness by rending his clothes, and crying, 'Unclean, unclean,' Lev. 13:45. And backsliding Israel, before God heals them, are brought to 'acknowledge that they have sinned, and have not obeyed the voice of the Lord,' and to see that 'they lie down in their shame, and that confusion covers them,' and 'that in vain is salvation hoped for from the hills, and from the multitude of mountains,' and that God only can save them, Jer. 3:23, 24, 25. Joseph, who was sold by his brethren, and therein was a type of Christ, brings his brethren into great perplexity and distress, and brings them to reflect on their sin, and to say, We are verily guilty; and at last to resign up themselves entirely into his hands for bondmen; and then reveals himself to them, as their brother and their savior.

And if we consider those extraordinary manifestations which God made of himself to saints of old, we shall find that he commonly first manifested himself in a way which was terrible, and then by those things that were comfortable. So it was with Abraham; first, a horror of great darkness fell upon him, and then God revealed himself to him in sweet promises, Gen. 15:12, 13. So it was with Moses at Mount Sinai; first, God appeared to him in all the terrors of his dreadful Majesty, so that Moses said, 'I exceedingly fear and quake,' and then he made all his goodness to pass before him, and proclaimed his name, 'The Lord God gracious and merciful,' etc. So it was with Elijah; first, there is a stormy wind, and earthquakes and devouring fire, and then a still, small, sweet voice, 1 Kgs 19. So it was with Daniel; he first saw Christ's countenance as lightning, that terrified him, and caused him to faint away; and then he is strengthened and refreshed with such comfortable words as these, 'O Daniel, a man greatly beloved,' Dan. 10. So it was with the apostle John, Rev. 1. And there is an analogy observable in God's dispensations and deliverances which he works for his people, and the manifestations which he makes of himself to them, both ordinary and extraordinary.

But there are many things in Scripture which do more directly show, that this is God's ordinary manner in working salvation for the souls of men, and in the manifestations God makes of himself and of his mercy in Christ, in the ordinary works of his grace on the hearts of sinners. The servant that owed his prince ten thousand talents, is first held to his debt, and the king pronounces sentence of condemnation upon him, and commands him to be sold, and his wife and children, and payment to be made; and thus he humbles him, and brings him to own the whole of the debt to be just, and then forgives him all. The prodigal son spends all he has, and is brought to see himself in extreme circumstances, and to humble himself, and own his unworthiness, before he is relieved and feasted by his father, Luke 15. Old inveterate wounds must be searched to the bottom, in order to healing: and the Scripture compares sin, the wound of the soul, to this, and speaks of healing this wound without thus searching of it, as vain and deceitful, Jer. 7:11. Christ, in the work of his grace on the hearts of men, is compared to rain on the new mown grass, grass that is cut down with a scythe, Ps. 72:6, representing his refreshing, comforting influences on the wounded spirit. Our first parents, after they had sinned, were first terrified with God's majesty and justice, and had their sin, with its aggravations, set before them by their Judge, before they were relieved by the promise of the seed of the woman. Christians are spoken of as those 'that have fled for refuge to lay hold on the hope set before them,' Heb. 6:18, which representation implies great fear and sense of danger, preceding. To the like purpose, Christ is called 'a hiding place from the wind, and a covert from the tempest, and as rivers of water in a dry place, and as the shadow of a great rock in a weary land,' Isa. 32 at the beginning. And it seems to be the natural import of the word gospel, glad tidings, that it is news of deliverance and salvation, after great fear and distress. There is also reason to suppose, that God deals with particular believers, as he dealt with his church, which he first made to hear his voice in the law, with terrible thunders and lightning and kept her under that schoolmaster to prepare her for Christ; and then comforted her with the joyful sound of the gospel from Mount Zion. So likewise John the Baptist came to prepare the way for Christ, and prepare men's hearts for his reception, by showing them their sins, and by bringing the self-righteous Jews off from their own righteousness, telling them that they were 'a generation of vipers,' and showing them their danger of 'the wrath to come,' telling them that 'the axe was laid at the root of the trees,' etc.

And if it be indeed God's manner (as I think the foregoing considerations show that it undoubtedly is), before he gives men the comfort of a deliverance from their sin and misery, to give them a considerable sense of the greatness and dreadfulness of those evils, and their extreme wretchedness by reason of them; surely it is not unreasonable to suppose, that persons, at least oftentimes, while under these views, should have great distresses and terrible apprehensions of mind; especially if it be considered what these evils are that they have a view of; which are no other than great and manifold sins, against the infinite majesty of the great Jehovah, and the suffering of the fierceness of his wrath to all eternity. And the more so still, when we have many plain instances in Scripture of persons that have actually been brought into great distress, by such convictions, before they have received saving consolations: as the multitude at Jerusalem, who were 'pricked in their heart, and said unto Peter and the rest of the apostles, Men and brethren, what shall we do?' And the apostle Paul, who trembled and was astonished, before he was comforted; and the gaoler, when 'he called for a light, and sprang in, and came trembling, and fell down before Paul and Silas, and said, Sirs, what must I do to be saved?'

From these things it appears to be very unreasonable in professing Christians to make this an objection against the truth and spiritual nature of the comfortable and joyful affections which any have, that they follow such awful apprehensions and distresses as have been mentioned.

And, on the other hand, it is no evidence that comforts and joys are right, because they succeed great terrors, and amazing fears of hell. This seems to be what some persons lay a great weight upon; esteeming great terrors an evidence of the great work of the law as wrought on the heart, well preparing the way for solid comfort; not considering that terror and a conviction of conscience are different things. For though convictions of conscience do often cause terror; yet they do not consist in it; and terrors do often arise from other causes. Convictions of conscience, through the influences of God's Spirit, consist in conviction of sinfulness of heart and practices and of the dreadfulness of sins as committed against a God of terrible majesty, infinite holiness and hatred of sin, and strict justice in punishing of it. But there are some persons that have frightful apprehensions of hell, a dreadful pit ready to swallow them up, and flames just ready to lay hold of them, and devils around them, ready to seize them; who at the same time seem to have very little proper enlightenings of conscience really convincing them of their sinfulness of heart and life. The devil, if permitted, can terrify men as well as the Spirit of God, it is a work natural to him, and he has many ways of doing it, in a manner tending to no good.

He may exceedingly affright persons, by impressing on them images and ideas of many external things, of a countenance frowning, a sword drawn, black clouds of vengeance, words of an awful doom pronounced, hell gaping, devils coming, and the like, not to convince persons of things that are true, and revealed in the word of God, but to lead them to vain and groundless determinations; as that their day is past, that they are reprobated, that God is implacable, that he has come to a resolution immediately to cut them off, etc.

And the terrors which some persons have, are very much owing to the particular constitution and temper they are of. Nothing is more manifest than that some persons are of such a temper and frame, that their imaginations are more strongly impressed with everything they are affected with, than others; and the impression on the imagination reacts on the affection, and raises that still higher; and so affection and imagination act reciprocally, one on another, till their affection is raised to a vast height, and the person is swallowed up, and loses as possession of himself.

And some speak of a great sight they have of their wickedness, who really, when the matter comes to be well examined into and thoroughly weighted, are found to have little or no convictions of conscience. They tell of a dreadful hard heart, and how their heart lies like a stone; when truly they have none of those things in their minds or thoughts, wherein the hardness of men's heart does really consist. They tell of a dreadful load and sink of sin, a heap of black and loathsome filthiness within them; when, if the matter be carefully inquired into, they have not in view anything wherein the corruption of nature does truly consist, nor have they any thought of any particular thing wherein their hearts are sinfully defective, or fall short of what ought to be in them, or any exercises at all of corruption in them. And many think also they have great convictions of their actual sins, who truly have none. They tell how their sins are set in order before them, they see them stand encompassing them round in a row, with a dreadful, frightful appearance; when really they have not so much as one of the sins they have been guilty of in the course of their lives, coming into view, that they are affected with the aggravations of.

And if persons have had great terrors which really have been from the awakening and convincing influences of the Spirit of God, it doth not thence follow that their terrors must needs issue in true comfort. The unmortified corruption of the heart may quench the Spirit of God (after he has been striving) by leading men to presumptuous, and self-exalting hopes and joys, as well as otherwise. It is not every woman who is really in travail, that brings forth a real child; but it may be a monstrous production, without anything of the form or properties of human nature belonging to it. Pharaoh's chief baker after he had lain in the dungeon with Joseph, had a vision that raised his hopes and he was lifted out of the dungeon, as well as the chief butler; but it was to be hanged.

But if comforts and joys do not only come after great terrors and awakenings, but there be an appearance of such preparatory convictions and humiliations, and brought about very distinctly, by such steps, and in such a method as has frequently been observable in true converts; this is no certain sign that the light and comforts which follow are true and saving. And for these following reasons:

First, As the devil can counterfeit all the saving operations and graces of the Spirit of God, so he can counterfeit those operations that are preparatory to grace. If Satan can counterfeit those effects of God's Spirit, which are special, divine and sanctifying, so that there shall be a very great resemblance, in all that can be observed by others; much more easily may he imitate those works of God's Spirit which are common, and which men, while they are yet his own children, are the subjects of. These works are in no wise so much above him as the other. There are no works of God that are so high and divine, and above the powers of nature, and out of reach of the power of all creatures, as those works of his Spirit, whereby he forms the creature in his own image, and makes it to be a partaker of the divine nature. But if the devil can be the author of such resemblances of these as have been spoken of, without doubt he may of those that are of an infinitely inferior kind. And it is abundantly evident in fact, that there are false humiliations and false submissions, as well as false comforts. How far was Saul brought, though a very wicked man, and of a haughty spirit, when he (though a great king) was brought, in conviction of his sin, as it were to fall down, all in tears, weeping aloud, before David his own subject (and one that he had for a long time mortally hated, and openly treated as an enemy), and condemn himself before him, crying out, 'Thou art more righteous than I: for thou hast rewarded me good, whereas I have rewarded thee evil.' And at another time,

'I have sinned, I have played the fool, I have erred exceedingly,' 1 Sam. 24:16, 17, and chap. 26:21. And yet Saul seems then to have had very little of the influences of the Spirit of God, it being after God's Spirit had departed from him, and given him up, and an evil spirit from the Lord troubled him. And if this proud monarch, in a pang of affection, was brought to humble himself so low before a subject that he hated, and still continued an enemy to, there doubtless may be appearances of great conviction and humiliation in men, before God, while they yet remain enemies to him, and though they finally continue so. There is oftentimes in men who are terrified through fears of hell, a great appearance of their being brought off from their own righteousness, when they are not brought off from it in all ways, although they are in many ways that are more plain and visible. They have only exchanged some ways of trusting in their own righteousness, for others that are more secret and subtle. Oftentimes a great degree of discouragement, as to many things they used to depend upon, is taken for humiliation: that is called a submission to God, which is no absolute submission, but has some secret bargain in it, that it is hard to discover.

Secondly, If the operations and effects of the Spirit of God, in the convictions, and comforts of true converts, may be sophisticated, then the order of them may be imitated. If Satan can imitate the things themselves, he may easily put them one after another, in such a certain order. If the devil can make A, B, and C, it is as easy for him to put A first, and B next, and C next, as to range them in a contrary order. The nature of divine things is harder for the devil to imitate, than their order. He cannot *exactly* imitate divine operations in their nature, though his counterfeits may be very much like them in external appearance, but he can exactly imitate their order. When counterfeits are made, there is no divine power needful in order to the placing one of them first, and another last. And therefore no order or method of operations and experiences is any certain sign of their divinity. That only is to be trusted to, as a certain evidence of grace, which Satan cannot do, and which it is impossible should be brought to pass by any power short of divine.

Thirdly, We have no certain rule to determine how far God's own Spirit may go in those operations and convictions which in themselves are not spiritual and saving, and yet the person that is the subject of them never be converted, but fall short of salvation at last. There is no necessary connection in the nature of things, between anything that a natural man may experience while in a state of nature, and the saving grace of God's Spirit. And if there be no connection in the nature of things, then there can be no known and certain connection at all, unless it be by divine revelation. But there is no revealed certain connection between a state of salvation, and anything that a natural man can be the subject of, before he believes in Christ. God has revealed no certain connection between salvation, and any qualifications in men, but only grace and its fruits. And therefore we do not find any legal convictions, or comforts, following these legal convictions, in any certain method or order, ever once mentioned in the Scripture, as certain signs of grace, or things peculiar to the saints; although we do find gracious operations and effects themselves, so mentioned, thousands of times. Which should be enough with Christians who are willing to have the word of God, rather than their own philosophy, and experiences and conjectures, as their sufficient and sure guide in things of this nature.

Fourthly, Experience does greatly confirm, that persons seeming to have convictions and comforts following one another in such a method and order, as is frequently observable in true converts, is no certain sign of grace. I appeal to all those ministers in this land, who have had much occasion of dealing with souls in the late extraordinary season, whether there have not been many who do not prove well, that have given a fair account of their experiences, and have seemed to be converted according to rule, i.e., with convictions and affections, succeeding distinctly and exactly, in that order and method, which has been ordinarily insisted on, as the order of the operations of the Spirit of God in conversion.

And as a seeming to have this distinctness as to steps and method, is no certain sign that a person is converted; so a being without it, is no evidence that a person is not converted. For though it might be made evident to a demonstration, on Scripture principles, that a sinner cannot be brought heartily to receive Christ as his Savior, who is not convinced of his sin and misery, and of his own emptiness and helplessness, and his just desert of eternal condemnation; and that therefore such convictions must be some way implied in what is wrought in his soul; yet nothing proves it to be necessary, that all those things which are implied or presupposed in an act of faith in Christ, must be plainly and distinctly wrought in the soul, in so many successive and separate works of the Spirit, that shall be each one plain and manifest, in all who are truly converted. On the contrary (as Mr Shepard observes), sometimes the change made in a saint, at first work, is like a confused chaos; so that the saints know not what to make of it. The manner of the Spirit's proceeding in them that are born of the Spirit, is very often exceeding mysterious and unsearchable; we, as it were, hear the sound of it, the effect of it is discernible; but no man can tell whence it came, or whither it went. And it is oftentimes as difficult to know the way of the Spirit in the new birth, as in the first birth; Eccl. 11:5, 'Thou knowest not what is the way of the Spirit, or how the bones do grow in the womb of her that is with child; even so thou knowest not the works of God, that worketh all.' The ingenerating of a principle of grace in the soul, seems in Scripture to be compared to the conceiving of Christ in the womb, Gal. 4:19. And therefore the Church is called Christ's mother, Cant. 3:11. And so is every particular believer, Matt. 12:49, 50. And the conception of Christ in the womb of the blessed virgin, by the power of the Holy Ghost, seems to be a designed resemblance of the conception of Christ in the soul of a believer, by the power of the same Holy Ghost. And we know not what is the way of the Spirit, nor how the bones do grow, either in the womb, or heart that conceives this holy child. The new creature may use that language in Ps. 139:14, 15, 'I am fearfully and wonderfully made; marvellous are thy works, and that my soul knoweth right well. My substance was not hid from thee, when I was made in secret.' Concerning the generation of Christ, both in his person, and also in the hearts of his people, it may be said, as in Isa. 53:8, 'Who can declare his generation?' We know not the works of God, that worketh all. 'It is the glory of God to conceal a thing' (Prov. 25:2), and to have 'his path as it were in the mighty waters, that his footsteps may not be known;' and especially in the works of his Spirit on the hearts of men, which are the highest and chief of his works. And therefore it is said, Isa. 40:13, 'Who hath directed the Spirit of the Lord, or being his counselor hath taught him?' It is to be feared that some have gone too far towards directing the Spirit of the Lord, and marking out his footsteps for him, and limiting him to certain steps and methods. Experience plainly shows, that God's Spirit is unsearchable and untraceable, in some of the best of Christians, in the method of his operations, in their conversion. Nor does the Spirit of God proceed discernibly in the steps of a particular established scheme, one half so often as is imagined.

A scheme of what is necessary, and according to a rule already received and established by common opinion, has a vast (though to many a very insensible) influence in forming persons' notions of the steps and method of their own experiences. I know very well what their way is; for I have had much opportunity to observe it. Very often, at first, their experiences appear like a confused chaos, as Mr Shepard expresses it: but then those passages of their experience are picked out, that have most of the appearance of such particular steps that are insisted on; and these are dwelt upon in the thoughts, and these are told of from time to time, in the relation they give: these parts grow brighter and brighter in their view; and others, being neglected, grow more and more obscure: and what they have experienced is insensibly strained to bring all to an exact conformity to the scheme that is established. And it becomes natural for ministers, who have to deal with them, and direct them that insist upon distinctness and clearness of method, to do so too. But yet there has been so much to be seen of the operations of the Spirit of God, of late, that they who have had much to do with souls, and are not blinded with a seven-fold veil of prejudice, must know that the Spirit is so exceeding various in the manner of his operating, that in many cases it is impossible to trace him, or find out his way.

What we have principally to do with, in our inquiries into our own state, or directions we give to others, is the nature of the effect that God has brought to pass in the soul. As to the steps which the Spirit of God took to bring that effect to pass, we may leave them to him. We are often in Scripture expressly directed to try ourselves by the nature of the fruits of the Spirit; but nowhere by the Spirit's method of producing them. Many do greatly err in their notions of a clear work of conversion; calling that a clear work, where the successive steps of influence, and method of experience are clear: whereas that indeed is the clearest work (not where the order of doing is clearest, but) where the spiritual and divine nature of the work done, and effect wrought, is most clear.

9. *It is no certain sign that the religious affections which persons have are such as have in them the nature of true religion, or that they have not, that they dispose persons to spend much time in religion, and to be zealously engaged in the external duties of worship.*

This has, very unreasonably of late, been looked upon as an argument against the religious affections which some have had, that they spend so much time in reading, praying, singing, hearing sermons, and the like. It is plain from the Scripture, that it is the tendency of true grace to cause persons to delight in such religious exercises. True grace had this effect on Anna the prophetess: Luke 2:27, 'She departed not from the temple, but served God with fastings and prayers night and day.' And grace had this effect upon the primitive Christians in Jerusalem: Acts 2:46, 47, 'And they continuing daily with one accord in the temple, and breaking bread from house to house, did eat their meat with gladness and singleness of heart, praising God.' Grace made Daniel delight in the duty of prayer, and solemnly to attend it three times a day, as it also did David: Ps. 55:17, 'Evening, morning, and at noon will I pray.' Grace makes the saints delight in singing praises to God: Ps. 135: 3, 'Sing praises unto his name, for it is pleasant.' And 147:1, 'Praise ye the Lord; for it is good to sing praises unto our God; for it is pleasant, and praise is comely.' It also causes them to delight to hear the word of God preached: it makes the gospel a joyful sound to them, Ps. 89:15, and makes the feet of those who publish these good tidings to be beautiful: Isa. 52:7, 'How beautiful upon the mountains are the feet of him that bringeth good tidings!' etc. It makes them love God's public worship: Ps. 26:8, 'Lord, I have loved the habitation of thy house, and the place where thine honor dwelleth.' And 27:4, 'One thing have I desired of the Lord, that will I seek after, that I may dwell in the house of the Lord all the days of my life, to behold the beauty of the Lord, and to inquire in his temple.' Ps. 84:1, 2, etc. 'How amiable are thy tabernacles, O Lord of hosts! My soul longeth, yea, even fainteth for the courts of the Lord. – Yea, the sparrow hath found a house and the swallow a nest for herself, where she may lay her young, even thine altars, O Lord of hosts, my King and my God. Blessed are they that dwell in thy house: they will be still praising thee. Blessed is the man in whose heart are the ways of them, who passing through the valley of Baca – go from strength to strength, everyone of them in Zion appeareth before God.' V. 10, 'A day in thy courts is better than a thousand.'

This is the nature of true grace. But yet, on the other hand, persons' being disposed to abound and to be zealously engaged in the external exercises of religion, and to spend much time in them, is no sure evidence of grace; because such a disposition is found in many that have no grace. So it was with the Israelites of old, whose services were abominable to God; they attended the 'new moons, and Sabbaths, and calling of assemblies, and spread forth their hands, and made many prayers,' Isa. 1:12-15. So it was with the Pharisees; they 'made long prayers, and fasted twice a week.' False religion may cause persons to be loud and earnest in prayer: Isa. 58: 4, 'Ye shall not fast as ye do this day, to cause your voice to be heard on high.' That religion which is not spiritual and saving, may cause men to delight in religious duties and ordinances: Isa. 58:2, 'Yet they seek me daily, and delight to know my ways, as a nation that did righteousness, and forsook not the ordinance of their God: they ask of me the ordinances of justice: they take delight in approaching to God.' It may cause them to take delight in hearing the word of God preached, as it was with Ezekiel's hearers: Ezek. 33:31, 32, 'And they come unto thee as the people cometh, and they sit before thee as my people, and they hear thy words, but they will not do them: for with their mouth they show much love, but their heart goeth after their covetousness. And lo, thou art unto them as a very lovely song of one that hath a pleasant voice, and can play well on an instrument: for they hear thy words, but they do them not.' So it was with Herod; he heard John the Baptist gladly, Mark 6:20. So it was with others of his hearers, 'for a season they rejoiced in his light,' John 5:35. So the stony ground hearers heard the word with joy.

Experience shows, that persons, from false religion, may be inclined to be exceeding abundant in the external exercises of religion; yea, to give themselves up to them, and devote almost their whole time to them. Formerly a sort of people were very numerous in the Romish church, called recluses, who forsook the world, and utterly abandoned the society of mankind, and shut themselves up close in a narrow cell, with a vow never to stir out of it, nor to see the face of any of mankind any more (unless that they might be visited in case of sickness), to spend all their days in the exercise of devotion and converse with God. There were also in old time, great multitudes called Hermits and Anchorites, that left the world to spend all their days in lonesome deserts, to give themselves up to religious contemplations and exercises of devotion; some sorts of them having no dwellings, but the caves and vaults of the mountains, and no food, but the spontaneous productions of the earth. I once lived, for many months, next door to a Jew (the houses adjoining one to another), and had much opportunity daily to observe him; who appeared to me the devoutest person that I ever saw in my life; great part of his time being spent in acts of devotion, at his eastern window, which opened next to mine, seeming to be most earnestly engaged, not only in the daytime, but sometimes whole nights.

10. *Nothing can be certainly known of the nature of religious affections by this, that they much dispose persons with their mouths to praise and glorify God.*

This indeed is implied in what has been just now observed, of abounding and spending much time in the external exercises of religion, and was also hinted before; but because many seem to look upon it as a bright evidence of gracious affection, when persons appear greatly disposed to praise and magnify God, to have their mouths full of his praises, and affectionately to be calling on others to praise and extol him, I thought it deserved a more particular consideration.

No Christian will make it an argument against a person, that he seems to have such a disposition. Nor can it reasonably be looked upon as an evidence for a person, if those things that have been already observed and proved, be duly considered, viz., that persons, without grace, may have high affections towards God and Christ, and that their affections, being strong, may fill their mouths and incline them to speak much, and very earnestly, about the things they are affected with, and that there may be counterfeits of all kinds of gracious affection. But it will appear more evidently and directly, that this is no certain sign of grace, if we consider what instances the Scripture gives us of it in those that were graceless. We often have an account of this, in the multitude that were present when Christ preached and wrought miracles; Mark 2:12, 'And immediately he arose, took up his bed, and went forth before them all, insomuch that they were all amazed, and glorified God, saying, We never saw it on this fashion.' So Matt. 9:8, and Luke 5:26. Also Matt. 15:31, 'Insomuch that the multitude wondered, when they saw the dumb to speak, the maimed to be whole, the lame to walk, and the blind to see: and they glorified the God of Israel.' So we are told, that on occasion of Christ's raising the son of the widow of Nain, Luke 7:16, 'There came a fear on all: and they glorified God, saying, That a great prophet is risen up among us; and, That God hath visited his people.' So we read of their glorifying Christ, or speaking exceeding highly of him: Luke 4:15, 'And he taught in their synagogues, being glorified of all.' And how did they praise him, with loud voices, crying, 'Hosanna to the Son of David; hosanna in the highest; blessed is he that cometh in the name of the Lord,' a little before he was crucified! And after Christ's ascension, when the apostles had healed the impotent man, we are told, that all men glorified God for that which was done, Acts 4:21. When the Gentiles in Antioch of Pisidia, heard from Paul and Barnabas, that God would reject the Jews, and take the Gentiles to be his people in their room, they were affected with the goodness of God to the Gentiles, 'and glorified the word of the Lord': but all that did so were not true believers; but only a certain elect number of them; as is intimated in the account we have of it, Acts 13:48: 'And when the Gentiles heard this, they were glad, and glorified the word of the Lord: and as many as were ordained to eternal life, believed.' So of old the children of Israel at the Red Sea, 'sang God's praise; but soon forgat his works.' And the Jews in Ezekiel's time, 'with their mouth showed much love, while their heart went after their covetousness.' And it is foretold of false professors and real enemies of religion, that they should show a forwardness to glorify God: Isa. 66:5, 'Hear the word of the Lord, ye that tremble at his word. Your brethren that hated you, that cast you out for my name's sake, said, Let the Lord be glorified.'

It is no certain sign that a person is graciously affected, if, in the midst of his hopes and comforts, he is greatly affected with God's unmerited mercy to him that is so unworthy, and seems greatly to extol and magnify free grace. Those that yet remain with unmortified pride and enmity against God, may, when they imagine that they have received extraordinary kindness from God, cry out of their unworthiness, and magnify God's undeserved goodness to them, from no other conviction of their ill deservings, and from no higher principle than Saul had, who, while he yet remained with unsubdued pride and enmity against David, was brought, though a king, to acknowledge his unworthiness, and cry out, 'I have played the fool, I have erred exceedingly,' and with great affection and admiration, to magnify and extol David's unmerited and unexampled kindness to him, 1 Sam. 25:16-19, and 26:21, and from no higher principle than that from whence Nebuchadnezzar was affected with God's dispensations, that he saw and was the subject of, and praises, extols and honors the King of heaven; and both he, and Darius, in their high affections, call upon all nations to praise God, Dan. 3:28, 29, 30, and 4:1, 2, 3, 34, 35, 37, and 6:25, 26, 27.

11. *It is no sign that affections are right, or that they are wrong, that they make persons that have them exceeding confident that what they experience is divine, and that they are in a good estate.*

It is an argument with some, against persons, that they are deluded if they pretend to be assured of their good estate, and to be carried beyond all doubting of the favor of God; supposing that there is no such thing to be expected in the church of God, as a full and absolute assurance of hope; unless it be in some very extraordinary circumstances; as in the case of martyrdom; contrary to the doctrine of Protestants, which has been maintained by their most celebrated writers against the Papists; and contrary to the plainest Scripture evidence. It is manifest, that it was a common thing for the saints that we have a history or particular account of in Scripture, to be assured. God, in the plainest and most positive manner, revealed and testified his special favor to Noah, Abraham, Isaac, Jacob, Moses, Daniel, and others. Job often speaks of his sincerity and uprightness with the greatest imaginable confidence and assurance, often calling God to witness to it; and says plainly, 'I know that my Redeemer liveth, and that I shall see him for myself, and not another,' Job 19:25, etc. David, throughout the book of Psalms, almost everywhere speaks without any hesitancy, and in the most positive manner, of God as his God glorying in him as his portion and heritage, his rock and confidence, his shield; salvation, and high tower, and the like. Hezekiah appeals to God, as one that knew that he had walked before him in truth, and with a perfect heart, 2 Kgs 20:3. Jesus Christ, in his dying discourse with his eleven disciples, in the 14th, 15th, and 16th chapters of John (which was as it were Christ's last will and testament to his disciples, and to his whole church), often declares his special and everlasting love to them in the plainest and most positive terms and promises them a future participation with him in his glory, in the most absolute manner; and tells them at the same time that he does so, to the end that their joy might be full: John 15:11, 'These things have I spoken unto you, that my joy might remain in you, and that your joy might be full.' See also at the conclusion of his whole discourse, chap. 16:33: 'These things have I spoken unto you, that in me ye might have peace. In the world ye shall have tribulation: but be of good cheer, I have overcome the world.' Christ was not afraid of speaking too plainly and positively to them; he did not desire to hold them in the least suspense. And he concluded that last discourse of his with a prayer in their presence, wherein he speaks positively to his Father of those eleven disciples, as having all of them savingly know him, and believed in him, and received and kept his word; and that they were not of the world; and that for their sakes he sanctified himself; and that his will was, that they should be with him in his glory; and tells his Father, that he spake those things in his prayer, to the end, that his joy might be fulfilled in them, v. 13. By these things it is evident, that it is agreeable to Christ's designs, and the contrived ordering and disposition Christ makes of things in his church, that there should be sufficient and abundant provision made, that his saints might have full assurance of their future glory.

The Apostle Paul, through all his epistles speaks in an assured strain; ever speaking positively of his special relation to Christ, his Lord, and Master, and Redeemer, and his interest in, and expectation of the future reward. It would be endless to take notice of all places that might be enumerated; I shall mention but three or four: Gal. 2:20, 'Christ liveth in me; and the life which I now live in the flesh, I live by the faith of the Son of God, who loved me, and gave himself for me'; Phil. 1:21, 'For me to live is Christ, and to die is gain'; 2 Tim. 1:12, 'I know whom I have believed, and I am persuaded that he is able to keep that which I have committed unto him against that day'; 2 Tim. 4:7, 8, 'I have fought a good fight, I have finished my course, I have kept the faith. Henceforth there is laid up for me a crown of righteousness, which the Lord, the righteous Judge, will give me at that day.'

And the nature of the covenant of grace, and God's declared ends in the appointment and constitution of things in that covenant, do plainly show it to be God's design to make ample provision for the saints having an assured hope of eternal life, while living here upon earth. For so are all things ordered and contrived in that covenant, that everything might be made sure on God's part. 'The covenant is ordered in all things and sure': the promises are most full, and very often repeated, and various ways exhibited; and there are many witnesses, and many seals; and God has confirmed his promises with an oath. And God's declared design in all this, is, that the heirs of the promises might have an undoubting hope and full joy, in an assurance of their future glory. Heb. 6:17, 18, 'Wherein God, willing more abundantly to show unto the heirs of promise the immutability of his counsel, confirmed it by an oath: that by two immutable things, in which it was impossible for God to lie, we might have a strong consolation, who have fled for refuge to lay hold on the hope set before us.' But all this would be in vain, to any such purpose, as the saints' strong consolation, and hope of their obtaining future glory, if their interest in those sure promises in ordinary cases was not ascertainable. For God's promises and oaths, let them be as sure as they will, cannot give strong hope and comfort to any particular person, any further than he can know that those promises are made to him. And in vain is provision made in Jesus Christ, that believers might be perfect as pertaining to the conscience, as is signified, Heb. 9:9, if assurance of freedom from the guilt of sin is not attainable.

It further appears that assurance is not only attainable in some very extraordinary cases, but that all Christians are directed to give all diligence to make their calling and election sure, and are told how they may do it, 2 Pet. 1:5-8. And it is spoken of as a thing very unbecoming Christians, and an argument of something very blamable in them, not to know whether Christ be in them or no: 2 Cor. 13:5, 'Know ye not your own selves, how that Jesus Christ is in you, except ye be reprobates?' And it is implied that it is an argument of a very blamable negligence in Christians, if they practise Christianity after such a manner as to remain uncertain of the reward, in 1 Cor. 9:26: 'I therefore so run, as not uncertainly.' And to add no more, it is manifest, that Christians' knowing their interest in the saving benefits of Christianity is a thing ordinarily attainable, because the apostle tells us by what means Christians (and not only the apostles and martyrs) were wont to know this: 1 Cor. 2:12, 'Now we have received, not the spirit of the world, but the Spirit which is of God; that we might know the things that are freely given to us of God.' And 1 John 2:3, 'And hereby we do know that we know him, if we keep his commandments.' And v. 5, 'Hereby know we that we are in him.' Chap. 3:14, 'We know that we have passed from death unto life, because we love the brethren'; ver. 19, 'Hereby we know that we are of the truth, and shall assure our hearts before him;' ver. 24, 'Hereby we know that he abideth in us, by the Spirit which he hath given us.' So chap. 4:13, and chap. 5:2, and v. 19.

Therefore it must needs be very unreasonable to determine, that persons are hypocrites, and their affections wrong, because they seem to be out of doubt of their own salvation, and the affections they are the subjects of seem to banish all fears of hell.

On the other hand, it is no sufficient reason to determine that men are saints, and their affections gracious, because the affections they have are attended with an exceeding confidence that their state is good, and their affections divine. Nothing can be certainly argued from their confidence, how great and strong soever it seems to be. If we see a man that boldly calls God his Father, and commonly speaks in the most bold, familiar, and appropriating language in prayer, 'My Father, my dear Redeemer, my sweet Savior, my Beloved,' and the like; and it is a common thing for him to use the most confident expressions before men, about the goodness of his state; such as, I know certainly that God is my Father; I know so surely as there is a God in heaven, that he is my God; I know I shall go to heaven, as well as if I were there; I know that God is now manifesting himself to my soul, and is now smiling upon me'; and seems to have done forever with any inquiry or examination into his state, as a thing sufficiently known, and out of doubt, and to contemn all that so much as intimate or suggest that there is some reason to doubt or fear whether all is right; such things are no signs at all that it is indeed so as he is confident it is. Such an overbearing, high-handed, and violent sort of confidence as this, so affecting to declare itself with a most glaring show in the sight of men, which is to be seen in many, has not the countenance of a true Christian assurance: it savors more of the spirit of the Pharisees, who never doubted but that they were saints, and the most eminent of saints, and were bold to go to God, and come up near to him, and lift up their eyes, and thank him for the great distinction he had made between them and other men; and when Christ intimated that they were blind and graceless, despised the suggestion: John 9:40, 'And some of the Pharisees which were with him, heard these words, and said unto him, Are we blind also?' If they had more of the spirit of the publican, with their confidence, who, in a sense of his exceeding unworthiness, stood afar off, and durst not so much as lift up his eyes to heaven, but smote on his breast, and cried out of himself as a sinner, their confidence would have more of the aspect of the confidence of one that humbly trusts and hopes in Christ, and has no confidence in himself.

If we do but consider what the hearts of natural men are, what principles they are under the dominion of, what blindness and deceit, what self-flattery, self-exaltation, and self-confidence reign there, we need not at all wonder that their high opinion of themselves, and confidence of their happy circumstances, be as high and strong as mountains, and as violent as a tempest, when once conscience is blinded, and convictions killed, with false high affections, and those forementioned principles let loose, fed up and prompted by false joys and comforts, excited by some pleasing imaginations, impressed by Satan, transforming himself into an angel of light.

When once a hypocrite is thus established in a false hope, he has not those things to cause him to call his hope in question, that oftentimes are the occasion of the doubting of true saints; as, *first,* he has not that cautious spirit, that great sense of the vast importance of a sure foundation, and that dread of being deceived. The comforts of the true saints increase awakening and caution, and a lively sense how great a thing it is to appear before an infinitely holy, just and omniscient Judge. But false comforts put an end to these things and dreadfully stupify the mind. *Secondly,* The hypocrite has not the knowledge of his own blindness, and the deceitfulness of his own heart, and that mean opinion of his own understanding that the true saint has. Those that are deluded with false discoveries and affections, are evermore highly conceited of their light and understanding. *Thirdly,* The devil does not assault the hope of the hypocrite, as he does the hope of a true saint. The devil is a great enemy to a true Christian hope, not only because it tends greatly to the comfort of him that hath it, but also because it is a thing of a holy, heavenly nature, greatly tending to promote and cherish grace in the heart, and a great incentive to strictness and diligence in the Christian life. But he is no enemy to the hope of a hypocrite, which above all things establishes his interest in him that has it. A hypocrite may retain his hope without opposition, as long as he lives, the devil never disturbing it, nor attempting to disturb it. But there is perhaps no true Christian but what has his hope assaulted by him. Satan assaulted Christ himself upon this, whether he were the Son of God or no: and the servant is not above his Master, nor the disciple above his Lord; it is enough for the disciple, that is most privileged in this world, to be as his Master. *Fourthly,* He who has a false hope, has not that sight of his own corruptions, which the saint has. A true Christian has ten times so much to do with his heart and its corruptions, as a hypocrite: and the sins of his heart and practice, appear to him in their blackness; they look dreadful; and it often appears a very mysterious thing, that any grace can be consistent with such corruption, or should be in such a heart. But a false hope hides corruption, covers it all over, and the hypocrite looks clean and bright in his own eyes.

There are two sorts of hypocrites: ones that are deceived with their outward morality and external religion; many of whom are professed Arminians, in the doctrine of justification: and the others, are those that are deceived with false discoveries and elevations; who often cry down works, and men's own righteousness, and talk much of free grace; but at the same time make a righteousness of their discoveries and of their humiliation, and exalt themselves to heaven with them. These two kinds of hypocrites, Mr Shepard, in his exposition of the Parable of the Ten Virgins, distinguishes by the name of *legal* and *evangelical* hypocrites; and often speaks of the latter as the worst. And it is evident that the latter are commonly by far the most confident in their hope, and with the most difficulty brought off from it: I have scarcely known the instance of such a one, in my life, that has been undeceived. The chief grounds of the confidence of many of them, are the very same kind of impulses and supposed revelations (sometimes with texts of Scripture, and sometimes without) that so many of late have had concerning future events; calling these impulses about their good estate, the witness of the

Spirit; entirely misunderstanding the nature of the witness of the Spirit, as I shall show here-after. Those that have had visions and impulses about other things, it has generally been to reveal such things as they are desirous and fond of: and no wonder that persons who give heed to such things, have the same sort of visions or impressions about their own eternal salvation, to reveal to them that their sins are forgiven them, that their names are written in the book of life, that they are in high favor with God, etc., and especially when they earnestly seek, expect, and wait for evidence of their election and salvation this way, as the surest and most glorious evidence of it. Neither is it any wonder, that when they have such a supposed revelation of their good estate, it raises in them the highest degree of confidence of it. It is found by abundant experience, that those who are led away by impulses and imagined revelations, are extremely confident: they suppose that the great Jehovah has declared these and those things to them; and having his immediate testimony, a strong confidence is the highest virtue. Hence they are bold to say, I know this or that – I know certainly – I am as sure as that I have a being, and the like; and they despise all argument and inquiry in the case. And above all things else, it is easy to be accounted for, that impressions and impulses about that which is so pleasing, so suiting their self-love and pride, as their being the dear children of God, distinguished from most in the world in his favor, should make them strongly confident; especially when with their impulses and revelations they have high affections, which they take to be the most eminent exercises of grace. I have known of several persons, that have had a fond desire of something of a temporal nature, through a violent passion that has possessed them; and they have been earnestly pursuing the thing they have desired should come to pass, and have met with great difficulty and many discouragements in it, but at last have had an impression, or supposed revelation, that they should obtain what they sought; and they have looked upon it as a sure promise from the Most High, which has made them most ridiculously confident, against all manner of reason to convince them to the contrary, and all events working against them. And there is nothing hinders, but that persons who are seeking their salvation, may be deceived by the like delusive impressions, and be made confident of that, the same way.

The confidence of many of this sort of hypocrites, that Mr Shepard calls *evangelical hypocrites*, is like the confidence of some mad men, who think they are kings; they will maintain it against all manner of reason and evidence. And in one sense, it is much more immovable than a truly gracious assurance; a true assurance is not upheld, but by the soul's being kept in a holy frame, and Grace maintained in lively exercise. If the actings of grace do much decay in the Christian, and he falls into a lifeless frame, he loses his assurance: but this kind of confidence of hypocrites will not be shaken by sin; they (at least some of them) will maintain their boldness in their hope, in the most corrupt frames and wicked ways; which is a sure evidence of their delusion.

And here I cannot but observe, that there are certain doctrines often preached to the people, which need to be delivered with more caution and explanation than they frequently are; for, as they are by many understood, they tend greatly to establish this delusion and false confidence of hypocrites. The doctrines I speak of are those of 'Christians living by faith, not by sight; their giving glory to God, by trusting him in the dark; living upon Christ, and not upon experiences; not making their good frames the foundation of their faith': which are excellent and important doctrines indeed, rightly understood, but corrupt and destructive, as many understand them. The Scripture speaks of living or walking by faith, and not by sight, in no other way than these, viz., a being governed by a respect to eternal things, that are the objects of faith, and are not seen, and not by a respect to temporal things, which are seen; and believing things revealed, that we never saw with bodily eyes; and also living by faith in the promise of future things, without yet seeing or enjoying the things promised, or knowing the way how they can be fulfilled. This will be easily evident to anyone who looks over the Scriptures, which speak of *faith* in opposition to *sight*; as 2 Cor. 4:18, and 5:7, Heb. 11:1, 8, 13, 17, 27, 29, Rom. 8:24, John 20:29. But this doctrine, as it is understood by many, is, that Christians ought firmly to believe and trust in Christ, without spiritual sight or light, and although they are in a dark dead frame, and, for the present, have no spiritual experiences or discoveries. And it is truly the duty of those who are thus in darkness, to come out of darkness into light and believe. But that they should confidently believe and trust, while they yet remain without spiritual light or sight, is an anti-scriptural and absurd doctrine. The Scripture is ignorant of any such faith in Christ of the operation of God, that is not founded in a spiritual sight of Christ. That believing on Christ, which accompanies a title to everlasting life, is a 'seeing the Son, and believing on him,' John 6:40. True faith in Christ is never exercised, any further than persons 'behold as in a glass the glory of the Lord, and have the knowledge of the glory of God in the face of Jesus Christ,' 2 Cor. 3:18, and 4:6. They into whose minds 'the light of the glorious gospel of Christ, who is the image of God, does not shine, believe not,' 2 Cor. 4:5. That faith, which is without spiritual light, is not the faith of the children of the light, and of the day; but the presumption of the children of darkness. And therefore to press and urge them to believe, without any spiritual light or sight, tends greatly to help forward the delusions of the prince of darkness. Men not only cannot exercise faith without some spiritual light, but they can exercise faith only just in such proportion as they have spiritual light. Men will trust in God no further than they know him; and they cannot be in the exercise of faith in him one ace further than they have a sight of his fullness and faithfulness in exercise. Nor can they have the exercise of trust in God, any further than they are in a gracious frame. They that are in a dead carnal frame, doubtless ought to trust in God; because that would be the same thing as coming out of their bad frame, and turning to God; but to exhort men confidently to trust in God, and so hold up their hope and peace, though they are not in a gracious frame, and continue still to be so, is the same thing in effect, as to exhort them confidentially to trust in God, but not with a gracious trust: and what is that but a wicked presumption? It is just as impossible for men to have a strong or lively trust in God, when they have no lively exercises of grace, or sensible Christian experiences, as it is for them to be in the lively exercises of grace, without the exercises of grace.

It is true, that it is the duty of God's people to trust in him when in darkness, and though they remain still in darkness, in that sense, that they ought to trust in God when the aspects of his providence are dark, and look as though God had forsaken them, and did not hear their prayers, and many clouds gather, and many enemies surround them, with a formidable aspect, threatening to swallow them up, and all events of providence seem to be against them, all circumstances seem to render the promises of God difficult to be fulfilled, and God must be trusted out of sight, i.e., when we cannot see which way it is possible for him to fulfill his word; everything but God's mere word makes it look unlikely, so that if persons believe, they must hope against hope. Thus the ancient Patriarchs, and Job, and the Psalmist, and Jeremiah, Daniel, Shadrach, Meshech, and Abednego, and the Apostle Paul, gave glory to God by trusting in God in darkness. And we have many instances of such a glorious victorious faith in the eleventh of Hebrews. But how different a thing is this, from trusting in God, without spiritual sight, and being at the same time in a dead and carnal frame!

There is also such a thing as spiritual light's being let into the soul in one way, when it is not in another; and so there is such a thing as the saints trusting in God, and also knowing their good estate, when they are destitute of some kinds of experience. As for instance, they may have clear views of God's sufficiency and faithfulness, and so confidently trust in him, and know that they are his children; and at the same time, not have those clear and sweet ideas of his love as at other times: for it was thus with Christ himself in his last passion. And they may have views of much of God's sovereignty, holiness, and all sufficiency, enabling them quietly to submit to him, and exercise a sweet and most encouraging hope in God's fullness, when they are not satisfied of their own good estate. But how different things are these, from confidently trusting in God, without spiritual light or experience!

Those that thus insist on persons living by faith, when they have no experience, and are in very bad frames, are also very absurd in their notions of faith. What they mean by faith is, believing that they are in a good estate. Hence they count it a dreadful sin for them to doubt of their state, whatever frames they are in, and whatever wicked things they do, because it is the great and heinous sin of unbelief; and he is the best man, and puts most honor upon God, that maintains his hope of his good estate the most confidently and immovably, when he has the least light or experience; that is to say, when he is in the worst and most wicked frame and way; because, forsooth, that is a sign that he is strong in faith, giving glory to God, and against hope believes in hope. But what Bible do they learn this notion of faith out of, that it is a man's confidently believing that he is in a good estate? If this be faith, the Pharisees had faith in an eminent degree; some of which, Christ teaches, committed the unpardonable sin against the Holy Ghost. The Scripture represents faith as that by which men are brought into a good estate; and therefore it cannot be the same thing as believing that they are already in a good estate. To suppose that faith consists in persons believing that they are in a good estate, is in effect the same thing, as to suppose that faith consists in a person's believing that he has faith, or believing that he believes.

Indeed persons doubting of their good estate, may in several respects arise from unbelief. It may be from unbelief, or because they have so little faith that they have so little evidence of their good estate: if they had more experience of the actings of faith, and so more experience of the exercise of grace, they would have clearer evidence that their state was good; and so their doubts would be removed. And then their doubting of their state may be from unbelief thus, when, though there be many things that are good evidences of a work of grace in them, yet they doubt very much whether they are really in a state of favor with God, because it is they, those that are so unworthy, and have done so much to provoke God to anger against them. Their doubts in such a case arise from unbelief, as they arise from want of a sufficient sense of, and reliance on, the infinite riches of God's grace, and the sufficiency of Christ for the chief of sinners. They may also be from unbelief, when they doubt of their state, because of the mystery of God's dealings with them; they are not able to reconcile such dispensations with

God's favor to them; or when they doubt whether they have any interest in the promises, because the promises from the aspect of providence appear so unlikely to be fulfilled; the difficulties that are in the way are so many and great. Such doubting arises from want of dependence upon God's almighty power, and his knowledge and wisdom, as infinitely above theirs. But yet, in such persons, their unbelief, and their doubting of their state, are not the same thing; though one arises from the other.

Persons may be greatly to blame for doubting of their state, on such grounds as these last mentioned; and they may be to blame, that they have no more grace, and no more of the present exercises and experiences of it, to be an evidence to them of the goodness of their state: men are doubtless to blame for being in a dead, carnal frame; but when they are in such a frame, and have no sensible experience of the exercises of grace, but on the contrary, are much under the prevalence of lusts and an unchristian spirit, they are not to blame for doubting their state. It is as impossible, in the nature of things, that a holy and Christian hope be kept alive, in its clearness and strength, in such circumstances, as it is to keep the light in the room, when the candle is put out; or to maintain the bright sunshine in the air, when the sun is gone down. Distant experiences, when darkened by present prevailing lust and corruption, never keep alive a gracious confidence and assurance; but that sickens and decays upon it, as necessarily as a little child by repeated blows on the head with a hammer. Nor is it at all to be lamented, that persons doubt of their state in such circumstances: but, on the contrary, it is desirable and every way best that they should. It is agreeable to that wise and merciful constitution of things, which God hath established, that it should be so. For so hath God contrived and constituted things, in his dispensations towards his own people, that when their love decays, and the exercises of it fail, or become weak, fear should arise; for then they need it to restrain them from sin, and to excite them to care for the good of their souls, and so to stir them up to watchfulness and diligence in religion: but God hath so ordered, that when love rises, and is in vigorous exercise, then fear should vanish, and be driven away; for then they need it not, having a higher and more excellent principle in exercise, to restrain them from sin, and stir them up to their duty. There are no other principles, which human nature is under the influence of, that will ever make men conscientious, but one of these two, *fear* or *love*; and therefore, if one of these should not prevail as the other decays, God's people, when fallen into dead and carnal frames, when love is asleep, would be lamentably exposed indeed: and therefore God has wisely ordained, that these two opposite principles of love and fear should rise and fall, like the two opposite scales of a balance; when one rises the other sinks. As light and darkness necessarily and unavoidably succeed each other; if light prevails, so much does darkness cease, and no more; and if light decays, so much does darkness prevail; so it is in the heart of a child of God: if divine love decays and falls asleep, and lust prevails, the light and joy of hope go out, and dark fear and doubting arises; and if, on the contrary, divine love prevails and comes into lively exercise, this brings in the brightness of hope, and drives away black lust, and fear with it. Love is the spirit of adoption, or the childlike principle; if that slumbers, men fall under fear, which is the spirit of bondage, or the servile principle; and so on the contrary. And if it be so, that love, or the spirit of adoption, be carried to a great height, it quite drives away all fear, and gives full assurance; agreeable to that of the apostle, 1 John 4:18, 'There is no fear in love, but perfect love casts out fear.' These two opposite principles of lust and holy love, bring hope and fear into the hearts of God's children, in proportion as they prevail; that is, when left to their own natural influence, without something adventitious, or accidental intervening; as the distemper of melancholy, doctrinal ignorance, prejudices of education, wrong instruction, false principles, peculiar temptations, etc.

Fear is cast out by the Spirit of God, no other way than by the prevailing of love; nor is it ever maintained by his Spirit but when love is asleep. At such a time, in vain is all the saint's self-examinations, and poring on past experience, in order to establish his peace, and get assurance. For it is contrary to the nature of things, as God hath constituted them, that he should have assurance at such a time.

They therefore do directly thwart God's wise and gracious constitution of things, who exhort others to be confident in their hope, when in dead frames; under a notion of 'living by faith, and not by sight, and trusting God in the dark, and living upon Christ, and not upon experiences'; and warn them not to doubt of their good estate, lest they should be guilty of the dreadful sin of unbelief. And it has a direct tendency to establish the most presumptuous hypocrites, and to prevent their ever calling their state in question, how much soever wickedness rages, and reigns in their hearts, and prevails in their lives; under a notion of honoring God, by hoping against hope, and confidently trusting in God, when things look very dark. And doubtless vast has been the mischief that has been done this way.

Persons cannot be said to forsake Christ, and live on their experiences of the exercises of grace, merely because they take them and use them as evidences of grace; for there are no other evidences that they can or ought to take. But then may persons be said to live upon their experiences, when they make a righteousness of them, and instead of keeping their eye on God's glory and Christ's excellency, they turn their eyes off these objects without them, on to themselves, to entertain their minds, by viewing their own attainments, and high experiences, and the great things they have met with, and are bright and beautiful in their own eyes, and are rich and increased with goods in their own apprehensions, and think that God has as admiring an esteem of them, on the same account, as they have of themselves: this is living on experiences, and not on Christ; and is more abominable in the sight of God, than the gross immoralities of those who make no pretenses to religion. But this is a far different thing from a mere improving experiences as evidences of an interest in a glorious Redeemer.

But to return from this digression, I would mention one thing more under the general head that I am upon.

12. *Nothing can be certainly concluded concerning the nature of religious affections, that any are the subjects of, from this, that the outward manifestations of them, and the relation persons give of them, are very affecting and pleasing to the truly godly, and such as greatly gain their charity, and win their hearts.*

The true saints have not such a spirit of discerning that they can certainly determine who are godly, and who are not. For though they know experimentally what true religion is, in the internal exercises of it; yet these are what they can neither feel, nor see, in the heart of another. There is nothing in others, that comes within their view, but outward manifestations and appearances; but the Scripture plainly intimates, that this way of judging what is in men by outward appearances, is at best uncertain, and liable to deceit: 1 Sam. 16:7, 'The Lord seeth not as man seeth; for man looketh on the outward appearance, but the Lord looketh on the heart.'

Isa. 11:3, 'He shall not judge after the sight of his eyes, neither reprove after the hearing of his ears.' They commonly are but poor judges, and dangerous counselors in soul cases, who are quick and peremptory in determining persons' states, vaunting themselves in their extraordinary faculty of discerning and distinguishing, in these great affairs; as though all was open and clear to them. They betray one of these three things: either that they have had but little experience; or are persons of a weak judgment; or that they have a great degree of pride and self-confidence, and so ignorance of themselves. Wise and experienced men will proceed with great caution in such an affair.

When there are many probable appearances of piety in others, it is the duty of the saints to receive them cordially into their charity, and to love them and rejoice in them, as their brethren in Christ Jesus. But yet the best of men may be, when the appearances seem to them exceeding fair and bright, as entirely to gain their charity, and conquer their hearts. It has been a common thing in the church of God, for such bright professors, that are received as eminent saints, among the saints, to fall away and come to nothing. And this we need not wonder at, if we consider the things that have been already observed; what things it has been shown may appear in men who are altogether graceless. Nothing hinders but that all these things may meet together in men, and yet they be without a spark of grace in their hearts. They may have religious affections of many kinds together; they may have a sort of affection towards God, that bears a great resemblance of dear love to him; and so a kind of love to the brethren, and great appearances of admiration of God's perfections and works, and sorrow for sin, and reverence, submission, self-abasement, gratitude, joy, religious longings, and zeal for religion and the good of souls. And these affections may come after great awakenings and convictions of conscience; and there may be great appearances of a work of humiliation: and counterfeit love and joy, and other affections may seem to follow these, and one another, just in the same order that is commonly observable in the holy affections of true converts. And these religious affections may be carried to a great height, and may cause abundance of tears, yea, may overcome the nature of those who are the subjects of them, and may make them affectionate, and fervent, and fluent, in speaking of the things of God, and dispose them to be abundant in it; and may be attended with many sweet texts of Scripture, and precious promises, brought with great impression on their minds; and may dispose them with their mouths to praise and glorify God, in a very ardent manner, and fervently to call upon others to praise him, crying out of their unworthiness, and extolling free grace. And may, moreover, dispose them to abound in the external duties of religion, such as prayer, hearing the word preached, singing, and religious conference; and these things attended with a great resemblance of a Christian assurance, in its greatest height, when the saints mount on eagles' wings, above all darkness and doubting. I think it has been made plain, that there may be all these things, and yet there be nothing more than the common influences of the Spirit of God, joined with the delusions of Satan, and the wicked and deceitful heart. To which I may add, that all these things may be attended with a sweet natural temper, and a good doctrinal knowledge of religion, and a long acquaintance with the saints' way of talking, and of expressing their affections and experiences, and a natural ability and subtlety in accommodating their expressions and manner of speaking to the dispositions and notions of the hearers, and a taking decency of expression and behavior, formed by a good education. How great therefore may the resemblance be, as to all outward expressions and appearances, between a hypocrite and a true saint! Doubtless it is the glorious prerogative of the omniscient God, as the great searcher of hearts, to be able well to separate between sheep and goats. And what an indecent self-exaltation and arrogance it is, in poor, fallible, dark mortals, to pretend that they can determine and know, who are really sincere and upright before God, and who are not!

Many seem to lay great weight on that, and to suppose it to be what may determine them with respect to others' real piety, when they not only tell a plausible story, but when, in giving an account of their experiences, they make such a representation, and speak after such a manner, that they feel their talk; that is to say, when their talk seems to harmonize with their own experience, and their hearts are touched and affected and delighted, by what they hear them say, and drawn out by it, in dear love to them. But there is not that certainty in such things, and that full dependence to be had upon them, which many imagine. A true saint greatly delights in holiness; it is a most beautiful thing in his eyes; and God's work, in savingly renewing and making holy and happy, a poor, and before perishing soul, appears to him a most glorious work: no wonder, therefore, that his heart is touched, and greatly affected, when he hears another give a probable account of this work, wrought on his own heart, and when he sees in him probable appearances of holiness; whether those pleasing appearances have anything real to answer them, or no. And if he uses the same words, which are commonly made use of, to express the affections of true saints, and tells of many things following one another in an order, agreeable to the method of the experience of him that hears him, and also speaks freely and boldly, and with an air of assurance; no wonder the other thinks his experiences harmonize with his own. And if, besides all this, in giving his relation, he speaks with much affection; and, above all, if in speaking he seems to show much affection to him to whom he speaks, such an affection as the Galatians did to the Apostle Paul; these things will naturally have a powerful influence, to affect and draw his hearer's heart, and open wide the doors of his charity towards him. David speaks as one who had felt Ahithophel's talk, and had once a sweet savor and relish of it. And therefore exceeding great was his surprise and disappointment, when he fell; it was almost too much for him: Ps. 55:12, 13, 14, 'It was not an enemy – then I could have borne it; but it was thou, a man, mine equal, my guide, and mine acquaintance: we took sweet counsel together, and walked unto the house of God in company.'

It is with professors of religion, especially such as become so in a time of outpouring of the Spirit of God, as it is with blossoms in the spring; there are vast numbers of them upon the trees, which all look fair and promising; but yet many of them never come to anything. And many of those, that in a little time wither up, and drop off, and rot under the trees; yet for a while look as beautiful and gay as others; and not only so, but smell sweet, and send forth a pleasant odor; so that we cannot, by any of our senses, certainly distinguish those blossoms which have in them that secret virtue, which will afterwards appear in the fruit, and that inward solidity and strength which shall enable them to bear, and cause them to be perfected by the hot summer sun, that will dry up the others. It is the mature fruit which comes afterwards, and not the beautiful colors and smell of the blossoms, that we must judge by. So new converts (professedly so), in their talk about things of religion, may appear fair, and be very savory, and the saints may think they talk feelingly. They may relish their talk, and imagine they perceive a divine savor in it, and yet all may come to nothing.

It is strange how hardly men are brought to be contented with the rules and directions Christ has given them, but they must needs go by other rules of their counsels which Christ ever delivered more plainly, than the rule. I know of no directions or councils which Christ ever delivered more plainly, than the rule he has given us, to guide our judging of others' sincerity, viz., that we should judge of the tree chiefly by the fruit: but yet this will not do; but other ways are found out, which are imagined to be more distinguishing and certain. And woeful have been the mischievous consequences of this arrogant setting up men's wisdom above the wisdom of Christ. I believe many saints have gone much out of the way of Christ's word, in this respect: and some of them have been chastised with whips, and (I had almost said) scorpions, to bring them back again. But many things which have lately appeared, and do now appear, may convince that ordinarily those who have gone farthest this way, that have been most highly conceited of their faculty of discerning, and have appeared most forward, peremptorily and suddenly to determine the state of men's souls, have been hypocrites, who have known nothing of true religion.

In the parable of the wheat and tares, it is said, Matt. 13:26, 'When the blade was sprung up, and brought forth fruit, then appeared the tares also.' As though the tares were not discerned, nor distinguishable from the wheat, until then, as Mr Flavel observes, who mentions it as an observation of Jerome's, that 'wheat and tares are so much alike, until the blade of the wheat comes to bring forth the ear, that it is next to impossible to distinguish them.' And then Mr Flavel adds, 'How difficult soever it be to discern the difference between wheat and tares; yet doubtless the eye of sense can much easier discriminate them, than the most quick and piercing eye of man can discern the difference between special and common grace. For all saving graces in the saints, have their counterfeits in hypocrites; there are similar works in those, which a spiritual and very judicious eye may easily mistake for the saving and genuine effects of a sanctifying spirit.'

As it is the ear of the fruit which distinguishes the wheat from the tares, so this is the true Shibboleth, that he who stands as judge at the passages of Jordan, makes use of to distinguish those that shall pass over Jordan into the true Canaan, from those that should be slain at the passages. For the Hebrew word Shibboleth signifies an ear of corn. And perhaps the more full pronunciation of Jephthah's friends, Shibboleth, may represent a full ear with fruit in it, typifying the fruits of the friends of Christ, the antitype of Jephthah; and the more lean pronunciation of the Ephraimites, his enemies, may represent their empty ears, typifying the show of religion in hypocrites, without substance and fruit. This is agreeable to the doctrine we are abundantly taught in Scripture, viz., that he who is set to judge those that pass through death, whether they have a right to enter into the heavenly Canaan or no, or whether they should not be slain, will judge every man according to his works.

We seem to be taught the same things, by the rules given for the priest's discerning the leprosy. In many cases it was impossible for the priest to determine whether a man had the leprosy, or whether he were clean, by the most narrow inspection of the appearances that were upon him, until he had waited to see what the appearances would come to, and had shut up the person who showed himself to him, one seven days after another; and when he judged, he was to determine by the hair, which grew out of the spot that was showed him, which was as it were the fruit that it brought forth.

And here, before I finish what I have to say under this head, I would say something to a strange notion some have of late been led away with, of certainly knowing the good estate that others are in, as though it were immediately revealed to them from heaven, by their love flowing out to them in an extraordinary manner. They argue thus, that their love being very sensible and great, it may be certainly known by them who feel it, to be a true Christian love: and if it be a true Christian love, the Spirit of God must be the author of it: and inasmuch as the Spirit of God who knows certainly, whether others are the children of God or no, and is a spirit of truth, is pleased by an uncommon influence upon them, to cause their love to flow out, in an extraordinary manner, towards such a person as a child of God; it must needs be, that this infallible Spirit, who deceives none, knows that that person is a child of God. But such persons might be convinced of the falseness of their reasoning, if they would consider whether or no it be not their duty, and what God requires of them, to love those as the children of God whom they think are the children of God, and whom they have no reason to think otherwise of, from all that they can see in them, though God, who searches the hearts, knows them not to be his children.

If it be their duty, then it is good, and the want of it sin; and therefore surely the Spirit of God may be the author of it: the Spirit of God, without being a spirit of falsehood, may in such a case assist a person to do his duty, and keep him from sin. But then they argue from the uncommon degree and special manner, in which their love flows out to the person, which they think the Spirit of God never would cause, if he did not know the object to be a child of God. But then I would ask them, whether or no it is not their duty to love all such as they are bound to think are the children of God, from all that they can see in them, to a very great degree, though God, from other things which he sees, that are out of sight to them, knows them not to be so. It is men's duty to love all whom they are bound in charity to look upon as the children of God, with a vastly dearer affection than they commonly do. As we ought to love Christ to the utmost capacity of our nature, so it is our duty to love those whom we think are so near and dear to him as his members, with an exceeding dear affection, as Christ has loved us; and therefore it is sin in us not to love them so. We ought to pray to God that he would by his Spirit keep us from sin, and enable us to do our duty: and may not his Spirit answer our prayers, and enable us to do our duty, in a particular instance, without lying? If he cannot, then the Spirit of God is bound not to help his people to do their duty in some instances, because he cannot do it without being a spirit of falsehood. But surely God is so sovereign as that comes to, that he may enable us to do our duty when he pleases, and on what occasion he pleases. When persons think others are his children, God may have other ends in causing their exceedingly endeared love to flow out to them, besides revealing to them whether their opinion of them be right or no: he may have that merciful end in it to enable them to know their duty, and to keep them from that dreadful infinite evil, sin. And will they say God shall not show them that mercy in such a case? If I am at a distance from home, and hear, that in my absence my house is burnt, but my family have, in some extraordinary manner, all escaped the flames; and everything in the circumstances of the story, as I hear it, makes it appear very credible, it would be sin in me, in such a case, not to feel a very great degree of gratitude to God, though the story indeed be not true. And is not God so sovereign, that he may, if he pleases, show me that mercy on that occasion, and enable me to do my duty in a much further degree than I used to do it, and yet not incur the charge of deceitfulness in confirming a falsehood?

It is exceeding manifest, that error or mistake may be the occasion of a gracious exercise, and consequently a gracious influence of the Spirit of God by Rom. 14:6: 'He that eateth to the Lord he eateth, and giveth God thanks; and he that eateth not to the Lord he eateth not, and giveth God thanks!' The apostle is speaking of those, who through erroneous and needless scruples, avoided eating legally unclean meats. By this it is very evident, that there may be true exercises of grace, a true respect to the Lord, and particularly, a true thankfulness, which may be occasioned, both by an erroneous judgment and practice. And consequently, an error may be the occasion of those true holy exercises that are from the infallible Spirit of God. And if so, it is certainly too much for us to determine, to how great a degree the Spirit of God may give this holy exercise, on such an occasion.

This notion, of certainly discerning another's state, by love flowing out, is not only not founded on reason or Scripture, but it is anti-scriptural, it is against the rules of Scripture; which say not a word of any such way of judging the state of others as this, but direct us to judge chiefly by the fruits that are seen in them. And it is against the doctrines of Scripture, which do plainly teach us, that the state of others' souls towards God cannot be known by us, as in Rev. 2:17: 'To him that overcometh will I give to eat of the hidden manna, and I will give him a white stone, and in the stone a new name written, which no man knoweth, saving he that receiveth it.' And Rom. 2:29, 'He is a Jew, which is one inwardly; and circumcision is that of the heart, in the spirit, and not in the letter, whose praise is not of men, but of God.' That by this last expression, 'whose praise is not of men, but of God,' the apostle has respect to the insufficiency of men to judge concerning him, whether he be inwardly a Jew or no (as they could easily see by outward marks, whether men were outwardly Jews), and would signify, that it belongs to God alone to give a determining voice in this matter, is confirmed by the same apostle's use of the phrase, in 1 Cor. 4:5: 'Therefore judge nothing before the time, until the Lord come, who both will bring to light the hidden things of darkness, and will make manifest the counsels of the heart:' and then shall every man have praise of God. The apostle, in the two foregoing verses, says, 'But with me it is a very small thing that I should be judged of you, or of man's judgment: yea, I judge not mine own self. For I know nothing by myself, yet am I not hereby justified; but he that judgeth me is the Lord.' And again, it is further confirmed, because the apostle, in this second chapter to the Romans, directs his speech especially to those who had a high conceit of their own holiness, made their boast of God, and were confident of their own discerning, and that they knew God's will, and approved the things which were excellent, or tried the things that differ (as it is in the margin), v. 19: 'And were confident that they were guides of the blind, and a light to them which are in darkness, instructors of the foolish, teachers of babes; and so took upon them to judge others.' See vv. 1, and 17, 18, 19, 20.

And how arrogant must the notion be, that they have, who imagine they can certainly know others' godliness, when that great Apostle Peter pretends not to say any more concerning Sylvanus, than that he was a faithful brother, as he supposed! 1 Pet. 5:12. Though this Sylvanus appears to have been a very eminent minister of Christ, and an evangelist, and a famous light in God's church at that day, and an intimate companion of the apostles. See 2 Cor. 1:19, 1 Thess. 1:1, and 2 Thess. 1:1.

✣ PART III ✣

SHOWING WHAT ARE DISTINGUISHING SIGNS OF TRULY GRACIOUS AND HOLY AFFECTIONS

I COME now to the second thing appertaining to the trial of religious affections, which was proposed, viz., to take notice of some things, wherein those affections that are spiritual and gracious, do differ from those that are not so.

But before I proceed directly to the distinguishing characters, I would previously mention some things which I desire may be observed, concerning the marks I shall lay down.

a.   That I am far from undertaking to give such signs of gracious affections, as shall be sufficient to enable any certainly to distinguish true affection from false in others; or to determine positively which of their neighbors are true professors, and which are hypocrites. In so doing, I should be guilty of that arrogance which I have been condemning. Though it be plain that Christ has given rules to all Christians, to enable them to judge of professors of religion, whom they are concerned with, so far as is necessary for their own safety, and to prevent their being led into a snare by false teachers, and false pretenders to religion; and though it be also beyond doubt, that the Scriptures do abound with rules, which may be very serviceable to ministers, in counseling and conducting souls committed to their care, in things appertaining to their spiritual and eternal state; yet it is also evident, that it was never God's design to give us any rules, by which we may certainly know, who of our fellow-professors are his, and to make a full and clear separation between sheep and goats; but that, on the contrary, it was God's design to reserve this to himself, as his prerogative. And therefore no such distinguishing signs as shall enable Christians or ministers to do this, are ever to be expected to the world's end: for no more is ever to be expected from any signs, that are to be found in the word of God, or gathered from it, than Christ designed them for.

b.   No such signs are to be expected, that shall be sufficient to enable those saints certainly to discern their own good estate, who are very low in grace, or are such as have much departed from God, and are fallen into a dead, carnal, and unchristian frame. It is not agreeable to God's design (as has been already observed), that such should know their good estate: nor is it desirable that they should; but, on the contrary, every way best that they should not; and we have reason to bless God, that he has made no provision that such should certainly know the state that they are in, any other way than by first coming out of the ill frame and way they are in. Indeed it is not properly through the defect of the signs given in the word of God, that every saint living, whether strong or weak, and those who are in a bad frame, as well as others, cannot certainly know their good estate by them. For the rules in themselves are certain and infallible, and every saint has, or has had those things in himself, which are sure evidences of grace; for every, even the least act of grace is so. But it is through his defect to whom the signs are given. There is a twofold defect in that saint who is very low in grace, or in an ill frame, which makes it impossible for him to know certainly that he has true grace, by the best signs and rules which can be given him. First, a defect in the object, or the qualification to be viewed and examined. I do not mean an essential defect; because I suppose the person to be a real saint; but a defect in degree: grace being very small, cannot be clearly and certainly discerned and distinguished.

Things that are very small, we cannot clearly discern their form, or distinguish them one from another; though, as they are in themselves, their form may be very different. There is doubtless a great difference between the body of man, and the bodies of other animals, in the first conception in the womb: but yet if we should view the different embryos, it might not be possible for us to discern the difference, by reason of the imperfect state of the object; but as it comes to greater perfection, the difference becomes very plain. The difference between creatures of very contrary qualities, is not so plainly to be seen while they are very young; even after they are actually brought forth, as in their more perfect state. The difference between doves and ravens, or doves and vultures, when they first come out of the egg, is not so evident; but as they grow to their perfection, it is exceeding great and manifest. Another defect attending the grace of those I am speaking of is its being mingled with so much corruption, which clouds and hides it, and makes it impossible for it certainly to be known. Though different things that are before us, may have in themselves many marks thoroughly distinguishing them one from another; yet if we see them only in a thick smoke, it may nevertheless be impossible to distinguish them. A fixed star is easily distinguishable from a comet, in a clear sky; but if we view them through a cloud, it may be impossible to see the difference. When true Christians are in an ill frame, guilt lies on the conscience; which will bring fear, and so prevent the peace and joy of an assured hope.

Secondly, there is in such a case a defect in the eye. As the feebleness of grace and prevalence of corruption, obscures the object; so it enfeebles the sight; it darkens the sight as to all spiritual objects, of which grace is one. Sin is like some distempers of the eyes, that make things to appear of different colors from those which properly belong to them, and like many other distempers, that put the mouth out of taste so as to disenable it from distinguishing good and wholesome food from bad, but everything tastes bitter.

Men in a corrupt and carnal frame, have their spiritual senses in but poor plight for judging and distinguishing spiritual things.

For these reasons no signs that can be given, will actually satisfy persons in such a case: let the signs that are given be never so good and infallible, and clearly laid down, they will not serve them. It is like giving a man rules, how to distinguish visible objects in the dark; the things themselves may be very different, and their difference may be very well and distinctly described to him; yet all is insufficient to enable him to distinguish them, because he is in the dark. And therefore many persons in such a case spend time in a fruitless labor, in poring on past experiences, and examining themselves by signs they hear laid down from the pulpit, or that they read in books; when there is other work for them to do, that is much more expected of them; which, while they neglect, all their self-examinations are like to be in vain if they should spend never so much time in them. The accursed thing is to be destroyed from their camp, and Achan to be slain; and until this be done they will be in trouble. It is not God's design that men should obtain assurance in any other way, than by mortifying corruption, and increasing in grace, and obtaining the lively exercises of it. And although self-examination be a duty of great use and importance, and by no means to be neglected; yet it is not the principal means, by which the saints do get satisfaction of their good estate. Assurance is not to be obtained so much by self-examination, as by action. The Apostle Paul sought assurance chiefly this way, even by 'forgetting the things that were behind, and reaching forth unto those things that were before, pressing towards the mark for the prize of the high calling of God in Christ Jesus; if by any means he might attain unto the resurrection of the dead.' And it was by this means chiefly that he obtained assurance: 1 Cor. 9:26, 'I therefore so run, not as uncertainly.' He obtained assurance of winning the prize, more by running, than by considering. The swiftness of his pace did more towards his assurance of a conquest, than the strictness of his examination. Giving all diligence to grow in grace, by adding to faith, virtue, etc., is the direction that the Apostle Peter gives us, for 'making our calling and election sure, and having an entrance ministered to us abundantly, into Christ's everlasting kingdom'; signifying to us, that without this, our eyes will be dim, and we shall be as men in the dark, that cannot plainly see things past or to come, either the forgiveness of our sins past, or our heavenly inheritance that is future, and far off, 2 Pet. 1:5–11.

Therefore, though good rules to distinguish true grace from counterfeit, may tend to convince hypocrites, and be of great use to the saints, in many respects; and among other benefits may be very useful to them to remove many needless scruples, and establish their hope; yet I am far from pretending to lay down any such rules, as shall be sufficient of themselves, without other means, to enable all true saints to see their good estate, or as supposing they should be the principal means of their satisfaction.

c.   Nor is there much encouragement, in the experience of present or past times, to lay down rules or marks to distinguish between true and false affections, in hopes of convincing any considerable number of that sort of hypocrites, who have been deceived with great false discoveries and affections, and are once settled in a false confidence, and high conceit of their own supposed great experiences and privileges. Such hypocrites are so conceited of their own wisdom, and so blinded and hardened with a very great self-righteousness (but very subtle and secret, under the disguise of great humility), and so invincible a fondness of their pleasing conceit of their great exaltation, that it usually signifies nothing at all to lay before them the most convincing evidences of their hypocrisy. Their state is indeed deplorable, and next to those who have committed the unpardonable sin. Some of this sort of persons seem to be most out of the reach of means of conviction and repentance. But yet the laying down good rules may be a means of preventing such hypocrites, and of convincing many of other kinds of hypocrites; and God is able to convince even this kind, and his grace is not to be limited, nor means to be neglected. And besides, such rules may be of use to the true saints, to detect false affections, which they may have mingled with true; and be a means of their religion's becoming more pure, and like gold tried in the fire.

Having premised these things, I now proceed directly to take notice of those things in which true religious affections are distinguished from false.

1.   *Affections that are truly spiritual and gracious, do arise from those influences and operations on the heart, which are spiritual, supernatural and divine.*

I will explain what I mean by these terms, whence will appear their use to distinguish between those affections which are spiritual, and those which are not so.

We find that true saints, or those persons who are sanctified by the Spirit of God, are in the New Testament called spiritual persons. And their being spiritual is spoken of as their peculiar character, and that wherein they are distinguished from those who are not sanctified. This is evident, because those who are spiritual are set in opposition to natural men, and carnal men.

Thus the spiritual man and the natural man are set in opposition one to another, 1 Cor. 2:14, 15: 'The natural man receiveth not the things of the Spirit of God; for they are foolishness unto him; neither can he know them, because they are spiritually discerned. But he that is spiritual judgeth all things.' The Scripture explains itself to mean an ungodly man, or one that has no grace, by a natural man: thus the Apostle Jude, speaking of certain ungodly men, that had crept in unawares among the saints, v. 4, of his epistle, says, 5:19, 'These are sensual, having not the Spirit.' This the apostle gives as a reason why they behaved themselves in such a wicked manner as he had described. Here the word translated *sensual*, which in those verses in 1 Cor. chap. 2 is translated *natural*. In the like manner, in the continuation of the same discourse, in the next verse but one, spiritual men are opposed to carnal men; which the connection plainly shows mean the same, as spiritual men and natural men, in the foregoing verses; 'And I, brethren, could not speak unto you, as unto spiritual, but as unto carnal'; i.e., as in a great measure unsanctified. That by carnal the apostle means corrupt and unsanctified, is abundantly evident, by Rom. 7:25, and 8:1, 4, 5, 6, 7, 8, 9, 19, 13, Gal. 5:16, to the end, Col. 2:18. Now therefore, if by natural and carnal in these texts, be intended unsanctified, then doubtless by spiritual, which is opposed thereto, is meant sanctified and gracious.

And as the saints are called spiritual in Scripture, so we also find that there are certain properties, qualities, and principles, that have the same epithet given them. So we read of a 'spiritual mind,' Rom. 8:6, 7, and of 'spiritual wisdom,' Col. 1:9, and of 'spiritual blessings,' Eph. 1:3.

Now it may be observed, that the epithet *spiritual*, in these and other parallel texts of the New Testament, is not used to signify any relation of persons or things to the spirit or soul of man, as the spiritual part of man, in opposition to the body, which is the material part. Qualities are not said to be spiritual, because they have their seat in the soul, and not in the body: for there are some properties that the Scripture calls *carnal* or *fleshly*, which have their seat as much in the soul, as those properties that are called *spiritual*. Thus it is with pride and self-righteousness, and a man's trusting to his own wisdom, which the apostle calls *fleshly*, Col. 2:18. Nor are things called spiritual, because they are conversant about those things that are immaterial, and not corporeal. For so was the wisdom of the wise men, and princes of this world, conversant about spirits, and immaterial beings; which yet the apostle speaks of as natural men, totally ignorant of those things that are spiritual, 1 Cor. chap. 2. But it is with relation to the Holy Ghost, or Spirit of God, that persons or things are termed spiritual in the New Testament. Spirit, as the word is used to signify the third person in the Trinity, is the substantive, of which is formed the adjective spiritual, in the holy Scriptures. Thus Christians are called spiritual persons, because they are born of the Spirit, and because of the indwelling and holy influences of the Spirit of God in them. And things are called spiritual as related to the Spirit of God; 1 Cor. 2:13, 14, 'Which things also we speak, not in the words which man's wisdom teacheth, but which the Holy Ghost teacheth, comparing spiritual things with spiritual. But the natural man receiveth not the things of the Spirit of God.' Here the apostle himself expressly signifies, that by spiritual things, he means the things of the Spirit of God, and things which the Holy Ghost teacheth. The same is yet more abundantly apparent by viewing the whole context. Again, Rom. 8:6, 'To be carnally minded, is death; to be spiritually minded, is life and peace.' The apostle explains what he means by being carnally and spiritually minded in what follows in the 9th verse, and shows that by being spiritually minded, he means a having the indwelling and holy influences of the Spirit of God in the heart: 'But ye are not in the flesh, but in the Spirit, it so be the Spirit of God dwell in you. Now if any man have not the Spirit of Christ, he is none of his.' The same is evident by all the context. But time would fail to produce all the evidence there is of this, in the New Testament.

And it must be here observed, that although it is with relation to the Spirit of God and his influences, that persons and things are called spiritual; yet not all those persons who are subject to any kind of influence of the Spirit of God, are ordinarily called spiritual in the New Testament. They who have only the common influences of God's Spirit, are not so called, in the places cited above, but only those who have the special, gracious, and saving influences of God's Spirit; as is evident, because it has been already proved, that by spiritual men is meant godly men, in opposition to natural, carnal, and unsanctified men. And it is most plain, that the apostle by spiritually minded, Rom. 8:6, means graciously minded. And though the extra-ordinary gifts of the Spirit, which natural men might have, are sometimes called spiritual, because they are from the Spirit; yet natural men, whatever gifts of the Spirit they had, were not, in the usual language of the New Testament, called spiritual persons. For it was not by men's having the gifts of the Spirit, but by their having the virtues of the Spirit, that they were called spiritual; as is apparent by Gal. 6:1: 'Brethren, if any man be overtaken in a fault, ye which are spiritual, restore such a one in the spirit of meekness.' Meekness is one of those virtues which the apostle had just spoken of, in the verses next preceding, showing what are the fruits of the Spirit. Those qualifications are said to be spiritual in the language of the New Testament, which are truly gracious and holy, and peculiar to the saints.

Thus, when we read of spiritual wisdom and understanding (as in Col. 1:9, 'We desire that ye may be filled with the knowledge of his will, in all wisdom and spiritual understanding'), hereby is intended that wisdom which is gracious, and from the sanctifying influences of the Spirit of God. For, doubtless, by spiritual wisdom is meant that which is opposite to what the Scripture calls natural wisdom; as the spiritual man is opposed to the natural man. And there-fore spiritual wisdom is doubtless the same with that wisdom which is from above, that the Apostle James speaks of, Jas 3:17: 'The wisdom that is from above, is first pure, then peaceable, gentle,' etc., for this the apostle opposes to natural wisdom, v. 15: 'This wisdom descendeth not from above, but is earthly, sensual' – the last word in the original is the same that is translated *natural*, in 1 Cor. 2:14.

So that although natural men may be the subjects of many influences of the Spirit of God, as is evident by many Scriptures, as Num. 24:2, 1 Sam. 10:10, and 11:6, and 16:14, 1 Cor. 13:1, 2, 3, Heb. 6:4, 5, 6, and many others; yet they are not, in the sense of the Scripture, spiritual persons; neither are any of those effects, common gifts, qualities, or affections, that are from the influence of the Spirit of God upon them, called spiritual things. The great difference lies in these two things.

a. The Spirit of God is given to the true saints to dwell in them, as his proper lasting abode; and to influence their hearts, as a principle of new nature or as a divine supernatural spring of life and action. The Scriptures represent the Holy Spirit not only as moving, and occasionally influencing the saints, but as dwelling in them as his temple, his proper abode, and everlasting dwelling place, 1 Cor. 3:16, 2 Cor. 6:16, John 14:16, 17. And he is represented as being there so

A *Treatise Concerning Religious Affections* ✦

united to the faculties of the soul, that he becomes there a principle or spring of new nature and life.

So the saints are said to live by Christ living in them, Gal. 2:20. Christ by his Spirit not only *is* in them, but *lives* in them; and so that they live by his life; so is his Spirit united to them, as a principle of life in them; they do not only drink living water, but this 'living water becomes a well or fountain of water,' in the soul, 'springing up into spiritual and everlasting life,' John 4:14, and thus becomes a principle of life in them. This living water, this evangelist himself explains to intend the Spirit of God, chap. 7:38, 39. The light of the Sun of righteousness does not only shine upon them, but is so communicated to them that they shine also, and become little images of that Sun which shines upon them; the sap of the true vine is not only conveyed into them, as the sap of a tree may be conveyed into a vessel, but is conveyed as sap is from a tree into one of its living branches, where it becomes a principle of life. The Spirit of God being thus communicated and united to the saints, they are from thence properly denominated from it, and are called *spiritual*.

On the other hand, though the Spirit of God may many ways influence natural men; yet because it is not thus communicated to them, as an indwelling principle, they do not derive any denomination or character from it: for, there being no union, it is not their own. The light may shine upon a body that is very dark or black; and though that body be the subject of the light, yet, because the light becomes no principle of light in it, so as to cause the body to shine, hence that body does not properly receive its denomination from it, so as to be called a lightsome body. So the Spirit of God acting upon the soul only, without communicating itself to be an active principle in it, cannot denominate it spiritual. A body that continues black, may be said not to have light, though the light shines upon it: so natural men are said 'not to have the Spirit,' Jude 19, sensual or natural (as the word is elsewhere rendered), having not the Spirit.

b. Another reason why the saints and their virtues are called spiritual (which is the principal thing) is, that the Spirit of God, dwelling as a vital principle in their souls, there produces those effects wherein he exerts and communicates himself in his own proper nature. Holiness is the nature of the Spirit of God, therefore he is called in Scripture the Holy Ghost. Holiness, which is as it were the beauty and sweetness of the divine nature, is as much the proper nature of the Holy Spirit, as heat is the nature of fire, or sweetness was the nature of that holy anointing oil, which was the principal type of the Holy Ghost in the Mosaic dispensation; yea, I may rather say, that holiness is as much the proper nature of the Holy Ghost, as sweetness was the nature of the sweet odor of that ointment. The Spirit of God so dwells in the hearts of the saints, that he there, as a seed or spring of life, exerts and communicates himself, in this his sweet and divine nature, making the soul a partaker of God's beauty and Christ's joy, so that the saint has truly fellowship with the Father, and with his Son Jesus Christ, in thus having the communion or participation of the Holy Ghost. The grace which is in the hearts of the saints, is of the same nature with the divine holiness, as much as it is possible for that holiness to be, which is infinitely less in degree; as the brightness that is in a diamond which the sun shines upon, is of the same nature with the brightness of the sun, but only that it is as nothing to it in degree. Therefore Christ says, John 3:6, 'That which is born of the Spirit, is spirit;' i.e., the grace that is begotten in the hearts of the saints, is something of the same nature with that Spirit, and so is properly called a spiritual nature; after the same manner as that which is born of the flesh is flesh, or that which is born of corrupt nature is corrupt nature.

But the Spirit of God never influences the minds of natural men after this manner. Though he may influence them many ways, yet he never, in any of his influences, communicates himself to them in his own proper nature. Indeed he never acts disagreeably to his nature, either on the minds of saints or sinners: but the Spirit of God may act upon men agreeably to his own nature, and not exert his proper nature in the acts and exercises of their minds: the Spirit of God may act so, that his actions may be agreeable to his nature, and yet may not at all communicate himself in his proper nature, in the effect of that action. Thus, for instance, the Spirit of God moved upon the face of the waters, and there was nothing disagreeable to his nature in that action; but yet he did not at all communicate himself in that action, there was nothing of the proper nature of the Holy Spirit in that motion of the waters. And so he may act upon the minds of men many ways, and not communicate himself any more than when he acts on inanimate things.

Thus not only the manner of the relation of the Spirit, who is the operator, to the subject of his operations, is different; as the Spirit operates in the saints, as dwelling in them, as an abiding principle of action, whereas he doth not so operate upon sinners; but the influence and operation itself is different, and the effect wrought exceeding different. So that not only the persons are called *spiritual*, as having the Spirit of God dwelling in them; but those qualifications, affections, and experiences, that are wrought in them by the Spirit, are also *spiritual*, and therein differ vastly in their nature and kind from all that a natural man is or can be the subject of, while he remains in a natural state; and also from all that men or devils can be the authors of. It is a spiritual work in this high sense; and therefore above all other works is peculiar to the Spirit of God. There is no work so high and excellent; for there is no work wherein God doth so much communicate himself, and wherein the mere creature hath, in so high a sense a participation of God; so that it is expressed in Scripture by the saints 'being made partakers of the divine nature,' 2 Pet. 1:4, and 'having God dwelling in them, and they in God,' 1 John 4:12, 15, 16, and chap. 3:21; 'and having Christ in them,' John 17:21, Rom. 8:10; 'being the temples of the living God,' 2 Cor. 6:16; 'living by Christ's life,' Gal. 2:20; 'being made partakers of God's holiness,' Heb. 12:10; 'having Christ's love dwelling in them,' John 17:26; 'having his joy fulfilled in them,' John 17:13; 'seeing light in God's light, and being made to drink of the river of God's pleasures,' Ps. 36:8, 9; 'having fellowship with God, or communicating and partaking with him (as the word signifies),' 1 John 1:3. Not that the saints are made partakers of the essence of God, and so are *godded* with God, and *christed* with Christ, according to the abominable and blasphemous language and notions of some heretics: but, to use the Scripture phrase, they are made partakers of God's fullness, Eph. 3:17, 18, 19, John 1:16, that is, of God's spiritual beauty and happiness, according to the measure and capacity of a creature; for so it is evident the word *fullness* signifies in Scripture language. Grace in the hearts of the saints, being therefore the most glorious work of God, wherein he communicates of the goodness of his nature, it is doubtless his peculiar work, and in an eminent manner above the power of all creatures. And the influences of the Spirit of God in this, being thus peculiar to God, and being those wherein God does, in so high a manner, communicate himself, and make the creature partaker of the divine nature (the Spirit of God communicating itself in its own proper nature); this is what I mean by those influences that are divine, when I say that 'truly gracious affections do arise from those influences that are spiritual and divine.'

The true saints only have that which is spiritual; others have nothing which is divine, in the sense that has been spoken of. They not only have not these communications of the Spirit of God in so high a degree as the saints, but have nothing of that nature or kind. For the Apostle James tells us, that natural men have not the Spirit; and Christ teaches the necessity of a new birth, or of being born of the Spirit, from this, that he that is born of the flesh, has only flesh, and no spirit, John 3:6. They have not the Spirit of God dwelling in them in any degree; for the apostle teaches, that all who have the Spirit of God dwelling in them, are some of his, Rom. 8:9-11. And a having the Spirit of God is spoken of as a certain sign that persons shall have the eternal inheritance; for it is spoken of as the earnest of it, 2 Cor. 1:29, and 5:5, Eph. 1:14; and a having anything of the Spirit is mentioned as a sure sign of being in Christ, 1 John 4:13: 'Hereby know we that we dwell in him, because he hath given us of his Spirit.' Ungodly men not only have not so much of the divine nature as the saints, but they are not partakers of it; which implies that they have nothing of it; for a being partaker of the divine nature is spoken of as the peculiar privilege of the true saints, 2 Pet. 1:4. Ungodly men are not 'partakers of God's holiness,' Heb. 12:10. A natural man has no experience of any of those things that are spiritual: the apostle teaches us, that he is so far from it, that he knows nothing about them, he is a perfect stranger to them, the talk about such things is all foolishness and nonsense to him, he knows not what it means; 1 Cor. 2:14, 'The natural man receiveth not the things of the Spirit of God; for they are foolishness to him: neither can he know them, because they are spiritually discerned.' And to the like purpose Christ teaches us that the world is wholly unacquainted with the Spirit of God, John 14:17: 'Even the Spirit of truth, whom the world cannot receive, because it seeth him not, neither knoweth him.' And it is further evident, that natural men have nothing in them of the same nature with the true grace of the saints, because the apostle teaches us, that those of them who go farthest in religion have no charity, or true Christian love, 1 Cor. chap. 13. So Christ elsewhere reproves the Pharisees, those high pretenders to religion, that they 'had not the love of God in them,' John 5:42. Hence natural men have no communion or fellowship with Christ, or participation with him (as these words signify), for this is spoken of as the peculiar privilege of the saints, 1 John 1:3, together with vv. 6, 7, and 1 Cor. 1:8, 9. And the Scripture speaks of the actual being of a gracious principle in the soul, though in its first beginning, as a seed there planted, as inconsistent with a man's being a sinner, 1 John 3:9. And natural men are represented in Scripture, as having no spiritual light, no spiritual life, and no spiritual being; and therefore conversion is often compared to opening the eyes of the blind, raising the dead, and a work of creation (wherein creatures are made entirely new), and becoming new-born children.

From these things it is evident, that those gracious influences which the saints are subjects of, and the effects of God's Spirit which they experience, are entirely above nature, altogether of a different kind from anything that men find within themselves by nature, or only in the exercise of natural principles; and are things which no improvement of those qualifications, or principles that are natural, no advancing or exalting them to higher degrees, and no kind of composition of them, will ever bring men to; because they not only differ from what is natural, and from everything that natural men experience, in degree and circumstances, but also in kind; and are of a nature vastly more excellent. And this is what I mean, by supernatural, when I say that gracious affections are from those influences that are supernatural.

From hence it follows, that in those gracious exercises and affections which are wrought in the minds of the saints, through the saving influences of the Spirit of God, there is a new inward perception or sensation of their minds, entirely different in its nature and kind, from anything that ever their minds were the subjects of before they were sanctified. For doubtless if God by his mighty power produces something that is new, not only in degree and circumstances, but in its whole nature, and that which could be produced by no exalting, varying, or compounding of what was there before, or by adding anything of the like kind; I say, if God produces something thus new in a mind, that is a perceiving, thinking, conscious thing; then doubtless something entirely new is felt, or perceived, or thought; or, which is the same thing, there is some new sensation or perception of the mind, which is entirely of a new sort and which could be produced by no exalting, varying, or compounding of that kind of perception or sensation which the mind had before; or there is what some metaphysicians call a new simple idea. If grace be, in the sense above described, an entirely new kind of principle, then the exercises of it are also entirely a new kind of exercise. And if there be in the soul a new sort of exercise which it is conscious of, which the soul knew nothing of before, and which no improvement, composition, or management of what it was before conscious or sensible of, could produce, or anything like it; then it follows that the mind has an entirely new kind of perception or sensation; and here is, as it were, a new spiritual sense that the mind has, or a principle of a new kind of perception or spiritual sensation, which is in its whole nature different from any former kinds of sensation of the mind, as tasting is diverse from any of the other senses; and something is perceived by a true saint, in the exercise of this new sense of mind, in spiritual and divine things, as entirely diverse from anything that is perceived in them, by natural men, as the sweet taste of honey is diverse from the ideas men have of honey by only looking on it, and feeling of it. So that the spiritual perceptions which a sanctified and spiritual person has, are not only diverse from all that natural men have after the manner that the ideas or perceptions of the same sense may differ one from another, but rather as the ideas and sensations of different senses do differ. Hence the work of the Spirit of God in regeneration is often in Scripture compared to the giving a new sense, giving eyes to see, and ears to hear, unstopping the ears of the deaf, and opening the eyes of them that were born blind, and turning from darkness unto light. And because this spiritual sense is immensely the most noble and excellent, and that without which all other principles of perception, and all our faculties are useless and vain; therefore the giving this new sense, with the blessed fruits and effects of it in the soul, is compared to a raising the dead, and to a new creation.

This new spiritual sense, and the new dispositions that attend it, are no new faculties, but are new principles of nature. I use the word principles for want of a word of a more determinate signification. By a principle of nature in this place, I mean that foundation which is laid in nature, either old or new, for any particular manner or kind of exercise of the faculties of the soul; or a natural habit or foundation for action, giving a personal ability and disposition to exert the faculties in exercises of such a certain kind; so that to exert the faculties in that kind of exercise may be said to be his nature. So this new spiritual sense is not a new faculty of understanding, but it is a new foundation laid in the nature of the soul, for a new kind of exercise of the same faculty of understanding. So that new holy disposition of heart that attends this new sense is not a new faculty of will, but a foundation laid in the nature of the soul, for a new kind of exercise of the same faculty of will.

The Spirit of God, in all his operations upon the minds of natural men, only moves, impresses, assists, improves, or some way acts upon natural principles; but gives no new spiritual principle. Thus when the Spirit of God gives a natural man visions, as he did Balaam, he only impresses a natural principle, viz., the sense of seeing, immediately exciting ideas of that sense; but he gives no new sense; neither is there anything supernatural, spiritual, or divine in it. So if the Spirit of God impresses on a man's imagination, either in a dream, or when he is awake, any outward ideas of any of the senses, either voices, or shapes and colors, it is only exciting ideas of the same kind that he has by natural principles and senses. So if God reveals to any natural man any secret fact: as, for instance, something that he shall hereafter see or hear; this is not infusing or exercising any new spiritual principle, or giving the ideas of any new spiritual sense; it is only impressing, in an extraordinary manner, the ideas that will hereafter be received by sight and hearing. So in the more ordinary influences of the Spirit of God on the hearts of sinners, he only assists natural principles to do the same work to a greater degree, which they do of themselves by nature. Thus the Spirit of God by his common influences may assist men's natural ingenuity, as he assisted Bezaleel and Aholiab in the curious works of the tabernacle: so he may assist men's natural abilities in political affairs, and improve their courage and other natural qualifications, as he is said to have put his spirit on the seventy elders, and on Saul, so as to give him another heart: so God may greatly assist natural men's reason, in their reasoning about secular things, or about the doctrines of religion, and may greatly advance the clearness of their apprehensions and notions of things of religion in many respects, without giving any spiritual sense. So in those awakenings and convictions that natural men may have, God only assists conscience, which is a natural principle, to do that work in a further degree, which it naturally does. Conscience naturally gives men an apprehension of right and wrong, and suggests the relation there is between right and wrong, and a retribution: the Spirit of God assists men's consciences to do this in a greater degree, helps conscience against the stupifying influence of worldly objects and their lusts. And so many other ways might be mentioned wherein the Spirit acts upon, assists, and moves natural principles; but after all it is no more than nature moved, acted and improved; here is nothing supernatural and divine. But the Spirit of God in his spiritual influences on the hearts of his saints, operates by infusing or exercising new, divine, and supernatural principles; principles which are indeed a new and spiritual nature, and principles vastly more noble and excellent than all that is in natural men.

From what has been said it follows, that all spiritual and gracious affections are attended with and do arise from some apprehension, idea, or sensation of mind, which is in its whole nature different, yea, exceeding different, from all that is, or can be in the mind of a natural man; and which the natural man discerns nothing of, and has no manner of idea of (agreeable to 1 Cor. 2:14), and conceives of no more than a man without the sense of tasting can conceive of the sweet taste of honey, or a man without the sense of hearing can conceive of the melody of a tune, or a man born blind can have a notion of the beauty of the rainbow.

But here two things must be observed, in order to the right understanding of this.

i. On the one hand it must be observed, that not everything which in any respect appertains to spiritual affections, is new and entirely different from what natural men can conceive of, and do experience; some things are common to gracious affections with other affections; many circumstances, appendages and effects are common. Thus a saint's love to God has a great many things appertaining to it, which are common with a man's natural love to a near relation; love to God makes a man have desires of the honor of God, and a desire to please him; so does a natural man's love to his friend make him desire his honor, and desire to please him; love to God causes a man to delight in the thoughts of God, and to delight in the presence of God, and to desire conformity to God, and the enjoyment of God; and so it is with a man's love to his friend; and many other things might be mentioned which are common to both. But yet that idea which the saint has of the loveliness of God, and that sensation, and that kind of delight he has in that view, which is as it were the marrow and quintessence of his love, is peculiar, and entirely diverse from anything that a natural man has, or can have any notion of. And even in those things that seem to be common, there is something peculiar; both spiritual and natural love cause desires after the object beloved; but they be not the same sort of desires: there is a sensation of soul in the spiritual desires of one that loves God, which is entirely different from all natural desires: both spiritual love and natural love are attended with delight in the object beloved; but the sensations of delight are not the same, but entirely and exceedingly diverse. Natural men may have conceptions of many things about spiritual affections; but there is something in them which is as it were the nucleus, or kernel of them, that they have no more conception of, than one born blind, has of colors.

It may be clearly illustrated by this: we will suppose two men; one is born without the sense of tasting, the other has it; the latter loves honey, and is greatly delighted in it, because he knows the sweet taste of it; the other loves certain sounds and colors; the love of each has many things that appertain to it, which is common; it causes both to desire and delight in the object beloved, and causes grief when it is absent, etc., but yet that idea or sensation which he who knows the taste of honey has of its excellency and sweetness, that is the foundation of his love, is entirely different from anything the other has or can have; and that delight which he has in honey is wholly diverse from anything that the other can conceive of, though they both delight in their beloved objects. So both these persons may in some respects love the same object: the one may love a delicious kind of fruit, which is beautiful to the eye, and of a delicious taste; not only because he has seen its pleasant colors, but knows its sweet taste; the other, perfectly ignorant of this, loves it only for its beautiful colors: there are many things seen, in some respect, to be common to both; both love, both desire, and both delight; but the love and desire, and delight of the one, is altogether diverse from that of the other. The difference between the love of a natural man and a spiritual man is like to this; but only it must be observed, that in one respect it is vastly greater, viz., that the kinds of excellency which are perceived in spiritual objects, by these different kinds of persons, are in themselves vastly more diverse than the different kinds of excellency perceived in delicious fruit, by a tasting and a tasteless man; and in another respect it may not be so great, viz., as the spiritual man may have a spiritual sense or taste, to perceive that divine and most peculiar excellency but in small beginnings, and in a very imperfect degree.

ii. On the other hand, it must be observed that a natural man may have those religious apprehensions and affections, which may be in many respects very new and surprising to him, and what before he did not conceive of; and yet what he experiences be nothing like the exercises of a principle of new nature, or the sensations of a new spiritual sense; his affections may be very new, by extraordinarily moving natural principles in a very new degree, and with a great many new circumstances, and a new co-operation of natural affections, and a new composition of ideas; this may be from some extraordinary powerful influence of Satan, and some great delusion; but there is nothing but nature extraordinarily acted. As if a poor man that had always dwelt in a cottage and, had never looked beyond the obscure village where he was born, should in a jest be taken to a magnificent city and prince's court, and there arrayed in princely robes, and set on the throne, with the crown royal on his head, peers and nobles bowing before him, and should be made to believe that he was now a glorious monarch; the ideas he would have, and the affections he would experience, would in many respects be very new, and such as he had no imagination of before; but all this is no more than extraordinarily raising and exciting natural principles, and newly exalting, varying, and compounding such sort of ideas, as he has by nature; here is nothing like giving him a new sense.

Upon the whole, I think it is clearly manifest, that all truly gracious affections do arise from special and peculiar influences of the Spirit, working that sensible effect or sensation in the souls of the saints, which are entirely different from all that is possible a natural man should experience, not only different in degree and circumstances, but different in its whole nature; so that a natural man not only cannot experience that which is individually the same, but cannot experience anything but what is exceeding diverse, and immensely below it, in its kind; and that which the power of men or devils is not sufficient to produce the like of, or anything of the same nature.

I have insisted largely on this matter, because it is of great importance and use evidently to discover and demonstrate the delusions of Satan, in many kinds of false religious affections, which multitudes are deluded by, and probably have been in all ages of the Christian church; and to settle and determine many articles of doctrine, concerning the operations of the Spirit of God, and the nature of true grace.

Now, therefore, to apply these things to the purpose of this discourse.

From hence it appears, that impressions which some have made on their imagination, or the imaginary ideas which they have of God or Christ, or heaven, or anything appertaining to religion, have nothing in them that is spiritual, or of the nature of true grace. Though such things may attend what is spiritual, and be mixed with it, yet in themselves they have nothing that is spiritual, nor are they any part of gracious experience.

Here, for the sake of common people, I will explain what is intended by impressions on the imagination and imaginary ideas. The imagination is that power of the mind whereby it can have a conception, or idea of things of an external or outward nature (that is, of such sort of things as are the objects of the outward senses) when those things are not present, and be not perceived by the senses. It is called imagination from the word image; because thereby a person can have an image of some external thing in his mind, when that thing is not present in reality, nor anything like it. All such things as we perceive by our five external senses, seeing, hearing, smelling, tasting, and feeling, are external things: and when a person has an idea or image of any of these sorts of things in his mind, when they are not there, and when he does not really see, hear, smell, taste, nor feel them; that is to have an imagination of them, and these ideas are imaginary ideas: and when such kinds of ideas are strongly impressed upon the mind, and the image of them in the mind is very lively, almost as if one saw them, or heard them, etc., that is called an impression on the imagination. Thus colors and shapes, and a form of countenance, they are outward things; because they are those sorts of things which are the objects of the outward sense of seeing; and therefore when any person has in his mind a lively idea of any shape, or color, or form of countenance; that is to have an imagination of those things. So if he has an idea, of such sort of light or darkness, as he perceives by the sense of seeing; that is to have an idea of outward light, and so is an imagination. So if he has an idea of any marks made on paper, suppose letters and words written in a book; that is to have an external and imaginary idea of such kinds of things as we sometimes perceive by our bodily eyes. And when we have the ideas of those kinds of things which we perceive by any of the other senses, as of any sounds or voices, or words spoken; this is only to have ideas of outward things, viz., of such kinds of things as are perceived by the external sense of hearing, and so that also is imagination: and when these ideas are livelily impressed, almost as if they were really heard with the ears, this is to have an impression on the imagination. And so I might go on, and instance in the ideas of things appertaining to the other three senses of smelling, tasting, and feeling.

Many who have had such things have very ignorantly supposed them to be of the nature of spiritual discoveries. They have had lively ideas of some external shape, and beautiful form of countenance; and this they call spiritually seeing Christ. Some have had impressed upon them ideas of a great outward light; and this they call a spiritual discovery of God's or Christ's glory. Some have had ideas of Christ's hanging on the cross, and his blood running from his wounds; and this they call a spiritual sight of Christ crucified, and the way of salvation by his blood. Some have seen him with his arms open ready to embrace them; and this they call a discovery of the sufficiency of Christ's grace and love. Some have had lively ideas of heaven, and of Christ on his throne there, and shining ranks of saints and angels; and this they call seeing heaven opened to them. Some from time to time have had a lively idea of a person of a beautiful countenance smiling upon them; and this they call a spiritual discovery of the love of Christ to their souls, and tasting the love of Christ. And they look upon it a sufficient evidence that these things are spiritual discoveries, and that they see them spiritually because they say they do not see these things with their bodily eyes, but in their hearts; for they can see them when their eyes are shut. And in like manner, the imaginations of some have been impressed with ideas of the sense of hearing; they have had ideas of words, as if they were spoken to them, sometimes they are the words of Scripture, and sometimes other words: they have had ideas of Christ's speaking comfortable words to them. These things they have called having the inward call of Christ, hearing the voice of Christ spiritually in their hearts, having the witness of the Spirit, and the inward testimony of the love of Christ, etc.

The common and less considerate and understanding sort of people, are the more easily led into apprehensions that these things are spiritual things, because spiritual things being invisible, and not things that can be pointed forth with the finger, we are forced to use figurative expressions in speaking of them, and to borrow names from external and sensible objects to signify them by. Thus we call a clear apprehension of things spiritual by the name of *light*; and a having such an apprehension of such or such things, by the name of *seeing* such things;

and the conviction of the judgment, and the persuasion of the will by the word of Christ in the gospel, we signify by spiritually hearing the call of Christ: and the Scripture itself abounds with such like figurative expressions. Persons hearing these often used, and having pressed upon them the necessity of having their eyes opened, and having a discovery of spiritual things, and seeing Christ in his glory and having the inward call, and the like, they ignorantly look and wait for some such external discoveries, and imaginary views as have been spoken of; and when they have them are confident, that now their eyes are opened, now Christ has discovered himself to them, and they are his children; and hence are exceedingly affected and elevated with their deliverance and happiness, and many kinds of affections are at once set in a violent motion in them.

But it is exceedingly apparent that such ideas have nothing in them which is spiritual and divine, in the sense wherein it has been demonstrated that all gracious experiences are spiritual and divine. These external ideas are in no wise of such a sort, that they are entirely, and in their whole nature diverse from all that men have by nature, perfectly different from, and vastly above any sensation which it is possible a man should have by any natural sense or principle, so that in order to have them, a man must have a new spiritual and divine sense given him, in order to have any sensations of that sort: so far from this, that they are ideas of the same sort which we have by the external senses, that are some of the inferior powers of the human nature: they are merely ideas of external objects, or ideas of that nature, of the same outward, sensitive kind: the same sort of sensations of mind (differing not in degree, but only in circumstances) that we have by those natural principles which are common to us with the beasts, viz., the five external senses. This is a low, miserable notion of spiritual sense, to suppose that it is only a conceiving or imagining those sorts of ideas which we have by our animal senses, which senses the beasts have in as great perfection as we; it is, as it were, a turning Christ, or the divine nature in the soul, into a mere animal. There is nothing wanting in the soul, as it is by nature, to render it capable of being the subject of all these external ideas, without any new principles. A natural man is capable of having an idea, and a lively idea of shapes, and colors, and sounds, when they are absent, and as capable as a regenerate man is: so there is nothing supernatural in them. And it is known by abundant experience, that it is not the advancing or perfecting human nature, which makes persons more capable of having such lively and strong imaginary ideas, but that on the contrary, the weakness of body and mind, and distempers of body, make persons abundantly more susceptive of such impressions.

As to a truly spiritual sensation, not only is the manner of its coming into the mind extraordinary, but the sensation itself is totally diverse from all that men have, or can have, in a state of nature, as has been shown. But as to these external ideas, though the way of their coming into the mind is sometimes unusual, yet the ideas in themselves are not the better for that; they are still of no different sort from what men have by their senses; they are of no higher kind, nor a whit better. For instance, the external idea a man has now of Christ hanging on the cross, and shedding his blood, is no better in itself, than the external idea that the Jews his enemies had, who stood round his cross, and saw this with their bodily eyes. The imaginary idea which men have now of an external brightness and glory of God, is no better than the idea the wicked congregation in the wilderness had of the external glory of the Lord at Mount Sinai, when they saw it with their bodily eyes; or any better than that idea which millions of cursed reprobates will have of the external glory of Christ at the day of judgment, who shall see, and have a very lively idea of ten thousand times greater external glory of Christ, than ever yet was conceived in any man's imagination: yea, the image of Christ, which men conceive in their imaginations, is not in its own nature of any superior kind to the idea the Papists conceive of Christ, by the beautiful and affecting images of him which they see in their churches (though the way of their receiving the idea may not be so bad); nor are the affections they have, if built primarily on such imaginations, any better than the affections raised in the ignorant people, by the sight of those images, which oftentimes are very great; especially when these images, through the craft of the priests, are made to move, and speak, and weep, and the like. Merely the way of persons receiving these imaginary ideas, does not alter the nature of the ideas themselves that are received; let them be received in what way they will, they are still but external ideas, or ideas of outward appearances, and so are not spiritual. Yea, if men should actually receive such external ideas by the immediate power of the most high God upon their minds, they would not be spiritual, they would be no more than a common work of the Spirit of God; as is evident in fact, in the instance of Balaam, who had impressed on his mind, by God himself, a clear and lively outward representation or idea of Jesus Christ, as 'the Star rising out of Jacob, when he heard the words of God, and knew the knowledge of the Most High, and saw the vision of the Almighty, falling into a trance,' Num. 24:16, 17, but yet had no manner of spiritual discovery of Christ; that Day Star never spiritually rose in his heart, he being but a natural man.

And as these external ideas have nothing divine or spiritual in their nature and nothing but what natural men, without any new principles, are capable of; so there is nothing in their nature which requires that peculiar, inimitable and unparalleled exercise of the glorious power of God, in order to their production, which it has been shown there is in the production of true grace. There appears to be nothing in their nature above the power of the devil. It is certainly not above the power of Satan to suggest thoughts to men; because otherwise he could not tempt them to sin. And if he can suggest any thoughts or ideas at all, doubtless imaginary ones, or ideas of things external, are not above his power; for the external ideas men have are the lowest sort of ideas. These ideas may be raised only by impressions made on the body, by moving the animal spirits, and impressing the brain. Abundant experience does certainly show, that alterations in the body will excite imaginary or external ideas in the mind; as often, in the case of a high fever, melancholy, etc. These external ideas are as much below the more intellectual exercises of the soul, as the body is a less noble part of man than the soul.

And there is not only nothing in the nature of these external ideas or imaginations of outward appearances, from whence we can infer that they are above the power of the devil; but it is certain also that the devil can excite, and often hath excited such ideas. They were external ideas which he excited in the dreams and visions of the false prophets of old, who were under the influence of lying spirits, that we often read of in Scripture, as Deut. 13:1., 1 Kgs 22:22, Isa. 33:7, Ezek. 13:7. And they were external ideas that he often excited in the minds of the heathen priests, magicians and sorcerers, in their visions and ecstasies, and they were external ideas that he excited in the mind of the man Christ Jesus, when he showed him all the kingdoms of the world, with the glory of them, when those kingdoms were not really in sight.

And if Satan or any created being, has power to impress the mind with outward representations, then no particular sort of outward representations can be any evidence of a divine power. Almighty power is no more requisite to represent the shape of man to the imagination, than the shape of anything else: there is no higher kind of power necessary to form in the brain one bodily shape or color than another: it needs a no more glorious power to represent the form of the body of a man, than the form of a chip or block; though it be of a very beautiful human body, with a sweet smile in his countenance, or arms open, or blood running from the hands, feet and side: that sort of power which can represent black or darkness to the imagination, can also represent white and shining brightness: the power and skill which can well and exactly paint a straw, or a stick of wood, on a piece of paper or canvas; the same in kind, only perhaps further improved, will be sufficient to paint the body of a man, with great beauty and in royal majesty, or a magnificent city, paved with gold, full of brightness, and a glorious throne, etc. So it is no more than the same sort of power that is requisite to paint one as the other of these on the brain. The same sort of power that can put ink upon paper, can put on leaf gold. So that it is evident to a demonstration, if we suppose it to be in the devil's power to make any sort of external representation at all on the fancy (as without doubt it is, and never anyone questioned it who believed there was a devil, that had any agency with mankind): I say, if so, it is demonstrably evident, that a created power may extend to all kinds of external appearances and ideas in the mind. From hence it again clearly appears, that no such things have anything in them that is spiritual, supernatural, and divine, in the sense in which it has been proved that all truly gracious experiences have. And though external ideas, through man's make and frame, do ordinarily in some degree attend spiritual experiences, yet these ideas are no part of their spiritual experience, any more than the motion of the blood, and beating of the pulse, that attend experiences, are a part of spiritual experience. And though undoubtedly, through men's infirmity in the present state, and especially through the weak constitution of some persons, gracious affections which are very strong, do excite lively ideas in the imagination; yet it is also undoubted, that when persons' affections are founded on imaginations, which is often the case, those affections are merely natural and common, because they are built on a foundation that is not spiritual; and so are entirely different from gracious affections, which, as has been proved, do evermore arise from those operations that are spiritual and divine.

These imaginations do oftentimes raise the carnal affections of men to an exceeding great height: and no wonder, when the subjects of them have an ignorant, but undoubting persuasion, that they are divine manifestations, which the great Jehovah immediately makes to their souls, therein giving them testimonies in an extraordinary manner, of his high and peculiar favor.

Again, it is evident from what has been observed and proved of the manner in which gracious operations and effects in the heart are spiritual, supernatural and divine, that the immediate suggesting of the words of Scripture to the mind has nothing in it which is spiritual.

I have had occasion to say something of this already; and what has been said may be sufficient to evince it; but if the reader bears in mind what has been said concerning the nature of spiritual influences and effects, it will be more abundantly manifest that this is no spiritual effect. For I suppose there is no person of common understanding, who will say or imagine that the bringing words (let them be what words they will) to the mind is an effect of that nature which it is impossible the mind of a natural man, while he remains in a state of nature, should be the subject of, or anything like it; or that it requires any new divine sense in the soul;

or that the bringing sounds or letters to the mind, is an effect of so high, holy, and excellent a nature, that it is impossible any created power should be the cause of it.

As the suggesting words of Scripture to the mind, is only the exciting in the mind ideas of certain sounds or letters; so it is only one way of exciting ideas in the imagination; for sounds and letters are external things, that are the objects of the external senses of seeing and hearing. Ideas of certain marks upon paper, such as any of the twenty-four letters, in whatever order, or any sounds of the voice, are as much external ideas, as of any other shapes or sounds whatsoever; and therefore, by what has been already said concerning these external ideas, it is evident they are nothing spiritual; and if at any time the Spirit of God suggests these letters or sounds to the mind, this is a common, and not any special or gracious influence of that Spirit. And therefore it follows from what has been already proved, that those affections which have this effect for their foundation, are no spiritual or gracious affections. But let it be observed what it is that I say, viz., when this effect, even the immediate and extraordinary manner of words of Scripture's coming to the mind, is that which excites the affections, and is properly the foundation of them, then these affections are not spiritual. It may be so, that persons may have gracious affections going with Scriptures which come to their minds, and the Spirit of God may make use of those Scriptures to excite them; when it is some spiritual sense, taste or relish they have of the divine and excellent things contained in those Scriptures, that is the thing which excites their affections, and not the extraordinary and sudden manner of words being brought to their minds. They are affected with the instruction they receive from the words, and the view of the glorious things of God or Christ, and things appertaining to them, that they contain and teach; and not because the words came suddenly, as though some person had spoken them to them, thence concluding that God did as it were immediately speak to them. Persons oftentimes are exceedingly affected on this foundation; the words of some great and high promises of Scripture came suddenly to their minds, and they look upon the words as directed immediately by God to them, as though the words that moment proceeded out of the mouth of God as spoken to them: so that they take it as a voice from God, immediately revealing to them their happy circumstances, and promising such and such great things to them: and this it is that affects and elevates them. There is no near spiritual understanding of the divine things contained in the Scripture, or new spiritual sense of the glorious things taught in that part of the Bible going before their affection, and being the foundation of it. All the new understanding they have, or think they have, to be the foundation of their affection, is this, that the words are spoken to them, because they come so suddenly and extraordinarily. And so this affection is built wholly on the sand! Because it is built on a conclusion for which they have no foundation. For, as has been shown, the sudden coming of the words to their minds, is no evidence that the bringing them to their minds in that manner was from God. And if it was true that God brought the words to their minds, and they certainly knew it, that would not be spiritual knowledge; it may be without any spiritual sense: Balaam might know that the words which God suggested to him, were indeed suggested to him by God, and yet have no spiritual knowledge. So that these affections which are built on that notion, that texts of Scripture are sent immediately from God, are built on no spiritual foundation, and are vain and delusive. Persons who have their affections thus raised, if they should be inquired of, whether they have any new sense of the excellency of things contained in those Scriptures, would probably say, Yes, without hesitation: but it is true no otherwise than thus, that then they have taken up that notion, that the words are spoken immediately to them, that makes them seem sweet to them, and they own the things which these Scriptures say to them, for excellent things and wonderful things. As for instance supposing these were the words which were suddenly brought to their minds, *Fear not, it is your Father's good pleasure to give you the kingdom*; they having confidently taken up a notion that the words were as it were immediately spoken from heaven to them, as an immediate revelation that God was their Father, and had given the kingdom to them, they are greatly affected by it, and the words seem sweet to them; and oh, they say, 'they are excellent things that are contained in those words!' But the reason why the promise seems excellent to them, is only because they think it is made to them immediately; all the sense they have of any glory in them, is only from self-love, and from their own imagined interest in the words; not that they had any view or sense of the holy and glorious nature of the kingdom of heaven and the spiritual glory of that God who gives it, and of his excellent grace to sinful men, it offering and giving them this kingdom, of his own good pleasure preceding their imagined interest in these things, and their being affected by them, and being the foundation of their affection, and hope of an interest in them. On the contrary, they first imagine they are interested, and then are highly affected with that, and then can own these things to be excellent. So that the sudden and extraordinary way of the Scripture's coming to their mind is plainly the first foundation of the whole; which is a clear evidence of the wretched delusion they are under.

The first comfort of many persons, and what they call their conversion, is after this manner: after awakening and terror, some comfortable sweet promise comes suddenly and wonderfully to their minds; and the manner of its coming makes them conclude it comes from God to them; and this is the very thing that is all the foundation of their faith, and hope, and comfort: from hence they take their first encouragement to trust in God and in Christ, because they think that God, by some Scripture so brought, has now already revealed to them that he loves them, and has already promised them eternal life, which is very absurd; for every one of common knowledge of the principles of religion, knows that it is God's manner to reveal his love to men, and their interest in the promises, after they have believed, and not before, because they must first believe before they have any interest in the promises to be revealed. The Spirit of God is a Spirit of truth and not of lies: he does not bring Scriptures to men's minds, to reveal to them that they have an interest in God's favor and promises, when they have none, having not yet believed: which would be the case, if God's bringing texts of Scripture to men's minds, to reveal to them that their sins were forgiven, or that it was God's pleasure to give them the kingdom, or anything of that nature, went before, and was the foundation of their first faith. No promise of the covenant of grace belongs to any man, until he has first believed in Christ; for it is by faith alone that we become interested in Christ, and the promises of the new covenant made in him: and therefore whatever spirit applies the promises of that covenant to a person who has not first believed, as being already his, must be a lying spirit, and that faith which is first built on such an application of promises is built upon a lie. God's manner is not to bring comfortable texts of Scripture to give men assurance of his love, and that they shall be happy, before they have had a faith of dependence. And if the Scripture which comes to a person's mind, be not so properly a promise, as an invitation; yet if he makes the sudden or unusual manner of the invitations coming to his mind, the ground on which he believes that he is invited, it is not true faith; because it is built on that which is not the true ground of faith. True faith is built on no precarious foundation: but a determination that the words of such a particular text were, by the immediate power of God, suggested to the mind, at such a time, as though then spoken and directed by God to him, because the words came after such a manner, is wholly an uncertain and precarious determination, as has been now shown; and therefore is a false and sandy foundation for faith; and accordingly that faith which is built upon it is false. The only certain foundation which any person has to believe that he is invited to partake of the blessings of the gospel, is, that the word of God declares that persons so qualified as he is, are invited, and God who declares it, is true, and cannot lie. If a sinner be once convinced of the veracity of God, and that the Scriptures are his word, he will need no more to convince and satisfy him that he is invited; for the Scriptures are full of invitations to sinners, to the chief of sinners, to come and partake of the benefits of the gospel; he will not want any never speaking of God to him; what he hath spoken already will be enough with him.

As the first comfort of many persons, and their affections at the time of their supposed conversion, are built on such grounds as these which have been mentioned; so are their joys and hopes and other affections, from time to time afterwards. They have often particular words of Scripture, sweet declarations and promises suggested to them, which by reason of the manner of their coming, they think are immediately sent from God to them, at that time, which they look upon as their warrant to take them, and which they actually make the main ground of their appropriating them to themselves, and of the comfort they take in them, and the confidence they receive from them. Thus they imagine a kind of conversation is carried on between God and them; and that God, from time to time, does, as it were, immediately speak to them, and satisfy their doubts, and testifies his love to them, and promises them supports and supplies, and his blessing in such and such cases, and reveals to them clearly their interest in eternal blessings. And thus they are often elevated, and have a course of a sudden and tumultuous kind of joys, mingled with a strong confidence, and high opinion of themselves; when indeed the main ground of these joys, and this confidence, is not anything contained in, or taught by these Scriptures, as they lie in the Bible, but the manner of their coming to them; which is a certain evidence of their delusion. There is no particular promise in the word of God that is the saint's, or is any otherwise made to him, or spoken to him, than all the promises of the covenant of grace are his, and are made to him and spoken to him; though it be true that some of these promises may be more peculiarly adapted to his case than others, and God by his Spirit may enable him better to understand some than others, and to have a greater sense of the preciousness, and glory, and suitableness of the blessings contained in them.

But here some may be ready to say, What, is there no such thing as any particular spiritual application of the promises of Scripture by the Spirit of God? I answer, there is doubtless such a thing as a spiritual and saving application of the invitations and promises of Scripture to the souls of men; but it is also certain, that the nature of it is wholly misunderstood by many persons, to the great ensnaring of their own souls, and the giving Satan a vast advantage against them, and against the interest of religion, and the church of God. The spiritual application of a Scripture promise does not consist in its being immediately suggested to the thoughts by some extrinsic agent, and being borne into the mind with this strong apprehension, that it is particularly spoken and directed to them at that time; there is nothing of the evidence of the hand of God in this effect, as events have proved, in many notorious instances; and it is a mean notion of a spiritual application of Scripture; there is nothing in the nature of it at all beyond the power of the devil, if he be not restrained by God; for there is nothing in the nature of the effect that is spiritual, implying any vital communication of God. A truly spiritual application of the word of God is of a vastly higher nature; as much above the devil's power, as it is, so to apply the word of God to a dead corpse, as to raise it to life; or to a stone, to turn it into an angel. A spiritual application of the word of God consists in applying it to the heart, in spiritually enlightening, sanctifying influences. A spiritual application of an invitation or offer of the gospel consists, in giving the soul a spiritual sense or relish of the holy and divine blessings offered, and the sweet and wonderful grace of the offerer, in making so gracious an offer, and of his holy excellency and faithfulness to fulfill what he offers, and his glorious sufficiency for it; so leading and drawing forth the heart to embrace the offer; and thus giving the man evidence of his title to the thing offered. And so a spiritual application of the promises of Scripture, for the comfort of the saints, consists in enlightening their minds to see the holy excellency and sweetness of the blessings promised, and also the holy excellency of the promiser, and his faithfulness and sufficiency; thus drawing forth their hearts to embrace the promiser, and thing promised; and by this means, giving the sensible actings of grace, enabling them to see their grace, and so their title to the promise. An application not consisting in this divine sense and enlightening of the mind, but consisting only in the word's being borne into the thoughts, as if immediately then spoken, so making persons believe, on no other foundation, that the promise is theirs, is a blind application, and belongs to the spirit of darkness, and not of light.

When persons have their affections raised after this manner, those affections are really not raised by the word of God; the Scripture is not the foundation of them; it is not anything contained in those Scriptures which come to their minds, that raise their affections; but truly that effect, viz., the strange manner of the word's being suggested to their minds, and a proposition from thence taken up by them, which indeed is not contained in that Scripture, nor any other; as that his sins are forgiven him, or that it is the Father's good pleasure to give him in particular the kingdom, or the like. There are propositions to be found in the Bible, declaring that persons of such and such qualifications are forgiven and beloved of God: but there are no propositions to be found in the Bible declaring that such and such particular persons, independent on any previous knowledge of any qualifications, are forgiven and beloved of God: and therefore, when any person is comforted, and affected by any such proposition, it is by another word, a word newly coined, and not any word of God contained in the Bible. And thus many persons are vainly affected and deluded.

Again, it plainly appears from what has been demonstrated, that no revelation of secret facts by immediate suggestion, is anything spiritual and divine, in that sense wherein gracious effects and operations are so.

By secret facts, I mean things that have been done, or are come to pass, or shall hereafter come to pass, which are secret in that sense that they do not appear to the senses, nor are known by any argumentation, or any evidence to reason, nor any other way, but only by that revelation by immediate suggestion of the ideas of them to the mind. Thus for instance, if it should be revealed to me, that the next year this land would be invaded by a fleet from France, or that such and such persons would then be converted, or that I myself should then be converted; not by enabling me to argue out these events from anything which now appears in providence, but immediately suggesting and bearing in upon my mind, in an extraordinary manner, the apprehension or ideas of these facts, with a strong suggestion or impression on my mind, that I had no hand in myself, that these things would come to pass: or if it should be revealed to me, that this day there is a battle fought between the armies of such and such powers in Europe; or that such a prince in Europe was this day converted, or is now in a converted state, having been converted formerly, or that one of my neighbors is converted, or that I myself am converted; not by having any other evidence of any of these facts, from whence I argue them, but an immediate extraordinary suggestion or excitation of these ideas, and a strong impression of them upon my mind: this is a revelation of secret facts by immediate suggestion, as much as if the facts were future; for the facts being past, present, or future, alters not the case, as long as they are secret and hidden from my senses and reason, and not spoken of in Scripture, nor known by me any other way than by immediate suggestion. If I have it revealed to me, that such a revolution is come to pass this day in the Ottoman Empire, it is the very same sort of revelation, as if it were revealed to me that such a revolution would come to pass there this day come twelvemonth; because, though one is present and the other future, yet both are equally hidden from me, any other way than by immediate revelation. When Samuel told Saul that the asses which he went to seek were found, and that his father had left caring for the asses and sorrowed for him; this was by the same kind of revelation, as that by which he told Saul, that in the plain of Tabor there should meet him three men going up to God to Bethel (1 Sam. 10:2, 3), though one of these things was future, and the other was not. So when Elisha told the king of Israel the words that the king of Syria spake in his bedchamber, it was by the same kind of revelation with that by which he foretold many things to come.

It is evident that this revelation of secret facts by immediate suggestions, has nothing of the nature of a spiritual and divine operation, in the sense forementioned; there is nothing at all in the nature of the perceptions or ideas themselves, which are excited in the mind, that is divinely excellent, and so, far above all the ideas of natural men; though the manner of exciting the ideas be extraordinary. In those things which are spiritual, as has been shown, not only the manner of producing the effect, but the effect wrought is divine, and so vastly above all that can be in an unsanctified mind. Now simply the having an idea of facts, setting aside the manner of producing those ideas, is nothing beyond what the minds of wicked men are susceptible of, without any goodness in them; and they all, either have or will have, the knowledge of the truth of the greatest and most important facts, that have been, are, or shall be.

And as to the extraordinary manner of producing the ideas or perception of facts, even by immediate suggestion, there is nothing in it, but what the minds of natural men, while they are yet natural men, are capable of, as is manifest in Balaam, and others spoken of in the Scripture. And therefore it appears that there is nothing appertaining to this immediate suggestion of secret facts that is spiritual, in the sense in which it has been proved that gracious operations are so. If there be nothing in the ideas themselves, which is holy and divine, and so nothing but what may be in a mind not sanctified, then God can put them into the mind by immediate power without sanctifying it. As there is nothing in the idea of a rainbow itself that is of a holy and divine nature; so that nothing hinders but that an unsanctified mind may receive that idea; so God, if he pleases, and when he pleases, immediately, and in an extraordinary manner, may excite that idea in an unsanctified mind. So also, as there is nothing in the idea or knowledge that such and such particular persons are forgiven and accepted of God, and entitled to heaven, but what unsanctified minds may have and will have concerning many at the day of judgment; so God can, if he pleases, extraordinarily and immediately, suggest this to, and impress it upon an unsanctified mind now: there is no principle wanting in an unsanctified mind, to make it capable of such a suggestion or impression, nor is there anything in it to exclude, or necessarily to prevent such a suggestion.

And if these suggestions of secret facts be attended with texts of Scripture, immediately and extraordinarily brought to mind, about some other facts that seem in some respects similar, that does not make the operation to be of a spiritual and divine nature. For that suggestion of words of Scripture is no more divine, than the suggestion of the facts themselves; as has been just now demonstrated: and two effects together, which are neither of them spiritual cannot make up one complex effect, that is spiritual.

Hence it follows, from what has been already shown, and often repeated, that those affections which are properly founded on such immediate suggestions, or supposed suggestions, of secret facts, are not gracious affections. Not but that it is possible that such suggestions may be the occasion, or accidental cause of gracious affections; for so may a mistake and delusion; but it is never properly the foundation of gracious affections: for gracious affections, as has been shown, are all the effects of an influence and operation which is spiritual, supernatural, and divine. But there are many affections, and high affections, which some have, that have such kind of suggestions or revelations for their very foundation: they look upon these as spiritual discoveries, which is a gross delusion, and this delusion is truly the spring whence their affections flow.

Here it may be proper to observe, that it is exceedingly manifest from what has been said, that what many persons call the witness of the Spirit, that they are the children of God, has nothing in it spiritual and divine; and consequently that the affections built upon it are vain and delusive. That which many call the witness of the Spirit, is no other than an immediate suggestion and impression of that fact, otherwise secret, that they are converted, or made the children of God, and so that their sins are pardoned, and that God has given them a title to heaven. This kind of knowledge, viz., knowing that a certain person is converted, and delivered from hell, and entitled to heaven, is no divine sort of knowledge in itself. This sort of fact, is not that which requires any higher or more divine kind of suggestion, in order to impress it on the mind, than any other fact which Balaam had impressed on his mind. It requires no higher sort of idea or sensation, for a man to have the apprehension of his own conversion impressed upon him, than to have the apprehension of his neighbor's conversion, in like manner impressed: but God, if he pleased, might impress the knowledge of this fact, that he had forgiven his neighbor's sins, and given him a title to heaven, as well as any other fact, without any communication of his holiness: the excellency and importance of the fact, do not at all hinder a natural man's mind being susceptible of an immediate suggestion and impression of it. Balaam had as excellent, and important, and glorious facts as this, immediately impressed on his mind, without any gracious influence; as particularly, the coming of Christ, and his setting up his glorious kingdom, and the blessedness of the spiritual Israel in his peculiar favor, and their happiness living and dying. Yea, Abimelech, king of the Philistines, had God's special favor to a particular person, even Abraham, revealed to him, Gen. 20:6, 7. So it seems that he revealed to Laban his special favor to Jacob, see Gen. 31:24, and Ps. 105:15. And if a truly good man should have an immediate revelation or suggestion from God, after the like manner concerning his favor to his neighbor or himself; it would be no higher kind of influence; it would be no more than a common sort of influence of God's Spirit; as the gift of prophecy, and all revelation by immediate suggestion is; see 1 Cor. 13:2. And though it be true, that it is not possible that a natural man should have that individual suggestion from the Spirit of God, that he is converted, because it is not true; yet that does not arise from the nature of the influence, or because that kind of influence which suggests such excellent facts, is too high for him to be the subject of; but purely from the defect of a fact to be revealed. The influence which immediately suggests this fact, when it is true, is of no different kind from that which immediately suggests other true facts: and so the kind and nature of the influence is not above what is common to natural men, with good men.

But this is a mean, ignoble notion of the witness of the Spirit of God given to his dear children, to suppose that there is nothing in the kind and nature of that influence of the Spirit of God, in imparting this high and glorious benefit, but what is common to natural men, or which men are capable of, and be in the mean time altogether unsanctified and the children of hell; and that therefore the benefit or gift itself has nothing of the holy nature of the Spirit of God in it, nothing of a vital communication of that Spirit. This notion greatly debases that high and most exalted kind of influence and operation of the Spirit, which there is in the true witness of the Spirit. That which is called the witness of the Spirit, Rom. 8, is elsewhere in the New Testament called the seal of the Spirit, 2 Cor. 1:22, Eph. 1:13, and 4:13, alluding to the seal of princes, annexed to the instrument, by which they advanced any of their subjects to some high honor and dignity, or peculiar privilege in the kingdom, as a token of their special favor. Which is an evidence that the influence of the Spirit, of the Prince of princes, in sealing his favorites, is far from being of a common kind; and that there is no effect of God's Spirit whatsoever, which is in its nature more divine; nothing more holy, peculiar, inimitable and distinguishing of divinity: as nothing is more royal than the royal seal; nothing more sacred, that belongs to a prince, and more peculiarly denoting what belongs to him; it being the very end and design of it, to be the most peculiar stamp and confirmation of the royal authority, and great note of distinction, whereby that which proceeds from the king, or belongs to him, may be known from everything else. And therefore undoubtedly the seal of the great King of heaven and earth enstamped on the heart, is something high and holy in its own nature, some excellent communication from the infinite fountain of divine beauty and glory; and not merely a making known a secret fact by revelation or suggestion; which is a sort of influence of the Spirit of God, that the children of the devil have often been the subjects of. The seal of the Spirit is a kind of effect of the Spirit of God on the heart, which natural men, while such, are so far from a capacity of being the subjects of; that they can have no manner of notion or idea of it, agreeable to Rev. 2:17: 'To him that overcometh will I give to eat of the hidden manna, and I will give him a white stone, and in the stone a new name written, which no man knoweth, saving he that receiveth it.' There is all reason to suppose that what is here spoken of, is the same mark, evidence, or blessed token of special favor, which is elsewhere called the seal of the Spirit.

What has misled many in their notion of that influence of the Spirit of God we are speaking of, is the word *witness*, its being called the witness of the Spirit. Hence they have taken it, not to be any effect or work of the Spirit upon the heart, giving evidence, from whence men may argue that they are the children of God; but an inward immediate suggestion, as though God inwardly spoke to the man, and testified to him, and told him that he was his child, by a kind of a secret voice, or impression: not observing the manner in which the word witness, or testimony, is often used in the New Testament, where such terms often signify, not only a mere declaring and asserting a thing to be true, but holding forth evidence from whence a thing may be argued, and proved to be true. Thus Heb. 2:4, God is said to 'bear witness, with signs and wonders and divers miracles, and gifts of the Holy Ghost.' Now these miracles, here spoken of, are called God's witness, not because they are of the nature of assertions, but evidences and proofs. So Acts 14:3: 'Long time therefore abode they speaking boldly in the Lord, which gave testimony unto the word of his grace, and granted signs and wonders to be done by their hands.' And John 5:36: 'But I have greater witness than that of John: for the works which the Father hath given me to finish, the same works that I do, bear witness of me, that the Father hath sent of me.' Again, chap. 10:25: 'The works that I do in my Father's name, they bear witness of me.' So the water and the blood are said to bear witness, 1 John 5:8, not that they spoke or asserted anything, but they were proofs and evidences. So God's works of providence, in the rain and fruitful seasons, are spoken of as witnesses of God's being and goodness, i.e., they are evidences of these things. And when the Scripture speaks of the seal of the Spirit, it is an expression which properly denotes, not an immediate voice or suggestion, but some work or effect of the Spirit, that is left as a divine mark upon the soul, to be an evidence by which God's children might be known. The seals of princes were the distinguishing marks of princes: and thus God's seal is spoken of as God's mark, Rev. 7:3: 'Hurt not the earth, neither the sea, nor the trees, till we have sealed the servants of our God in their foreheads,' together with Ezek. 9:4, 'Set a mark upon the foreheads of the men that sigh and that cry for all the abominations that are done in the midst thereof.' When God sets his seal on a man's heart by his Spirit, there is some holy stamp, some image impressed and left upon the heart by the Spirit, as by the seal upon the wax. And this holy stamp, or impressed image, exhibiting clear evidence to the conscience, that the subject of it is the child of God, is the very thing which in Scripture is called the seal of the Spirit, and the witness, or evidence of the Spirit. And this image enstamped by the Spirit on God's children's hearts, is his own image; that is the evidence by which they are known to be God's children, that they have the image of their Father stamped upon their hearts by the Spirit of adoption. Seals anciently had engraven on them two things, viz., the image and the name of the person whose seal it was. Therefore when Christ says to his spouse, Cant. 8:6, 'Set me as a seal upon thine heart, as a seal upon thine arm,' it is as much as to say, let my name and image remain impressed there. The seals of princes were wont to bear their image; so that what they set their seal and royal mark upon, had their image left on it. It was the manner of princes of old to have their image engraven on their jewels and precious stones; and the image of Augustus engraven on a precious stone, was used as the seal of the

Roman emperors, in Christ's and the Apostle's times. And the saints are the jewels of Jesus Christ, the great potentate, who has the possession of the empire of the universe; and these jewels have his image enstamped upon them by his royal signet, which is the Holy Spirit. And this is undoubtedly what the Scripture means by the seal of the Spirit; especially when it is stamped in so fair and clear a manner, as to be plain to the eye of conscience; which is what the Scripture calls our spirit. This is truly an effect that is spiritual, supernatural and divine. This is in itself of a holy nature, being a communication of the divine nature and beauty. That kind of influence of the Spirit which gives and leaves this stamp upon the heart, is such that no natural man can be the subject of anything of the like nature with it. This is the highest sort of witness of the Spirit, which it is possible the soul should be the subject of: if there were any such thing as a witness of the Spirit by immediate suggestion or revelation, this would be vastly more noble and excellent, and as much above it as the heaven is above the earth. This the devil cannot imitate; as to an inward suggestion of the Spirit of God, by a kind of secret voice speaking, and immediately asserting and revealing a fact, he can do that which is a thousand times so like to this, as he can to that holy and divine effect, or work of the Spirit of God, which has now been spoken of.

Another thing which is a full proof that the seal of the Spirit is no revelation of any fact by immediate suggestion, but is grace itself in the soul, is, that the seal of the Spirit is called in the Scripture, the earnest of the Spirit. It is very plain that the seal of the Spirit is the same thing with the *earnest of the Spirit*, by 2 Cor. 1:22: 'Who hath also sealed us, and given the earnest of the Spirit in our hearts,' and Eph. 1:13, 14, 'In whom, after that ye believed, ye were sealed with that Holy Spirit of promise, which is the earnest of our inheritance, until the redemption of the purchased possession unto the praise of his glory.' Now the earnest is part of the money agreed for, given in hand, as a token of the whole, to be paid in due time; a part of the promised inheritance granted now, in token of full possession of the whole hereafter. But surely that kind of communication of the Spirit of God, which is of the nature of eternal glory, is the highest and most excellent kind of communication, something that is in its own nature spiritual, holy and divine, and far from anything that is common: and therefore high above anything of the nature of inspiration, or revelation of hidden facts by suggestion of the Spirit of God, which many natural men have had. What is the earnest, and beginning of glory, but grace itself, especially in the more lively and clear exercises of it? It is not prophecy, nor tongues, nor knowledge, but that more excellent divine thing, 'charity that never faileth,' which is a prelibation and beginning of the light, sweetness and blessedness of heaven, that world of love or charity. It is grace that is the seed of glory and dawning of glory in the heart, and therefore it is grace that is the earnest of the future inheritance. What is it that is the beginning or earnest of eternal life in the soul, but spiritual life; and what is that but grace? The inheritance that Christ has purchased for the elect, is the Spirit of God; not in any extraordinary gifts, but in his vital indwelling in the heart, exerting and communicating himself there, in his own proper, holy, or divine nature; and this is the sum total of the inheritance that Christ purchased for the elect. For so are things constituted in the affair of our redemption, that the Father provides the Savior or purchaser, and the purchase is made of him; and the Son is the purchaser and the price; and the Holy Spirit is the great blessing or inheritance purchased, as is intimated, Gal. 3:13, 14; and hence the Spirit often is spoken of as the sum of the blessings promised in the gospel, Luke 24:49, Acts 1:4, and chap. 2:38, 39, Gal. 3:14, Eph. 1:13. This inheritance was the grand legacy which Christ left his disciples and church, in his last will and testament, John chap. 14, 15, 16. This is the sum of the blessings of eternal life, which shall be given in heaven. (Compare John 7:37, 38, 39, and John 4:14, with Rev. 21:6, and 22:1, 17.) It is through the vital communications and indwelling of the Spirit that the saints have all their light, life, holiness, beauty, and joy in heaven; and it is through the vital communications and indwelling of the same Spirit that the saints have all light, life, holiness, beauty and comfort on earth; but only communicated in less measure. And this vital indwelling of the Spirit in the saints, in this less measure and small beginning is, 'the earnest of the Spirit, the earnest of the future inheritance, and the first fruits of the Spirit,' as the apostle calls it, Rom. 8:22, where, by 'the first fruits of the Spirit,' the apostle undoubtedly means the same vital, gracious principle that he speaks of in all the preceding part of the chapter, which he calls Spirit, and sets in opposition to flesh or corruption. Therefore this earnest of the Spirit, and first fruits of the Spirit, which has been shown to be the same with the seal of the Spirit, is the vital, gracious, sanctifying communication and influence of the Spirit, and not any immediate suggestion or revelation of facts by the Spirit.

And indeed the apostle, when in that, Rom. 8:16, he speaks of the Spirit's bearing witness with our spirit that we are the children of God, does sufficiently explain himself, if his words were but attended to. What is here expressed is connected with the two preceding verses, as resulting from what the apostle had said there as every reader may see. The three verses together are thus: 'For as many as are led by the Spirit of God, they are the sons of God: for ye have not received the spirit of bondage again to fear; but ye have received the spirit of adoption, whereby we cry, Abba, Father: the Spirit itself beareth witness with our spirits that we are the children of God.' Here, what the apostle says, if we take it together, plainly shows that what he has respect to, when he speaks of the Spirit's giving us witness or evidence that we are God's children, is his dwelling in us, and leading us, as a spirit of adoption, or spirit of a child, disposing us to behave towards God as to a Father. This is the witness or evidence which the apostle speaks of that we are children, that we have the spirit of children, or spirit of adoption. And what is that but the spirit of love? There are two kinds of spirits the apostle speaks of, the spirit of a slave or the spirit of bondage, that is fear; and the spirit of a child, or spirit of adoption, and that is love. The apostle says, we have not received the spirit of bondage, or of slaves, which is a spirit of fear; but we have received the more ingenuous noble spirit of children, a spirit of love, which naturally disposes us to go to God as children to a father, and behave towards God as children. And this is the evidence or witness which the Spirit of God gives us that we are his children. This is the plain sense of the apostle; and so undoubtedly he here is speaking of the very same way of casting out doubting and fear and the spirit of bondage, which the Apostle John speaks of, 1 John 4:18, viz., by the prevailing of love, that is the spirit of a child. The spirit of bondage works by fear, the slave fears the rod: but love cries, Abba, Father; it disposes us to go to God, and behave ourselves towards God as children; and it gives us clear evidence of our union to God as his children, and so casts out fear. So that it appears that the witness of the Spirit the apostle speaks of, is far from being any whisper, or immediate suggestion or revelation; but that gracious holy effect of the Spirit of God in the hearts of the saints, the disposition and temper of children, appearing in sweet childlike love to God, which casts out fear, or a spirit of a slave.

And the same thing is evident from all the context: it is plain the apostle speaks of the Spirit, over and over again, as dwelling in the hearts of the saints as a gracious principle, set in opposition to the flesh or corruption: and so he does in the words that immediately introduce this passage we are upon, v. 13, 'For if ye live after the flesh, ye shall die: but if ye through the Spirit do mortify the deeds of the flesh, ye shall live.'

Indeed it is past doubt with me, that the apostle has a more special respect to the spirit of grace, or the spirit of love, or spirit of a child, in its more lively actings; for it is perfect love, or strong love only, which so witnesses or evidences that we are children as to cast out fear, and wholly deliver from the spirit of bondage. The strong and lively exercises of a spirit of child-like, evangelical, humble love to God, give clear evidence of the soul's relation to God as his child; which does very greatly and directly satisfy the soul. And though it be far from being true, that the soul in this case, judges only by an immediate witness without any sign or evidence; for it judges and is assured by the greatest sign and clearest evidence; yet in this case the saint stands in no need of multiplied signs, or any long reasoning upon them. And though the sight of his relative union with God, and his being in his favor, is not without a medium, because he sees it by that medium, viz., his love; yet his sight of the union of his heart to God is immediate: love, the bond of union, is seen intuitively: the saint sees and feels plainly the union between his soul and God; it is so strong and lively, that he cannot doubt of it. And hence he is assured that he is a child. How can he doubt whether he stands in a childlike relation to God, when he plainly sees a childlike union between God and his soul, and hence does boldly, and as it were naturally and necessarily cry, Abba, Father?

And whereas the apostle says, the Spirit bears witness with our spirits; by our spirit here, is meant our conscience, which is called the spirit of man, Prov. 20:17, 'The spirit of man is the candle of the Lord, searching all the inward parts of the belly.' We elsewhere read of the witness of this spirit of ours: 2 Cor. 1:12, 'For our rejoicing is this, the testimony of our conscience.' And 1 John 3:19, 20, 21: 'And hereby we know that we are of the truth, and shall assure our hearts before him. For if our heart condemn us, God is greater than our heart, and knoweth all things. Beloved, if our heart condemn us not, then have we confidence towards God.' When the Apostle Paul speaks of the Spirit of God bearing witness with our spirit, he is not to be understood of two spirits that are two separate, collateral, independent witnesses; but it is by one that we receive the witness of the other: the Spirit of God gives the evidence by infusing and shedding abroad the love of God, the spirit of a child, in the heart, and our spirit, or our conscience, receives and declares this evidence for our rejoicing.

Many have been the mischiefs that have arisen from that false and delusive notion of the witness of the Spirit, that it is a kind of inward voice, suggestion, or declaration from God to man, that he is beloved of him, and pardoned, elected, or the like, sometimes with, and sometimes without a text of Scripture; and many have been the false and vain (though very high) affections that have arisen from hence. And it is to be feared that multitudes of souls have been eternally undone by it. I have therefore insisted the longer on this head.

THE TREASURY OF DAVID

by

 C. H. SPURGEON

CONTENTS

Psalm 1

Title

This Psalm may be regarded as THE PREFACE PSALM, having in it a notification of the contents of the entire Book. It is the Psalmist's desire to teach us the way to blessedness, and to warn us of the sure destruction of sinners. This, then, is the matter of the first Psalm, which may be looked upon, in some respects, as the text upon which the whole of the Psalms make up a divine sermon.

Division

This Psalm consists of two parts: in the first (from verse 1 to the end of the third) David sets out wherein the felicity and blessedness of a godly man consisteth, what his exercises are, and what blessings he shall receive from the Lord. In the second part (from verse 4 to the end) he contrasts the state and character of the ungodly, reveals the future, and describes, in telling language, his ultimate doom.

Exposition

Verse 1. 'BLESSED' – see how this Book of Psalms opens with a benediction, even as did the famous Sermon of our Lord upon the Mount! The word translated 'blessed' is a very expressive one. The original word is plural, and it is a controverted matter whether it is an adjective or a substantive. Hence we may learn the multiplicity of the blessings which shall rest upon the man whom God hath justified, and the perfection and greatness of the blessedness he shall enjoy. We might read it, 'Oh, the blessednesses!' and we may well regard it (as Ainsworth does) as a joyful acclamation of the gracious man's felicity. May the like benediction rest on us!

Here the gracious man is described both negatively (verse 1) and positively (verse 2). He is a man who does not walk in the counsel of the ungodly. He takes wiser counsel, and walks in the commandments of the Lord his God. To him the ways of piety are paths of peace and pleasantness. His footsteps are ordered by the Word of God, and not by the cunning and wicked devices of carnal men. It is a rich sign of inward grace when the outward walk is changed, and when ungodliness is put far from our actions. Note next, he standeth not in the way of sinners. His company is of a choicer sort than it was. Although a sinner himself, he is now a blood-washed sinner, quickened by the Holy Spirit, and renewed in heart. Standing by the rich grace of God in the congregation of the righteous, he dares not herd with the multitude that do evil. Again it is said, 'nor sitteth in the seat of the scornful.' He finds no rest in the atheist's scoffings. Let others make a mock of sin, of eternity, of hell and heaven, and of the Eternal God; this man has learned better philosophy than that of the infidel, and has too much sense of God's presence to endure to hear His name blasphemed. The seat of the scorner may be very lofty, but it is very near to the gate of hell; let us flee from it, for it shall soon be empty, and destruction shall swallow up the man who sits therein. Mark the gradation in the first verse:

He walketh not in the counsel of the ungodly,
Nor standeth in the way of sinners,
Nor SITTETH in the SEAT of SCORNFUL.

When men are living in sin they go from bad to worse. At first they merely walk in the counsel of the careless and ungodly, who forget God – the evil is rather practical than habitual – but after that, they become habituated to evil, and they stand in the way of open sinners who wilfully violate God's commandments; and if let alone, they go one step further, and become themselves pestilent teachers and tempters of others, and thus they sit in the seat of the scornful. They have taken their degree in vice, and as true Doctors of Damnation they are installed, and are looked up to by others as Masters in Belial. But the blessed man, the man to whom all the blessings of God belong, can hold no communion with such characters as these. He keeps himself pure from these lepers; he puts away evil things from him as garments spotted by the flesh; he comes out from among the wicked, and goes without the camp, bearing the reproach of Christ. O for grace to be thus separate from sinners.

And now mark his positive character. 'His delight is in the law of the Lord.' He is not under the law as a curse and condemnation, but he is in it, and he delights to be in it as his rule of life; he delights, moreover, to meditate in it, to read it by day, and think upon it by night. He takes a text and carries it with him all day long; and in the night-watches, when sleep forsakes his eyelids, he museth upon the Word of God. In the day of his prosperity he sings psalms out of the Word of God, and in the night of his affliction he comforts himself with promises out of the same book. 'The law of the Lord' is the daily bread of the true believer. And yet, in David's day, how small was the volume of inspiration, for they had scarcely anything save the first five books of Moses! How much more, then, should we prize the whole written Word which it is our privilege to have in all our houses! But, alas, what ill-treatment is given to this angel from heaven! We are not all Berean searchers of the Scriptures. How few among us can lay claim to the benediction of the text! Perhaps some of you can claim a sort of negative purity, because you do not walk in the way of the ungodly; but let me ask you – Is your delight in the law of God? Do you study God's Word? Do you make it the man of your right hand – your best companion and hourly guide? If not, this blessing belongeth not to you.

Verse 3. 'And he shall be like a tree planted' – not a wild tree, but 'a tree planted,' chosen, considered as property, cultivated and secured from the last terrible uprooting, for 'every plant which my heavenly Father hath not planted, shall be rooted up' Matthew 15:13. 'By the rivers of water;' so that even if one river should fail, he hath another. The rivers of pardon and the rivers of grace, the rivers of the promise and the rivers of communion with Christ, are never-failing sources of supply. He is 'like a tree planted by the rivers of water, that bringeth forth his fruit in his season;' not unseasonable graces, like untimely figs, which are never full-flavoured. But the man who delights in God's Word, being taught by it, bringeth forth patience in the time of suffering, faith in the day of trial, and holy joy in the hour of prosperity. Fruitfulness is an essential quality of a gracious man, and that fruitfulness should be seasonable. 'His leaf also shall not wither;' his faintest word shall be everlasting; his little deeds of love shall be had in remembrance. Not simply shall his fruit be preserved, but his leaf also. He shall neither lose his beauty nor his fruitfulness. 'And whatsoever he doeth shall prosper.' Blessed is the man who hath such a promise as this. But we must not always estimate the fulfilment of a promise by our own eye-sight. How often, my brethren, if we judge by feeble sense, may we come to the mournful conclusion of Jacob, 'All these things are against me!' For though we know our interest in the promise, yet we are so tried and troubled, that sight sees the very reverse of what that promise foretells. But to the eye of faith this word is sure, and by it we perceive that our works are prospered, even when everything seems to go against us. It is not outward prosperity which the Christian most desires and values; it is soul prosperity which he longs for. We often, like Jehoshaphat, make ships to go to Tarshish for gold, but they are broken at Ezion-geber; but even here there is a true prospering, for it is often for the soul's health that we would be poor, bereaved, and persecuted. Our worst things are often our best things. As there is a curse wrapped up in the wicked man's mercies, so there is a blessing concealed in the righteous man's crosses, losses, and sorrows. The trials of the saint are a divine husbandry, by which he grows and brings forth abundant fruit.

Verse 4. We have now come to the second head of the Psalm. In this verse the contrast of the ill estate of the wicked is employed to heighten the colouring of that fair and pleasant picture which precedes it. The more forcible translation of the Vulgate and of the Septuagint version is – 'Not so the ungodly, not so.' And we are hereby to understand that whatever good thing is said of the righteous is not true in the case of the ungodly. Oh! how terrible is it to have a double negative put upon the promises! and yet this is just the condition of the ungodly. Mark the use of the term 'ungodly,' for, as we have seen in the opening of the Psalm, these are the beginners in evil, and are the least offensive of sinners. Oh! if such is the sad state of those who quietly continue in their morality, and neglect their God, what must be the condition of open sinners and shameless infidels? The first sentence is a negative description of the ungodly, and the second is the positive picture. Here is their character – 'they are like chaff,' intrinsically worthless, dead, unserviceable, without substance, and easily carried away. Here, also, mark their doom, – 'the wind driveth away;' death shall hurry them with its terrible blast into the fire in which they shall be utterly consumed.

Verse 5. They shall stand there to be judged, but not to be acquitted. Fear shall lay hold upon them there; they shall not stand their ground; they shall flee away; they shall not stand in their own defence; for they shall blush and be covered with eternal contempt.

Well may the saints long for heaven, for no evil men shall dwell there, 'nor sinners in the congregation of the righteous.' All our congregations upon earth are mixed. Every Church hath one devil in it. The tares grow in the same furrows as the wheat. There is no floor which is as yet thoroughly purged from chaff. Sinners mix with saints, as dross mingles with gold. God's precious diamonds still lie in the same field with pebbles. Righteous Lots are this side heaven continually vexed by the men of Sodom. Let us rejoice then, that in 'the general assembly and church of the firstborn' above, there shall by no means be admitted a single unrenewed soul. Sinners cannot live in heaven. They would be out of their element. Sooner could a fish live upon a tree than the wicked in Paradise. Heaven would be an intolerable hell to an impenitent man, even if he could be allowed to enter; but such a privilege shall never be granted to the man who perseveres in his iniquities. May God grant that we may have a name and a place in his courts above!

Verse 6. Or, as the Hebrew hath it yet more fully, 'The Lord is knowing the way of the righteous.' He is constantly looking on their way, and though it may be often in mist and darkness, yet the Lord knoweth it. If it be in the clouds and tempest of affliction, he understandeth it. He numbereth the hairs of our head; he will not suffer any evil to befall us. 'He knoweth the way that I take: when He hath tried me, I shall come forth as gold' (Job 23:10). 'But the way of the ungodly shall perish.' Not only shall they perish themselves, but their way shall perish too. The righteous carves his name upon the rock, but the wicked writes his remembrance in the sand. The righteous man ploughs the furrows of earth, and sows a harvest here, which shall never be fully reaped till he enters the enjoyments of eternity; but as for the wicked, he ploughs the sea, and though there may seem to be a shining trail behind his keel, yet the waves shall pass over it, and the place that knew him shall know him no more for ever. The very 'way' of the ungodly shall perish. If it exist in remembrance, it shall be in the remembrance of the bad; for the Lord will cause the name of the wicked to rot, to become a stench in the nostrils of the good, and to be only known to the wicked themselves by its putridity.

May the Lord cleanse our hearts and our ways, that we may escape the doom of the ungodly, and enjoy the blessedness of the righteous!

Explanatory notes and quaint sayings

Whole Psalm. As the book of the Canticles is called the Song of Songs by a Hebraism, it being the most excellent, so this Psalm may not unfitly be entitled, the Psalm of Psalms, for it contains in it the very pith and quintessence of Christianity. What Jerome saith on St Paul's epistles, the same may I say of this Psalm; it is short as to the composure, but full of length and strength as to the matter. This Psalm carries blessedness in the frontpiece; it begins where we all hope to end: it may well be called a Christian's Guide, for it discovers the quicksands where the wicked sink down in perdition, and the firm ground on which the saints tread to glory. Thomas Watson's Saints' Spiritual Delight, 1660.

This whole Psalm offers itself to be drawn into these two opposite propositions: a godly man is blessed, a wicked man is miserable; which seem to stand as two challenges, made by the prophet: one, that he will maintain a godly man against all comers, to be the only Jason for winning the golden fleece of blessedness; the other, that albeit the ungodly make a show in the world of being happy, yet they of all men are most miserable. Sir Richard Baker, 1640.

I have been induced to embrace the opinion of some among the ancient interpreters (Augustine, Jerome, etc.), who conceive that the first Psalm is intended to be descriptive of the character and reward of the JUST ONE, i.e. the Lord Jesus. John Fry, B.A., 1842.

Verse 1. The psalmist saith more to the point about true happiness in this short Psalm than any one of the philosophers, or all of them put together; they did but beat the bush, God hath here put the bird into our hand. John Trapp, 1660.

Verse 1. Where the word blessed is hung out as a sign, we may be sure that we shall find a godly man within. Sir Richard Baker.

Verse 1. The seat of the drunkard is the seat of the scornful. Matthew Henry, 1662–1714.

Verse 1. 'Walketh NOT ... NOR standeth ... NOR sitteth,' etc. Negative precepts are in some cases more absolute and peremptory than affirmatives; for to say, 'that hath walketh in the counsel of the godly,' might not be sufficient; for, he might walk in the counsel of the godly, and yet walk in the counsel of the ungodly too; not both indeed at once, but both at several times; where now, this negative clears him at all times. Sir Richard Baker.

Verse 1. The word (Heb.) *haish* is emphatic, that man; that one among a thousand who lives for the accomplishment of the end for which God created him. Adam Clarke, 1844.

Verse 1. 'That walketh not in the counsel of the ungodly.' Mark certain circumstances of their differing characters and conduct. 1. The ungodly man has his counsel. 2. The sinner has his way. 3. The scorner has his seat. The ungodly man is unconcerned about religion; he is neither zealous for his own salvation nor for that of others; and he counsels and advises those with whom he converses to adopt his plan, and not trouble themselves about praying, reading, repentance, etc., etc.; 'there is no need for such things; live an honest life, make no fuss about religion, and you will fare well enough at last.' Now 'blessed is the man who walks not in this man's counsel,' who does not come into his measures, nor act according to his plan.

The sinner has his particular way of transgressing; one is a drunkard, another dishonest, another unclean. Few are given to every species of vice. There are many covetous men who abhor drunkenness, many drunkards who abhor covetousness; and so of others. Each has his easily besetting sin; therefore, says the prophet, 'Let the wicked forsake HIS WAY' (Isaiah 55:7). Now, blessed is he who stands not is such a man's WAY.

The scorner has brought, in reference to himself, all religion and moral feeling to an end. He has sat down – is utterly confirmed in impiety, and makes a mock at sin. His conscience is seared, and he is a believer in all unbelief. Now, blessed is the man who sits not down in his SEAT. Adam Clarke.

Verse 1. In the Hebrew, the word 'blessed' is a plural noun, *ashrey* (blessednesses), that is, all blessednesses are the portion of that man who has not gone away, etc.; as though it were said, 'All things are well with that man who,' etc. Why do you hold any dispute? Why draw vain conclusions? If a man has found that pearl of great price, to love the law of God and to be separate from the ungodly, all blessednesses belong to that man; but, if he does not find this jewel, he will seek for all blessednesses but will never find one! For as all things are pure unto the pure, so all things are lovely unto the loving, all things good unto the good; and, universally, such as thou art thyself, such is God himself unto thee, though he is not a creature. He is perverse unto the perverse, and holy unto the holy. Hence nothing can be good or saving unto him who is evil: nothing sweet unto him unto whom the law of God is not sweet. The word 'counsel' is without doubt here to be received as signifying decrees and doctrines, seeing that no society of men exists without being formed and preserved by decrees and laws. David, however, by this term strikes at the pride and reprobate temerity of the ungodly. First, because they will not humble themselves so far as to walk in the law of the Lord, but rule themselves by their own counsel. And then he calls it their 'counsel,' because it is their prudence, and the way that seems to them to be without error. For this is the destruction of the ungodly – their being prudent in their own eyes and in their own esteem, and clothing their errors in the garb of prudence and of the right way. For if they came to men in the open garb of error, it would not be so distinguishing a mark of blessedness not to walk with them. But David does not here say, 'in the folly of the ungodly,' or 'in the error of the ungodly;' and therefore he admonishes us to guard with all diligence against the appearance of what is right, that the devil transformed into an angel of light do not seduce us by his craftiness. And he contrasts the counsel of the wicked with the law of the Lord, that we may learn to beware of wolves in sheep's clothing, who are always ready to give counsel to all, to teach all, and to offer assistance unto all, when they are of all men least qualified to do so. The term 'stood' descriptively represents their obstinacy, and stiff-neckedness, wherein they harden themselves and make their excuses in words of malice, having become incorrigible in their ungodliness. For 'to stand,' in the figurative manner of Scripture expression, signifies to be firm and fixed: as in Romans 14:4, 'To his own master he standeth or falleth: yea, he shall be holden up, for God is able to make him stand.' Hence the word 'column' is by the Hebrew derived from their verb 'to stand,' as is the word 'statue' among the Latins. For this is the very self-excuse and self-hardening of the ungodly – their appearing to themselves to live rightly, and to shine in the eternal show of works above all others. With respect to the term 'seat,' to sit in the seat, is to teach, to act the instructor and teacher; as in Matthew 23:2, 'The scribes sit in Moses' chair.' They sit in the seat of pestilence, who fill the church with the opinions of philosophers, with the traditions of men, and with the counsels of their own brain, and oppress miserable consciences, setting aside, all the while, the word of God, by which alone the soul is fed, lives, and is preserved. Martin Luther, 1536–1546.

Verse 1. 'The scornful.' *Peccator cum in profundum venerit contemnet* – when a wicked man comes to the depth and worst of sin, he despiseth. Then the Hebrew will despise Moses (Exodus 2:14), 'Who made thee a prince and a judge over us?' Then Ahab will quarrel with Micaiah (1 Kings 22:18), because he doth not prophecy good unto him. Every child in Bethel will mock Elisha (2 Kings 2:23), and be bold to call him 'bald pate.' Here is an original drop of venom swollen to a main ocean of poison: as one drop of some serpent's poison, lighting on the hand, gets into the veins, and so spreads itself over all the body till it hath stifled the vital spirits. God shall 'laugh you to scorn' (Psalm 2:4), for laughing Him to scorn; and at last despise you that have despised him in us. That which a man spits against heaven, shall fall back on his own face. Your indignities done to your spiritual physicians shall sleep in the dust with your ashes, but stand up against your souls in judgment. Thomas Adams, 1614.

Verse 2. 'But his will is in the law of the Lord.' The 'will,' which is here signified, is that delight of heart, and that certain pleasure, in the law, which does not look at what the law promises, nor at what it threatens, but at this only; that 'the law is holy, and just, and good.' Hence it is not only a love of the law, but that loving delight in the law which no prosperity, nor adversity, nor the world, nor the prince of it, can either take away or destroy; for it victoriously bursts its way through poverty, evil report, the cross, death, and hell, and in the midst of adversities, shines the brightest. Martin Luther.

Verse 2. 'His delight is in the law of the Lord.' – This delight which the prophet here speaks of is the only delight that neither blushes nor looks pale; the only delight that gives a repast without an after reckoning; the only delight that stands in construction with all tenses; and like Æneas Anchyses, carries his parents upon his back. Sir Richard Baker.

Verse 2. 'In His law doth he meditate.' In the plainest text there is a world of holiness and spirituality; and if we in prayer and dependence upon God did sit down and study it, we should behold much more than appears to us. It may be, at once reading or looking, we see little or nothing; as Elijah's servant went once, and saw nothing; therefore he was commanded to look seven times. What now? says the prophet, 'I see a cloud rising, like a man's hand;' and by-and-by, the whole surface of the heavens was covered with clouds. So you may look lightly upon a Scripture and see nothing; meditate often upon it, and there you shall see a light, like the light of the sun. Joseph Caryl, 1647.

Verse 2. 'In His law doth he meditate day and night.' The good man doth meditate on the law of God day and night. The pontificians beat off the common people from this common treasury, by objecting this supposed difficulty. Oh, the Scriptures are hard to be understood, do not you trouble your heads about them; we will tell you the meaning of them. They might as well say, heaven is a blessed place, but it is a hard way to it; do not trouble yourselves, we will go thither for you. Thus in the great day of trial, when they should be saved by their book, alas! they have no book to save them. Instead of the Scriptures they can present images; these are the layman's books; as if they were to be tried by a jury of carvers and painters, and not by the twelve apostles. Be not you so cheated; but study the gospel as you look for comfort by the gospel. He that hopes for the inheritance, will make much of the conveyance. Thomas Adams.

Verse 2. To 'meditate,' as it is generally understood, signifies to discuss, to dispute; and its meaning is always confined to a being employed in words, as in Psalm 32:30, 'The mouth of the righteous shall meditate wisdom.' Hence Augustine has, in his translation, 'chatter;' and a beautiful metaphor it is – as chattering is the employment of birds, so a continual conversing in the law of the Lord (for talking is peculiar to man), ought to be the employment of man. But I cannot worthily and fully set forth the gracious meaning and force of this word; for this 'meditating' consists first in an intent observing of the words of the law, and then in a comparing of the different Scriptures; which is a certain delightful hunting, nay, rather a playing with stags in a forest, where the Lord furnishes us with the stags, and opens to us their secret coverts. And from this kind of employment, there comes forth at length a man well instructed in the law of the Lord to speak unto the people. Martin Luther.

Verse 2. 'In his law doth he meditate day and night.' The godly man will read the Word by day, that men, seeing his good works, may glorify his Father who is in heaven; he will do it in the night, that he may not be seen of men: by day, to show that he is not one of those who dread the light; by night, to show that he is one who can shine in the shade: by day, for that is the time for working – work whilst it is day; by night, lest his Master should come as a thief, and find him idle. Sir Richard Baker.

Verse 2. I have no rest, but in a nook, with the book. Thomas à Kempis, 1380–1471.

Verse 2. 'Meditate.' Meditation doth discriminate and characterise a man; by this he may take a measure of his heart, whether it be good or bad; let me allude to that; 'For as he thinketh in his heart, so is he' Proverbs 23:7. As the meditation is, such is the man. Meditation is the touchstone of a Christian; it shows what metal he is made of. It is a spiritual index; the index shows what is in the book, so meditation shows what is in the heart. Thomas Watson's Saints' Spiritual Delight.

Verse 2. Meditation chews the cud, and gets the sweetness and nutritive virtue of the Word into the heart and life: this is the way the godly bring forth much fruit. Bartholomew Ashwood's Heavenly Trade, 1688.

Verse 2. The naturalists observe that to uphold and accommodate bodily life, there are diverse sorts of faculties communicated, and these among the rest:

1. An attractive faculty, to assume and draw in the food;
2. A retentive faculty, to retain it when taken in;
3. As assimilating faculty to concoct the nourishment;
4. An augmenting faculty, for drawing to perfection.

Meditation is all these. It helps judgment, wisdom, and faith to ponder, discern, and credit the things which reading and hearing supply and furnish. It assists the memory to lock up the jewels of divine truth in her sure treasury. It has a digesting power, and turns special truth into spiritual nourishment; and lastly, it helps the renewed heart to grow upward and increase its power to know the things which are freely given to us of God. Condensed from Nathaniel Ranew, 1670.

Verse 3. 'A tree.' – There is one tree, only to be found in the valley of the Jordan, but too beautiful to be entirely passed over; the oleander, with its bright blossoms and dark green leaves, giving the aspect of a rich garden to any spot where it grows. It is rarely if ever alluded to in the Scriptures. But it may be the tree planted by the streams of water which bringeth forth his fruit in due season, and 'whose leaf shall not wither.' A. P. Stanley, D.D., in 'Sinai and Palestine.'

Verse 3. 'A tree planted by the rivers of water.' – This is an allusion to the Eastern method of cultivation, by which rivulets of water are made to flow between the rows of trees, and thus, by artificial means, the trees receive a constant supply of moisture.

Verse 3. 'His fruit in his season.' – In such a case expectation is never disappointed. Fruit is expected, fruit is borne, and it comes also in the time in which it should come. A godly education, under the influences of the divine Spirit, which can never be withheld where they are earnestly sought, is sure to produce the fruits of righteousness; and he who reads, prays, and meditates, will ever see the work which God has given him to do; the power by which he is to perform it; and the times, places, and opportunities for doing those things by which God can obtain most glory, his own soul most good, and his neighbour most edification. Adam Clarke.

Verse 3. 'In his season.' The Lord reckons the times which pass over us, and puts them to our account: let us, therefore, improve them, and with the impotent persons at the pool of Bethesda, step in when the angel stirs the water. Now the church is afflicted, it is a season of prayer and learning; now the church is enlarged, it is a season of praise; I am now at a sermon, I will hear what God will say; now in the company of a learned and wise man, I will draw some knowledge and counsel from him; I am under a temptation, now is a fit time to lean on the name of the Lord; I am in a place of dignity and power, let me consider what it is that God requireth of me in such a time as this. And thus as the tree of life bringeth fruit every month, so a wise Christian, as a wise husbandman, hath his distinct employments for every month, bringing forth his fruit in his season. John Spencer's Things New and Old, 1658.

Verse 3. 'In his season.' Oh, golden and admirable word! by which is asserted the liberty of Christian righteousness. The ungodly have their stated days, stated times, certain works, and certain places; to which they stick so closely, that if their neighbours were perishing with hunger, they could not be torn from them. But this blessed man, being free at all times, in all places, for every work, and to every person, will serve you whenever an opportunity is offered him; whatsoever comes into his hands to do, he does it. He is neither a Jew, nor a Gentile, nor a Greek, nor a barbarian, nor of any other particular person. He gives his fruit in his season, so often as either God or man requires his work. Therefore his fruits have no name, and his times have no name. Martin Luther.

Verse 3. 'His leaf also shall not wither.' He describes the fruit before he does the leaf. The Holy Spirit himself always teaches every faithful preacher in the church to know that the kingdom of God does not stand in word but in power. 1 Corinthians 4:20. Again, 'Jesus began both to do and to teach' Acts 1:1. And again, 'Which was a prophet mighty in deed and word' Luke 24:19. And thus, let him who professes the word of doctrine, first put forth the fruits of life, if he would not have his fruit to wither, for Christ cursed the fig tree which bore no fruit. And, as Gregory saith, that man whose life is despised is condemned by his doctrine, for he preaches to others, and is himself reprobated. Martin Luther.

Verse 3. 'His leaf also shall not wither.' The Lord's trees are all evergreens. No winter's cold can destroy their verdure; and yet, unlike evergreens in our country, they are all fruit bearers. C.H.S.

Verse 3. 'And whatsoever he doeth [or, maketh or taketh in hand], shall prosper.' And with regard to this 'prospering,' take heed that thou understandest not a carnal prosperity. This prosperity is hidden prosperity, and lies entirely secret in spirit; and therefore if thou hast not this prosperity that is by faith, thou shouldest rather judge thy prosperity to be the greatest adversity. For as the devil bitterly hates this leaf and the word of God, so does he also those who teach and hear it, and he persecutes such, aided by all the powers of the world. Therefore thou hearest of a miracle the greatest of all miracles, when thou hearest that all things prosper which a blessed man doeth. Martin Luther.

Verse 3. A critical journal has shown that instead of 'Whatsoever it doeth shall prosper,' the rendering might be, 'Whatsoever it produceth shall come to maturity.' This makes the figure entire, and is sanctioned by some MSS. and ancient versions.

Verse 3 (last clause). Outward prosperity, if it follow close walking with God, is very sweet; as the cipher, when it follows a figure, adds to the number, though it be nothing in itself. John Trapp.

Verse 4. 'Chaff.' Here, by the way, we may let the wicked know they have a thanks to give they little think of; that they may thank the godly for all the good days they live upon the earth, seeing it is for their sakes and not for their own that they enjoy them. For as the chaff while it is united and keeps close to the wheat, enjoys some privileges for the wheat's sake, and is laid up carefully in the barn; but as soon as it is divided, and parted from the wheat, it is cast out and scattered by the wind; so the wicked, whilst the godly are in company and live amongst them, partake for their sake of some blessedness promised to the godly; but if the godly forsake them or be taken from them, then either a deluge of water comes suddenly upon them, as it did upon the old world when Noah left it; or a deluge of fire, as it did upon Sodom, when Lot left it, and went out of the city. Sir Richard Baker.

Verse 4. 'Driveth away,' or tosseth away; the Chaldee translateth for 'wind,' 'whirlwind.' Henry Ainsworth, 1639.

This shows the vehement tempest of death, which sweeps away the soul of the ungodly.

Verse 5. 'Therefore the ungodly shall not stand in the judgment,' etc. And may not a reason also be conceived thus, why the ungodly can never come to be of the congregation of the righteous: the righteous go a way that God knows, and the wicked go a way that God destroys; and seeing that these ways can never meet, how should the men meet that go these ways? And to make sure work that they shall never meet indeed, the prophet expresseth the way of the righteous by the first link of the chain of God's goodness, which is his knowledge; but expresseth the way of the wicked by the last link of God's justice, which is his destroying; and though God's justice and his mercy do often meet, and are contiguous one to another, yet the first link of his mercy and the last link of his justice can never meet, for it never comes to destroying till God be heard to say *Nescio vos,* 'I know you not,' and *nescio vos* in God, and God's knowledge, can certainly never possibly meet together. Sir Richard Baker.

Verse 5. The Irish air will sooner brook a toad, or a snake, than heaven a sinner. John Trapp.

Verse 6. 'For the Lord knoweth the way of the righteous: but the way of the ungodly shall perish.' Behold how David here terrifies us away from all prosperous appearances, and commends to us various temptations and adversities. For this 'way' of the righteous all men utterly reprobate; thinking also, that God knoweth nothing about any such way. But this is the wisdom of the cross. Therefore, it is God alone that knoweth the way of the righteous, so hidden is it to the righteous themselves. For his right hand leads them on in a wonderful manner, seeing that it is a way, not of sense, nor of reason, but of faith only; even of that faith that sees in darkness, and beholds things that are invisible. Martin Luther.

Verse 6. 'The righteous.' They that endeavour righteous living in themselves and have Christ's righteousness imputed to them. Thomas Wilcocks, 1586.

Hints to the village preacher
Verse 1. May furnish an excellent text upon 'Progress in Sin,' or 'The Purity of the Christian,' or 'The Blessedness of the Righteous.' Upon the last subject speak of the believer as BLESSED –

1. By God;
2. In Christ;
3. With all blessings;
4. In all circumstances;
5. Through time and eternity;
6. To the highest degree.

Verse 1. Teaches a godly man to beware, (1) of the opinions, (2) of the practical life, and (3) of the company and association of sinful men. Show how meditation upon the Word will assist us in keeping aloof from these three evils.

The insinuating and progressive nature of sin. J. Morrison.

Verse 1. In connection with the whole Psalm. The wide difference between the righteous and the wicked.

Verse 2. THE WORD OF GOD.

1. The believer's delight in it.
2. The believer's acquaintance with it.

We long to be in the company of those we love.

Verse 2.

1. What is meant by 'the law of the Lord.'
2. What there is in it for the believer to delight in.
3. How he shows his delight, thinks of it, reads much, speaks of it, obeys it, does not delight in evil.

Verse 2 (last clause). The benefits, helps, and hindrances of meditation.

Verse 3. 'The fruitful tree.'

1. Where it grows.
2. How it came there.
3. What it yields.
4. How to be like it.

Verse 3. 'Planted by the rivers of water.'

1. The origination of Christian life, 'planted.'
2. The streams which support it.
3. The fruit expected from it.

Verse 3. Influence of religion upon prosperity. Blair.

The nature, causes, signs, and results of true prosperity.

'Fruit in his season;' virtues to be exhibited at certain seasons – patience in affliction; gratitude in prosperity; zeal in opportunity, etc.

'His leaf also shall not wither;' the blessing of retaining an unwithered profession.

Verses 3, 4. See No. 280 of 'Spurgeon's Sermons.' 'The Chaff Driven Away.'

Sin puts a negative on every blessing.

Verse 5. The sinner's double doom.

1. Condemned at the judgment-bar.
2. Separated from the saints.

Reasonableness of these penalties, 'therefore,' and the way to escape them.

'The congregation of the righteous' viewed as the church of the first-born above. This may furnish a noble topic.

Verse 6 (first sentence). A sweet encouragement to the tried people of God. The knowledge here meant.

1. Its character. – It is a knowledge of observation and approbation.
2. Its source. – It is caused by omniscience and infinite love.
3. Its results. – Support, deliverance, acceptance, and glory at last.

Verse 6 (last clause). His way of pleasure, of pride, of unbelief, of profanity, of persecution, of procrastinating, of self-deception, etc.: all these shall come to an end.

Psalm 4

Title

This Psalm is apparently intended to accompany the third, and make a pair with it. If the last may be entitled THE MORNING PSALM, this from its matter is equally deserving of the title of THE EVENING HYMN. May the choice words of the eighth verse be our sweet song of rest as we retire to our repose!

> Thus with my thoughts composed to peace,
> I'll give mine eyes to sleep;
> Thy hand in safety keeps my days,
> And will my slumbers keep.

The Inspired title runs thus: 'To the chief Musician on Neginoth, a Psalm of David.' The chief musician was the master or director of the sacred music of the sanctuary. Concerning this person carefully read 1 Chronicles 6:31,32; 15:16–22; 25: 1, 7. In these passages will be found much that is interesting to the lover of sacred song, and very much that will throw a light upon the mode of praising God in the temple. Some of the titles of the Psalms are, we doubt not, derived from the names of certain renowned singers, who composed the music to which they were set.

On Neginoth, that is, on stringed instruments, or hand instruments, which were played on with the hand alone, as harps and cymbals. The joy of the Jewish church was so great that they needed music to set forth the delightful feelings of their souls. Our holy mirth is none the less overflowing because we prefer to express it in a more spiritual manner, as becometh a more spiritual dispensation. In allusion to these instruments to be played on with the hand, Nazianzen says, 'Lord, I am an instrument for thee to touch.' Let us lay ourselves open to the Spirit's touch, so shall we make melody. May we be full of faith and love, and we shall be living instruments of music.

Hawker says: 'The Septuagint read the word which we have rendered in our translation chief musician Lamenetz, instead of Lamenetzoth, the meaning of which is unto the end. From whence the Greek and Latin fathers imagined, that all psalms which bear this inscription refer to the Messiah, the great end. If so, this Psalm is addressed to Christ; and well it may, for it is all of Christ, and spoken by Christ, and hath respect only to his people as being one with Christ. The Lord the Spirit give the reader to see this, and he will find it most blessed.

Division

In the first verse David pleads with God for help. In the second he expostulates with his enemies, and continues to address them to the end of verse 5. Then from verse 6 to the close he delightfully contrasts his own satisfaction and safety with the disquietude of the ungodly in their best estate. The Psalm was most probably written upon the same occasion as the preceding, and is another choice flower from the garden of affliction. Happy is it for us that David was tried, or probably we should never have heard these sweet sonnets of faith.

Exposition

Verse 1. This is another instance of David's common habit of pleading past mercies as a ground for present favour. Here he reviews his Ebenezers and takes comfort from them. It is not to be imagined that he who has helped us in six troubles will leave us in the seventh. God does nothing by halves, and he will never cease to help us until we cease to need. The manna shall fall every morning until we cross the Jordan.

Observe, that David speaks first to God and then to men. Surely we should all speak the more boldly to men if we had more constant converse with God. He who dares to face his Maker will not tremble before the sons of men.

The name by which the Lord is here addressed, 'God of my righteousness,' deserves notice, since it is not used in any other part of Scripture. It means, Thou art the author, the witness, the maintainer, the judge, and the rewarder of my righteousness; to thee I appeal from the calumnies and harsh judgments of men. Herein is wisdom, let us imitate it and always take our suit, not to the petty courts of human opinion, but into the superior court, the King's Bench of heaven.

'Thou hast enlarged me when I was in distress.' A figure taken from an army enclosed in a defile, and hardly pressed by the surrounding enemy. God hath dashed down the rocks and given me room; he hath broken the barriers and set me in a large place. Or, we may understand it thus: 'God hath enlarged my heart with joy and comfort, when I was like a man imprisoned by grief and sorrow.' God is a never-failing comforter.

'Have mercy upon me.' Though thou mayest justly permit my enemies to destroy me, on account of my many and great sins, yet I flee to thy mercy, and I beseech thee hear my prayer, and bring thy servant out of his troubles. The best of men need mercy as truly as the worst of men. All the deliverances of saints, as well as the pardons of sinners, are the free gifts of heavenly grace.

Verse 2. In this second division of the Psalm, we are led from the closet of prayer into the field of conflict. Remark the undaunted courage of the man of God. He allows that his enemies are great men (for such is the import of the Hebrew words translated 'sons of men'), but still he believes them to be foolish men, and therefore chides them, as though they were but children. He tells them that they love vanity, and seek after leasing, that is, lying, empty fancies, vain conceits, wicked fabrications. He asks them how long they mean to make his honour a jest, and his fame a mockery? A little of such mirth is too much, why need they continue to indulge in it? Had they not been long enough upon the watch for his halting? Had not repeated disappointments convinced them that the Lord's anointed was not to be overcome by all their calumnies? Did they mean to jest their souls into hell, and go on with their laughter until swift vengeance should turn their merriment into howling? In the contemplation of their perverse continuance in their vain and lying pursuits, the Psalmist solemnly pauses and inserts a Selah. Surely we too may stop awhile, and meditate upon the deep-seated folly of the wicked, their continuance in evil, and their sure destruction; and we may learn to admire that grace which has made us to differ, and taught us to love truth, and seek after righteousness.

Verse 3. 'But know.' Fools will not learn, and therefore they must again and again be told the same thing, especially when it is such a bitter truth which is to be taught them, viz., the fact that the godly are the chosen of God, and are, by distinguishing grace, set apart and separated from among men. Election is a doctrine which unrenewed men cannot endure, but nevertheless, it is a glorious and well-attested truth, and one which should comfort the tempted believer. Election is the guarantee of complete salvation, and an argument for success at the throne of grace. He who chose us for himself will surely hear our prayer. The Lord's elect shall not be condemned, nor shall their cry be unheard. David was king by divine decree, and we are the Lord's people in the same manner: let us tell our enemies to their faces, that they fight against God and destiny, when they strive to overthrow our souls. O beloved, when you are on your knees, the fact of your being set apart as God's own peculiar treasure, should give you courage and inspire you with fervency and faith. 'Shall not God avenge his own elect, which cry day and night unto him?' Since he chose to love us he cannot but choose to hear us.

Verse 4. 'Tremble and sin not.' How many reverse this counsel and sin but tremble not. O that men would take the advice of this verse and commune with their own hearts. Surely a want of thought must be one reason why men are so mad as to despite Christ and hate their own mercies. O that for once their passions would be quiet and let them be still, that so in solemn silence they might review the past, and meditate upon their inevitable doom. Surely a thinking man might have enough sense to discover the vanity of sin and the worthlessness of the world. Stay, rash sinner, stay, ere thou take the last leap. Go to thy bed and think upon thy ways. Ask counsel of thy pillow, and let the quietude of night instruct thee! Throw not away thy soul for nought! Let reason speak! Let the clamorous world be still awhile, and let thy poor soul plead with thee to bethink thyself before thou seal its fate, and ruin it for ever! Selah. O sinner! pause while I question thee awhile in the words of a sacred poet:

> Sinner, is thy heart at rest?
> Is thy bosom void of fear?
> Art thou not by guilt oppress'd?
> Speaks not conscience in thine ear?

Can this world afford thee bliss?
Can it chase away thy gloom?
Flattering, false, and vain it is;
Tremble at the worldling's doom!

Think, O sinner, on thy end,
See the judgment-day appear,
Thither must thy spirit wend,
There thy righteous sentence hear.

Wretched, ruin'd, helpless soul,
To a Saviour's blood apply;
He alone can make thee whole,
Fly to Jesus, sinner, fly!

Verse 5. Provided that the rebels had obeyed the voice of the last verse, they would now be crying, 'What shall we do to be saved?' And in the present verse, they are pointed to the sacrifice, and exhorted to trust in the Lord. When the Jew offered sacrifice righteously, that is, in a spiritual manner, he thereby set forth the Redeemer, the great sin-atoning Lamb; there is, therefore, the full gospel in this exhortation of the Psalmist. O sinners, flee ye to the sacrifice of Calvary, and there put your whole confidence and trust, for he who died for men is the LORD JEHOVAH.

Verse 6. We have now entered upon the third division of the Psalm, in which the faith of the afflicted one finds utterance in sweet expressions of contentment and peace.

There were many, even among David's own followers, who wanted to see rather than to believe. Alas! this is the tendency of us all! Even the regenerate sometimes groan after the sense and sight of prosperity, and are sad when darkness covers all good from view. As for worldlings, this is their unceasing cry. 'Who will shew us any good?' Never satisfied, their gaping mouths are turned in every direction, their empty hearts are ready to drink in any fine delusion which impostors may invent; and when these fail, they soon yield to despair, and declare that there is no good thing in either heaven or earth. The true believer is a man of a very different mould. His face is not downward like the beasts', but upward like the angels'. He drinks not from the muddy pools of Mammon, but from the fountain of life above. The light of God's countenance is enough for him. This is his riches, his honour, his health, his ambition, his ease. Give him this, and he will ask no more. This is joy unspeakable, and full of glory. Oh, for more of the indwelling of the Holy Spirit, that our fellowship with the Father and with his Son Jesus Christ may be constant and abiding!

Verse 7. 'It is better,' said one, 'to feel God's favour one hour in our repenting souls, than to sit whole ages under the warmest sunshine that this world affordeth.' Christ in the heart is better than corn in the barn, or wine in the vat. Corn and wine are but fruits of the world, but the light of God's countenance is the ripe fruit of heaven. 'Thou art with me,' is a far more blessed cry than 'Harvest home.' Let my granary be empty, I am yet full of blessings if Jesus Christ smiles upon me; but if I have all the world, I am poor without him.

We should not fail to remark that this verse is the saying of the righteous man, in opposition to the saying of the many. How quickly doth the tongue betray the character! 'Speak, that

I may see thee!' said Socrates to a fair boy. The metal of a bell is best known by its sound. Birds reveal their nature by their song. Owls cannot sing the carol of the lark, nor can the nightingale hoot like the owl. Let us, then, weigh and watch our words, lest our speech should prove us to be foreigners, and aliens from the commonwealth of Israel.

Verse 8. Sweet Evening Hymn! I shall not sit up to watch through fear, but I will lie down; and then I will not lie awake listening to every rustling sound, but I will lie down in peace and sleep, for I have nought to fear. He that hath the wings of God above him needs no other curtain. Better than bolts or bars is the protection of the Lord. Armed men kept the bed of Solomon, but we do not believe that he slept more soundly than his father, whose bed was the hard ground, and who was haunted by blood-thirsty foes. Note the word 'only', which means that God alone was his keeper, and that though alone, without man's help, he was even then in good keeping, for he was 'alone with God.' A quiet conscience is a good bedfellow. How many of our sleepless hours might be traced to our untrusting and disordered minds. They slumber sweetly whom faith rocks to sleep. No pillow so soft as a promise; no coverlet so warm as an assured interest in Christ.

O Lord, give us this calm repose on thee, that like David we may lie down in peace, and sleep each night while we live; and joyfully may we lie down in the appointed season, to sleep in death, to rest in God!

Dr Hawker's reflection upon this Psalm is worthy to be prayed over and fed upon with sacred delight. We cannot help transcribing it.

'Reader! let us never lose sight of the Lord Jesus while reading this Psalm. He is the Lord our righteousness; and therefore, in all our approaches to the mercy seat, let us go there in a language corresponding to this which calls Jesus the Lord our righteousness. While men of the world, from the world are seeking their chief good, let us desire his favour which infinitely transcends corn and wine, and all the good things which perish in the using. Yes, Lord, thy favour is better than life itself. Thou causest them that love thee to inherit substance, and fillest all their treasure.

'Oh! thou gracious God and Father, hast thou in such a wonderful manner set apart one in our nature for thyself? Hast thou indeed chosen one out of the people? Hast thou beheld him in the purity of his nature, as one in every point Godly? Hast thou given him as the covenant of the people? And hast thou declared thyself well pleased in him? Oh! then, well may my soul be well pleased in him also. Now do I know that my God and Father will hear me when I call upon him in Jesus' name, and when I look up to him for acceptance for Jesus' sake! Yes, my heart is fixed, O Lord, my heart is fixed; Jesus is my hope and righteousness; the Lord will hear me when I call. And henceforth will I both lay me down in peace and sleep securely in Jesus, accepted in the Beloved; for this is the rest wherewith the Lord causeth the weary to rest, and this is the refreshing.'

Explanatory notes and quaint sayings

Verse 1. 'Hear me when I call,' etc. Faith is a good orator and a noble disputer in a strait; it can reason from God's readiness to hear: 'Hear me when I call, O God.' And from the everlasting righteousness given to the man in the justification of his person: 'O God of my righteousness.' And from God's constant justice in defending the righteousness of his servant's cause: 'O God of my righteousness.' And from both present distresses and those that are by-past, wherein he hath been, and from by-gone mercies received: 'Thou hast enlarged me when I was in distress.' And from God's grace, which is able to answer all objections from the man's unworthiness or ill-deserving: 'Have mercy upon me, and hear my prayer.' David Dickson, 1653.

Verse 1. 'Hear me.' The great Author of nature and of all things does nothing in vain. He instituted not this law, and, if I may so express it, art of praying, as a vain and insufficient thing, but endows it with wonderful efficacy for producing the greatest and happiest consequences. He would have it to be the key by which all the treasures of heaven should be opened. He has constructed it as a powerful machine, by which we may, with easy and pleasant labour, remove from us the most dire and unhappy machinations of our enemy, and may with equal ease draw to ourselves what is most propitious and advantageous. Heaven and earth, and all the elements, obey and minister to the hands which are often lifted up to heaven in earnest prayer. Yea, all works, and, which is yet more and greater, all the words of God obey it. Well known in the sacred Scriptures are the examples of Moses and Joshua, and that which James (5:17) particularly mentions of Elijah, a man subject to like infirmities with ourselves, that he might illustrate the admirable force of prayer, by the common and human weakness of the person by whom it was offered. And that Christian legion under Antonius is well known and justly celebrated, which for the singular ardour and efficacy of its prayers, obtained the name of *keraunoboloz*, the thundering legion. Robert Leighton, D.D., Archbishop of Glasgow, 1611–1684.

Verse 2. 'O ye sons of men, how long will ye turn my glory into shame? how long will ye love vanity, and seek after leasing? Selah.' Prayer soars above the violence and impiety of men, and with a swift wing commits itself to heaven, with happy omen, if I may allude to what the learned tell us of the augury of the ancients, which I shall not minutely discuss. Fervent prayers stretch forth a strong, wide-extended wing, and while the birds of night hover beneath, they mount aloft, and point out, as it were, the proper seats to which we should aspire. For certainly there is nothing that cuts the air so swiftly, nothing that takes so sublime, so happy, so auspicious a flight as prayer, which bears the soul on its pinions, and leaves far behind all the dangers, and even the delights of this low world of ours. Behold this holy man, who just before was crying to God in the midst of distress, and with urgent importunity entreating that he might be heard, now, as if he were already possessed of all he had asked, taking upon him boldly to rebuke his enemies, how highly soever they were exalted, and how potent soever they might be even in the royal palace. Robert Leighton, D.D.

Verse 2. 'O ye sons of men, how long will ye turn my glory into shame?' etc. We might imagine every syllable of this precious Psalm used by our Master some evening, when about to leave the temple for the day, and retiring to his wonted rest at Bethany (verse 8), after another fruitless expostulation with the men of Israel. And we may read it still as the very utterance of his heart, longing over man, and delighting in God. But, further, not only is this the utterance of the Head, it is also the language of one of his members in full sympathy with him in holy feeling. This is a Psalm with which the righteous may make their dwellings resound, morning and evening, as they cast a sad look over a world that rejects God's grace. They may sing it while they cling more and more every day to Jehovah, as their all-sufficient heritage, now and in the age to come. They may sing it, too, in the happy confidence of faith and hope, when the evening of the world's day is coming, and may then fall asleep in the certainty of what shall greet their eyes on the resurrection morning –

> Sleeping embosomed in his grace,
> Till morning-shadows flee.
> Andrew A. Bonar, 1859

Verse 2. 'Love vanity.' They that love sin, love vanity; they chase a bubble, they lean upon a reed, their hope is as a spider's web.

'Leasing.' This is an old Saxon word signifying falsehood.

Verse 2. 'How long will ye love vanity, and seek after leasing?' 'Vanity of vanities, and all is vanity.' This our first parents found, and therefore named their second son Abel, or vanity. Solomon, that had tried these things, and could best tell the vanity of them, he preacheth this sermon over again and again. 'Vanity of vanities, and all is vanity.' It is sad to think how many thousands there be that can say with the preacher, 'Vanity of vanities, all is vanity;' nay, swear it, and yet follow after these things as if there were no other glory, nor felicity, but what is to be found in these things they call vanity. Such men will sell Christ, heaven, and their souls, for a trifle, that call these things vanity, but do not cordially believe them to be vanity, but set their hearts upon them as if they were their crown, the top of all their royalty and glory. Oh! let your souls dwell upon the vanity of all things here below, till your hearts so thoroughly convinced and persuaded of the vanity of them, as to trample upon them, and make them a footstool for Christ to get up, and ride in a holy triumph in your hearts.

Gilemex, king of Vandals, led in triumph by Belisarius, cried out, 'Vanity of vanities, all is vanity.' The fancy of Lucian, who placeth Charon on the top of a high hill, viewing all the affairs of men living, and looking on their greatest cities as little bird's nests, is very pleasant. Oh, the imperfection, the ingratitude, the levity, the inconstancy, the perfidiousness of those creatures we most servilely affect! Ah, did we but weigh man's pain with his payment, his crosses with his mercies, his miseries with his pleasures, we should then see that there is nothing got by the bargain, and conclude, 'Vanity of vanities, all is vanity.' Chrysostom said once, 'That if he were the fittest in the world to preach a sermon to the whole world, gathered together in one congregation, and had some high mountain for his pulpit, from whence he might have a prospect of all the world in his view, and were furnished with a voice of brass, a voice as loud as the trumpets of the archangel, that all the world might hear him, he would choose to preach upon no other text than that in the Psalms, O mortal men, 'How long will ye love vanity, and follow after leasing?'' Thomas Brooks, 1608–1680.

Verse 2. 'Love vanity.' Men's affections are according to their principles; and every one loves that most without him which is most suitable to somewhat within him: liking is founded in likeness, and has therefore that word put upon it. It is so in whatsoever we can imagine; whether in temporals or spirituals, as to the things of this life, or of a better. Men's love is according to some working and impression upon their own spirits. And so it is here in the point of vanity; those which are vain persons, they delight in vain things; as children, they love such matters as are most agreeable to their childish dispositions, and as do suit them in that particular. Out of the heart comes all kind of evil. Thomas Horton, 1675.

Verse 3. 'The Lord hath set apart him that is godly for himself.' When God chooseth a man, he chooseth him for himself; for himself to converse with, to communicate himself unto him as a friend, a companion, and his delight. Now, it is holiness that makes us fit to live with the holy God for ever, since without it we cannot see him (Hebrews 12:14), which is God's main aim, and more than our being his children; as one must be supposed a man, one of mankind, having a soul reasonable, ere we can suppose him capable of adoption, or to be another man's heir. As therefore it was the main first design in God's eye, before the consideration of our happiness, let it be so in ours. Thomas Goodwin, 1600–1679.

Verse 3. What rare persons the godly are: 'The righteous is more excellent than his neighbour.' Proverbs 12:26. As the flower of the sun, as the wine of Lebanon, as the sparkling upon Aaron's breastplate, such is the orient splendour of a person embellished with godliness ... The godly are precious, therefore they are set apart for God, 'Know that the Lord hath set apart him that is godly for himself.' We set apart things that are precious; the godly are set apart as God's peculiar treasure (Psalm 135:4); as his garden of delight (Canticles 4:12); as his royal diadem (Isaiah 43:3); the godly are the excellent of the earth (Psalm 16:3); comparable to fine gold (Lamentations 4:2); double refined (Zechariah 13:9). They are the glory of the creation. (Isaiah 46:13). Origen compares the saints to sapphires and crystals: God calls them jewels (Malachi 3:17). Thomas Watson.

Verse 3. 'The Lord will hear when I call unto him.' Let us remember that the experience of one of the saints concerning the verity of God's promises, and of the certainty of the written privileges of the Lord's people, is a sufficient proof of the right which all his children have to the same mercies, and a ground of hope that they also shall partake of them in their times of need. David Dickson, 1653.

Verse 4. 'Stand in awe and sin not.' Jehovah is a name of great power and efficacy, a name that hath in it five vowels, without which no language can be expressed; a name that hath in it also three syllables, to signify the Trinity of persons, the eternity of God, One in Three and Three in One; a name of such dread and reverence amongst the Jews, that they tremble to name it, and therefore they use the name *Adonai* (Lord) in all their devotions. And thus ought every one to 'stand in awe, and sin not,' by taking the name of God in vain; but to sing praise, and honour, to remember, to declare, to exalt, to praise and bless it; for holy and reverend, only worthy and excellent is his name. Rayment, 1630.

Verse 4. 'Commune with your own heart.' The language is similar to that which we use when we say, 'Consult your better judgment,' or 'Take counsel of your own good sense.' Albert Barnes, in loc.

Verse 4. If thou wouldst exercise thyself to godliness in solitude, accustom thyself to soliloquies, I mean to conference with thyself. He needs never be idle that hath so much business to do with his own soul. It was a famous answer which Antisthenes gave when he was asked what fruit he reaped by all his studies. By them, saith he, I have learned both to live and talk with myself. Soliloquies are the best disputes; every good man is best company for himself of all the creatures. Holy David enjoineth this to others, 'Commune with your own hearts upon your bed, and be still.' 'Commune with your own hearts;' when ye have none to speak with, talk to yourselves. Ask yourselves for what end ye were made, what lives ye have led, what times ye have lost, what love ye have abused, what wrath ye have deserved. Call yourselves to a reckoning, how ye have improved your talents, how true or false ye have been to your trust, what provision ye have laid in for an hour of death, what preparation ye have made for a great day of account. 'Upon your beds.' Secrecy is the best opportunity for this duty. The silent night is a good time for this speech. When we have no outward objects to disturb us, and to call our eyes, as the fools' eyes are always, to the ends of the earth; then our eyes, as the eyes of the wise, may be in our heads; and then our minds, like the windows in Solomon's temple, may be broad inwards. The most successful searches have been made in the night season; the soul is then wholly shut up in the earthly house of the body, and hath no visits from strangers to disquiet its thoughts. Physicians have judged dreams a probable sign whereby they might find out the distempers of the body. Surely, then, the bed is no bad place to examine and search into the state of the soul. 'And be still.' Self-communion will much help to curb your headstrong, ungodly passions. Serious consideration, like the casting up of earth amongst bees, will allay inordinate affections when they are full of fury, and make such a hideous noise. Though sensual appetites and unruly desires are, as the people of Ephesus, in an uproar, pleading for their former privilege, and expecting their wonted provisions, as in the days of their predominancy, if conscience use its authority, commanding them in God's name, whose officer it is, to keep the king's peace, and argue it with them, as the town-clerk of Ephesus, 'We are in danger to be called in question for this day's uproar, there being no cause whereby we may give an account of this day's concourse;' all is frequently by this means hushed, and the tumult appeased without any further mischief. George Swinnock, 1627–1673.

Verse 4. 'Commune with your own heart upon your bed, and be still.' When we are most retired from the world, then we are most fit to have, and usually have, most communion with God. If a man would but abridge himself of sleep, and wake with holy thoughts, when deep sleep falleth upon sorrowful labouring men, he might be entertained with visions from God, though not such visions as Eliphaz and others of the saints have had, yet visions he might have. Every time God communicates himself to the soul, there is a vision of love, or mercy, or power, somewhat of God in his nature, or in his will, is showed unto us. David shows us divine work when we go to rest. The bed is not all for sleep: 'Commune with your own heart upon your bed, and be still.' Be still or quiet, and then commune with your hearts; and if you will commune with your hearts, God will come and commune with your hearts, too, his Spirit will give you a loving visit and visions of his love. Joseph Caryl.

Verse 4. 'Stand in awe.'

With sacred awe pronounce his name,
Whom words nor thoughts can reach.
John Needham, 1768.

Verse 6. Where Christ reveals himself there is satisfaction in the slenderest portion, and without Christ there is emptiness in the greatest fullness. Alexander Grosse, on enjoying Christ, 1632.

Verse 6. 'Many,' said David. 'ask who will shew us any good?' meaning riches, and honour, and pleasure, which are not good. But when he came to godliness itself, he leaves out 'many,' and prayeth in his own person, 'Lord, lift thou up the light of thy countenance upon us;' as if none would join with him. Henry Smith.

Verse 6. 'Who will shew us any good?' This is not a fair translation. The word *any* is not in the text, nor anything equivalent to it; and not a few have quoted it, and preached upon the text, placing the principal emphasis upon this illegitimate. The place is sufficiently emphatic. There are multitudes who say, Who will shew us good? Man wants good; he hates evil as evil, because he has pain, suffering, and death through it; and he wishes to find that supreme good which will content his heart, and save him from evil. But men mistake this good. They look for a good that is to gratify their passions; they have no notion of any happiness that does not come to them through the medium of their senses. Therefore they reject spiritual good, and they reject the Supreme God, by whom alone all the powers of the soul of man can be gratified. Adam Clarke.

Verse 6. 'Lift thou up,' etc. This was the blessing of the high priest and is the heritage of all the saints. It includes reconciliation, assurance, communion, benediction, in a word, the fulness of God. Oh, to be filled therewith! C. H. S.

Verses 6, 7. Lest riches should be accounted evil in themselves, God sometimes gives them to the righteous; and lest they should be considered as the chief good, he frequently bestows them on the wicked. But they are more generally the portion of his enemies than his friends. Alas! what is it to receive and not be received? to have none other dews of blessing than such as shall be followed by showers of brimstone? We may compass ourselves with sparks of security, and afterwards be secure in eternal misery. This world is a floating island, and so sure as we cast anchor upon it, we shall be carried away by it. God, and all that he has made, is not more than God without anything that he has made. He can never want treasure who has such a golden mine. He is enough without the creature, but the creature is not anything without him. It is, therefore, better to enjoy him without anything else, than to enjoy everything else without him. It is better to be a wooden vessel filled with wine, than a golden one filled with water. William Secker's Nonsuch Professor, 1660.

Verse 7. What madness and folly is it that the favourites of heaven should envy the men of the world, who at best do but feed upon the scraps that come from God's table! Temporals are the bones; spirituals are the marrow. Is it below a man to envy the dogs, because of the bones? And is it not much more below a Christian to envy others for temporals, when himself enjoys spirituals? Thomas Brooks.

Verse 7. 'Thou hast put gladness in my heart.' The comforts which God reserves for his mourners are filling comforts (Romans 15:13); 'The God of hope fill you with joy' (John 16:24); 'Ask that your joy may be full.' When God pours in the joys of heaven they fill the heart, and make it run over (2 Corinthians 7:4); 'I am exceeding joyful;' the Greek is, I overflow with joy, as a cup that is filled with wine till it runs over. Outward comforts can no more fill the heart than a triangle can fill a circle. Spiritual joys are satisfying (Psalm 63:5); 'My heart shall be satisfied as with marrow and fatness; and my mouth shall praise thee with joyful lips;' 'Thou hast put gladness in my heart.' Worldly joys do put gladness into the face, but the spirit of God puts gladness into the heart; divine joys are heart joys (Zechariah 10:7; John 16:22); 'Your heart shall rejoice' (Luke 1:47); 'My spirit rejoiced in God.' And to show how filling these comforts are, which are of a heavenly extraction, the psalmist says they create greater joy than when 'corn and wine increase.' Wine and oil may delight but not satisfy; they have their vacuity and indigence. We may say, as Zechariah 10:2, 'They comfort in vain;' outward comforts do sooner cloy than cheer, and sooner weary that fill. Xerxes offered great rewards to him that could find out a new pleasure; but the comforts of the Spirit are satisfactory, they recruit the heart (Psalm 94:19), 'Thy comforts delight my soul.' There is as much difference between heavenly comforts and earthly, as between a banquet that is eaten, and one that is painted on the wall. Thomas Watson.

Verse 8. It is said of the husbandman, that having cast his seed into the ground, he sleeps and riseth day and night, and the seed springs and grows he knoweth not how. Mark 4:26,27. So a good man having by faith and prayer cast his care upon God, he resteth night and day, and is very easy, leaving it to his God to perform all things for him according to his holy will. Matthew Henry.

Verse 8. When you have walked with God from morning until night, it remaineth that you conclude the day well, when you would give yourself to rest at night. Wherefore, first, look back and take a strict view of your whole carriage that day past. Reform what you find amiss; and rejoice, or be grieved, as you find you have done well or ill, as you have advanced or declined in grace that day. Secondly, since you cannot sleep in safety if God, who is your keeper (Psalm 121:4, 5), do not wake and watch for you (Psalm 127:1); and though you have God to watch when you sleep, you cannot be safe, if he that watcheth be your enemy. Wherefore it is very convenient that at night you renew and confirm your peace with God by faith and prayer, commending and committing yourself to God's tuition by prayer (Psalm 3:4, 5; Psalm 92:2), with thanksgiving before you go to bed. Then shall you lie down in safety. Psalm 4:8. All this being done, yet while you are putting off your apparel, when you are lying down, and when you are in bed, before you sleep, it is good that you commune with your own heart. Psalm 4:4. If possibly you can fall asleep with some heavenly meditation, then will your sleep be more sweet (Proverbs 3:21, 24, 25); and more secure (Proverbs 6:21, 22); your dreams fewer, or more comfortable; your head will be fuller of good thoughts (Proverbs 6:22), and your heart will be in a better frame when you awake, whether in the night or in the morning. Condensed from Henry Scudder's Daily Walk, 1633.

Verse 8. 'I will both,' etc. We have now to retire for a moment from the strife of tongues and the open hostility of foes, into the stillness and privacy of the chamber of sleep. Here, also, we find the 'I will' of trust. 'I will both lay me down in peace, and sleep; for thou, Lord, only makest me dwell in safety.' God is here revealed to us as exercising personal care in the still chamber. And there is something here which should be inexpressibly sweet to the believer, for this shows the minuteness of God's care, the individuality of his love; how it condescends and stoops, and acts, not only in great, but also in little spheres; not only where glory might be procured from great results, but where nought is to be had save the gratitude and love of a poor feeble creature, whose life has been protected and preserved, in a period of helplessness and sleep. How blessed would it be if we made larger recognition of God in the still chamber; if we thought of him as being there in all hours of illness, of weariness, and pain; if we believed that his interest and care are as much concentrated upon the feeble believer there as upon his people when in the wider battle field of the strife of tongues. There is something inexpressibly touching in this 'lying down' of the Psalmist. In thus lying down he voluntarily gave up any guardianship of himself; he resigned himself into the hands of another; he did so completely, for in the absence of all care he slept; there was here a perfect trust. Many a believer lies down, but it is not to sleep. Perhaps he feels safe enough so far as his body is concerned, but cares and anxieties invade the privacy of his chamber; they come to try his faith and trust; they threaten, they frighten, and alas! prove too strong for trust. Many a poor believer might say, 'I will lay me down, but not to sleep.' The author met with a touching instance of this, in the case of an aged minister whom he visited in severe illness. This worthy man's circumstances were narrow, and his family trials were great; he said, 'The doctor wants me to sleep, but how can I sleep with care sitting on my pillow?' It is the experience of some of the Lord's people, that although equal to an emergency or a continued pressure, a re-action sets in afterwards; and when they come to be alone their spirits sink, and they do not realise that strength from God, or feel that confidence in him which they felt while the pressure was exerting its force ... There is a trial in stillness; and oftentimes the still chamber makes a larger demand upon loving trust than the battle field. O that we could trust God more and more with personal things! O that he were the God of our chamber, as well as of our temples and houses! O that we could bring him more and more into the minutiae of daily life! If we did thus, we should experience a measure of rest to which we are, perhaps, strangers now; we should have less dread of the sick chamber; we should have that unharassed mind which conduces most to repose, in body and soul; we should be able to say, 'I will lie down and sleep, and leave to-morrow with God!' Ridley's brother offered to remain with him during the night preceding his martyrdom, but the bishop declined, saying, that 'he meant to go to bed, and sleep as quietly as ever he did in his life.' Philip Bennett Power's 'I Wills' of the Psalms.

Verse 8. Due observation of Providence will both beget and secure inward tranquillity in your minds amidst the vicissitudes and revolutions of things in this unstable vain world. 'I will both lay me down in peace, and sleep; for the Lord only maketh me dwell in safety.' He resolves that sinful fears of events shall not rob him of his inward quiet, nor torture his thoughts with anxious presages; he will commit all his concerns into that faithful fatherly hand that had hitherto wrought all things for him; and he means not to lose the comfort of one night's rest, nor bring the evil of to-morrow upon the day; but knowing in whose hand he was, wisely enjoys the sweet felicity of a resigned will. Now this tranquillity of our minds is as much begotten and preserved by a due consideration of providence as by anything whatsoever. John Flavel, 1627–1691.

Verse 8. Happy is the Christian, who having nightly with this verse, committed himself to his bed as to his grave, shall at last, with the same words, resign himself to his grave as to his bed, from which he expects in due time to arise, and sing a morning hymn with the children of the resurrection. George Horne, D.D., 1776.

Verse 8. 'Sleep.'

How blessed was that sleep
The sinless Saviour knew!
In vain the storm-sands blew,
Till he awoke to others' woes,
And hushed the billows to repose.

How beautiful is sleep –
The sleep that Christians know!
Ye mourners! cease your woe,
While soft upon his Saviour's breast,
The righteous sinks to endless rest.
Mrs. M'Cartree.

Hints to the village preacher

Verse 1. Is full of matter for a sermon upon, past mercies a plea for present help. The first sentence shows that believers desire, expect, and believe in a God that heareth prayer. The title 'God of my righteousness' may furnish a text (see exposition), and the last sentence may suggest a sermon upon, 'The best of saints must still appeal to God's mercy and sovereign grace.'

Verse 2. Depravity of man as evinced

1. by continuance in despising Christ,
2. by loving vanity in his heart, and
3. seeking lies in his daily life.

Verse 2. The length of the sinner's sin. 'How long?' May be bounded by repentance, shall be by death, and yet shall continue in eternity.

Verse 3. Election. Its aspects toward God, our enemies, and ourselves.

Verse 3. 'The Lord will hear when I call unto him.' Answers to prayer certain to special persons. Mark out those who can claim the favour.

Verse 3. The gracious Separatist. Who is he? Who separated him? With what end? How to make men know it?

Verse 4. The sinner directed to review himself, that he may be convinced of sin. Andrew Fuller, 1754–1815.

Verse 4. 'Be still.' Advice – good, practical, but hard to follow. Times when seasonable. Graces needed to enable one to be still. Results of quietness. Persons who most need the advice. Instances of its practice. here is much material for a sermon.

Verse 5. The nature of those sacrifices of righteousness which the Lord's people are expected to offer. William Ford Vance, 1827.

Verse 6. The cry of the world and the church contrasted. *Vox populi* not always *Vox Dei*.

Verse 6. The cravings of the soul all satisfied in God.

Verses 6, 7. An assurance of the Saviour's love, the source of unrivalled joy.

Verse 7. The believer's joys.

1. Their source, 'Thou;'
2. Their season – even now – 'Thou hast;'
3. Their position, 'in my heart;'
4. Their excellence, 'more than in the time that their corn and their wine increased.'

Another excellent theme suggests itself – 'The superiority of the joys of grace to the joys of earth;' or, 'Two sorts of prosperity – which is to be the more desired?'

Verse 8. The peace and safety of the good man. Joseph Lathrop, D.D., 1805.

Verse 8. A bedchamber for believers, a vesper song to sing in it, and a guard to keep the door.

Verse 8. The Christian's good night.

Verses 2 to 8. The means which a believer should use to win the ungodly to Christ.

1. Expostulation, verse 2.
2. Instruction, verse 3.
3. Exhortation, verses 4, 5.
4. Testimony to the blessedness of true religion as in verses 6, 7.
5. Exemplification of that testimony by the peace of faith, verse 8.

Psalm 6

Title

This Psalm is commonly known as the first of the PENITENTIAL PSALMS (the other six are 32, 38, 51, 102, 130, 143) and certainly its language well becomes the lip of a penitent, for it expresses at once the sorrow (verses 3, 6, 7), the humiliation (verses 2 and 4), and the hatred of sin (verse 8), which are the unfailing marks of the contrite spirit when it turns to God. O Holy Spirit, beget in us the true repentance which needeth not to be repented of. The title of this Psalm is 'To the chief Musician on Neginoth upon Sheminith (1 Chronicle 15:21), A Psalm of David,' that is, to the chief musician with stringed instruments, upon the eighth, probably the octave. Some think it refers to the bass or tenor key, which would certainly be well adapted to this mournful ode. But we are not able to understand these old musical terms, and even the term 'Selah,' still remains untranslated. This, however, should be no difficulty in our way. We probably lose but very little by our ignorance, and it may serve to confirm our faith. It is a proof of the high antiquity of these Psalms that they contain words, the meaning of which is lost even to the best scholars of the Hebrew language. Surely these are but incidental (accidental I might almost say, if I did not believe them to be designed by God), proofs of their being, what they profess to be, the ancient writings of King David of olden times.

Division

You will observe that the Psalm is readily divided into two parts. First, there is the Psalmist's plea in his great distress, reaching from the first to the end of the seventh verse. Then you have, from the eighth to the end, quite a different theme. The Psalmist has changed his note. He leaves the minor key, and betakes himself to sublimer strains. He tunes his note to the high key of confidence, and declares that God hath heard his prayer, and hath delivered him out of all his troubles.

Exposition

Verse 1. Having read through the first division, in order to see it as a whole, we will now look at it verse by verse. 'O Lord, rebuke me not in thine anger.' The Psalmist is very conscious that he deserves to be rebuked, and he feels, moreover, that the rebuke in some form or other must come upon him, if not for condemnation, yet for conviction and sanctification. 'Corn is cleaned with wind, and the soul with chastenings.' It were folly to pray against the golden hand which enriches us by its blows. He does not ask that the rebuke may be totally withheld, for he might thus lose a blessing in disguise; but, 'Lord, rebuke me not in thine anger.' If thou remindest me of my sin, it is good; but, oh, remind me not of it as one incensed against me, lest thy servant's heart should sink in despair. Thus saith Jeremiah, 'O Lord, correct me, but with judgment; not in thine anger, lest thou bring me to nothing.' I know that I must be chastened, and though I shrink from the rod yet do I feel that it will be for my benefit; but, oh, my God, 'chasten me not in thy hot displeasure,' lest the rod become a sword, and lest in smiting, thou shouldest also kill. So may we pray that the chastisements of our gracious God, if they may not be entirely removed, may at least be sweetened by the consciousness that they are 'not in anger, but in his dear covenant love.'

Verse 2. 'Have mercy upon me, O Lord; for I am weak.' Though I deserve destruction, yet let thy mercy pity my frailty. This is the right way to plead with God if we would prevail. Urge not your goodness or your greatness, but plead your sin and your littleness. Cry, 'I am weak,' therefore, O Lord, give me strength and crush me not. Send not forth the fury of thy tempest against so weak a vessel. Temper the wind to the shorn lamb. Be tender and pitiful to a poor withering flower, and break it not from its stem. Surely this is the plea that a sick man would urge to move the pity of his fellow if he were striving with him, 'Deal gently with me, 'for I am weak.'' A sense of sin had so spoiled the Psalmist's pride, so taken away his vaunted strength, that he found himself weak to obey the law, weak through the sorrow that was in him, too weak, perhaps, to lay hold on the promise. 'I am weak.' The original may be read, 'I am one who droops,' or withered like a blighted plant. Ah! beloved, we know what this means, for we, too, have seen our glory stained, and our beauty like a faded flower.

Verse 3. 'O Lord, heal me; for my bones are vexed.' Here he prays for healing, not merely the mitigation of the ills he endured, but their entire removal, and the curing of the wounds which had arisen therefrom. His bones were 'shaken,' as the Hebrew has it. His terror had become so great that his very bones shook; not only did his flesh quiver, but the bones, the solid pillars of the house of manhood, were made to tremble. 'My bones are shaken.' Ah, when the soul has a sense of sin, it is enough to make the bones shake; it is enough to make a man's hair stand up on end to see the flames of hell beneath him, an angry God above him, and danger and doubt surrounding him. Well might he say, 'My bones are shaken.' Lest, however, we should imagine that it was merely bodily sickness – although bodily sickness might be the outward sign – the Psalmist goes on to say, 'My soul is also sore vexed.' Soul-trouble is the very soul of trouble. It matters not that the bones shake if the soul be firm, but when the soul itself is also sore vexed this is agony indeed. 'But thou, O Lord, how long?' This sentence ends abruptly, for words failed, and grief drowned the little comfort which dawned upon him. The Psalmist had still, however, some hope; but that hope was only in his God. He therefore cries, 'O Lord, how long?' The coming of Christ into the soul in his priestly robes of grace is the grand hope of the penitent soul; and, indeed, in some form or other, Christ's appearance is, and ever has been, the hope of the saints.

Calvin's favourite exclamation was '*Domine usquequo*' - 'O Lord, how long?' Nor could his sharpest pains, during a life of anguish, force from him any other word. Surely this is the cry of the saints under the altar, 'O Lord, how long?' And this should be the cry of the saints waiting for the millennial glories, 'Why are his chariots so long in coming; Lord, how long?' Those of us who have passed through conviction of sin knew what it was to count our minutes hours, and our hours years, while mercy delayed its coming. We watched for the dawn of grace, as they that watch for the morning. Earnestly did our anxious spirits ask, 'O Lord, how long?'

Verse 4. 'Return, O Lord; deliver my soul.' As God's absence was the main cause of his misery, so his return would be enough to deliver him from his trouble. 'Oh save me for thy mercies' sake.' He knows where to look, and what arm to lay hold upon. He does not lay hold on God's left hand of justice, but on his right hand of mercy. He knew his iniquity too well to think of merit, or appeal to anything but the grace of God.

'For thy mercies' sake.' What a plea that is! How prevalent it is with God! If we turn to justice, what plea can we urge? but if we turn to mercy we may still cry, notwithstanding the greatness of our guilt, 'Save me for thy mercies' sake.'

Observe how frequently David here pleads the name of Jehovah, which is always intended where the word LORD is given in capitals. Five times in four verses we here meet with it. Is not this a proof that the glorious name is full of consolation to the tempted saint? Eternity, Infinity, Immutability, Self-existence, are all in the name Jehovah, and all are full of comfort.

Verse 5. And now David was in great fear of death – death temporal, and perhaps death eternal. Read the passage as you will, the following verse is full of power. 'For in death there is no remembrance of thee; in the grave who shall give thee thanks?' Churchyards are silent places; the vaults of the sepulchre echo not with songs. Damp earth covers dumb mouths. 'O Lord!' saith he, 'if thou wilt spare me I will praise thee. If I die, then must my mortal praise at least be suspended; and if I perish in hell, then thou wilt never have any thanksgiving from me. Songs of gratitude cannot rise from the flaming pit of hell. True, thou wilt doubtless be glorified, even in my eternal condemnation, but then O Lord, I cannot glorify thee voluntarily; and among the sons of men, there will be one heart the less to bless thee.' Ah! poor trembling sinners, may the Lord help you to use this forcible argument! It is for God's glory that a sinner should be saved. When we seek pardon, we are not asking God to do that which will stain his banner, or put a blot on his escutcheon. He delighteth in mercy. It is his peculiar, darling attribute. Mercy honours God. Do not we ourselves say, 'Mercy blesseth him that gives, and him that takes?' And surely, in some diviner sense, this is true of God, who, when he gives mercy, glorifies himself.

Verse 6. The Psalmist gives a fearful description of his long agony: 'I am weary with my groaning.' He has groaned till his throat was hoarse; he had cried for mercy till prayer became a labour. God's people may groan, but they may not grumble. Yea, they must groan, being burdened, or they will never shout in the day of deliverance. The next sentence, we think, is not accurately translated. It should be, 'I shall make my bed to swim every night' (when nature needs rest, and when I am most alone with my God). That is to say, my grief is fearful even now, but if God do not soon save me, it will not stay of itself, but will increase, until my tears will be so many, that my bed itself shall swim. A description rather of what he feared would be, than of what had actually taken place. May not our forebodings of future woe become arguments which faith may urge when seeking present mercy?

Verse 7. 'I water my couch with my tears. Mine eye is consumed because of grief; it waxeth old because of all my enemies.' As an old man's eye grows dim with years, so, says David, my eye is grown red and feeble through weeping. Conviction sometimes has such an effect upon the body, that even the outward organs are made to suffer. May not this explain some of the convulsions and hysterical attacks which have been experienced under convictions in the revivals in Ireland? Is it surprising that some souls be smitten to the earth, and begin to cry aloud; when we find that David himself made his bed to swim, and grew old while he was under the heavy hand of God? Ah! brethren, it is no light matter to feel one's self a sinner, condemned at the bar of God. The language of this Psalm is not strained and forced, but perfectly natural to one in so sad a plight.

Verse 8. Hitherto, all has been mournful and disconsolate, but now –

Your harps, ye trembling saints,
Down from the willows take.

Ye must have your times of weeping, but let them be short. Get ye up, get ye up, from your dunghills! Cast aside your sackcloth and ashes! Weeping may endure for a night, but joy cometh in the morning.

David has found peace, and rising from his knees he begins to sweep his house of the wicked. 'Depart from me, all ye workers of iniquity.' The best remedy for us against an evil man is a long space between us both. 'Get ye gone; I can have no fellowship with you.' Repentance is a practical thing. It is not enough to bemoan the desecration of the temple of the heart, we must scourge out the buyers and sellers, and overturn the tables of the money changers. A pardoned sinner will hate the sins which cost the Saviour his blood. Grace and sin are quarrelsome neighbours, and one or the other must go to the wall.

'For the Lord hath heard the voice of my weeping.' What a fine Hebraism, and what grand poetry it is in English! 'He hath heard the voice of my weeping.' Is there a voice in weeping? Does weeping speak? In what language doth it utter its meaning? Why, in that universal tongue which is known and understood in all the earth, and even in heaven above. When a man weeps, whether he be a Jew or Gentile, Barbarian, Scythian, bond or free, it has the same meaning in it. Weeping is the eloquence of sorrow. It is an unstammering orator, needing no interpreter, but understood of all. Is it not sweet to believe that our tears are understood even when words fail? Let us learn to think of tears as liquid prayers, and of weeping as a constant dropping of importunate intercession which will wear its way right surely into the very heart of mercy, despite the stony difficulties which obstruct the way. My God, I will 'weep' when I cannot plead, for thou hearest the voice of my weeping.

Verse 9. 'The Lord hath heard my supplication.' The Holy Spirit had wrought into the Psalmist's mind the confidence that his prayer was heard. This is frequently the privilege of the saints. Praying the prayer of faith, they are often infallibly assured that they have prevailed with God. We read of Luther that, having on one occasion wrestled hard with God in prayer, he came leaping out of his closet crying, *Vicimus, vicimus*; that is, We have conquered, we have prevailed with God.' Assured confidence is no idle dream, for when the Holy Ghost bestows it upon us, we know its reality, and could not doubt it, even though all men should deride our boldness. 'The Lord will receive my prayer.' Here is past experience used for future encouragement. He hath, he will. Note this, O believer, and imitate its reasoning.

Verse 10. 'Let all mine enemies be ashamed and sore vexed.' This is rather a prophecy than an imprecation, it may be read in the future, 'All my enemies shall be ashamed and sore vexed.'

They shall return and be ashamed instantaneously – in a moment; – their doom shall come upon them suddenly. Death's day is doom's day, and both are sure and may be sudden. The Romans were wont to say, 'The feet of the avenging Deity are shod with wool.' With noiseless footsteps vengeance nears its victim, and sudden and overwhelming shall be its destroying stroke. If this were an imprecation, we must remember that the language of the old dispensation is not that of the new. We pray for our enemies, not against them. God have mercy on them, and bring them into the right way.

Thus the Psalm, like those which precede it, shews the different estates of the godly and the wicked. O Lord, let us be numbered with thy people, both now and forever!

Explanatory notes and quaint sayings

Whole Psalm. David was a man that was often exercised with sickness and troubles from enemies, and in all the instances almost that we meet with in the Psalms of these his afflictions, we may observe the outward occasions of trouble brought him under the suspicion of God's wrath and his own iniquity; so that he was seldom sick, or persecuted, but this called on the disquiet of conscience, and brought his sin to remembrance; as in this Psalm, which was made on the occasion of his sickness, as appears from verse 8, wherein he expresseth the vexation of his soul under the apprehension of God's anger; all his other griefs running into this channel, as little brooks, losing themselves in a great river, change their name and nature. He that at first was only concerned for his sickness, is now wholly concerned with sorrow and smart under the fear and hazard of his soul's condition; the like we may see in Psalm 38, and many places more. Richard Gilpin, 1677.

Verse 1. 'Rebuke me not.' God hath two means by which he reduceth his children to obedience; his word, by which he rebukes them; and his rod, by which he chastiseth them. The word precedes, admonishing them by his servants whom he hath sent in all ages to call sinners to repentance: of the which David himself saith, 'Let the righteous rebuke me;' and as a father doth first rebuke his disordered child, so doth the Lord speak to them. But when men neglect the warnings of his word, then God as a good Father, takes up the rod and beats them. Our Saviour wakened the three disciples in the garden three times, but seeing that served not, he told them that Judas and his band were coming to awaken them whom his own voice could not waken. A. Symson, 1638.

Verse 1. 'Jehovah, rebuke me not in thine anger,' etc. He does not altogether refuse punishment, for that would be unreasonable; and to be without it, he judged would be more hurtful than beneficial to him; but what he is afraid of is the wrath of God, which threatens sinners with ruin and perdition. To anger and indignation David tacitly opposes fatherly and gentle chastisement, and this last he was willing to bear. John Calvin, 1509–1564.

Verse 1. 'O Lord, rebuke me not in thine anger.'

The anger of the Lord? Oh, dreadful thought!
How can a creature frail as man endure
The tempest of his wrath? Ah, whither flee
To 'scape the punishment he well deserves?
Flee to the cross! the great atonement there

Will shield the sinner, if he supplicate
For pardon with repentance true and deep,
And faith that questions not. Then will the frown
Of anger pass from off the face of God,
Like a black tempest cloud that hides the sun.
Anon.

Verse 1. 'Lord, rebuke me not in thine anger,' etc.; that is, do not lay upon me that thou hast threatened in thy law; where anger is not put for the decree nor the execution, but for the denouncing. So (Matthew 3:11, and so Hosea 11:9), 'I will not execute the fierceness of mine anger,' that is, I will not execute my wrath as I have declared it. Again, it is said, he executes punishment on the wicked; he declares it not only, but executeth it, so anger is put for the execution of anger. Richard Stock, 1641.

Verse 1. 'Neither chasten me in thine hot displeasure.'

O keep up life and peace within,
If I must feel thy chastening rod!
Yet kill not me, but kill my sin,
And let me know thou art my God.
O give my soul some sweet foretaste
Of that which I shall shortly see!
Let faith and love cry to the last,
'Come, Lord, I trust myself with thee!'
Richard Baxter, 1615–1691.

Verse 2. 'Have mercy upon me, O Lord.' To fly and escape the anger of God, David sees no means in heaven or in earth, and therefore retires himself to God, even to him that wounded him that he might heal him. He flies not with Adam to the bush, nor with Saul to the witch, nor with Jonah to Tarshish; but he appeals from an angry and just God to a merciful God, and from himself to himself. The woman who was condemned by King Philip, appealed from Philip being drunken to Philip being sober. But David appeals from one virtue, justice, to another, mercy. There may be appellation from the tribunal of man to the justice-seat of God; but when thou art indicted before God's justice-seat, whither or to whom wilt thou go but to himself and his mercy-seat, which is the highest and last place of appellation? 'I have none in heaven but thee, nor in earth besides thee' . . . David, under the name of mercy, includeth all things, according to that of Jacob to his brother Esau, 'I have gotten mercy, and therefore I have gotten all things.' Desirest thou any thing at God's hands? Cry for mercy, out of which fountain all good things will spring to thee. A. Symson.

Verse 2. 'For I am weak.' Behold what rhetoric he useth to move God to cure him, 'I am weak,' an argument taken from his weakness, which indeed were a weak argument to move any man to show his favour, but is a strong argument to prevail with God. If a diseased person would come to a physician, and only lament the heaviness of his sickness, he would say, God help thee; or an oppressed person come to a lawyer, and show him the estate of his action and ask his advice, that is a golden question; or to a merchant to crave raiment, he will either have present money or a surety; or a courtier favour, you must have your reward ready in your hand. But coming before God, the most forcible argument that you can use is your necessity, poverty, tears, misery, unworthiness, and confessing them to him, it shall be an open door to furnish you with all things that he hath ... The tears of our misery are forcible arrows to pierce the heart of our heavenly Father, to deliver us and pity our hard case. The beggars lay open their sores to the view of the world, that the more they may move men to pity them. So let us deplore our miseries to God, that he, with the pitiful Samaritan, at the sight of our wounds, may help us in due time. A. Symson.

Verse 2. 'Heal me,' etc. David comes not to take physic upon wantonness, but because the disease is violent, because the accidents are vehement; so vehement, so violent, as that it hath pierced *ad ossa*, and *ad animam*, 'My bones are vexed, and my soul is sore troubled,' therefore 'heal me;' which is the reason upon which he grounds this second petition, 'Heal me, because my bones are vexed,' etc. John Donne.

Verse 2. 'My bones are vexed.' The Lord can make the strongest and most insensible part of a man's body sensible of his wrath when he pleaseth to touch him, for here David's bones are vexed. David Dickson.

Verse 2. The term 'bones' frequently occurs in the Psalms, and if we examine we shall find it used in three different senses. 1. It is sometimes applied literally to our blessed Lord's human body, to the body which hung upon the cross, as, 'They pierced my hands and my feet; I may tell all my bones.' 2. It has sometimes also a further reference to his mystical body the church. And then it denotes all the members of Christ's body that stand firm in the faith, that cannot be moved by persecutions, or temptations, however severe, as, 'All my bones shall say, Lord, who is like unto thee?' 3. In some passages the term 'bones' is applied to the soul, and not to the body, to the inner man of the individual Christian. Then it implies the strength and fortitude of the soul, the determined courage which faith in God gives to the righteous. This is the sense in which it is used in the second verse of Psalm 6,. 'O Lord, heal me; for my bones are vexed.' Augustine, Ambrose, and Chrysostom; quoted by F. H. Dunwell, B.A., in 'Parochial Lectures on the Psalms,' 1855.

Verse 3. 'My soul.' Yokefellows in sin are yokefellows in pain; the soul is punished for informing, the body for performing, and as both the informer and performer, the cause and the instrument, so shall the stirrer up of sin and the executor of it be punished. John Donne.

Verse 3. 'O Lord, how long?' Out of this we have three things to observe; first, that there is an appointed time which God hath measured for the crosses of all his children, before which time they shall not be delivered, and for which they must patiently attend, not thinking to prescribe time to God for their delivery, or limit the Holy One of Israel. The Israelites remained in Egypt till the complete number of four hundred and thirty years were accomplished. Joseph was three years and more in the prison till the appointed time of his delivery came. The Jews remained seventy years in Babylon. So that as the physician appointeth certain times to the patient, both wherein he must fast, and be dieted, and wherein he must take recreation, so God knoweth the convenient times both of our humiliation and exaltation. Next, see the impatience of our nature in our miseries, our flesh still rebelling against the Spirit, which oftentimes forgetteth itself so far, that it will enter into reasoning with God, and quarrelling with him, as we may read in Job, Jonas, etc., and here also of David. Thirdly, albeit the Lord delay his coming to relieve his saints, yet hath he great cause if we could ponder it; for when we were in the heat of our sins, many times he cried by the mouth of his prophets and servants, 'O fools, how long will you continue in your folly?' And we would not hear; and therefore when we are in the heat of our pains, thinking long, yea, every day a year till we be delivered, no wonder is it if God will not hear; let us consider with ourselves the just dealing of God with us; that as he cried and we would not hear, so now we cry, and he will not hear. A. Symson.

Verse 3. 'O Lord, how long?' As the saints in heaven have their *usque quo*, how long, Lord, holy and true, before thou begin to execute judgment? So, the saints on earth have their *usque quo*. How long, Lord, before thou take off the execution of this judgment upon us? For, our deprecatory prayers are not mandatory, they are not directory, they appoint not God his ways, nor times; but as our postulatory prayers are, they also are submitted to the will of God, and have all in them that ingredient, that herb of grace, which Christ put into his own prayer, yet not my will, but thy will be fulfilled; and they have that ingredient which Christ put into our prayer, thy will be done in earth as it is in heaven; in heaven there is no resisting of his will; yet in heaven there is a soliciting, a hastening, an accelerating of the judgment, and the glory of the resurrection; so though we resist not his corrections here upon the earth, we may humbly present to God the sense which we have of his displeasure, for this sense and apprehension of his corrections is one of the principal reasons why he sends them; he corrects us therefore that we might be sensible of his corrections; that when we, being humbled under his hand, have said with his prophet, 'I will bear the wrath of the Lord, because I have sinned against him' (Micah 7:9), he may be pleased to say to his correcting angel, as he did to his destroying angel, This is enough, and so burn his rod now, as he put up his sword then. John Donne.

Verse 4. 'Return, O Lord, deliver my soul,' etc. In this his besieging of God, he brings up his works from afar off, closer; he begins in this Psalm, at a deprecatory prayer; he asks nothing, but that God would do nothing, that he would forbear him – rebuke me not, correct me not. Now, it costs the king less to give a pardon than to give a pension, and less to give a reprieve than to give a pardon, and less to connive, not to call in question, than either reprieve, pardon, or pension; to forbear is not much. But then as the mathematician said, that he could make an engine, a screw, that should move the whole frame of the world, if he could have a place assigned him to fix that engine, that screw upon, that so it might work upon the world; so prayer, when one petition hath taken hold upon God, works upon God, moves God, prevails with God, entirely for all. David then having got this ground, this footing in God, he brings his works closer; he comes from the deprecatory to a postulatory prayer; not only that God would do nothing against him, but that he would do something for him. God hath suffered man to see the secrets of his state, how he governs – he governs by precedent; by precedents of his predecessors, he cannot, he hath none; by precedents of other gods he cannot, there are none; and yet he proceeds by precedents, by his own precedents, he does as he did before, to him that hath received he gives more, and is willing to be wrought and prevailed upon, and pressed with his own example. And, as though his doing good were but to learn how to do good better, still he writes after his own copy, and *nulla dies sine linea*. He writes something to us, that is, he doth something for us every day. And then, that which is not often seen in other masters, his copies are better than the originals; his latter mercies larger than his former; and in this postulatory prayer, larger than the deprecatory, enters our text, 'Return, O Lord; deliver my soul: O save me,' etc. John Donne.

Verse 5. 'For in death there is no remembrance of thee, in the grave who will give thee thanks?' Lord, be thou pacified and reconciled to me ... for shouldest thou now proceed to take away my life, as it were a most direful condition for me to die before I have propitiated thee, so I may well demand what increase of glory or honour will it bring unto thee? Will it not be infinitely more glorious for thee to spare me, till by true contrition I may regain thy favour? – and then I may live to praise and magnify thy mercy and thy grace: thy mercy in pardoning so great a sinner, and then confess thee by vital actions of all holy obedience for the future, and so demonstrate the power of thy grace which hath wrought this change in me; neither of which will be done by destroying me, but only thy just judgments manifested in thy vengeance on sinners, Henry Hammond, D.D., 1659.

Verse 6. 'I fainted in my mourning.' It may seem a marvellous change in David, being a man of such magnitude of mind, to be thus dejected and cast down. Prevailed he not against Goliath, against the lion and the bear, through fortitude and magnanimity? But now he is sobbing, sighing, and weeping as a child! The answer is easy; the diverse persons with whom he hath to do occasioneth the same. When men and beasts are his opposites, then he is more than a conqueror; but when he hath to do with God against whom he sinned, then he is less than nothing.

Verse 6. 'I caused my bed to swim' ... Showers be better than dews, yet it is sufficient if God at least hath bedewed our hearts, and hath given us some sign of a penitent heart. If we have not rivers of waters to pour forth with David, neither fountains flowing with Mary Magdalen, nor as Jeremy, desire to have a fountain in our head to weep day and night, nor with Peter weep bitterly; yet if we lament that we cannot lament, and mourn that we cannot mourn: yea, if we have the smallest sobs of sorrow and tears of compunction, if they be true and not counterfeit, they will make us acceptable to God; for as the woman with the bloody issue that touched the hem of Christ's garment, was no less welcome to Christ than Thomas, who put his fingers in the print of the nails; so, God looketh not at the quantity, but the sincerity of our repentance.

Verse 6. 'My bed.' The place of his sin is the place of his repentance, and so it should be; yea, when we behold the place where we have offended, we should be pricked in the heart, and there again crave him pardon. As Adam sinned in the garden, and Christ sweat bloody tears in the garden. 'Examine your hearts upon your beds, and convert unto the Lord;' and whereas ye have stretched forth yourselves upon your bed to devise evil things, repent there and make them sanctuaries to God. Sanctify by your tears every place which ye have polluted by sin. And let us seek Christ Jesus on our own bed, with the spouse in the Canticles, who saith, 'By night on my bed I sought him whom my soul loveth.' A. Symson.

Verse 6. 'I water my couch with tears.' Not only I wash, but also I water. The faithful sheep of the great Shepherd go up from the washing place, every one bringeth forth twins, and none barren among them. Canticles 4:2. For so Jacob's sheep, having conceived at the watering troughs, brought forth strong and partly-coloured lambs. David likewise, who before had erred and strayed like a lost sheep making here his bed a washing-place, by so much the less is barren in obedience, by how much the more he is fruitful in repentance. In Solomon's temple stood the caldrons of brass, to wash the flesh of those beasts which were to be sacrificed on the altar.

Solomon's father maketh a water of his tears, a caldron of his bed, an altar of his heart, a sacrifice, not of the flesh of unreasonable beasts, but of his own body, a living sacrifice, which is his reasonable serving of God. Now the Hebrew word here used signifies properly, to cause to swim, which is more than simply to wash. And thus the Geneva translation readeth it, I cause my bed every night to swim. So that as the priests used to swim in the molten sea, that they might be pure and clean, against they performed the holy rites and services of the temple, in like manner the princely prophet washeth his bed, yea, he swimmeth in his bed, or rather he causeth his bed to swim in tears, as in a sea of grief and penitent sorrow for his sin. Thomas Playfere, 1604.

Verse 6. 'I water my couch with my tears.' Let us water our bed every night with our tears. Do not only blow upon it with intermissive blasts, for then like fire, it will resurge and flame the more. Sin is like a stinking candle newly put out, it is soon lighted again. It may receive a wound, but like a dog it will easily lick itself whole; a little forbearance multiplies it like Hydra's heads. Therefore, whatsoever aspersion the sin of the day has brought upon us, let the tears of the night wash away. Thomas Adams.

Verses 6, 7. Soul-trouble is attended usually with great pain of body too, and so a man is wounded and distressed in every part. There is no soundness in my flesh, because of thine anger, says David. 'The arrows of the Almighty are within me, the poison whereof drinketh up my spirit.' Job 6:4. Sorrow of heart contracts the natural spirits, making all their motions slow and feeble; and the poor afflicted body does usually decline and waste away; and, therefore, saith Heman, 'My soul is full of troubles, and my life draweth nigh unto the grave.' In this inward distress we find our strength decay and melt, even as wax before the fire; for sorrow darkeneth the spirits, obscures the judgment, blinds the memory, as to all pleasant things, and beclouds the lucid part of the mind, causing the lamp of life to burn weakly. In this troubled condition the person cannot be without a countenance that is pale, and wan, and dejected, like one that is seized with strong fear and consternation; all his motions are sluggish, and no sprightliness nor activity remains. A merry heart doth good, like a medicine; but a broken spirit drieth the bones. Hence come those frequent complaints in Scripture: My moisture is turned into the drought of the summer: I am like a bottle in the smoke; my soul cleaveth unto the dust: my face is foul with weeping, and on my eyelid is the shadow of death. Job 16:16, 30:17,18–19. 'My bones are pierced in me, in the night seasons, and my sinews take no rest; by the great force of my disease is my garment changed. He hath cast me into the mire, and I am become like dust and ashes. Many times indeed the trouble of the soul does begin from the weakness and indisposition of the body. Long affliction, without any prospect of remedy, does, in process of time, begin to distress the soul itself. David was a man often exercised with sickness and the rage of enemies; and in all the instances almost that we meet with him in the Psalms, we may observe that the outward occasions of trouble brought him under an apprehension of the wrath of God for his sin. (Psalm 6:1, 2; and the reasons given, verses 5 and 6.) All his griefs running into this most terrible thought, that God was his enemy. As little brooks lose themselves in a great river, and change their name and nature, it most frequently happens that when our pain is long and sharp, and helpless and unavoidable, we begin to question the sincerity of our estate toward God, though at its first assault we had few doubts or fears about it. Long weakness of body makes the soul more susceptible of trouble, and uneasy thoughts. Timothy Rogers on Trouble of Mind.

Verse 7. 'Mine eye is consumed.' Many make those eyes which God hath given them, as it were two lighted candles to let them see to go to hell; and for this God in justice requiteth them, seeing their minds are blinded by the lust of the eyes, the lust of the flesh, and the pride of life, God, I say, sendeth sickness to debilitate their eyes which were so sharp-sighted in the devil's service, and their lust now causeth them to want the necessary sight of their body.

Verse 7. 'Mine enemies.' The pirates seeing an empty bark, pass by it; but if she be loaded with precious wares, then they will assault her. So, if a man have no grace within him, Satan passeth by him as not a convenient prey for him; but being loaded with graces, as the love of God, his fear, and such other spiritual virtues, let him be persuaded that according as he knows what stuff is in him, so will he not fail to rob him of them, if in any case he may. A. Symson.

Verse 7. That eye of his that had looked and lusted after his neighbour's wife is now dimmed and darkened with grief and indignation. He has wept himself almost blind. John Trapp.

Verse 8. 'Depart from me,' etc., i.e., you may now go your way; for that which you look for, namely, my death, you shall not have at this present; for the Lord hath heard the voice of my weeping, i.e., has graciously granted me that which with tears I asked of him. Thomas Wilcocks.

Verse 8. 'Depart from me, all ye workers of iniquity.' May not too much familiarity with profane wretches be justly charged upon church members? I know man is a sociable creature, but that will not excuse saints as to their carelessness of the choice of their company. The very fowls of the air, and beasts of the field, love not heterogeneous company. 'Birds of a feather flock together.' I have been afraid that many who would be thought eminent, of a high stature in grace and godliness, yet see not the vast difference there is between nature and regeneration, sin and grace, the old and the new man, seeing all company is alike unto them. Lewis Stuckley's 'Gospel Glass', 1667.

Verse 8. 'The voice of my weeping.' Weeping hath a voice, and as music upon the water sounds farther and more harmoniously than upon the land, so prayers, joined with tears, cry louder in God's ears, and make sweeter music than when tears are absent. When Antipater had written a large letter against Alexander's mother unto Alexander, the king answered him, 'One tear from my mother will wash away all her faults.' So it is with God. A penitent tear is an undeniable ambassador, and never returns from the throne of grace unsatisfied. Spencer's Things New and Old.

Verse 8. The wicked are called, 'workers of iniquity,' because they are free and ready to sin, they have a strong tide and bent of spirit to do evil, and they do it not to halves but thoroughly; they do not only begin or nibble at the bait a little (as a good man often doth), but greedily swallow it down, hook and all; they are fully in it, and do it fully; they make a work of it, and so are 'workers of iniquity'. Joseph Caryl.

Verse 8. Some may say, 'My constitution is such that I cannot weep; I may as well go to squeeze a rock, as think to get a tear.' But if thou canst not weep for sin, canst thou grieve? Intellectual mourning is best; there may be sorrow where there are no tears, the vessel may be full though it wants vent; it is not so much the weeping eye God respects as the broken heart; yet I would be loath to stop their tears who can weep. God stood looking on Hezekiah's tears (Isaiah 38:5), 'I have seen thy tears.' David's tears made music in God's ears, 'The Lord hath heard the voice of my weeping.' It is a sight fit for angels to behold, tears as pearls dropping from a penitent eye. T. Watson.

Verse 8. 'The Lord hath heard the voice of my weeping.' God hears the voice of our looks, God hears the voice of our tears sometimes better than the voice of our words; for it is the Spirit itself that makes intercession for us. Romans 8:26. *Gemitibus inenarrabilibus,* in those groans, and so in those tears, which we cannot utter; *ineloquacibus,* as Tertullian reads that place, devout, and simple tears, which cannot speak, speak aloud in the ears of God; nay, tears which we cannot utter; not only utter the force of the tears, but not utter the very tears themselves. As God sees the water in the spring in the veins of the earth before it bubble upon the face of the earth, so God sees tears in the heart of a man before they blubber his face; God hears the tears of that sorrowful soul, which for sorrow cannot shed tears. From this casting up of the eyes, and pouring out the sorrow of the heart at the eyes, at least opening God a window through which he may see a wet heart through a dry eye; from these overtures of repentance, which are as those imperfect sounds of words, which parents delight in, in their children, before they speak plain, a penitent sinner comes to a verbal and a more expressive prayer. To these prayers, these vocal and verbal prayers from David, God had given ear, and from this hearing of those prayers was David come to this thankful confidence, 'The Lord hath heard, the Lord will hear'. John Donne.

Verse 8. What a strange change is here all of a sudden! Well might Luther say, 'Prayer is the leech of the soul, that sucks out the venom and swelling thereof.' 'Prayer,' saith another, 'is an exorcist with God, and an exorcist against sin and misery.' Bernard saith, 'How oft hath prayer found me despairing almost, but left me triumphing, and well assured of pardon!' The same in effect saith David here, 'Depart from me, all ye workers of iniquity; for the Lord hath heard the voice of my weeping.' What a word is that to his insulting enemies! Avaunt! come out! vanish! These be words used to devils and dogs, but good enough for a Doeg or a Shimei. And the Son of David shall say the same to his enemies when he comes to judgment. John Trapp.

Verse 9. 'The Lord hath heard my supplication,' etc. The psalmist three times expresses his confidence of his prayers being heard and received, which may be either in reference to his having prayed so many times for help, as the apostle Paul did (2 Corinthians 12:8); and as Christ his antitype did (Matthew 26:39, 42, 44); or to express the certainty of it, the strength of his faith in it, and the exuberance of his joy on account of it. John Gill, D.D., 1697–1771.

Verse 10. 'Let all mine enemies be ashamed,' etc. If this were an imprecation, a malediction, yet it was medicinal, and had *rationem boni,* a charitable tincture and nature in it; he wished the men no harm as men. But it is rather *prædictorium,* a prophetical vehemence, that if they will take no knowledge of God's declaring himself in the protection of his servants, if they would not consider that God had heard, and would hear, had rescued, and would rescue his children, but would continue their opposition against him, heavy judgments would certainly fall upon them; their punishment should be certain, but the effect should be uncertain; for God only knows whether his correction shall work upon his enemies to their mollifying, or to their obduration ... In the second word, 'Let them be sore vexed,' he wishes his enemies no worse than himself had been, for he had used the same word of himself before, *Ossa turbata,* My bones are vexed; and *Anima turbata,* My soul is vexed; and considering that David had found this vexation to be his way to God, it was no malicious imprecation to wish that enemy the same physic that he had taken, who was more sick of the same disease than he was. For this is like a troubled sea after a tempest; the danger is past, but yet the billow is great still; the danger was in the calm, in the security, or in the tempest, by misinterpreting God's correction to our obduration, and to a remorseless stupefication; but when a man is come to this holy vexation, to be troubled, to be shaken with the sense of the indignation of God, the storm is past, and the indignation of God is blown over. That soul is in a fair and near way of being restored to a calmness, and to reposed security of conscience that is come to this holy vexation. John Donne.

Verse 10. 'Let all mine enemies [or all mine enemies shall] be ashamed, and sore vexed', etc. Many of the mournful Psalms end in this manner, to instruct the believer that he is continually to look forward, and solace himself with beholding that day, when his warfare shall be accomplished; when sin and sorrow shall be no more; when sudden and everlasting confusion shall cover the enemies of righteousness; when the sackcloth of the penitent shall be exchanged for a robe of glory, and every tear becomes a sparkling gem in his crown; when to sighs and groans shall succeed the songs of heaven, set to angels' harps, and faith shall be resolved into the vision of the Almighty. George Horne.

Hints to the village preacher
Verse 1. A sermon for afflicted souls.

I. God's twofold dealings:
   1. Rebuke, by a telling sermon, a judgment on another, a slight trial in our own person, or a solemn monition in our conscience by the Spirit.
   2. Chastening. This follows the other when the first is disregarded. Pain, losses, bereavements, melancholy, and other trials.
II. The evils in them to be most dreaded, anger and hot displeasure.
III. The means to avert these ills. Humiliation, confession, amendment, faith in the Lord, etc.

Verse 1. The believer's greatest dread, the anger of God. What this fact reveals in the heart? Why is it so? What removes the fear?
Verse 2. The *argumentum ad misericordiam.*
Verse 2 (first sentence). – Divine healing.
   1. What precedes it, my bones are vexed.
   2. How it is wrought.
   3. What succeeds it.

Verse 3. The impatience of sorrow; its sins, mischief, and cure.
Verse 3. A fruitful topic may be found in considering the question, How long will God continue afflictions to the righteous?
Verse 4. 'Return, O Lord.' A prayer suggested by a sense of the Lord's absence, excited by grace, attended with heart searching and repentance, backed by pressing danger, guaranteed as to its answer, and containing a request for all mercies.
Verse 4. The praying of the deserted saint.

1. His state: his soul is evidently in bondage and danger;
2. His hope: it is in the Lord's return.
3. His plea: mercy only.

Verse 5. The final suspension of earthly service considered in various practical aspects.

Verse 5. The duty of praising God while we live.

Verse 6. Saint's tears in quality, abundance, influence, assuagement, and final end.

Verse 7. The voice of weeping. What it is.

Verse 8. The pardoned sinner forsaking his bad companions.

Verse 9. Past answers the ground of present confidence. He hath, he will.

Verse 10. The shame reserved for the wicked.

Psalm 11

Subject

Charles Simeon gives an excellent summary of this Psalm in the following sentences: 'The Psalms are a rich repository of experimental knowledge. David, at the different periods of his life, was placed in almost every situation in which a believer, whether rich or poor, can be placed; in these heavenly compositions he delineates all the workings of the heart. He introduces, too, the sentiments and conduct of the various persons who were accessory either to his troubles or his joys; and thus sets before us a compendium of all that is passing in the hearts of men throughout the world. When he penned this Psalm he was under persecution from Saul, who sought his life, and hunted him 'as a partridge upon the mountains.' His timid friends were alarmed for his safety, and recommended him to flee to some mountain where he had a hiding-place, and thus to conceal himself from the rage of Saul. But David, being strong in faith, spurned the idea of resorting to any such pusillanimous expedients, and determined confidently to repose his trust in God.'

To assist us to remember this short, but sweet Psalm, we will give it the name of 'THE SONG OF THE STEADFAST.'

Division

From 1 to 3, David describes the temptation with which he was assailed, and from 4 to 7, the arguments by which his courage was sustained.

Exposition

Verse 1. These verses contain an account of a temptation to distrust God, with which David was, upon some unmentioned occasion, greatly exercised. It may be, that in the days when he was in Saul's court, he was advised to flee at a time when this flight would have been charged against him as a breach of duty to the king, or a proof of personal cowardice. His case was like that of Nehemiah, when his enemies, under the garb of friendship, hoped to entrap him by advising him to escape for his life. Had he done so, they could then have found a ground of accusation. Nehemiah bravely replied, 'Shall such a man as I flee?' and David, in a like spirit, refuses to retreat, exclaiming, 'In the Lord put I my trust: how say ye to my soul, Flee as a bird to your mountain?' When Satan cannot overthrow us by presumption, how craftily will he seek to ruin us by distrust! He will employ our dearest friends to argue us out of our confidence, and he will use such plausible logic, that unless we once for all assert our immovable trust in Jehovah, he will make us like the timid bird which flies to the mountain whenever danger presents itself.

Verse 2. How forcibly the case is put! The bow is bent, the arrow is fitted to the string: 'Flee, flee, thou defenceless bird, thy safety lies in flight; begone, for thine enemies will send their shafts into thy heart; haste, haste, for soon wilt thou be destroyed!' David seems to have felt the force of the advice, for it came home to his soul; but yet he would not yield, but would rather dare the danger than exhibit a distrust in the Lord his God. Doubtless the perils which encompassed David were great and imminent; it was quite true that his enemies were ready to shoot privily at him.

Verse 3. It was equally correct that the very foundations of law and justice were destroyed under Saul's unrighteous government: but what were all these things to the man whose trust was in God alone? He could brave the dangers, could escape the enemies, and defy the injustice which surrounded him. His answer to the question 'What can the righteous do?' would be the counter-question, 'What cannot they do?' When prayer engages God on our side, and when faith secures the fulfilment of the promise, what cause can there be for flight, however cruel and mighty our enemies? With a sling and a stone, David had smitten a giant before whom the whole hosts of Israel were trembling, and the Lord, who delivered him from the uncircumcised Philistine, could surely deliver him from King Saul and his myrmidons. There is no such word as 'impossibility' in the language of faith; that martial grace knows how to fight and conquer, but she knows not how to flee.

Verse 4. David here declares the great source of his unflinching courage. He borrows his light from heaven – from the great central orb of deity. The God of the believer is never far from him; he is not merely the God of the mountain fastnesses, but of the dangerous valleys and battle plains.

'Jehovah is in his holy temple.' The heavens are above our heads in all regions of the earth, and so is the Lord ever near to us in every state and condition. This is a very strong reason why we should not adopt the vile suggestions of distrust. There is one who pleads his precious blood in our behalf in the temple above, and there is one upon the throne who is never deaf to the intercession of his Son. Why, then, should we fear? What plots can men devise which Jesus will not discover? Satan has doubtless desired to have us, that he may sift us as wheat, but Jesus is in the temple praying for us, and how can our faith fail? What attempts can the wicked make which Jehovah shall not behold? And since he is in his holy temple, delighting in the sacrifice of his Son, will he not defeat every device, and send us a sure deliverance?

'Jehovah's throne is in the heavens;' he reigns supreme. Nothing can be done in heaven, or earth, or hell, which he doth not ordain and over-rule. He is the world's great Emperor. Wherefore, then, should we flee? If we trust this King of kings, is not this enough? Cannot he deliver us without our cowardly retreat? Yes, blessed be the Lord our God, we can salute him as Jehovah-nissi; in his name we set up our banners, and instead of flight, we once more raise the shout of war.

'His eyes behold.' The eternal Watcher never slumbers; his eyes never know a sleep. 'His eyelids try the children of men:' he narrowly inspects their actions, words, and thoughts. As men, when intently and narrowly inspecting some very minute object, almost close their eyelids to exclude every other object, so will the Lord look all men through and through. God sees each man as much and as perfectly as if there were no other creature in the universe. He sees us always; he never removes his eye from us; he sees us entirely, reading the recesses of the soul as readily as the glances of the eye. Is not this a sufficient ground of confidence, and an abundant answer to the solicitations of despondency? My danger is not hid from him; he knows my extremity, and I may rest assured that he will not suffer me to perish while I rely alone on him. Wherefore, then, should I take wings of a timid bird, and flee from the dangers which beset me?

Verse 5. 'The Lord trieth the righteous:' he doth not hate them, but only tries them. They are precious to him, and therefore he refines them with afflictions. None of the Lord's children may hope to escape from trial, nor, indeed, in our right minds, would any of us desire to do so, for trial is the channel of many blessings.

> Tis my happiness below
> Not to live without the cross;
> But the Saviour's power to know,
> Sanctifying every loss.
>
> Trials make the promise sweet;
> Trials give new life to prayer;
> Trials bring me to his feet –
> Lay me low, and keep me there.
>
> Did I meet no trials here –
> No chastisement by the way –
> Might I not, with reason, fear
> I should prove a cast-away?
>
> Bastards may escape the rod,
> Sunk in earthly vain delight;
> But the true-born child of God
> Must not – would not, if he might.
> William Cowper.

Is not this a very cogent reason why we should not distrustfully endeavour to shun a trial? – for in so doing we are seeking to avoid a blessing.

Verse 6. 'But the wicked and him that loveth violence his soul hateth:' why, then, shall I flee from these wicked men? If God hateth them, I will not fear them. Haman was very great in the palace until he lost favour, but when the king abhorred him, how bold were the meanest attendants to suggest the gallows for the man at whom they had often trembled! Look at the black mark upon the faces of our persecutors, and we shall not run away from them. If God is in the quarrel as well as ourselves, it would be foolish to question the result, or avoid the conflict. Sodom and Gomorrah perished by a fiery hail, and by a brimstone shower from heaven; so shall all the ungodly. They may gather together like Gog and Magog to battle, but the Lord will rain upon them 'an overflowing rain, and great hailstones, fire, and brimstone' Ezekiel 38:22. Some expositors think that in the term 'horrible tempest,' there is in the Hebrew an allusion to that burning, suffocating wind, which blows across the Arabian deserts, and is known by the name of Simoom. 'A burning storm,' Lowth calls it, while another great commentator reads it 'wrathwind;' in either version the language is full of terrors. What a tempest will that be which shall overwhelm the despisers of God! Oh! what a shower will that be which shall pour out itself for ever upon the defenceless heads of impenitent sinners in hell! Repent, ye rebels, or this fiery deluge shall soon surround you. Hell's horrors shall be your inheritance, your entailed estate, 'the portion of your cup.' The dregs of that cup you shall wring out, and drink for ever. A drop of hell is terrible, but what must a full cup of torment be? Think of it – a cup of misery, but not a drop of mercy. O people of God, how foolish is it to fear the faces of men who shall soon be faggots in the fire of hell! Think of their end, their fearful end, and all fear of them must be changed into contempt of their threatenings, and pity for their miserable estate.

Verse 7. The delightful contrast of the last verse is well worthy of our observation, and it affords another overwhelming reason why we should be steadfast, unmoveable, not carried away with fear, or led to adopt carnal expedients in order to avoid trial. 'For the righteous Lord loveth righteousness.' It is not only his office to defend it, but his nature to love it. He would deny himself if he did not defend the just. It is essential to the very being of God that he should be just; fear not, then, the end of all your trials, but 'be just, and fear not.' God approves, and, if men oppose, what matters it? 'His countenance doth behold the upright.' We need never be out of countenance, for God countenances us. He observes, he approves, he delights in the upright. He sees his own image in them, an image of his own fashioning, and therefore with complacency he regards them. Shall we dare to put forth our hand unto iniquity in order to escape affliction? Let us have done with by-ways and short turnings, and let us keep to that fair path of right along which Jehovah's smile shall light us. Are we tempted to put our light under a bushel, to conceal our religion from our neighbours? Is it suggested to us that there are ways of avoiding the cross, and shunning the reproach of Christ? Let us not hearken to the voice of the charmer, but seek an increase of faith, that we may wrestle with principalities and powers, and follow the Lord, fully going without the camp, bearing his reproach. Mammon, the flesh, the devil, will all whisper in our ear, 'Flee as a bird to your mountain;' but let us come forth and defy them all. 'Resist the devil, and he will flee from you.' There is no room or reason for retreat. Advance! Let the vanguard push on! To the front! all ye powers and passions of our soul. On! on! in God's name, on! for 'the Lord of hosts is with us; the God of Jacob is our refuge.'

Explanatory notes and quaint sayings
Whole Psalm. The most probable account of the occasion of this Psalm is that given by Amyraldus. He thinks it was composed by David while he was in the court of Saul, at a time when the hostility of the king was beginning to show itself, and before it had broken out into open persecution. David's friends, or those professing to be so, advised him to flee to his native mountains for a time, and remain in retirement, till the king should show himself more favourable. David does not at that time accept the counsel, though afterwards he seems to have followed it. This Psalm applies itself to the establishment of the church against the calumnies

of the world and the compromising counsel of man, in that confidence which is to be placed in God the Judge of all. W. Wilson, D.D., in loc., 1860.

Whole Psalm. If one may offer to make a modest conjecture, it is not improbable this Psalm might be composed on the sad murder of the priests by Saul (1 Samuel 22:19), when after the slaughter of Abimelech, the high priest, Doeg, the Edomite, by command from Saul, 'slew in one day fourscore and five persons which wore a linen ephod.' I am not so carnal as to build the spiritual church of the Jews on the material walls of the priests' city at Nob (which then by Doeg was smitten with the edge of the sword), but this is most true, that 'knowledge must preserve the people;' and (Malachi 2:7), 'The priests' lips shall preserve knowledge;' and then it is easy to conclude, what an earthquake this massacre might make in the foundations of religion. Thomas Fuller.

Whole Psalm. Notice how remarkably the whole Psalm corresponds with the deliverance of Lot from Sodom. This verse, with the angel's exhortation, 'Escape to the mountains, lest thou be consumed,' and Lot's reply, 'I cannot escape to the mountains, lest some evil take me and I die' Genesis 19:17–19. And again, 'The Lord's seat is in heaven, and upon the ungodly he shall rain snares, fire, brimstone, storm and tempest,' with 'Then the Lord rained upon Sodom and Gomorrah brimstone and fire out of heaven:' and again 'His countenance will behold the thing that is just,' with 'Delivered just Lot ... for that righteous man vexed his righteous soul with their ungodly deeds' 2 Peter 2: 7, 8. Cassidorus (A.D., 560) in John Mason Neal's 'Commentary on the Psalms, from Primitive and Mediaeval Writers,' 1860.

Whole Psalm. The combatants at the Lake Thrasymene are said to have been so engrossed with the conflict that neither party perceived the convulsions of nature that shook the ground –

An earthquake reeled unheedingly away,
None felt stern nature rocking at his feet.

From a nobler cause, it is thus with the soldiers of the Lamb. They believe, and, therefore, make no haste; nay, they can scarcely be said to feel earth's convulsions as other men, because their eager hope presses forward to the issue at the advent of the Lord. Andrew A. Bonar.

Verse 1. 'I trust in the Lord: how do ye say to my soul, Swerve on to your mountain like a bird?' (others, 'O thou bird.') Saul and his adherents mocked and jeered David with such taunting speeches, as conceiving that he knew no other shift or refuge, but so betaking himself unto wandering and lurking on the mountains; hopping, as it were, from one place to another like a silly bird; but they thought to ensnare and take him well enough for all that, not considering God who was David's comfort, rest and refuge. Theodore Haak's 'Translation of the Dutch Annotations, as ordered by the Synod of Dort, in 1618.' London, 1657.

Verse 1. 'With Jehovah I have taken shelter; how say ye to my soul, Flee, sparrows, to your hill?' 'Your hill,' that hill from which you say your help cometh: a sneer. Repair to that boasted hill, which may indeed give you the help which it gives the sparrow: a shelter against the inclemencies of a stormy sky, no defence against our power. Samuel Horsley, in loc.

Verse 1. 'In the Lord put I my trust: how say ye to my soul, Flee as a bird to your mountain?' The holy confidence of the saints in the hour of great trial is beautifully illustrated by the following ballad which Anne Askew, who was burned at Smithfield in 1546, made and sang when she was in Newgate:

> Like as the armed knight,
> Appointed to the field,
> With this world will I fight,
> And Christ shall be my shield.
>
> Faith is that weapon strong,
> Which will not fail at need:
> My foes, therefore, among,
> Therewith will I proceed.
>
> As it is had in strength
> And force of Christ's way,
> It will prevail at length,
> Though all the devils say nay.
>
> Faith in the fathers old
> Obtained righteousness;
> Which makes me very bold
> To fear no world's distress.
>
> I now rejoice in heart,
> And hope bids me do so;
> For Christ will take my part,
> And ease me of my woe.
>
> Thou say'st Lord, whoso knock,
> To them wilt thou attend:
> Undo therefore the lock,
> And thy strong power send.
>
> More enemies now I have
> Than hairs upon my head:
> Let them not me deprave,
> But fight thou in my stead.
>
> On thee my care I cast,
> For all their cruel spite:
> I set not by their haste;
> For thou art my delight.
>
> I am not she that list
> My anchor to let fall
> For every drizzling mist,
> My ship substantial.

Not oft use I to write,
In prose, nor yet in rhyme;
Yet will I shew one sight
That I saw in my time.

I saw a royal throne,
Where justice should have sit,
But in her stead was one
Of moody, cruel wit.

Absorbed was righteousness,
As of the raging flood:
Satan, in his excess,
Sucked up the guiltless blood.

Then thought I, Jesus Lord,
When thou shall judge us all,
Hard it is to record
On these men what will fall.

Yet, Lord, I thee desire,
For that they do to me,
Let them not taste the hire
Of their iniquity.

Verse 1. 'How say ye to my soul, Flee as a bird to your mountain?' We may observe, that David is much pleased with the metaphor in frequently comparing himself to a bird, and that of several sorts: first, to an eagle (Psalm 103:5), 'My youth is renewed like the eagle's;' sometimes to an owl (Psalm 102:6), 'I am like an owl in the desert;' sometimes to a pelican, in the same verse, 'Like a pelican in the wilderness;' sometimes to a sparrow (Psalm 102:7), 'I watch, and am as a sparrow;' sometimes to a partridge, 'As when one doth hunt a partridge.' I cannot say that he doth compare himself to a dove, but he would compare himself (Psalm 55:6), 'O that I had the wings of a dove, for then I would flee away and be at rest.' Some will say, How is it possible that birds of so different a feather should all so fly together as to meet in the character of David? To whom we answer, That no two men can more differ one from another, that the same servant of God at several times differeth from himself. David in prosperity, when commanding, was like an eagle; in adversity, when contemned, like an owl; in devotion, when retired, like a pelican; in solitariness, when having no company (of Saul), like a partridge. This general metaphor of a bird, which David so often used on himself, his enemies in the first verse of this Psalm used on him, though not particularising the kind thereof: 'Flee as a bird to your mountain;' that is, speedily betake thyself to thy God, in whom thou hopest for succour and security.

Seeing this counsel was both good in itself, and good at this time, why doth David seem so angry and displeased thereat? Those his words, 'Why say you to my soul, Flee as a bird to your mountain?' import some passion, at leastwise, a disgust of the advice. It is answered, David was not offended with the counsel, but with the manner of the propounding thereof. His enemies did it ironically in a gibing, jeering way, as if his flying thither were to no purpose, and he unlikely to find there the safety he sought for. However, David was not hereby put out of conceit with the counsel, beginning this Psalm with this his firm resolution, 'In the Lord put I my trust: how say ye then to my soul,' etc. Learn we from hence, when men give us good counsel in a jeering way, let us take the counsel, and practise it; and leave them the jeer to be punished for it. Indeed, corporal cordials may be envenomed by being wrapped up in poisoned papers; not so good spiritual advice where the good matter receives no infection from the ill manner of the delivery thereof. Thus, when the chief priests mocked our Saviour (Matthew 27:43), 'He trusted in God, let him deliver him now if he will have him.' Christ trusted in God. Otherwise, if men's mocks should make us to undervalue good counsel, we might in this age be mocked out of our God, and Christ, and Scripture, and heaven; the apostle Jude, verse 18, having foretold that in the last times there should be mockers, walking after their own lusts. Thomas Fuller.

Verse 1. It is as great an offence to make a new, as to deny the true God. 'In the Lord put I my trust;' how then 'say ye unto my soul' (ye seducers of souls), 'that she should fly unto the mountains as a bird;' to seek unnecessary and foreign helps, as if the Lord alone were not sufficient? 'The Lord is my rock, and my fortress, and he that delivereth me, my God, and my strength; in him will I trust: my shield, the horn of my salvation, and my refuge. I will call upon the Lord, who is worthy to be praised, so shall I be safe from mine enemies.' 'Whom have I in heaven but thee,' amongst those thousands of angels and saints, what Michael or Gabriel, what Moses or Samuel, what Peter, what Paul? 'and there is none in earth that I desire in comparison of thee.' John King, 1608.

Verse 1. In temptations of inward trouble and terror, it is not convenient to dispute the matter with Satan. David in Psalm 42:11, seems to correct himself for his mistake; his soul was cast down within him, and for the cure of that temptation, he had prepared himself by arguments for a dispute; but perceiving himself in a wrong course, he calls off his soul from disquiet to an immediate application to God and the promises, 'Trust still in God, for I shall yet praise him;' but here he is more aforehand with his work; for while his enemies were acted by Satan to discourage him, he rejects the temptation at first, before it settled upon his thoughts, and chaseth it away as a thing that he would not give ear to. 'In the Lord put I my trust: how say ye to my soul, Flee as a bird to your mountain?' And there are weighty reasons that should dissuade us from entering the lists with Satan in temptation of inward trouble. Richard Gilpin.

Verse 1. The shadow will not cool except in it. What good to have the shadow though of a mighty rock, when we sit in the open sun? To have almighty power engaged for us, and we to throw ourselves out of it, by bold sallies in the mouth of temptation! The saints' falls have been when they have run out of their trench and stronghold; for, like the conies, they are a weak people in themselves, and their strength lies in the rock of God's almightiness, which is their habitation. William Gurnall.

Verse 1. The saints of old would not accept deliverances on base terms. They scorned to fly away for the enjoyment of rest except it were with the wings of a dove, covered with silver innocence. As willing were many of the martyrs to die as to dine. The tormentors were tired in torturing Blandina. 'We are ashamed, O Emperor! The Christians laugh at your cruelty, and grow the more resolute,' said one of Julian's nobles. This the heathen counted obstinacy; but they knew not the power of the Spirit, nor the secret armour of proof, which saints wear about their hearts. John Trapp.

Verse 2. 'For, lo, the wicked bend their bow,' etc. This verse presents an unequal combat betwixt armed power, advantaged with policy, on the one side; and naked innocence on the other. First, armed power: 'They bend their bows, and make ready their arrows,' being all the artillery of that age; secondly, advantaged with policy: 'that they may privily shoot,' to surprise them with an ambush unawares, probably pretending amity and friendship unto them; thirdly, naked innocence: if innocence may be termed naked, which is its own armour; 'at the upright in heart.' Thomas Fuller.

Verse 2. 'For, lo, the ungodly bend their bow, and make ready their arrows within the quiver: that they may privily shoot at them which are true of heart.' The plottings of the chief priests and Pharisees that they might take Jesus by subtlety and kill him. They bent their bow, when they hired Judas Iscariot for the betrayal of his Master; they made ready their arrows within the quiver when they sought 'false witnesses against Jesus to put him to death' Matthew 26:59. 'Them which are true of heart.' Not alone the Lord himself, the only true and righteous, but his apostles, and the long line of those who should faithfully cleave to him from that time to this. And as with the Master, so with the servants: witness the calumnies and the revilings that from the time of Joseph's accusation by his mistress till the present day, have been the lot of God's people. Michael Ayguan, 1416, in J. M. Neale's Commentary.

Verse 2. 'That they may secretly shoot at them which are upright in heart.' They bear not their bows and arrows as scarecrows in a garden of cucumbers, to fray, but to shoot, not at stakes, but men; their arrows are *jacula mortifera* (Psalm 7), deadly arrows, and lest they should fail to hit, they take advantage of the dark, of privacy and secrecy; they shoot privily. Now this is the covenant of hell itself. For what created power in the earth is able to dissolve that work which cruelty and subtlety, like Simeon and Levi, brothers in evil, are combined and confederate to bring to pass? Where subtlety is ingenious, insidious to invent, cruelty barbarous to execute, subtlety giveth counsel, cruelty giveth the stroke. Subtlety ordereth the time, the place, the means, accommodateth circumstances; cruelty undertaketh the act: subtlety hideth the knife, cruelty cutteth the throat: subtlety with a cunning head layeth the ambush, plotteth the train, the stratagem; and cruelty with as savage a heart, sticketh not at the dreadfullest, direfullest objects, ready to wade up to the ankles, the neck, in a whole red sea of human, yea, country blood: how fearful is their plight that are thus assaulted! John King.

Verse 3. 'If the foundations be destroyed, what can the righteous do?' But now we are met with a giant objection, which with Goliath must be removed, or else it will obstruct our present proceedings. Is it possible that the foundations of religion should be destroyed? Can God be in so long a sleep, yea, so long a lethargy, as patiently to permit the ruins thereof? If he looks on, and yet doth not see these foundations when destroyed, where then is his omnisciency? If he seeth it, and cannot help it, where then is his omnipotency? If he seeth it, can help it, and will not, where then is his goodness and mercy? Martha said to Jesus (John 11:21), 'Lord, if thou hadst been here, my brother had not died.' But many will say, Were God effectually present in the world with his aforesaid attributes, surely the foundations had not died, had not been destroyed. We answer negatively, that it is impossible that the foundations of religion should ever be totally and finally destroyed, either in relation to the church in general, or in reference to every true and lively member thereof. For the first, we have an express promise of Christ, Matthew 16:18: 'The gates of hell shall not prevail against it.' And as for every particular Christian (2 Timothy 2:19), 'Nevertheless, the foundation of God standeth sure, having this seal, the Lord knoweth them that are his.' However, though for the reasons aforementioned in the objections (the inconsistency thereof with the attributes of God's omnipotency, omni-sciency, and goodness), the foundations can never totally and finally, yet may they partially be destroyed in a fourfold degree, as followeth. First, in the desires and utmost endeavours of wicked men, they bring their

1. Hoc velle,
2. Hoc agere,
3. Totum posse.

If they destroy not the foundations, it is no thanks to them, seeing all the world will bear them witness they have done their best (that is, their worst), what their might and malice could perform. Secondly, in their own vainglorious imaginations: they may not only vainly boast, but also verily believe that they have destroyed the foundations. Applicable to this purpose, is that high rant of the Roman emperor (Luke 2:1): 'And it came to pass in those days, that there went out a decree from Caesar Augustus, that all the world should be taxed.' All the world! whereas he had, though much, not all in Europe, little in Asia, less in Africa, none in America, which was so far from being conquered, it was not so much as known to the Romans. But hyperbole is not a figure, but the ordinary language of pride; because indeed Augustus had very much he proclaimeth himself to have all the world . . . Thirdly, the foundations may be destroyed as to all outward visible illustrious apparition. The church in persecution is like unto a ship in a tempest; down go all their masts, yea, sometimes for the more speed they are forced to cut them down: not a piece of canvas to play with the winds, no sails to be seen; they lie close knotted to the very keel, that the tempest may have the less power upon them, though when the storm is over, they can hoist up their sails as high, and spread their canvas as broad as ever before. So the church in the time of persecution feared, but especially felt, loseth all gayness and gallantry which may attract and allure the eyes of beholders, and contenteth itself with its own secrecy. In a word, on the work-days of affliction she weareth her worst clothes, whilst her best are laid up in her wardrobe, in sure and certain hope that God will give her a holy and happy day, when with joy she shall wear her best garments. Lastly, they may be destroyed in the jealous apprehensions of the best saints and servants of God, especially in their melancholy fits. I will instance in no puny, but in a star of the first magnitude and greatest eminency, even Elijah himself complaining (1 Kings 19:10): 'And I, even I only, am left; and they seek my life, to take it away.' Thomas Fuller.

Verse 3. 'If.' It is the only word of comfort in the text, that what is said is not positive, but suppositive; not thetical, but hypothetical. And yet this comfort which is but a spark (at which we would willingly kindle our hopes), is quickly sadded with a double consideration. First, impossible suppositions produce impossible consequences, 'As is the mother, so is the daughter.' Therefore, surely God's Holy Spirit would not suppose such a thing but what was feasible and possible, but what either had, did, or might come to pass. Well, it is good to know the worst of things, that we may provide ourselves accordingly; and therefore let us behold this doleful case, not as doubtful, but as done; not as feared, but felt; not as suspected, but at this time really come to pass. Thomas Fuller.

Verse 3. 'If the foundations,' etc. My text is an answer to a tacit objection which some may raise; namely, that the righteous are wanting to themselves, and by their own easiness and inactivity (not daring and doing so much as they might and ought), betray themselves to that bad condition. In whose defence David shows, that if God in his wise will and pleasure seeth it fitting, for reasons best known to himself, to suffer religion to be reduced to terms of extremity, it is not placed in the power of the best man alive to remedy and redress the same. 'If the foundations be destroyed, what can the righteous do?' My text is hung about with mourning, as for a funeral sermon, and contains: First, a sad case supposed, 'If the foundations be destroyed.' Secondly, a sad question propounded, 'What can the righteous do?' Thirdly, a sad answer implied, namely, that they can do just nothing, as to that point of re-establishing the destroyed foundation. Thomas Fuller.

Verse 3. 'If the foundations be destroyed,' etc. The civil foundation of a nation or people, is their laws and constitutions. The order and power that's among them, that's the foundation of a people; and when once this foundation is destroyed, 'What can the righteous do?' What can the best, the wisest in the world, do in such a case? What can any man do, if there be not a foundation of government left among men? There is no help nor answer in such a case but that which follows in the fourth verse of the Psalm, 'The Lord is in his holy temple, the Lord's throne is in heaven: his eyes behold, his eyelids try, the children of men;' as if he had said, in the midst of these confusions, when as it is said (Psalm 82:5), 'All the foundations of the earth are out of course;' yet God keeps his course still, he is where he was and as he was, without variableness or shadow of turning. Joseph Caryl.

Verse 3. 'The righteous.' The righteous indefinitely, equivalent to the righteous universally; not only the righteous as a single arrow, but in the whole sheaf; not only the righteous in their personal, but in their diffusive capacity. Were they all collected into one body, were all the righteous living in the same age wherein the foundations are destroyed, summoned up and modelled into one corporation, all their joint endeavours would prove ineffectual to the re-establishing of the fallen foundations, as not being man's work, but only God's work to perform. Thomas Fuller.

Verse 3. 'The foundations.' Positions, the things formerly fixed, placed, and settled. It is not said, if the roof be ruinous, or if the side walls be shattered, but if the foundations.

Verse 3. 'Do.' It is not said, What can they think? It is a great blessing which God hath allowed injured people, that though otherwise oppressed and straitened, they may freely enlarge themselves in their thoughts. Thomas Fuller.

Verse 3. Sinning times have ever been the saints' praying times: this sent Ezra with a heavy heart to confess the sin of his people, and to bewail their abominations before the Lord. Ezra 9. And Jeremiah tells the wicked of his degenerate age, that 'his soul should weep in secret places for their pride.' Jeremiah 13:17. Indeed, sometimes sin comes to such a height, that this is almost all the godly can do, to get into a corner, and bewail the general pollutions of the age. 'If the foundations be destroyed, what can the righteous do?' Such dismal days of national confusion our eyes have seen, when foundations of government were destroyed, and all hurled into military confusion. When it is thus with a people, 'What can the righteous do?' Yes, this they may, and should do, 'fast and pray.' There is yet a God in heaven to be sought to, when a people's deliverance is thrown beyond the help of human policy or power. Now is the fit time to make their appeal to God, as the words following hint: 'The Lord is in his holy temple, the Lord's throne is in heaven;' in which words God is presented sitting in heaven as a temple, for their encouragement, I conceive, in such a desperate state of affairs, to direct their prayers thither for deliverance. And certainly this hath been the engine that hath been instrumental, above any, to restore this poor nation again, and set it upon the foundation of that lawful government from which it had so dangerously departed. William Gurnall.

Verse 4. The infinite understanding of God doth exactly know the sins of men; he knows so as to consider. He doth not only know them, but intently behold them: 'His eyelids try the children of men,' a metaphor taken from men, that contract the eyelids when they would accurately behold a thing: it is not a transient and careless look. Stephen Charnock.

Verse 4. 'His eyes behold,' etc. God searcheth not as man searcheth, by enquiring into that which before was hid from him; his searching is no more but his beholding; he seeth the heart, he beholdeth the reins; God's very sight is searching. Hebrews 4:13. 'All things are naked, and opened unto his eyes,' dissected or anatomised. He hath at once as exact a view of the most hidden things, the very entrails of the soul, as if they had been with never so great curiosity anatomised before him. Richard Alleine, 1611–1681.

Verse 4. 'His eyes behold,' etc. Consider that God not only sees into all you do, but he sees it to that very end that he may examine and search into it. He doth not only behold you with a common and indifferent look, but with a searching, watchful, and inquisitive eye: he pries into the reasons, the motives, the ends of all your actions. 'The Lord's throne is in heaven: his eyes behold, his eyelids try, the children of men' Revelation 1:14, where Christ is described, it is said, his eyes are as a flame of fire: you know the property of fire is to search and make trial of those things which are exposed unto it, and to separate the dross from the pure metal: so, God's eye is like fire, to try and examine the actions of men: he knows and discerns how much your very purest duties have in them of mixture, and base ends of formality, hypocrisy, distractedness, and deadness: he sees through all your specious pretenses, that which you cast as a mist before the eyes of men when yet thou art but a juggler in religion: all your tricks and sleights of outward profession, all those things that you use to cozen and delude men withal, cannot possibly impose upon him: he is a God that can look through all those fig-leaves of outward profession, and discern the nakedness of your duties through them. Ezekiel Hopkins, D.D.

Verse 4. 'His eyes behold,' etc. Take God into thy counsel. Heaven overlooks hell. God at any time can tell thee what plots are hatching there against thee. William Gurnall.

Verse 4. 'His eyes behold, his eyelids try, the children of men.' When an offender, or one accused for any offence, is brought before a judge, and stands at the bar to be arraigned, the judge looks upon him, eyes him, sets his eye upon him, and he bids the offender look up in his face: 'Look upon me,' saith the judge, 'and speak up:' guiltiness usually clouds the forehead and clothes the brow; the weight of guilt holds down the head! the evil doer hath an ill look, or dares not look up; how glad is he if the judge looks off him. We have such an expression here, speaking of the Lord, the great Judge of heaven and earth: 'His eyelids try the children of men,' as a judge tries a guilty person with his eye, and reads the characters of his wickedness printed in his face. Hence we have a common speech in our language, such a one looks suspiciously, or, he hath a guilty look. At that great gaol-delivery described in Revelation 6:16, all the prisoners cry out to be hid from the face of him that sat upon the throne. They could not look upon Christ, and they could not endure Christ should look upon them; the eyelids of Christ try the children of men . . . Wickedness cannot endure to be under the observation of any eye much less of the eye of justice. Hence the actors of it say, 'Who seeth us?' It is very hard not to show the guilt of the heart in the face, and it is as hard to have it seen there. Joseph Caryl.

Verse 5. 'The Lord trieth the righteous.' Except our sins, there is not such plenty of anything in all the world as there is of troubles which come from sin, as one heavy messenger came to Job after another. Since we are not in paradise, but in the wilderness, we must look for one trouble after another. As a bear came to David after a lion, and a giant after a bear, and a king after a giant, and Philistines after a king, so, when believers have fought with poverty. they shall fight with envy; when they have fought with envy, they shall fight with infamy; when the have fought with infamy, they shall fight with sickness; they shall be like a labourer who is never out of work. Henry Smith.

Verse 5. 'The Lord trieth the righteous.' Times of affliction and persecution will distinguish the precious from the vile, it will difference the counterfeit professor from the true. Persecution is a Christian's touchstone, it is a *lapis lydius* that will try what metal men are made of, whether they be silver or tin, gold or dross, wheat or chaff, shadow or substance, carnal or spiritual, sincere or hypocritical. Nothing speaks out more soundness and uprightness than a pursuing after holiness, even then when holiness is most afflicted, pursued, and persecuted in the world: to stand fast in fiery trials argues much integrity within. Thomas Brooks.

Verse 5. Note the singular opposition of the two sentences. God hates the wicked, and therefore in contrast he loves the righteous; but it is here said that he tries them: therefore it follows that to try and to love are with God the same thing. C. H. S.

Verse 6. 'Upon the wicked he shall rain snares.' Snares to hold them; then if they be not delivered, follow fire and brimstone, and they cannot escape. This is the case of a sinner if he repent not; if God pardon not, he is in the snare of Satan's temptation, he is in the snare of divine vengeance; let him therefore cry aloud for his deliverance, that he may have his feet in a large room. The wicked lay snares for the righteous, but God either preventeth them that their souls ever escape them, or else he subverteth them: 'The snares are broken and we are delivered.' No snares hold us so fast as those of our own sins; they keep down our heads, and stoop us that we cannot look up: a very little ease they are to him that hath not a seared conscience. Samuel Page, 1646.

Verse 6. 'He shall rain snares.' As in hunting with the lasso, the huntsman casts a snare from above upon his prey to entangle its head or feet, so shall the Lord from above with many twistings of the line of terror, surround, bind, and take captive the haters of his law. C. H. S.

Verse 6. 'He shall rain snares,' etc. He shall rain upon them when they least think of it, even in the midst of their jollity, as rain falls on a fair day. Or, he shall rain down the vengeance when he sees good, for it rains not always. Though he defers it, yet it will rain. William Nicholson, Bishop of Gloucester, in 'David's Harp Strung and Tuned,' 1662.

Verse 6. 'Upon the wicked he shall rain snares, fire and brimstone, and an horrible tempest.' The strange dispensation of affairs in this world is an argument which doth convincingly prove that there shall be such a day wherein all the entanglements of providence shall be clearly unfolded. Then shall the riddle be dissolved, why God hath given this and that profane wretch so much wealth, and so much power to do mischief: is it not that they might be destroyed for ever? Then shall they be called to a strict account for all that plenty and prosperity for which they are now envied; and the more they have abused, the more dreadful will their condemnation be. Then it will be seen that God gave them not as mercies, but as 'snares.' It is said that God 'will rain on the wicked snares, fire and brimstone, and an horrible tempest:' when he scatters abroad the desirable things of this world, riches, honours, pleasures, etc., then he rains 'snares' upon them; and when he shall call them to an account for these things, then he will rain upon them 'fire and brimstone, and an horrible tempest' of his wrath and fury. Dives, who caroused on earth, yet, in hell could not obtain so much as one poor drop of water to cool his scorched and flaming tongue: had not his excess and intemperance been so great in his life, his fiery thirst had not been so tormenting after death; and therefore, in that sad item that Abraham gives him (Luke 16:25), he bids him 'remember that thou, in thy lifetime, receivedst thy good things, and likewise Lazarus evil things; but now he is comforted, and thou art tormented.' I look upon this as a most bitter and a most deserved sarcasm; upbraiding him for his gross folly, in making the trifles of this life his good things. Thou hast received thy good things, but now thou art tormented. Oh, never call Dives' purple and delicious fare good things, if they thus end in torments! Was it good for him to be wrapped in purple who is now wrapped in flames? Was it good for him to fare deliciously who was only thereby fatted up against the day of slaughter? Ezekiel Hopkins.

Verse 6. 'Snares, fire and brimstone, storm and tempest: this shall be the portion of their cup.' After the judgment follows the condemnation: pre-figured as we have seen, by the overthrow of Sodom and Gomorrah. 'Snares:' because the allurements of Satan in this life will be their worst punishments in the next; the fire of anger, the brimstone of impurity, the tempest of pride, the lust of the flesh, the lust of the eyes, and the pride of life. 'This shall be their portion;' compare it with the psalmist's own saying, 'The Lord himself is the portion of my inheritance and my cup' Psalm 16:5. Cassidorus, in J. M. Neale's Commentary.

Verse 6. 'The portion of their cup.' Hebrew, the allotment of their cup. The expression has reference to the custom of distributing to each guest his mess of meat. William French and George Skinner, 1842.

Verse 7. That God may give grace without glory is intelligible; but to admit a man to communion with him in glory without grace, is not intelligible. It is not agreeable to God's holiness to make any inhabitant of heaven, and converse freely with him in a way of intimate love, without such a qualification of grace: 'The righteous Lord loveth righteousness; his countenance doth behold the upright;' he looks upon him with a smiling eye, and therefore he cannot favourably look upon an unrighteous person; so that this necessity is not founded only in the command of God that we should be renewed, but in the very nature of the thing, because God, in regard to his holiness, cannot converse with an impure creature. God must change his nature, or the sinner's nature must be changed. There can be no friendly communion between two of different natures without the change of one of them into the likeness of the other. Wolves and sheep, darkness and light, can never agree. God cannot love a sinner as a sinner, because he hates impurity by a necessity of nature as well as a choice of will. It is as impossible for him to love it as to cease to be holy. Stephen Charnock.

Hints to the village preacher

Verse 1. Faith's bold avowal, and brave refusal.

Verse 1. Teacheth us to trust in God, how great soever our dangers be; also that we shall be many times assaulted to make us put far from us this trust, but yet that we must cleave unto it, as the anchor of our souls, sure and steadfast. Thomas Wilcocks.

Verse 1. The advice of cowardice, and the jeer of insolence, both answered by faith. Lesson – Attempt no other answer.

Verse 2. The craftiness of our spiritual enemies.

Verse 3. This may furnish a double discourse:

1. If God's oath and promise could remove, what could we do? Here the answer is easy.

2. If all earthly things fail, and the very State fall to pieces, what can we do? We can suffer joyfully, hope cheerfully, wait patiently, pray earnestly, believe confidently, and triumph finally.

Verse 3. Necessity of holding and preaching foundation truths.

Verse 4. The elevation, mystery, supremacy, purity, everlastingness, invisibility, etc., of the throne of God.

Verses 4, 5. In these verses mark the fact that the children of men, as well as the righteous, are tried; work out the contrast between the two trials in their designs and results, etc.

Verse 5. 'The Lord trieth the righteous.'

1. Who are tried?
2. What in them is tried? – Faith, love, etc.
3. In what manner? – Trials of every sort.
4. How long?
5. For what purpose?

Verse 5. 'His soul hateth.' The thoroughness of God's hatred of sin. Illustrate by providential judgments, threatenings, sufferings of the Surety, and the terrors of hell.

Verse 5. The trying of the gold, and the sweeping out of the refuse.

Verse 6. 'He shall rain.' Gracious rain and destroying rain.

Verse 6. The portion of the impenitent.

Verse 7. The Lord possesses righteousness as a personal attribute, loves it in the abstract, and blesses those who practise it.

Psalm 14

Title

This admirable ode is simply headed 'To the Chief Musician, by David.' The dedication to the Chief Musician stands at the head of fifty-three of the Psalms, and clearly indicates that such psalms were intended, not merely for the private use of believers, but to be sung in the great assemblies by the appointed choir at whose head was the overseer, or superintendent, called in our version, 'the Chief Musician,' and by Ainsworth, 'the Master of the Music.' Several of these psalms have little or no praise in them, and were not addressed directly to the Most High, and yet were to be sung in public worship; which is a clear indication that the theory of Augustine lately revived by certain hymn-book makers, that nothing but praise should be sung, is far more plausible than scriptural. Not only did the ancient Church chant hallowed doctrine and offer prayer amid her spiritual songs, but even the wailing notes of complaint were put into her mouth by the sweet singer of Israel who was inspired of God. Some persons grasp at any nicety which has a gloss of apparent correctness upon it, and are pleased with being more fancifully precise than others; nevertheless it will ever be the way of plain men, not only to magnify the Lord in sacred canticles, but also, according to Paul's precept, to teach and admonish one another in psalms and hymns and spiritual songs, singing with grace in their hearts unto the Lord.

As no distinguishing title is given to this Psalm, we would suggest as an assistance to the memory, the heading CONCERNING PRACTICAL ATHEISM. The many conjectures as to the occasion upon which it was written are so completely without foundation, that it would be a waste of time to mention them at length. The apostle Paul, in Romans 3, has shown incidentally that the drift of the inspired writer is to show that both Jews and Gentiles are all under sin; there was, therefore, no reason for fixing upon any particular historical occasion, when all of history reeks with terrible evidence of human corruption. With instructive alterations, David has given us in Psalm 53 a second edition of this humiliating psalm, being moved of the Holy Ghost thus doubly to declare a truth which is ever distasteful to carnal minds.

Division
The world's foolish creed (verse 1); its practical influence in corrupting morals, 1, 2, 3. The persecuting tendencies of sinners, 4; their alarms, 5; their ridicule of the godly, 6; and a prayer for the manifestation of the Lord to his people's joy.

Exposition
Verse 1. 'The fool.' The Atheist is the fool pre-eminently, and a fool universally. He would not deny God if he were not a fool by nature, and having denied God it is no marvel that he becomes a fool in practice. Sin is always folly, and as it is the height of sin to attack the very existence of the Most High, so it is also the greatest imaginable folly. To say there is no God is to belie the plainest evidence, which is obstinacy; to oppose the common consent of mankind, which is stupidity; to stifle consciousness, which is madness. If the sinner could by his atheism destroy the God whom he hates there were some sense, although much wickedness, in his infidelity; but as denying the existence of fire does not prevent its burning a man who is in it, so doubting the existence of God will not stop the Judge of all the earth from destroying the rebel who breaks his laws; nay, this atheism is a crime which much provokes heaven, and will bring down terrible vengeance on the fool who indulges it. The proverb says, 'A fool's tongue cuts his own throat,' and in this instance it kills both soul and body for ever: would to God the mischief stopped even there, but alas! one fool makes hundreds, and a noisy blasphemer spreads his horrible doctrines as lepers spread the plague. Ainsworth, in his 'Annotations,' tells us that the word here used is Nabal, which has the signification of fading, dying, or falling away, as a

withered leaf or flower; it is a title given to the foolish man as having lost the juice and sap of wisdom, reason, honesty, and godliness. Trapp hits the mark when he calls him 'that sapless fellow, that carcase of a man, that walking sepulchre of himself, in whom all religion and right reason is withered and wasted, dried up and decayed'. Some translate it the apostate, and others the wretch. With what earnestness should we shun the appearance of doubt as to the presence, activity, power and love of God, for all such mistrust is of the nature of folly, and who among us would wish to be ranked with the fool in the text? Yet let us never forget that all unregenerate men are more or less such fools.

The fool 'hath said in his heart.' May a man with his mouth profess to believe, and yet in heart say the reverse? Had he hardly become audacious enough to utter his folly with his tongue? Did the Lord look upon his thoughts as being in the nature of words to Him though not to man? Is this where man first becomes an unbeliever? – in his heart, not in his head? And when he talks atheistically, is it a foolish heart speaking, and endeavouring to clamour down the voice of conscience? We think so. If the affections were set upon truth and righteousness, the understanding would have no difficulty in settling the question of a present personal Deity, but as the heart dislikes the good and the right, it is no wonder that it desires to be rid of that Elohim, who is the great moral Governor, the Patron of rectitude and the Punisher of iniquity. While men's hearts remain what they are, we must not be surprised at the prevalence of scepticism; a corrupt tree will bring forth corrupt fruit. 'Every man,' says Dickson, 'so long as he lieth unrenewed and unreconciled to God is nothing in effect but a madman.' What wonder then if he raves? Such fools as those we are now dealing with are common to all time, and all countries; they grow without watering, and are found all the world over. The spread of mere intellectual enlightenment will not diminish their number, for since it is an affair of the heart, this folly and great learning will often dwell together. To answer sceptical cavillings will be labour lost until grace enters to make the mind willing to believe; fools can raise more objections in an hour than wise men can answer in seven years, indeed it is their mirth to set stools for wise men to stumble over. Let the preacher aim at the heart, and preach the all-conquering love of Jesus, and he will by God's grace win more doubters to the faith of the gospel than any hundred of the best reasoners who only direct their arguments to the head.

'The fool hath said in his heart, There is no God,' or 'no God.' So monstrous is the assertion, that the man hardly dared to put it as a positive statement, but went very near to doing so. Calvin seems to regard this saying, 'no God,' as hardly amounting to a syllogism, scarcely reaching to a positive, dogmatical declaration; but Dr Alexander clearly shows that it does. It is not merely the wish of the sinner's corrupt nature, and the hope of his rebellious heart, but he manages after a fashion to bring himself to assert it, and at certain seasons he thinks that he believes it. It is a solemn reflection that some who worship God with their lips may in their hearts be saying, 'no God.' It is worthy of observation that he does not say there is no Jehovah, but there is no Elohim; Deity in the abstract is not so much the object of attack, as the covenant, personal, ruling and governing presence of God in the world. God as ruler, lawgiver, worker, Saviour, is the butt at which the arrows of human wrath are shot. How impotent the malice! How mad the rage which raves and foams against Him in whom we live and move and have our being! How horrible the insanity which leads a man who owes his all to God to cry out, 'No God'! How terrible the depravity which makes the whole race adopt this as their hearts' desire, 'no God!'

'They are corrupt.' This refers to all men, and we have the warrant of the Holy Ghost for so saying; see the third chapter of the epistle to the Romans. Where there is enmity to God, there is deep, inward depravity of mind. The words are rendered by eminent critics in an active sense, 'they have done corruptly:' this may serve to remind us that sin is not only in our nature passively as the source of evil, but we ourselves actively fan the flame and corrupt ourselves, making that blacker still which was black as darkness itself already. We rivet our own chains by habit and continuance.

'They have done abominable works.' When men begin with renouncing the Most High God, who shall tell where they will end? When the Master's eyes are put out, what will not the servants do? Observe the state of the world before the flood, as portrayed in Genesis 6:12, and remember that human nature is unchanged. He who would see a terrible photograph of the world without God must read that most painful of all inspired Scriptures, the first chapter of the epistle to the Romans.

'There is none that doeth good.' Sins of omission must abound where transgressions are rife. Those who do the things which they ought not to have done, are sure to leave undone those things which they ought to have done. What a picture of our race is this! Save only where grace reigns, there is none that doeth good; humanity, fallen and debased, is a desert without an oasis, a night without a star, a dunghill without a jewel, a hell without a bottom.

Verse 2. 'The Lord looked down from heaven upon the children of men.' As from a watch-tower, or other elevated place of observation, the Lord is represented as gazing intently upon men. He will not punish blindly, nor like a tyrant command an indiscriminate massacre because a rumour of rebellion has come up to his ears. What condescending interest and impartial justice are here imaged! The case of Sodom, visited before it was overthrown, illustrates the careful manner in which Divine Justice beholds the sin before it avenges it, and searches out the righteous that they perish not with the guilty. Behold then the eyes of Omniscience ransacking the globe, and prying among every people and nation, 'to see if there were any that did understand and seek God.' He who is looking down knows the good, is quick to discern it, would be delighted to find it; but as he views all the unregenerate children of men his search is fruitless, for of all the race of Adam, no unrenewed soul is other than an enemy to God and goodness. The objects of the Lord's search are not wealthy men, great men, or learned men; these, with all they can offer, cannot meet the demands of the great Governor: at the same time, he is not looking for superlative eminence in virtue, he seeks for any that understand themselves, their state, their duty, their destiny, their happiness; he looks for any that seek God, who, if there be a God, are willing and anxious to find him out. Surely this is not too great a matter to expect; for if men have not yet known God, if they have any right understanding, they will seek him. Alas! even this low degree of good is not to be found even by him who sees all things: but men love the hideous negation of 'No God,' and with their backs to their Creator, who is the sun of their life, they journey into the dreary region of unbelief and alienation, which is a land of darkness as darkness itself, and of the shadow of death without any order and where the light is as darkness.

Verse 3. 'They are all gone aside.' Without exception, all men have apostatised from the Lord their Maker, from his laws, and from all the eternal principles of right. Like stubborn heifers they have sturdily refused to receive the yoke, like errant sheep they have found a gap and left the right field. The original speaks of the race as a whole, as a totality; and humanity as a whole has become depraved in heart and defiled in life. 'They have altogether become filthy;' as a whole they are spoiled and soured like corrupt leaven, or, as some put it, they have become putrid and even stinking. The only reason why we do not more clearly see this foulness is because we are accustomed to it, just as those who work daily among offensive odours at last cease to smell them. The miller does not observe the noise of his own mill, and we are slow to discover our own ruin and depravity. But are there no special cases, are all men sinful? 'Yes,' says the Psalmist, in a manner not to be mistaken, 'they are.' He has put it positively, he repeats it negatively, 'There is none that doeth good, no, not one.' The Hebrew phrase is an utter denial concerning any mere man that he of himself doeth good. What can be more sweeping? This is the verdict of the all-seeing Jehovah, who cannot exaggerate or mistake. As if no hope of finding a solitary specimen of a good man among the unrenewed human family might be harboured for an instant. The Holy Spirit is not content with saying all and altogether, but adds the crushing threefold negative, 'none, no, not one.' What say the opponents to the doctrine of natural depravity to this? Rather what do we feel concerning it? Do we not confess that we by nature are corrupt, and do we not bless the sovereign grace which has renewed us in the spirit of our minds, that sin may no more have dominion over us, but that grace may rule and reign?

Verse 4. Hatred of God and corruptness of life are the motive forces which produce persecution. Men who having no saving knowledge of divine things, enslave themselves to become workers of iniquity, have no heart to cry to the Lord for deliverance, but seek to amuse themselves with devouring the poor and despised people of God. It is hard bondage to be a 'worker of iniquity;' a worker at the galleys, or in the mines of Siberia, is not more truly degraded and wretched; the toil is hard and the reward dreadful: those who have no knowledge choose such slavery, but those who are taught of God cry to be rescued from it. The same ignorance which keeps men bondsmen to evil, makes them hate the freeborn sons of God; hence they seek to eat them up 'as they eat bread,' – daily, ravenously, as though it were an ordinary, usual, everyday matter to oppress the saints of God. As pikes in a pond eat up little fish, as eagles prey on smaller birds, as wolves rend the sheep of the pasture, so sinners naturally and as a matter of course, persecute, malign, and mock the followers of the Lord Jesus. While thus preying, they forswear all praying, and in this act consistently, for how could they hope to be heard while their hands are full of blood?

Verse 5. Oppressors have it not all their own way, they have their fits of trembling and their appointed seasons of overthrow. There – where they denied God and hectored against his people; there – where they thought of peace and safety, they were made to quail. 'There were they' – these very loud-mouthed, iron-handed, proud-hearted Nimrods and Herods, those heady, high-minded sinners – 'there were they in great fear.' A panic terror seized them: 'they feared a fear,' as the Hebrew puts it; an undefinable, horrible, mysterious dread crept over them. The most hardened of men have their periods when conscience casts them into a cold sweat of alarm. As cowards are cruel, so all cruel men are at heart cowards. The ghost of past sin is a terrible spectre to haunt any man, and though unbelievers may boast as loudly as they will, a sound is in their ears which makes them ill at ease.

'For God is in the generation of the righteous.' This makes the company of godly men so irksome to the wicked because they perceive that God is with them. Shut their eyes as they may, they cannot but perceive the image of God in the character of his truly gracious people, nor can they fail to see that he works for their deliverance. Like Haman, they instinctively feel a trembling when they see God's Mordecais. Even though the saint may be in a mean position, mourning at the gate where the persecutor rejoices in state, the sinner feels the influence of the believer's true nobility and quails before it, for God is there. Let scoffers beware, for they persecute the Lord Jesus when they molest his people; the union is very close between God and his people, it amounts to a mysterious indwelling, for God is in the generation of the righteous.

Verse 6. Notwithstanding their real cowardice, the wicked put on the lion's skin and lord it over the Lord's poor ones. Though fools themselves, they mock at the truly wise as if the folly were on their side; but this is what might be expected, for how should brutish minds appreciate excellence, and how can those who have owl's eyes admire the sun? The special point and butt of their jest seems to be the confidence of the godly in their Lord. What can your God do for you now? Who is that God who can deliver out of our hand? Where is the reward of all your praying and beseeching? Taunting questions of this sort they thrust into the faces of weak but gracious souls, and tempt them to feel ashamed of their refuge. Let us not be laughed out of our confidence by them, let us scorn their scorning and defy their jeers; we shall need to wait but a little, and then the Lord our refuge will avenge his own elect, and ease himself of his adversaries, who once made so light of him and of his people.

Verse 6. Natural enough is this closing prayer, for what would so effectually convince atheists, overthrow persecutors, stay sin, and secure the godly, as the manifest appearance of Israel's great Salvation? The coming of Messiah was the desire of the godly in all ages, and though he has already come with a sin-offering to purge away iniquity, we look for him to come a second time, to come without a sin-offering unto salvation. O that these weary years would have an end! Why tarries he so long? He knows that sin abounds and that his people are down-trodden; why comes he not to the rescue? His glorious advent will restore his ancient people from literal captivity, and his SPIRITUAL seed from spiritual sorrow. Wrestling Jacob and prevailing Israel shall alike rejoice before him when he is revealed as their salvation. O that he were come! What happy, holy, halcyon, heavenly days should we then see! But let us not count him slack, for behold he comes, he comes quickly! Blessed are all they that wait for him.

Explanatory notes and quaint sayings

Whole Psalm. There is a peculiar mark put upon this Psalm, in that it is twice in the Book of psalms. The fourteenth Psalm and the fifty-third Psalm are the same, with the alteration of one or two expressions at most. And there is another mark put upon it, that the apostle transcribes a great part of it. Romans 3:10–12.

It contains a description of a most deplorable state of things in the world – ay, in Israel; a most deplorable state, by reason of the general corruption that was befallen all sorts of men, in their principles, and in their practices, and in their opinions.

First, it was a time when there was a mighty prevalent principle of atheism got into the world, got among the great men of the world. Saith he, 'That is their principle, they say in their hearts, 'There is no God." It is true, they did not absolutely profess it; but it was the principle whereby all their actings were regulated, and which they conformed unto. 'The fool,' saith he, 'hath said in his heart, There is no God.' Not this or that particular man, but the fool – that is, those foolish men; for in the next word he tells you, 'They are corrupt;' and verse 3, 'They are all gone aside.' 'The fool' is taken indefinitely for the great company and society of foolish men, to intimate that whatsoever they were divided about else, they were all agreed in this. 'They are all a company of atheists,' saith he, 'practical atheists.'

Secondly, their affections were suitable to this principle, as all men's affections and actions are suitable to their principles. What are you to expect from men whose principle is, that there is no God? Why, saith he, for their affections, 'They are corrupt;' which he expresseth again (verse 3), 'They are all gone aside, they are altogether become filthy.' 'All gone aside.' The word in the original is, 'They are all grown sour;' as drink, that hath been formerly of some use, but when grown vapid – lost all its spirits and life – it is an insipid thing, good for nothing. And, saith he, 'They are altogether become filthy' – 'become stinking,' as the margin hath it. They have corrupt affections, that have left them no life, no savour; but stinking, corrupt lusts prevail in them universally. They say, 'There is no God;' and they are filled with stinking, corrupt lusts.

Thirdly, if this be their principle and these their affections, let us look after their actions, to see if they be any better. But consider their actions. They be of two sorts: 1. How they act in the world, 2. How they act toward the people of God.

1.   How do they act in the world? Why, consider that, as to their duties which they omit, and as to the wickednesses which they perform. What good do they do? Nay, saith he, 'None of them doeth good.' Yea, some of them. 'No, not one.' Saith he, verses 1, 3, 'There is none that doeth good, no, not one.' If there was any one among them that did attend to what was really good, and useful in the world, there was some hope. 'No,' saith he, 'their principle is atheism, their affections are corrupt; and for good, there is not one of them doeth any good – they omit all duties.'

What do they do for evil? Why, saith he, 'They have done abominable works' – 'works,' saith he, 'not to be named, not to be spoken of – works which God abhors, which all good men abhor.' 'Abominable works,' saith he, 'such as the very light of nature would abhor;' and give me leave to use the expression of the psalmist – 'stinking, filthy works.' So he doth describe the state and condition of things under the reign of Saul, when he wrote this Psalm.

2.   'If thus it be with them, and if thus it be with their own ways, yet they let the people of God alone; they will not add that to the rest of their sins.' Nay, it is quite otherwise, saith he, 'They eat up my people as they eat bread.' 'Those workers of iniquity have no knowledge, who eat up my people as they eat bread, and call not upon the Lord.' What is the reason why he brings it in in that manner? Why could he not say, 'They have no knowledge that do such abominable things;' but brings it in thus, 'They have no knowledge who eat up my people as they eat bread?' 'It is strange, that after all my dealings with them and declaration of my will, they should be so brutish as not to know this would be their ruin. Don't they know this will devour them, destroy them, and be called over again in a particular manner? In the midst of all the sins, and greatest and highest provocations that are in the world, God lays a special weight upon the eating of his people. They may feed upon their own lusts what they will; but, 'Have they no knowledge, that they eat up my people as they eat bread?'

There are very many things that might be observed from all this; but I aim to give but a few hints from the Psalms.

Well, what is the state of things now? You see what it was with them. How was it with the providence of God in reference unto them? Which is strange, and a man would scarce believe it in such a course as this is, he tells you (verse 5), notwithstanding all this, they were in great fear. 'There were they in great fear,' saith he. May be so, for they saw some evil coming upon them. No, there was nothing but the hand of God in it; for in Psalm 53:5, where these words are repeated, it is, 'There were they in great fear, where no fear was' – no visible cause of fear yet they were in great fear.

God by his providence seldom gives an absolute, universal security unto men in their height of sin, and oppression, and sensuality, and lusts; but he will secretly put them in fear where no fear is: and though there be nothing seen that should cause them to have any fear, they shall act like men at their wits' end with fear.

But whence should this fear arise? Saith he, it ariseth from hence, 'For God is in the generation of the righteous.' Plainly they see their work doth not go on; their meat doth not digest with them; their bread doth not go well down. 'They were eating and devouring my people, and when they came to devour them, they found God was among them (they could not digest their bread); and this put them in fear; quite surprised them.' They came, and thought to have found them a sweet morsel: when engaged, God was there filling their mouth and teeth with gravel; and he began to break out the jawbone of the terrible ones when they came to feed upon them. Saith he, 'God was there' (verse 5).

The Holy Ghost gives an account of the state of things that was between those two sorts of people he had described – between the fool and the people of God – them that were devouring, and them that had been utterly devoured, had not God been among them. Both were in fear – they that were to be devoured, and those that did devour. And they took several ways for their relief; and he showeth what those ways were, and what judgment they made upon the ways of one another. Saith he, 'Ye have shamed the counsel of the poor, because the Lord is his refuge.'

There are the persons spoken of – they are 'the poor;' and that is those who are described in the verses foregoing, the people that were ready to be eaten up and devoured.

And there is the hope and refuge that these poor had in such a time as this, when all things were in fear; and that was 'the LORD.' The poor maketh the Lord his refuge.

And you may observe here, that as he did describe all the wicked as one man, 'the fool,' so he describes all his own people as one man, 'the poor' – that is, the poor man: 'Because the LORD is his refuge.' He keeps it in the singular number. Whatsoever the people of God may differ in, they are all as one man in this business.

And there is the way whereby these poor make God their refuge. They do it by 'counsel,' saith he. It is not a thing they do by chance, but they look upon it as their wisdom. They do it upon consideration, upon advice. It is a thing of great wisdom.

Well, what thoughts have the others concerning this acting of theirs? The poor make God their refuge; and they do it by counsel. What judgment, now, doth the world make of this counsel of theirs? Why, they 'shame it;' that is, they cast shame upon it, contemn it as a very foolish thing, to make the Lord their refuge. 'Truly, if they could make this or that great man their refuge, it were something; but to make the Lord their refuge, this is the foolishest thing in the world,' say they. To shame men's counsel, to despise their counsel as foolish, is as great contempt as they can lay upon them.

Here you see the state of things as they are represented in this Psalm, and spread before the Lord: which being laid down, the psalmist showeth what our duty is upon such a state of things – what is the duty of the people of God, things thus being stated. Saith he, 'Their way is to go to prayer:' verse 7, 'O that the salvation of Israel were come out of Zion! when the Lord bringeth back the captivity of his people, Jacob shall rejoice, and Israel shall be glad.' If things are thus stated, then cry, then pray, 'O that the salvation of Israel were come out of Zion,' etc. There shall a revenue of praise come to God out of Zion, to the rejoicing of his people. John Owen.

Verse 1. 'The fool.' That sapless fellow, that carcase of a man, that walking sepulchre of himself, in whom all religion and right reason is withered and wasted, dried up and decayed. That apostate in whom natural principles are extinct, and from whom God is departed, as when the prince is departed, hangings are taken down. That mere animal that hath no more than a reasonable soul, and for little other purpose than as salt, to keep his body from putrefying. That wicked man hereafter described, that studieth atheism. John Trapp.

Verse 1. 'The fool,' etc. The world we live in is a world of fools. The far greater part of mankind act a part entirely irrational. So great is their infatuation, that they prefer time to eternity, momentary enjoyments to those that shall never have an end, and listen to the testimony of Satan in preference to that of God. Of all folly, that is the greatest, which relates to eternal objects, because it is the most fatal, and when persisted in through life, entirely remediless. A mistake in the management of temporal concerns may be afterwards rectified. At any rate, it is comparatively of little importance. But an error in spiritual and eternal matters, as it is in itself of the greatest moment, if carried through life, can never be remedied; because after death there is no redemption. The greatest folly that any creature is capable of, is that of denying or entertaining unjust apprehensions of the being and perfections of the great Creator. Therefore in a way of eminence, the appellation of fool is given by the Spirit of God, to him who is chargeable with this guilt. 'The fool hath said in his heart, There is no God.' John Jamieson, M.A., 1789.

Verse 1. 'The fool,' a term in Scripture signifying a wicked man, used also by the heathen philosophers to signify a vicious person, (Heb.) as coming from (Heb.) signifies the extinction of life in men, animals, and plants; so the word (Heb.) is taken Isaiah 40:7, (Heb.) 'the flower fadeth' (Isaiah 28:1), a plant that hath lost all that juice that made it lovely and useful. So, a fool is one that hath lost his wisdom and right notion of God and divine things, which were communicated to man by creation; one dead in sin, yet one not so much void of rational faculties, as of grace in those faculties; not one that wants a reason, but abuses his reason. Stephen Charnock.

Verse 1. 'The fool hath said,' etc. This folly is bound up in every heart. It is bound, but it is not tongue-tied; it speaks blasphemous things against God, it says there is 'no God.' There is a difference indeed in the language: gross sins speak this louder, there are crying sins; but though less sins speak it not so loud, they whisper it. But the Lord can hear the language of the heart, the whisperings of its motions, as plainly as we hear one another in our ordinary discourse. Oh, how heinous is the least sin, which is so injurious to the very being of the great God! David Clarkson.

Verse 1. 'The fool hath said in his heart, There is no God.' If you will turn over some few leaves, as far as the fifty-third Psalm, you shall not only find my text, but this whole Psalm, without any alteration, save only in the fifth verse, and that not at all in the sense neither. What shall we say? Took the Holy Spirit of God such especial particular notice of the sayings and deeds of a fool, that one expression of them would not serve the turn? Or, does that babbling and madness of a fool so much concern us, as that we need to have them urged upon us once and again, and a third time in the third of the Romans? Surely not any one of us present here, is this fool! Nay, if one of us could but tell where to find such a fool as this, that would offer to say, though in his heart, 'There is no God,' he should not rest in quiet, he should soon perceive we were not of his faction. We that are able to tell David an article or two of faith more than ever he was acquainted with! Nay, more; can we with any imaginable ground of reason be supposed liable to any suspicion of atheism, that are able to read to David a lecture out of his own Psalms, and explain the meaning of his own prophecies much clearer than himself which held the pen to the Holy Spirit of God? Though we cannot deny but that in other things there may be found some spice of folly and imperfection in us, but it cannot be imagined that we, who are almost cloyed with heavenly manna of God's word, that can instruct our teachers, and are able to maintain opinions and tenets, the scruples whereof not both the universities in this land, nor the whole clergy are able to resolve, that it should be possible for us ever to come to that perfection and excellency of folly and madness, as to entertain thought that there is no God: nay, we are not so uncharitable as to charge a Turk or an infidel with such a horrible imputation as this.

Beloved Christians, be not wise in your own conceits: if you will seriously examine the third of Romans (which I mentioned before), you shall find that Paul, out of this Psalm, and the like words of Isaiah, doth conclude the whole posterity of Adam (Christ only excepted), under sin and the curse of God; which inference of his were weak and inconcluding, unless every man of his own nature were such a one as the prophet here describes; and the same apostle in another place expresses, 'Even altogether without God in the world,' i.e., not maintaining it as an opinion which they would undertake by force of argument to confirm. That there is no God: for we read not of above three or four among the heathens, that were of any fashion, which went this far; but such as though in their discourse and serious thoughts they do not question a deity, but would abhor any man that would not liberally allow unto God all his glorious attributes, yet in their hearts and affections they deny him; they live as if there was no God, having no respect at all to him in all their projects, and therefore, indeed and in God's esteem, become formally, and in strict propriety of speech, very atheists. William Chillingworth, 1602–1643.

Verse 1. 'The fool hath said in his heart, There is no God.' Why do men resist God's authority, against which they cannot dispute? and disobey his commands, unto which they cannot devise to frame an exception? What but the spirit of enmity, can make them regret 'so easy a yoke,' reject so 'light a burden,' shun and fly off from so peaceful and pleasant paths? yea, and take ways that so manifestly 'take hold of hell, and lead down to the chambers of death,' rather choosing to perish than obey? Is not this the very height of enmity? What further proof would we seek of a disaffected and implacable heart? Yet to all this we may cast in that fearful addition, their saying in their heart, 'No God;' as much as to say, 'O that there were none!' This is enmity not only to the highest pitch of wickedness, to wish their common parent extinct, the author of their being, but even unto madness itself. For in the forgetful heat of this transport, it is not thought on that they wish the most absolute impossibility; and that, if it were possible, they wish, with his, the extinction of their own and of all being; and that the sense of their hearts, put into words, would amount to no less than a direful and most horrid execration and curse upon God and the whole creation of God at once! As if, by the blasphemy of their poisonous breath, they would wither all nature, blast the whole universe of being, and make it fade, languish, and drop into nothing. This is to set their mouth against heaven and earth, themselves, and all things at once, as if they thought their feeble breath should overpower the omnipotent Word, shake and shiver the adamantine pillars of heaven and earth, and the Almighty fiat be defeated by their nay, striking at the root of all! So fitly is it said, 'The fool hath in his heart' muttered thus. Nor are there few such fools; but this is plainly given us as the common character of apostate man, the whole revolted race, of whom it is said in very general terms, 'They are all gone back, there is none that doeth good.' This is their sense, one and all, that is, comparatively; and the true state of the case being laid before them, it is more their temper and sense to say, 'No God,' than to repent, 'and turn to him.' What mad enmity is this! Nor can we devise into what else to resolve it. John Howe.

Verse 1. 'The fool hath said in his heart, there is no God.' He that shall deny there is a God, sins with a very high hand against the light of nature; for every creature, yea, the least gnat and fly, and the meanest worm that crawls upon the ground will confute and confound that man that disputes whether there be a God or no. The name of God is written in such full, fair, and shining characters upon the whole creation, that all men may run and read that there is a God. The notion of a deity is so strongly and deeply impressed upon the tables of all men's hearts, that to deny a God is to quench the very principles of common nature; yea, it is formally a killing of God, as much a sin the creature lies. There are none of these atheists in hell, for the devils believe and tremble. James 2:19. The Greek word *priddoudi*, that is here used, signifies properly the roaring of the sea; it implies such an extreme fear, as causeth not only trembling, but also a roaring and screeching out. Mark 6:49; Acts 16:29. The devils believe and acknowledge four articles of our faith. Matthew 8:29: 1. They acknowledge God; 2. Christ; 3. The day of judgment; (4) That they shall be tormented then; so that he doth not believe that there is a God, is more vile than a devil. To deny there is a God, is a sort of atheism that is not to be found in hell.

> On earth are atheists many,
> In hell there is not any.

Augustine, speaking of atheists, saith, 'That albeit there be some who think, or would persuade themselves, that there is no God, yet the most vile and desperate wretch that ever lived would not say, there was no God.' Seneca hath a remarkable speech, *Mentiuntur qui dicunt se non sentire Deum esse: nam etsi tibi affirmant interdi – noctu tamen dubitant.* They lie, saith he, who say they perceive not there is a God; for although they affirm it to thee in the daytime, yet by night they doubt of it. Further, saith the same author, I have heard of some that deny that there was a God; yet never knew the man, but when he was sick he would seek unto God for help; therefore they do but lie that say there is no God; they sin against the light of their own consciences; they who most studiously go about to deny God, yet cannot do it but some check of conscience will fly in their faces. Tully would say that there was never any nation under heaven so barbarous as to deny that there was a God. T. Brooks.

Verse 1. 'The fool hath said in his heart, There is no God.' Popery has not won to itself so great wits as atheism; it is the superfluity of wit that makes atheists. These will not be beaten down with impertinent arguments; disordered hail-shot of Scriptures will never scare them; they must be convinced and beaten by their own weapons. 'Hast thou appealed to Caesar? To Caesar thou shalt go.' Have they appealed to reason? Let us bring reason to them, that we may bring them to reason. We need not fear the want of weapons in that armoury, but our own ignorance and want of skill to use them. There is enough even in philosophy to convince atheism, and make them confess, 'We are foiled with our own weapons;' for with all their wit atheists are fools. Thomas Adams.

Verse 1. As there is no wound more mortal than that which plucketh forth man's heart or soul; so, likewise, is there no person or pestilence of greater force suddenly in men to kill all faith, hope, and charity, with the fear of God, and consequently to cast them headlong into the pit of hell, than to deny the principle and foundation of all religion – namely, that there is a God. Robert Cawdray's 'Treasury or Storehouse of Similes,' 1609.

Verse 1. 'The fool hath said in his heart, There is no God.' Who in the world is a verier fool, a more ignorant, wretched person, than he that is an atheist? A man may better believe there is no such man as himself, and that he is not in being, than that there is no God; for himself can cease to be, and once was not, and shall be changed from what he is, and in very many periods of his life knows not that he is; and so it is every night with him when he sleeps; but none of these can happen to God; and if he knows it not, he is a fool. Can anything in this world be more foolish than to think that all this rare fabric of heaven and earth can come by chance, when all the skill of art is not able to make an oyster? To see rare effects, and no cause; an excellent government and no prince; a motion without an immovable; a circle without a centre; a time without eternity; a second without a first; a thing that begins not from itself, and therefore, not to perceive there is something from whence it does begin, which must be without beginning; these things are so against philosophy and natural reason, that he must needs be a beast in his understanding that does not assent to them; this is the atheist: 'The fool hath said in his heart, There is no God.' That is his character; the thing framed, says that nothing framed it; the tongue never made itself to speak, and yet talks against him that did; saying, that which is made, is, and that which made it, is not. But this folly is as infinite as hell, as much without light or bound, as the chaos or the primitive nothing. Jeremy Taylor, 1613–1667.

Verse 1. 'The fool hath said in his heart, There is no God.' A wise man, that lives up to the principles of reason and virtue, if one considers him in his solitude as taking in the system of the universe, observing the mutual dependence and harmony by which the whole frame of it hangs together, beating down his passions, or swelling his thoughts with magnificent ideas of providence, makes a nobler figure in the eye of an intelligent being, than the greatest conqueror amidst the pomp and solemnities of a triumph. On the contrary, there is not a more ridiculous animal than an atheist in his retirement. His mind is incapable of rapture or elevation: he can only consider himself as an insignificant figure in a landscape, and wandering up and down in a field or a meadow, under the same terms as the meanest animals about him, and as subject to as total a mortality as they, with this aggravation, that he is the only one amongst them who lies under the apprehension of it. In distresses he must be of all creatures the most helpless and forlorn; he feels the whole pressure of a present calamity, without being relieved by the memory of anything that is past, or the prospect of anything that is to come. Annihilation is the greatest blessing that he proposes to himself, and a halter or a pistol the only refuge he can fly to. But if you would behold one of these gloomy miscreants in his poorest figure, you must consider him under the terrors or at the approach of death. About thirty years ago, I was a shipboard with one of these vermin, when there arose a brisk gale, which could frighten nobody but himself. Upon the rolling of the ship he fell upon his knees, and confessed to the chaplain, that he had been a vile atheist, and had denied a Supreme Being ever since he came to his estate. The good man was astonished, and a report immediately ran through the ship, that there was an atheist upon the upper deck. Several of the common seamen, who had never heard the word before, thought it had been some strange fish; but they were more surprised when they saw it was a man, and heard out of his own mouth, 'That he never believed till that day that there was a God.' As he lay in the agonies of confession, one of the honest tars whispered to the boatswain, 'That it would be a good deed to heave him overboard.' But we were now within sight of a port, when of a sudden the wind fell, and the penitent relapsed, begging all of us that were present, as we were gentlemen, not to say anything of what had passed. He had not been ashore above two days, when one of the company began to rally him upon his devotion on shipboard, which the other denied in so high terms, that it produced the lie on both sides, and ended in a duel. The atheist was run through the body, and after some loss of blood, became as good a Christian as he was at sea, till he found that his wound was not mortal. He is at present one of the free-thinkers of the age, and now writing a pamphlet against several received opinions concerning the existence of fairies. Joseph Addison (1671–1719), in 'The Tattler.'

Verse 1:

The owlet, Atheism,
Sailing on obscene wings across the noon,
Drops his blue-fringed lids, and shuts them close,
And, hooting at the glorious sun in heaven,
Cries out, 'Where is it'
Samuel Taylor Coleridge, 1772–1834.

Verse 1. 'They are corrupt, they have done abominable works.' Sin pleaseth the flesh. Corruption inherent is nourished by the accession of corrupt actions. Judas's covetousness is sweetened with unjust gain. Joab is heartened and hardened with blood. 1 Kings 2:5. Theft is fitted to and fatted in the thievish heart with obvious booties. Pride is fed with the officious compliments of observant grooms. Extortion battens in the usurer's affections by the trolling in of his moneys. Sacrilege thrives in the church-robber by the pleasing distinctions of those sycophant priests, and helped with their not labourious profit. Nature is led, is fed with sense. And when the citadel of the heart is once won, the turret of the understanding will not long hold out. As the suffumigations of the oppressed stomach surge up and cause the headache, or as the thick spumy mists, which vapour up from the dark and foggy earth, do often suffocate the brighter air, and to us more than eclipse the sun, the black and corrupt affections, which ascend out of the nether part of the soul, do no less darken and choke the understanding. Neither can the fire of grace be kept alive at God's altar (man's heart), when the clouds of lust shall rain down such showers of impiety on it. Farewell the perspicuity of judgment, when the matter is put to the partiality of affection. Thomas Adams.

Verse 1. 'They are corrupt, they have done abominable things: there is none that doeth good.' 'Men,' says Bernard, 'because they are corrupt in their minds, become abominable in their doings: corrupt before God, abominable before men. There are three sorts of men of which none doeth good. There are those who neither understand nor seek God, and they are the dead: there are others who understand him, but seek him not, and they are the wicked. There are others that seek him but understand him not, and they are the fools.' 'O God,' cries a writer of the middle ages, 'how many are here at this day who, under the name of Christianity, worship idols, and are abominable both to thee and to men! For every man worships that which he most loves. The proud man bows down before the idol of worldly power; the covetous man before the idol of money; the adulterer before the idol of beauty; and so of the rest.' And of such, saith the apostle, 'They profess that they know God, but in works deny him, being abominable and disobedient, and unto every good work reprobate' Titus 1:16. 'There is none that doeth good.' Notice how Paul avails himself of this testimony of the psalmist, among those which he heaps together in the third chapter of the epistle to the Romans, where he is proving concerning 'both Jews and Gentiles, that they are all under sin' Romans 3:9. John Mason Neale, in loc.

Verse 1. The argument of my text is the atheist's divinity, the brief of his belief couched all in one article, and that negative too, clean contrary to the fashion of all creeds, 'There is no God.' The article but one; but so many absurdities tied to the train of it, and itself so irreligious, so prodigiously profane, that he dares not speak it out, but saith it softly to himself, in secret, 'in his heart.' So the text yields these three points; Who is he? A 'fool.' What he saith, 'no God.' How he speaks it, 'in his heart.' A fool, his bolt, and his draught. I will speak of them severally ... There is a child in years, and there is a child in manners, *aetate et moribus*, saith Aristotle. There is a fool in wit, and there is a fool in life; a witless and a graceless fool. The latter is worthy of the title as the first; both void of reason; not of the faculty but of the use. Yea, the latter fool is indeed the more kindly of the twain; for the sot would use his reason if he could; the sinner will not though he may. It is not the natural, but the moral fool that David means, the wicked and ungracious person, for so is the sense of the original term ... It is time we leave the person, and come unto the act. What hath this fool done? Surely nothing; he hath only said. What hath he said? Nay, nothing either; he hath only thought: for to say in heart, is but to think. There are two sorts of saying in the Scripture, one meant indeed so properly, the other but in hope; one by word of mouth, the other by thought of heart. You see the psalmist means here the second sort. The bolt the fool here shoots is atheism: he makes no noise at the loss of it, as bowmen use; he draws and delivers closely, and stilly, out of sight, and without sound: he saith 'God is not,' but 'in heart.' The heart hath a mouth; *intus est os cordis*, saith Augustine. God, saith Cyprian, is *cordis auditor*, he hears the heart; then belike it hath some speech. When God said to Moses, *quare clamas?* why criest thou? we find no words he uttered: *silens auditor*, saith Gregory, he is heard through saying nothing. There is a silent speech (Psalm 4:4), 'Commune with your own heart,' saith David, 'and be still.' Speech is not the heart's action, no more than meditation is the mouth's. But sometimes the heart and mouth exchange offices; *lingua mea meditabitur*, saith David. Psalm 35:28. There is *lingua meditans*, a musing tongue; here is *cor loquens*, a speaking heart. And to say the truth, the philosopher saith well, it is the heart doth all things, *mens videt, mens audit, mens loquitur*. It is the heart that speaks, the tongue is but the instrument to give the sound. It is but the heart's echo to repeat the words after it. Except when the tongue doth run before the wit, the heart doth dictate to the mouth; it suggests what it shall say. The heart is the soul's herald: look what she will have proclaimed, the heart reads it, and the mouth cries it. The tongue saith nought but what the heart saith first. Nay, in very deed, the truest and kindest speech is the heart's. The tongue and lips are Jesuits, they lease, and lie, and use equivocations: flattery, or fear, or other by-respect, other wry respect adulterate their words. But the heart speaks as it means, worth twenty mouths, if it could speak audibly. Richard Clerke, D.D., 1634 (one of the translators of our English Bible).

Verses 1, 4. The Scripture gives this as a cause of the notorious courses of wicked men, that 'God is not in all their thoughts' Psalm 10:4. They forget there is a God of vengeance and a day of reckoning. 'The fool' would needs enforce upon his heart, that 'there is no God,' and what follows: 'Corrupt they are, there is none doth good: they eat up my people as bread,' etc. They make no more bones of devouring men and their estates, than they make conscience of eating a piece of bread. What a wretched condition hath sin brought man unto, that the great God who 'filleth heaven and earth' (Jeremiah 23:24) should yet have no place in the heart which he hath especially made for himself! The sun is not so clear as this truth, that God is, for all things in the world are because God is. If he were not, nothing could be. It is from him that wicked men have that strength they have to commit sin, therefore sin proceeds from atheism, especially these plotting sins; for if God were more thought on, he would take off the soul from sinful contrivings, and fix it upon himself. Richard Sibbes.

Verse 2. To see if there were any that did understand ... seek God.' None seek him aright, and as he ought to be sought, nor can do while they live in sin: for men in seeking God fail in many things: as, First, men seek him not for himself. Secondly, they seek him not alone, but other things with him. Thirdly, they seek other things before him, as worldlings do. Fourthly, they seek him coldly or carelessly. Fifthly, they seek him inconstantly; example of Judas and Demas. Sixthly, they seek him not in his word, as heretics do. Seventhly, they seek him not in all his word, as hypocrites do. Lastly, they seek him not seasonably and timely, as profane, impenitent sinners do; have no care to depend upon God's word, but follow their own lusts and fashions of this world. Thomas Wilson, 1653.

Verses 2, 3. What was the issue of God's so looking upon men? 'They are all gone aside,' that is, from him and his ways; 'They are altogether become filthy;' their practices are such as make then stink; 'There is none that doeth good, no, not one;' of so many millions of men that are upon the earth, there is not one doeth good. There were men of excellent parts then in the world, men of soul, but not one of them did know God, or seek after God: Paul therefore hath laid it down for a universal maxim, that the animal, natural, or intellectual man, receives not the things of the Spirit of God, for they are foolishness unto him, and so are rejected by him. William Greenhill.

Verse 3. The ungodly are 'vile' persons (Nahum 1:14). 'I will make thy grave; for thou art vile.' Sin makes men base, it blots their name, it taints their blood: 'They are altogether become filthy;' in the Hebrew it is, they are become stinking. Call wicked men ever so bad, you cannot call them out of their name; they are 'swine' (Matthew 7:6); 'vipers' (Matthew 3:7); 'devils'

(John 6:70). The wicked are the dross and refuse (Psalms 119:119); and heaven is too pure to have any dross mingle with it. Thomas Watson.

Verse 3. 'Altogether become filthy.' Thus the Roman satirist describes his own age:

Nothing is left, nothing, for future times
To add to the full catalogue of crimes;
The baffled sons must feel the same desires,
And act the same mad follies as their sires,
Vice has attained its zenith.
Juvenal, Sat. 1.

Verse 3. 'There is none that doeth good, no, not one.' Origen maketh a question, how it could be said that there was none, neither among the Jews nor Gentiles, that did any good; seeing there were many among them which did clothe the naked, feed the hungry, and did other good things: he hereunto maketh this answer: That like as one that layeth a foundation, and buildeth upon it a wall or two, yet cannot be said to have built a house till he have finished it; so although these might do some good things, yet they attained not unto perfect goodness, which was only to be found in Christ. But this is not the apostle's meaning only to exclude men from the perfection of justice; for even the faithful and believers were short of that perfection which is required; he therefore showeth what men are by nature, all under sin and in the same state of damnation, without grace and faith in Christ: if any perform any good work, either it is of grace, and so not of themselves, or if they did it by the light of nature, they did it not as they ought, and so it was far from a good work indeed. Andrew Willet (1562–1621), on Romans 3:10.

Verse 4. 'Have the workers of iniquity no knowledge?' Men's ignorance is the reason why they fear not what they should fear. Why is it that the ungodly fear not sin? Oh, it's because they know it not. 'Have the workers of iniquity no knowledge?' Sure enough they have none, for 'they eat up my people as they eat bread;' such morsels would scald their mouths, they would not dare to be such persecutors and destroyers of the people of God; they would be afraid to touch them if they did but know what they did. Richard Alleine.

Verse 4. 'Who eat up my people as they eat bread.' That is, daily, saith Austin; as duly as they eat bread; or, with the same eagerness and voracity. These man-eaters, cruel cannibals, make no more conscience to undo a poor man, than to eat a good meal when they are hungry. Like pickerels in a pond, or sharks in the sea, they devour the poorer, as those do the lesser fishes; and that many times with a plausible, invisible consumption; as the usurer, who like the ostrich, can digest any metal; but especially money. John Trapp.

Verse 4. 'Who eat up my people as they eat bread.' Oh, how few consult and believe the Scriptures setting forth the enmity of wicked men against God's people! The Scripture tells us 'they eat up God's people as bread,' which implies a strange inclination in them to devour the saints, and that they take as great delight therein as a hungry man in eating, and that it is natural to them to molest them. The Scripture compares them, for their hateful qualities, to the lions, and bears, to foxes for subtlety, to wild bulls, to greedy swine, to scorpions, to briers and thorns (grievous and vexing things). The Scripture represents them as industrious and unwearied in their bloody enterprises, they cannot sleep without doing mischief. Herodias had rather have the blood of a saint than half a kingdom. Haman would pay a great fine to the king that the scattered Jews (who keep not the king's laws) may be cut off. Wicked men will run the hazard of damning their own souls, rather than not fling a dagger at the apple of God's eye. Though they know what one word – aha!! – cost, yet they will break through all natural, civil, and moral obligations, to ruin God's people. The Holy Ghost calls them 'implacable' men, fierce and headstrong; they are like the hot oven for fury, like the sea for boundless rage; yet, 'who hath believed' this Scripture 'report?' Did we believe what enemies all wicked men are unto all saints, we should not lean to our own prudence and discretion to secure us from any danger by these men; we would get an ark to secure us from the deluge of their wrath; if at any time we be cast among them and delivered, we would bless God with the three children that the hot fiery oven did not consume us; we would not wonder when we hear of any of their barbarous cruelty, but rather wonder at God's restraining them every day; we would be suspicious of receiving hurt when cast among light and frothy companions; we would shun their company as we do lions and scorpions; we would never commit any trust or secret into their hands; we would not be light-hearted whilst in their society; we would not rely on their promises any more than we would on the promise of the devil, their father; we would long for heaven, to be delivered from 'the tents of Kedar;' we would not count any of the saints secured from danger, though related to any great wicked man; we would not twist ourselves with them by matching ourselves or children to these sons and daughters of Belial; neither would we make choice of devils to be our servants. Lewis Stuckley.

Verse 4. This is an evil world. It hates the people of God. 'Because ye are not of the world, therefore the world hateth you' John 15:19. Haman's hatred was against the whole seed of the Jews. When you can find a serpent without a sting, or a leopard without spots, then may you expect to find a wicked world without hatred to the saints. Piety is the target which is aimed at. 'They are mine adversaries because I follow the thing that good is' Psalm 38:20. The world pretends to hate the godly for something else, but the ground of their quarrel is holiness. The world's hatred is implacable: anger may be reconciled, hatred cannot. You may as soon reconcile heaven and hell as the two seeds. If the world hated Christ, no wonder that it hates us. 'The world hated me before it hated you' John 15:18. Why should any hate Christ? This blessed Dove had no gall, this rose of Sharon did send forth a most sweet perfume; but this shows the world's baseness, it is a Christ-hating and a saint-eating world. Thomas Watson.

Verse 5. 'There were they in great fear.' That we may not mistake the meaning of the point, we must understand that this faintheartedness and cowardliness doth not always come upon presumptuous sinners when they behold imminent dangers, for though none of them have true courage and fortitude, yet many of them have a kind of desperate stoutness and resolution when they do, as it were, see death present before their faces; which proceedeth from a kind of deadness, that is upon their hearts, and a brawniness that hath overgrown their consciences to their greater condemnation. But when it pleaseth the Lord to waken them out of the dead slumber, and to set the worm of conscience awork within them, then this doctrine holdeth true without any exception, that the boldest sinners prove at length the basest cowards: and they that have been most audacious in adventuring upon the most mischievous evils, do become of all others most timorous when God's revenging hand seizeth upon them for the same. John Dod, 1547–1645.

Verse 5. 'God is in the generation of the righteous;' that is, he favours that generation or sort of men; God is in all generations, but such he delights in most: the wicked have cause enough to fear those in whom God delights. Joseph Caryl.

Verse 5. The King of Glory cannot come into the heart (as he is said to come into the hearts of his people as such; Psalm 24:9,10), but some glory of himself will appear; and as God doth accompany the word with majesty because it is his word, so he doth accompany his own children, and their ways, with majesty, yea, even in their greatest debasements. As when Stephen was brought before the council, as a prisoner at the bar for his life, then God manifested his presence to him, for it is said, 'His face shone as the face of an angel of God' (Acts 6:15); in a proportionable manner it is ordinarily true what Solomon says of all righteous men, 'A man's wisdom makes his face to shine' Ecclesiastes 8:1. Thus Peter also speaks (1 Peter 4:14): 'If you be reproached for the name of Christ, happy are you, for the Spirit,' not only of God, or of grace, but 'of glory, resteth upon you.' And so in the martyrs; their innocency, and carriage, and godly behaviour, what majesty had it with it! What an amiableness in the sight of the people, which daunted, dashed, and confounded their most wretched oppressors; so that although the wicked persecutors 'did eat up God's people as bread' (verse 4), yet it is added that they were in great fear upon this very account, that 'God is in the generation of the just.' God stands, as it were, astonished at their dealings: 'Have the workers of iniquity no knowledge,' (so in the words afore) 'that they eat up my people as bread,' and make no more ado of it that a man doth that heartily eats of his meat? They seem to do thus, they would carry it and bear it out; but for all that they are in great fear whilst they do thus, and God strikes their hearts with terror when they most insult. Why? For, 'God is in the generation of, or dwelleth in the just,' and God gives often some glimmerings, hints, and warnings to the wicked (such as Pilate had concerning Christ), that his people are righteous. And this you may see in Philippians 1:28: 'And in nothing terrified by your adversaries, which is to them an evident token of perdition, but to you of salvation, and that of God.' In that latter passage, I observe that an assurance of salvation, and a spirit of terror, and that of God, is given either. In the Old Testament it is recorded of David (1 Samuel 18:12), that although Saul hated him (verse 9), and sought to destroy him (verses 10,11), 'yet Saul was afraid of David, because the Lord was with him, and was departed from Saul;' which is the reason in hand. God manifested his presence in David, and struck Saul's conscience with his godly and wise carriage, and that made him afraid. Thomas Goodwin.

Verse 6. 'Ye have shamed the counsel of the poor, because the Lord is his refuge.' In the fifty-third Psalm it is, 'Thou hast put them to shame, because God hath despised them.' Of course, the allusion is totally different in each; in this Psalm it is the indignant remonstrance of the Psalmist with 'the workers of iniquity' for undervaluing and putting God's poor to shame; the other affirms the final shame and confusion of the ungodly, and the contempt in which the Lord holds them. In either case it sweetly illustrates God's care of his poor, not merely the poor in spirit, but literally the poor and low ones, the oppressed and the injured. It is this character of God which is so conspicuously delineated in his word. Barton Bouchier.

Verse 6. 'Ye have shamed.' Every fool that saith in his heart there is no God, hath out of the same quiver a bolt to shoot at goodness. Barren Michal hath too many sons, who, like their mother, jeer at holy David. John Trapp.

Verse 6. 'Ye have shamed,' saith he, 'the counsel of the poor.' There is nothing that wicked men do so despise as the making God a refuge – nothing which they scorn in their hearts like it. 'They shame it,' saith he, 'It is a thing to be cast out of all consideration. The wise man trusts in his wisdom, the strong man in his strength, the rich man in his riches; but this trusting in God is the foolishest thing in the world.' The reasons of it are – 1. They know not God; and it is a foolish thing to trust one knows not whom. 2. They are enemies to God, and God is their enemy; and they account it a foolish thing to trust their enemy. 3. They know not the way of God's assistance and help. And – 4. They seek for such help, such assistance, such supplies, as God will not give; to be delivered, to serve their lusts; to be preserved, to execute their rage, filthiness, and folly. They have no other design or end of these things; and God will give none of them. And it is a foolish thing in any man to trust God to be preserved in sin. It is true, their folly is their wisdom, considering their state and condition. It is a folly to trust in God to live in sin, and despise the counsel of the poor. John Owen.

Verse 6. 'Ye have made a mock of the counsel of the poor:' and why? 'because the Lord is his trust.' This is the very true cause, whatsoever other pretenses there be. Whence observe this doctrine; that true godliness is that which breeds the quarrel between God's children and the wicked. Ungodly men may say what they list, as, namely, that they hate and dislike them for that they are proud and saucy in meddling with their betters; for that they are so scornful and disdainful towards their neighbours; for that they are malcontent, and turbulent, and I know not what; but the true reason is yielded by the Lord in this place, to wit, because they make him their stay and their confidence, and will not depend upon lying vanities as the men of the world do. John Dod.

Verse 6. 'The Lord is his refuge.' Be persuaded actually to hide yourselves with Jesus Christ. To have a hiding-place and not to use it, is as bad as to want one; fly to Christ; run into the holes of this Rock. Ralph Robinson, 1656.

Verse 7. 'O that salvation,' etc. Like as when we be in quiet, we do pray either nothing at all, or very coldly unto God; so in adversity and trouble, our spirit is stirred up and enkindled to prayer, whereof we do find examples everywhere in the Psalms of David; so that affliction is as it were the sauce of prayer, as hunger is unto meat. Truly their prayer is usually unsavoury who are without afflictions, and many of them do not pray truly, but do rather counterfeit a prayer, or pray for custom. Wolfgang Musculus, 1497–1563.

Verse 7. 'Out of Zion.' Zion, the church is no Saviour, neither dare we trust in her ministers or ordinances, and yet salvation comes to men through her. The hungry multitudes are fed by the hands of the disciples, who delight to act as the servitors of the gospel feast. Zion becomes the site of the fountain of healing waters which shall flow east and west till all nations drink thereat. What a reason for maintaining in the utmost purity and energy all the works of the church of the living God! C. H. S.

Verse 7. 'When the Lord turneth the captivity of his people: then shall Jacob rejoice, and Israel shall be glad.' Notice that by Israel we are to understand those other sheep which the Lord has that are not of this fold, but which he must also bring, that they may hear his voice. For it is Israel, not Judah; Sion, not Jerusalem. 'When the Lord turneth the captivity of his people.' 'Then,' as it is in the parallel passage, 'were we like unto them that dream.' A glorious dream indeed, in which, fancy what we may, the half of the beauty, the half of the splendour, will not be reached by our imagination. 'The captivity' of our souls to the law of concupiscence, of our bodies to the law of death; the captivity of our senses to fear; the captivity, the conclusion of which is so beautifully expressed by one of our greatest poets: namely, Giles Fletcher (1588–1623), in his 'Christ's Triumph over Death.'

Hints to the village preacher

Verse 1 (first clause). The folly of atheism.

Verse 1. Atheism of the heart. Jamieson's Sermons on the Heart.

Verse 1 (whole verse). Describe:

I. The creed of the fool.

II. The fool who holds the creed: or thus, Atheism.

1. Its source: 'the heart.'
2. Its creed: 'no God.'
3. Its fruits: 'corrupt,' etc.

Verse 1.

1. The great source of sin – alienation from God.
2. Its place of dominion – the heart.
3. Its effect upon the intellect – makes man a fool.
4. Its manifestations in the life – acts of commission and omission.

Verse 1 (last clause). The lantern of Diogenes. Hold it up upon all classes, and denounce their sins.

Verse 2.

1. Condescending search.
2. Favoured subjects.
3. Generous intentions.

Verse 2. What God looks for, and what we should look for. Men usually are quick to see things congruous to their own character.

Verses 2, 3. God's search for a naturally good man; the result; lessons to be learned therefrom.

Verse 3. Total depravity of the race.

Verse 4. 'Have all the workers of iniquity no knowledge?' If men rightly knew God, his law, the evil of sin, the torment of hell, and other great truths, would they sin as they do? Or if they know these and yet continue in their iniquities, how guilty and foolish they are! Answer the question both positively and negatively, and it supplies material for a searching discourse.

Verse 4 (first clause). The crying sin of transgressing against light and knowledge.

Verse 4 (last clause). Absence of prayer, a sure mark of a graceless state.

Verse 5. The foolish fears of those who have no fear of God.

Verse 5. The Lord's nearness to the righteous, its consequences to the persecutor, and its encouragement to saints.

Verse 6. The wisdom of making the Lord our refuge. John Owen.

Verse 6. Describes:

1. The poor man here intended.
2. His counsel.
3. His reproach.
4. His refuge.

Verse 6. Trust in God, a theme for mockery to fools only. Show its wisdom.
Verse 7. Longings for the advent.
Verse 7. 'Out of Zion.' The church, the channel of blessings to men.
Verse 7. Discourse to promote revival.

1. Frequent condition of the church, 'captivity.'
2. Means of revival – the Lord's coming in grace.
3. Consequences, 'rejoice,' 'be glad.'

Verse 7. Captivity of soul. What it is. How provided for. How accomplished. With what results.

Psalm 15

Subject
This Psalm of David bears no dedicatory title at all indicative of the occasion upon which it was written, but it is exceedingly probable that, together with the twenty-fourth Psalm, to which it bears a striking resemblance, its composition was in some way connected with the removal of the ark to the holy hill of Zion. Who should attend upon the ark was a matter of no small consequence, for because unauthorised persons had intruded into the office, David was unable on the first occasion to complete his purpose of bringing the ark to Zion. On the second attempt he is more careful, not only to allot the work of carrying the ark to the divinely appointed Levites (1 Chronicles 15:2), but also to leave it in charge of the man whose house the Lord had blessed, even Obed-edom, who, with his many sons, ministered in the house of the Lord. (1 Chronicles 26:8, 12.) Spiritually we have here a description of the man who is a child at home in the Church of God on earth, and who will dwell in the house of the Lord for ever above. He is primarily Jesus, the perfect man, and in him all who through grace are conformed to his image.

Division
The first verse asks the question; the rest of the verses answer it. We will call the Psalm THE QUESTION AND ANSWER.

Exposition
Verse 1. THE QUESTION. Jehovah. Thou high and holy One, who shall be permitted to have fellowship with thee? The heavens are not pure in thy sight, and thou chargest thine angels with folly, who then of mortal mould shall dwell with thee, thou dread consuming fire? A sense of the glory of the Lord and of the holiness which becomes his house, his service, and his attendants, excites the humble mind to ask the solemn question before us. Where angels bow

with veiled faces, how shall man be able to worship at all? The unthinking many imagine it to be a very easy matter to approach the Most High, and when professedly engaged in his worship they have no questionings of heart as to their fitness for it; but truly humbled souls often shrink under a sense of utter unworthiness, and would not dare to approach the throne of the God of holiness if it were not for him, our Lord, our Advocate, who can abide in the heavenly temple, because his righteousness endureth for ever. 'Who shall abide in thy tabernacle?' Who shall be admitted to be one of the household of God, to sojourn under his roof and enjoy communion with himself? 'Who shall dwell in thy holy hill?' Who shall be a citizen of Zion, and an inhabitant of the heavenly Jerusalem? The question is raised, because it is a question. All men have not this privilege, nay, even among professors there are aliens from the commonwealth, who have no secret intercourse with God. On the grounds of law no mere man can dwell with God, for there is not one upon earth who answers to the just requirements mentioned in the succeeding verses. The questions in the text are asked of the Lord, as if none but the Infinite Mind could answer them so as to satisfy the unquiet conscience. We must know from the Lord of the tabernacle what are the qualifications for his service, and when we have been taught of him, we shall clearly see that only our spotless Lord Jesus, and those who are conformed unto his image, can ever stand with acceptance before the Majesty on high.

Impertinent curiosity frequently desires to know who and how many shall be saved; if those who thus ask the question, 'Who shall dwell in thy holy hill?' would make it a soul-searching enquiry in reference to themselves they would act much more wisely. Members of the visible church, which is God's tabernacle of worship, and hill of eminence, should diligently see to it, that they have the preparation of heart which fits them to be inmates of the house of God. Without the wedding-dress of righteousness in Christ Jesus, we have no right to sit at the banquet of communion. Without uprightness of walk we are not fit for the imperfect church on earth, and certainly we must not hope to enter the perfect church above.

Verse 2. THE ANSWER. The Lord in answer to the question informs us by his Holy Spirit of the character of the man who alone can dwell in his holy hill. In perfection this holiness is found only in the Man of Sorrows, but in a measure it is wrought in all his people by the Holy Ghost. Faith and the graces of the Spirit are not mentioned, because this is a description of outward character, and where fruits are found the root may not be seen, but it is surely there. Observe the accepted man's walk, work, and word. 'He that walketh uprightly,' he keeps himself erect as those do who traverse high ropes; if they lean on one side over they must go, or as those who carry precious but fragile ware in baskets on their heads, who lose all if they lose their perpendicular. True believers do not cringe as flatterers, wriggle as serpents, bend double as earth-grubbers, or crook on one side as those who have sinister aims; they have the strong backbone of the vital principle of grace within, and being themselves upright, they are able to walk uprightly. Walking is of far more importance than talking. He only is right who is upright in walk and downright in honesty. 'And worketh righteousness.' His faith shows itself by good works, and therefore is no dead faith. God's house is a hive for workers, not a nest for drones. Those who rejoice that everything is done for them by another, even the Lord Jesus, and therefore hate legality, are the best doers in the world upon gospel principles. If we are not positively serving the Lord, and doing his holy will to the best of our power, we may seriously debate our interest in divine things, for trees which bear no fruit must be hewn down and cast into the fire. 'And speaketh the truth in his heart.' The fool in the last psalm spoke falsely in his heart; observe both here and elsewhere in the two psalms, the striking contrast. Saints not only desire to love and speak truth with their lips, but they seek to be true within; they will not lie even in the closet of their hearts, for God is there to listen; they scorn double meanings, evasions, equivocations, white lies, flatteries, and deceptions. Though truths, like roses, have thorns about them, good men wear them in their bosoms. Our heart must be the sanctuary and refuge of truth, should it be banished from all the world beside, and hunted from among men; at all risk we must entertain the angel of truth, for truth is God's daughter. We must be careful that the heart is really fixed and settled in principle, for tenderness of conscience toward truthfulness, like the bloom on a peach, needs gentle handling, and once lost it were hard to regain it. Jesus was the mirror of sincerity and holiness. Oh, to be more and more fashioned after his similitude!

Verse 3. After the positive comes the negative. 'He that backbiteth not with his tongue.' There is a sinful way of backbiting with the heart when we think too hardly of a neighbour, but it is the tongue which does the mischief. Some men's tongues bite more than their teeth. The tongue is not steel, but it cuts, and its wounds are very hard to heal; its worst wounds are not with its edge to our face, but with its back when our head is turned. Under the law, a night hawk was an unclean bird, and its human image is abominable everywhere. All slanderers are the devil's bellows to blow up contention, but those are the worst which blow at the back of the fire. 'Nor doeth evil to his neighbour.' He who bridles his tongue will not give a licence to his hand. Loving our neighbour as ourselves will make us jealous of his good name, careful not to injure his estate, or by ill example to corrupt his character. 'Nor taketh up a reproach against his neighbour.' He is a fool if not a knave who picks up stolen goods and harbours them; in slander as well as robbery, the receiver is as bad as the thief. If there were not gratified hearers of ill reports, there would be an end of the trade of spreading them. Trapp says, that 'the tale-bearer carrieth the devil in his tongue, and the tale-hearer carries the devil in his ear.' The original may be translated, 'endureth;' implying that it is a sin to endure or tolerate tale-bearers. 'Show that man out!' we should say of a drunkard, yet it is very questionable if his unmanly behaviour will do us so much mischief as the tale-bearers insinuating story. 'Call for a policeman!' we say if we see a thief at his business; ought we to feel no indignation when we hear a gossip at her work? Mad dog! Mad dog!! is a terrible hue and cry, but there are few curs whose bite is so dangerous as a busybody's tongue. Fire! fire!! is an alarming note, but the tale-bearer's tongue is set on fire of hell, and those who indulge it had better mend their manners, or they may find that there is fire in hell for unbridled tongues. Our Lord spake evil of no man, but breathed a prayer for his foes; we must be like him, or we shall never be with him.

Verse 4. 'In whose eyes a vile person is contemned; but he honoureth them that fear the Lord.' We must be as honest in paying respect as in paying our bills. Honour to whom honour is due. To all good men we owe a debt of honour, and we have no right to hand over what is their due to vile persons who happen to be in high places. When base men are in office, it is our duty to respect the office; but we cannot so violate our consciences as to do otherwise than contemn the men; and on the other hand, when true saints are in poverty and distress, we must sympathise with their afflictions and honour the men none the less. We may honour the roughest cabinet for the sake of the jewels, but we must not prize false gems because of their setting.

A sinner in a gold chain and silken robes is no more to be compared with a saint in rags than a rushlight in a silver candlestick with the sun behind a cloud. The proverb says, that 'ugly women, finely dressed, are the uglier for it,' and so mean men in high estate are the more mean because of it. 'He that sweareth to his own hurt, and changeth not.' Scriptural saints under the New Testament rule 'swear not at all,' but their word is as good as an oath: those men of God who think it right to swear, are careful and prayerful lest they should even seem to overshoot the mark. When engagements have been entered into which turn out to be unprofitable, 'the saints are men of honour still.' Our blessed Surety swore to his own hurt, but how gloriously he stood to his suretyship! what a comfort to us that he changeth not, and what an example to us to be scrupulously and precisely exact in fulfilling our covenants with others! The most far-seeing trader may enter into engagements which turn out to be serious losses, but whatsoever else he loses, if he keeps his honour, his losses will be bearable; if that be lost all is lost.

Verse 5. 'He that putteth not out his money to usury.' Usury was and is hateful both to God and man. That a lender should share with the borrower in gains made by his money is most fitting and proper; but that the man of property should eat up the poor wretch who unfortunately obtained a loan of him is abominable. Those who grind poor tradesmen, needy widows, and such like, by charging them interest at intolerable rates, will find that their gold, and their silver are cankered. The man who shall ascend into the hill of the Lord must shake off this sin as Paul shook the viper into the fire. 'Nor taketh reward against the innocent.' Bribery is a sin both in the giver and the receiver. It was frequently practised in Eastern courts of justice; that form of it is now under our excellent judges almost an unheard-of thing; yet the sin survives in various forms, which the reader needs not that we should mention; and under every shape it is loathsome to the true man of God. He remembers that Jesus instead of taking reward against the innocent died for the guilty.

Verse 5. 'He that doeth these things shall never be moved.' No storm shall tear him from his foundations, drag him from his anchorage, or uproot him from his place. Like the Lord Jesus, whose dominion is everlasting, the true Christian shall never lose his crown. He shall not only be on Zion, but like Zion, fixed and firm. He shall dwell in the tabernacle of the Most High, and neither death nor judgment shall remove him from his place of privilege and blessedness.

Let us betake ourselves to prayer and self-examination, for this Psalm is as fire for the gold, and as a furnace for silver. Can we endure its testing power?

Explanatory notes and quaint sayings

Verse 1. 'Lord, who shall abide in thy tabernacle?' In that the church of Christ upon earth is a 'tabernacle,' we may note, that neither the church itself, nor the members of it, have any fixed or firm seat of habitation in this world: 'Arise, depart, for this is not your rest' Micah 2:10. 'Here have we no continuing city, but we seek one to come' Hebrews 13:14. God's tabernacle, being a movable temple, wandered up and down, sometimes in the desert, sometimes in Shiloh, sometimes among the Philistines, sometimes in Kerjathjearim, and never found any settled place till it was translated into the mountain of God: even so the church of God wandereth as a straggler and a stranger in the wilderness of this world, being destitute, tormented, and afflicted on every side, persecuted from this city to that, and never enjoying any constant habitation of sound and sure rest until it be translated unto 'God's holy hill.' The verb (Heb.) *gur* (as the learned in Hebrew note) signifying to dwell as a stranger, or a sojourner, imports that a citizen of heaven is a pilgrim on earth ... In that the church is a tabernacle, we may see that it is not a fort, compassed about with any strong walls, armed with any human forces; and yet such as keep within her are defended from heat of sun, and hurt of storms. Her strength is not here, but from above, for Christ her Head is in all her troubles a present help, a refuge against the tempest, a shadow against the heat. Isaiah 35:4. The church on earth is indeed a tabernacle, but it is God's tabernacle, wherein he dwelleth as in his house; 'Lord, who shall abide in thy tabernacle?' for to this end the Lord commanded the tabernacle to be made, that he might dwell among them, the blessed apostle construeth it of his dwelling among them. 2 Corinthians 6:16. 'You are,' saith he, 'the temple of the living God, as God hath said, I will dwell in them, and walk in them.' To the same purpose, God is said elsewhere to dwell in Sion, and to walk in the midst of the seven golden candlesticks, that is, in the midst of the seven churches, in the midst of his city (Psalm 46:5), in the midst of his people. Isaiah 12:6. John Boys, D.D., Dean of Canterbury, 1571–1625.

Verse 1. 'Lord, who shall abide,' etc. If David, a man endued with an excellent and divine spirit, one in whom singular wisdom, rare knowledge, and deep understanding of hidden secrets appeared, who being taught of God in heavenly things, far surpassed and exceeded in wisdom all his teachers and counsellors, did notwithstanding desire to know the sheep from the goats, the good from the bad, the saints from the hypocrites, the true worshippers of God from dissemblers, the true inhabitants of the holy tabernacle from the intruders of the wicked, lest therein he should be deceived; how great cause have we, in whom neither the like spirit, neither such wisdom, nor equal knowledge, nor comparable understanding, by many degrees appeareth, to fear our own weakness, to doubt of our own judgments, to confess our own infirmity, and to suspect the subtle sleights and coloured pretenses of men: and for further knowledge in hidden, deep, and secret things, with David to demand and ask this question, 'Lord, who shall abide in thy tabernacle? who shall dwell in thy holy hill?' ... Where David saith, 'Who shall abide in thy holy hill?' he giveth us to understand that there is no true and sound rest but in the holy hill of the Lord, which is the church. Then the wicked and ungodly which are not of God's house, of his holy hill, of the church, have no quiet, rest, nor sound peace; but they are in continual perplexity, continual torment, continual disquietness of their minds. Richard Turnbull, 1606.

Verse 1. 'Abide in the tabernacle,' etc. The worshippers in the outer court only will get their eternal abode without among the dogs, sorcerers, etc; but they that shall be inhabitants of heaven, come further in, even unto the tabernacle itself: their souls are fed at his table, they find the smell of his garments as of myrrh, aloes, and cassia; and if they miss it at any time, it is the grief of their souls, and they are never at rest till they recover it again. Thomas Boston.

Verse 1. 'Who shall dwell,' etc.

Now who is he? Say, if ye can,
Who so shall gain the firm abode?
Pilate shall say, 'Behold the Man!'
And John, 'Behold the Lamb of God!'
John Barclay

Verse 1. 'Holy hill.' Heaven is aptly compared to a hill, hell to a hole. Now who shall ascend unto this holy mount? None but those whom this mount comes down unto, that have sweet communion with God in this life present, whose conversation is in heaven, though their life be for awhile upon earth, who do here eat, and drink, and sleep, eternal life. John Trapp.

Verses 1, 2. The disguising and counterfeiting of hypocrites in all ages, occasioned haply this query: for, as Paul speaks, 'all are not Israel that are of Israel,' a great many living in the church are not of the church, according to that of the doctors upon this place, *multi sunt corpore qui non sunt fide, multi nomine qui non sunt nomine.* Wherefore, David, here perceiving that sundry people were shuffled into God's tabernacle like goats among the sheep, and tares among the corn, being Jews outwardly, but not inwardly, deceiving others often, and, sometimes, themselves also, with a bare profession of religion, and false opinion of true piety, cometh unto God (as to the searcher and trier of the hearts of men, acquainted with all secrets, and best understanding who are his own), saying unto him, O Lord, forsomuch as there is so much unsoundness and hypocrisy reigning among those that dwell in thy tabernacle, professing thy word, and frequenting the places of thy worship; I beseech thee most humbly, to declare to thy people some tokens and cognizances by which a true subject of thy kingdom may be discerned from the children of this world. Here then, observe, that an external profession of faith, and outward communion with the church of God, is not sufficient unto salvation, unless we lead an incorrupt life correspondent to the same, doing the thing which is right, and speaking the truth in our heart. And, therefore, the silly Papist is exceedingly deceived in relying so much upon the church's outside, to wit, upon the succession of Roman bishops, upon the multitude of Roman Catholics, upon the power and pomp of the Roman synagogue, crying as the Jews in old time, 'The temple of the Lord, the temple of the Lord,' our church is the temple of the Lord. The carnal and careless gospeller is deceived also, placing all his religion in the formal observation of outward service, for a mere verbal Christian is a real atheist, according to that of Paul (Titus 1:16), 'In word they profess that they know God, but in their works they deny him;' and so many who seem to sojourn in God's tabernacle for a time, shall never rest upon his 'holy hill;' and this assertion is expressly confirmed by Christ himself: 'Not every one (saith he) that saith unto me, Lord, Lord, shall enter into the kingdom of heaven; but he that doeth the will of my Father which is in heaven. Many will say to me in that day, Lord, Lord, have we not prophesied in thy name? and in thy name have cast out devils? and in thy name done many wonderful works? And then will I profess unto them, I never knew you: depart from me, ye that work iniquity' Matthew 7:21–23. Consider this, all ye which are Christians in lip only but not in life, making a mask of religion, or rather a very vizard, with eyes, and mouth, and nose, fairly painted and proportioned to all pretenses and purposes. O think on this, all ye that forget God, he that dwelleth on high, and beholds the things here below, suffers none to rest upon the mountain of his holiness but such as walk uprightly, doing that which is just, and speaking that which is true. John Boys.

Verse 2. 'He that walketh uprightly,' etc. If neither the golden reason of excellency can move us, nor the silver reason of profit allure us, then must the iron reason of necessity enforce us to integrity and uprightness of heart. For first, such is the necessity thereof, that without integrity the best graces we seem to have are counterfeit, and, therefore, but glorious sins; the best worship we can perform is but hypocrisy, and therefore abominable in God's sight. For uprightness is the soundness of all grace and virtues, as also of all religion and worship of God, without which they are unsound and nothing worth. And first, as touching graces, if they be not joined with uprightness of heart, they are sins under the masks or vizards of virtue, yea, as it may seem, double sins. Feigned equity is double iniquity, both because it is iniquity, and because it is feigning. George Downame, D.D., 1604.

Verse 2. 'He that walketh uprightly.' Here two questions are moved; First. Why David describes a sound member of the church, and inheritor of heaven, by works rather than by faith, seeing the kingdom of heaven is promised unto faith, and the profession thereof also maketh one a member of the visible church? Secondly. Why, among all the fruits of faith, almost innumerable, he makes choice of those duties especially which concern our neighbours? To the first, answer may be, that in this, and in all other places in Holy Scripture, where good works are commanded or commended in any, faith is ever presupposed, according to that apostolical maxim, 'Whatsoever is not of faith is sin;' 'Without me,' saith our blessed Saviour, 'ye can do nothing' (John 15:5); and without faith in him it is impossible to please God (Hebrews 11:6); *fides est operum fomes*, as Paulinus wittily: 'Faith (as our church speaks), is the nest of good works; albeit our birds be never so fair, though haply we do that which is right, and speak that which is true, yet all these will be lost, except it be brought forth in a true belief.' Aristides was so just in his government that he would not tread awry for any respect to friend or despite of foe. Pomponius is said to have been so true, that he never made lie himself, nor suffered a lie in other. Curtius at Rome, Menaeceus at Thebes, Codrus at Athens, exposed themselves unto voluntary death, for the good of their neighbours and country: yet, because they wanted the rest of true faith in the world's Saviour, where to lay their young, we cannot (if we speak with our prophet here from God's oracle), say that they shall ever rest upon his holy hill. Another answer may be, that faith is an inward and hidden grace, and many deceive themselves and others with a feigned profession thereof, and therefore the Holy Spirit will have every man's faith to be tried and known by their fruits, and howsoever, eternal life be promised to faith, and eternal damnation be threatened against infidelity, yet the sentence of salvation and condemnation shall be pronounced according to works, as the clearest evidence of both. It is truly said, out of Bernard, that although our good works are not *causa regnandi*, yet they be *via regni*, the causeway wherein, although not the cause wherefore, we must ascend God's holy hill. To the second demand, why the duties immediately belonging to God, are not mentioned here, but only such as concern our brother? Answer is made, that this question is propounded of such as, living in the visible church, openly profess the faith, and would seem to be devout, hearing the word of God, and calling upon his name; for of such as are profane atheists, and so not so much as make a semblance of holiness, there is no question to be made, for, without all doubt, there can be no resting place for such in the kingdom of heaven. Now that we may discern aright which of those that profess religion are sound, and which unsound; the marks are not to be taken from an outward hearing of the word, or receiving of the sacraments, and much less from a formal observation of human traditions in God's tabernacle (For all these things hypocrites usually perform), but from the duties of righteousness, giving every man his due, because the touchstone of piety towards God is charity towards our brother. 'Herein,' saith John, 'are the children of God known, and the children of the devil: whosoever doth not righteousness is not of God, neither he that loveth not his brother.' John Boys.

Verse 2. There is no ascertaining the quality of a tree but by its fruits. When the wheels of a clock move within, the hand on the dial will move without. When the heart of a man is sound in conversion, then the life will be fair in profession. When the conduit is walled in, how shall we judge of the spring but by the waters which run through the pipes? William Secker.

Verse 2. 'And worketh righteousness.' A man must first be righteous before he can work righteousness of life. 'He that doeth righteousness is righteous, even as he is righteous.' 1 John 3:7. The tree makes the fruit, not the fruit the tree; and therefore the tree must be good before the fruit can be good. Matthew 7:18. A righteous man may make a righteous work, but no work of an unrighteous man can make him righteous. Now we become righteous only by faith, through the righteousness of Christ imputed to us. Romans 5:1 ... Wherefore let men work as they will, if they be not true believers in Christ, they are not workers of righteousness; and, consequently, they will not be dwellers in heaven. Ye must then close with Christ in the first place, and by faith receive the gift of imputed righteousness, or ye will never truly bear this character of a citizen of Zion. A man shall as soon force fruit out of a branch broken off from the tree and withered, as work righteousness without believing in, and uniting with Christ. These are two things by which those that hear the gospel are ruined. Thomas Boston.

Verse 2. 'Worketh righteousness.' Jacob's ladder had stairs, upon which he saw none standing still, but all either ascending, or else descending by it. Ascend you likewise to the top of the ladder, to heaven, and there you shall hear one say, 'My Father doth now work, and I work also.' Whereupon Basil noteth that King David having first said, 'Lord, who shall dwell in thy tabernacle?' adds then, not he that hath wrought righteousness heretofore, but he that doth now work righteousness, even as Christ saith, 'My Father doth now work, and I work also.' Thomas Playfere.

Verse 2. But here observe, David saith, 'that worketh righteousness;' not that talks about, thinks about, or hears of, righteousness; because, 'not the hearers of the law, but the doers of the law, shall be justified.' What then do we owe unto others? That which Christ saith (Matthew 7), 'Whatsoever ye would that men should do unto you, do ye also unto them,' even unto your enemies: that is, to injure no one, to succour those that suffer injury, and to do good unto all men. But these things, I say, are spoken especially unto those who have respect of persons; as if he has said, It is not because thou art a priest, nor because thou art of a religious order, not because thou prayest much, nor because thou doest miracles, nor because thou teachest excellently, nor because thou art dignified with the title of father, nor because thou art the doer of any work (except righteousness), that thou shalt rest in the holy hill of the Lord; for if thou be destitute of the works of righteousness, neither all thy good works, nor thy indulgences, nor thy votes and suffrages, nor thy intercessions, shall avail thee anything. Therefore, the truth is firm; that it is the walker without spot, and the doer of righteousness, that shall rest in the tabernacles of the Lord. Yet how many are there, who build, increase and adorn churches, monasteries, altars, vessels, garments, etc., who, all the while, never so much as think of the works of righteousness; nay, who tread righteousness under foot that they may work these their own works, and because of them hope to gain the pardon of their unrighteousness, while thousands are deceived by these means! Hence, in the last day, Christ will say, 'I was an hungered, I was thirsty, I was naked, I was in prison, I was a stranger.' He will not say one word about those works which are done and admired at this day. And, on the other hand, it is of no account against thee that thou art a layman, or poor, or sick, or contemptible, or how vile soever thou art, if thou workest righteousness, thou shalt be saved. The only work that we must hope will be considered and accounted of, is the work of righteousness: all other works that either urge or allure us on under a show of godliness, are a thing of naught. Martin Luther.

Verse 2. 'And speaketh the truth in his heart.' Anatomists have observed that the tongue in man is tied with a double string to the heart. And so in truth spoken there is necessary a double agreement of our words. 1. With our heart. That is, to the speaking of truth, it is necessary our words agree with our mind and thoughts about the thing. We must speak as we think, and our tongues must be faithful interpreters of our mind: otherwise we lie, not speaking as we think. So what is truth in itself may be spoken by a man, and yet he be a liar; namely, if he does not think as he speaks. 2. With the thing as it is in itself. Though we think a thing to be so, which is not so, we lie, when we affirm it; because it is not as we say, though we really think it is so. For our mistaken notions of things can never stamp lies to pass current for truths. 2 Thessalonians 2:11. Thomas Boston.

Verse 2. I this day heard a sermon from Psalm 15:2, 'And speaketh the truth in his heart' . . . O my soul, receive the admonition that has been given thee! Study truth in the inward parts; let integrity and truth always accompany thee, and preserve thee: speak the truth in thy heart. I am thankful for any conviction and sense I have of the evil of lying; Lord, increase my abhorrence of it: as a further assistance and help against this mean, sordid, pernicious vice, I would endeavour, and resolve, in pursuit of the directions laid before us in the sermon, to mortify those passions and corruptions from whence this sin of lying more ordinarily flows, and which are the chief occasion of it, as 'out of the heart proceed evil thoughts' (Matthew 15:19); so, from the same fountain proceed evil words. And I would, with the greatest zeal, set myself against such corruptions as upon observation I find more commonly betray me into this iniquity: pride often indites our speech, and coins many a lie; so envy, covetousness, malice, etc. I would endeavour to cleanse myself from all this filthiness: there never will be a mortified tongue while there is an unmortified heart. If I love the world inordinately, it is a thousand to one I shall be often stretching a point to promote a worldly interest; and if I hate my brother, it is the same odds I shall reproach him. Lord, help me to purge the fountain, and then the streams will be pure. When the spring of a clock, and all of the movements are right, the hand will go right; and so it is here. The tongue follows the inward inclination. I would resolve to do nothing that may need a lie. If Gehazi's covetousness had not shamed him, he had not wanted a lie to excuse him, 'He that walks uprightly, walks surely' and safely in this, as well as other respects. Proverbs 10:9. May I do nothing that is dishonourable and mean, nothing that cannot bear the light, and then I shall have little temptation to lying. I would endeavour for a lively sense of the eye of God upon me, acting and speaking in his presence. Lord, I desire to set thee always before me; thou understandest my thoughts as perfectly as others do my words. I would consider before I speak, and not speak much or rashly. Proverbs 29:20. I would often think of the severity of a future judgment, when every secret shall be made manifest, and the hypocrite and liar exposed before angels and men. Lastly, I would frequently beg divine assistance herein. Psalm 119:29; Proverbs 30:8. O my God, help me in my future conduct, remove from me the way of lying; may the law of kindness and truth be in my tongue; may I take heed to my ways, that I sin not with my tongue. I bewail my past miscarriages in this respect, and flee to thy mercy through the blood of Christ; bless to me the instructions that have been this day given me; let no iniquity prevail against me; 'Keep back thy servant from presumptuous sins, and cleanse me from secret faults.' I commit my thoughts, desires, and tongue, to thy conduct and government; may I think and act in thy fear, and always speak the truth in my heart. Benjamin Bennet's 'Christian Oratory,' 1728.

Verses 2, 5. As the eagle casteth off her beak, and so reneweth her youth, and the snake strippeth off her old skin, and so maketh herself smooth: even so he that will enter into the joys of God, and rest upon his holy mountain, must, as the Scripture speaks, put off the old man and put on the new, which, after God, is created in righteousness and true holiness, repenting truly speedily, steadily. Robert Cawdray.

Verse 3. 'He that backbiteth not with his tongue, nor doeth evil to his neighbour.' Lamentation for the gross neglect of this duty, or the frequent commission of this sin. What tears are sufficient to bewail it? How thick do censures and reproaches fly in all places, at all tables, in all conventions! And this were the more tolerable, if it were only the fault of ungodly men, of strangers and enemies to religion; for so saith the proverb, 'Wickedness proceedeth from the wicked.' When a man's heart is full of hell, it is not unreasonable to expect his tongue should be set on fire of hell; and it is no wonder to hear such persons reproach good men, yea, even for their goodness. But alas! the disease doth not rest here, this plague is not only among the Egyptians but Israelites too. It is very doleful to consider how professors sharpen their tongues like swords against professors; and one good man censures and reproaches another, and one minister traduceth another; and who can say, 'I am clean from this sin?' O that I could move your pity in this case! For the Lord's sake pity yourselves, and do not pollute and wound your consciences with this crime. Pity your brethren; let it suffice that godly ministers and Christians are loaded with reproaches by wicked men – there is no need that you should combine with them in this diabolical work. You should support and strengthen their hands against the reproaches of the ungodly world, and not add affliction to the afflicted. O pity the world, and pity the church which Christ hath purchased with his own blood, which methinks bespeaks you in these words, 'Have pity upon me, have pity upon me, O ye my friends; for the hand of God hath touched me' Job 19:21. Pity the mad and miserable world, and help it against this sin; stop the bloody issue; restrain this wicked practice amongst men as much as possibly you can, and lament it before God, and for what you cannot do yourselves, give God no rest until he shall please to work a cure. Matthew Poole, 1624–1679.

Verse 3. 'He that backbiteth not,' etc. Detraction or slander is not lightly to be passed over, because we do so easily fail in this point. For the good name of a man, as saith Solomon, is a precious thing to every one, and to be preferred before much treasure, insomuch that it is no less grievous to hurt a man with the tongue than with a sword: nay, ofttimes the stroke of a tongue is grievouser than the wound of a spear, as it is in the French proverb. And therefore the tongue must be bridled, that we hurt not in any wise the good name of our neighbour; but preserve it unto him safe and sound, as much as in us shall lie. That which he addeth touching evil or injury not to be done to our neighbour, is like unto that which we have seen already concerning the working or exercising of righteousness. He would have us therefore so to exercise all upright dealing, that we might be far from doing any damage or wrong to our neighbours. And by the name of neighbour, is meant every man and woman, as it is plain and evident. For we are all created of God, and placed in this world that we might live uprightly and sincerely together. And therefore he breaketh the law of human society (for we are all tied and bound by this law of nature) that doth hurt or injury to another. The third member of this verse is, nor that reproacheth another, or, that maintaineth not a false report give one against another; which latter particle seemeth to be the better, since he had spoken before expressly, touching the good name of another, not to be hurt or wronged with our tongue. To the which fault this is next in degree, wherewith we are too much encumbered, and which we scarce acknowledge to be a fault, when we further and maintain the slanders devised and given out by another against a man, either by hearing them or telling them forth to others, as we heard them. For why? It seemeth for the most part to be enough for us if we can say, that we feign not this or that, nor make it of our own heads, but only tell it forth as we heard it of others, without adding anything of our own brain. But as oft as we do this we fail in our duty doing, in not providing for our neighbour's credit, as were requisite for the things, which being uttered by others ought to be passed over in silence and to lie dead, we gather up, and by telling them forth, disperse them abroad, which whether it be a sin or no, when as we ought by all means possible to wish and do well unto our neighbours, all men do see. And therefore thou that travellest towards eternal life, must not only not devise false reports and slanders against other men, but also not so much as have them in thy mouth being devised by others, neither by any means assist or maintain them in slandering; but by all honest and lawful means, provide for the credit and estimation of thy neighbour, so much as in thee lieth. Peter Baro, D.D., 1560.

Verse 3. 'He that backbiteth not with his tongue.' The Hebrew word signifieth to play the spy, and by a metaphor, to backbite or slander, for backbiters and whisperers, after the manner of spies, go up and down dissembling their malice, that they may espy the faults and defects of others, whereof they may make a malicious relation to such as will give ear to their slanders. So that backbiting is a malicious defamation of a man behind his back ... And that the citizen of heaven doth and ought to abhor from backbiting, the horrible wickedness of this sin doth evince. For first, Leviticus 19:16, where it is straightly forbidden, the 'tale-bearer' is compared to a pedlar: 'Thou shalt not walk about with tales and slanders, as it were a pedlar among thy people.' So much (Heb.) signifieth. For as the pedlar having bought his wares of some one or more goeth about from house to house that he may sell the same to others; so backbiters and tale-bearers, gathering together tales and rumours, as it were wares, go from one to another, that such wares as either themselves have invented, or have gathered by report, they may utter in the absence of their neighbour to his infamy and disgrace. Likewise Psalm 50:20, it is condemned as a notable crime, which God will not suffer to go unpunished; Ezekiel 22:9, it is reckoned among the abominations of Jerusalem, for which destruction is denounced against it; and Romans 1:29, 30, among the crimes of the heathen, given over unto a reprobate sense, this is placed: they were 'whisperers and backbiters.' George Downame.

Verse 3. 'He that backbiteth not.' He that is guilty of backbiting, that speaks evil of another behind his back, if that which he speaks be false, is guilty of lying, which is prejudicial to salvation. If that which he speaks be true, yet he is void of charity in seeking to defame another. For as Solomon observes, 'Love covereth all sins.' Proverbs 10:12. Where there is love and charity, there will be a covering and concealing of men's sins as much as may be. Now where charity is wanting, their salvation is not to be expected. 1 Corinthians 13:1, etc.; 1 John 3:14,15. Christopher Cartwright, 1602–1658.

Verse 3. 'Backbiteth not.' This crime is a conjugation of evils, and is productive of infinite mischiefs; it undermines peace, and saps the foundation of friendship; it destroys families, and rends in pieces the very heart and vitals of charity; it makes an evil man party, and witness, and judge, and executioner of the innocent. Bishop Taylor.

Verse 3. 'Backbiteth.' The scorpion hurteth none but such as he toucheth with the tip of his tail; and the crocodile and basilisk slay none but such as either the force of their sight, or strength of their breath reacheth. The viper woundeth none but such as it biteth; the venomous herbs or roots kill none but such as taste, or handle, or smell them, and so come near unto them; but the poison of slanderous tongues is much more rank and deadly; for that hurteth and slayeth, woundeth and killeth, not only near, but afar off; not only at hand, but by distance of place removed; not only at home, but abroad; not only in our own nation, but in foreign countries; and spareth neither quick nor dead. Richard Turnbull.

Verse 3. 'Backbiteth.' The word here used comes from a root signifying foot, and denotes a person who goes about from house to house, speaking things he should not (1 Timothy 5:13); and a word from this root siginifies spies; and the phrase here may point at persons who creep into houses, pry into the secrets of families, divulge them, and oftentimes represent them in a false light. Such are ranked among the worst of men, and are very unfit to be in the society of saints, or in the Church of Christ. See Romans 1:30. John Gill.

Verse 3. 'Nor taketh up a reproach against his neighbour.' The saints of God must not be too light of hearing, much less of believing all tales, rumours, and reports of their brethren; and charity requireth that we do not only stop and stay them, but that we examine them before we believe them. Saul, the king, too light of belief in this point, believed the slanderous and false reports of David's enemies, who put into Saul's head that David imagined evil against him. Yea, David himself showed his great infirmity in that, that without due examination and proof of the matter, he believed the false report of Ziba, against Mephibosheth, the son of Jonathan; of whom to David the king, persecuted by Absalom his son, Ziba reported falsely, that he should say, 'This day shall the house of Israel restore unto me the kingdom of my father.' The example of whose infirmity in Scripture reproved, must not we follow; but let us rather embrace the truth of that heavenly doctrine which, through God's Spirit, here he preacheth, that we believe not false reports against our neighbours. Richard Turnbull.

Verse 3. Despise not thy neighbour, but think thyself as bad a sinner, and that the like defects may befall thee. If thou canst not excuse his doing, excuse his intent which may be good; or if the deed be evil, think it was done of ignorance; if thou canst no way excuse him, think some great temptation befell him, and that thou shouldst be worse if the like temptation befell thee; and give God thanks that the like as yet hath not befallen thee. Despise not a man being a sinner, for though he be evil to-day, he may turn to-morrow. William Perkins, 1558–1602.

Verses 3, 4, 5. They that cry down moral honesty, cry down that which is a great part of religion, my duty towards God, and my duty towards man. What care I to see a man run after a sermon, if he cozens and cheats as soon as he comes home? On the other side, morality must not be without religion, for if so, it may change as I see convenience. Religion must govern it.

He that has not religion to govern his morality, is not a dram better than my mastiff-dog; so long as you stroke him, and please him, and do not pinch him, he will play with you as finely as may be, he is a very good moral mastiff; but if you hurt him, he will fly in your face, and tear out your throat. John Seldon, 1584–1654.

Verse 4. 'In whose eyes a vile person is contemned,' etc. When wicked Jehoram, king of Israel, came to Eliseus, the prophet, to ask counsel of the Lord, and to entreat for waters, having in company Jehoshaphat, the king of Judah, being virtuous; the prophet showeth his contempt to the one, being wicked, and his reverence to the other, being godly, faithful and virtuous, said, 'As the Lord of hosts liveth, before whom I stand, were it not that I regard the presence of Jehoshaphat, the king of Judah, I would not look toward thee, nor see thee' 2 Kings 3:14. Thus was the wicked vile in his sight; thus did he not flatter the ungodly. In like manner godly Mordecai, the Jew, having Haman the ambitious and proud Agagite in contempt, would in no wise bow the knee unto him in sign of honour, as the rest of the people did; for which cause he was extremely hated, menaced, and molested of proud and wicked Haman. To wink at their wickedness, to uphold them in their iniquity, to fawn upon them and flatter them, to praise them when they deserve just reproof, is, as it were, an honouring of them; to which, as to a most grievous sin, the prophet denounces a most bitter curse: 'Woe unto them that call evil good, and good evil; that put darkness for light, and light for darkness; that put bitter for sweet, and sweet for bitter!' Isaiah 5:20. Richard Turnbull.

Verse 4. 'In whose eyes a vile person is contemned.' To contemn the wicked and honour the godly, are opposite the one to the other. But the former may seem not to be sufficiently beseeming to a godly man. For why should he contemn or despise others, who is commanded by all means to care for the credit of others, as we heard even now? Nay, a godly man, letting others go, ought to search into himself, and to accuse himself, but not to judge of others. But this saying of the prophet is to be understood rather of the faults than of the person. As every man therefore is to be loved, so are the faults of every man to be hated of the godly. For so is God himself, whom we desire to be like unto, that we might dwell with him, affected and disposed. For why? he hateth no man, nay, he hateth nothing at all in this whole universal world, but only sin. For he is the author and preserver of all things that be; and therefore doth good and wisheth well to all; only of sin he is not the author, but the free and unconstrained will of man and Satan. Notwithstanding God doth so greatly hate sin, that by reason thereof he doth sometimes neglect and forsake men, yea, and have them in contempt. So then a godly man, nor contemneth any; but yet notwithstanding he disliketh sin in sinful men, and that he sticketh not to let them perceive either by reproving them, or shunning their company, or by doing of some other thing, whereby they may know they are misliked of good men for their enormities, and see themselves to be contemned of others for their wicked and ungodly life. A good man therefore must not flatter the ungodly in their ungracious attempts, but must freely declare that he disalloweth their course and conversation. Peter Baro.

Verse 4. 'In whose eyes a vile person is contemned.' Augustine, as Posidonius writeth, showing what hatred he had to tale-bearers and false reporters of others, had two verses written over his table; by translation these:

He that doth love with bitter speech the absent to defame,
Must surely know that at this board no place is for the same.
Richard Turnbull.

Verse 4. 'He honoureth them that fear the Lord.' Though the godly some way or other be injurious unto us, we ought nevertheless to honour and not to despise them. So Joseph did Mary, though he supposed her to have dealt injuriously with him; and she had done so, indeed, if it had been with her as he imagined. Calvin's resolution concerning Luther was very admirable in this respect. They differed much about the presence of Christ in the sacrament; and Luther being of a vehement spirit, wrote bitterly against those who did hold otherwise in that point than himself did. This enforced some, who were more nearly concerned in the business, to prepare to answer Luther; which Calvin understanding, and fearing lest they being provoked by Luther's tartness, should deal with him in the like kind, he wrote unto Bullinger, a prime man among them, persuading and exhorting him to carry the business so as to show all due respect unto Luther, considering what worth and excellency there was in him, however he had demeaned himself in that particular. And he adds, that he often used to say, that although Luther should call him devil, yet he would do him that honour, to acknowledge him a choice servant of God. Christopher Cartwright.

Verse 4. 'He honoureth them that fear the Lord.' I have read of one that said, If he should meet a preacher and an angel together, he would first salute the preacher and then the angel. Charles Bradbury's 'Cabinet of Jewels,' 1785.

Verse 4. 'He that sweareth to his own hurt, and changeth not.'

His words are bonds, his oaths are oracles;
His love sincere, his thoughts immaculate;
His tears pure messengers, sent from his heart;
His heart as far from fraud as heaven from earth.
William Shakspere.

Verse 5. The Puritanic divines are almost all of them against the taking of any interest upon money, and go to the length of saying that one penny per cent. per annum will shut a man out of heaven if persisted in. It appeared to me to be useless to quote opinions in which I cannot agree, especially as this would occupy space better employed. The demanding of excessive and grinding interest is a sin to be detested; the taking of the usual and current interest in a commercial country is not contrary to the law of love. The Jews were not engaged in commerce, and to lend money even at the lowest interest to their fellow farmers in times of poverty would have been usurious; but they might lend to strangers, who would usually be occupied in commerce, because in the commercial world, money is a fruitful thing, and the lender has a right to a part of its products; a loan to enable a non-trader to live over a season of want is quite another matter. C. H. S.

Verse 5. 'He that putteth not out his money to usury.' By usury is generally understood the gain of anything above the principal, or that which was lent, exacted only in consideration of the loan, whether it be in money, corn, wares, or the like. It is most commonly taken for an unlawful profit which a person makes of his money or goods. The Hebrew word for usury signifies biting. The law of God prohibits rigorous imposing conditions of gain for the loan of money or goods, and exacting them without respect to the condition of the borrower, whether he gain or lose; whether poverty occasioned his borrowing, or a visible prospect of gain by employing the borrowed goods. It is said in Exodus 22:25,26, 'If thou lend money to any of my people that is poor by thee, thou shalt not be to him an usurer, neither shalt thou lay upon him usury,' etc. And in Leviticus 25:35,36,37, 'If thy brother be waxen poor, and fallen into decay with thee, then thou shalt relieve him; yea, though he be a stranger, or a sojourner, that he may live with thee: take thou no usury of him,' etc. This law forbids the taking usury from a brother that was poor, an Israelite reduced to poverty, or from a proselyte; but in Deuteronomy 23:20, God seems to tolerate usury towards strangers; 'Unto a stranger thou mayest lend upon usury.' By strangers, in this passage, some understand the Gentiles in general, or all such as were not Jews, excepting proselytes. Others think that by strangers are meant the Canaanites, and the other people that were devoted to slavery and subjection; of these the Hebrews were permitted to exact usury, but not of such strangers with whom they had no quarrel, and against whom the Lord had not denounced his judgments. The Hebrews were plainly commanded in Exodus 22:25, etc., not to receive usury for money from any that borrowed from necessity, as in that case in Nehemiah 5:5,7. And such provision the law made for the preserving of estates to their families by the year of jubilee; for a people that had little concern in trade, could not be supposed to borrow money but out of necessity: but they were allowed to lend upon usury to strangers, whom yet they must not oppress. This law, therefore, in the strictness of it, it obligeth us to show mercy to those we have advantage against, and to be content to share with those we lend to in loss, as well as profit, if Providence cross them. And upon this condition, a valuable commentator says, It seems as lawful for me to receive interest for money, which another takes pains with, improves, but runs the hazard of in trade, as it is to receive rent for my land, which another takes pains with, improves, but runs the hazard of in husbandry.' Alexander Cruden, 1701–1770.

Verse 5. 'He that putteth not out his money to usury.' 'If thou lend money to any of my people that is poor by thee.' Exodus 22:25. Rather, according to the letter of the original, 'If thou lend money to my people, even to a poor man with thee.' The Israelites were a people but little engaged in commerce, and therefore could not in general be supposed to borrow money but from sheer necessity; and of that necessity the lender was not to take advantage by usurious exactions. The law is not to be understood as a prohibition of interest at any rate whatever, but of excessive interest or usury. The clause, 'Thou shalt not be to him as an usurer,' is equivalent to saying, 'Thou shalt not domineer and lord it over him rigorously and cruelly.' That this class of men were peculiarly to be extortionate and oppressive in their dealings with debtors would seem to be implied by the etymology of the original term for usury (Heb. *neshek*), which comes from a root signifying to bite; and in Nehemiah 5:2–5, we have a remarkable case of the bitter and grinding effects resulting from the creditor's rights over the debtor. A large portion of the people had not only mortgaged their lands, vineyards, and houses, but had actually sold their sons and daughters into bondage, to satisfy the claims of their grasping creditors. In this emergency Nehemiah espoused the cause of the poor, and compelled the rich, against whom he called the people together, to remit the whole of their dues; and, moreover, exacted from them an oath that they would never afterwards oppress their poor brethren for the payment of those debts. This was not because every part of those proceedings had been contrary to the letter of the Mosaic law, but because it was a flagrant breach of equity under the circumstances. It was taking a cruel and barbarous advantage of the necessities of their brethren, at which God was highly indignant, and which his servants properly rebuked. From this law the Hebrew canonists have gathered a general rule, that 'Whoso exacteth of a poor man, and knoweth that he hath not aught to pay him, he transgresseth against this prohibition, Thou shalt not be to him as an exacting creditor.' (Maimonides, in Ainsworth.) We nowhere learn from the institutes delivered by Moses that the simple taking of interest, especially from the neighbouring nations (Deuteronomy 23:19,20), was forbidden to the Israelites; but the divine law would give no countenance to the griping and extortionate practices to which miserly money-lenders are always prone. The deserving and industrious poor might sometimes be reduced to such straits, that pecuniary accommodations might be very desirable to them; and towards such God would inculcate a mild, kind, and forbearing spirit, and the precept is enforced by the relation which they sustained to him: 'Remember that you are lending to my people, my poor; and therefore, take no advantage of their necessities. Trust me against the fear of loss, and treat them kindly and generously.' George Bush, in 'Notes on the Book of Exodus,' 1856.

Verse 5. 'He that putteth not out his money to usury.' With respect to the first clause, as David seems to condemn all kinds of usury in general, and without exception, the very name has been everywhere held in detestation. But crafty men have invented specious names under which to conceal the vice; and thinking by this artifice to escape, they have plundered with greater excess than if they had lent on usury avowedly and openly. God, however, will not be dealt with and imposed upon by sophistry and false pretenses. He looks upon the thing as it really is. There is no worse species of usury than an unjust way of making bargains, where equity is disregarded on both sides. Let us, then, remember that all bargains, in which the one party unrighteously strives to make gain by the loss of the other party, whatever name may be given to them, are here condemned. It may be asked, whether all kinds of usury are to be put into this denunciation, and regarded as alike unlawful? If we condemn all without distinction, there is a danger lest many, seeing themselves brought into such a strait as to find that sin must be incurred, in whatever way they can turn themselves, may be rendered bolder by despair, and may rush headlong into all kinds of usury without choice or discrimination. On the other hand, whenever we concede that something may be lawfully done in this way, many will give themselves loose reins, thinking that a liberty to exercise usury, without control or moderation, has been granted them. In the first place, therefore, I would, above all things, counsel my readers to beware of ingeniously contriving deceitful pretexts by which to take advantage of their fellow men, and let them not imagine that anything can be lawful to them which is grievous and hurtful to others ... It is not without cause that God has in Leviticus 25:35, 36, forbidden usury, adding this reason: 'And if thy brother be waxen poor, and fallen in decay with thee; then thou shalt relieve him: yea, though he be a stranger, or a sojourner; that he may live with thee. Take thou no usury of him, or increase.' We see that the end for which the law was framed was that man should not cruelly oppress the poor, who ought rather to receive sympathy and compassion. This was, indeed, a part of the judicial law which God appointed for the Jews in particular; but it is a common principle of justice, which extends to all nations, and to all ages, that we should keep ourselves from plundering and devouring the poor who are in distress and want. Whence it follows, that the gain which he who lends his money upon interest acquires, without doing injury to any one, is not to be included under the head of unlawful usury. The Hebrew word *neshek*, which David employs, being derived from another word which signifies to bite, sufficiently shows that usuries are condemned in so far as they involve in them, or lead to, a license of robbing, or plundering our fellow men. Ezekiel, indeed (chapters 18:17, and 22:12), seems to condemn the taking of any interest whatever upon money lent; but he, doubtless, has an eye to the unjust and crafty arts of gaining by which the rich devoured the poor people. In short, provided we had engraven on our hearts the rule of equity which Christ prescribes in Matthew 7:12, 'Therefore, all things whatsoever ye would that men should do to you, do ye even so to them,' it would not be necessary to enter into lengthened disputes concerning usury. John Calvin, in loc.

Verse 5 (first clause). The Mosaic law forbids the lending of money for interest to an Israelite. Exodus 22:25; Leviticus 25:37; Deuteronomy 23:19; Proverbs 28:8; Ezekiel 18:8. In several of the passages referred to, it is expressly supposed that money is lent only to the poor, a supposition which has its ground in the simple relations of the Mosaic times, in which lending, for the purpose of speculation and gain, had no existence. Such lending ought only to be a work of brotherly love; and it is a great violation of that if any one, instead of helping his neighbour, takes advantage of his need to bring him into still greater straits. The Mosaic regulation in question has, accordingly, its import also for New Testament times. With the interest-lending of capitalists, who borrow for speculation, it has nothing to do. This belongs to a quite different matter, as is implied even by the name (Heb.), according to which only such usury can be meant as plagues and impoverishes a neighbour. By unseasonable comparison with our modes of speech, many would expound, 'His money he puts not to interest.' E. W. Hengstenberg.

Verse 5 (first clause). The worm called in Latin *teredo*, whereof Pliny hath reported something in his story, breeding in wood, to the touch as soft yet it hath such teeth as endeavoureth and consumeth the hard timber. So the usurer is a soft beast at first to handle, but in continuance of time the hardness of his teeth will eat thee up, both flesh and bone, if thou beware not. He pleadeth love, but not for thy sake, but for his own; for as the ivy colleth and claspeth the oak as a lover, but thereby it groweth up and over toppeth the oak, and sucketh out the juice and sap thereof, that it cannot thrive nor prosper; so the usurer colleth, embraceth, and claspeth in arms the borrower, that thereby himself may grow richer, and suck all wealth, goods, and riches from him, that he never thriveth or prospereth after. The pleasure the usurer showeth is like the playing of the cat with the silly mouse: the cat playeth with the mouse, but the play of the cat is the death of the mouse. The usurer pleasureth the borrower; but the pleasure of the usurer is the undoing of the borrower. The fox through craft slideth and tumbleth and maketh much pastime till he come to the prey, then he devoureth: the usurer maketh many fair speeches, giveth out many fair promises, pretendeth very great kindness, until he have got thee within his compass, then he crusheth thee. The usurer preyeth upon the poor, he waxeth rich at the penury of his brother, he clotheth himself with the coat of the naked, he feedeth himself of the bread of the hungry, and devoureth his poor brother, as the beasts do the smaller; than which, saith Ambrose, there is no greater inhumanity and cruelty, no greater wretchedness and iniquity, as Chrysostom in many places, and Basil upon this Psalm, have well observed. Richard Turnbull.

Verse 5. The rich make the poor to fill them; for usurers feed upon the poor, even as great fishes devour the small. Therefore, he which said, Let there not be a beggar in Israel (Deuteronomy 15:4), said too, Let there not be an usurer in Israel. For if there be usurers in Israel there will be beggars in Israel; for usurers make beggars, even as lawyers make quarrellers ... It is a miserable occupation to live by sin, and a great comfort to a man when he looketh upon his gold and silver, and his heart telleth him, All this is well gotten; and when he lieth upon his death-bed, and must leave all to his children, he can say unto them, I leave you mine own; but the usurer cannot say, I leave you mine own, but I leave you other men's; therefore the usurer can never die in peace, because if he die before he maketh restitution, he dieth in his sin. Henry Smith.

Verse 5. Biting usurers were so abhorred in the primitive church, that as they condemned the usurer himself, so they made the scribes, who wrote the bonds, and also the witnesses, incapable of any benefit; and that no testament or latter will, written by such should be valid. The house of the usurer was called *domus Satanae*, the house of the devil; and they ordained that no man should eat or drink with such usurer, nor fetch fire from them; and after they were dead that they should not be buried in Christian burial. The conclusion of this is (Ezekiel 18:13), this sin is matched with theft; and verse ll, with adultery; and verse 12, with violence; it is the daughter of oppression and sister to idolatry, and he that doth these things shall not dwell in God's holy hill. Albeit, these worldlings think themselves more honest than thieves and adulterers, yet the Lord maketh their case all alike. John Weemse, 1636.

Verse 5. 'Taketh reward against the innocent.' I am sure this is *scala inferni*, the right way to hell, to be covetous, to take bribes, and pervert justice. If a judge should ask me the way to hell, I should show him this way: First, let him be a covetous man; let his heart be poisoned with covetousness. Then let him go a little further and take bribes; and, lastly, pervert judgments. Lo, here is the mother, and the daughter, and the daughter's daughter. Avarice is the mother; she brings forth bribe-taking, and bribe-taking perverting of judgment. There lacks a fourth thing to make up the mess, which, so help me God, if I were judge, should be *hangum tuum*, a Tyburn tippet to take with him; an it were the judge of the King's Bench, my Lord Chief Judge of England, yea, an it were my Lord Chancellor himself, to Tyburn with him. Hugh Latimer.

Verse 5. Taketh reward against the innocent.' I come to corrupt lawyers and advocates, who so often take rewards against the innocent, as they do take upon them the defence of such causes as they in their own conscience are persuaded to be evil and unjust. Which being so common a fault among lawyers, as that very few which plead causes, either in civil or ecclesiastical courts, do seem to make any conscience thereof, to whom all is fish that cometh to their nets; therefore all lawyers are to be exhorted to apply this note unto themselves. George Downame.

Verse 5. 'He that doeth.' 'Tis not said he that professes this or that, or he that believes thus and thus, or he that is of such or such an opinion or way of worship, or he that sets up new lights, and pretends the Spirit for his immediate guide; 'tis not he that hears much or talks much of religion; no, nor he that preaches and prays much, nor he that thinks much of these things, and means well; but 'tis he that 'doeth these things' – that is actually employed about them – that is the religious and truly godly man. 'Tis not, I say, a formal professor, a confidant, a wild opinionist, a high-flown perfectist; it is not a constant hearer, or a mighty talker, or a labourious teacher, or a gifted brother, or a simple well-wisher must pass; but 'tis the honest and sincere doer of these things, that will abide the test and stand the trial; when all other flashy pretences shall, in those searching flames, be burnt and consumed like 'hay and stubble,' as the apostle expresses it. To wear Christ's livery and to do him no service is but to mock a gracious Master; to own him in our profession and deny him in our practice, is, with Judas, to betray him with a kiss of homage; with the rude soldiers to bow the knee before him, and, in the meantime to beat his sacred head with his reeden sceptre, and with Pilate to crown him with thorns, to crucify the Lord and write over his head, 'King of the Jews:' in a word, to grieve him with our honours, and wound him with our acknowledgments. A Christian profession without a life answerable, will be so far from saving any one, that 'twill highly aggravate his condemnation; when a dissembled friendship at the great day of discoveries shall be looked upon as the worst of enmities. A mere outside formality of worship, is at best but Prometheus's sacrifice, a skeleton of bones and a religious cheat . . . The harmless humour of meaning well is not enough to approve a man's spiritual state, to acquit obligations, or to ascertain his expectations. For he that bids us 'eschew evil' does immediately subjoin, that we must 'follow' and 'hold fast that which is good.' It will be no good account not to have done evil, unless we make it appear that we have been doing good too; since the non-commission of great sins will not excuse our omission of great duties. In the best commonwealth of bees, the drone without a sting, as she has no weapon for mischief, so, wanting a tool for employ, is deservedly cashiered the hive. Condensed from Adam Littleton, D.D., 1627–1694.

Verse 5. 'He that doeth these things shall never be moved.' Mark how the prophet saith not, he that readeth these things, or he that heareth these things, but he that doth them, shall never be removed. For were it enough to read or hear these precepts, then should an infinite number of vain and wicked persons enter into, and continue in the church, which notwithstanding have no place therein; for there are very few, or none at all, which have not read, or at least have not heard these things, yet they will not do them. Neither doth he say, he that talketh of these things, but he that doth them; for many now in these days can talk gloriously of uprightness, justice, truth, in whom notwithstanding, there is neither upright dealings, nor sound righteousness, nor unfeigned truth to be found. Many can say that slander is sin, injury is iniquity, to receive false reports is uncharitable, that it becometh not the saints to flatter the wicked, that to break promise and falsify their oaths is unseemly, to give upon usury is oppression, to receive bribes against the innocent is extreme cruelty; yet themselves backbite and hurt their neighbour, they themselves believe every tale that is brought them, they flatter and fawn upon the wicked for advantage, they swear and forswear for commodity, they oppress through usury, and receive gifts of bribery against the innocent; and so in word they speak of these things, but do them not indeed . . . Neither doth David say he that preacheth these, 'shall never be removed,' for then not only many other wicked persons, which can speak of, yea, many ungodly men which can also preach of virtue, should have the place in the Lord's tabernacle, and rest upon his holy hill; but also among others, even Balaam the covetous prophet, should have a sure place in God's tabernacle; for he could say, 'If Balak would give me his house full of silver and gold, I cannot go beyond the word of the Lord my God, to do less or more' (Numbers

22:18); yet he took rewards; yet he was carried away with covetousness, as much as in him lay, to work the destruction of Israel, the innocent people of the Lord. Richard Turnbull.

Verse 5. 'Shall never be moved.' Moved he may be for a time, but not removed for ever. His soul is bound up in the bundle of life, near unto the throne of glory; when the souls of the wicked are restless as a stone in the midst of a sling, saith the Targum in 1 Samuel 25. John Trapp.

Verse 5 (last clause). The holy soul is the love of God, the joy of angels; her eyes dare look upon the glorious Judge whom she knows to be her Saviour. Her heart is courageous; she dares stand the thunder; and when guilty minds creep into corners, she is confident in him that will defend her. She challengeth the whole world to accuse her of injustice, and fears not the subornation of false witnesses, because she knows the testimony of her own conscience. Her language is free and bold, without the guiltiness of broken stops. Her forehead is clear and smooth, as the brow of heaven. Her knees are ever bent to the throne of grace; her feet travelling toward Jerusalem; her hands weaving the web of righteousness. Good men bless her; good angels guard her; the Son of God doth kiss her; and when all the world shall be turned to a burning pile, she shall be brought safe to the mountain of joy, and set in a throne of blessedness for ever. Thomas Adams.

Hints to the village preacher

Verse 1. Qualifications for church membership on earth and in heaven. A subject for self-examination.

Verse 1.

1. Comparison of the church to the tabernacle. God's presence manifested, sacrifice offered, and vessels of grace preserved in it; mean externally, glorious within.
2. Comparison of its double position to that of the tabernacle. Moving in the wilderness, and fixed on the hill.
3. Enquire into qualification for admittance into church and tabernacle. Parallel with the priests, etc.

Verse 1. The great question. Asked by idle curiosity, despair, godly fear, earnest enquirer, soul troubled by falls of others, holy faith. Give answer to each.

Verse 1. The citizen of Zion described. Thomas Boston's Sermons.

Verse 1. Anxiety to know the true saints, how far lawful and profitable.

Verse 1. God the only infallible discerner of true saints.

Verse 2. 'He that walketh uprightly.'

1. What he must be. He must be upright in heart. A man himself bent double cannot walk uprightly.
2. How he must act. Neither from impulse, ambition, gain, fear, or flattery. He must not be warped in any direction, but stand perpendicularly.
3. What he must expect. Snares, etc., to trip him.
4. Where he must walk. Path of duty, the only one in which he can walk uprightly.
5. Where he must look. Up, right-up, and then he will be upright.

Verse 2. 'Speaketh the truth in his heart.' Subject: – Heart falsehood and heart truth.

Verse 2 (first clause). The citizen of Zion, an upright walker.

Verse 2 (middle clause). The citizen of Zion, a worker of righteousness.

Verse 2 (last clause). The citizen of Zion, a speaker of truth. Four Sermons in Thomas Boston's Works.

Verse 3. The evils of detraction. It affects three persons here mentioned: the backbiter, the suffering neighbour, and the taker-up of the reproach.

Verse 3. 'Nor taketh up a reproach.' The sin of being too ready to believe ill reports. Common, cruel, foolish, injurious, wicked.

Verse 4. The duty of practically honouring those who fear the Lord. Commendation, deference, assistance, imitation, etc.

Verse 4. The sin of estimating persons other than by their practical characters.

Verse 4 (last clause). The Lord Jesus as our unchanging Surety, his oath and his hurt.

Verse 5. The evidences and privileges of godly men.

Verse 5 (last clause). The fixedness and safety of the godly.

Psalm 19

Subject

It would be idle to enquire into the particular period when this delightful poem was composed, for their is nothing in its title or subject to assist us in the enquiry. The heading, 'To the Chief Musician, a Psalm of David,' informs us that David wrote it, and that it was committed to the Master of the service of song in the sanctuary for the use of the assembled worshippers. In his earliest days the psalmist, while keeping his father's flock, had devoted himself to the study of God's two great books – nature and Scripture; and he had so thoroughly entered into the spirit of these two only volumes in his library that he was able with a devout criticism to compare and contrast them, magnifying the excellency of the Author as seen in both. How foolish and wicked are those who instead of accepting the two sacred tomes, and delighting to behold the same divine hand in each, spend all their wits in endeavouring to find discrepancies and contradictions. We may rest assured that the true 'Vestiges of Creation' will never contradict Genesis, nor will a correct 'Cosmos' be found at variance with the narrative of Moses. He is wisest who reads both the world-book, and the Word-book as two volumes of the same work, and feels concerning them, 'My Father wrote them both.'

Division

This song very distinctly divides itself into three parts, very well described by the translators in the ordinary heading of our version. The creatures show God's glory, 1–6. The word showeth his grace, 7–11. David prayeth for grace, 12–14. Thus praise and prayer are mingled, and he who here sings the work of God in the world without, pleads for a work of grace in himself within.

Exposition

Verse 1. 'The heavens declare the glory of God.' The book of nature has three leaves, heaven, earth, and sea, of which heaven is the first and the most glorious, and by its aid we are able to see the beauties of the other two. Any book without its first page would be sadly imperfect, and especially the great Natural Bible, since its first pages, the sun, moon, and stars, supply light to the rest of the volume, and are thus the keys, without which the writing which follows would be dark and undiscerned. Man walking erect was evidently made to scan the skies, and he who begins to read creation by studying the stars begins the book at the right place.

The heavens are plural for their variety, comprising the watery heavens with their clouds of countless forms, the aerial heavens with their calms and tempests, the solar heavens with all the glories of the day, and the starry heavens with all the marvels of the night; what the Heaven of heavens must be hath not entered into the heart of man, but there in chief all things are telling the glory of God. Any part of creation has more instruction in it than human mind will ever exhaust, but the celestial realm is peculiarly rich in spiritual lore. The heavens declare, or are declaring, for the continuance of their testimony is intended by the participles employed; every moment God's existence, power, wisdom and goodness, are being sounded abroad by the heavenly heralds which shine upon us from above. He who would guess at divine sublimity should gaze upward into the starry vault; he who would imagine infinity must peer into the boundless expanse; he who desires to see divine wisdom should consider the balancing of the orbs; he who would know divine fidelity must mark the regularity of the planetary motions; and he who would attain some conceptions of divine power, greatness, and majesty, must estimate the forces of attraction, the magnitude of the fixed stars, and the brightness of the whole celestial train. It is not merely glory that the heavens declare, but the 'glory of God,' for they deliver to us such unanswerable arguments for a conscious, intelligent, planning, controlling, and presiding Creator, that no unpredjudiced person can remain unconvinced by them. The testimony given by the heavens is no mere hint, but a plain, unmistakable declaration; and it is a declaration of the most constant and abiding kind. Yet for all this, to what avail is the loudest declaration to a deaf man, or the clearest showing to one spiritually blind? God the Holy Ghost must illuminate us, or all the suns in the milky way never will.

'The firmament sheweth his handy-work;' not handy in the vulgar use of that term, but hand-work. The expanse is full of the works of the Lord's skilful, creating hands; hands being attributed to the great creating Spirit to set forth his care and workmanlike action, and to meet the poor comprehension of mortals. It is humbling to find that even when the most devout and elevated minds are desirous to express their loftiest thoughts of God, they must use words and metaphors drawn from the earth. We are children, and must each confess, 'I think as a child, I speak as a child.' In the expanse above us God flies, as it were, his starry flag to show that the King is at home, and hangs out his escutcheon that atheists may see how he despises their denunciations of him. He who looks up to the firmament and then writes himself down an atheist, brands himself at the same moment as an idiot or a liar. Strange is it that some who love God are yet afraid to study the God-declaring book of nature; the mock-spirituality of some believers, who are too heavenly to consider the heavens, has given colour to the vaunts of infidels that nature contradicts revelation. The wisest of men are those who with pious eagerness trace the goings forth of Jehovah as well in creation as in grace; only the foolish have any fears lest the honest study of the one should injure our faith in the other. Dr M'Cosh has well said, 'We have often mourned over the attempts made to set the works of God against the Word of God, and thereby excite, propagate, and perpetuate jealousies fitted to separate parties that ought to live in closest union. In particular, we have always regretted that endeavours should have been made to depreciate nature with a view of exalting revelation; it has always appeared to us to be nothing else than the degrading of one part of God's work in the hope thereby of exalting and recommending another. Let not science and religion be reckoned as opposing citadels, frowning defiance upon each other, and their troops brandishing their armour in hostile attitude. They have too many common foes, if they would but think of it, in ignorance and prejudice, in passion and vice, under all their forms, to admit of their lawfully wasting their strength in a useless warfare with each other. Science has a foundation, and so has religion; let them unite their foundations, and the basis will be broader, and they will be two compartments of one great fabric reared to the glory of God. Let one be the outer and the other the inner court. In the one, let all look, and admire and adore; and in the other, let those who have faith kneel, and pray, and praise. Let the one be the sanctuary where human learning may present its richest incense as an offering to God, and the other the holiest of all, separated from it by a veil now rent in twain, and in which, on a blood-sprinkled mercy-seat, we pour out the love of a reconciled heart, and hear the oracles of the living God.'

Verse 2. 'Day unto day uttereth speech, and night unto night sheweth knowledge.' As if one day took up the story where the other left it, and each night passed over the wondrous tale to the next. The original has in it the thought of pouring out or welling over, with speech; as though days and nights were but as a fountain flowing evermore with Jehovah's praise. Oh to drink often at the celestial well, and learn to utter the glory of God! The witnesses above cannot be slain or silenced; from their elevated seats they constantly preach the knowledge of God, unawed and unbiased by the judgment of men. Even the changes of alternating night and day are mutely eloquent, and light and shade equally reveal the Invisible One; let the vicissitudes of our circumstances do the same, and while we bless the God of our days of joy, let us also extol him who giveth 'songs in the night.'

The lesson of day and night is one which it were well if all men learned. It should be among our day-thoughts and night-thoughts, to remember the flight of time, the changeful character of earthly things, the brevity both of joy and sorrow, the preciousness of life, our utter powerlessness to recall the hours once flown, and the irresistible approach of eternity. Day bids us labour, night reminds us to prepare for our last time; day bids us work for God, and night invites us to rest in him; day bids us look for endless day, and night warns us to escape from everlasting night.

Verse 3. 'There is no speech nor language, where their voice is not heard.' Every man may hear the voices of the stars. Many are the languages of terrestrials, to celestials there is but one, and that one may be understood by every willing mind. The lowest heathen are without excuse, if they do not discover the invisible things of God in the works which he has made. Sun, moon, and stars are God's travelling preachers; they are apostles upon their journey confirming those who regard the Lord, and judges on circuit condemning those who worship idols.

The margin gives us another rendering, which is more literal, and involves less repetition; 'no speech, no words, their voice is not heard;' that is to say, their teaching is not addressed to the ear, and is not uttered in articulate sounds; it is pictorial, and directed to the eye and heart; it touches not the sense by which faith comes, for faith cometh by hearing. Jesus Christ is called the Word, for he is a far more distinct display of Godhead than all the heavens can afford; they are, after all, but dumb instructors; neither star nor sun can arrive at a word, but Jesus is the express image of Jehovah's person, and his name is the Word of God.

Verse 4. 'Their line is gone out through all the earth, and their words to the end of the world.' Although the heavenly bodies move in solemn silence, yet in reason's ear they utter precious teachings. They give forth no literal words, but yet their instruction is clear enough to be so described. Horne says that the phrase employed indicates a language of signs, and thus we are told that the heavens speak by their significant actions and operations. Nature's words are like those of the deaf and dumb, but grace tells us plainly of the Father. By their line is probably meant the measure of their domain which, together with their testimony, has gone out to the utmost end of the habitable earth. No man living beneath the copes of heaven dwells beyond the bounds of the diocese of God's Court-preachers; it is easy to escape from the light of ministers, who are as stars in the right hand of the Son of Man; but even then men, with a conscience yet unseared, will find a Nathan to accuse them, a Jonah to warn them, and an Elijah to threaten them in the silent stars of night. To gracious souls the voices of the heavens are more influential far, they feel the sweet influences of the Pleiades, and are drawn towards their Father God by the bright bands of Orion.

'In them hath he set a tabernacle for the sun.' In the heavens the sun encamps, and marches like a mighty monarch on his glorious way. He has no fixed abode, but as a traveller pitches and removes his tent, a tent which will soon be taken down and rolled together as a scroll. As the royal pavilion stood in the centre of the host, so the sun in his place appears like a king in the midst of attendant stars.

Verse 5. 'Which is as a bridegroom coming out of his chamber.' A bridegroom comes forth sumptuously apparelled, his face beaming with a joy which he imparts to all around; such, but with a mighty emphasis, is the rising Sun. 'And rejoiceth as a strong man to run a race.' As a champion girt for running cheerfully addresses himself to the race, so does the sun speed onward with matchless regularity and unwearying swiftness in his appointed orbit. It is but mere play to him; there are no signs of effort, flagging, or exhaustion. No other creature yields such joy to the earth as her bridegroom the sun; and none, whether they be horse or eagle, can for an instant compare in swiftness with that heavenly champion. But all his glory is but the glory of God; even the sun shines in light borrowed from the Great Father of Lights.

Thou sun, of this great world both eye and soul,
Acknowledge Him thy greater; sound his praise
Both when thou climb'st, and when high noon hast gained,
And when thou fall'st.

Verse 6. 'His going forth is from the end of the heaven, and his circuit unto the ends of it.' He bears his light to the boundaries of the solar heavens, traversing the zodiac with steady motion, denying his light to none who dwell within his range. 'And there is nothing hid from the heat thereof.' Above, beneath, around, the heat of the sun exercises an influence. The bowels of the earth are stored with the ancient produce of the solar rays, and even yet earth's inmost caverns feel their power. Where light is shut out, yet heat and other more subtle influences find their way.

There is no doubt a parallel intended to be drawn between the heaven of grace and the heaven of nature. God's way of grace is sublime and broad, and full of his glory; in all its displays it is to be admired and studied with diligence; both its lights and its shades are instructive; it has been proclaimed, in a measure, to every people, and in due time shall be yet more completely published to the ends of the earth. Jesus, like a sun, dwells in the midst of revelation, tabernacling among men in all his brightness; rejoicing, as the Bridegroom of his church, to reveal himself to men; and, like a champion, to win unto himself renown. He makes a circuit of mercy, blessing the remotest corners of the earth; and there are no seeking souls, however degraded and depraved, who shall be denied the comfortable warmth and benediction of his love – even death shall feel the power of his presence, and resign the bodies of the saints, and this fallen earth shall be restored to its pristine glory.

In the three following verses (7, 8, 9) we have a brief but instructive *hexapla* containing six descriptive titles of the word, six characteristic qualities mentioned and six divine effects declared. Names, nature, and effect are well set forth.

Verse 7. 'The law of the Lord is perfect;' by which he means not merely the law of Moses but the doctrine of God, the whole run and rule of sacred Writ. The doctrine revealed by God he declares to be perfect, and yet David had but a very small part of the Scriptures, and if a fragment, and that the darkest and most historical portion, be perfect, what must the entire volume be? How more than perfect is the book which contains the clearest possible display of divine love, and gives us an open vision of redeeming grace. The gospel is a complete scheme or law of gracious salvation, presenting to the needy sinner everything that his terrible necessities can possibly demand. There are no redundancies and no omissions in the Word of God, and in the plan of grace; why then do men try to paint this lily and gild this refined gold? The gospel is perfect in all its parts, and perfect as a whole: it is a crime to add to it, treason to alter it, and felony to take from it.

'Converting the soul.' Making the man to be returned or restored to the place from which sin had cast him. The practical effect of the Word of God is to turn the man to himself, to his God, and to holiness; and the turn or conversion is not outward alone, 'the soul' is moved and renewed. The great means of the conversion of sinners is the Word of God, and the more closely we keep to it in our ministry the more likely we are to be successful. It is God's Word rather than man's comment on God's Word which is made mighty with souls. When the law drives and the gospel draws, the action is different but the end is one, for by God's Spirit the soul is made to yield, and cries, 'Turn me, and I shall be turned.' Try men's depraved nature with philosophy and reasoning, and it laughs your efforts to scorn, but the Word of God soon works a transformation.

'The testimony of the Lord is sure.' God bears his testimony against sin, and on behalf of righteousness; he testifies of our fall and of our restoration; this testimony is plain, decided, and infallible, and is to be accepted as sure. God's witness in his Word is so sure that we may draw solid comfort from it both for time and eternity, and so sure that no attacks made upon it however fierce or subtle can ever weaken its force. What a blessing that in a world of uncertainties we have something sure to rest upon! We hasten from the quicksands of human speculations to the *terra firma* of Divine Revelation.

'Making wise the simple.' Humble, candid, teachable minds receive the word, and are made wise unto salvation. Things hidden from the wise and prudent are revealed unto babes. The persuadable grow wise, but the cavillers continue fools. As a law or plan the Word of God converts, and then as a testimony it instructs; it is not enough for us to be converts, we must continue to be disciples; and if we have felt the power of truth, we must go on to prove its certainty by experience. The perfection of the gospel converts, but its sureness edifies; if we would be edified it becomes us not to stagger at the promise through unbelief, for a doubted gospel cannot make us wise, but truth of which we are assured will be our establishment.

Verse 8. 'The statutes of the Lord are right.' His precepts and decrees are founded in right-eousness, and are such as are right or fitted to the right reason of man. As a physician gives the right medicine, and a counsellor the right advice, so does the Book of God. 'Rejoicing the heart.' Mark the progress; he who was converted was next made wise and is now made happy; that truth which makes the heart right then gives joy to the right heart. Free-grace brings heart-joy. Earthborn mirth dwells on the lip, and flushes the bodily powers; but heavenly delights satisfy the inner nature, and fill the mental faculties to the brim. There is no cordial of comfort like that which is poured from the bottle of Scripture.

Retire and read thy Bible to be happy.

'The commandment of the Lord is pure.' No mixture of error defiles it, no stain of sin pollutes it; it is the unadulterated milk, the undiluted wine. 'Enlightening the eyes,' purging away by its own purity the earthly grossness which mars the intellectual discernment: whether the eye be dim with sorrow or with sin, the Scripture is a skilful occulist, and makes the eye clear and bright. Look at the sun and it puts out your eyes, look at the more than sunlight of Revelation and it enlightens them; the purity of snow causes snow-blindness to the Alpine traveller, but the purity of God's truth has the contrary effect, and cures the natural blindness of the soul. It is well again to observe the gradation; the convert becomes a disciple and next a rejoicing soul, he now obtains a discerning eye and as a spiritual man discerneth all things, though he himself is discerned of no man.

Verse 9. 'The fear of the Lord is clean.' The doctrine of truth is here described by its spiritual effect, viz., inward piety, or the fear of the Lord; this is clean in itself, and cleanses out the love of sin, sanctifying the heart in which it reigns. Mr Godly-fear is never satisfied till every street, lane, and alley, yea, and every house and every corner of the town of Mansoul is clean rid of the Diablolonians who lurk therein. 'Enduring for ever.' Filth brings decay, but cleanness is the great foe of corruption. The grace of God in the heart being a pure principle, is also an abiding and incorruptible principle, which may be crushed for a time, but cannot be utterly destroyed. Both in the Word and in the heart, when the Lord writes, he says with Pilate, 'What I have written, I have written;' he will make no erasures himself, much less suffer others to do so. The revealed will of God is never changed; even Jesus came not to destroy but to fulfil, and even the ceremo-nial law was only changed as to its shadow, the substance intended by it is eternal. When the governments of nations are shaken with revolution, and ancient constitutions are being repealed, it is comforting to know that the throne of God is unshaken, and his law unaltered.

'The judgments of the Lord are true and righteous altogether;' – jointly and severally the words of the Lord are true; that which is good in detail is excellent in the mass; no exception may be taken to a single clause separately, or to the book as a whole. God's judgments, all of them together, or each of them apart, are manifestly just, and need no labourious excuses to justify them. The judicial decisions of Jehovah, as revealed in the law, or illustrated in the history of his providence, are truth itself, and commend themselves to every truthful mind; not only is their power invincible, but their justice is unimpeachable.

Verse 10. 'More to be desired are they than fine gold, yea, than much fine gold.' Bible truth is enriching to the soul in the highest degree; the metaphor is one which gathers force as it is brought out; – gold – fine gold – much fine gold; it is good, better, best, and therefore it is not only to be desired with a miser's avidity, but with more than that. As spiritual treasure is more noble than mere material wealth, so should it be desired and sought after with greater eagerness. Men speak of solid gold, but what is so solid as solid truth? For love of gold pleasure is forsworn, ease renounced, and life endangered; shall we not be ready to do as much for love of truth? 'Sweeter also than honey and the honeycomb.' Trapp says, 'Old people are all for profit, the young for pleasure; here's gold for the one, yea, the finest gold in great quantity; here's honey for the other, yea, live honey dropping from the comb.' The pleasures arising from a right understanding of the divine testimonies are of the most delightful order; earthly enjoyments are utterly contemptible, if compared with them. The sweetest joys, yea, the sweetest of the sweetest falls to his portion who has God's truth to be his heritage.

Verse 11. 'Moreover by them is thy servant warned.' We are warned by the Word both of our duty, our danger, and our remedy. On the sea of life there would be many more wrecks, if it were not for the divine storm-signals, which give to the watchful a timely warning. The Bible should be our Mentor, our Monitor, our Memento Mori, our Remembrancer, and the Keeper of our Conscience. Alas, that so few men will take the warning so graciously given; none but servants of God will do so, for they alone regard their Master's will. Servants of God not only find his service delightful in itself, but they receive good recompense; 'In keeping of them there is great reward.' There is a wage, and a great one; though we earn no wages of debt, we win great wages of grace. Saints may be losers for a time, but they shall be glorious gainers in the long run, and even now a quiet conscience is in itself no slender reward for obedience. He who wears the herb called heart's-ease in his bosom is truly blessed. However, the main reward is yet to come, and the word here used hints as much, for it signifies the heel, as if the reward would come to us at the end of life when the work was done; – not while the labour was in hand, but when it was gone and we could see the heel of it. Oh the glory yet to be revealed! It is enough to make a man faint for joy at the prospect of it. Our light affliction, which is but for a moment, is not worthy to be compared with the glory which shall be revealed in us. Then shall we know the value of the Scriptures when we swim in that sea of unutterable delight to which their streams will bear us, if we commit ourselves to them.

Verse 12. 'Who can understand his errors?' A question which is its own answer. It rather requires a note of exclamation than of interrogation. By the law is the knowledge of sin, and in the presence of divine truth, the psalmist marvels at the number and heinousness of his sins. He best knows himself who best knows the Word, but even such an one will be in a maze of wonder as to what he does not know, rather than on the mount of congratulation as to what he does know. We have heard of a comedy of errors, but to a good man this is more like a tragedy. Many books have a few lines of errata at the end, but our errata might well be as large as the volume if we could but have sense enough to see them. Augustine wrote in his older days a series of Retractations; ours might make a library if we had enough grace to be convinced of our mistakes and to confess them. 'Cleanse thou me from secret faults.' Thou canst mark in me faults entirely hidden from myself. It were hopeless to expect to see all my spots; therefore, O Lord, wash away in the atoning blood even those sins which my conscience has been unable to detect. Secret sins, like private conspirators, must be hunted out, or they may do deadly mischief; it is well to be much in prayer concerning them. In the Lateran Council of the Church of Rome, a decree was passed that every true believer must confess his sins, all of them, once a year to the priest, and they affixed to it this declaration, that there is no hope of pardon but in complying with that decree. What can equal the absurdity of such a decree as that? Do they suppose that they can tell their sins as easily as they can count their fingers? Why, if we could receive pardon for all our sins by telling every sin we have committed in one hour, there is not one of us who would be able to enter heaven, since, besides the sins that are known to us and that we may be able to confess, there are a vast mass of sins, which are as truly sins as those which we lament, but which are secret, and come not beneath our eye. If we had eyes like those of God, we should think very differently of ourselves. The transgressions which we see and confess are but like the farmer's small samples which he brings to market, when he has left his granary full at home. We have but a very few sins which we can observe and detect, compared with those which are hidden from ourselves and unseen by our fellow-creatures.

Verse 13. 'Keep back thy servant also from presumptuous sins; let them not have dominion over me.' This earnest and humble prayer teaches us that saints may fall into the worst of sins unless restrained by grace, and that therefore they must watch and pray lest they enter into temptation. There is a natural proneness to sin in the best of men, and they must be held back as a horse is held back by the bit or they will run into it. Presumptuous sins are peculiarly dangerous. All sins are great sins, but yet some sins are greater than others. Every sin has in it the very venom of rebellion, and is full of the essential marrow of traitorous rejection of God; but there be some sins which have in them a greater development of the essential mischief of rebellion, and which wear upon their faces more of the brazen pride which defies the Most High. It is wrong to suppose that because all sins will condemn us, that therefore one sin is not greater than another. The fact is, that while all transgression is a greatly grievous and sinful thing, yet there are some transgressions which have a deeper shade of blackness, and a more double scarlet-dyed hue of criminality than others. The presumptuous sins of our text are the chief and worst of all sins; they rank head and foremost in the list of iniquities. It is remarkable that though an atonement was provided under the Jewish law for every kind of sin, there was this one exception: 'But the soul that sinneth presumptuously shall have no atonement; it shall be cut off from the midst of the people.' And now under the Christian dispensation, although in the sacrifice of our blessed Lord there is a great and precious atonement for presumptuous sins, whereby sinners who have erred in this manner are made clean, yet without doubt, presumptuous sinners, dying without pardon, must expect to receive a double portion of the wrath of God, and a more terrible portion of eternal punishment in the pit that is digged for the wicked. For this reason is David so anxious that he may never come under the reigning power of these giant evils. 'Then shall I be upright, and I shall be innocent from the great transgression.' He shudders at the thought of the unpardonable sin. Secret sin is a stepping-stone to presumptuous sin, and that is the vestibule of 'the sin which is unto death.' He who is not wilful in his sin, will be in a fair way to be innocent so far as poor sinful man can be; but he who tempts the devil to tempt him is in a path which will lead him from bad to worse, and from the worse to the worst.

Verse 14. 'Let the words of my mouth, and the meditation of my heart, be acceptable in thy sight, O Lord, my strength, and my Redeemer.' A sweet prayer, and so spiritual that it is almost as commonly used in Christian worship as the apostolic benediction. Words of the mouth are mockery if the heart does not meditate; the shell is nothing without the kernel; but both together are useless unless accepted; and even if accepted by man, it is all vanity if not acceptable in the sight of God. We must in prayer view Jehovah as our strength enabling, and our Redeemer saving, or we shall not pray aright, and it is well to feel our personal interest so as to use the word my, or our prayers will be hindered. Our near Kinsman's name, our *goel* or Redeemer, makes a blessed ending to the Psalm; it began with the heavens, but it ends with him whose glory fills heaven and earth. Blessed Kinsman, give us now to meditate acceptably upon thy most sweet love and tenderness.

Explanatory notes and quaint sayings

Whole Psalm. The magnificent scenery to which the poem alludes is derived entirely from a contemplation of nature, in a state of pastoral seclusion; and a contemplation indulged in, at noontide or in the morning, when the sun was travelling over the horizon, and eclipsing all the other heavenly bodies by his glory. On which account it forms a perfect contrast with the eighth Psalm, evidently composed in the evening, and should be read in connection with it, as it was probably written nearly at the same time; and as both are songs of praise derived from natural phenomena, and therefore peculiarly appropriate to rural or pastoral life. John Mason Good.

Whole Psalm. The world resembleth a divinity-school, saith Plutarch, and Christ, as the Scripture telleth, is our doctor, instructing us by his works, and by his words. For as Aristotle had two sorts of writings, one called exoterical, for his common auditors, another acromatical, for his private scholars and familiar acquaintance: so God hath two sorts of books, as David intimates in this Psalm; namely, the book of his creatures, as a common-place book for all men in the world: 'The heavens declare the glory of God' verses 1–6; the book of his Scriptures as a statute-book for his domestic auditory, the church: 'The law of the Lord is an undefiled law' verses 7, 8. The great book of the creatures in folio, may be termed aptly the shepherd's kalendar, and the ploughman's alphabet, in which even the most ignorant may run (as the prophet speaks) and read. It is a letter patent, or open epistle for all, as David, in our text, Their sound is gone out into all lands, and their words unto the ends of the world; there is neither speech nor language but have heard of their preaching. For albeit, heaven, and the sun in heaven, and the light in the sun are mute, yet their voices are well understood, catechising plainly the first elements of religion, as, namely, that there is a God, and that this God is but one God, and that this one God excelleth all other things infinitely both in might and majesty. *Universus mundus* (as one pithily) *nihil aliud est quam Deus explicatus*: the whole world is nothing else but God expressed. So St Paul, Romans 1:20: God's invisible things, as his eternal power and Godhead, 'are clearly seen' by the creation of the world, 'being understood by the things that are made.' The heavens declare this, and the firmament showeth this, and the day telleth this, and the night certifieth this, the sound of the thunder proclaimeth, as it were, this in all lands, and the words of the whistling wind unto the ends of the world. More principally the sun, which as a bridegroom cometh out of his chamber, and rejoiceth as a giant to run his course. The body thereof (as mathematicians have confidently delivered) is one hundred and sixty-six times bigger than the whole earth, and yet it is every day carried by the finger of God so great a journey, so long a course, that if it were to be taken on the land, it should run every several hour of the day two hundred and twenty-five German miles. It is true that God is incapable to sense, yet he makes himself, as it were, visible in his works; as the divine poet (Du Bartas) sweetly:

Therein our fingers feel, our nostrils smell,
Our palates taste his virtues that excel,
He shows him to our eyes, talks to our ears,
In the ordered motions of the spangled spheres.

So 'the heavens declare,' that is, they make men declare the glory of God, by their admirable structure, motions, and influence. Now the preaching of the heavens is wonderful in three respects: 1. As preaching all the night and all the day without intermission: verse 2. One day telleth another, and one night certifieth another. 2. As preaching in every kind of language: verse 3. There is neither speech, nor language, but their voices are heard among them. 3. As preaching in every part of the world, and in every parish of every part, and in every place of every parish: verse 4. Their sound is gone into all lands, and their words unto the ends of the world. They be diligent pastors, as preaching at all times; and learned pastors, as preaching in all tongues; and catholic pastors, as preaching in all towns. Let us not then in this University (where the voices of so many great doctors are heard), be like to truants in other schools, who gaze so much upon the babies, (the pictures or illustrations of a book), and gilded cover, and painted margent of their book, that they neglect the text and lesson itself. This is God's primer, as it were, for all sorts of people; but he hath another book proper only for his domestic auditory the church: 'He sheweth his word unto Jacob, his statutes and his judgments unto Israel. He hath not dealt so with any nation, neither have the heathen knowledge of his laws' Psalm 147:19,20. Heathen men read in his primer, but Christian men are well acquainted with his Bible. The primer is a good book, but it is imperfect; for after a man hath learned it he must learn more; but 'the law of the Lord,' that is, the body of the Holy Scriptures, is a most absolute canon of all doctrines appertaining either to faith or good manners; it is a perfect law, converting the soul, giving wisdom to the simple, sure, pure, righteous, and rejoicing the heart,' etc. John Boys.

Whole Psalm. Saint Chrysostom conjectures that the main intention of the greatest part of this Psalm consists in the discovery of divine providence, which manifests itself in the motions and courses of the heavenly bodies, concerning which the psalmist speaketh much, from verse 1 to verse 7. Saint Austin upon the place, is of a quite different opinion, who conjectures that Christ is the whole subject of this Psalm; whose person is compared to the sun for excellency and beauty, and the course of whose doctrine was dispersed round about the world by his apostles to which Saint Paul alludes (Romans 10:18); 'Have they not heard? Yes, verily, their sound went into all the earth,' etc., and the efficacy of whose gospel is like the heat of the sun, which pierceth into the very heart of the earth, so that into the secrets of the soul. I confess this allegorical exposition is not altogether impertinent, neither is that literal exposition of Saint Chrysostom to be blamed, for it hath its weight. But to omit all variety of conjecture, this Psalm contains in it:

1.   A double kind of the knowledge of God, of which one is by the book of the creature; and this divines call a natural knowledge: there is not any one creature but it is a leaf written all over with the description of God; his eternal power and Godhead may be understood by the things that are seen, saith the apostle. Romans 1:20. And, as every creature, so especially 'the heavens' do lead us to the knowledge of a God; so verse 1 of this Psalm: 'The heavens declare the glory of God, and the firmament sheweth his handiwork;' they are the theatres, as it were, of his wisdom, and power, and glory. Another is by the book of Scripture; and this knowledge is far more distinct and explicit: with the other even the heathen do grope after a deity, but with this Christians do behold God, as it were, with open face. The characters here are now fresh, spiritual, complete, and lively. The word of God is the singular means to know God aright. Look, as the light which comes from the sun, so that word of God, which is light, is the clearest way to know God who is light itself. Hence it is that the psalmist stands much upon this from verse 7 to verse 12, where he sets open the word in its several encomiums and operations; namely, in its perfection, its certainties, and firmness; its righteousness, and purity, and truth; and then in its efficacy – that it is a converting word, an enlightening word, an instructing word, a rejoicing word, a desirable word, a warning word, and a rewarding word.

2.   A singular and experimental knowledge of himself. – So it seemeth, that that word which David did so much commend, he did commend it from an experimental efficacy; he had found it to be a righteous, and holy, and pure, and discovering word, laying open, not only visible and gross transgressions, but also, like the light of the sun, those otherwise unobserved and secret atoms of senses flying within the house; I mean in the secret chambers of the soul. Obadiah Sedgwick, 1660.

Verse 1. 'The heavens declare the glory of God,' etc. – The eminent saints of ancient times were watchful observers of the objects and operations of nature. In every event they saw the agency of God; and, therefore, they took delight in its examination. For they could not but receive pleasure from witnessing the manifestations of his wisdom and beneficence, whom they adored and loved. They had not learned, as we have in modern times, to interpose unbending laws between the Creator and his works; and then, by giving inherent power to these laws, virtually to remove God away from his creation into an ethereal *extramundane* sphere of repose and happiness. I do not say that this is the universal feeling of the present day. But it prevails extensively in the church, and still more in the world. The ablest philosophers of modern times do, indeed, maintain that a natural law is nothing more than the uniform mode in which God acts; and that, after all, it is not the efficiency of the law, but God's own energy, that keeps all nature in motion; that he operates immediately and directly, not remotely and indirectly, in bringing about every event, and that every natural change is as really the work of God as if the eye of sense could see his hand turning round the wheels of nature. But, although the ablest philosophy of modern times has reached this conclusion, the great mass of the community, and even of Christians, are still groping in the darkness of that mechanical system which ascribes the operation of this natural world to nature's laws instead of nature's God. By a sort of figure, indeed, it is proper, as the advocates of this system admit, to speak of God as the author of its natural events, because he originally ordained the laws of nature. But they have no idea that he exerts any direct and immediate agency in bringing them about; and, therefore, when they look upon these events they feel no impression of the presence and active agency of Jehovah.

But how different, as already remarked, were the feeling of ancient saints. The psalmist could not look up to heaven without exclaiming, 'The heavens declare the glory of God; and the firmament sheweth his handiwork. Day unto day uttereth speech, and night unto night sheweth knowledge. There is no speech nor language where their voice is not heard.' When he cast his eyes abroad upon the earth, his full heart cried out, 'O Lord, how manifold are thy works! In wisdom hast thou made them all; the earth is full of thy riches.' In his eye everything was full of God. It was God who 'sent springs into the valleys, which run among the hills.' When the thunder-storm passed before him, it was 'God's voice in the heavens, and his lightnings that lighted the world.' When he heard the bellowings, and saw the smoke of the volcano, it was 'God who looketh on the earth, and it trembleth; he toucheth the hills, and they smoke.' Edward Hitchcock, D.D., LL.D., 1867.

Verse 1. 'The heavens declare,' etc. Man has been endued by his Creator with mental powers capable of cultivation. He has employed them in the study of the wonderful works of God which the universe displays. His own habitation has provided a base which has served him to measure the heavens. He compares his own stature with the magnitude of the earth on which he dwells; the earth, with the system in which it is placed; the extent of the system, with the distance of the nearest fixed stars; and that distance again serves as a unit of measurement for other distances which observation points out. Still no approach is made to any limit. How extended these wonderful works of the Almighty may be no man can presume to say. The sphere of creation appears to extend around us indefinitely on all sides; 'to have its centre everywhere, its circumference nowhere.' These are considerations which from their extent almost bewilder our minds. But how should they raise our ideas toward their great Creator, when we consider that all these were created from nothing, by a word, by a mere volition of the Deity. 'Let them be,' said God, and they were. 'By the word of the Lord were the heavens made, and all the host of them by the breath of his mouth.' 'For he spake, and it was done. He commanded, and it stood fast' Psalm 33:6, 9. What must be that power, which so formed worlds on worlds; worlds in comparison of which this earth which we inhabit sinks into utter nothingness! Surely when we thus lift up our thoughts to the heavens, the moon and the stars which he hath ordained, we must feel, if we can ever feel, how stupendous and incomprehensible is that Being who formed them all; that 'the heavens' do indeed 'declare the glory of God;' and the firmament sheweth his handiwork.' Temple Chevallier, in 'The Hulsean Lectures for 1827.'

Verse 1. I have often been charmed and awed at the sight of the nocturnal heavens, even before I knew how to consider them in their proper circumstances of majesty and beauty. Something like magic has struck my mind, on transient and unthinking survey of the aethreal vault, tinged throughout with the purest azure, and decorated with innumerable starry lamps. I have felt, I know not what, powerful and aggrandising impulse, which seemed to snatch me from the low entanglements of vanity, and prompted an ardent sigh for sublimer objects. Methought I heard, even from the silent spheres, a commanding call to spurn the abject earth, and pant after unseen delights. Henceforth I hope to imbibe more copiously this moral emanation of the skies, when, in some such manner as the preceding, they are rationally seen, and the sight is duly improved. The stars, I trust, will teach as well as shine, and help to dispel both nature's gloom and my intellectual darkness. To some people they discharge no better a service than that of holding a flambeau to their feet, and softening the horrors of their night. To me and my friends may they act as ministers of a superior order, as counsellors of wisdom, and guides to happiness! Nor will they fail to execute this nobler office, if they gently light our way into the knowledge of their adored Maker – if they point out with their silver rays our path to his beatific presence. James Hervey, A.M., 1713–1758.

Verse 1. Should a man live underground, and there converse with the works of art and mechanism, and should afterwards be brought up into the open day, and see the several glories of the heaven and earth, he would immediately pronounce them the work of such a Being as we define God to be. Aristotle.

Verse 1. When we behold 'the heavens,' when we contemplate the celestial bodies, can we fail of conviction? Must we not acknowledge that there is a Divinity, a perfect Being, a ruling intelligence, which governs; a God who is everywhere and directs all by his power? Anybody who doubts this may as well deny there is a sun that lights us. Time destroys all false opinions, but it confirms those which are formed by nature. For this reason, with us as well as with other nations, the worship of the gods, and the holy exercises of religion, increase in purity and extent every day. Cicero.

Verse 1. 'The heavens declare the glory of God,' etc. They discover his wisdom, his power, his goodness; and so there is not any one creature, though never so little, but we are to admire the Creator in it. As a chamber hung round about with looking-glasses represents the face upon every turn, thus all the world doth the mercy and the bounty of God; though that be visible, yet it discovers an invisible God and his invisible properties. Anthony Burgess, 1656.

Verse 1. None of the elect are in that respect so unwise as to refuse to hear and consider the works and words of God as not appertaining unto him. God forbid. No man in the world doth with more fervency consider the works of God, none more readily lift up their ears to hear God speak than even they who have the inward revelation of the Holy Spirit. Wolfgang Musculus.

Verse 1. During the French revolution Jean Bon St André, the Vendean revolutionist, said to a peasant, 'I will have all your steeples pulled down, that you may no longer have any object by which you may be reminded of your old superstitions.' 'But,' replied the peasant, 'you cannot help leaving us the stars.' John Bate's 'Cyclopaedia of Moral and Religious Truths,' 1865.

Verse 1. 'The heavens declare the glory of God.'

How beautiful this dome of sky,
And the vast hills in fluctuation fixed
At thy command, how awful! Shall the soul,
Human and rational, report of Thee
Even less than these? Be mute who will, who can,
Yet I will praise thee with impassioned voice.

My lips, that may forget thee in the crowd,
Cannot forget thee here, where thou hast built
For thine own glory, in the wilderness!
William Wordsworth, 1770–1850.

Verse 1. 'The firmament sheweth his handiwork.'

The glitt'ring stars
By the deep ear of meditation heard,
Still in their midnight watches sing of him.
He nods a calm. The tempest blows his wrath:
The thunder is his voice; and the red flash
His speedy sword of justice. At his touch
The mountains flame. He shakes the solid earth,
And rocks the nations. Nor in these alone –
In ev'ry common instance God is seen.
James Thompson.

These are thy glorious works, Parent of good,
Almighty! Thine this universe frame,
Thus wondrous fair; Thyself how wondrous then!
Unspeakable, who sitt'st above these heavens
To us invisible, or dimly seen
In these thy lowest works; yet these declare
Thy goodness beyond thought, and power divine.
John Milton.

Verses 1, 2. In order more fully to illustrate the expressive richness of the Hebrew, I would direct the attention of my reader to the beautiful phraseology of the nineteenth Psalm. The literal reading of the first and second verses may be thus given:

The heavens are telling the glory of God,
The firmament displaying the work of his hands;
Day unto day welleth forth speech,
Night unto night breatheth out knowledge.

Thus the four distinct terms in the original are preserved in the translation; and the overflowing fulness with which day unto day pours forth divine instruction, and the gentle whisperings of the silent night, are contrasted as in the Hebrew. Henry Craik, 1860.

Verses 1–4. Though all preachers on earth should grow silent, and every human mouth cease from publishing the glory of God, the heavens above will never cease to declare and proclaim his majesty and glory. They are for ever preaching; for, like an unbroken chain, their message is delivered from day to day and from night to night. At the silence of one herald another takes up his speech. One day, like the other, discloses the same spectacles of his glory, and one night, like the other, the same wonders of his majesty. Though nature be hushed and quiet when the sun in his glory has reached the zenith on the azure sky – though the world keep her silent festival, when the stars shine brightest at night – yet, says the psalmist, they speak; ay, holy silence itself is a speech, provided there be the ear to hear it. Augustus T. Tholuck.

Verses 1–4. 'The heavens declare the glory of God, and the firmament sheweth his handiwork.' If the heavens declare the glory of God, we should observe what that glory is which they declare. The heavens preach to us every day . . . 'Their line is gone out through all the earth, and their words to the end of the world.' Sun, moon, and stars are preachers; they are universal, they are natural apostles. The world is their charge; 'their words,' saith the Psalm, 'go to the end of the world.' We may have good doctrine from them, especially this doctrine in the text, of the wisdom and power of God. And it is very observable that the apostle alludes to this text in the Psalm for a proof of gospel preaching to the whole world. Romans 10:18. The gospel, like the sun, casts his beams over, and sheds his light into all the world. David in the Psalm saith, 'Their line is gone out,' etc. By which word he shows that the heavens, being so curious a fabric, made, as it were, by a line and level, do clearly, though silently, preach the skill and perfection of God. Or, that we may read divine truths in them as a line formed by a pen into words and sentences (the original signifies both a measuring line and a written line), letters and words in writing being nothing but lines drawn into several forms or figures. But the Septuagint, whose translation the apostle citeth, for *kavam*, their line, read *kolam*, their sound; either misreading the word or studiously mollifying the sense into a nearer compliance with the latter clause of the verse, 'And their words to the end of the world.' Joseph Caryl.

Verses 1–4. Like as the sun with his light beneficially comforteth all the world, so Christ, the Son of God, reacheth his benefits unto all men, so that they will receive them thankfully, and not refuse them disobediently. Robert Cawdray.

Verse 2. 'Day unto day,' etc. But what is the meaning of the next word – One day telleth another, and one night certifieth another? Literally, *dies diem dicit*, is nothing else but *dies diem docet*. One day telleth another, is one day teacheth another. The day past is instructed by the day present: every new day doth afford new doctrine. The day is a most apt time to learn by reading and conference; the night a most fit time for invention and meditation. Now that which thou canst not understand this day thou mayest haply learn the next, and that which is not found out in one night may be gotten in another. Mystically (saith Hierem), Christ is this 'day,' who saith of himself, 'I am the light of the world,' and his twelve apostles are the twelve hours of the day; for Christ's Spirit revealed by the mouths of his apostles the mysteries of our salvation, in other ages not so fully known unto the sons of men. One day telleth another, that is, the spiritual utter this unto the spiritual; and one night certifieth another, that is, Judas insinuates as much unto the Jews in the night of ignorance, saying, 'Whomsoever I shall kiss, that is he, lay hold on him' Matthew 26:28. Or, the Old Testament only shadowing Christ is the night, and the New Testament plainly showing Christ is the day. John Boys.

Verse 2. 'Day unto day,' or day after day; the vicissitude or continual succession of day and night speaketh much divine knowledge. The assiduity and constancy without any intermission by the heavens preaching is hereby expressed. John Richardson.

Verse 2. 'Uttereth,' poureth forth abundantly; 'sheweth' demonstrates clearly and effectively, without ambiguity. Job 36:2. Many in the full light of gospel day, hear not that speech, who yet in the night of affliction and trouble, or in the conviction of their natural darkness, have that knowledge communicated to them which enables them to realise the joy that cometh in the morning. W. Wilson.

Verse 2. 'Sheweth knowledge.' We may illustrate the differing measures in which natural objects convey knowledge to men of differing mental and spiritual capacity by the story of our great English artist. He is said to have been engaged upon one of his immortal works, and a lady of rank looking on remarked, 'But Mr Turner, I do not see in nature all that you describe there.' 'Ah, Madam,' answered the painter, 'do you not wish you could?' C. H. S.

Verse 3. 'There is no speech,' etc. The sunset was one of the most glorious I ever beheld, and the whole earth seemed so still that the voice of neither God nor man was heard. There was not a ripple upon the waters, not the leaf of a tree, nor even of a blade of grass moving, and the rocks upon the opposite shore reflected the sun's 'after-glow,' and were again themselves reflected from or in the river during the brief twilight, in a way I do not remember ever to have beheld before. No! I will not say the voice of God was not heard; it spoke in the very stillness as loud as in roaring thunder, in the placid scene as in rocks and cliffs impassable, and louder still in the heavens and in the firmament, and in the magnificent prospect around me. His wondrous works declared him to be near, and I felt as if the very ground upon which I was treading was holy. John Gadsby.

Verse 4. 'Their line is gone out,' etc. 'Their sound went,' etc. Romans 10:18. The relations which the gospel of Christ Jesus hath to the Psalms of David I find to be more than to all the Bible besides, that seldom anything is written in the New Testament, but we are sent to fetch our proofs from these. The margin here sends me to the Psalm, and the Psalm sends me back to this again; showing that they both speak one thing. How comes it then that it is not one, for 'line' and 'sound' are not one thing? Is there not some mistake here? Answer – To fetch a proof from a place is one thing, an allusion is another. Sometimes the evangelists are enforced to bring their proofs for what they write out of the Old Testament, else we should never believe them, and then they must be very sure of the terms, when they say, 'This was done that it might be fulfilled which was spoken,' etc. But the apostle was not now upon that account; only showing to the Romans the marvellous spreading of the gospel, alluding to this passage of David discoursing of 'the heavens,' to which the prophet compared the publication of the word; the sun and moon and stars not only shining through, but round all the earth. The same subject Paul was now upon, and for his purpose makes use of a term fitter to express the preaching of the gospel, by the word 'sound,' than that other word expressing the limitations of the law, by the word 'line:' both of these agreeing that there is no fitter comparison to be fetched from anything in nature than from 'the heavens,' their motions, revolutions, influences upon sublunary bodies; also in their eclipses, when one text seems to darken another, as if it were put out altogether by crossing and opposing, which is but seemingly so to the ignorant, they agree sweetly enough in themselves; no bridegroom can agree better with his bride, nor rejoice more to run his course. So they both conclude in this, that the sun never saw that nation yet where the word of truth, in one degree or other (all the world, you must think, cannot be right under the meridian) hath not shined. William Streat, in 'The Dividing of the Hoof,' 1654.

Verse 4. 'Unto the end of the world.' Venantius Fortunatus eleven hundred years ago witnesses to the peregrinations of Paul the apostle.

He passed the ocean's curled wave,
As far as islands harbours have;
As far as Britain yields a bay,
Or Iceland's frozen shore a stay.
John Cragge, 1557.

Verse 4. 'Their line is gone out through all the earth,' etc. The molten sea did stand upon twelve oxen, that is, as Paul doth interpret it, upon twelve apostles (1 Corinthians 9:10); which in that they looked four ways, east, west, north, and south, they did teach all nations. And in that they looked three and three together, they did represent the blessed Trinity. Not only teaching all nations, but also in that sea of water, baptising them in the name of the Father, and of the Son, and of the Holy Ghost. Wherefore, though the two kine which carried the ark wherein were the tables of the law, went straight and kept one path, turning neither to the right hand nor to the left; yet these twelve oxen which carried the molten sea, signifying the doctrine of the gospel, went not straight, neither kept one path, but turned into the way of the Gentiles; yea, they looked all manner of ways, east, west, north, and south. And these two kine stood still and lowed no more when they came to the field of Joshua, dwelling in Bethshemesh, that is, the house of the sun. To note, that all the kine, and calves, and sacrifices, and ceremonies of the old law were to cease and stand still when they came to Jesus, who is the true Joshua, dwelling in heaven, which is the true Bethshemesh. But these twelve oxen were so far from leaving off, either to go, or to low, when they came to Christ, that even then they went much faster and lowed much louder; so that now 'their sound is gone out into all lands, and their words to the end of the world;' and 'in them hath God set' Bethshemesh, that is, a house or 'tabernacle for the sun.' Therefore, as the material sun, through the twelve signs of the Zodiac, goeth forth from the uttermost parts of the heaven, and runneth about to the end of it again: in like sort, the spiritual Sun of Righteousness, by the twelve apostles, as by twelve signs, hath been borne round about the world, that he might be not only 'the glory of his people Israel,' but also 'a light to lighten the Gentiles;' and that all, 'all the ends of the earth might see the salvation of our God.' Thomas Playfere.

Verses 4–6. It appears to me very likely that the Holy Ghost in these expressions which he most immediately uses about the rising of the sun, has an eye to the rising of the Sun of Righteousness from the grave, and that the expressions that the Holy Ghost here uses are conformed to such a view. The times of the Old Testament are times of night in comparison of the gospel day, and are so represented in Scripture, and therefore the approach of the day of the New Testament dispensation in the birth of Christ, is called the day-spring from on high visiting the earth (Luke 1:78), 'Through the tender mercy of our God; whereby the dayspring from on high hath visited us;' and the commencing of the gospel dispensation as it was introduced by Christ, is called the Sun of Righteousness rising. Malachi 4:2. But this gospel dispensation commences with the resurrection of Christ. Therein the Sun of Righteousness rises from under the earth, as the sun appears to do in the morning, and comes forth as a bridegroom. He rose as the joyful, glorious bridegroom of his church; for Christ, especially as risen again, is the proper bridegroom, or husband, of his church, as the apostle teaches (Romans 7:4), 'Wherefore, my brethren, ye also are become dead to the law by the body of Christ; that ye should be married to another, even to him who is raised from the dead, that we should bring forth fruit unto God.' He that was covered with contempt, and overwhelmed in a deluge of sorrow, has purchased and won his spouse, for he loved the church, and gave himself for it, that he might present it to himself; now he comes forth as a bridegroom to bring home his purchased spouse to him in spiritual marriage, as he soon after did in the conversion of such multitudes, making his people willing in the day of his power, and hath also done many times since, and will do in a yet more glorious degree. And as the sun when it rises comes forth like a bridegroom gloriously adorned, so Christ in his resurrection entered on his state of glory. After his state of sufferings, he rose to shine forth in ineffable glory as the King of heaven and earth, that he might be a glorious bridegroom, in whom his church might be unspeakably happy. Here the psalmist says that God has placed a tabernacle for the sun in the heavens: so God the Father had prepared an abode in heaven for Jesus Christ; he had set a throne for him there, to which he ascended after he rose. The sun after it is risen ascends up to the midst of heaven, and then at that end of its race descends again to the earth; so Christ when he rose from the grave ascended up to the height of heaven, and far above all heavens, but at the end of the gospel day will descend again to the earth. It is here said that the risen sun 'rejoiceth as a strong man to run a race.' So Christ, when he rose, rose as a man of war, as the Lord strong and mighty, the Lord mighty in battle; he rose to conquer his enemies, and to show forth his glorious power in subduing all things to himself, during that race which he had to run, which is from his resurrection to the end of the world, when he will return to the earth again ... That the Holy Ghost here has a mystical meaning, and has respect to the light of the Sun of Righteousness, and not merely the light of the natural sun, is confirmed by the verses that follow, in which the psalmist himself seems to apply them to the word of God, which is the light of that Sun, even of Jesus Christ, who himself revealed the word of God: see the very next words, 'The law of the Lord is perfect,' etc. Jonathan Edwards, 1703–1758.

Verse 5. 'Which is as a bridegroom,' etc. The sun is described like a bridegroom coming out of his chamber, dressed and prepared, and as a giant rejoicing to run his race; but though the sun be thus prepared, and dressed, and ready, yet if the Lord send a writ and a prohibition to the sun to keep within his chamber, he cannot come forth, his journey is stopped. Thus also he stops man in his nearest preparation for any action. If the Lord will work, who shall let it? Isaiah 43:13. That is, there is no power in heaven or earth which can hinder him. But if the Lord will let, who shall work? Neither sun, nor stars, nor men, nor devils, can work, if he forbids them. The point is full of comfort. Joseph Caryl.

Verse 5. 'Which is as a bridegroom,' etc. The Sun of Righteousness appeared in three signs especially; Leo, Virgo, Libra. 1. In Leo, roaring as a lion, in the law; so that the people could not endure his voice. 2. In Virgo, born of a pure virgin in the gospel. 3. In Libra, weighing our works in his balance at the day of judgment. Or as Bernard distinguisheth his threefold coming aptly – *venit ad homines, venit in homines, venit contra homines*: in the time past he came unto men as upon this day (the Nineteenth Psalm is one 'appointed to be read' on Christmas Day); in the time present, he comes by his spirit into men every day; in the time future, he shall come against men at the last day. The coming here mentioned is his coming in the flesh – for so the fathers usually gloss the text – he came forth of the virgin's womb, 'as a bridegroom out of his chamber.' As a bridegroom, for the King of heaven at this holy time made a great wedding for his Son. Matthew 22:1. Christ is the bridegroom, man's nature the bride, the conjunction and blessed union of both in one person is his marriage. The best way to reconcile two disagreeing families is to make some marriage between them: even so, the Word became flesh, and dwelt among us in the world that he might hereby make our peace, reconciling God to man and man to God. By this happy match the Son of God is become the Son of Man, even flesh of our flesh, and bone of our bones; and the sons of men are made the sons of God, 'of his flesh and of his bones,' as Paul saith, Ephesians 5:30. So that now the church being Christ's own spouse, saith, 'I am my Beloved's, and my Beloved is mine' Canticles 6:3. My sin is his sin, and his righteousness is my righteousness. He who knew no sin, for my sake was made sin; and I, contrariwise, having no good thing, am made the righteousness of God in him: I which am brown by persecution, and black by nature (Canticles 1:5), so foul as the sow that walloweth in the mire, through his favour am comely, without spot or wrinkle, so white as the snow, like a lily among thorns, even the fairest among women. Canticles 2:2. This happy marriage is not a mar age, but it makes a merry age, being 'the consolation of Israel,' and comfort of Jerusalem's heart. Indeed, Christ our husband doth absent himself from us in his body for a time; but when he did ascend into heaven he took with him our pawn, namely his flesh; and he gave us his pawn, namely, his Spirit, assuring us that we shall one day, when the world is ended, enter with him into the wedding chamber, and there feast with him, and enjoy his blessed company for evermore. John Boys.

Verse 6. 'There is nothing hid from the heat thereof.' This is literally the case. The earth receives its heat from the sun, and by conduction, a part of it enters the crust of our globe. By convection, another portion is carried to the atmosphere, which it warms. Another portion is radiated into space, according to laws yet imperfectly understood, but which are evidently connected with the colour, chemical composition, and mechanical structure of parts of the earth's surface. At the same time the ordinary state of the air, consisting of gases and vapour, modifies the heat-rays and prevents scorching. Thus, the solar heat is equalised by the air. Nothing on earth or in air is hid from the heat of the sun ... Even the colour of some bodies is changed by heat ... Heat also is in bodies in a state which is not sensible, and is therefore called latent heat, or heat of fluidity, because it is regarded as the cause of fluidity in ponderable substances. It can fuse every substance it does not decompose below the melting point, as in the case of wood. Every gas may be regarded as consisting of heat, and some basis of ponderable matter, whose cohesion it overcomes, imparting a tendency to great expansion, when no external obstacle prevents, and this expansive tendency is their elasticity or tension. Certain gases have been liquified under great pressure, and extreme cold. Heat, also, at certain temperatures, causes the elasticity of vapours to overcome the atmospheric pressure which can no longer restrain them. An example of this is the boiling point of water; and, indeed, in every case the true instance is the boiling point. Philosophers are agreed that the affinity of heat for any ponderable substance is superior to all other forces acting upon it. No ponderable matters can combine without disengagement of heat ... And the same occurs from every mechanical pressure and condensation of a body. In all these cases, and many more, there are like evidences of the presence and influence of heat; but the facts now advanced are sufficient to show us the force of the expression, that in terrestrial things nothing is hid from, or can by any possibility escape the agency of heat. Edwin Sidney, A.M., in 'Conversations on the Bible and Science,' 1866.

Verse 6 (last clause). 'There is nothing hid from the heat,' nothing from the light of Christ. It is not solely on the mountain top that he shines, as in the day before he was fully risen, when his rays, although unseen by the rest of the world, formed a glory round the heads of his prophets, who saw him while to the chief part of mankind he was still lying below the horizon. Now, however, that he is risen, he pours his light through the valley, as well as over the mountain; nor is there any one, at least in these countries, who does not catch some gleams of that light, except those who burrow and hide themselves in the dark caverns of sin. But it is not light alone that Christ sheds from his heavenly tabernacle. As nothing is hid from his light, neither is anything hid from his heat. He not only enlightens the understanding, so that it shall see and know the truth; he also softens and melts, and warms the heart, so that it shall love the truth, and calls forth fruit from it, and ripens the fruit he has called forth; and that too on the lowliest plant which creeps along the ground, as well as the loftiest tree...

Though while he was on earth, he had fullest power of bestowing every earthly gift, yet, in order that he should be able to bestow heavenly gifts with the same all-healing power, it was necessary that he should go up into heaven. When he had done so, when he had ascended into his tabernacle in the heavens, then, he promises his disciples, he would send down the Holy Spirit of God, who should bring them heavenly gifts, yea, who should enter into their hearts, and make them bring forth all the fruits of the Spirit in abundance; should make them abound in love, in peace, in longsuffering, in gentleness, in goodness, in faith, in meekness, in temperance. These are the bright heavenly rays, which, as it were, make up the pure light of Christ; and from this heat nothing is hid. Even the hardest heart may be melted by it; even the foulest may be purified. Julias Charles Hare, M.A., 1841.

Verse 7. 'The law of the Lord is perfect, converting the soul.' To man fallen, the law only convinceth of sin, and bindeth over to death, it is nothing but a killing letter; but the gospel, accompanied by the power of the Spirit, bringeth life. Again, it is said, 'The law of the Lord is perfect, converting the soul;' therefore it seems the law may also be a word of salvation to the creature. I answer; by the law there, is not meant only that part of the word which we call the covenant of works, but there it is put for the whole word, for the whole doctrine of the covenant of life and salvation; as Psalm 1:2: 'His delight is in the law of the Lord; and in his law doth he meditate day and night.' And if you take it in that stricter sense, then it converteth the soul but by accident, as it is joined with the gospel, which is the misery of life and righteousness, but in itself it is the law of sin and death. Look, as a thing taken simply, would be poison and deadly in itself, yet mixed with other wholesome medicines, it is of great use, is an excellent physical ingredient; so the law is of great use as joined with the gospel, to awaken and startle the sinner, to show him his duty, to convince him of sin and judgment; but it is the gospel properly that pulls in the heart. Thomas Manton.

Verse 7. The law, or doctrine, an orderly manner of instruction, an institution or disposition, called in Hebrew *torah*, which implies both doctrine and an orderly disposition of the same. Therefore where one prophet, relating David's words, saith the law of man (2 Samuel 7:19), another saith, the orderly estate, or course of man. 1 Corinthians 17:17. The Holy Ghost, in Greek, calls it *nomos*, a law (Hebrews 8:10), from Jeremiah 31:33. This name is most commonly ascribed to the precepts given by Moses at Mount Sinai (Deuteronomy 32:4; Malachi 4:4; John 1:17, and 7:19); it is also largely used for all his writings. For the history of Genesis is called law

(Galatians 4:21), from Genesis 16. And though sometimes the law be distinguished from the Psalms and Prophets (Luke 16:16, and 24:24), yet the other prophets' books are called law (1 Corinthians 14:21), from Isaiah 28:11; the Psalms are also thus named (John 10:24 and 15:25), from Psalm 82:6 and 35:19. Yea, one Psalm is called a law (Psalm 78:1); and the many branches of Moses' doctrine as the law of the sin-offering, etc. Leviticus 6:25. And generally it is used for any doctrine, as the law of works, the law of faith, etc. Romans 3:27. Henry Ainsworth.

Verse 7. 'Converting the soul.' This version conveys a sense good and true in itself, but is not in accordance with the design of the psalmist, which is, to express the divine law on the feelings and affections of good men. The Hebrew terms properly mean, 'bringing back the spirit,' when it is depressed by adversity, by refreshing and consoling it; like food, it restores the faint, and communicates vigour to the disconsolate.' William Walford, 1837.

Verse 7. 'Converting the soul.' The heart of man is the most free and hard of anything to work upon, and to make an impression and stamp upon this hard heart, this heart that is so stony, adamantine, 'harder than the nether millstones,' as the Scripture teacheth. To compel this free-will, this *Domina sui actus*, the queen in the soul, the empress, it cannot be without a divine power, without a hand that is omnipotent; but the ministers do this by the Word – they mollify, and wound, and break this heart, they incline, and bow, and draw this free-will whither the spirit listeth. And Clemens Alexandrinus is not afraid to say, that if the fables of Orpheus and Amphion were true – that they drew birds, beasts, and stones, with their ravishing melody – yet the harmony of the Word is greater, which translates men from Hellicon to Zion, which softens the hard heart of man obdurate against the truth, that 'raises up children to Abraham of stones,' that is (as he interprets), of unbelievers, which he calls stocks and stones, that put their trust in stones and stocks; which metamorphoses men that are beastlike, wild birds for their lightness and vanity, serpents for their craft and subtlety, lions for their wrath and cruelty, swine for voluptuousness and luxury, etc.; and charms them so that of wild beasts they become tame men; that makes living stones (as he did others) come of their own accord to the building of the walls of Jerusalem (as he of Thebes), to the building of a living temple to the everlasting God. This must needs be a truly persuasive charm, as he speaks. John Stoughton's 'Choice Sermons,' 1640.

Verse 7. 'Making wise the simple.' The apostle Paul, in Ephesians 1:8, expresseth conversion, and the whole work inherently wrought in us, by the making of a man wise. It is usual in the Scriptures, and you may ofttimes meet with it; 'converting the soul,' 'making wise the simple.' The beginning of conversion, and so all along, the increase of all grace to the end, is expressed by wisdom entering into a man's heart, 'If wisdom enter into thy heart,' and so goes on to do more and more; not unto thy head only – a man may have all that, and be a fool in the end, but when it entereth into the heart, and draws all the affections after it, and along with it, 'when knowledge is pleasant to thy soul,' then a man is converted; when God breaks open a man's heart, and makes wisdom fall in, enter in, and make a man wise. Thomas Goodwin.

Verse 7. This verse, and the two next following, which treat of God's law, are in Hebrew, written each of them with ten words, according to the number of the ten commandments, which are called the ten words. Exodus 34:28. Henry Ainsworth.

Verses 7, 8. 'The testimony of the Lord is sure, enlightening the eyes,' revealing the object, ennobling the organ. Richard Stock.

Verse 7–11. All of us are by nature the children of wrath; our souls are like the porches of Bethesda (John 5), in which are lodged a great many 'sick folk, blind, halt, withered;' and the Scriptures are like the pool of Bethesda, into which whoever entereth, after God's Holy Spirit hath a little stirred the water, is 'made whole of whatsoever disease he hath.' He that hath anger's frenzy, being as furious as a lion, by stepping into this pool shall in good time become as gentle as a lamb; he that hath the blindness of intemperance, by washing in this pool shall easily see his folly; he that hath envy's rust, avarice's leprosy, luxury's palsy, shall have means and medicines here for the curing of his maladies. The word of God is like the drug catholicon, that is instead of all purges; and like the herb panaces, that is good for all diseases. Is any man heavy? the statutes of the Lord rejoice the heart: is any man in want? the judgments of the Lord are more to be desired than gold, yea, than much fine gold, and by keeping of them there is great reward: is any man ignorant? the testimonies of the Lord give wisdom to the simple, that is, to little ones, both in standing and understanding. In standing, as unto little Daniel, little John the evangelist, little Timothy: to little ones in understanding; for the great philosophers who were the wizards of the world, because they were not acquainted with God's law became fools while they professed themselves wise. Romans 1:22. But our prophet saith, 'I have more understanding than all my teachers, because thy testimonies are my meditation,' and my study. Psalm 119:99. To conclude, whatsoever we are by corruption of nature, God's law converteth us, and maketh us to speak with new tongues, and to sing new songs unto the Lord, and to become new men and new creatures in Christ. 2 Corinthians 5:17. J. Boys.

Verse 8. 'The statutes.' Many divines and critics, and Castalio in particular, have endeavoured to attach a distinct shade of meaning to the words, law, testimony, the statutes, commandments, fear, judgments, occurring in this context (Heb.), the law, has been considered to denote the perceptive part of revelation (Heb.), the testimony, has been restricted to the doctrinal part (Heb.), the statutes, has been regarded as relating to such things as have been given in charge (Heb.), the commandment, has been taken to express the general body of the divine law and doctrine (Heb.), religious fear (Heb.), the judgments, the civil statutes of the Mosaic law, more particularly the penal sanctions. John Morison.

Verse 8. 'The statutes of the Lord are right, rejoicing the heart.' How odious is the profaneness of those Christians who neglect the Holy Scriptures, and give themselves to reading other books! How many precious hours do many spend, and that not only on work days, but holy days, in foolish romances, fabulous histories, lascivious poems! And why this, but that they may be cheered and delighted, when as full joy is only to be had in these holy books. Alas! the joy you find in those writings is perhaps pernicious, such as tickleth your lust, and promoteth contemplative wickedness. At the best it is but vain, such as only pleaseth the fancy and affecteth the wit; whereas those holy writings (to use David's expression), are 'right, rejoicing the heart.' Again, are there not many who more set by Plutarch's morals, Seneca's epistles, and such like books, than they do by the Holy Scriptures? It is true, beloved, there are excellent truths in those moral writings of the heathen, but yet they are far short of these sacred books. Those may comfort against outward trouble, but not against inward fears; they may rejoice the mind, but cannot quiet the conscience; they may kindle some flashy sparkles of joy, but they cannot warm the soul with a lasting fire of solid consolations. And truly, brethren, if ever God give you a spiritual ear to judge of things aright, you will then acknowledge there are no bells like to those of Aaron's, no harp like to that of David's, no trumpet like to that of Isaiah's, no pipes like to those of the apostle's; and, you will confess with Petrus Damianus, that those writings of heathen orators, philosophers, poets, which formerly were so pleasing, are now dull and harsh in comparison of the comfort of the Scriptures. Nathanael Hardy, D.D., 1618–1670.

Verse 10. 'Sweeter than honey and the honeycomb.' Love the word written. Psalm 119:97. 'Oh, how love I thy law!' 'Lord,' said Augustine, 'let the holy Scriptures be my chaste delight.' Chrysostom compares the Scripture to a garden, every truth is a fragrant flower, which we should wear, not on our bosom, but in our heart. David counted the word 'sweeter than honey and the honeycomb.' There is that in Scripture which may breed delight. It shows us the way to riches: Deuteronomy 28:5, Proverbs 3:10; to long life: Psalm 34:12; to a kingdom: Hebrews 12:28. Well, then, may we count those the sweetest hours which are spent in reading the holy Scriptures; well may we say with the prophet (Jeremiah 15:16), 'Thy words were found and I did eat them; and they were the joy and rejoicing of my heart.' Thomas Watson.

Verse 10. 'Sweeter than honey and the honeycomb.' There is no difference made amongst us between the delicacy of honey in the comb and that which is separated from it. From the information of Dr Halle, concerning the diet of the Moors of Barbary, we learn that they esteem honey a very wholesome breakfast, 'and the most delicious that which is in the comb with the young bees in it, before they come out of their cases, whilst they still look milk-white' (Miscellanea Curiosa vol. iii. p. 382). The distinction made by the psalmist is then perfectly just and conformable to custom and practice, at least of more modern, and probably, equally so of ancient times. Samuel Burder, A.M., in 'Oriental Customs,' 1812.

Verse 11. 'Moreover by them is thy servant warned.' A certain Jew had formed a design to poison Luther, but was disappointed by a faithful friend, who sent Luther a portrait of the man, with a warning against him. By this, Luther knew the murderer and escaped his hands. Thus the word of God, O Christian, shows thee the face of those lusts which Satan employs to destroy thy comforts and poison thy soul. G. S. Bowes, B.A., in 'Illustrative Gatherings for Preachers and Teachers.'

Verse 11. 'In keeping of them there is great reward.' This 'keeping of them' implies great carefulness to know, to remember, and to observe; and the 'reward' (literally 'the end'), i.e., the recompense, is far beyond anticipation. W. Wilson.

Verse 11. 'In keeping of them there is great reward.' Not only for keeping, but in keeping of them, there is great reward. The joy, the rest, the refreshing, the comforts, the contents, the smiles, the incomes that saints now enjoy, in the ways of God, are so precious and glorious in their eyes, that they would not exchange them for ten thousand worlds. Oh! if the vails (gratuities, presents) be thus sweet and glorious before pay-day comes, what will be that glory that Christ will crown his saints with for cleaving to his service in the face of all difficulties, when he shall say to his Father, 'Lo, here am I, and the children which thou hast given me' Isaiah 8:18. If there be so much to be had in the wilderness, what then shall be had in paradise! Thomas Brooks.

Verse 11. 'In keeping of them there is great reward.' Not only for keeping but in keeping of them. As every flower hath its sweet smell, so every good action hath its sweet reflection upon the soul: and as Cardan saith, that every precious stone hath some egregious virtue; so here, righteousness is its own reward, though few men think so, and act accordingly. Howbeit, the chief reward is not till the last cast, till we come home to heaven. The word here rendered 'reward,' signifieth the heel, and by a metaphor, the end of a work, and the reward of it, which is not till the end. John Trapp.

Verse 11. 'Reward.' Though we should not serve God for a reward, yet we shall have a reward for our service. The time is coming when ungodliness shall be as much prosecuted by justice, as in times past godliness had been persecuted by injustice. Though our reward be not for our good works, yet we shall have our good works rewarded, and have a good reward for our works. Though the best of men (they being at the best but unprofitable servants) deserve nothing at the hands of God, yet they may deserve much at the hands of men; and if they have not the recompense they deserve, yet it is a kind of recompense to have deserved. As he said, and nobly, 'I had rather it should be said, Why doth not Cato's image stand here? than it should be said, Why doth it stand here?' Ralph Venning. 1620–1673.

Verse 12. 'Who can understand his errors?' After this survey of the works and word of God, he comes at last to peruse the third book, his conscience; a book which though wicked men may keep shut up, and naturally do not love to look into it, yet will one day be laid open before the great tribunal in the view of the whole world, to the justifying of God when he judges, and to impenitent sinners' eternal confusion. And what finds he here? A foul, blurred copy that he is puzzled how to read; 'who,' says he, 'can understand his errors?' Those notions which God had with his own hand imprinted upon conscience in legible characters, are partly defaced and slurred with scribble, and interlinings of 'secret faults;' partly obliterated and quite razed out with capital crimes, 'presumptuous sins.' And yet this manuscript cannot be so abused, but it will still give in evidence for God; there being no argument in the world that can with more force extort an acknowledgment of God from any man's conscience than the conviction of guilt itself labours under. For the sinner cannot but know he has transgressed a law, and he finds within him, if he is not past all sense, such apprehensions that though at present he 'walk in the ways of his heart and in the sight of his eyes' (as the wise man ironically advises the young man to do, Ecclesiastes 11:9), yet he knows (as the same wise man there from his own experience tells him) that 'for all these things God will bring him into judgment.' The conscience being thus convicted of sin, where there is any sense of true piety the soul will, with David, here address itself to God for pardon, that it may be 'cleansed from secret faults;' and for grace, that by its restraints, and preventions, and assistances, it may be 'kept back from presumptuous sins,' and if unhappily engaged, that it may be freed at least from the 'dominion' of them – 'Keep back thy servant also from presumptuous sins; let them not have dominion over me,' etc. Adam Littleton.

Verse 12. The prophet saith, 'Who can understand his own faults?' No man can, but God can; therefore reason after this manner, as Saint Bernard saith: I know and am known; I know but in part, but God knows me and knows me wholly; but what I know I know but in part. So the apostle reasons; 'I know nothing of myself, yet am I not hereby justified.' Admit that thou keepest thyself so free, and renewest thy repentance so daily that thou knowest nothing by thyself, yet mark what the apostle adds further; 'Notwithstanding, I do not judge myself; I am not hereby justified, but he that judges me is the Lord.' This is the condition of all men; he that is infinite knows them; therefore they should not dare to judge themselves, but with the prophet David, in Psalm 19, entreat the Lord that he would cleanse them from their secret sins. Richard Stock.

Verse 12. 'Who can understand his own errors?' None can to the depth and bottom. In this question there are two considerables: 1. A concession; 2. A confession. He makes a grant that our life is full of errors; and the Scriptures say the same, while they affirm that 'All we like sheep have gone astray' (Isaiah 53:6); 'I have gone astray like a lost sheep' Psalm 119:176; that the 'house of Israel' hath 'lost sheep' Matthew 10:6. I need not reckon up the particulars, as the errors of our senses, understandings, consciences, judgments, wills, affections, desires, actions, and occurrences. The whole man in nature is like a tree nipped at root, which brings forth worm-eaten fruits. The whole man in life is like an instrument out of tune, which jars at every stroke. If we cannot understand them, certainly they are very many. Robert Abbot, 1646.

Verse 12. 'Who can understand his errors?' By 'errors' he means his unwitting and inconsiderate mistakes. There are sins, some of which are committed when the sun shines – i.e., with light and knowledge; and then, as it is with colours when the sun shines, you may see them; so these, a man can see, and know, and confess them particularly to be transgressions. There are other sins which are committed either in the times of ignorance, or else (if there be knowledge), yet with unobservance. Either of these may be so heaped up in the particular number of them, that as a man did when he did commit them, take no notice of them; so now, after the commission, if he should take the brightest candle to search all the records of his soul, yet many of them would escape his notice. And, indeed, this is a great part of our misery, that we cannot understand all our debts. We can easily see too many, yet many more lie, as it were, dead and out of sight. To sin is one great misery, and then to forget our sins is a misery too. If in repentance we could set the battle in array, point to every individual sin in the true and particular times of acting and re-acting, oh, how would our hearts be more broken with shame and sorrow, and how would we adore the richness of the treasure of mercy which must have a multitude in it to pardon the multitude of our infinite errors and sins. But this is the comfort; though we cannot understand every particular sin, or time of sinning, yet if we be not idle to search and cast over the books, and if we be heartily grieved for these sins which we have found out, and can by true repentance turn from them unto God, and by faith unto the blood of Jesus Christ, I say that God, who knows our sins better than we can know them, and who understands the true intentions and dispositions of the heart – that if it did see the unknown sins it would be answerably carried against them – he will for his own mercy sake forgive them, and he, too, will not remember them. Nevertheless, though David saith, 'Who can understand his errors?' as the prophet Jeremiah spake also, 'The heart of man is desperately wicked, who can know it?' yet must we bestir ourselves at heaven to get more and more heavenly light, to find out more and more of our sinnings. So the Lord can search the heart; and, though we shall never be able to find out all our sins which we have committed, yet it is proper and beneficial for us to find out yet more sins than yet we do know. And you shall find these in your own experience; that as soon as ever grace entered your hearts, you saw sin in another way than you ever saw it before; yea, and the more grace hath traversed and increased in the soul, the more full discoveries hath it made of sins. It hath shown new sins as it were; new sins, not for their being, not as if they were not in the heart and life before, but for their evidence and our apprehension. We do now see such wages and such inclinations to be sinful which we did not think to be so before. As physic brings those humours which had their residence before now more to the sense of the patient, or as the sun makes open the motes of dust which were in the room before, so doth the light of the word discover more corruption. Obadiah Sedgwick.

Verse 12. 'Who can understand his errors?' Who can tell how oft he offendeth? No man. The hairs of a man's head may be told, the stars appear in multitudes, yet some have undertaken to reckon them; but no arithmetic can number our sins. Before we can recount a thousand we shall commit ten thousand more; and so rather multiply by addition than divide by subtraction; there is no possibility of numeration. Like Hydra's head, while we are cutting off twenty by repentance, we find a hundred more grown up. It is just, then, that infinite sorrows shall follow infinite sins. Thomas Adams.

Verse 12. 'Cleanse thou me from secret faults.' It is the desire of a holy person to be cleansed, not only from public, but also from private and secret sins. Romans 7:24. 'O wretched man (saith Paul), who shall deliver me?' Why, O blessed apostle! what is it that holds thee? What is it that molests thee? Thy life, thou sayest, was unblamable before thy conversion, and since thy conversion. Philippians 3. Thou hast exercised thyself to have always a conscience void of offence toward God and toward men. Acts 24:16. And yet thou criest out, 'O wretched man,' and yet thou complainest, 'Who shall deliver me?' Verily, brethren, it was not sin abroad, but at home: it was not sin without, but at this time sin within; it was not Paul's sinning with man, but Paul's sinning within Paul: oh! that 'law of his members warring (secretly within him) against the law of his mind;' this, this made that holy man so to cry out, so to complain. As Rebekah was weary of her life, not as we read for any foreign disquietments, but because of domestic troubles: 'The daughters of Heth' within the house made her 'weary of her life;' so the private and secret birth of corruption within Paul – the workings of that – that was the cause of his trouble, that was the ground of his exclamation and desires, 'Who shall deliver me?' I remember that the same Paul adviseth the Ephesians as 'to put off the former conversation' so 'to put on the renewed spirit of the mind' (Ephesians 4:22, 23); intimating that there are sins lurking within as well as sins walking without; and that true Christians must not only sweep the door, but wash the chamber; my meaning is, not only come off from the sins which lie open in the conversation, but also labour to be cleansed from sin and sinning which remain secret and hidden in the spirit and inward disposition. Obadiah Sedgwick.

Verse 12. 'Cleanse thou me from secret faults.' Learn to see thy spots. Many have unknown sins, as a man may have a mole on his back and himself never know it. Lord, cleanse me from my secret faults. But have we not spots whereof we are not ignorant? In diseases sometimes nature is strong enough to put forth spots, and there she cries to us by these outward declarations that we are sick. Sometimes she cannot do it but by the force of cordials. Sometimes conscience of herself shows us our sins; sometimes she cannot but by medicines, arguments that convince us out of the holy word. Some can see, and will not, as Balaam; some would see, and cannot, as the eunuch; some neither will nor can, as Pharaoh; some both can and will, as David ... We have many spots which God does not hear from us, because we see them not in ourselves. Who will acknowledge that error, whereof he does not know himself guilty? The sight of sins is a great happiness, for it causeth an ingenuous confession. Thomas Adams.

Verse 12. 'Cleanse thou me from secret faults.' The law of the Lord is so holy that forgiveness must be prayed for, even for hidden sins. (Note – This was a principal text of the Reformers against the auricular confession of the Roman Catholics.) T. C. Barth's 'Bible Manual,' 1865.

Verse 12. 'Secret faults.' Sins may be termed 'secret' either, 1. When they are coloured and disguised – though they do fly abroad, yet not under that name, but apparelled with some semblance of virtues. Cyprian complains of such tricks in his second epistle, which is to Donatus. 2. When they are kept off from the stage of the world; they are like fire in the chimney; though you do not see it, yet it burns. So many a person, like those in Ezekiel, 'commit abominations in secret' – that is, so as the public eye is not upon them. He is sinful, and acts it with the greatest vileness; all the difference betwixt another sinner and him is this – that he is, and the other saith he is, a sinner. Just as 'twixt a book shut and a book opened; that which is shut hath the same lines and words, but the other being opened every man may see and read them. 3. When they are kept, not only from the public eye, but from any mortal eye; that is, the carnal eye of him who commits the sins sees them not; he doth, indeed, see them with the eye of conscience, but not with the eye of natural sense. Even those persons with whom he doth have converse, and who highly commend the frame of his ways, cannot yet see the secret discoursings and actings of sin in his mind and heart. For, brethren, all the actings of sin are not without, they are not visible; but there are some, yes, the most dangerous actings within the soul, where corruption lies as a fountain and root. The heart of man is a scheme of wickedness; nay, a man saith that in his heart which he dares not speak with his tongue, and his thought will do that which his hands dare not to execute. Well, then, sin may be called 'secret' when it is sin, and acted as sin, even there, where none but God and conscience can see. Methinks sin is like a candle in a lantern, where the shining is first within and then bursting out at the windows; or like evils and ulcerous humours, which are scabs and scurvy stuff, first within the skin, and afterwards they break out to the view on the outside. So it is with sin; it is a malignant humour and a fretting leprosy, diffusing itself into several secret acts and workings within the mind, and then it breaks abroad and dares adventure the practice of itself to the eye of the world; and be it that it may never see the light, that it may be like a child born and buried in the womb, yet as that child is a man, a true man there closeted in that hidden frame of nature, so sin is truly sin, though it never gets out beyond the womb which did conceive and enliven it. Obadiah Sedgwick.

Verse 12. 'Secret faults.' 'Secret sins' are more dangerous to the person in some respects than open sins. For a man doth, by his art of sinning, deprive himself of the help of his sinfulness. Like him who will carry his wound covered, or who bleeds inwardly, help comes not in because the danger is not descried or known. If a man's sin breaks out there is a minister at hand, a friend near, and others to reprove, to warn, to direct; but when he is the artificer of his lusts, he bars himself of all public remedy, and takes great order and care to damn his soul, by covering his 'secret sins' with some plausible varnish which may beget a good opinion in others of his ways. A man does by his secrecy give the reins unto corruption: the mind is fed all the day long either with sinful contemplations or projectings, so that the very strength of the soul is wasted and corrupted. Nay, secret actings do but heat and inflame natural corruption. As in shouldering in a crowd, when one hath got out of the door, two or three are ready to fall out after; so when a man hath given his heart leave to act a secret sin, this begets a present, and quick, and strong flame in corruption to repeat and multiply and throng out the acts. Sinful acts are not only fruits of sin, but helps and strengths, all sinning being more sinful by more sinning, not only in the effects but in the cause: the spring and cause of sin will grow mad and insolent hereby, and more corrupt; this being a truth, that if the heart gives way for one sin, it will be ready for the next; if it will yield to bring forth once at the devil's pleasure, it will bring forth twice by its own motion. A man by 'secret sins' doth but polish and square the hypocrisy of his heart: he doth strive to be an exact hypocrite; and the more cunning he is in the palliating of his sinnings, the more perfect he is in his hypocrisy. Obadiah Sedgwick.

Verse 12. 'Secret faults.' Beware of committing acts which it will be necessary to conceal. There is a singular poem by Hood, called 'The Dream of Eugene Aram' – a most remarkable piece it is indeed, illustrating the point on which we are now dwelling. Aram had murdered a man, and cast his body into the river – 'a sluggish water, black as ink, the depth was so extreme.' The next morning he visited the scene of his guilt:

> And sought the black accursed pool,
> With a wild misgiving eye;
> And he saw the dead in the river bed,
> For the faithless stream was dry.

Next he covered the corpse with heaps of leaves, but a mighty wind swept through the wood and left the secret bare before the sun –

> Then down I cast me on my face,
> And first began to weep,
> For I knew my secret then was one
> That earth refused to keep:
> On land or sea though it should be
> Ten thousand fathoms deep.

In plaintive notes he prophesies his own discovery. He buried his victim in a cave, and trod him down with stones, but when years had run their weary round, the foul deed was discovered and the murderer put to death.

Guilt is a 'grim chamberlain,' even when his fingers are not bloody red. Secret sins bring fevered eyes and sleepless nights, until men burn out their consciences, and become in very deed ripe for the pit. Hypocrisy is a hard game to play at, for it is one deceiver against many observers; and for certain it is a miserable trade, which will earn at last, as its certain climax, a tremendous bankruptcy. Ah! ye who have sinned without discovery, 'Be sure your sin will find you out;' and bethink you, it may find you out ere long. Sin, like murder, will come out; men will even tell tales about themselves in their dreams. God has made men to be so wretched in their consciences that they have been obliged to stand forth and confess the truth. Secret sinner! if thou wantest the foretaste of damnation upon earth, continue in thy secret sins; for no man is more miserable than he who sinneth secretly, and yet trieth to preserve a character. Yon stag, followed by the hungry hounds, with open mouths, is far more happy than the man who is pursued by his sins. Yon bird, taken in the fowler's net, and labouring to escape, is far more happy than he who hath weaved around himself a web of deception, and labours to escape from it, day by day making the toils more thick and the web more strong. Oh the misery of secret sins! One may well pray, 'Cleanse thou me from secret faults.' Spurgeon's Sermons, No. 116, 'Secret Sins.'

Verse 12. The sin through ignorance (Heb.) is the same that David prays against in Psalm 19:12, 'Who can understand his errors (Heb.)? cleanse thou me from secret things!' These are not sins of omission, but acts committed by a person, when at the time, he did not suppose that what he did was sin. Although he did the thing deliberately, yet he did not perceive the sin of it. So deceitful is sin, we may be committing that abominable thing which casts angels into an immediate and an eternal hell, and yet at the moment be totally unaware! Want of knowledge of the truth, and too little tenderness of conscience hide it from us. Hardness of heart and a corrupt nature cause us to sin unperceived. But here again the form of the Son of Man appears! Jehovah, God of Israel, institutes sacrifice for sins of ignorance, and thereby discovers the same compassionate and considerate heart that appears in our High Priest, 'who can have compassion on the ignorant!' Hebrews 5:2. Amidst the types of this tabernacle, we recognize the presence of Jesus – it is his voice that shakes the curtains, and speaks in the ear of Moses, 'If a soul shall sin through ignorance!' The same yesterday, to-day, and for ever! Andrew A. Bonar, in 'Commentary on Leviticus,' ch. iv. v. 2.

Verse 12 (last clause). This is a singular difference between pharisaical and real sanctity: that is curious to look abroad, but seeth nothing at home: so that Pharisee condemned the Publican, and saw nothing in himself worthy of blame; but this careful to look at home, and searcheth into the secret corners, the very spirit of the mind. So did good David when he prayed, 'Cleanse thou me from secret faults.' Nathanael Hardy.

Verse 12. Our corruptions have made us such combustible matter, that there is scarce a dart thrown at us in vain: when Satan tempts us, it is but like the casting of fire into tinder, that presently catcheth: our hearts kindle upon the least spark that falls; as a vessel that is brimful of water, upon the least jog, runs over. Were we but true to ourselves, though the devil might knock by his temptations, yet he could never burst open the everlasting doors of our hearts by force or violence; but alas! we ourselves are not all of one heart and one mind: Satan hath got a strong party within us, that, as soon as he knocks, opens to him, and entertains him. And hence it is, that many times, small temptations and very petty occasions draw forth great corruptions: as a vessel, that is full of new liquor, upon the least vent given, works over into foam and froth; so truly, our hearts, almost upon every slight and trivial temptation, make that inbred corruption that lodgeth there, swell and boil, and run over into abundance of scum and filth in our lives and conversations. Ezekiel Hopkins.

Verse 12. Sins are many times hid from the godly man's eye, though he commits them, because he is not diligent and accurate in making a search of himself, and in an impartial studying of his own ways. If any sin be hid, as Saul was behind the stuff, or as Rahab had hid the spies, unless a man be very careful to search, he shall think no sin is there where it is. Hence it is that the Scripture doth so often command that duty of searching and trying, of examining and communing with our hearts. Now what need were there of this duty, but that it is supposed many secret and subtle lusts lie lurking in our hearts, which we take no notice of? If then the godly would find out their hidden lusts, know the sins they not yet know, they must more impartially judge themselves; they must take time to survey and examine themselves; they must not in an overly and slight manner, but really and industriously look up and down as they would search for thieves; and they must again and again look into this dark corner, and that dark corner of their hearts, as the woman sought for the lost groat. This self-scrutiny, and self-judging, this winnowing and sifting of ourselves, is the only way to see what is chaff and what is wheat, what is mere refuse and what is enduring. Anthony Burgess.

Verse 12. Sin is of a growing and advancing nature. From weakness to willfulness, from ignorance to presumption, is its ordinary course and progress. The cloud that Elijah's man saw, was at first no bigger than a hand's-breadth, and it threatened no such thing as a general tempest; but yet, at last, it overspread the face of the whole heavens; so truly, a sin that at first ariseth in the soul but as a small mist, and is scarcely discernable; yet, if it be not scattered by the breath of prayer, it will at length overspread the whole life, and become most tempestuous and raging. And therefore, David, as one experienced in the deceitfulness of sin, doth thus digest and methodise his prayer: first against secret and lesser sins; and then against the more gross and notorious; as knowing the one proceeds and issues from the other: Lord, cleanse me from my secret faults; and this will be a most effectual means to preserve and keep thy servant from presumptuous sins. Ezekiel Hopkins.

Verse 12, 13. That there is a difference betwixt infirmities and presumptuous sins is not to be denied; it is expressly in the holy Scripture. Papists say that the man who doth a mortal sin is not in the state of grace; but for venials, a man may commit (in their divinity) who can tell how many of them, and yet be in Christ for all that! I hope there is no such meaning in any of our divines as to tie up men's consciences, to hang on such a distinction of sins; since it is beyond the wit of man to set down a distinct point between mortal and venial sins. Now when it is an impossible matter punctually to set down to the understanding of man which is, and which is not a venial sin, they must pardon me for giving the least way to such divinity as must needs leave the conscience of a man in a maze and labyrinth. I find that the nature of infirmities doth so depend upon circumstances, that that is an infirmity in one man which is a gross sin in another; and some men plead for themselves that the things they do are but infirmities. He that will sin, and when he hath done will say – not to comfort his soul against Satan, but – to flatter himself in his sin, that it is but an infirmity; for aught I know, he may go to hell for his infirmities. Besides, if that be good divinity, that a man who is in the state of grace may do infirmities, but not commit gross sins, then I would I could see a man that would undertake to find us out some rule out of the word, by which a sinner may find by his sin, when he is in Christ and when out of Christ; at what degree of sinning – where lies the mathematical point and stop – that a man may say, 'Thus far may I go and yet be in grace; but if I step a step farther, then I am none of Christ's.' We all know that sins have their latitude; and for a man to hang his conscience on such a distinction as hath no rule to define where the difference lies, is not safe divinity. The conscience on the rack will not be laid and said with forms. The best and nearest way to quiet the heart of man is to say, that be the sin a sin of infirmity when we strive and strive but yield at last; or, of precipitancy, when we be taken in haste, as he was who said in his haste, 'All men are liars;' or, a mere gross sin in the matter: ay, say it be a presumptuous sin, yet if we allow it not, it hinders not but we are in Christ, though we do with reluctancy act and commit it. And I say that we do resist it if we do not allow it. For let us not go about to deny that a godly man during his being a godly man may possibly commit gross and presumptuous sins; and for infirmities, if we allow them and like them that we know to be sins, then we do not resist them; and such a man who allows himself in one is guilty of all, and is none of Christ's as yet. Be the sin what it will, James makes no distinction; and, where the law distinguisheth not, we must not distinguish. I speak not of doing a sin, but allowing; for a man may do it, and yet allow it not; as in Paul (Romans 7:15,16), 'That which I would not, that I do;' and he that allows not sin doth resist it. Therefore, a man may resist it, hate it, and yet do it. All the difference that I know is this: 1. That a man may live after his conversion all his days, and yet never fall into a gross sin. By gross here I mean presumptuous sins also. So David saith not 'cleanse,' but 'KEEP BACK thy servant from presumptuous sins.' We may, then, be kept from them. I speak not that all are, but some be; and, therefore, in itself all might be. 2. For lesser sins, 'secret faults,' we cannot live without them – they are of daily and almost hourly incursion; but yet we must be cleansed from them, as David speaks. Daily get your pardon; there is a pardon, of course, for them; they do not usually distract and plague the conscience, but yet we must not see them and allow them; if we do our case is to be pitied, we are none of Christ's as yet. 3. Great staring sins a man cannot usually and commonly practise, but he shall allow them. So Psalm 19:13, 'Keep back thy servant from presumptuous sins; let them not have dominion over me,' implying that except we be kept back from them they will have dominion over us. It follows, 'then shall I be upright;' so that the man in whom gross or presumptuous sins or sins have no dominion, he is an upright man. Richard Capel.

Verses 12, 13. The psalmist was sensible of sin's force and power; he was weary of sin's dominion; he cries unto God to deliver him from the reign of all the sins he knew; and those sins which were secret and concealed from his view, he begs that he might be convinced of them, and thoroughly cleansed from them. The Lord can turn the heart perfectly to hate the sin that was most of all beloved; and the strength of sin is gone when once 'tis hated; and as the hatred grows stronger and stronger, sin becomes weaker and weaker daily. Nathaniel Vincent, 1695.

Verse 13. 'Keep back thy servant also from all presumptuous sins.' He doth desire absolutely to be kept from 'presumptuous sins;' but then, he adds by way of supposition and reserve, that if he could not by reason of his naughty heart be kept from them, yet that they might not have full power and dominion over him. Thomas Manton.

Verse 13. 'Keep back thy servant.' It is an evil man's cross to be restrained, and a good man's joy to be kept back from sin. When sin puts forth itself, the evil man is putting forth his hand to the sin; but when sin puts forth itself, the good man is putting forth his hand to heaven; if he finds his heart yielding, out he cries, O keep back thy servant. An evil man is kept back from sin, as a friend from a friend, as a lover from his lover, with knit affections and projects of meeting; but a good man is kept back from sin, as a man from his deadly enemy, whose presence he hates, and with desires of his ruin and destruction. It is the good man's misery that he hath yet a heart to be more tamed and mastered; it is an evil man's vexation and discontent, that still, or at any time, he is held in by cord or bridle. And thus you see what David aims at in desiring to be kept back from presumptuous sins, namely, not a mere suspension, but a mortification, not a not acting only, but a subduing of the inclination; not for a time, but for ever. Obadiah Sedgwick.

Verse 13. 'Keep back thy servant,' etc. Even all the people of God, were they not kept by God's grace and power, they would every moment be undone both in soul and body. It is not our grace, our prayer, our watchfulness keeps us, but it is in the power of God, his right arm, supports us; we may see David praying to God that he would 'keep' him in both these respects from temporal dangers (Psalm 18:8,9; 'keep me'), etc.; where he doth not only pray to be kept, but he doth insinuate how carefully God keeps his people, and in what precious account their safety is, even as 'the apple of the eye,' and for spiritual preservation he often begs it. Though David be God's 'servant' yet he will, like a wild horse, run violently, and that into 'presumptuous sins,' if God 'keep' him not 'back,' yea, he prayeth that God would 'keep' the particular parts of his body that they sin not: 'keep the door of my lips' (Psalm 141:3); he entreateth God to 'keep' his lips and to set a watch about his mouth, as if he were not able to set guard sure enough: thus much more are we to pray that God would 'keep' our hearts, our minds, our wills, our affections, for they are more masterful. Anthony Burgess.

Verse 13. 'Keep back thy servant.' God keeps back his servants from sin, 1. By preventing grace, which is, by infusing such a nature as is like a bias into a bowl, drawing it aside another way; 2. By assisting grace, which is a further strength superadded to that first-implanted nature of holiness; like a hand upon a child holding him in; 3. By quickening grace, which is, when God doth enliven our graces to manifest themselves in actual opposition; so that the soul shall not yield, but keep off from entertaining the sin; 4. By directing grace, which is, when God confers that effectual wisdom to the mind, tenderness to the conscience, watchfulness to the heart, that his servants become greatly solicitous of his honour, scrupulously jealous of their own strength, and justly regardful of the honour of their holy profession; 5. By doing grace, which is, when God effectually inclines the hearts of his servants to the places and ways of their refuge, safeties, and preservations from sin, by enlarging the spirit of supplication, and framing the heart to the reverent and affectionate use of his ordinances. Condensed from Obadiah Sedgwick.

Verse 13. 'Thy servant:' as if he had said, 'O God, thou art my Lord, I have chosen thee, to whom I will give obedience; thou art he whom I will follow; I bestow all that I am on thee. Now a lord will help his servant against an enemy, who for the lord's service is the servant's enemy. O my Lord, help me! I am not able by my own strength to uphold myself, but thou art All-sufficiency' – 'Keep back thy servant from presumptuous sins' ... Beloved, it is a great thing to stand in near relations to God; and then it is a good thing to plead by them with God, forso-much as nearer relations have strongest force with all. The servant can do more than a stranger, and the child than a servant, and the wife than a child ... There be many reasons against sinning ... Now this also may come in, namely, the specialty of our relation to God, that we are his children, and he is our Father; we are his servants, and he is our Lord: though the common obligations are many and sufficient, yet the special relations are also a further tie: the more near a person comes to God, the more careful he should be not to sin against God. Obadiah Sedgwick.

Verse 13. 'Presumptuous sins.' The Rabbins distinguish all sins unto those committed (Heb.) ignorantly, and (Heb.) presumptuously. Benjamin Kennicott, D.D., 1718–1783.

Verse 13. 'Presumptuous sins.' When sin grows up from act to delight, from delight to new acts, from repetition of sinful acts to vicious indulgence, to habit and custom and a second nature, so that anything that toucheth upon it is grievous, and strikes to the man's heart; when it is got into God's place, and requires to be loved with the whole strength, makes grace strike sail, and other vices do it homage, demands all his concerns to be sacrificed to it and to be served with his reputation, his fortunes, his parts, his body, and soul, to the irreparable loss of his time and eternity both – this is the height of its dominion – then sin becomes 'exceedingly sinful,' and must needs make strange and sad alterations in the state of saints themselves, and be great hindrances to them in their way to Heaven, having brought them so near to Hell. Adam Littleton.

Verse 13. 'Presumptuous sins.' David prays that God would keep him back from 'presumptuous sins,' from known and evident sins, such as proceed from the choice of the perverse will against the enlightened mind, which are committed with deliberation, with design, resolution, and eagerness, against the checks of conscience, and the motions of God's spirit: such sins are direct rebellion against God, a despising of his command, and they provoke his pure eyes. Alexander Cruden.

Verse 13. 'Then shall I be innocent from the great transgression.' It is in the motions of a tempted soul to sin, as in the motions of a stone falling from the brow of a hill; it is easily stopped at first, but when once it is set a-going, who shall stay it? And therefore it is the greatest wisdom in the world to observe the first motions of the heart, to check and stop it there. G. H. Salter.

Verse 13. 'The great transgression.' Watch very diligently against all sin; but above all, take special heed of those sins that come near to the sin against the Holy Ghost; and these are, hypocrisy, taking only the outward profession of religion, and so dissembling and mocking of God; sinning wilfully against conviction of conscience, and against great light and knowledge, sinning presumptuously, with a high hand. These sins, though none of them are the direct sin against the Holy Ghost, yet they will come very near to it: therefore take special heed of them, lest they, in time, should bring you to the committing of that unpardonable sin. Robert Russel, 1705.

Verse 13. 'Let them not have dominion over me.' Any small sin may get the upper-hand of the sinner and bring him under in time, and after that is once habituated by long custom so as he cannot easily shake off the yoke, neither redeem himself from under the tyranny thereof. We see the experiment of it but too often, and too evidently in our common swearers and drunkards. Yet do such kind of sins, for the most part, grow on by little and little, steal into the throne insensibly, and do not exercise dominion over the enslaved soul till they have got strength by many and multiplied acts. But a presumptuous sin worketh a great alteration in the state of the soul at once, and by one single act advanceth marvellously, weakening the spirit, and giving a mighty advantage to the flesh, even to the hazard of a complete conquest. Robert Sanderson.

Verse 13. To sin presumptuously is the highest step. So in David's account; for first he prays, 'Lord, keep me from secret sins,' which he maketh sins of ignorance, and then next he prays against 'presumptuous sins,' which, as the opposition shows, are sins against knowledge; for says he, 'if they get dominion over me, I shall not be free from that great offence,' that is, that unpardonable sin which shall never be forgiven: so as these are nearest it of any other, yet not so as that every one that falls into such a sin commits it, but he is nigh to it, at the next step to it. For to commit that sin, but two things are required – light in the mind, and malice in the heart; not malice alone, unless there be light, for then that apostle had sinned it, so as knowledge is the parent of it, it is 'after receiving the knowledge of the truth.' Hebrews 10:27,28. Thomas Goodwin.

Verse 13. Happy souls, who, under a sense of peace through the blood of Jesus, are daily praying to be kept by the grace of the Spirit. Such truly know themselves, see their danger of falling, will not, dare not palliate or lessen the odious nature, and hateful deformity of their sin. They will not give a softer name to sin than it deserves, lest they depreciate the infinite value of that precious blood which Jesus shed to atone its guilt. Far will they be from flattering themselves into a deceitful notion that they are perfect, and have no sin in them. The spirit of truth delivers them from such errors; he teacheth them as poor sinners to look to the Saviour, and to beseech him to 'keep back' the headstrong passions, the unruly lusts and evil concupiscences which dwell in their sinful natures. Alas! the most exalted saint, the most established believer, if left to himself, how soon might the blackest crimes, the most 'presumptuous sins,' get the 'dominion' over him! David had woeful experience of this for a season. He prays from a heartfelt sense of past misery, and the dread of future danger, and he found the blessing of that covenant-promise: 'Sin shall not have dominion over you; for ye are not under the law, but under grace' Romans 6:14. William Mason, 1719–1791, in 'A Spiritual Treasury for the Children of God.'

Verse 14. 'Let the words of my mouth, and the meditation of my heart, be acceptable in thy sight, O Lord,' was David's prayer. David could not bear it, that a word, or a thought of his should miss acceptance with God. It did not satisfy him that his actions were well witnessed unto men on earth, unless his very thoughts were witnessed to by the Lord in heaven. Joseph Caryl.

Verse 14. 'Let the words of my mouth,' etc. The best of men have their failing, and an honest Christian may be a weak one; but weak as he may be, the goodness and sincerity of his heart will entitle him to put the petition of this verse, which no hypocrite or cunning deceiver can ever make use of. Thomas Sherlock (Bishop), 1676–1761.

Verse 14. 'Let the words of my mouth, and the meditation of my heart be acceptable in thy sight, O Lord, my strength and my Redeemer.' Fast and pray; Lord, I do fast, and I would pray; for to what end do I withhold sustenance from my body if it be not the more to cheer up my soul? my hungry, my thirsty soul? But the bread, the water of life, both which I find nowhere but in thy word, I partake not but by exercising my soul therein. This I begin to do, and fain would do it well, but in vain shall I attempt except thou do bless: bless me then, O Lord; bless either part of me, both are thine, and I would withhold neither part from thee. Not my body; I would set my tongue on work to speak of thee; not my soul, I would exercise my heart in thinking on thee; I would join them in devotion which thou hast joined in creation. Yea, Lord, as they have conspired to sin against thee, so do they nor consort to do their duty to thee; my tongue is ready, my heart is ready; I would think, I would speak; think upon thee, speak to thee. But, Lord, what are my words? what are my thoughts? Thou knowest the thoughts of men, that they are altogether vanity, and our words are but the blast of such thoughts; both are vile. It were well it were no more; both are wicked, my heart a corrupt fountain, and my tongue an unclean stream; and shall I bring such a sacrifice to God? The halt, the lame, the blind, though otherwise the beasts be clean, yet are they sacrifices abominable to God: how much more if we offer those beasts which are unclean? And yet, Lord, my sacrifice is no better, faltering words, wandering thoughts, are neither of them presentable to thee; how much less evil thoughts and idle words? Yet such are the best of mine. What remedy? If any, it is in thee, O Lord, that I must find it, and for it now do I seek unto thee. Thou only, O Lord, canst hallow my tongue, and hallow my heart that my tongue may speak, and my heart think that which may 'be acceptable unto thee,' yea, that which may be thy delight. Do not I lavish? Were it not enough that God should bear with, that he should not publish, the defects of my words, of my thoughts? May I presume that God shall accept of me? nay, delight in me? Forget I who the Lord is? Of what majesty? Of what felicity? Can it stand with his Majesty to vouchsafe acceptance? with his felicity to take content in the words of a worm? in the thoughts of a wretch? And, Lord, I am too proud that vilify myself so little, and magnify thee no more. But see whither the desire of thy servant doth carry him; how, willing to please, I consider not how hard it is for dust and ashes to please God, to do that wherein God should take content. But Lord, here is my comfort that I may set God to give content unto God; God is mine, and I cannot want access unto God, if God may approach himself. Let me be weak, yet God is strong; O Lord, thou art 'my strength.' Let me be a slave to sin, God is a Saviour; O Lord, thou art my Saviour; thou hast redeemed me from all that woeful state whereunto Adam cast me, yea, thou hast built me upon a rock, strong and sure, that the gates of hell might never prevail against me. These two things hast thou done for me, O Lord, and what may not he presume of for whom thou hast done these things! I fear not to come before thee. I presume my devotion shall content thee; be thine eyes never such all-seeing eyes, I will be bold to present my inward, my outward man before thee; be thy eyes never so holy eyes, I will not fly with Adam to hide my nakedness from thee, for I am able to keep my ground; seeing I am supported by my Lord, I doubt not but to prove a true Israelite, and to prevail with God. For all my woe, for all my sin, I will not shrink, nay, I will approach, approach to thee, for thou art 'My Redeemer.' The nearer I come to thee, the freer shall I be both from sin and woe. Oh, blessed state of man who is so weak, so strong; so wretched, and so happy; weak in himself, strong in God; most happy in God, though in himself a sinful wretch. And now, my soul, thou wouldst be devout; thou mayest be what thou wouldst: sacrifice to God thy words, sacrifice to God thy thoughts, make thyself a holocaust, doubt not but thou shalt be accepted, thou shalt content even the most glorious, the most holy eyes of God. Only presume not of thyself, presume on him; build thy words, build thy thoughts upon thy Rock, they shall not be shaken; free thy words, free thy thoughts (thoughts and words enthralled to sin), by thy Saviour, and thy sacrifice shall be accepted. So let me build on thee, so let me be enlarged by thee, in soul, in body, that 'The words of my mouth, and the meditation of my heart, be acceptable in thy sight, O Lord, my strength, and my Redeemer.' Arthur Lake (Bishop), in 'Divine Meditations,' 1629.

Hints to the village preacher

Verse 1. 'Chalmers' Astronomical Discourses' will suggest to the preacher many ways of handling this theme. The power, wisdom, goodness, punctuality, faithfulness, greatness, and glory of God are very visible in the heavens.

Verses 1–5. Parallel between the heavens and the revelation of Scripture, dwelling upon Christ as the central Sun of Scripture.

Verse 1. 'The heavens declare the glory of God.' Work in which we may unite, the nobility, pleasure, usefulness, and duty of such service.

Verse 2. Voices of the day and of the night. Day and night thoughts.

Verse 3. The marginal reading, coupled with verse four, suggests the eloquence of an unobtrusive life – silent, yet heard.

Verse 4. In what sense God is revealed to all men.

Verses 4, 5, 6. The Sun of Righteousness.

1. His tabernacle.
2. His appearance as a Bridegroom.
3. His joy as a champion.
4. His circuit and his influence.

Verse 5. 'Rejoiceth as a strong man,' etc. The joy of strength, the joy of holy labour, the joy of the anticipated reward.

Verse 6. The permeating power of the gospel.

Verse 7 (first clause). Holy Scripture.

1. What it is – 'law.'
2. Whose it is – 'of the Lord.'
3. What is its character – 'perfect.'
4. What its result – 'converting the soul.'

Verse 7 (second clause).

1. Scholars.
2. Class-book.
3. Teacher.
4. Progress.

Verse 7 (last clause). The wisdom of a simple faith.

Verse 8 (first clause). The heart-cheering power of the Word.

1. Founded in its righteousness.
2. Real in its quality.
3. Constant in its operation.

Verse 8 (second clause). Golden ointment for the eyes.

Verse 9. The purity and permanence of true religion, and the truth and justice of the principles upon which it is founded.

Verse 10. Two arguments for loving God's statutes – Profit and Pleasure.

Verse 10. The inexpressible delights of meditation on Scripture.

Verse 11 (first clause).

1. What? 'Warned.'
2. How? 'By them.'
3. Who? 'Thy servant.'
4. When? 'Is' – present.

Verse 11 (second clause). Evangelical rewards – 'In,' not for keeping.

Verse 12. See 'Spurgeon's Sermons,' No. 116, 'Secret Sins.'

Verses 12, 13. The three grades of sin – secret, presumptuous, unpardonable.

Verse 13 (last clause). 'The great transgression.' What it is not, may be, involves, and suggests.

Verse 14. A prayer concerning our holy things.

Verse 14. All wish to please. Some please themselves. Some please men. Some seek to please God. Such was David.

1. The prayer shows his humility.
2. The prayer show his affection.
3. The prayer shows a consciousness of duty.
4. The prayer shows a regard to self-interest.
   William Jay.

Verse 14. The harmony of heart and lips needful for acceptance.

Psalm 22

Title

'To the chief Musician upon Aijeleth Shahar. A Psalm of David.' This ode of singular excellence was committed to the most excellent of the temple songsters; the chief among ten thousand is worthy to be extolled by the chief Musician; no meaner singer must have charge of such a strain; we must see to it that we call up our best abilities when Jesus is the theme of praise. The words Aijeleth Shahar are enigmatical, and their meaning is uncertain; some refer them to a musical instrument used upon mournful occasions, but the majority adhere to the translation of our margin, 'Concerning the kind of the morning.' This last interpretation is the subject of much enquiry and conjecture. Calmet believed that the psalm was addressed to the music master who presided over the band called the 'Morning Hind,' and Adam Clarke thinks this to be the most likely of all the conjectural interpretations, although he himself inclines to the belief that no interpretation should be attempted, and believes that it is a merely arbitrary and unmeaning title, such as Orientals have always been in the habit of appending to their songs. Our Lord Jesus is so often compared to a hind, and his cruel huntings are so pathetically described in this most affecting psalm, that we cannot but believe that the title indicates the Lord Jesus under a well-known poetical metaphor; at any rate, Jesus is the Hind of the morning concerning whom David here sings.

Subject

This is beyond all others THE PSALM OF THE CROSS. It may have been actually repeated word by word by our Lord when hanging on the tree; it would be too bold to say that it was so, but even a casual reader may see that it might have been. It begins with, 'My God, my God, why hast thou forsaken me?' and ends, according to some, in the original with 'It is finished.' For plaintive expressions uprising from unutterable depths of woe we may say of this psalm, 'there is none like it.' It is the photograph of our Lord's saddest hours, the record of his dying words, the lachrymatory of his last tears, the memorial of his expiring joys. David and his afflictions may be here in a very modified sense, but, as the star is concealed by the light of the sun, he who sees Jesus will probably neither see nor care to see David. Before us we have a description both of the darkness and of the glory of the cross, the sufferings of Christ and the glory which shall follow. Oh for grace to draw near and see this great sight! We should read reverently, putting off our shoes from off our feet, as Moses did at the burning bush, for if there be holy ground anywhere in Scripture it is in this psalm.

Division

From the commencement to the twenty-first verse is a most pitiful cry for help, and from verse 21 to 31 is a most precious foretaste of deliverance. The first division may be subdivided at the tenth verse, from verse 1 to 10 being an appeal based upon covenant relationship; and from verse 10 to 21 being an equally earnest plea derived from the imminence of his peril.

Exposition

Verse 1. 'My God, my God, why hast thou forsaken me?' This was the startling cry of Golgotha: *Eloi, Eloi, lama sabacthani.* The Jews mocked, but the angels adored when Jesus cried this exceeding bitter cry. Nailed to the tree we behold our great Redeemer in extremities, and what see we? Having ears to hear let us hear, and having eyes to see let us see! Let us gaze with holy wonder, and mark the flashes of light amid the awful darkness of that midday-midnight. First, our Lord's faith beams forth and deserves our reverent imitation; he keeps his hold upon his God with both hands and cries twice, 'My God, my God!' The spirit of adoption was strong within the suffering Son of Man, and he felt no doubt about his interest in his God. Oh that we could imitate this cleaving to an afflicting God! Nor does the sufferer distrust the power of God to sustain him, for the title used – 'El' – signifies strength, and is the name of the Mighty God. He knows the Lord to be the all-sufficient support and succour of his spirit, and therefore appeals to him in the agony of grief, but not in the misery of doubt. He would fain know why he is left, he raises that question and repeats it, but neither the power nor the faithfulness of God does he mistrust. What an enquiry is this before us! 'Why hast thou forsaken me?' We must lay the emphasis on every word of this saddest of all utterances. 'Why?' what is the great cause of such a strange fact as for God to leave his own Son at such a time and in such a plight? There was no cause in him, why then was he deserted? 'Hast:' it is done, and the Saviour is feeling its dread effect as he asks the question; it is surely true, but how mysterious! It was no threatening of forsaking which made the great Surety cry aloud, he endured that forsaking in very deed. 'Thou:' I can understand why traitorous Judas and timid Peter should be gone, but thou, my God, my faithful friend, how canst thou leave me? This is worst of all, yea, worse than all put together. Hell itself has for its fiercest flame the separation of the soul from God. 'Forsaken:' if thou hadst chastened I might bear it, for thy face would shine; but to forsake me utterly, ah! why is this? 'Me:' thine innocent, obedient, suffering Son, why leavest thou me to perish? A sight of self seen by penitence, and of Jesus on the cross seen by faith will best expound this question. Jesus is forsaken because our sins had separated between us and our God.

'Why art thou so far from helping me, and from the words of my roaring?' The Man of Sorrows had prayed until his speech failed him, and he could only utter moanings and groanings as men do in severe sicknesses, like the roarings of a wounded animal. To what extremity of grief was our Master driven? What strong crying and tears were those which made him too hoarse for speech! What must have been his anguish to find his own beloved and trusted Father standing afar off, and neither granting help nor apparently hearing prayer! This was good cause to make him 'roar.' Yet there was reason for all this which those who rest in Jesus as their Substitute well know.

Verse 2. 'O my God, I cry in the daytime, but thou hearest not.' For our prayers to appear to be unheard is no new trial, Jesus felt it before us, and it is observable that he still held fast his believing hold on God, and cried still, 'My God.' On the other hand his faith did not render him less importunate, for amid the hurry and horror of that dismal day he ceased not his cry, even as in Gethsemane he had agonized all through the gloomy night. Our Lord continued to pray even though no comfortable answer came, and in this he set us an example of obedience to his own words, 'men ought always to pray, and not to faint.' No daylight is too glaring, and no midnight too dark to pray in; and no delay or apparent denial, however grievous, should tempt us to forbear from importunate pleading.

Verse 3. 'But thou art holy, O thou that inhabitest the praises of Israel.' However ill things may look, there is no ill in thee, O God! We are very apt to think and speak hardly of God when we are under his afflicting hand, but not so the obedient Son. He knows too well his Father's goodness to let outward circumstances libel his character. There in no unrighteousness with the God of Jacob, he deserves no censure; let him do what he will, he is to be praised, and to reign enthroned amid the songs of his chosen people. If prayer be unanswered it is not because God is unfaithful, but for some other good and weighty reason. If we cannot perceive any ground for the delay, we must leave the riddle unsolved, but we must not fly in God's face in order to invent an answer. While the holiness of God is in the highest degree acknowledged and adored, the afflicted speaker in this verse seems to marvel how the holy God could forsake him, and be silent to his cries. The argument is, thou art holy, Oh! why is it that thou dost disregard thy holy One in his hour of sharpest anguish? We may not question the holiness of God, but we may argue from it, and use it as a plea in our petitions.

Verse 4. 'Our fathers trusted in thee: they trusted, and thou didst deliver them.' This is the rule of life with all the chosen family. Three times over is it mentioned, they trusted, and trusted, and trusted, and never left off trusting, for it was their very life; and they fared well too, for thou didst deliver them. Out of all their straits, difficulties, and miseries faith brought them by calling their God to the rescue; but in the case of our Lord it appeared as if faith would bring no assistance from heaven, he alone of all the trusting ones was to remain without deliverance. The experience of other saints may be a great consolation to us when in deep waters if faith can be sure that their deliverance will be ours; but when we feel ourselves sinking, it is poor comfort to know that others are swimming. Our Lord here pleads the past dealings of God with his people as a reason why he should not be left alone; here again he is an example to us in the skilful use of the weapon of all prayer. The use of the plural pronoun 'our' shows how one with his people Jesus was even on the cross. We say, 'Our Father which art in heaven,' and he calls those 'our fathers' through whom we came into the world, although he was without father as to the flesh.

Verse 5. 'They cried unto thee, and were delivered: they trusted in thee, and were not confounded.' As if he had said, 'How is it that I am now left without succour in my overwhelming griefs, while all others have been helped? We may remind the Lord of his former loving kindnesses to his people, and beseech him to be still the same. This is true wrestling; let us learn the art. Observe, that ancient saints cried and trusted, and that in trouble we must do the same; and the invariable result was that they were not ashamed of their hope, for deliverance came in due time; this same happy portion shall be ours. The prayer of faith can do the deed when nothing else can. Let us wonder when we see Jesus using the same pleas as ourselves, and immersed in griefs far deeper than our own.

Verse 6. 'But I am a worm, and no man.' This verse is a miracle in language. How could the Lord of glory be brought to such abasement as to be not only lower than the angels, but even lower than men. What a contrast between 'I AM' and 'I am a worm'! yet such a double nature was found in the person of our Lord Jesus when bleeding upon the tree. He felt himself to be comparable to a helpless, powerless, down-trodden worm, passive while crushed, and unnoticed and despised by those who trod upon him. He selects the weakest of creatures, which is all flesh; and becomes, when trodden upon, writhing, quivering flesh, utterly devoid of any might except strength to suffer. This was a true likeness of himself when his body and soul had become a mass of misery – the very essence of agony – in the dying pangs of crucifixion. Man by nature is but a worm; but our Lord puts himself even beneath man, on account of the scorn that was heaped upon him and the weakness which he felt, and therefore he adds, 'and no man.' The privileges and blessings which belonged to the fathers he could not obtain while deserted by God, and common acts of humanity were not allowed him, for he was rejected of men; he was outlawed from the society of earth, and shut out from the smile of heaven. How utterly did the Saviour empty himself of all glory, and become of no reputation for our sakes! 'A reproach of men' – their common butt and jest; a byword and a proverb unto them: the sport of the rabble, and the scorn of the rulers. Oh the caustic power of reproach, to those who endure it with patience, yet smart under it most painfully! 'And despised of the people.' The *vox populi* was against him. The very people who would once have crowned him then contemned him, and they who were benefited by his cures sneered at him in his woes. Sin is worthy of all reproach and contempt, and for this reason Jesus, the Sinbearer, was given up to be thus unworthily and shamefully entreated.

Verse 7. 'All they that see me laugh me to scorn.' Read the evangelistic narrative of the ridicule endured by the Crucified One, and then consider, in the light of this expression, how it grieved him. The iron entered into his soul. Mockery has for its distinctive description 'cruel mockings;' those endured by our Lord were of the most cruel kind. The scornful ridicule of our Lord was universal; all sorts of men were unanimous in the derisive laughter, and vied with each other in insulting him. Priests and people, Jews and Gentiles, soldiers and civilians, all united in the general scoff, and that at the time when he was prostrate in weakness and ready to die. Which shall we wonder at the most, the cruelty of man or the love of the bleeding Saviour? How can we ever complain of ridicule after this?

'They shoot out the lip, they shake the head.' These were gestures of contempt. Pouting, grinning, shaking of the head, thrusting out of the tongue, and other modes of derision were endured by our patient Lord; men made faces at him before whom angels vail their faces and adore. The basest signs of disgrace which disdain could devise were maliciously cast at him. They punned upon his prayers, they made matter for laughter of his sufferings, and set him utterly at nought. Herbert sings of our Lord as saying,

Shame tears my soul, my body many a wound;
Sharp nails pierce this, but sharper that confound;
Reproaches which are free, while I am bound.
Was ever grief like mine?

Verse 8. 'Saying, He trusted on the Lord that he would deliver him: let him deliver him, seeing he delighted in him.' Here the taunt is cruelly aimed at the sufferer's faith in God, which is the tenderest point in a good man's soul, the very apple of his eye. They must have learned the diabolical art from Satan himself, for they made rare proficiency in it. According to Matthew 27:39–44, there were five forms of taunt hurled at the Lord Jesus; this special piece of mockery is probably mentioned in this psalm because it is the most bitter of the whole; it has a biting, sarcastic irony in it, which gives it a peculiar venom; it must have stung the Man of Sorrows to the quick. When we are tormented in the same manner, let us remember him who endured such contradiction of sinners against himself, and we shall be comforted. On reading these verses one is ready, with Trapp, to ask, Is this a prophecy or a history? for the description is so accurate. We must not lose sight of the truth which was unwittingly uttered by the Jewish scoffers. They themselves are witnesses that Jesus of Nazareth trusted in God: why then was he permitted to perish? Jehovah had aforetime delivered those who rolled their burdens upon him: why was this man deserted? Oh that they had understood the answer! Note further, that their ironical jest, 'seeing he delighted in him,' was true. The Lord did delight in his dear Son, and when he was found in fashion as a man, and became obedient unto death, he still was well pleased with him. Strange mixture! Jehovah delights in him, and yet bruises him; is well pleased, and yet slays him.

Verse 9. 'But thou art he that took me out of the womb.' Kindly providence attends with the surgery of tenderness at every human birth; but the Son of Man, who was marvellously begotten of the Holy Ghost, was in an especial manner watched over by the Lord when brought forth by Mary. The destitute state of Joseph and Mary, far away from friends and home, led them to see the cherishing hand of God in the safe delivery of the mother, and the happy birth of the child; that Child now fighting the great battle of his life, uses the mercy of his nativity as an argument with God. Faith finds weapons everywhere. He who wills to believe shall never lack reasons for believing. 'Thou didst make me hope when I was upon my mother's breasts.' Was our Lord so early a believer? Was he one of those babes and sucklings out of whose mouths strength is ordained? So it would seem; and if so, what a plea for help! Early piety gives peculiar comfort in our after trials, for surely he who loved us when we were children is too faithful to cast us off in our riper years. Some give the text the sense of 'gave me cause to trust, by keeping me safely,' and assuredly there was a special providence which preserved our Lord's infant days from the fury of Herod, the dangers of travelling, and the ills of poverty.

Verse 10. 'I was cast upon thee from the womb.' Into the Almighty arms he was first received, as into those of a loving parent. This is a sweet thought. God begins his care over us from the earliest hour. We are dandled upon the knee of mercy, and cherished in the lap of goodness; our cradle is canopied by divine love, and our first totterings are guided by his care. 'Thou art my God from my mother's belly.' The psalm begins with 'My God, my God,' and here, not only is the claim repeated, but its early date is urged. Oh noble perseverance of faith, thus to continue pleading with holy ingenuity of argument! Our birth was our weakest and most perilous period of existence; if we were then secured by Omnipotent tenderness, surely we have no cause to suspect that divine goodness will fail us now. He who was our God when we left our mother, will be with us till we return to mother earth, and will keep us from perishing in the belly of hell.

Verses 11–21. The crucified Son of David continues to pour out his complaint and prayer. We need much grace that while reading we may have fellowship with his sufferings. May the blessed Spirit conduct us into a most clear and affecting sight of our Redeemer's woes.

Verse 11. 'Be not far from me.' This is the petition for which he has been using such varied and powerful pleas. His great woe was that God had forsaken him, his great prayer is that he would be near him. A lively sense of the divine presence is a mighty stay to the heart in times of distress. 'For trouble is near; for there is none to help.' There are two 'fors,' as though faith gave a double knock at mercy's gate; that is a powerful prayer which is full of holy reasons and thoughtful arguments. The nearness of trouble is a weighty motive for divine help; this moves our heavenly Father's heart, and brings down his helping hand. It is his glory to be our very present help in trouble. Our Substitute had trouble in his inmost heart, for he said, 'the waters have come in, even unto my soul;' well might he cry, 'be not far from me.' The absence of all other helpers is another telling plea. In our Lord's case none either could or would help him, it was needful that he should tread the winepress alone; yet was it a sore aggravation to find that all his disciples had forsaken him, and lover and friend were put far from him. There is an awfulness about absolute friendlessness which is crushing to the human mind, for man was not made to be alone, and is like a dismembered limb when he has to endure heart-loneliness.

Verse 12. 'Many bulls have compassed me: strong bulls of Bashan have beset me round.' The mighty ones in the crowd are here marked by the tearful eye of their victim. The priests, elders, scribes, Pharisees, rulers, and captains bellowed round the cross like wild cattle, fed in the fat and solitary pastures of Bashan, full of strength and fury; they stamped and foamed around the innocent One, and longed to gore him to death with their cruelties. Conceive of the Lord Jesus as a helpless, unarmed, naked man, cast into the midst of a herd of infuriated wild bulls. They were brutal as bulls, many, and strong, and the Rejected One was all alone, and bound naked to the tree. His position throws great force into the earnest entreaty, 'Be not far from me.'

Verse 13. 'They gaped upon me with their mouths, as a ravening and a roaring lion.' Like hungry cannibals they opened their blasphemous mouths as if they were about to swallow the man whom they abhorred. They could not vomit forth their anger fast enough through the ordinary aperture of their mouths, and therefore set the doors of their lips wide open like those who gape. Like roaring lions they howled out their fury, and longed to tear the Saviour in pieces, as wild beasts raven over their prey. Our Lord's faith must have passed through a most severe conflict while he found himself abandoned to the tender mercies of the wicked, but he came off victorious by prayer; the very dangers to which he was exposed being used to add prevalence to his entreaties.

Verse 14. Turning from his enemies, our Lord describes his own personal condition in language which should bring the tears into every loving eye. 'I am poured out like water.' He was utterly spent, like water poured upon the earth; his heart failed him, and had no more firmness in it than running water, and his whole being was made a sacrifice, like a libation poured out before the Lord. He had long been a fountain of tears; in Gethsemane his heart welled over in sweat, and on the cross he gushed forth with blood; he poured out his strength and spirit, so that he was reduced to the most feeble and exhausted state. 'All my bones are out of joint,' as if distended upon a rack. Is it not most probable that the fastenings of the hands and feet, and the jar occasioned by fixing the cross in the earth, may have dislocated the bones of the Crucified One? If this is not intended, we must refer the expression to that extreme weakness which would occasion relaxation of the muscles and a general sense of parting asunder throughout the whole system. 'My heart is like wax; it is melted in the midst of my bowels.' Excessive debility and intense pain made his inmost life to feel like wax melted in the heat. The Greek liturgy uses the expression, 'thine unknown sufferings,' and well it may. The fire of Almighty wrath would have consumed our souls for ever in hell; it was no light work to bear as a substitute the heat of an anger so justly terrible. Dr Gill wisely observes, 'if the heart of Christ, the Lion of the tribe of Judah, melted at it, what heart can endure, or hands be strong, when God deals with them in his wrath?'

Verse 15. 'My strength is dried up like a potsherd.' Most complete debility is here portrayed; Jesus likens himself to a broken piece of earthenware, or an earthen pot, baked in the fire till the last particle of moisture is driven out of the clay. No doubt a high degree of feverish burning afflicted the body of our Lord. All his strength was dried up in the tremendous flames of avenging justice, even as the paschal lamb was roasted in the fire. 'My tongue cleaveth to my jaws;' thirst and fever fastened his tongue to his jaws. Dryness and a horrible clamminess tormented his mouth, so that he could scarcely speak. 'Thou hast brought me into the dust of death;' so tormented in every single part as to feel dissolved into separate atoms, and each atom full of misery; the full price of our redemption was paid, and no part of the Surety's body or soul escaped its share of agony. The words may set forth Jesus as having wrestled with Death until he rolled into the dust with his antagonist. Behold the humiliation of the Son of God! The Lord of Glory stoops to the dust of death. Amid the mouldering relics of mortality Jesus condescends to lodge!

Bishop Mant's version of the two preceding verses is forcible and accurate:

Pour'd forth like water is my frame;
My bones asunder start;
As wax that feels the searching flame,
Within me melts my heart.
My wither'd sinews shrink unstrung
Like potsherd dried and dead:
Cleaves to my jaws my burning tongue
The dust of death my bed.

Verse 16. We are to understand every item of this sad description as being urged by the Lord Jesus as a plea for divine help; and this will give us a high idea of his perseverance in prayer. 'For dogs have compassed me.' Here he marks the more ignoble crowd, who, while less strong than their brutal leaders, were not less ferocious, for there they were howling and barking like unclean and hungry dogs. Hunters frequently surround their game with a circle, and gradually encompass them with an ever-narrowing ring of dogs and men. Such a picture is before us. In the centre stands, not a panting stag, but a bleeding, fainting man, and around him are the enraged and unpitying wretches who have hounded him to his doom. Here we have the 'hind of the morning' of whom the psalm so plaintively sings, hunted by bloodhounds, all thirsting to devour him. The assembly of the wicked have inclosed me: thus the Jewish people were unchurched, and that which called itself an assembly of the righteous is justly for its sins marked upon the forehead as an assembly of the wicked. This is not the only occasion when professed churches of God have become synagogues of Satan, and have persecuted the Holy One and the Just. They pierced my hands and my feet. This can by no means refer to David, or to any one but Jesus of Nazareth, the once crucified but now exalted Son of God. Pause, dear reader, and view the wounds of thy Redeemer.

Verse 17. So emaciated was Jesus by his fastings and sufferings that he says, 'I may tell all my bones.' He could count and recount them. The posture of the body on the cross, Bishop Horne thinks, would so distend the flesh and skin as to make the bones visible, so that they might be numbered. The zeal of his Father's house had eaten him up; like a good soldier he had endured hardness. Oh that we cared less for the body's enjoyment and ease and more for our Father's business! It were better to count the bones of an emaciated body than to bring leanness into our souls.

'They look and stare upon me.' Unholy eyes gazed insultingly upon the Saviours's nakedness, and shocked the sacred delicacy of his holy soul. The sight of the agonizing body ought to have ensured sympathy from the throng, but it only increased their savage mirth, as they gloated their cruel eyes upon his miseries. Let us blush for human nature, and mourn in sympathy with our Redeemer's shame. The first Adam made us all naked, and therefore the second Adam became naked that he might clothe our naked souls.

Verse 18. 'They part my garments among them, and cast lots upon my vesture.' The garments of the executed were the perquisites of the executioners in most cases, but it was not often that they cast lots at the division of the spoil; this incident shows how clearly David in vision saw the day of Christ, and how surely the Man of Nazareth is he of whom the prophets spake: 'these things, therefore, the soldiers did.' He who gave his blood to cleanse us gave his garments to clothe us. As Ness says, 'this precious Lamb of God gave up his golden fleece for us.' How every incident of Jesus' griefs is here stored up in the treasury of inspiration, and embalmed in the amber of sacred song; we must learn hence to be very mindful of all that concerns our Beloved, and to think much more of everything which has a connection with him. It may be noted that the habit of gambling is of all others the most hardening, for men could practise it even at the cross-foot while besprinkled with the blood of the Crucified. No Christian will endure the rattle of the dice when he thinks of this.

Verse 19. 'But be thou not far from me, O Lord.' Invincible faith returns to the charge, and uses the same means, viz., importunate prayer. He repeats the petition so piteously offered before. He wants nothing but his God, even in his lowest state. He does not ask for the most comfortable or nearest presence of God, he will be content if he is not far from him; humble requests speed at the throne. 'O my strength, haste thee to help me.' Hard cases need timely aid: when necessity justifies it we may be urgent with God as to time, and cry, 'make haste;' but we must not do this out of willfulness. Mark how in the last degree of personal weakness he calls the Lord 'my strength;' after this fashion the believer can sing, 'when I am weak, then am I strong.'

Verse 20. 'Deliver my soul from the sword.' By the sword is probably meant entire destruction, which as a man he dreaded; or perhaps he sought deliverance from the enemies around him, who were like a sharp and deadly sword to him. The Lord had said, 'Awake, O sword,' and now from the terror of that sword the Shepherd would fain be delivered as soon as justice should see fit. 'My darling from the power of the dog.' Meaning his soul, his life, which is most dear to every man. The original is, 'my only one,' and therefore is our soul dear, because it is our only soul. Would that all men made their souls their darlings, but many treat them as if they were not worth so much as the mire of the streets. The dog may mean Satan, that infernal Cerberus, that cursed and cursing cur; or else the whole company of Christ's foes, who though many in number were as unanimous as if there were but one, and with one consent sought to rend him in pieces. If Jesus cried for help against the dog of hell, much more may we. *Cave canem*, beware of the dog, for his power is great, and only God can deliver us from him. When he fawns upon us, we must not put ourselves in his power; and when he howls at us, we may remember that God holds him with a chain.

Verse 21. 'Save me from the lion's mouth: for thou hast heard me from the horns of the unicorns.' Having experienced deliverance in the past from great enemies, who were strong as the unicorns, the Redeemer utters his last cry for rescue from death, which is fierce and mighty as the lion. This prayer was heard, and the gloom of the cross departed. Thus faith, though sorely beaten, and even cast beneath the feet of her enemy, ultimately wins the victory. It was so in our Head, it shall be so in all the members. We have overcome the unicorn, we shall conquer the lion, and from both lion and unicorn we shall take the crown.

Verses 22–31. The transition is very marked; from a horrible tempest all is changed into calm. The darkness of Calvary at length passed away from the face of nature, and from the soul of the Redeemer, and beholding the light of his triumph and its future results the Saviour smiled. We have followed him through the gloom, let us attend him in the returning light. It will be well still to regard the words as a part of our Lord's soliloquy upon the cross, uttered in his mind during the last few moments before his death.

Verse 22. 'I will declare thy name unto my brethren.' The delights of Jesus are always with his church, and hence his thoughts, after much distraction, return at the first moment of relief to their usual channel; he forms fresh designs for the benefit of his beloved ones. He is not ashamed to call them brethren, 'Saying, I will declare thy name unto my brethren, in the midst of the church will I sing praise unto thee.' Among his first resurrection words were these, 'Go to my brethren.' In the verse before us, Jesus anticipates happiness in having communication with his people; he purposes to be their teacher and minister, and fixes his mind upon the subject of his discourse. The name, i.e., the character and conduct of God are by Jesus Christ's gospel proclaimed to all the holy brotherhood; they behold the fulness of the Godhead dwelling bodily in him, and rejoice greatly to see all the infinite perfections manifested in one who is bone of their bone and flesh of their flesh. What a precious subject is the name of our God! It is the only one worthy of the only Begotten, whose meat and drink it was to do the Father's will. We may learn from this resolution of our Lord, that one of the most excellent methods of showing our thankfulness for deliverances is to tell to our brethren what the Lord has done for us. We mention our sorrows readily enough; why are we so slow in declaring our deliverances? 'In the midst of the congregation will I praise thee.' Not in a little household gathering merely does our Lord resolve to proclaim his Father's love, but in the great assemblies of his saints, and in the general assembly and church of the first-born. This the Lord Jesus is always doing by his representatives, who are the heralds of salvation, and labour to praise God. In the great universal church Jesus is the One authoritative teacher, and all others, so far as they are worthy to be called teachers, are nothing but echoes of his voice. Jesus, in this second sentence, reveals his object in declaring the divine name, it is that God may be praised; the church continually magnifies Jehovah for manifesting himself in the person of Jesus, and Jesus himself leads the song, and is both precentor and preacher in his church. Delightful are the seasons when Jesus communes with our hearts concerning divine truth; joyful praise is the sure result.

Verse 23. 'Ye that fear the Lord praise him.' The reader must imagine the Saviour as addressing the congregation of the saints. He exhorts the faithful to unite with him in thanksgiving. The description of 'fearing the Lord' is very frequent and very instructive; it is the beginning of wisdom, and is an essential sign of grace. 'I am a Hebrew and I fear God' was Jonah's confession of faith. Humble awe of God is so necessary a preparation for praising him that none are fit to sing to his honour but such as reverence his word; but this fear is consistent with the highest joy, and is not to be confounded with legal bondage, which is a fear which perfect love casteth out. Holy fear should always keep the key of the singing pew. Where Jesus leads the tune none but holy lips may dare to sing. 'All ye the seed of Jacob glorify him.' The genius of the gospel is praise. Jew and Gentile saved by sovereign grace should be eager in the blessed work of magnifying the God of our salvation. All saints should unite in the song; no tongue may be silent, no heart may be cold. Christ calls us to glorify God, and can we refuse? 'And fear him, all ye the seed of Israel.' The spiritual Israel all do this, and we hope the day will come when Israel after the flesh will be brought to the same mind. The more we praise God the more reverently shall we fear him, and the deeper our reverence the sweeter our songs. So much does Jesus value praise that we have it here under his dying hand and seal that all the saints must glorify the Lord.

Verse 24. 'For he hath not despised nor abhorred the affliction of the afflicted.' Here is good matter and motive for praise. The experience of our covenant Head and Representative should encourage all of us to bless the God of grace. Never was man so afflicted as our Saviour in body and soul from friends and foes, by heaven and hell, in life and death; he was the foremost in the ranks of the afflicted, but all those afflictions were sent in love, and not because his Father despised and abhorred him. 'Tis true that justice demanded that Christ should bear the burden which as a substitute he undertook to carry, but Jehovah always loved him, and in love laid that load upon him with a view to his ultimate glory and to the accomplishment of the dearest wish of his heart. Under all his woes our Lord was honourable in the Father's sight, the matchless jewel of Jehovah's heart. 'Neither hath he hid his face from him.' That is to say, the hiding was but temporary, and was soon removed; it was not final and eternal. 'But when he cried unto him, he heard.' Jesus was heard in that he feared. He cried *in extremis* and *de profundis*, and was speedily answered; he therefore bids his people join him in singing a *Gloria in excelsis*.

Every child of God should seek refreshment for his faith in this testimony of the Man of Sorrows. What Jesus here witnesses is as true to-day as when it was first written. It shall never be said that any man's affliction or poverty prevented his being an accepted suppliant at Jehovah's throne of grace. The meanest applicant is welcome at mercy's door:

> None that approach his throne shall find
> A God unfaithful or unkind.

Verse 25. 'My praise shall be of thee in the great congregation.' The one subject of our Master's song is the Lord alone. The Lord and the Lord only is the theme which the believer handleth when he gives himself to imitate Jesus in praise. The word in the original is 'from thee,' – true praise is of celestial origin. The rarest harmonies of music are nothing unless they are sincerely consecrated to God by hearts sanctified by the Spirit. The clerk says, 'Let us sing to the praise and glory of God;' but the choir often sing to the praise and glory of themselves. Oh when shall our service of song be a pure offering? Observe in this verse how Jesus loves the public praises of the saints, and thinks with pleasure of the great congregation. It would be wicked on our part to despise the twos and threes; but, on the other hand, let not the little companies snarl at the greater assemblies as though they were necessarily less pure and less approved, for Jesus loves the praise of the great congregation. 'I will pay my vows before them that fear him.' Jesus dedicates himself anew to the carrying out of the divine purpose in fulfilment of his vows made in anguish. Did our Lord when he ascended to the skies proclaim amid the redeemed in glory the goodness of Jehovah? And was that the vow here meant? Undoubtedly the publication of the gospel is the constant fulfilment of covenant engagements made by our Surety in the councils of eternity. Messiah vowed to build up a spiritual temple for the Lord, and he will surely keep his word.

Verse 26. 'The meek shall eat and be satisfied.' Mark how the dying Lover of our souls solaces himself with the result of his death. The spiritually poor find a feast in Jesus, they feed upon him to the satisfaction of their hearts, they were famished until he gave himself for them, but now they are filled with royal dainties. The thought of the joy of his people gave comfort to our expiring Lord. Note the characters who partake of the benefit of his passion; 'the meek,' the humble and lowly. Lord, make us so. Note also the certainty that gospel provisions shall not be wasted, 'they shall eat;' and the sure result of such eating, 'and be satisfied.' 'They shall praise the Lord that seek him.' For a while they may keep a fast, but their thanksgiving days must and shall come. 'Your heart shall live for ever.' Your spirits shall not fail through trial, you shall not die of grief, immortal joys shall be your portion. Thus Jesus speaks even from the cross to the troubled seeker. If his dying words are so assuring, what consolation may we not find in the truth that he ever liveth to make intercession for us! They who eat at Jesus' table receive the fulfilment of the promise, 'Whosoever eateth of this bread shall live for ever.'

Verse 27. In reading this verse one is struck with the Messiah's missionary spirit. It is evidently his grand consolation that Jehovah will be known throughout all places of his dominion. 'All the ends of the world shall remember and turn unto the Lord.' Out from the inner circle of the present church the blessing is to spread in growing power until the remotest parts of the earth shall be ashamed of their idols, mindful of the true God, penitent for their offences, and unanimously earnest for reconciliation with Jehovah. Then shall false worship cease, 'and all the kindreds of the nations shall worship before thee,' O thou only living and true God. This hope which was the reward of Jesus is a stimulus to those who fight his battles.

It is well to mark the order of conversion as here set forth; they shall 'remember' – this is reflection, like the prodigal who came unto himself; 'and turn unto Jehovah' – this is repentance, like Manasseh who left his idols and 'worship' – this is holy service, as Paul adored the Christ whom once he abhorred.

Verse 28. 'For the kingdom is the Lord's.' As an obedient Son the dying Redeemer rejoiced to know that his Father's interests would prosper through his pains. 'The Lord reigneth' was his song as it is ours. He who by his own power reigns supreme in the domains of creation and providence, has set up a kingdom of grace, and by the conquering power of the cross that kingdom will grow until all people shall own its sway and proclaim that 'he is the governor among the nations.' Amid the tumults and disasters of the present the Lord reigneth; but in the halcyon days of peace the rich fruit of his dominion will be apparent to every eye. Great Shepherd, let thy glorious kingdom come.

Verse 29. 'All they that be fat upon earth,' the rich and great are not shut out. Grace now finds the most of its jewels among the poor, but in the latter days the mighty of the earth 'shall eat,' shall taste of redeeming grace and dying love, and shall 'worship' with all their hearts the God who deals so bountifully with us in Christ Jesus. Those who are spiritually fat with inward prosperity shall be filled with the marrow of communion, and shall worship the Lord with peculiar fervour. In the covenant of grace Jesus has provided good cheer for our high estate, and he has taken equal care to console us in our humiliation, for the next sentence is, 'all they that go down to the dust shall bow before him.' There is relief and comfort in bowing before God when our case is at its worst; even amid the dust of death prayer kindles the lamp of hope.

While all who come to God by Jesus Christ are thus blessed, whether they be rich or poor, none of those who despise him may hope for a blessing. 'None can keep alive his own soul.' This is the stern counterpart of the gospel message of 'look and live.' There is no salvation out of Christ. We must hold life, and have life as Christ's gift, or we shall die eternally. This is very solid evangelical doctrine, and should be proclaimed in every corner of the earth, that like a great hammer it may break in pieces all self-confidence.

Verse 30. 'A seed shall serve him.' Posterity shall perpetuate the worship of the Most High. The kingdom of truth on earth shall never fail. As one generation is called to its rest, another will arise in its stead. We need have no fear for the true apostolic succession; that is safe enough. 'It shall be accounted to the Lord for a generation.' He will reckon the ages by the succession of the saints, and set his accounts according to the families of the faithful. Generations of sinners come not into the genealogy of the skies. God's family register is not for strangers, but for the children only.

Verse 31. 'They shall come.' Sovereign grace shall bring out from among men the blood bought ones. Nothing shall thwart the divine purpose. The chosen shall come to life, to faith, to pardon, to heaven. In this the dying Saviour finds a sacred satisfaction. Toiling servant of God, be glad at the thought that the eternal purpose of God shall suffer neither let nor hindrance. 'And shall declare his righteousness unto a people that shall be born.' None of the people who shall be brought to God by the irresistible attractions of the cross shall be dumb, they shall be able to tell forth the righteousness of the Lord, so that future generations shall know the truth. Fathers shall teach their sons, who shall hand it down to their children; the burden of the story always being 'that he hath done this,' or, that 'It is finished.' Salvation's glorious work is done, there is peace on earth, and glory in the highest. 'It is finished,' these were the expiring words of the Lord Jesus, as they are the last words of this Psalm. May we by living faith be enabled to see our salvation finished by the death of Jesus!

Explanatory notes and quaint sayings

Title. The title of the twenty-second Psalm is Aijeleth Shahar – the morning hart. The whole Psalm refers to Christ, containing much that cannot be applied to another: parting his garments, casting lots for his vesture, etc. He is described as a kindly, meek and beautiful hart, started by the huntsman at the dawn of the day. Herod began hunting him down as soon as he appeared. Poverty, the hatred of men, and the temptation of Satan, joined in the pursuit. There always was some 'dog,' or 'bull,' or 'unicorn,' ready to attack him. After his first sermon the huntsmen gathered about him, but he was too fleet of foot, and escaped. The church had long seen the Messiah 'like a roe, or a young hart, upon the mountains,' had 'heard the voice of her Beloved,' and had cried out, 'Behold, he cometh, leaping upon the mountains, skipping upon the hills;' sometimes he was even seen, with the dawn of the day, in the neighbourhood of the temple, and beside the enclosures of the vineyards. The church requested to see him 'on the mountains of Bether,' and upon 'the mountains of spices.' The former probably signifying the place of his sufferings, and the latter the sublime acclivities of light, glory, and honour, where the 'hart' shall be hunted no more. But in the afternoon, the huntsmen who had been following the 'young roe' from early day-break, had succeeded in driving him to the mountains of Bether. Christ found Calvary a craggy, jagged, and fearful hill – 'a mountain of division.' Here he was driven by the huntsmen to the edges of the awful precipices yawning destruction from below, while he was surrounded and held at bay by all the beasts of prey and monsters of the infernal forest. The 'unicorn,' and the 'bulls of Bashan,' gored him with their horns; the great 'lion' roared at him; and the 'dog' fastened himself upon him. But he foiled them all. In his own time he bowed his head and gave up the ghost. He was buried in a new grave; and his assailants reckoned upon complete victory. They had not considered that he was a 'morning hart.' Surely enough, at the appointed time, did he escape from the hunter's net, and stand forth on the mountains of Israel ALIVE, and never, NEVER to die again. Now he is with Mary in the garden, giving evidence of his own resurrection; in a moment he is at Emmaus, encouraging the too timid and bewildered disciples. Nor does it cost him any trouble to go thence to Galilee to his friends, and again to the Mount of Olives, 'on the mountains of spices,' carrying with him the day-dawn, robed in life and beauty for ever more.' Christmas Evans, 1766–1838.

Title. It will be very readily admitted that the hind is a very appropriate emblem of the suffering and persecuted righteous man who meets us in this Psalm ... That the hind may be a figurative expression significant of suffering innocence, is put beyond a doubt by the fact, that the wicked and the persecutors in this Psalm, whose peculiar physiognomy is marked by emblems drawn from the brute creation, are designed by the terms dogs, lions, bulls, etc. E. W. Hengstenberg.

Title. 'The hind.' Much extraordinary symbolism has by old authors been conjured up and clustered around the hind. According to their curious natural history, there exists a deadly enmity between the deer and the serpent, and the deer by its warm breath draws serpents out of their holes in order to devour them. The old grammarians derived Elaphas, or hart, from *elaunein tous opheis*, that is, of driving away serpents. Even the burning a portion of the deer's horns was said to drive away all snakes. If a snake had escaped the hart after being drawn out by the hart by its breath, it was said to be more vehemently poisonous than before. The timidity of the deer was ascribed to the great size of its heart, in which they thought was a bone shaped like a cross. Condensed from Wood's 'Bible Animals,' by C. H. S.

Whole Psalm. This is a kind of gem among the Psalms, and is peculiarly excellent and remarkable. It contains those deep, sublime, and heavy sufferings of Christ, when agonising in the midst of the terrors and pangs of divine wrath and death, which surpass all human thought and comprehension. I know not whether any Psalm throughout the whole book contains matter more weighty, or from which the hearts of the godly can so truly perceive those sighs and groans, inexpressible by man, which their Lord and Head, Jesus Christ, uttered when conflicting for us in the midst of death, and in the midst of the pains and terrors of hell. Wherefore this Psalm ought to be most highly prized by all who have any acquaintance with temptations of faith and spiritual conflicts. Martin Luther.

Whole Psalm. This Psalm, as it sets out the sufferings of Christ to the full, so also his three great offices. His sufferings are copiously described from the beginning of the Psalm to verse 22. The prophetical office of Christ, from verse 22 to verse 25. That which is foretold about his vows (verse 25), hath respect to his priestly function. In the rest of the Psalm the kingly office of Christ is set forth. William Gouge, D.D. (1575–1653), in 'A Commentary on the whole Epistle to the Hebrews,' (reprinted in Nichol's Series of Commentaries).

Whole Psalm. This Psalm seems to be less a prophecy than a history. Cassiodorus.

Whole Psalm. This Psalm must be expounded, word for word, entire and in every respect, of Christ only; without any allegory, trope, or anagoge. Bakius, quoted by F. Delitzsch, D.D., on Hebrews, ii. 12.

Whole Psalm. A prophecy of the passion of Christ, and of the vocation of the Gentiles. Eusebius of Cæsarea.

Verse 1. 'My God, my God, why hast thou forsaken me?' We contrast this with John 16:32, 'I am not alone, because the Father is with me.' That these words in David were notwithstanding the words of Christ, there is no true believer ignorant; yet how cross our Lord's words in John! Answer: It is one thing to speak out of present sense of misery, another thing to be confident of a never-separated Deity. The condition of Christ in respect of his human state (not the divine), is in all outward appearances, like ours; we conceive the saints' condition very lamentable at times, as if God were for ever gone. And Christ (to teach us to cry after God the Father, like children after the mother, whose very stepping but at the door, ofttimes makes the babe believe, and so saith that his father is gone for ever), presents in his own sufferings how much he is sensible of ours in that case. As for his divine nature, he and his Father can never sunder in that, and so at no time is he alone, but the Father is always with him. William Streat, in 'The Dividing of the Hoof,' 1654.

Verse 1. 'My God, my God,' etc. There is a tradition that our Lord, hanging on the cross, began, as we know from the gospel, this Psalm; and repeating it and those that follow, gave up his most blessed spirit when he came to the sixth verse of the thirty-first Psalm. However that may be, by taking these first words on his lips, he stamped the Psalm as belonging to himself. Ludolph, the Carthusian (c.1350), in J. M. Neale's Commentary.

Verse 1. 'My God, my God,' etc. It was so sharp, so heavy an affliction to Christ's soul, that it caused him who was meek under all other sufferings as a lamb, to roar under this like a lion. For so much those words of Christ signify, 'My God, my God, why hast thou forsaken me? why art thou so far from helping me, and from the words of my roaring?' It comes from a root that signifies to howl or roar as a lion, and rather signifies the noise made by a wild beast than the voice of a man. And it is as much as if Christ had said, O my God, no words can express my anguish, I will not speak, but roar, howl out my complaints. Pour it out in volleys of groans. I roar as a lion. It's no small matter will make that majestic creature to roar. And sure so great a spirit as Christ's would not have roared under a slight burden.

Did God really forsake Jesus Christ upon the cross? then from the desertion of Christ singular consolation springs up to the people of God; yea, manifold consolation. Principally it's a support in these two respects, as it is preventive of your final desertion, and a comfortable pattern to you in your present sad desertions. 1. Christ's desertion is preventive of your final desertion. Because he was forsaken for a time you shall not be forsaken for ever. For he was forsaken for you. It is every way as much for the dear Son of God, the darling delight of his soul, to be forsaken of God for a time, as if such a poor inconsiderable thing as thou art shouldst be cast off to eternity. Now, this being equivalent and borne in thy room, must needs give thee the highest security in the world that God will never finally withdraw from thee. 2. Moreover, this sad desertion of Christ becomes a comfortable pattern to poor deserted souls in divers respects; and the proper business of such souls, at such times, is to eye it believingly. Though God deserted Christ, yet at the same time he powerfully supported him. His omnipotent arms were under him, though his pleased face was hid from him. He had not indeed his smiles, but he had his supportations. So, Christian, just so shall it be with thee. Thy God may turn away his face, he will not pluck away his arm. When one asked of holy Mr Baines how the case stood with his soul, he answered, 'Supports I have, though suavities I want.' Our Father in this deals with us as we ourselves sometimes do with a child that is stubborn and rebellious. We turn him out of doors and bid him begone out of our sight, and there he sighs and weeps; but however for the humbling of him, we will not presently take him into house and favour; yet we order, at least permit the servants to carry him meat and drink: here is fatherly care and support, though no former smiles or manifested delights … Though God forsook Christ, yet at that time he could justify God. So you read, 'O my God (saith he), I cry in the day time; but thou hearest not, and in the night season, and am not silent; but thou art holy.' Is not thy spirit according to thy measure, framed like Christ's in this; canst thou not, say even when he writes bitter things against thee, he is a holy, faithful and good God for all this! I an deserted but not wronged. There is not one drop of injustice in all the sea of my sorrows. Though he condemned me I must and will justify him: this also is Christ-like. John Flavel.

Verse 1. 'My God, my God.' The repetition is expressive of fervent desire – 'My God,' in an especial sense, as in his words after the resurrection to Mary Magdalene, 'I ascend unto my God, and your God;' 'My God,' not as the Son of God only, but in that nature which he hath assumed, as the beloved Son in whom the Father is well pleased; who is loved of the Father and who loveth the Father more than the whole universe. It is observed that this expression, 'My God,' is three times repeated. Dionysius, quoted by Isaac Williams.

Verse 1. 'My God.' It was possible for Christ by faith to know that he was beloved of God, and he did know that he was beloved of God, when yet as to sense and feeling he tasted of God's wrath. Faith and the want of sense are not inconsistent; there may be no present sense of God's love, nay, there may be a present sense of his wrath, and yet there may be faith at the same time. John Row's 'Emmanuel,' 1680.

Verse 1. This word, 'My God,' takes in more than all the philosophers in the world could draw out of it. Alexander Wedderburn, 1701.

Verse 1. That there is something of a singular force, meaning, and feeling in these words is manifest from this – the evangelists have studiously given us this verse in the very words of the Hebrew, in order to show their emphatic force. And moreover I do not remember any one other place in the Scriptures where we have this repetition, ELI, ELI. Martin Luther.

Verse 1. 'Why?' Not the 'why' of impatience or despair, not the sinful questioning of one whose heart rebels against his chastening, but rather the cry of a lost child who cannot understand why his father has left him, and who longs to see his father's face again. J. J. Stewart Perowne.

Verse 1. 'My roaring.' (Heb.), seems primarily to denote the roaring of a lion; but, as applied to intelligent beings, it is generally expressive of profound mental anguish poured forth in audible and even vehement strains. Psalm 38:9; 33:3; Job 3:24. Thus did the suffering Messiah pour forth strong crying and tears, to him that was able to save him from death. Hebrews 5:7. John Morison.

Verse 1. When Christ complains of having been forsaken by God, we are not to understand that he was forsaken by the First Person, or that there was a dissolution of the hypostatic union, or that he lost the favour and friendship of the Father; but he signifies to us that God permitted his human nature to undergo those dreadful torments, and to suffer an ignominious death, from which he could, if he chose, most easily deliver him. Nor did such complaints proceed either from impatience or ignorance, as if Christ were ignorant of the cause of his suffering, or was not most willing to bear such abandonment in his suffering; such complaints were only a declaration of his most bitter sufferings. And whereas, through the whole course of his passion, with such patience did our Lord suffer, as not to let a single groan or sigh escape from him, so now, lest the bystanders may readily believe that he was rendered impassible by some superior power; therefore, when his last moments were nigh he protests that he is true man, truly possible; forsaken by his Father in his sufferings, the bitterness and acuteness of which he then intimately felt. Robert Bellarmine (Cardinal), 1542–1621.

Verse 1. Divines are wont commonly to say, that Christ, from the moment of his conception, had the sight of God, his human soul being immediately united to the Deity, Christ from the very moment of his conception had the sight of God. Now for our Saviour, who had known experimentally how sweet the comfort of his Father's face had been, and had lived all his days under the warm beams and influences of the Divinity, and had had his soul all along refreshed with the sense of the Divine presence, for him to be left in that horror and darkness, as to have no taste of comfort, no glimpse of the Divinity breaking in upon his human soul, how great an affliction must that needs be unto him! John Row.

Verse 1. Desertion is in itself no sin; for Christ endured its bitterness, ay, he was so deep in it, that when he died, he said, 'Why hast thou forsaken me?' A total, a final desertion ours is not;

partial the best have had and have. God turns away his face, David himself is troubled: 'The just shall live by faith,' and not by feeling. Richard Capel.

Verse 1. Oh! how will our very hearts melt with love, when we remember that as we have been distressed for our sins against him; so he was in greater agonies for us? We have had gall and wormwood, but he tasted a more bitter cup. The anger of God has dried up our spirits, but he was scorched with a more flaming wrath. He was under violent pain in the garden, and on the cross; ineffable was the sorrow that he felt, being forsaken of his Father, deserted by his disciples, affronted and reproached by his enemies, and under a curse for us. This Sun was under a doleful eclipse, this living Lord was pleased to die, and in his death was under the frowns of an angry God. That face was then hid from him that had always smiled before; and his soul felt that horror and that darkness which it had never felt before. So that there was no separation between the divine and human nature, yet he suffered pains equal to those which we had deserved to suffer in hell for ever. God so suspended the efficacies of his grace that it displayed in that hour none of its force and virtue on him. He had no comfort from heaven, none from his angels, none from his friends, even in that sorrowful hour when he needed comfort most. Like a lion that is hurt in the forest, so he roared and cried out, though there was no despair in him; and when he was forsaken, yet there was trust and hope in these words, 'My God, my God.' Timothy Rogers.

Verse 1. Here is comfort to deserted souls; Christ himself was deserted; therefore, if thou be deserted, God dealeth no otherwise with thee than he did with Christ. Thou mayest be beloved of God and not feel it; Christ was so, he was beloved of the Father, and yet he had no present sense and feeling of his love. This may be a great comfort to holy souls under the suspension of those comforts and manifestations which sometimes they have felt; Christ himself underwent such a suspension, therefore such a suspension of divine comfort may consist with God's love. Thou mayest conclude possibly, 'I am a hypocrite, and therefore God hath forsaken me;' this is the complaint of some doubting Christians, 'I am a hypocrite, and therefore God hath forsaken me;' but thou hast no reason so to conclude: there was no failure in Christ's obedience, and yet Christ was forsaken in point of comfort; therefore desertion, in point of comfort, may consist with truth of grace, yea, with the highest measure of grace; so it did in our Saviour. John Row.

Verse 1. Lord, thou knowest what it is for a soul to be forsaken, it was sometime thine own case when thou complainedst, 'My God, why hast thou forsaken me?' not, O my Lord! but that thou hadst a divine supportment, but thou hadst not (it seemeth) that inward joy which at other times did fill thee; now thou art in thy glory, pity a worm in misery, that mourns and desires more after thee than all things: Lord, thou paidst dear for my good, let good come unto me. Joseph Symonds, 1658.

Verse 1. The first verse expresses a species of suffering that never at any other time was felt in this world, and never will be again – the vengeance of the Almighty upon his child – 'MY God, why hast thou forsaken me?' R. H. Ryland.

Verse 2. 'O my God, I cry in the daytime, but thou hearest not,' etc. How like is this expostulation to that of a human child with its earthly parent! It is based on the ground of relationship – 'I am thine; I cry day and night, yet I am not heard. Thou art my God, yet nothing is done to silence me. In the daytime of my life I cried; in this night season of my death I intreat. In the garden of Gethsemane I occupied the night with prayers; with continual ejaculations have I passed through this eventful morning. O my God, thou hast not yet heard me, therefore am I not yet silent; I cannot cease till thou answerest.' Here Christ urges his suit in a manner which none but filial hearts adopt. The child knows that the parent yearns over him. His importunity is strengthened by confidence in paternal love. He keeps not silence, he gives him no rest because he confides in his power and willingness to grant the desired relief. This is natural. It is the argument of the heart, an appeal to the inward yearnings of our nature. It is also scriptural, and is thus stated, 'If ye then being evil, know how to give good gifts unto your children, how much more shall your heavenly Father give the Holy Spirit to them that ask him?' Luke 11:13. John Stevenson, in 'Christ on the Cross,' 1842.

Verse 2. The princely prophet says, 'Lord, I cry unto thee in the daytime, but thou hearest not, also in the night time, and yet this is not to be thought folly to me.' (Septuagint version.) Some perhaps would think it a great point of folly for a man to cry and call unto him who stops his ears, and seems not to hear. Nevertheless, this folly of the faithful is wiser than all the wisdom of the world. For we know well enough, that howsoever God seem at the first not to hear, yet the Lord is a sure refuge in due time – in affliction. Psalm 9:9. Thomas Playfere.

Verses 2, 3. Well, what hears God from him, now he hears nothing from God, as to the deliverance prayed for? No murmuring at God's proceedings; nay, he hears quite the contrary, for he justifies and praises God: 'But thou art holy, O thou that inhabitest the praises of Israel.' Observe whether thou canst not gather something from the manner of God's denying the thing prayed for, which may sweeten it to thee! Haply thou shalt find he denies thee, but it is with a smiling countenance, and ushers it in with some expressions of grace and favour, that may assure thee his denial proceeds not from displeasure. As you would do with a dear friend, who, may be, comes to borrow a sum of money of you; lend it you dare not, because you see plainly it is not for his good; but in giving him the denial, lest he should misinterpret it, as proceeding from want of love and respect, you preface it with some kind of language of your hearty affection to him, as that you love him, and therefore deny him, and shall be ready to do for him more than that comes to. Thus God sometimes wraps up his denials in such sweet intimations of love, as prevents all jealousies arising in the hearts of his people. William Gurnall.

Verses 2, 3. They that have conduit-water come into their houses, if no water come they do not conclude the spring to be dry, but the pipes to be stopped or broken. If prayer speed not, we must be sure that the fault is not in God, but in ourselves; were we but ripe for mercy, he is ready to extend it to us, and even waits for the purpose. John Trapp.

Verse 3. 'But thou art holy.' Here is the triumph of faith – the Saviour stood like a rock in the wide ocean of temptation. High as the billows rose, so did his faith, like the coral rock, wax greater and stronger till it became an island of salvation to our shipwrecked souls. It is as if he had said, 'It matters not what I endure. Storms may howl upon me; men despise; devils tempt; circumstances overpower; and God himself forsake me, still God is holy; there is no unrighteousness in him.' John Stevenson.

Verse 3. 'But thou art holy.' Does it seem strange that the heart in its darkness and sorrow should find comfort in this attribute of God? No, for God's holiness is but another aspect of his faithfulness and mercy. And in that remarkable name, 'the Holy One of Israel,' we are taught that he who is the 'holy' God is also the God who has made a covenant with his chosen. It would be impossible for an Israelite to think of God's holiness without thinking also of that covenant relationship. 'Be ye holy; for I, the Lord your God am holy,' were the words in which Israel was reminded of their relation to God. See especially Leviticus 19:1. We see something of this feeling in such passages as Psalm 89:16–19; 99:5–9; Hosea 11:8, 9; Isaiah 41:14; 47:4. J. J. Stewart Perowne.

Verse 3. Were temptations never so black, faith will not hearken to an ill word spoken against God, but will justify God always. David Dickson.

Verses 4, 5. Those who look upon this Psalm as having a primary reference to the King of Israel, attribute great beauty to these words, from the very pleasing conjecture that David was, at the time of composing them, sojourning at Mahanaim, where Jacob, in his distress, wrestled with the angel, and obtained such signal blessings. That, in a place so greatly hallowed by associations of the past, he should make his appeal to the God of his fathers, was alike the dictate of patriarchal feeling and religion. John Morison, D.D., in 'Morning Meditations.'

Verse 5. 'Thou didst deliver them,' but thou wilt not deliver me; nay, rather thou didst deliver them because thou wilt not deliver me. Gerhohus.

Verse 6. 'But I am a worm, and no man.' A fisherman, when he casts his angle into the river, doth not throw the hook in bare, naked and uncovered, for then he knows the fish will never bite, and therefore he hides the hook within a worm, or some other bait, and so, the fish, biting at the worm, is caught by the hook. Thus Christ, speaking of himself, saith, *Ego vermis et non homo.* He, coming to perform the great work of our redemption, did cover and hide his Godhead within the worm of his human nature. The grand water-serpent, Leviathan, the devil, thinking to swallow the worm of his humanity, was caught upon the hook of his divinity. This hook stuck in his jaws, and tore him very sore. By thinking to destroy Christ, he destroyed his own kingdom, and lost his own power for ever. Lancelot Andrewes.

Verse 6. 'I am a worm.' Christ calls himself 'a worm' . . . on account of the opinion that men of the world had of him . . . the Jews esteemed Christ as a worm, and treated him as such; he was loathsome to them and hated by them; every one trampled upon him, and trod him under foot as men do worms . . . The Chaldee paraphrase renders it here a weak worm; and though Christ is the mighty God, and is also the Son of man, whom God made strong for himself; yet there was a weakness in his human nature, and he was crucified through it, 2 Corinthians 13:4: and it has been observed by some, that the word (Heb.) there used signifies the scarlet worm, or the worm that is in the grain or berry with which scarlet is dyed: and like this scarlet worm did our Lord look, when by way of mockery he was clothed with a scarlet robe; and especially when he appeared in his dyed garments, and was red in his apparel, as one that treadeth in the wine fat; when his body was covered with blood when he hung upon the cross, which was shed to make crimson and scarlet sins as white as snow. John Gill.

Verse 6. 'I am a worm.' An humble soul is emptied of all swelling thoughts of himself. Bernard calls humility a self-annihilation. Job 22:29. 'Thou wilt save the humble;' in the Hebrew it is, 'Him that is of low eyes.' An humble man has lower thoughts of himself than others can have of him; David, though a king, yet looked upon himself as 'a worm:' 'I am a worm, and no man.' Bradford, a martyr, yet subscribes himself 'a sinner' Job 10:15. 'If I be righteous, yet will I not lift up my head:' like the violet a sweet flower, but hangs down the head. Thomas Watson.

Verse 6. 'A worm.' So trodden under foot, trampled on, maltreated, buffeted and spit upon, mocked and tormented, as to seem more like a worm than a man. Behold what great contempt hath the Lord of Majesty endured, that his confusion may be our glory; his punishment our heavenly bliss! Without ceasing impress this spectacle, O Christian, on thy soul! *Dionysius, quoted by Isaac Williams.*

Verse 7. 'All they that see me laugh me to scorn,' etc. Imagine this dreadful scene. Behold this motley multitude of rich and poor, of Jews and Gentiles! Some stand in groups and gaze. Some recline at ease and stare. Others move about in restless gratification at the event. There is a look of satisfaction on every countenance. None are silent. The velocity of speech seems tardy. The theme is far too great for one member to utter. Every lip, and head, and finger, is now a tongue. The rough soldiers, too, are busied in their coarse way. The work of blood is over. Refreshment has become necessary. Their usual beverage of vinegar and water is supplied to them. As they severally are satisfied, they approach the cross, hold some forth to the Saviour, and bid him drink as they withdraw it. Luke 23:36. They know he must be suffering an intense thirst, they therefore aggravate it with the mockery of refreshment. Cruel Romans! and ye, O regicidal Jews! Was not death enough? Must mockery and scorn be added? On this sad day Christ made you one indeed! Dreadful unity – which constituted you the joint mockers and murderers of the Lord of glory! *John Stevenson.*

Verse 7. 'All they that see me, laugh me to scorn,' etc. There have been persons in our own days, whose crimes have excited such detestation that the populace would probably have torn them in pieces, before, and even after their trial, if they could have had them in their power. Yet when these very obnoxious persons have been executed according to their sentence, if, perhaps, there was not one spectator who wished them to escape, yet neither was one found so lost to sensibility as to insult them in their dying moments. But when Jesus suffers, all that see him laugh him to scorn; they shoot out the lip, they shake the head; they insult his character and his hope. *John Newton.*

Verse 7. 'They shoot out the lip.' To protrude the lower lip is, in the East, considered a very strong indication of contempt. Its employment is chiefly confined to the lower orders. *Illustrated Commentary.*

Verses 7, 8. It was after his crucifixion, and during the hours that he hung upon the cross, that his sufferings in this way – the torment of beholding and hearing the scorn and mockery which was made of the truth of his person and doctrine – exceedingly abounded, and in such and so many kinds of mockery and insult that some consider this to have been the chiefest pain and sorrow which he endured in his most sacred passion. For as, generally, those things are considered the most painful to endure of which we are most sensible, so it seems to these persons, that sufferings of this kind contain in them more cause for feeling than any other sufferings. And, therefore, although all the torments of the Lord were very great, so that each one appears the greatest, and no comparison can be made between them; yet, nevertheless, this kind of suffering appears to be the most painful. Because in other troubles, not only the pain and suffering of them, but the troubles themselves, in themselves, may be desired by us, and such as we suffer for love's sake, in order by them to evince that love. Wherefore, the stripes, the crown of thorns, the buffetings, the cross, the gall, the vinegar, and other bodily torments, besides that they torment the body, are often a means for promoting the divine honour, which it holds in esteem above all else. But to blaspheme God, to give the lie to eternal truths, to deface the supreme demonstration of the divinity and majesty of the Son of God (although God knoweth how to extract from these things the good which he intends), nevertheless are, in their nature, things, which, from their so greatly affecting the divine honour, although they may be, for just considerations, endured, can never be desired by any one, but must be abhorrent to all. Our Lord then, being, of all, the most zealous for the divine honour, for which he also died, found in this kind of suffering, more than in all other, much to abhor and nothing to desire. Therefore with good reason it may be held to be the greatest of all, and that in which, more than in all other, he exhibited the greatest suffering and patience. Fra Thomé de Jesu, in 'The Sufferings of Jesus,' 1869.

Verse 8. Here are recorded some of those very words, by which the persecutors of our Lord expressed their mockery and scorn. How remarkable to find them in a Psalm written so many hundred years before! John Stevenson.

Verses 9, 10. Faith is much strengthened by constant evidences of God's favour. Herewith did he support his faith that said to God, 'Thou art he that took me out of the womb: thou didst make me hope when I was upon my mother's breasts. I was cast upon thee from the womb: thou art my God from my mother's belly.' 'Thou art my trust from my youth. By thee have I been holden up from the womb: thou art he that took me out of my mother's bowels' Psalm 71:5,6. It was not only the disposition of Obadiah towards God, but also the evidence that thereby he had of God's affection towards him, that made him with confidence say to Elijah, 'I fear the Lord from my youth' 1 Kings 18:12. By long continuance of ancient favour, many demonstrations are given of a fast, fixed, and unremovable affection. So as if, by reason of temptations, one or more evidences should be questioned, yet others would remain to uphold faith, and to keep it from an utter languishing, and a total falling away. As when a house is supported by many pillars, though some be taken away, yet by the support of them which remain, the house will stand. William Gouge.

Verses 9, 10. David acknowledges ancient mercies, those mercies which had been cast upon him long ago, these were still fresh and new in his memory, and this is one affection and disposition of a thankful heart – to remember those mercies which another would have quite forgotten, or never thought of. Thus does David here; the mercies of his infancy, and his childhood, and his younger years, which one would have imagined, that now in his age had been quite out of his mind; yet these does he here stir up himself to remember and bring to his thoughts. 'Took me out of the womb:' when was that? It may have been threescore years ago when David penned the Psalms. He thinks of those mercies which God vouchsafed him when he was not capable of thinking, nor considering what was bestowed upon him; and so are we taught hence to do, in an imitation of this holy example which is here set before us: those mercies which God hast bestowed in our minority, we are to call to mind and acknowledge in our riper years. Thomas Horton.

Verses 9, 10. Here the tribulation begins to grow lighter, and hope inclines towards victory; a support, though small, and sought out with deep anxiety, is now found. For after he had felt that he had suffered without any parallel or example, so that the wonderful works of God as displayed toward the fathers afforded him no help, he comes to the wonderful works of God toward himself, and in these he finds the goodwill of God towards him, and which was displayed towards him alone in so singular a way. Martin Luther.

Verses 9, 10. The bitter severity of the several taunts with which his enemies assailed our Lord, had no other effect than to lead the Saviour to make a direct appeal to his Father ... That appeal is set before us in these two verses. It is of an unusual and remarkable nature. The argument on which it is founded is most forcible and conclusive. At the same time, it is the most seasonable and appropriate that can be urged. We may thus paraphrase it, 'I am now brought as a man to my last extremity. It is said that God disowns me; but it cannot be so. My first moment of existence he tenderly cared for. When I could not even ask for, or think of his kindness, he bestowed it upon me. If, of his mere good pleasure he brought me into life at first, he will surely not forsake me when I am departing out of it. In opposition, therefore, to all their taunts, I can and I will appeal to himself. Mine enemies declare, O God, that thou hast cast me off – but thou art he that took me out of the womb. They affirm that I do not, and need not trust in thee; but thou didst make me hope (or, keptest me in safety, margin) when I was upon my mother's breasts. They insinuate that thou wilt not acknowledge me as thy Son; but I was cast upon thee from the womb; thou art my God from my mother's belly.' John Stevenson.

Verse 10. 'I was cast upon thee from the womb: thou art my God from my mother's belly.' There is a noble passage in Eusebius, in which he shows the connection between our Lord's incarnation and his passion: that he might well comfort himself while hanging on the cross by the remembrance that the very same body then 'marred more than any man, and his form more than the sons of men' (Isaiah 52:14), was that which had been glorified by the Father with such singular honour, when the Holy Ghost came upon Mary, and the power of the Highest overshadowed her. That this body, therefore, though now so torn and so mangled, as it had once been the wonder, so it would for ever be the joy, of the angels; and having put on immortality, would be the support of his faithful people to the end of time. J. M. Neale, in loc.

Verse 10. I was like one forsaken by his parent, and wholly cast upon Providence. I had no father upon earth, and my mother was poor and helpless. Matthew Poole.

Verse 12. 'Strong bulls of Bashan have beset me round.' These animals are remarkable for the proud, fierce, and sullen manner in which they exercise their great strength. Such were the persecutors who now beset our Lord. These were first, human, and secondly, spiritual foes; and both were alike distinguished by the proud, fierce, and sullen manner in which they assaulted him. John Stevenson.

Verses 12, 13. 'Bashan' was a fertile country (Numbers 32:4), and the cattle there fed were fat and 'strong' Deuteronomy 32:14. Like them, the Jews, in that good land, 'waxed fat and kicked,' grew proud, and rebelled; forsook God 'that made them, and lightly esteemed the rock of their salvation.' George Horne.

Verse 13. A helpless infant, or a harmless lamb, surrounded by furious bulls, and hungry lions, aptly represented the Saviour encompassed by his insulting and bloody persecutors. Thomas Scott, 1747–1821.

Verse 14. 'I am poured out like water, and all my bones are out of joint: my heart is like wax; it is melted in the midst of my bowels.' He was faint. Such a feeling of languor and faintness supervened that language fails to express it, and the emblem of 'water poured out' is employed to represent it. As the water falls from the vessel to the earth, see how its particles separate farther and farther from each other. Its velocity increases as it falls. It has no power to stay itself midway, much less to return to its place. It is the very picture of utter weakness. So did our Lord feel himself to be when hanging on the cross. He was faint with weakness. The sensations experienced when about to faint away are very overpowering. We appear to our own consciousness to be nothing but weakness, as water poured out. All our bones feel relaxed and out of joint; we seem as though we had none. The strength of bone is gone, the knitting of the joints is loosened, and the muscular vigour fled. A sickly giddiness overcomes us. We have no power to bear up. All heart is lost. Our strength disappears like that of wax, of melting wax, which drops upon surrounding objects, and is lost. Daniel thus describes his sensations on beholding the great vision, 'There remained no strength in me: for my vigour was turned into corruption, and I retained no strength.' Daniel 10:8. In regard, however, to the faintness which our Lord experienced, we ought to notice this additional and remarkable circumstance, that he did not altogether faint away. The relief of insensibility he refused to take. When consciousness ceases, all perception of pain is necessarily and instantly terminated. But our Lord retained his full consciousness throughout the awful scene; and patiently endured for a considerable period, those, to us, insupportable sensations which precede the actual swoon. John Stevenson.

Verse 14. 'I am poured out like water:' that is, in the thought of my enemies I am utterly destroyed. 'For we must needs die, and are as water spilt on the ground, which cannot be gathered up again.' 2 Samuel 14:14. 'What marvel,' asks St Bernard, 'that the name of the Bridegroom should be as ointment poured forth, when he himself, for the greatness of his love, was poured forth like water!' J. M. Neale.

Verse 14. 'I am poured out like water,' i.e., I am almost past all recovery, as water spilt upon the ground. John Trapp.

Verse 14. 'All my bones are out of joint.' The rack is devised as a most exquisite pain, even for terror. And the cross is a rack, whereon he was stretched till, saith the Psalm, 'all his bones were out of joint.' But even to stand, as he hung, three long hours together, holding up but the arms at length, I have heard it avowed of some that have felt it, to be a pain scarce credible. But the hands and the feet being so cruelly nailed (part, of all other, most sensible, by reason of the texture of sinews there in them most) it could not but make his pain out of measure painful. It was not for nothing, that *dolores acerrimi dicuntur cruciatus* (saith the heathen man), that the most sharp and bitter pains of all other have their name from hence, and are called *cruciatus* – pains like those of the cross. It had a meaning, that they gave him, that he had (for his welcome to the cross) a cup mixed with gall or myrrh; and (for his farewell) a sponge of vinegar; to show by the one the bitterness, and by the other the sharpness of the pains of this painful death. Lancelot Andrewes.

Verse 14. 'All my bones are out of joint.' We know that the greatest and most intolerable pain that the body can endure, is that arising from a bone out of its place, or dislocated joint. Now when the Lord was raised up upon the cross, and his sacred body hung in the air from the nails, all the joints began to give, so that the bones were parted the one from the other so visibly that, in very truth (as David had prophesied) they might tell all his bones, and thus, throughout the whole body, he endured acute torture. Whilst our Lord suffered these torments, his enemies, who had so earnestly desired to see him crucified, far from pitying him, were filled with delight, as though celebrating a victory. Fra Thomé de Jesu.

Verse 15. 'My strength is dried up,' etc. Inflammation must have commenced early and violently in the wounded parts – then been quickly imparted to those that were strained, and have terminated in a high degree of feverish burning over the whole body. The animal juices would be thus dried up, and the watery particles of the blood absorbed. The skin parched by the scorching sun till midday would be unable to supply or to imbibe any moisture. The loss of blood at the hands and feet would hasten the desiccation. Hence our Lord says, 'My strength is dried up like a potsherd, and my tongue cleaveth to my jaws.' The fever would devour his small remaining strength. And THIRST, that most intolerable of all bodily privations, must have been overpowering. His body appeared to his feeling like a potsherd that had been charred in the potter's kiln. It seemed to have neither strength nor substance left in it. So feeble had he become, so parched and dried up that CLAMMINESS OF THE MOUTH, one of the forerunners of immediate dissolution, had already seized him; 'My tongue cleaveth to my jaws, and thou hast brought me into the dust of death.' John Stevenson.

Verse 15. 'My strength is dried up;' not as in the trial of gold and silver, but 'like a potsherd,' as the earthen vessel dried up by the heat, spoken in humiliation. Isaac Williams, in loc.

Verse 15. 'A potsherd' (Heb.) rendered potsherd, is a word which denotes a piece of earthenware, frequently in a broken state. As employed in the verse under consideration, it seems to derive considerable illustration from the corresponding word in ARABIC, which expresses roughness of skin, and might well convey to the mind the idea of the bodily appearance of one in whom the moisture of the fluids had been dried up by the excess of grief. John Morison.

Verse 15. That hour what his feelings were is dangerous to define: we know them not; we may be too bold to determine of them. To very good purpose it was that the ancient Fathers of the Greek church in their liturgy, after they had recounted all the particular pains, as they are set down in his passion, and by all and by everyone of them called for mercy, do, after all, shut up with this *Di agnwstwn kopwn basanwn elehson ki swson emas.* By thine unknown sorrows and sufferings, felt by thee, but not distinctly known by us, have mercy upon us and save us. Lancelot Andrewes.

Verse 16. 'Dogs have compassed me.' So great and varied was the malignity exhibited by the enemies of our Lord, that the combined characteristics of two species of ferocious animals were not adequate to its representation. Another emblematical figure is therefore introduced. The assembly of the wicked is compared to that of 'dogs' who haunt about the cities, prowl in every corner, snarl over the carrion, and devour it all with greediness – like 'dogs,' with their wild cry in full pursuit, with unfailing scent tracking their victim, with vigilant eye on all its movements, and with a determination which nothing can falter, they run it on to death. The Oriental mode of hunting, both in ancient and modern times, is murderous and merciless in the extreme. A circle of several miles in circumference is beat round; and the men, driving all before them, and narrowing as they advance, inclose the prey on every side. Having thus made them prisoners, the cruel hunters proceed to slaughter at their own convenience. So did the enemies of our Lord: long before his crucifixion it is recorded that they used the most treacherous plans to get him into their power. John Stevenson.

Verse 16. 'Dogs have compassed me.' At the hunting of the lion, a whole district is summoned to appear, who, forming themselves first into a circle, enclose a space of four or five miles in compass, according to the number of the people and the quality of the ground which is pitched upon for the scene of action. The footmen advance first, running into the thickets with their dogs and spears, to put up the game; while the horsemen, keeping a little behind, are always ready to charge upon the first sally of the wild beast. In this manner they proceed, still contracting their circle, till they all at last close in together, or meet with some other game to divert them. Dr Shaw's Travels, quoted in Paxton's 'Illustrations of Scripture.'

Verse 16. 'They pierced my hands and my feet;' namely, when they nailed Christ to the cross. Matthew 27:35; John 20:25. Where let me simulate, saith a learned man, the orator's gradation, *Facinus vincire civem Romanum*, etc. It was much for the Son of God to be bound, more to be beaten, most of all to be slain; *Quid dicam in crucem tolle?* but what shall I say to this, that he was crucified? That was the most vile and ignominious; it was also a cruel and cursed kind of death, which yet he refused not; and here we have a clear testimony for his cross. John Trapp.

Verse 16. 'They pierced my hands and my feet.' Of all sanguinary punishments, that of crucifixion is one of the most dreadful – no vital part is immediately affected by it. The hands and the feet which are furnished with the most numerous and sensitive organs, are perforated with nails, which must necessarily be of some size to suit their intended purpose. The tearing asunder of the tender fibres of the hands and feet, the lacerating of so many nerves, and bursting so many blood-vessels, must be productive of intense agony. The nerves of the hand and foot are intimately connected, through the arm and leg, with the nerves of the whole body; their laceration therefore must be felt over the entire frame. Witness the melancholy result of even a needle's puncture in even one of the remotest nerves. A spasm is not unfrequently produced by it in the muscles of the face, which locks the jaws inseparably. When, therefore the hands and feet of our blessed Lord were transfixed with nails, he must have felt the sharpest pangs shoot through every part of his body. Supported only by his lacerated limbs, and suspended from his pierced hands, our Lord had nearly six hours' torment to endure. John Stevenson.

Verse 16. 'They pierced my hands and my feet.' That evangelical prophet testifies it, 'Behold, I have graven thee upon the palms of my hands' Isaiah 49:16. Were we not engraven there when his hands were pierced for us? 'They digged my hands and my feet.' And they digged them so deep, that the very prints remained after his resurrection, and their fingers were thrust into them for evidence sake. Some have thought that those scars remain still in his glorious body, to be showed at his second appearing: 'They shall see him whom they have pierced.' That is improbable, but this is certain; there remains still an impression upon Christ's hands and his heart, the sealing and wearing of the elect there, as precious jewels. Thomas Adams.

Verse 17. 'I may tell all my bones: they look and stare upon me.' The skin and flesh were distended by the posture of the body on the cross, that the bones, as through a thin veil, became visible, and might be counted. George Horne.

Verse 17. 'I may tell all my bones.' For, as the first Adam by his fall, lost the robe of inno-cence, and thenceforth needed other garments, so the second Adam vouchsafed to be stripped of his earthly vestments, to the end it might hereafter be said to us, 'Bring forth the first robe, and put it on him' Luke 15:22. Gerhohus, quoted by J. M. Neale.

Verse 17. 'They look and stare upon me.' Sensitively conscious of his condition upon the cross, the delicate feelings of the holy Saviour were sorely pained by the gaze of the multitude. With impudent face they looked upon him. To view him better they halted as they walked. With deliberate insolence they collected in groups, and made their remarks to each other on his conduct and appearance. Mocking his naked, emaciated, and quivering body, they 'looked and stared upon him.' John Stevenson.

Verse 17. 'They look and stare upon me.' Oh, how different is that look which the awakened sinner directs to Calvary, when faith lifts up her eye to him who agonised, and bled, and died, for the guilty! And what gratitude should perishing men feel, that from him that hangs upon the accursed tree there is heard proceeding the inviting sound, 'Look unto me, and be ye saved, all ye ends of the earth, for I am God, and besides me there is none else. John Morison.

Verse 18. 'They part my garments,' etc. Perfectly naked did the *cruciarii* hang upon the cross, and the executioners received their clothes. There is nothing to show that there was a cloth even round the loins. The clothes became the property of the soldiers, after Roman usage. The outer garment was divided probably into four, by ripping up the seams. Four soldiers were counted off as a guard, by the Roman code. The under garment could not be divided being woven; and this led the soldiers to the dice-throwing. J. P. Lange, D.D., on Matthew, 27:35.

Verse 18. 'They part my garments,' etc. Instruments will not be wanting to crucify Christ, if it were but for his old clothes, and those but little worth; for these soldiers crucify him, though they got but his garments for their reward. Christ did submit to suffer naked, hereby to teach us: 1. That all flesh are really naked before God by reason of sin (Exodus 32:25; 2 Chronicles 28:19), and therefore our Surety behoved to suffer naked. 2. That he offered himself a real captive in his sufferings, that so he might fully satisfy justice by being under the power of his enemies, till he redeemed himself by the strong hand, having fully paid the price; for therefore did he submit to be stripped naked, as conquerors use to do with prisoners. 3. That by thus suffering naked he would expiate our abuse of apparel, and purchase to us a liberty to make use of suitable raiment, and such as becometh us in our station. 4. That by this suffering naked he would purchase unto them who flee to him, to be covered with righteousness and glory, and to walk with him in white for ever, and would point out the nakedness of those, who, not being found clothed with his righteousness, shall not be clothed upon with immortality and glory. 2 Corinthians 5:2–3. He would also by this, teach all his followers to resolve on nakedness in their following of him, as a part of their conformity with their Head (1 John 4:17; Romans 8:35; Hebrews 11:37), and that therefore they should not dote much on their apparel when they have it. George Hutcheson, 1657.

Verse 18. 'And cast lots upon my vesture.' Trifling as this act of casting the lot for our Lord's vesture may appear, it is most significant. It contains a double lesson. It teaches us how greatly that seamless shirt was valued; how little he to whom it had belonged. It seemed to say, this garment is more valuable than its owner. As it was said of the thirty pieces of silver, 'A goodly price at which I was prized at of them;' so may we say regarding the casting of the lot, 'How cheaply Christ was held!' John Stevenson.

Verse 20. 'My darling' had better be rendered 'my lonely, or solitary one.' For he wishes to say that his soul was lonely and forsaken by all, and that there was no one who sought after him as a friend, or cared for him, or comforted him: as we have it, Psalm 142:4, 'Refuge failed me; no one cared for my soul; I looked on my right hand, but there was no one who would know me;' that is, solitude is of itself a certain cross, and especially so in such great torments, in which it is most grievous to be immersed without an example and without a companion. And yet, in such a state, everyone of us must be, in some suffering or other, and especially in that of death; and we must be brought to cry out with Psalm 25:16, 'Turn thee unto me, and have mercy upon me, for I am desolate and afflicted.' Martin Luther.

Verse 20. 'The dog.' It is scarcely possible for a European to form an idea of the intolerable nuisance occasioned in the villages and cities of the East, by the multitudes of dogs that infest the streets. The natives, accustomed from their earliest years to the annoyance, come to be regardless of it; but to a stranger, these creatures are the greatest plague to which he is subjected; for as they are never allowed to enter a house, and do not constitute the property of any particular owner, they display none of those habits of which the domesticated species among us are found susceptible, and are destitute of all those social qualities which often render the dog the trusty and attached friend of man ... The race seems wholly to degenerate in the warm regions of the East, and to approximate to the character of beasts of prey, as in disposition they are ferocious, cunning, bloodthirsty, and possessed of the most insatiable voracity: and even in their very form there is something repulsive; their sharp and savage features; their wolf-like eyes; their long hanging ears; their straight and pointed tails; their lank and emaciated forms, almost entirely without a belly, give them an appearance of wretchedness and degradation, that stands in sad contrast with the general condition and qualities of the breed in Europe ... These hideous creatures, dreaded by the people for their ferocity, or avoided by them as useless and unclean, are obliged to prowl about everywhere in search of a precarious existence ... They generally run in bands, and their natural ferocity, inflamed by hunger, and the consciousness of strength, makes them the most troublesome and dangerous visitors to the stranger who unexpectedly finds himself in their neighbourhood, as they will not scruple to seize whatever he may have about him, and even, in the event of his falling, and being otherwise defenceless, to attack and devour him ... These animals, driven by hunger, greedily devour everything that comes in their way; they glut themselves with the most putrid and loathsome substances that are thrown about the cities, and of nothing are they so fond as of human flesh, a repast, with which the barbarity of the despotic countries of Asia frequently supplies them, as the bodies of criminals slain for murder, treason, or violence, are seldom buried, and lie exposed till the mangled fragments are carried off by the dogs. From 'Illustrations of Scripture, by the late Professor George Paxton, D.D., revised and enlarged by Robert Jamieson,' 1843.

Verse 21. 'Save me from the lion's mouth.' Satan is called a lion, and that fitly; for he hath all the properties of the lion: as bold as a lion, as strong as a lion, as furious as a lion, as terrible as the roaring of a lion. Yea, worse: the lion wants subtlety and suspicion; herein the devil is beyond the lion. The lion will spare the prostrate, the devil spares none. The lion is full and forbears, the devil is full and devours. He seeks all; let not the simple say, He will take no notice of me; nor the subtle, He cannot overreach me; nor the noble say, He will not presume to meddle with me; nor the rich, He dares not contest with me; for he seeks to devour all. He is our common adversary, therefore let us cease all quarrels amongst ourselves, and fight with him. Thomas Adams.

Verse 21. 'Save me ... from the horns of the unicorns.' Those who are in great trouble from the power or cruelty of others, often cry out to their gods, 'Ah! save me from the tusk of the elephant! from the mouth of the tiger and the tusks of the boar, deliver me, deliver me!' Who will save me from the horn of the Kändam?' This animal is now extinct in these regions, and it is not easy to determine what it was; the word in the Sathur – Agaräthe – is rendered 'jungle cow.' Joseph Roberts.

Verse 22. 'I will declare thy name unto my brethren.' Having thus obtained relief from the oppressive darkness, and regained conscious possession of the joy and light of his Father's countenance, the thoughts and desires of the Redeemer flow into their accustomed channel. The glory of God in the salvation of his church. John Stevenson.

Verse 22. 'My brethren.' This give evidence of the low condescension of the Son of God, and also of the high exaltation of sons of men; for the Son of God to be a brother to sons of men is a great degree of humiliation, and for the sons of men to be made brethren with the Son of God is a high degree of exaltation; for Christ's brethren are in that respect sons of God, heirs of heaven, or kings, not earthly, but heavenly; not temporary, but everlasting kings … This respect of Christ to his brethren is a great encouragement and comfort to such as are despised and scorned by men of this world for Christ's professing of them. William Gouge.

Verse 24. 'For he hath not despised nor abhorred the prayer of the poor, neither hath he hid his face from me; but when I cried unto him, he heard me.' Let him, therefore, that desires to be of the seed of Israel, and to rejoice in the grace of the gospel, become poor, for this is a fixed truth, our God is one that has respect unto the poor! And observe the fulness and diligence of the prophet. He was not content with having said 'will not despise,' but adds, 'and will not abhor;' and, again, 'will not turn away his face;' and again, 'will hear.' And then he adds himself as an example, saying, 'When I cried,' as our translation has it. As if he had said, 'Behold ye, and learn by my example, who have been made the most vile of all men, and numbered among the wicked; when I was despised, cast out, rejected, behold! I was held in the highest esteem, and taken up, and heard. Let not this state of things, therefore, after this, my encouraging example, frighten you; the gospel requires a man to be such a character before it will save him. These things, I say, because our weakness requires so much exhortation, that it might not dread being humbled, nor despair when humbled, and thus might, after the bearing of the cross, receive the salvation. Martin Luther.

Verse 25. 'My praise shall be of thee in the great congregation,' etc. The joy and gratitude of our adorable Lord rise to such a height at this great deliverance, his heart so overflows with fresh and blessed consciousness of his heavenly Father's nearness, that he again pours forth the expression of his praise. By its repetition, he teaches us that this is not a temporary burst of gratitude, but an abiding determination, a full and settled resolution. John Stevenson.

Verse 25. 'In the great congregation.' Saints are fittest witnesses of sacred duties. That which, in Psalm 116:14, is implied under this particle of restraint, 'his,' in 'the presence of all his people,' is in Psalm 22:25, more expressly noted by a more apparent description, thus: 'I will pay my vows before them that fear him.' None but true saints do truly fear God. 1. This property of God's people, that they fear the Lord, showeth that they will make the best use of such sacred, solemn duties performed in their presence. They will glorify God for this your zeal; they will join their spirits with your spirit in this open performance of duty; they will become followers of you, and learn of you to vow and pay unto the Lord, and that openly, publicly. 2. As for others, they are no better than such hogs and dogs as are not meet to have such precious pearls and holy things cast before them, lest they trample them under their feet. William Gouge.

Verse 26. 'The meek shall eat and be satisfied: they shall praise the Lord that seek him; your heart shall live for ever.' A spiritual banquet is prepared in the church for the 'meek' and lowly in heart. The death of Christ was the sacrifice for sin; his flesh is meat indeed, and his blood is drink indeed. The poor in spirit feed on this provision, in their hearts by faith, and are satisfied; and thus, whilst they 'seek' the Lord, they 'praise' him also, and their 'hearts' (or souls), are preserved unto eternal life. Practical Illustrations of the Book of Psalms, 1826.

Verse 26. 'The meek.' Bonaventure engraved this sweet saying of our Lord, 'Learn of me, for I am meek and lowly in heart,' in his study. O that this saying was engraved upon all your foreheads, and upon all your hearts! Charles Bradbury.

Verse 26. 'They shall praise the Lord that seek him; your heart shall live for ever.' Now, I would fain know the man that ever went about to form such laws as should bind the hearts of men, or prepare such rewards as should reach the souls and consciences of men! Truly, if any mortal man should make a law that his subjects should love him with all their hearts and souls, and not dare, upon peril of his greatest indignation, to entertain a traitorous thought against his royal person, but presently confess it to him, or else he would be avenged on him, he would deserve to be more laughed at for his pride and folly, than Xerxes for casting his fetters into the Hellespont, to chain the waves into his obedience; or Caligula, that threatened the air, if it durst rain when he was at his pastimes, who durst not himself so much as look into the air when it thundered. Certainly a madhouse would be more fit for such a person than a throne, who should so far forfeit his reason, as to think that the thoughts and hearts of men were within his jurisdiction. William Gurnall.

Verse 26. 'Your heart,' that is, not your outward man, but the hidden man of the heart (Ezekiel 36:26); the new man which is created after the image of God in righteousness and true holiness, 'shall live for ever.' The life which animates it is the life of the Spirit of God. John Stevenson.

Verse 27. 'All the ends of the world shall remember and turn unto the Lord; and all the kindreds of the nations shall worship before him.' This passage is a prediction of the conversion of the Gentiles. It furnishes us with two interesting ideas; the nature of true conversion – and the extent of it under the reign of the Messiah. 1. The NATURE of true conversion: – It is to 'remember' – to 'turn to the Lord' – and to 'worship before him.' This is a plain and simple process. Perhaps the first religious exercise of mind of which we are conscious is reflection. A state of unregeneracy is a state of forgetfulness. God is forgotten. Sinners have lost all just sense of his glory, authority, mercy, and judgment; living as if there were no God, or as if they thought there was none. But if ever we are brought to be the subjects of true conversion, we shall be brought to remember these things. This divine change is fitly expressed by the case of the prodigal, who is said to have come to himself, or to his right mind. But further, true conversion consists not only in remembering, but in 'turning to the Lord.' This part of the passage is expressive of a cordial relinquishment of our idols, whatever they have been, and an acquiescence in the gospel way of salvation by Christ alone. Once more, true conversion to Christ will be accompanied with the 'worship' of him. Worship, as a religious exercise, is the homage of the heart, presented to God according to his revealed will ... 2. The EXTENT of conversion under the kingdom or reign of the Messiah: 'All the ends of the world shall remember and turn unto the Lord; and all the kindreds of the nations shall worship before him.' It was fit that the accession of the Gentiles should be reserved for the gospel day, that it might grace the triumph of Christ over his enemies, and appear to be what it is, 'the travail of his soul.' This great and good work, begun in the apostles' day, must go on, and 'must increase,' till 'All the ends of the world shall remember and turn,' and 'all the kindreds of the nations shall worship before him.' Conversion work has been individual; God has gathered sinners one by one. Thus it is at present with us; but it will not be thus always. People will flock to Zion as doves to their windows. Further, conversion work has hitherto been circumscribed within certain parts of the world. But the time will come when 'all the kindreds of the earth' shall worship. These hopes are not the flight of an ardent imagination; they are founded on the true sayings of God. Finally, while we are concerned for the world, let us not forget our own souls. So the whole world be saved and we lost, what will it avail us? Condensed from Andrew Fuller.

Verse 27. 'All the ends of the world shall REMEMBER' – this is a remarkable expression. It implies that man has forgotten God. It represents all the successive generations of the world as but one, and then it exhibits that one generation, as if it had been once in paradise, suddenly remembering the Lord whom it had known there, but had long forgotten . . . The converted nations, we learn by this verse, will not only obtain remembrance of their past loss, but will also be filled with the knowledge of present duty. John Stevenson.

Verse 27. 'All the nations of the world' (Heb. *jizkeru*, the same Hebrew root with *azkir*) 'shall remember;' why? what is that? or what shall they remember? Even this: they shall turn to the Lord, and worship him, in his name, in his ordinances; as is explained in the words following of this verse: 'And all the families of the nations' (Heb. *jishtachavu*, 'shall bow' down themselves, or) 'worship before thee,' etc. And so in Psalm 86:9, 'All nations whom thou hast made shall come' (Heb. *vejishtachavu*) 'and they shall worship before thee;' and how shall they do so? Even by recording, remembering, and making mention of the glory of thy name; as in the words following (Heb. *vicabbedu lishmecha*), 'and shall glorify thy name.' William Strong's 'Saints Communion with God,' 1656.

Verses 27, 28. The one undeviating object of the Son all through was, the glory of the Father: he came to do his will, and he fulfilled it with all the unvarying intensity of the most heavenly affection. What, then, will not be the exuberant joy of his heart, when in his glorious kingdom, he shall see the Father beyond all measure glorified? . . . The praise and honour and blessing which will be yielded to the Father in that day through him, so that God shall be all in all, will make him feel he underwent not a sorrow too much for such a precious consummation . . . Every note of thanksgiving which ascends to the Father, whether from the fowls of the air, or the beasts of the field, or the fishes of the sea, or the hills, or the mountains, or the trees of the forest, or the rivers of the valleys – all shall gladden his heart, as sweet in the ears of God, for the sake of him who redeemed even them from the curse, and restored to them a harmony more musical than burst from them on the birthday of their creation. And man! renewed and regenerated man! for whose soul the blood was spilt, and for the redemption of whose body death was overcome, how shall the chorus of his thanksgiving, in its intelligent and articulate hallelujahs, be the incense which that Saviour shall still love to present unto the Father, a sweet-smelling savour through himself, who, that he might sanctify his people by his own blood, suffered without the camp. How are the channels choked up or impaired in this evil world, wherein the praise and glory of our God should flow as a river! How will Christ then witness, to the delight of his soul, all cleared and restored! No chill upon the heart, no stammering in the tongue, in his Father's praises! No understanding dull, or eye feeble, in the apprehension of his glory! No hand unready, or foot stumbling, in the fulfilling of his commandments. God, the glory of his creatures: his glory their service and their love; and all this the reward to Jesus of once suffering himself. C. J. Goodhart, M.A., in 'Bloomsbury Lent Lectures,' 1848.

Verse 29. 'And they shall bow that go down into the dust; their soul liveth not:' that is, whose soul liveth not, by an Hebraism; it being meant, that he who is of most desperate condition, being without hope of life and salvation, his sins are so notorious, shall 'eat' also of this feast, and be turned to God to 'worship' and serve him; being thus plucked out of the jaws of death and everlasting destruction, as it were, being before this very hour ready to seize upon him. The new translation, 'None can keep alive his own soul,' as it agreeth not with the Hebrew, so it makes the sense more perplexed. By 'him that goeth down to the dust, whose soul liveth not,' some understand the most miserably poor, who have nothing to feed upon, whereby their life may be preserved, yet shall feed also of this feast as well as the rich, and praise God. Ainsworth is for either spiritually poor and miserable, because most wicked, or worldly poor; and there is an exposition of Basil's, understanding by the rich, the rich in faith and grace, touching which, or the rich properly so called, he is indifferent. But because it is said, 'The fat of the earth,' I prefer the former, and that the close of the verse may best answer to the first part; the latter by 'those that are going to the dust,' understand the miserably poor. So that there is a common-place of comfort for all, both richest and poorest, if they be subjects of God's kingdom of grace: their souls shall be alike fed by him and saved. John Mayer.

Verse 29. 'All they that go down to the dust;' either those who stand quivering on the brink of the grave, or those who occupy the humble, sequestered walks of life. As the great and opulent of the earth are intended in the first clause, it is not by any means unnatural to suppose that the image of going 'down to the dust,' is designed to represent the poor and mean of mankind, who are unable to support themselves, and to provide for their multiplied necessities. If the grave be alluded to, as is thought by many eminent divines, the beautiful sentiment of the verse will be, that multitudes of dying sinners shall be brought to worship Jehovah, and that those who cannot save or deliver themselves shall seek that shelter which none can find but those who approach the mercy-seat. 'Rich and poor,' as Bishop Horne observes, 'are invited' – that is, to 'worship God;' 'and the hour is coming when all the race of Adam, as many as sleep in the 'dust' of the earth, unable to raise themselves from thence, quickened and called forth by the voice of the Son of Man, must bow the knee to King Messiah.' John Morison.

Verse 29. To be brought to the dust, is, at first, a circumlocution or description of death: 'Shall the dust praise thee, shall it declare thy truth?' Psalm 30:9. That is, shall I praise thee when I am among the dead? 'What profit is there in my blood, when I go down to the pit?' Not that profit, sure, I cannot bring thee in the tribute of praise when my life's gone out. Secondly, to be brought to the dust is a description of any low and poor condition. 'All they that be fat upon the earth' (that is, the great and mighty), 'shall eat and worship' 'all they that go down to the dust' (that is, the mean and base), 'shall bow before him.' As if he had said, rich and poor, high and low, the king and the beggar, have alike need of salvation by Jesus Christ, and must submit unto him, that they may be saved, for, as it there follows, 'none can keep alive his own soul.' The captivity of the Jews in Babylon is expressed under those notions of death, and of dwelling in the dust (Isaiah 26:19); to show how low, that no power but his who can raise the dead, could work their deliverance. Joseph Caryl.

Verse 29. 'None can keep alive his own soul.' And yet we look back to our conversion, and its agonies of earnestness, its feelings of deep, helpless dependence – of Christ's being absolutely our daily, hourly need – supplier – as a past something – a stage of spiritual life which is over. And we are satisfied to have it so. The Spirit of God moved over our deadness, and breathed into us the breath of life. My soul became a living soul. But was this enough? God's word says, No. 'None can keep alive his own soul.' My heart says, No. Truth must ever answer to truth. I cannot (ah! have I not tried, and failed?) I cannot keep alive my own soul. We cannot live upon ourselves. Our physical life is kept up by supply from without – air, food, warmth. So must the spiritual life. Jesus gives, Jesus feeds us day by day, else must the life fade out and die. 'None can keep alive his own soul.' It is not enough to be made alive. I must be fed, and guided, and taught, and kept in life. Mother, who hast brought a living babe into the world, is your work done? Will you not nurse it, and feed it, and care for it, that it may be kept alive? Lord, I am this babe. I live indeed, for I can crave and cry. Leave me not, O my Saviour. Forsake not the work of thine own hands. In thee I live. Hold me, carry me, feed me, let me abide in thee. 'For thy kingdom is the Lord's: and he is the governor among the nations. All they that be fat upon earth shall eat and worship: all they that go down to the dust shall bow before him: and none can keep alive his own soul.' In our work for God, we need to remember this. Is not the conversion, the arousing of sinners, the great, and with many, the sole aim in working for God? Should it be so? Let us think of this other work. Let us help to keep alive. Perhaps it is less distinguished, as it may be less distinguished to feed a starving child than to rescue a drowning man. But let us walk less by sight, more by faith. Let us not indeed neglect to call to life those who are spiritually dead. But Oh! let us watch for the more hidden needs of the living – the fading, starving, fainting souls, which yet can walk and speak, and cover their want and sorrow. Let us be fellow-workers with God in all his work. And with a deep heart-feeling of the need of constant life supplies from above, let us try how often, how freely, we may be made the channels of those streams of the 'water of life,' – for 'none can keep alive his own soul.' Mary B. M. Duncan, in 'Bible Hours,' 1856.

Verse 29. Having considered the vastness and glory of the prospect, our Lord next contemplates the reality and minuteness of its accomplishment. He sets before his mind individual cases and particular facts. He appears to look upon this picture of the future as we do upon a grand historical painting of the past. It seems natural to gaze with silent admiration on the picture as a whole, then to fix the attention on particular groups, and testify our sense of the general excellence, by expatiating on the truth and beauty of the several parts. John Stevenson.

Verse 30. 'A seed shall serve him.' This figurative expression signifies Christ and his people, who yield true obedience to God – they are called by this name in a spiritual and figurative, but most appropriate sense. The idea is taken from the operations of the husbandman who carefully reserves every year a portion of his grain for seed. Though it be small, compared with all the produce of his harvest, yet he prizes it very highly and estimates it by the value of that crop which it may yield in the succeeding autumn. Nor does he look only to the quantity, he pays particular regard to the quality of the seed. He reserves only the best, nay, he will put away his own if spoiled, that he may procure better. The very smallest quantity of really good seed, is, to him, an object of great desire, and if by grievous failure of crops, he should not be able to procure more than a single grain, yet would he accept it thankfully, preserve it carefully, and plant it in the most favourable soil. Such is the source from which the metaphor is taken. John Stevenson.

Verse 31. 'And shall declare his righteousness.' The occupation of the seed is to 'declare,' to testify from their own experience, from their own knowledge and convictions, that grand subject, theme, or lesson, which they have learned ... They will declare the righteousness of God the Holy Ghost in his convictions of sin, in his reproofs of conscience, in his forsaking of the impenitent, and in his abiding with the believer. And in a special manner, they will declare the righteousness of God the Son, during his human life, in his sufferings, and death, as man's surety, by which he 'magnified the law, and made it honourable' (Isaiah 42:21), and on account of which they are able to address him by this name, 'The Lord our Righteousness' (Jeremiah 23:6) John Stevenson.

Verse 31. 'A people that shall be born.' What is this? What people is there that is not born? According to my apprehensions I think this is said for this reason – because the people of other kings are formed by laws, by customs, and by manners; by which, however, you can never move a man to true righteousness: it is only a fable of righteousness, and a mere theatrical scene or representation. For even the law of Moses could form the people of the Jews unto nothing but unto hypocrisy. But the people of this King are not formed by laws to make up an external appearance, but they are begotten by water and by the Spirit unto a new creature of truth. Martin Luther.

Hints to the village preacher

Whole Psalm. The volume entitled 'Christ on the Cross,' by Rev. J. Stevenson, has a sermon upon every verse. We give the headings, they are suggestive. Verse 1. The Cry. 2. The Complaint. 3. The Acknowledgment. 4–6. The Contrast. 6. The Reproach. 7. The Mockery. 8. The Taunt. 9, 10. The Appeal. 11. The Entreaty. 12, 13. The Assault. 14. The Faintness. 15. The Exhaustion. 16. The Piercing. 17. The Emaciation. 17. The Insulting Gaze. 18. The Partition of the Garments and Casting Lots. 19–21. The Importunity. 21. The Deliverance. 22. The Gratitude. 23. The Invitation. 24. The Testimony. 25. The Vow. 26. The Satisfaction of the Meek; the Seekers of the Lord Praising Him; the Eternal Life. 27. The Conversion of the World. 28. The Enthronement. 29. The Author of the Faith. 30. The Seed. 31. The Everlasting Theme and Occupation. The Finish of the Faith.

Verse 1. The Saviour's dying cry.

Verse 2. Unanswered prayer. Enquire the reason for it; encourage our hope concerning it; urge to continue in importunity.

Verse 3. Whatever God may do, we must settle it in our minds that he is holy and to be praised.

Verse 4. God's faithfulness in past ages a plea for the present.

Verses 4, 5. Ancient saints.

1. Their life. 'They trusted.'
2. Their practice. 'They cried.'

3. Their experience. 'Were not confounded.'
4. Their voice to us.

Verses 6–18. Full of striking sentences upon our Lord's suffering.

Verse 11. A saint's troubles, his arguments in prayer.

Verse 20. 'My darling.' A man's soul to be very dear to him.

Verse 21 (first clause). 'Lion's mouth.' Men of cruelty. The devil. Sin. Death. Hell.

Verse 22. Christ as a brother, a preacher, and a precentor.

Verse 22. A sweet subject, a glorious preacher, a loving relationship, a heavenly exercise.

Verse 23. A threefold duty, 'praise him, 'glorify him;' 'fear him;' towards one object, 'the Lord;' for three characters, 'ye that fear him, seed of Jacob, seed of Israel,' which are but one person.

Verse 23. Glory to God the fruit of the tree on which Jesus died.

Verse 24. A consoling fact in history attested by universal experience.

Verse 24. (first clause). A common fear dispelled.

Verse 25. Public praise.

1. A delightful exercise – 'praise.'
2. A personal participation – 'My praise.'
3. A fitting object – 'of thee.'
4. A special source – 'from thee.'
5. An appropriate place – 'in the great congregation.'

Verse 25. (second clause). Vows. What vows to make, when and how to make them, and the importance of paying them.

Verse 26. Spiritual feasting. The guests, the food, the host, and the satisfaction.

Verse 26. (second clause). Seekers who shall be singers. Who they are? What they shall do? When? and what is the reason for expecting that they shall?

Verse 27. (last clause). Life everlasting. What lives? Source of life. Manner of life. Why for ever? What occupation? What comfort to be derived from it?

Verse 27. Nature of true conversion, and extent of it under the reign of the Messiah. Andrew Fuller.

Verse 27. The universal triumph of Christianity certain.

Verse 27. The order of conversion. See the Exposition.

Verse 28. The empire of the King of kings as it is, and as it shall be.

Verse 29. Grace for the rich, grace for the poor, but all lost without it.

Verse 29 (last clause). A weighty text upon the vanity of self-confidence.

Verse 30. The perpetuity of the church.

Verse 30 (last clause). Church history, the marrow of all history.

Verse 31. Future prospects for the church.

1. Conversions certain.
2. Preachers promised.
3. Succeeding generations blest.
4. Gospel published.
5. Christ exalted.

Psalm 23

There is no inspired title to this psalm, and none is needed, for it records no special event, and needs no other key than that which every Christian may find in his own bosom. It is David's Heavenly Pastoral; a surpassing ode, which none of the daughters of music can excel. The clarion of war here gives place to the pipe of peace, and he who so lately bewailed the woes of the Shepherd tunefully rehearses the joys of the flock. Sitting under a spreading tree, with his flock around him, like Bunyan's shepherd-boy in the Valley of Humiliation, we picture David singing this unrivalled pastoral with a heart as full of gladness as it could hold; or, if the psalm be the product of his after-years, we are sure that his soul returned in contemplation to the lonely water-brooks which rippled among the pastures of the wilderness, where in early days she had been wont to dwell. This is the pearl of psalms whose soft and pure radiance delights every eye; a pearl of which Helicon need not be ashamed, though Jordan claims it. Of this delightful song it may be affirmed that its piety and its poetry are equal, its sweetness and its spirituality are unsurpassed.

The position of this psalm is worthy of notice. It follows the twenty-second, which is peculiarly the Psalm of the Cross. There are no green pastures, no still waters on the other side of the twenty-second psalm. It is only after we have read, 'My God, my God, why hast thou forsaken me?' that we come to 'The Lord is my Shepherd.' We must by experience know the value of blood-shedding, and see the sword awakened against the Shepherd, before we shall be able truly to know the Sweetness of the good Shepherd's care.

It has been said that what the nightingale is among birds, that is this divine ode among the psalms, for it has sung sweetly in the ear of many a mourner in his night of weeping, and has bidden him hope for a morning of joy. I will venture to compare it also to the lark, which sings as it mounts, and mounts as it sings, until it is out of sight, and even then is not out of hearing. Note the last words of the psalm – 'I will dwell in the house of the Lord for ever;' these are celestial notes, more fitted for the eternal mansions than for these dwelling places below the clouds. Oh that we may enter into the spirit of the psalm as we read it, and then we shall experience the days of heaven upon the earth!

Exposition

Verse 1. 'The Lord is my shepherd.' What condescension is this, that the infinite Lord assumes towards his people the office and character of a Shepherd! It should be the subject of grateful admiration that the great God allows himself to be compared to anything which will set forth his great love and care for his own people. David had himself been a keeper of sheep, and understood both the needs of the sheep and the many cares of a shepherd. He compares himself to a creature weak, defenceless, and foolish, and he takes God to be his Provider, Preserver, Director, and, indeed, his everything. No man has a right to consider himself the Lord's sheep unless his nature has been renewed for the scriptural description of unconverted men does not picture them as sheep, but as wolves or goats. A sheep is an object of property, not a wild animal; its owner sets great store by it, and frequently it is bought with a great price. It is well to know, as certainly David did, that we belong to the Lord. There is a noble tone of confidence about this sentence. There is no 'if' nor 'but,' nor even 'I hope so;' but he says, 'The

Lord is my shepherd.' We must cultivate the spirit of assured dependence upon our heavenly Father. The sweetest word of the whole is that monosyllable, 'My.' He does not say, 'The Lord is the shepherd of the world at large, and leadeth forth the multitude as his flock,' but 'The Lord is my shepherd;' if he be a Shepherd to no one else, he is a Shepherd to me; he cares for me, watches over me, and preserves me. The words are in the present tense. Whatever be the believer's position, he is even now under the pastoral care of Jehovah.

The next words are a sort of inference from the first statement – they are sententious and positive – 'I shall not want.' I might want otherwise, but when the Lord is my Shepherd he is able to supply my needs, and he is certainly willing to do so, for his heart is full of love, and therefore 'I shall not want.' I shall not lack for temporal things. Does he not feed the ravens, and cause the lilies to grow? How, then, can he leave his children to starve? I shall not want for spirituals, I know that his grace will be sufficient for me. Resting in him he will say to me, 'As thy day so shall thy strength be.' I may not possess all that I wish for, but 'I shall not want.' Others, far wealthier and wiser than I, may want, but 'I shall not.' 'The young lions do lack, and suffer hunger: but they that seek the Lord shall not want any good thing.' It is not only 'I do not want,' but 'I shall not want.' Come what may, if famine should devastate the land, or calamity destroy the city, 'I shall not want.' Old age with its feebleness shall not bring me any lack, and even death with its gloom shall not find me destitute. I have all things and abound; not because I have a good store of money in the bank, not because I have skill and wit with which to win my bread, but because 'The Lord is my shepherd.' The wicked always want, but the righteous never; a sinner's heart is far from satisfaction, but a gracious spirit dwells in the palace of content.

Verse 2. 'He maketh me to lie down in green pastures: he leadeth me beside the still waters.' The Christian life has two elements in it, the contemplative and the active, and both of these are richly provided for. First, the contemplative. 'He maketh me to lie down in green pastures.' What are these 'green pastures' but the Scriptures of truth – always fresh, always rich, and never exhausted? There is no fear of biting the bare ground where the grass is long enough for the flock to lie down in it. Sweet and full are the doctrines of the gospel; fit food for souls, as tender grass is natural nutriment for sheep. When by faith we are enabled to find rest in the promises, we are like the sheep that lie down in the midst of the pasture; we find at the same moment both provender and peace, rest and refreshment, serenity and satisfaction. But observe: 'He maketh me to lie down.' It is the Lord who graciously enables us to perceive the preciousness of his truth, and to feed upon it. How grateful ought we to be for the power to appropriate the promises! There are some distracted souls who would give worlds if they could but do this. They know the blessedness of it, but they cannot say that this blessedness is theirs. They know the 'green pastures,' but they are not made to 'lie down' in them. Those believers who have for years enjoyed a 'full assurance of faith' should greatly bless their gracious God.

The second part of a vigorous Christian's life consists in gracious activity. We not only think, but we act. We are not always lying down to feed, but are journeying onward toward perfection; hence we read, 'he leadeth me beside the still waters.' What are these 'still waters' but the influences and graces of his blessed Spirit? His Spirit attends us in various operations, like waters – in the plural – to cleanse, to refresh, to fertilise, to cherish. They are 'still waters,' for the Holy Ghost loves peace, and sounds no trumpet of ostentation in his operations. He may flow into our soul, but not into our neighbour's, and therefore our neighbour may not perceive the divine presence; and though the blessed Spirit may be pouring his floods into one heart, yet he that sitteth next to the favoured one may know nothing of it.

> In sacred silence of the mind
> My heaven, and there my God I find.

Still waters run deep. Nothing more noisy than an empty drum. That silence is golden indeed in which the Holy Spirit meets with the souls of his saints. Not to raging waves of strife, but to peaceful streams of holy love does the Spirit of God conduct the chosen sheep. He is a dove, not an eagle; the dew, not the hurricane. Our Lord leads us beside these 'still waters;' we could not go there of ourselves, we need his guidance, therefore it is said, 'he leadeth me.' He does not drive us. Moses drives us by the law, but Jesus leads us by his example, and the gentle drawing of his love.

Verse 3. 'He restoreth my soul.' When the soul grows sorrowful he revives it; when it is sinful he sanctifies it; when it is weak he strengthens it. 'He' does it. His ministers could not do it if he did not. His Word would not avail by itself. 'He restoreth my soul.' Are any of us low in grace? Do we feel that our spirituality is at its lowest ebb? He who turns the ebb into the flood can soon restore our soul. Pray to him, then, for the blessing – 'Restore thou me, thou Shepherd of my soul!'

'He leadeth me in the paths of righteousness for his name's sake.' The Christian delights to be obedient, but it is the obedience of love, to which he is constrained by the example of his Master. 'He leadeth me.' The Christian is not obedient to some commandments and neglectful of others; he does not pick and choose, but yields to all. Observe, that the plural is used – 'the paths of righteousness.' Whatever God may give us to do we would do it, led by his love. Some Christians overlook the blessing of sanctification, and yet to a thoroughly renewed heart this is one of the sweetest gifts of the covenant. If we could be saved from wrath, and yet remain unregenerate, impenitent sinners, we should not be saved as we desire, for we mainly and chiefly pant to be saved from sin and led in the way of holiness. All this is done out of pure free grace; 'for his name's sake.' It is to the honour of our great Shepherd that we should be a holy people, walking in the narrow way of righteousness. If we be so led and guided we must not fail to adore our heavenly Shepherd's care.

Verse 4. 'Yea, though I walk through the valley of the shadow of death, I will fear no evil: for thou art with me; thy rod and thy staff they comfort me.' This unspeakably delightful verse has been sung on many a dying bed, and has helped to make the dark valley bright times out of mind. Every word in it has a wealth of meaning. 'Yea, though I walk,' as if the believer did not quicken his pace when he came to die, but still calmly walked with God. To walk indicates the steady advance of a soul which knows its road, knows its end, resolves to follow the path, feels quite safe, and is therefore perfectly calm and composed. The dying saint is not in a flurry, he does not run as though he were alarmed, nor stand still as though he would go no further, he is not confounded nor ashamed, and therefore keeps to his old pace. Observe that it is not walking in the valley, but through the valley. We go through the dark tunnel of death and emerge into the light of immortality. We do not die, we do but sleep to wake in glory. Death is not the house but the porch, not the goal but the passage to it. The dying article is called a valley. The storm breaks on the mountain, but the valley is the place of quietude, and thus full often the last days of the Christian are the most peaceful of his whole career; the mountain is bleak and bare, but the valley is rich with golden sheaves, and many a saint has reaped more joy and knowledge when he came to die than he ever knew while he lived. And, then, it is not 'the valley of death,' but 'the valley of the shadow of death,' for death in its substance has been removed, and only the shadow of it remains. Some one has said that when there is a shadow there must be light somewhere, and so there is. Death stands by the side of the highway in which we have to travel, and the light of heaven shining upon him throws a shadow across our path; let us then rejoice that there is a light beyond. Nobody is afraid of a shadow, for a shadow cannot stop a man's pathway even for a moment. The shadow of a dog cannot bite; the shadow of a sword cannot kill; the shadow of death cannot destroy us. Let us not, therefore, be afraid. 'I will fear no evil.' He does not say there shall not be any evil; he had got beyond even that high assurance, and knew that Jesus had put all evil away; but 'I will fear no evil;' as if even his fears, those shadows of evil, were gone for ever. The worst evils of life are those which do not exist except in our imagination. If we had no troubles but real troubles, we should not have a tenth part of our present sorrows. We feel a thousand deaths in fearing one, but the psalmist was cured of the disease of fearing. 'I will fear no evil,' not even the Evil One himself; I will not dread the last enemy, I will look upon him as a conquered foe, an enemy to be destroyed, 'For thou art with me.' This is the joy of the Christian! 'Thou art with me.' The little child out at sea in the storm is not frightened like all the other passengers on board the vessel, it sleeps in its mother's bosom; it is enough for it that its mother is with it; and it should be enough for the believer to know that Christ is with him. 'Thou art with me; I have, in having thee, all that I can crave: I have perfect comfort and absolute security, for thou art with me.' 'Thy rod and thy staff,' by which thou governest and rulest thy flock, the ensigns of thy sovereignty and of thy gracious care – 'they comfort me.' I will believe that thou reignest still. The rod of Jesse shall still be over me as the sovereign succour of my soul.

Many persons profess to receive much comfort from the hope that they shall not die. Certainly there will be some who will be 'alive and remain' at the coming of the Lord, but is there so very much of advantage in such an escape from death as to make it the object of Christian desire? A wise man might prefer of the two to die, for those who shall not die, but who 'shall be caught up together with the Lord in the air,' will be losers rather than gainers. They will lose that actual fellowship with Christ in the tomb which dying saints will have, and we are expressly told that they shall have no preference beyond those who are asleep. Let us be of Paul's mind when he said that 'To die is gain,' and think of 'departing to be with Christ, which is far better.' This twenty-third psalm is not worn out, and it is as sweet in a believer's ear now as it was in David's time, let novelty-hunters say what they will.

Verse 5. 'Thou preparest a table before me in the presence of mine enemies.' The good man has his enemies. He would not be like his Lord if he had not. If we were without enemies we might fear that we were not the friends of God, for the friendship of the world is enmity to God. Yet see the quietude of the godly man in spite of, and in the sight of, his enemies. How refreshing is his calm bravery! 'Thou preparest a table before me.' When a soldier is in the presence of his enemies, if he eats at all he snatches a hasty meal, and away he hastens to the fight.

But observe: 'Thou preparest a table', just as a servant does when she unfolds the damask cloth and displays the ornaments of the feast on an ordinary peaceful occasion. Nothing is hurried, there is no confusion, no disturbance, the enemy is at the door, and yet God prepares a table, and the Christian sits down and eats as if everything were in perfect peace. Oh! the peace which Jehovah gives to his people, even in the midst of the most trying circumstances!

> Let earth be all in arms abroad,
> They dwell in perfect peace.

'Thou anointest my head with oil.' May we live in the daily enjoyment of this blessing, receiving a fresh anointing for every day's duties. Every Christian is a priest, but he cannot execute the priestly office without unction, and hence we must go day by day to God the Holy Ghost, that we may have our heads anointed with oil. A priest without oil misses the chief qualification for his office, and the Christian priest lacks his chief fitness for service when he is devoid of new grace from on high. 'My cup runneth over.' He had not only enough, a cup full, but more than enough, a cup which overflowed. A poor man may say this as well as those in higher circumstances. 'What, all this, and Jesus Christ too?' said a poor cottager as she broke a piece of bread and filled a glass with cold water. Whereas a man may be ever so wealthy, but if he be discontented his cup cannot run over; it is cracked and leaks. Content is the philosopher's stone which turns all it touches into gold; happy is he who has found it. Content is more than a kingdom, it is another word for happiness.

Verse 6. 'Surely goodness and mercy shall follow me all the days of my life.' This is a fact as indisputable as it is encouraging, and therefore a heavenly verily, or 'surely' is set as a seal upon it. This sentence may be read, 'only goodness and mercy', for there shall be unmingled mercy in our history. These twin guardian angels will always be with me at my back and my beck. Just as when great princes go abroad they must not go unattended, so it is with the believer. Goodness and mercy follow him always – 'all the days of his life' – the black days as well as the bright days, the days of fasting as well as the days of feasting, the dreary days of winter as well as the bright days of summer. Goodness supplies our needs, and mercy blots out our sins. 'And I will dwell in the house of the Lord for ever.' 'A servant abideth not in the house for ever, but the son abideth ever.' While I am here I will be a child at home with my God; the whole world shall be his house to me; and when I ascend into the upper chamber, I shall not change my company, nor even change the house; I shall only go to dwell in the upper storey of the house of the Lord for ever.

May God grant us grace to dwell in the serene atmosphere of this most blessed Psalm!

Explanatory notes and quaint sayings

Whole Psalm. David has left no sweeter Psalm than the short twenty-third. It is but a moment's opening of his soul; but, as when one, walking the winter street sees the door opened for some one to enter, and the red light streams a moment forth, and the forms of gay children are running to greet the comer, and genial music sounds, though the door shuts and leaves the night black, yet it cannot shut back again all that the eyes, the ear, the heart, and the imagination have seen – so in this Psalm, though it is but a moment's opening of the soul, are emitted truths of peace and consolation that will never be absent from the world. The twenty-third

Psalm is the nightingale of the Psalms. It is small, of a homely feather, singing shyly out of obscurity; but, oh! it has filled the air of the whole world with melodious joy, greater than the heart can conceive. Blessed be the day on which that Psalm was born! What would you say of a pilgrim commissioned of God to travel up and down the earth singing a strange melody, which, when one heard, caused him to forget whatever sorrows he had? And so the singing angel goes on his way through all lands, singing in the language of every nation, driving away trouble by the pulses of the air which his tongue moves with divine power. Behold just such an one! This pilgrim God has sent to speak in every language on the globe. It has charmed more griefs to rest than all the philosophy of the world. It has remanded to their dungeon more felon thoughts, more black doubts, more thieving sorrows, than there are sands on the sea-shore. It has comforted the noble host of the poor. It has sung courage to the army of the disappointed. It has poured balm and consolation into the heart of the sick, of captives in dungeons, of widows in their pinching griefs, of orphans in their loneliness. Dying soldiers have died easier as it was read to them; ghastly hospitals have been illuminated; it has visited the prisoner, and broken his chains, and, like Peter's angel, led him forth in imagination, and sung him back to his home again. It has made the dying Christian slave freer than his master, and consoled those whom, dying, he left behind mourning, not so much that he was gone, as because they were left behind, and could not go too. Nor is its work done. It will go singing to your children and my children, and to their children, through all the generations of time; nor will it fold its wings till the last pilgrim is safe, and time ended; and then it shall fly back to the bosom of God, whence it issued, and sound on, mingled with all those sounds of celestial joy which make heaven musical for ever. Henry Ward Beecher, in 'Life Thoughts.'

Whole Psalm. This Psalm may well be called David's *bucolic*, or pastoral, so daintily hath he struck upon the whole string, through the whole hymn. *Est Psalmis honorabilis*, saith Abenezra; it is a noble Psalm, written and sung by David, not when he fled into the forest of Hareth (1 Samuel 22:5), as some Hebrews will have it; but when as having overcome all his enemies, and settled his kingdom, he enjoyed great peace and quiet, and had one foot, as it were, upon the battlements of heaven. The Jews at this day use for most part to repeat this Psalm after they are sat down to meat. John Trapp.

Whole Psalm. Augustine is said to have beheld, in a dream, the one hundred and nineteenth Psalm rising before him as a tree of life in the midst of the paradise of God. This twenty-third may be compared to the fairest flowers that grew around it. The former has even been likened to the sun amidst the stars – surely this is like the richest of the constellations, even the Pleiades themselves! John Stoughton, in 'The Songs of Christ's Flock,' 1860.

Whole Psalm. Some pious souls are troubled because they cannot at all times, or often, use, in its joyous import, the language of this Psalm. Such should remember that David, though he lived long, never wrote but one twenty-third Psalm. Some of his odes do indeed express as lively a faith as this, and faith can walk in darkness. But where else do we find a whole Psalm expressive of personal confidence, joy, and triumph, from beginning to end? God's people have their seasons of darkness and their times of rejoicing. William S. Plumer.

Verse 1. 'The Lord is my shepherd; I shall not want.' Let them say that will, 'My lands shall keep me, I shall have no want, my merchandise shall be my help, I shall have no want;' let the soldier trust unto his weapons, and the husbandman unto his labour; let the artificer say unto his art, and the tradesman unto his trade, and the scholar unto his books, 'These shall maintain me, I shall not want.' Let us say with the church, as we both say and sing, 'The Lord is my keeper, I shall not want.' He that can truly say so, contemns the rest, and he that desires more than God, cannot truly say, the Lord is his, the Lord is this shepherd, governor and commander, and therefore I shall not want. John Hull, B.D., in 'Lectures on Lamentations,' 1617.

Verse 1. 'The Lord is my shepherd; I want nothing:' thus it may be equally well rendered, though in our version it is in the future tense. J. R. Macduff, D.D., in 'The Shepherd and his Flock,' 1866.

Verse 1. 'The Lord is my shepherd.' We may learn in general from the metaphor, that it is the property of a gracious heart to draw some spiritual use or other from his former condition. David himself having sometimes been a shepherd, as himself confesseth when he saith, 'he took David from the sheepfold from following the sheep,' etc., himself having been a shepherd, he beholds the Lord the same to him. Whatsoever David was to his flock – watchful over them, careful to defend them from the lion and the bear, and whatsoever thing else might annoy them, careful of their pasturage and watering, etc., the same and much more he beholds the Lord to himself. So Paul: 'I was a persecutor, and an oppressor: but the Lord had mercy on me.' This we may see in good old Jacob: 'With this staff,' saith he, 'I passed over Jordan;' and that now God had blessed him and multiplied him exceedingly. The doctrine is plain; the reasons are, first, because true grace makes no object amiss to gather some gracious instruction: it skills not what the object be, so that the heart be gracious; for that never wants matter to work upon. And secondly, it must needs be so, for such are guided by God's Spirit, and therefore are directed to a spiritual use of all things. Samuel Smith's 'Chief Shepherd,' 1625.

Verse 1. 'Shepherd.' May this sweet title persuade Japhet to dwell in the tents of Shem: my meaning is, that those who as yet never knew what it was to be enfolded in the bosom of Jesus, who as yet were never lambs nor ewes in Christ's fold, consider the sweetness of this Shepherd, and come in to him. Satan deals seemingly sweet, that he may draw you into sin, but in the end he will be really bitter to you. Christ, indeed, is seemingly bitter to keep you from sin, hedging up your way with thorns. But he will be really sweet if you come into his flock, even notwithstanding your sins. Thou lookest into Christ's fold, and thou seest it hedged and fenced all about to keep you in from sin, and this keeps thee from entering; but, oh! let it not. Christ, indeed, is unwilling that any of his should wander, and if they be unwilling too, it's well. And if they wander he'll fetch them in, it may be with his shepherd's dog (some affliction); but he'll not be, as we say, dogged himself. No, he is and will be sweet. It may be, Satan smiles, and is pleasant to you while you sin; but know, he'll be bitter in the end. He'll torment you and vex you, and be burning and bitterness to you. O come in therefore to Jesus Christ; let him be now the shepherd of thy soul. And know then, he'll be sweet in endeavouring to keep thee from sin before thou commit it; and he'll be sweet in delivering thee from sin after thou hast committed it. O that this thought – that Jesus Christ is sweet in his carriage unto all his members, unto all his flock, especially the sinning ones, might persuade the hearts of some sinners to come in unto his fold. John Durant, 1652.

Verse 1 (first clause). Feedeth me, or is my feeder, my pastor. The word comprehendeth all duties of a good herd, as together feeding, guiding, governing, and defending his flock. Henry Ainsworth.

Verse 1. 'The Lord is my shepherd.' Now the reasons of this resemblance I take to be these: First, one property of a good shepherd is, skill to know and judge aright of his sheep, and hence is it that it is a usual thing to set mark upon sheep, to the end that if they go astray (as of all creatures they are most subject to wander), the shepherd may seek them up and bring them home again. The same thing is affirmed of Christ, or rather indeed Christ affirmeth the same thing of himself, 'I know them, and they follow me' John 10:27. Yea, doubtless, he that hath numbered the stars, and calleth them all by their names, yea, the very hairs of our head, taketh special notice of his own children, 'the sheep of his pasture,' that they may be provided for and protected from all danger. Secondly, a good shepherd must have skill in the pasturing of his sheep, and in bringing them into such fruitful ground, as they may battle and thrive upon: a good shepherd will not suffer his sheep to feed upon rotten soil, but in wholesome pastures ... Thirdly, a good shepherd, knowing the straying nature of his sheep, is so much the more diligent to watch over them, and if at any time they go astray, he brings them back again. This is the Lord's merciful dealing towards poor wandering souls ... Fourthly, a good shepherd must have will to feed his sheep according to his skill: the Lord of all others is most willing to provide for his sheep. How earnest is Christ with Peter, to 'feed his sheep,' urging him unto it three several times! Fifthly, a good shepherd is provided to defend his flock ... The Lord is every way provided for the safety and defence of his sheep, as David confesseth in this Psalm (verse 4), 'Thy rod and thy staff they comfort me.' And again, 'I took unto me two staves' (saith the Lord), 'the one I called Beauty, and the other I called Bands; and I fed the flock' Zechariah 11:7. Sixthly, it is the property of a good shepherd, that if any of his sheep be weak and feeble, or his lambs young, for their safety and recovery he will bear them in his arms. The Lord is not wanting to us herein. Isaiah 40:11. And lastly, it is the property of a good shepherd to rejoice when the strayed sheep is brought home. The Lord doth thus rejoice at the conversion of a sinner. Luke 15:7. Samuel Smith.

Verse 1. 'The Lord is my shepherd.' I notice that some of the flock keep near the shepherd, and follow whithersoever he goes without the least hesitation, while others stray about on either side, or loiter far behind; and he often turns round and scolds them in a sharp, stern cry, or sends a stone after them. I saw him lame one just now. Not altogether unlike the good Shepherd. Indeed I never ride over these hills, clothed with flocks, without meditating upon this delightful theme. Our Saviour says that the good shepherd, when he putteth forth his own sheep, goeth before them, and they follow. John 10:4. This is true to the letter. They are so tame and so trained that they follow their keeper with the utmost docility. He leads them forth from the fold, or from their houses in the villages, just where he pleases. As there are many flocks in such a place as this, each one takes a different path, and it is his business to find pasture for them. It is necessary, therefore, that they should be taught to follow, and not to stray away into the unfenced fields of corn which lie so temptingly on either side. Any one that thus wanders is sure to get into trouble. The shepherd calls sharply from time to time to remind them of his presence. They know his voice, and follow on; but, if a stranger call, they stop short, lift up their heads in alarm, and, if it is repeated, they turn and flee, because they know not the voice of a stranger. This is not the fanciful costume of a parable, it is simple fact. I have made the experiment repeatedly. The shepherd goes before, not merely to point out the way, but to see that it is practicable and safe. He is armed in order to defend his charge, and in this he is very courageous. Many adventures with wild beasts occur, not unlike that recounted by David (1 Samuel 27:34–36), and in these very mountains; for though there are now no lions here, there are wolves in abundance; and leopards and panthers, exceeding fierce, prowl about the wild wadies. They not unfrequently attack the flock in the very presence of the shepherd, and he must be ready to do battle at a moment's warning. I have listened with intense interest to their graphic descriptions of downright and desperate fights with these savage beasts. And when the thief and the robber come (and come they do), the faithful shepherd has often to put his life in his hand to defend his flock. I have known more than one case in which he had literally to lay it down in the contest. A poor faithful fellow last spring, between Tiberias and Tabor, instead of fleeing, actually fought three Bedawin robbers until he was hacked to pieces with their *khanjars*, and died among the sheep he was defending. Some sheep always keep near the shepherd, and are his special favourites. Each of them has a name, to which it answers joyfully, and the kind shepherd is ever distributing to such, choice portions which he gathers for that purpose. These are the contented and happy ones. They are in no danger of getting lost or into mischief, nor do wild beasts or thieves come near them. The great body, however, are mere worldlings, intent upon their mere pleasures or selfish interests. They run from bush to bush, searching for variety or delicacies, and only now and then lift their heads to see where the shepherd is, or, rather where the general flock is, lest they get so far away as to occasion a remark in their little community, or rebuke from their keeper. Others, again, are restless and discontented, jumping into everybody's field, climbing into bushes, and even into leaning trees, whence they often fall and break their limbs. These cost the good shepherd incessant trouble. W. M. Thomson, D.D., in 'The Land and the Book.'

Verse 1. 'Shepherd.' As we sat the silent hillsides around us were in a moment filled with life and sound. The shepherds led their flocks forth from the gates of the city. They were in full view, and we watched them and listened to them with no little interest. Thousands of sheep and goats were there, grouped in dense, confused masses. The shepherds stood together until all came out. Then they separated, each shepherd taking a different path, and uttering as he advanced a shrill peculiar call. The sheep heard them. At first the masses swayed and moved, as if shaken by some internal convulsion; then points struck out in the direction taken by the shepherds; these became longer and longer until the confused masses were resolved into long, living streams, flowing after their leaders. Such a sight was not new to me, still it had lost none of its interest. It was perhaps one of the most vivid illustrations which human eyes could witness of that beautiful discourse of our Lord recorded by John, 'And the sheep hear the shepherd's voice: and he calleth his own sheep by name, and leadeth them out. And when he putteth forth his own sheep, he goeth before them, and the sheep follow him: for they know his voice. And a stranger will they not follow, but will flee from him: for they know not the voice of strangers,' chapter 10:3–5. The shepherds themselves had none of that peaceful and placid aspect which is generally associated with pastoral life and habits. They looked more like warriors marching to the battle-field – a long gun slung from the shoulder, a dagger and heavy pistols in the belt, a light battle-axe or ironheaded club in the hand. Such were the equipments; and their fierce flashing eyes and scowling countenances showed but too plainly that they were prepared to use their weapons at any moment. J. L. Porter, A.M., in 'The Giant Cities of Bashan,' 1867.

Verse 1. 'I shall not want.' You must distinguish 'twixt absence, and 'twixt indigence. Absence is when something is not present; indigence or want, is when a needful good is not present. If a man were to walk, and had not a staff, here were something absent. If a man were to walk, and had but one leg, here were something whereof he were indigent. It is confessed that there are many good things which are absent from a good person, but no good thing which he wants or is indigent of. If the good be absent and I need it not, this is no want; he that walks without his cloak, walks well enough, for he needs it not. As long as I can walk carefully and cheerfully in my general or particular calling, though I have not such a load of accessories as other men have, yet I want nothing, for my little is enough and serves the turn . . . Our corruptions are still craving, and they are always inordinate, they can find more wants than God needs to supply. As they say of fools, they can propose more questions than twenty wise men need to answer. They in James 4:3, did ask, but received not; and he gives two reasons for it: 1. This asking was but a lusting: 'ye lust and have not' (verse 4): another, they did ask to consume it upon their lusts (verse 3). God will see that his people shall not want; but withal, he will never engage himself to the satisfying of their corruptions, though he doth to the supply of their conditions. It is one thing what the sick man wants, another what his disease wants. Your ignorance, your discontents, your pride, your unthankful hearts, may make you to believe that you dwell in a barren land, far from mercies (as melancholy makes a person to imagine that he is drowning, or killing, etc.); whereas if God did open your eyes as he did Hagar's, you might see fountains and streams, mercies and blessings sufficient; though not many, yet enough, though not so rich, yet proper, and every way convenient for your good and comfort; and thus you have the genuine sense, so far as I can judge of David's assertion, 'I shall not want.' Obadiah Sedgwick.

Verse 1. 'I shall not want.' Only he that can want does not want; and he that cannot, does. You tell me that a godly man wants these and these things, which the wicked man hath; but I tell you he can no more be said to 'want' them than a butcher may be said to want Homer, or such another thing, because his disposition is such, that he makes no use of those things which you usually mean. 'Tis but only necessary things that he cares for, and those are not many. But one thing is necessary, and that he hath chosen, namely, the better part. And therefore if he have nothing at all of all other things, he does not want, neither is there anything wanting which might make him rich enough, or by absence whereof, his riches should be said to be deficient. A body is not maimed unless it have lost a principal part: only privative defects discommend a thing, and not those that are negative. When we say, there is nothing wanting to such-and-such a creature or thing that a man hath made, we mean that it hath all that belongs necessarily to it. We speak not of such things as may be added for compliments or ornaments or the like, such as are those things usually wherein wicked men excel the godly. Even so it is when we say that a godly man wanteth nothing. For though in regard of unnecessary goods he be 'as having nothing,' yet in regard of others he is as if he possessed all things. He wants nothing that is necessary either for his glorifying of God (being able to do that best in and by his afflictions), or for God's glorifying of him, and making him happy, having God himself for his portion and supply of his wants, who is abundantly sufficient at all times, for all persons, in all conditions. Zachary Bogan.

Verse 1. 'I shall not want.' To be raised above the fear of want by committing ourselves to the care of the Good Shepherd, or by placing our confidence in worldly property, are two distinct and very opposite things. The confidence in the former case, appears to the natural man to be hard and difficult, if not unreasonable and impossible: in the latter it appears to be natural, easy, and consistent. It requires, however, no lengthened argument to prove that he who relies on the promise of God for the supply of his temporal wants, possesses an infinitely greater security than the individual who confides in his accumulated wealth. The ablest financiers admit that there must be appended to their most choice investments, this felt or expressed proviso – 'So far as human affairs can be secure' . . . Since then no absolute security against want can be found on earth, it necessarily follows, that he who trusts in God is the most wise and prudent man. Who dare deny that the promise of the living God is an absolute security? John Stevenson.

Verse 1. 'I shall not want.' The sheep of Christ may change their pasture, but they shall never want a pasture. 'Is not the life more than meat, and the body than raiment?' Matthew 6:25. If he grant unto us great things, shall we distrust him for small things? He who has given us heavenly beings, will also give us earthly blessings. The great Husbandman never over-stocked his own commons. William Secker.

Verse 1. 'I shall not want.' Ever since I heard of your illness, and the Lord's mercy in sustaining and restoring, I have been intending to write, to bless the Lord with my very dear sister, and ask for some words to strengthen my faith, in detail of your cup having run over in the hour of need. Is it not, indeed, the bleating of Messiah's sheep, 'I shall not want'? 'shall not want,' because the Lord is our Shepherd! Our Shepherd the All-sufficient! nothing can unite itself to him; nothing mingle with him; nothing add to his satisfying nature; nothing diminish from his fulness. There is a peace and fulness of expression in this little sentence, known only to the sheep. The remainder of the Psalm is a drawing out of this, 'I shall not want.' In the unfolding we find repose, refreshment, restoring mercies, guidance, peace in death, triumph, an overflowing of blessings; future confidence, eternal security in life or death, spiritual or temporal, prosperity or adversity, for time or eternity. May we not say, 'The Lord is my Shepherd?' for we stand on the sure foundation of the twenty-third Psalm. How can we want, when united to him! we have a right to use all his riches. Our wealth is his riches and glory. With him nothing can be withheld. Eternal life is ours, with the promise that all shall be added; all he knows we want. Our Shepherd has learned the wants of his sheep by experience, for he was himself 'led as a sheep to the slaughter.' Does not this expression, dictated by the Spirit, imply a promise, and a full promise, when connected with his own words, 'I know my sheep,' by what painful discipline he was instructed in this knowledge, subjected himself to the wants of every sheep, every lamb of his fold, that he might be able to be touched with a feeling of their infirmities? The timid sheep has nothing to fear; fear not want, fear not affliction. fear not pain; 'fear not;' according to your want shall be your supply, 'The Lord is my portion, saith my soul; therefore will I trust in him.' Theodosia A. Howard, Viscountess Powerscourt (1830) in 'Letters,' etc., edited by Robert Daly, D.D., 1861.

Verse 1. 'I shall not want.' One of the poor members of the flock of Christ was reduced to circumstances of the greatest poverty in his old age, and yet he never murmured. 'You must be badly off,' said a kind-hearted neighbour to him one day as they met upon the road, 'you must be badly off; and I don't know how an old man like you can maintain yourself and your wife; yet you are always cheerful!' 'Oh no!' he replied, 'we are not badly off, I have a rich Father, and he does not suffer me to want.' 'What! your father not dead yet? he must be very old indeed!' 'Oh!' said he, 'my Father never dies, and he always takes care of me!' This aged Christian was a daily pensioner on the providence of his God. His struggles and his poverty were known to all; but his own declaration was, that he never wanted what was absolutely necessary. The days of his greatest straits were the days of his most signal and timely deliverances. When old age benumbed the hand of his industry, the Lord extended to him the hand of charity. And often has he gone forth from his scanty breakfast, not knowing from what earthly source his next meal was to be obtained. But yet with David he could rely on his Shepherd's care, and say, 'I shall not want;' and as certainly as he trusted in God, so surely, in some unexpected manner was his necessity supplied. John Stevenson.

Verse 1. In the tenth chapter of John's gospel, you will find six marks of Christ sheep: 1. They know their Shepherd; 2. They know his voice; 3. They hear him calling them each by name; 4. They love him; 5. They trust him; 6. They follow him. In 'The Shepherd's King,' by Mrs. Rogers, authoress of 'The Folded Lamb', 1856.

Verses 1–4. Come down to the river; there is something going forward worth seeing. Yon shepherd is about to lead his flock across; and as our Lord says of the good shepherd – you observe that he goes before, and the sheep follow. Not all in the same manner, however. Some enter boldly, and come straight across. These are the loved ones of the flock, who keep hard by the footsteps of the shepherd, whether sauntering through green meadows by the still waters, feeding upon the mountains, or resting at noon, beneath the shadow of great rocks. And now others enter, but in doubt and alarm. Far from their guide, they miss the ford, and are carried down the river, some more, some less; and yet, one by one, they all struggle over and make good their landing. Notice those little lambs. They refuse to enter, and must be driven into the stream by the shepherd's dog, mentioned by Job in his 'parable.' Poor things! how they leap, and plunge, and bleat in terror! That weak one yonder will be swept quite away, and perish in the sea. But no; the shepherd himself leaps into the stream, lifts it into his bosom, and bears it trembling to the shore. All safely over, how happy they appear! The lambs frisk and gambol about in high spirits, while the older ones gather round their faithful guide, and look up to him in subdued but expressive thankfulness. Now, can you watch such a scene, and not think of that Shepherd who leadeth Joseph like a flock; and of another river, which all his sheep must cross? He, too, goes before, and, as in the case of this flock, they who keep near him 'fear no evil.' They hear his sweet voice, saying, 'When thou passest through the waters, I will be with thee; and through the rivers, they shall not overflow thee' Isaiah 43:2. With eye fastened on him, they scarcely see the stream, or feel its cold and threatening waves. W. M. Thomson.

Verse 2. 'He maketh me to lie down in green pastures,' etc. Not only he hath 'green pastures' to lead me into, which shows his ability, but he leads me into them, which shows his goodness. He leads me not into pastures that are withered and dry, that would distaste me before I taste them; but he leads me into 'green pastures,' as well to please my eye with the verdure as my stomach with the herbage; and inviting me, as it were, to eat by setting out the meat in the best colour. A meat though never so good, yet if it look not handsomely, it dulls the appetite; but when besides the goodness, it hath also a good look, this gives the appetite another edge, and makes a joy before enjoying. But yet the goodness is not altogether in the greenness. Alas! green is but a colour, and colours are but deceitful things; they might be green leaves, or they might be green flags or rushes; and what good were to me in such a greenness? No, my soul; the goodness is in being 'green pastures,' for now they perform as much as they promise; and as in being green they were a comfort to me as soon as I saw them, so in being green 'pastures' they are a refreshing to me now as soon as I taste them. As they are pleasant to look on, so they are wholesome to feed on: as they are sweet to be tasted, so they are easy to be digested; that I am now, methinks, in a kind of paradise and seem not to want anything, unless perhaps a little water with which now and then to wash my mouth, at most to take sometimes a sip: for though sheep be not great drinkers, and though their pastures being green, and full of sap, make drink the less needful; yet some drink they must have besides. And now see the great goodness of this Shepherd, and what just cause there is to depend upon his providence; for he lets not his sheep want this neither, but 'he leadeth them besides still waters,' not waters that roar and make a noise, enough to fright a fearful sheep, but waters 'still' and quiet; that though they drink but little, yet they may drink that little without fear. And may I not justly say now, 'The Lord is my Shepherd; I shall not want?' And yet perhaps there will be want for all this; for is it enough that he lead them into green pastures and beside still waters? May he not lead them in, and presently take them out again before their bellies be half full; and so instead of making them happy, make them more miserable? set them in a longing with the sight, and then frustrate them of their expectation? No, my soul; the measure of this Shepherd's goodness is more than so. He not only leadeth them into green pastures, but 'he makes them to lie down' in them – he leads them not in to post over their meat as if they were to eat a passover, and to take it *in transita*, as dogs drink Nylus; but, 'he makes them to lie down in green pastures,' that they may eat their fill and feed at leisure; and when they have done, 'lie down' and take their ease, that their after-reckoning may be as pleasing as their repast. Sir Richard Baker.

Verse 2. 'He leadeth me,' etc. In ordinary circumstances the shepherd does not feed his flock, except by leading and guiding them where they may gather for themselves; but there are times when it is otherwise. Late in autumn, when the pastures are dried up, and in winter, in places covered with snow, he must furnish them food or they die. In the vast oak woods along the eastern sides of Lebanon, between Baalbek and the cedars, there are there gathered innumerable flocks, and the shepherds are all day long in the bushy trees, cutting down the branches, upon whose green leaves and tender twigs the sheep and goats are entirely supported. The same is true in all mountain districts, and large forests are preserved on purpose. W. M. Thomson.

Verse 2. 'Lie down' – 'leadeth.' Sitting Mary and stirring Martha are emblems of contemplation and action, and as they dwell in one house, so must these in one heart. Nathanael Hardy.

Verse 2. This short but touching epitaph is frequently seen in the catacombs at Rome, '*In Christo, in pace*' (In Christ, in peace). Realise the constant presence of the Shepherd of peace. 'HE maketh me to lie down!' 'HE leadeth me.' J. R. Macduff, D.D.

Verse 2 (last clause). 'Easily leadeth,' or 'comfortably guideth me:' it noteth a soft and gentle leading, with sustaining of infirmity. H. Ainsworth.

Verse 2. 'Green pastures.' Here are many pastures, and every pasture rich so that it can never be eaten bare; here are many streams, and every stream so deep and wide that it can never be drawn dry. The sheep have been eating in these pastures ever since Christ had a church on earth, and yet they are as full of grass as ever. The sheep have been drinking at these streams ever since Adam, and yet they are brim full to this very day, and they will so continue till the sheep are above the use of them in heaven! Ralph Robinson, 1656.

Verse 2. 'Green pastures ... beside the still waters.' From the top of the mound (of Arban on the Khabour) the eye ranged over a level country bright with flowers, and spotted with black tents, and innumerable flocks of sheep and camels. During our stay at Arban, the Collor of these great plains was undergoing a continual change. After being for some days of a golden yellow, a new family of flowers would spring up, and it would turn almost in a night to a bright scarlet, which would again as suddenly give way to the deepest blue. Then the meadows would be mottled with various hues, or would put on the emerald green of the most luxuriant of pastures. The glowing descriptions I had so frequently received from the Bedouins of the beauty and fertility of the banks of the Khabour were more than realised. The Arabs boast that its meadows bear three distinct crops of grass during the year, and the wandering tribes look upon its wooded banks and constant greensward as a paradise during the summer months, where man can enjoy a cool shade, and beast can find fresh and tender herbs, whilst all around is yellow, parched, and sapless. Austin H. Layard, 1853.

Verse 2. With guidance to 'green pastures,' the psalmist has, with good reason, associated guardianship beside 'still waters:' for as we can only appropriate the word through the Spirit, so we shall ordinarily receive the Spirit through the Word; not indeed only by hearing it, not only by reading it, not only by reflecting upon it. The Spirit of God, who is a most free agent, and who is himself the source of liberty, will come into the heart of the believer when he will, and how he will, and as he will. But the effect of his coming will ever be the realisation of some promise, the recognition of some principle, the attainment of some grace, the understanding of some mystery, which is already in the word, and which we shall thus find, with a deeper impression, and with a fuller development, brought home with power to the heart. Thomas Dale, M.A., in 'The Good Shepherd,' 1847.

Verse 2. 'Still waters;' which are opposed to great rivers, which both affright the sheep with their noise, and expose them to the danger of being carried away by their swift and violent streams, whilst they are drinking at them. Matthew Poole.

Verse 3. 'He restoreth my soul,' etc. The subjects experimentally treated in this verse are, first, the believer's liability to fall, or deviate even within the fold of the church, else wherefore should he need to be 'restored?' Next, the promptitude of the Good Shepherd to interpose for his rescue. 'He restoreth my soul.' Then Christ's subsequent care to 'lead him in the paths of righteousness;' and lastly, the reason assigned wherefore he will do this – resolving all into the spontaneousness, the supremacy, the omnipotence of grace. He will do all 'for his own name's sake.' Thomas Dale.

Verse 3. 'He restoreth my soul.' The same hand which first rescued us from ruin, reclaims us from all our subsequent aberrations. Chastisement itself is blended with tenderness; and the voice which speaks reproof, saying, 'They have perverted their way, and they have forsaken the Lord their God,' utters the kindest invitation, 'Return, ye backsliding children, and I will heal your backslidings.' Nor is the voice unheard, and the call unanswered or unfelt. 'Behold, we come unto thee; for thou art the Lord our God' Jeremiah 3:22. 'When thou saidst, Seek my face; my heart said unto thee, Thy face, Lord, will I seek.' J. Thornton's 'Shepherd of Israel,' 1826.

Verse 3. 'He restoreth my soul.' He restores it to its original purity, that was now grown foul and black with sin; for also, what good were it to have 'green' pastures and a black soul! He 'restores' it to its natural temper in affections, that was grown distempered with violence of passions; for alas! what good were it to have 'still' waters and turbulent spirits! He 'restores' it indeed to life, that was grown before in a manner quite dead; and who could 'restore my soul' to life, but he only that is the Good Shepherd and gave his life for his sheep? Sir Richard Baker.

Verse 3. 'He shall convert my soul;' turn me not only from sin and ignorance, but from every false confidence, and every deceitful refuge. 'He shall bring me forth in paths of right-eousness;' in those paths of imputed righteousness which are always adorned with the trees of holiness, are always watered with the fountains of consolation, and always terminate in ever-lasting rest. Some, perhaps, may ask, why I give this sense to the passage? Why may it not signify the paths of duty, and the way of our own obedience? Because such effects are here mentioned as never have resulted, and never can result, from any duties of our own. These are not 'green pastures,' but a parched and blasted heath. These are not 'still waters,' but a troubled and disorderly stream. Neither can these speak peace or administer comfort when we pass through the valley and shadow of death. To yield these blessings, is the exalted office of Christ, and the sole prerogative of his obedience. James Hervey.

Verse 3. 'He restoreth my soul:' Hebrew. 'He bringeth it back;' either, 1. From its errors or wandering; or, 2. Into the body, out of which it was even departing and fainting away. He reviveth or comforteth me. Matthew Poole.

Verse 3. 'Paths of righteousness.' Alas! O Lord, these 'paths of righteousness,' have a long time so little been frequented, that the prints of a path are almost clean worn out; that it is a hard matter now, but to find where the paths lie, and if we can find them, yet they are so narrow and so full of ruts, that without special assistance it is an impossible thing not to fall or go astray. Even so angels, and those no mean ones, were not able to go right in these 'paths of righteousness,' but for want of leading, went away and perished. O, therefore, thou the Great Shepherd of my soul, as thou art pleased of thy grace to lead me into them, so vouchsafe with thy grace to lead me in them; for though in themselves they be 'paths of righteousness,' yet to me they will be but paths of error if thou vouchsafe not, as well to lead me in them, as into them. Sir Richard Baker.

Verse 3. 'Paths.' In the wilderness and in the desert there are no raised paths, the paths being merely tracks; and sometimes there are six or eight paths running unevenly along side each other. No doubt this is what is figuratively referred to in Psalm 23:3, 'He leadeth me in the paths of righteousness,' all leading to one point. John Gadsby.

Verse 3. 'For his name's sake.' Seeing he hath taken upon him the name of a 'Good Shepherd,' he will discharge his part, whatever his sheep be. It is not their being bad sheep that can make him leave being a 'Good Shepherd,' but he will be 'good,' and maintain the credit of 'his name' in spite of all their badness; and though no benefit come to them of it, yet there shall glory accrue to him by it, and 'his name' shall nevertheless be magnified and extolled. Sir Richard Baker.

Verse 4. 'Yea, though I walk through the valley of the shadow of death, I will fear no evil.' To 'fear no evil,' then, 'in the valley of the shadow of death,' is a blessed privilege open to every true believer! For death shall be to him no death at all, but a very deliverance from death, from all pains, cares, and sorrows, miseries and wretchedness of this world, and the very entry into rest, and a beginning of everlasting joy: a tasting of heavenly pleasures, so great, that neither tongue is able to express, neither eyes to see, nor ear to hear them, no, nor any earthly man's heart to conceive them ... And to comfort all Christian persons herein, holy Scripture calleth this bodily death a sleep, wherein man's senses be, as it were, taken from him for a season, and yet, when he waketh, he is more fresh than when he went to bed! ... Thus is this bodily death a door or entering into life, and therefore not so much dreadful, if it be rightly considered, as it is comfortable; not a mischief, but a remedy for all mischief; no enemy, but a friend; not a cruel tyrant, but a gentle guide; leading us not to mortality, but to immortality! not to sorrow and pain, but to joy and pleasure, and that to endure for ever! Homily against the Fear of Death, 1547.

Verse 4. 'Yea, though I walk through the valley of the shadow of death, I will fear no evil.' Though I were called to such a sight as Ezekiel's vision, a valley full of dead men's bones; though the king of terrors should ride in awful pomp through the streets, slaying heaps upon heaps, and thousands should fall at my side, and ten thousands at my right hand, I will fear no evil. Though he should level his fatal arrows at the little circle of my associates, and put lover and friend far from me, and mine acquaintance into darkness, I will fear no evil. Yea, though I myself should feel his arrow sticking fast in me, the poison drinking up my spirits; though I should in consequence of that fatal seizure, sicken and languish, and have all the symptoms of approaching dissolution, still I will fear no evil. Nature, indeed, may start back and tremble, but I trust that he who knows the flesh to be weak, will pity and pardon these struggles. However I may be afraid of the agonies of dying, I will fear no evil in death. The venom of his sting is taken away. The point of his arrow is blunted, so that it can pierce no deeper than the body. My soul in invulnerable. I can smile at the shaking of his spear; look unmoved on the ravages which the unrelenting destroyer is making on my tabernacle; and long for the happy period when he shall have made a breach wide enough for my heaven-aspiring spirit to fly away and be at rest. Samuel Lavington.

Verse 4. 'Yea, though I walk through the valley of the shadow of death, I will fear no evil.' 'I want to talk to you about heaven,' said a dying parent (the late Rev. Hugh Stowell, Rector of Ballaugh, Isle of Man) to a member of his family. 'We may not be spared to each other long. May we meet around the throne of glory, one family in heaven!' Overpowered at the thought, his beloved daughter exclaimed, 'Surely you do not think there is any danger?' Calmly and beautifully he replied, 'Danger, my darling! Oh, do not use that word! There can be no danger to the Christian, whatever may happen! All is right! All is well! God is love! All is well! Everlastingly well! Everlastingly well!' John Stevenson.

Verse 4. 'Though I walk through the valley of the shadow of death, I will fear no evil.' What not fear then? Why, what friend is it that keeps up your spirits, that bears you company in that black and dismal region? He will soon tell you God was with him, and in those slippery ways he leaned upon his staff, and these were the cordials that kept his heart from fainting. I challenge all the gallants in the world, out of all their merry, jovial clubs, to find such a company of merry, cheerful creatures as the friends of God are. It is not the company of God, but the want of it, that makes sad. Alas! you know not what their comforts be, and strangers intermeddle not with their joy. You think they cannot be merry when their countenance is so grave; but they are sure you cannot be truly merry when you smile with a curse upon your souls. They know that he spoke that sentence which could not be mistaken, 'Even in laughter the heart is sorrowful; and the end of that mirth is heaviness' Proverbs 14:13. Then call your roaring, and your singing, and laughter, mirth; but the Spirit of God calls it madness. Ecclesiastes 2:2. When a carnal man's heart is ready to die within him, and, with Nabal, to become like a stone, how cheerfully then can those look that have God for their friend! Which of the valiant ones of the world can outface death, look joyfully into eternity? Which of them can hug a faggot, embrace the flames? This the saint can do, and more too; for he can look infinite justice in the face with a cheerful heart; he can hear of hell with joy and thankfulness; he can think of the day of judgment with great delight and comfort. I again challenge all the world to produce one out of all their merry companies, one that can do all this. Come, muster up all your jovial blades together; call for your harps and viols; add what you will to make the concert complete; bring in your richest wines; come, lay your heads together, and study what may still add to your comfort. Well, it is done? Now, come away, sinner, this night thy soul must appear before God. Well now, what say you, man? What! doth your courage fail you? Now call for your merry companions, and let them cheer thy heart. Now call for a cup, a whore; never be daunted, man. Shall one of thy courage quail, that could make a mock at the threatenings of the Almighty God? What, so boon and jolly but now, and now down in the mouth! Here's a sudden change indeed! Where are thy merry companions, I say again? All fled? Where are thy darling pleasures? Have all forsaken thee? Why shouldst thou be dejected; there's a poor man in rags that's smiling? What! art thou quite bereft of all comfort? What's the matter? There's a question with all my heart, to ask a man that must appear before God to-morrow morning. Well, then, it seems your heart misgives you. What then did you mean of talk of joys and pleasures? Are they all come to this? Why, there stands one that now hath his heart as full of comfort as ever it can hold, and the very thoughts of eternity, which do so daunt your soul, raise his! And would you know the reason? He knows he is going to his Friend; nay, his Friend bears him company through that dirty lane. Behold how good and how pleasant a thing it is for God and the soul to dwell together in unity! This it is to have God for a friend. 'Oh blessed is the soul that is in such a case; yea, blessed is the soul whose God is the Lord' Psalm 144:15. James Janeway.

Verse 4. 'Though I walk through the valley of the shadow of death.' Any darkness is evil, but darkness and the shadow of death is the utmost of evils. David put the worst of his case and the best of his faith when he said, 'Though I walk in the valley of the shadow of death, I will fear no evil;' that is, in the greatest evil I will fear no evil … Again, to be under the shadow of a thing, is to be under the power of a thing … Thus to be under the shadow of death, is to be so under the power or reach of death, that death may take a man and seize upon him when it pleaseth. 'Though I walk in the valley of the shadow of death,' that is, though I be so near death, that it seems to others death may catch me every moment, though I be under so many appearances and probabilities of extreme danger, that there appears an impossibility, in sense, to escape death, 'yet I will not fear.' Joseph Caryl.

Verse 4. 'Valley of the shadow of death.' A valley is a low place, with mountains on either side. Enemies may be posted on those mountains to shoot their arrows at the traveller, as ever was the case in the East; but he must pass through it. The psalmist, however, said he would fear no evil, not even the fiery darts of Satan, for the Lord was with him. The figure is not primarily, as is sometimes supposed, our dying moments, though it will beautifully bear that explanation; but it is the valley beset with enemies, posted on the hills. David was not only protected in that valley, but even in the presence of those enemies, his table was bountifully spread (verse 5). The Bedouin, at the present day often post themselves on the hills to harass travellers, as they pass along the valleys. John Gadsby.

Verse 4. 'Though art with me.' Do you know the sweetness, the security, the strength of 'Thou art with me'? When anticipating the solemn hour of death, when the soul is ready to halt and ask, How shall it then be? can you turn in soul-affection to your God and say, 'There is nothing in death to harm me, while thy love is left to me'? Can you say, 'O death, where is thy sting'? It is said, when a bee has left its sting in any one, it has no more power to hurt. Death has left its sting in the humanity of Christ, and has no more power to harm his child. Christ's victory over the grave is his people's. 'At that moment I am with you,' whispers Christ; 'the same arm you have proved strong and faithful all the way up through the wilderness, which has never failed, though you have been often forced to lean on it all your weakness.' 'On this arm,' answers the believer, 'I feel at home; with soul confidence, I repose on my Beloved; for he has supported through so many difficulties, from the contemplation of which I shuddered. He has carried over so many depths, that I know his arm to be the arm of love.' How can that be dark, in which God's child is to have the accomplishment of the longing desire of his life? How can it be dark to come in contact with the light of life? It is 'his rod,' 'his staff;' therefore they 'comfort.' Prove him – prove him now, believer! it is your privilege to do so. It will be precious to him to support your weakness; prove that when weak, then are you strong; that you may be secure, his strength shall be perfected in your perfect weakness. Omnipotent love must fail before one of his sheep can perish; for, says Christ, 'none shall pluck my sheep out of my hand.' 'I and my Father are one;' therefore we may boldly say, 'Yea, though I walk through the valley of the shadow of death, I will fear no evil: for thou art with me.' Viscountess Powerscourt.

Verse 4. 'Rod and staff.' The shepherd invariably carries a staff or rod with him when he goes forth to feed his flock. It is often bent or hooked at one end, which gave rise to the shepherd's crook in the hand of the Christian bishop. With this staff he rules and guides the flock to their green pastures, and defends them from their enemies. With it also he corrects them when disobedient, and brings them back when wandering. This staff is associated as inseparably with the shepherd as the goad is with the ploughman. W. M. Thomson.

Verse 4. The psalmist will trust, even though all be unknown. We find him doing this in Psalm 23:4: 'Yea, though I walk through the valley of the shadow of death, I will fear no evil.' Here, surely, there is trust the most complete. We dread the unknown far above anything that we can see; a little noise in the dark will terrify, when even great dangers which are visible do not affright: the unknown, with its mystery and uncertainty, often fills the heart with anxiety, if not with foreboding and gloom. Here, the psalmist takes the highest form of the unknown, the aspect which is most terrible to man, and says, that even in the midst if it he will trust. What could be so wholly beyond the reach of human experience or speculation, or even imagination, as 'the valley of the shadow of death,' with all that belonged to it? but the psalmist makes no reservation against it; he will trust where he cannot see. How often are we terrified at the unknown; even as the disciples were, 'who feared as they entered the cloud;' how often is the uncertainty of the future a harder trial to our faith than the pressure of some present ill! Many dear children of God can trust him in all known evils; but why those fears and forebodings, and sinkings of heart, if they trust him equally for the unknown? How much, alas! do we fall short of the true character of the children of God, in this matter of the unknown! A child practically acts upon the declaration of Christ that 'sufficient unto the day is the evil thereof,' we, in this respect far less wise than he, people the unknown with phantoms and speculations, and too often forget our simple trust in God. Philip Bennet Power.

Verse 4. 'For thou art with me; thy rod and thy staff comfort me. Thou shalt prepare a table before me, against them that trouble me. Thou hast anointed my head with oil, and my cup shall be full.' Seeing thou art with me, at whose power and will all troubles go and come, I doubt not but to have the victory and upper hand of them, how many and dangerous soever they are; for thy rod chasteneth me when I go astray, and thy staff stayeth me when I should fall – two things most necessary for me, good Lord; the one to call me from my fault and error, and the other to keep me in thy truth and verity. What can be more blessed than to be sustained and kept from falling by the staff and strength of the Most High? And what can be more profitable than to be beaten with his merciful rod when we go astray? For he chasteneth as many as he loveth, and beateth as many as he receiveth into his holy profession. Notwithstanding, while we are here in this life, he feeds us with the sweet pastures of the wholesome herbs of his holy word, until we come to eternal life; and when we put off these bodies, and come into heaven, and know the blessed fruition and riches of his kingdom, then shall we not only be his sheep, but also the guests of his everlasting banquet; which, Lord, thou settest before all them that love thee in this world, and dost so anoint and make glad our minds with thine Holy Spirit, that no adversities nor troubles can make us sorry. In this sixth part, the prophet declares the old saying amongst wise men, 'It is no less mastery to keep the thing that is won, than it was to win it.' King David perceives right well the same; and, therefore, as before in the Psalm he said, the Lord turned his soul, and led him into the pleasant pastures, where virtue and justice reigned, for his name's sake, and not for any righteousness of his own; so saith he now, that being brought into the pastures of truth, and into the favour of the Almighty, and accounted and taken for one of his sheep, it is only God that keeps and maintains him, in the same state, condition, and grace. For he could not pass through the troubles and shadow of death, as he and all God's elect people must do, but only by the assistance of God, and, therefore, he saith, he passes through all peril because he was with him. John Hooper (martyr), 1495–1555.

Verse 4. By the way, I note that David amidst his green pastures, where he wanted nothing, and in his greatest ease and highest excellency, recordeth the valley of misery and shade of death which might ensue, if God so would; and therewithal reckoneth of his safest harbour and firm repose, even in God alone. And this is true wisdom indeed, in fair weather to provide for a tempest; in health to think of sickness; in prosperity, peace, and quietness, to forecast the worst, and with the wise emmet, in summer to lay up for the winter following. The state of man is full of trouble, the condition of the godly man more. Sinners must be corrected, and sons chastised, there is no question. The ark was framed for the waters, the ship for the sea; and happy is the mariner that knoweth where to cast anchor; but, oh! blessed is the man that can take a right sanctuary, and knoweth whereupon to rely, and in whom to trust in the day of his need. 'I will not fear, for thou art with me.' In this Psalm, I take it, is rather vouched not what the prophet always performed, but what in duty must be performed, and what David's purpose was to endeavour unto for the time to come. For after so many pledges of God's infinite goodness, and by the guidance of his rod and stay of his sheep-hook, God willing, he would not fear, and this is the groundwork of his affiance. Peter in the gospel by our Saviour, in consideration of infirmity through fear denying his Master, is willed after his conversion by that favourable aspect of our Saviour, to confirm his brethren, and to train them in constancy; for verily God requireth settled minds, resolute men, and confirmed brethren. So upon occasions past, David found it true that he should not have been heretofore at any time, and therefore professeth, that for the time to come he would be no marigold-servant of the Lord, to open with the sun and shut with the dew – to serve him in calmer times only, and at a need, to shoot neck out of collar, fearfully and faithlessly to slip aside or shrink away. Good people, in all heartless imperfections, mark, I pray you, that they who fear every mist that ariseth, or cloud that appeareth – who are like the mulberry tree, that never shooteth forth or showeth itself till all hard weather be past – who, like standers-by and lookers on, neuters and internimists – who, like Metius Suffetius, dare not venture upon, nor enter into, nor endeavour any good action of greatest duty to God, prince, or country, till all be sure in one side – are utterly reproved by this ensample. John Prime, 1588.

Verse 4. The death of those who are under sin, is like a malefactor's execution: when he is panelled and justly convicted, one pulleth the hat doggedly from him, another his band, a third bindeth his hands behind his back; and the poor man, overcome with grief and fear, is dead before he die. But I look for the death of the righteous, and a peaceable end, that it shall be as a going to bed of an honest man: his servants with respect take off his clothes and lay them down in order; a good conscience the playing the page ordereth all, so that it confirmeth and increaseth his peace; it biddeth good night to Faith, Hope, and such other attending graces and gifts in the way – when we are come home to heaven there is no use of them – but it directeth Love, Peace, Joy, and other home graces, that as they conveyed us in the way, so they attend at death, and enter into the heavens with us. William Struther.

Verse 4. The Lord willeth us in the day of our troubles to call upon him, adding this promise – that he will deliver us. Whereunto the prophet David did so trust, feeling the comfortable truth thereof at sundry times in many and dangerous perils, that he persuaded himself (all fear set apart), to undergo one painful danger or other whatsoever; yea, if it were to 'walk in the valley of the shadow of death,' that he should not have cause to fear; comforting himself with this saying (which was God's promise made unto all), 'For thou art with me; thy rod and thy staff they comfort me.' Is God's 'staff' waxen so weak, that we dare not now lean too much thereon, lest it should break? or is he now such a changeling, that he will not be with us in our trouble according to his promise? Will he not give us this 'staff' to stay us by, and reach us his hand to hold us up, as he hath been wont to do? No doubt but that he will be most ready in all extremity to help, according to his promise. The Lord that created thee, O Jacob, and he that formed thee, O Israel, saith thus; Fear not, for I will defend thee,' etc. Isaiah 43. Thomas Tymme.

Verse 4. Not long before he died, he blessed God for the assurance of his love, and said, He could now as easily die as shut his eyes; and added, Here am I longing to be silent in the dust, and enjoying Christ in glory. I long to be in the arms of Jesus. It is not worth while to weep for me. Then, remembering how busy the devil had been about him, he was exceedingly thankful to God for his goodness in rebuking him. Memoir of James Janeway.

Verse 4. When Mrs. Hervey, the wife of a missionary in Bombay, was dying, a friend said to her, that he hoped the Saviour would be with her as she walked through the dark valley of the shadow of death. 'If this,' said she, 'is the dark valley, it has not a dark spot in it; all is light.' She had, during most of her sickness, bright views of the perfections of God. 'His awful holiness,' she said, 'appeared the most lovely of all his attributes.' At one time she said she wanted words to express her views of the glory and majesty of Christ. 'It seems,' said she, 'that if all other glory were annihilated and nothing left but his bare self, it would be enough; it would be a universe of glory!'

Verses 4, 5. A readiness of spirit to suffer gives the Christian the true enjoyment of life … The Christian, that hath this preparation of heart, never tastes more sweetness in the enjoyment of this life, than when he dips these morsels in the meditation of death and eternity. It is no more grief to his heart to think of the remove of these, which makes way for those far sweeter enjoyments, than it would be to one at a feast, to have the first course taken off, when he had fed well upon it, that the second course of all rare sweetmeats and banqueting stuff may come on, which it cannot till the other be gone. Holy David, in this place, brings in, as it were, a death's head with his feast. In the same breath almost, he speaks of his dying (verse 4), and of the rich feast he at present sat at through the bounty of God (verse 5), to which he was not so tied by the teeth, but if God, that gave him this cheer, should call him from it, to look death in the face, he could do it, and fear no evil when in the valley of the shadow of it. And what think you of the blessed apostle Peter? Had not he, think you, the true enjoyment of his life, when he could sleep so sweetly in a prison (no desirable place), fast bound between two soldiers (no comfortable posture), and this the very night before Herod would have brought him forth, in all probability, to his execution? no likely time, one would think, to get any rest; yet we find him, even there, thus, and then, so sound asleep, that the angel, who was sent to give him his gaol deliverance, smote him on the side to awaken him. Acts 12:6,7. I question whether Herod himself slept so well that night, as this his prisoner did. And what was the potion that brought this holy man so quietly to rest? No doubt this preparation of the gospel of peace – he was ready to die, and that made him able to sleep. Why should that break his rest in this world, which if it had been effected, would have brought him to his eternal rest in the other? William Gurnall.

Verses 4, 6. The psalmist expresseth an exceeding confidence in the midst of most inexpressible troubles and pressures. He supposes himself 'walking through the valley of the shadow of death.' As 'death' is the worst of evils, and comprehensive of them all, so the 'shadow' of death is the most dismal and dark representation of those evils into the soul, and the 'valley' of that shadow the most dreadful bottom and depth of that representation. This, then, the prophet supposed that he might be brought into. A condition wherein he may be overwhelmed with sad apprehensions of the coming of a confluence of all manner of evils upon him – and that not for a short season, but he may be necessitated to 'walk' in them, which denotes a state of some continuance, a conflicting with most dismal evils, and in their own nature tending to death – is in the supposal. What, then, would he do if he should be brought into this estate? Saith he, 'Even in that condition, in such distress, wherein I am, to my own and the eyes of others, hopeless, helpless, gone, and lost, 'I will fear no evil." A noble resolution, if there be a sufficient bottom and foundation for it, that it may not be accounted rashness and groundless confidence, but true spiritual courage and holy resolution. Saith he, 'It is because the Lord is with me.' But alas! what if the Lord should now forsake thee in this condition, and give thee up to the power of thine enemies, and suffer thee, by the strength of thy temptations, wherewith thou art beset, to fall utterly from him? Surely then thou wouldst be swallowed up for ever: the waters would go over thy soul, and thou must for ever lie down in the shades of death. 'Yea,' saith he, 'but I have an assurance to the contrary; 'Goodness and mercy shall follow me all the days of my life.' John Owen.

Verse 5. 'In the presence of mine enemies:' they seeing and envying and fretting at it, but not being able to hinder it. Matthew Poole.

Verse 5. 'Thou anointest my head with oil; my cup runneth over.' In the East the people frequently anoint their visitors with some very fragrant perfume; and give them a cup or glass of some choice wine, which they are careful to fill till it runs over. The first was designed to show their love and respect; the latter to imply that while they remained there, they should have an abundance of everything. To something of this kind the psalmist probably alludes in this passage. Samuel Burder.

Verse 5. 'Thou anointest my head with oil.' It is an act of great respect to pour perfumed oil on the head of a distinguished guest; the woman in the gospel thus manifested her respect for the Saviour by pouring 'precious ointment' on his head. An English lady went on board an Arabian ship which touched at Trincomalee, for the purpose of seeing the equipment of the vessel, and to make some little purchases. After she had been seated some time in the cabin, an Arabian female came and poured perfumed oil on her head. Joseph Roberts.

Verse 5. 'Thou anointest my head with oil.' In the East no entertainment could be without this, and it served, as elsewhere a bath does, for (bodily) refreshment. Here, however, it is naturally to be understood of the spiritual oil of gladness. T. C. Barth.

Verse 5. 'Thou anointest my head with oil.' Thou hast not confined thy bounty merely to the necessaries of life, but thou hast supplied me also with its luxuries. In 'A plain Explanation of Difficult Passages in the Psalms,' 1831.

Verse 5. 'Thou anointest my head with oil.' The unguents of Egypt may preserve our bodies from corruption, ensuring them a long duration in the dreary shades of the sepulchre, but, O Lord, the precious perfumed oil of thy grace which thou dost mysteriously pour upon our souls, purifies them, adorns them, strengthens them, sows in them the germs of immortality, and thus it not only secures them from a transitory corruption, but uplifts them from this house of bondage into eternal blessedness in thy bosom. Jean Baptiste Massillon, 1663–1742.

Verse 5. 'My cup runneth over.' He had not only a fulness of abundance, but of redundance. Those that have this happiness must carry their cup upright, and see that it overflows into their poor brethren's emptier vessels. John Trapp.

Verse 5. 'My cup runneth over.' Wherefore doth the Lord make you cup run over, but that other men's lips might taste the liquor? The showers that fall upon the highest mountains, should glide into the lowest valleys. 'Give, and it shall be given you,' is a maxim little believed. Luke 6:38. William Secker.

Verse 5. 'My cup runneth over.' Or as it is in the Vulgate: And my inebriating chalice, how excellent it is! With this cup were the martyrs inebriated, when, going forth to their passion, they recognised not those that belonged to them; not their weeping wife, not their children, not their relations; while they gave thanks and said, 'I will take the cup of salvation!' Augustine.

Verse 6. 'I will dwell in the house of the Lord for ever.' A wicked man, it may be, will turn into God's house, and say a prayer, etc., but the prophet would (and so all godly men must) dwell there for ever; his soul lieth always at the throne of grace, begging for grace. A wicked man prayeth as the cock croweth; the cock crows and ceaseth, and crows again, and ceaseth again, and thinks not of crowing till he crows again: so a wicked man prays and ceaseth, prays and ceaseth again; his mind is never busied to think whether his prayers speed or no; he thinks it is good religion for him to pray, and therefore he takes for granted that his prayers speed, though in very deed God never hears his prayers, nor no more respects them than he respects the lowing of oxen, or the grunting of hogs. William Fenner, B.D. (1600–1640), in 'The Sacrifice of the Faithful.'

Verse 6. 'I will dwell in the house of the Lord for ever.' This should be at once the crown of all our hopes for the future, and the one great lesson taught us by all the vicissitudes of life. The sorrows and the joys, the journeying and the rest, the temporary repose and the frequent struggles, all these should make us sure that there is an end which will interpret them all, to which they all point, for which they all prepare. We get the table in the wilderness here. It is as when the son of some great king comes back from foreign soil to his father's dominions, and is welcomed at every stage in his journey to the capital with pomp of festival and messengers from the throne, until at last he enters his palace home, where the travel-stained robe is laid aside, and he sits down with his father at his table. Alexander Maclaren, 1863.

Verse 6. Mark David's resolute persuasion, and consider how he came unto it, namely, by experience of God's favour at sundry times, and after sundry manners. For before he set down this resolution, he numbered up divers benefits received of the Lord; that he fed him in green pastures, and led him by the refreshing waters of God's word; that he restores him and leads him in the paths of righteousness; that he strengthened him in great dangers, even of death, and preserveth him; that in despite of his enemies, he enricheth him with many benefits. By means of all the mercies of God bestowed on him, he came to be persuaded of the continuance of the favour of God towards him. William Perkins.

Hints to the village preacher

Verse 1. Work out the similitude of a shepherd and his sheep. He rules, guides, feeds, and protects them; and they follow, obey, love and trust him. Examine as to whether we are sheep; show the lot of the goats who feed side by side with the sheep.

Verse 1. (second clause). The man who is beyond the reach of want for time and eternity.

Verse 2. (first clause). Believing rest.

1. Comes from God – 'He maketh.'
2. Is deep and profound – 'lie down.'
3. Has solid sustenance – 'in green pastures.'
4. Is subject for constant praise.

Verse 2. The contemplative and the active element provided for.

Verse 2. The freshness and richness of Holy Scripture.

Verse 2. (second clause). Onward. The Leader, the way, the comforts of the road, and the traveller in it.